Jane Austen's Textual Lives: From Aeschylus to Bollywood

KATHRYN SUTHERLAND

OXFORD
UNIVERSITY PRESS

Great Clarendon Street, Oxford OX2 6DP

Oxford University Press is a department of the University of Oxford.
It furthers the University's objective of excellence in research, scholarship,
and education by publishing worldwide in

Oxford New York

Auckland Cape Town Dar es Salaam Hong Kong Karachi
Kuala Lumpur Madrid Melbourne Mexico City Nairobi
New Delhi Shanghai Taipei Toronto

With offices in

Argentina Austria Brazil Chile Czech Republic France Greece
Guatemala Hungary Italy Japan Poland Portugal Singapore
South Korea Switzerland Thailand Turkey Ukraine Vietnam

Published in the United States
by Oxford University Press Inc., New York

First published 2005
First published in paperback 2007

British Library Cataloguing in Publication Data
Data available

Library of Congress Cataloging in Publication Data
Data available

Typeset by SPI Publisher Services, Pondicherry, India
Printed in Great Britain
on acid-free paper by
Biddles Ltd
King's Lynn, Norfolk

ISBN 978–0–19–925872–7 (Hbk.) 978–0–19–923428–8 (Pbk.)

1 3 5 7 9 10 8 6 4 2

Preface

This book traces three histories which impel one another with varying degrees of attention through the twentieth century. One is a history of Jane Austen's life and works through their textual dissemination; a second offers a picture of the development of English studies in which textual criticism's original and primary place is recovered; and a third is a more occasional investigation, by means of specific example, of the history of Oxford University Press and its role in shaping a canon of English texts. But first and foremost, this is a book about Jane Austen, an author who with very few others occupies a position within English-speaking cultures which is both popular and canonical, accessible and complexly inaccessible, fixed and certain, yet wonderfully amenable to shifts of sensibility and cultural assumptions. What we would now call her Regency production values—a pleasant blur of stately homes, English gardens, and empire-line dresses—coexist comfortably with a high critical appreciation of the modernist import of her technical innovations as a novelist; while the reassuringly limited preoccupations of her leisured middle classes combine effortlessly with lurid insights into sexual deviance and colonial misappropriation. Her novels' standing appears as decisively settled as our appetite for their reinvention is determinedly unappeased and unsettling. Since the mid-1990s, it seems, she has rarely been out of the newspapers, receiving the kind of media attention any living writer might envy.

My main enquiry in this world of familiar impermanence has been into those things we have taken for granted as permanent or prior to enquiry and interpretation—as simply *there*. By this I mean Jane Austen's texts. My subject is the ways in which Jane Austen is transmitted and transformed through texts: her manuscripts, the early published volumes, modern editions, biographies, continuations, and film versions; my concern is with the cultural context of each of these and with the kinds of authority invested in them.

Jane Austen's rise to celebrity status at the end of the nineteenth century was effectively managed by the family for whom the invention and preservation of a comfortable Victorian reputation for a disruptive and witty Regency novelist was of paramount importance. Between 1870, when James Edward

Austen-Leigh's biographical *Memoir* of his aunt first appeared, and 1913, the year in which William and Richard Arthur Austen-Leigh (James Edward's youngest son and grandson) published their expanded *Life and Letters*, Jane Austen was marketed sentimentally (and on occasion cynically) as the lady novelist of the Hampshire countryside. The image was maintained in part by the anxious family censorship and edited release or suppression of the manuscript writings left unpublished in Austen's lifetime—the irreverent juvenilia and the later experimental fiction. With R. W. Chapman's Clarendon Press edition of *The Novels of Jane Austen* in 1923 the pendulum swung to the opposite extreme, and a previously accessible and increasingly popular body of fiction was subjected to the kind of textual probing and proving reserved till then by scholars for Classical Greek and Roman authors obscured by centuries of attrition. Chapman's heavyweight intervention inaugurated simultaneously the modern textual critical engagement with Jane Austen and with the novel form, but it was to be almost fifty years before the Clarendon Press deemed it necessary to recalibrate the reputation of another popular English novelist in this way. Furthermore, with the Austen record settled according to a pre-First-World-War standard for Classical texts, Chapman's edition held the field for the rest of the twentieth century. Chapman's text was (and is) Jane Austen's text.

Until relatively recently, it has not been considered necessary or fashionable to think critically about the work that editing does. Yet editions of literary texts are textual performances as much as any other critical reading; and the cultural and interpretative identity of editing is as fundamental to the experience of producing and reading literature as it is to the performance and appreciation of music. We might go further and say that editing's critical performances effectively forestall subsequent encounters by establishing text as a selected and censored space whose workings are largely undeclared. Chapman's Austen text did massive ideological work scarcely recognized in the subsequent intensive critical industry of the second half of the twentieth century and oddly exempt from the cultural purposes that Austen's novels and Austen studies were at that time made to serve. So my concern is with Jane Austen's textual identities as a means to explore the wider issue of what text is and what it means to stabilize and destabilize particular definitions of text and particular texts. It seems at the very least worth considering how Austen studies have combined so successfully two contradictory impulses: one, a belief in the efficacy of close reading to deliver diverse interpretations; the other, an uncritical confidence in the authority of the text on the page to bear and resist this scrutiny. So my subject is editing as a prior critical activity, one that circumscribes every subsequent critical engagement; and it is an attempt to instil textual scepticism and broadmindedness. The integration of textual criticism as a usual and on occasion a leading activity within literary criticism extends far beyond the range of this book; but I hope the case for it is made here.

The first three chapters offer three specific encounters with three kinds of textual work and with the problems and clues they present: the cultural reparation served by Chapman's edition of the novels; the fractured and partisan record of a life provided by family biography; and the acts of writing performed by the manuscript hand. Each poses and attempts to address a particular question. In the case of Chapter 1 the basic question might be put like this: how good is the authoritative Chapman edition of Austen; but equally what are the values implicit in asking the question? In Chapter 2 I consider the resistant and repetitive material of the Austen biography industry. Jane Austen's enduring appeal as the subject for biography both defies and is fuelled by the paucity of the evidence; but what is the nature of the evidence, how has it been constructed and in response to what criteria, and in what sense might it be useful to think of the biographer as a textual critic? In particular, how might thinking about the textual origins of a life help dispel the notion that a life has an authentic text? Chapter 3 examines the evidence of the working manuscripts—the fragment of *The Watsons*, the cancelled ending to *Persuasion*, and the unfinished *Sanditon*—as challenges to our image of a writer constituted exclusively through print. The striking fact about the manuscripts is that they exist only for material Austen did not see through to publication; in the case of the later, working manuscripts there is the possibility that they will give us access to a creative process—the processes of writing and revision—otherwise denied us. What does the evidence of the working drafts suggest about Austen's practices as a writer? about the way her writing evolved and even about the form in which her manuscripts may have gone to press? about the difference between text in its manuscript and print states?

Chapters 4, 5, and 6 return to, resituate, and retextualize these initial encounters with edited text, biographical record, and acts of writing. The picture of Austen's writing life that emerges in Chapter 4 compares the difference between the familial context of her early writing up to the time she left Steventon in 1801 and what I suggest was the more private and uncounselled manner in which the mature novels took shape; it then considers how after her death the family re-annexed this private space through copyings, continuations, and living re-enactments of the fiction. Chapter 5 uses evidence of the working manuscripts and the probable early nineteenth-century publishing- and printing-house practices by which the novels were turned into print to reconsider the acts of intervention by which the Chapman edition was established. Here close attention to the 1814, first-edition text of *Mansfield Park*, which Chapman criticized as the 'worst printed' of her novels, leads to precise reflections on the importance of voice to meaning in Austen's writings and attempts to make the case for a fresh reading of the novels, in which an aural and oral (heard and spoken) element in the text, removed by well-meaning editorial attempts to present it in the approved form for written language, is shown to be essential. Finally, Chapter 6 sets side by side two extremes in the history of textual dissemination in the twentieth century: by the theorizing and practice of the one, scholarly editing, Austen's reputation and texts were fixed and accorded the highest cultural status; by the other, their adaptation for screen, they have been exuberantly unfixed and proved amenable to our most fickle contemporary imaginings.

While screen adaptation affirms the availability of Jane Austen's material social art to visual comprehension and pleasure, what has led me on through the book's argument has been an interest in sound and voice—a conviction that the voices talking around her in the private and public scenes of life became the voices talking inside her head that she couldn't stop herself from listening to; and that voices heard and the rhythms of conversation structure her mature novels as audio-experiences. There are important differences between our sense of texts as primarily visual or auditory forms, made starkly evident in cinema, where what we hear depends so much on what we see. The history of printed text, too, has been a steady suppression of the acoustic trace. What prompted my interest in Austen biography was the fact that her niece Anna Lefroy thought it worth recording on paper her memory of her grandfather, Jane's father, enquiring of Jane and Cassandra's whereabouts. 'I thought it so odd', Anna wrote, 'to hear Grandpapa speak of them as "the Girls". "Where are the Girls?" "Are the Girls gone out?"' In Jane Austen's case we miss something vital in her textual transmission if we lose those visual forms which keep her auditory depths alive.

Kathryn Sutherland
St Anne's College
Oxford

Acknowledgements

My work for this book has involved many debts of gratitude and it is a pleasure to acknowledge them here. A generous grant of a year's paid leave in 2003–4, funded by HEFCE and the Special Paid Leave Scheme of the University of Oxford, allowed me the time to complete the research and do much of the writing. I am grateful to the Humanities Division at Oxford for the award and to John Barnard, who cheerfully and expertly took up my teaching in the English Faculty Graduate School during my absence.

Projects pursued intensely, as this has been, attract new friendships and tax old ones. Once again Deirdre Le Faye shared with me her Jane Austen scholarship, responding with wonderful speed and kindness to my least enquiry. I could scarcely have contemplated this study without the assistance of David Gilson's monumental *Bibliography of Jane Austen* (corrected edition, 1997). It has been my constant companion for the past four years, while David himself has been generous and punctilious in offering advice. Claire Lamont and Jim McLaverty read a large part of the manuscript in first draft, providing detailed comment, encouragement, and much more. Claire began me thinking critically about Jane Austen's texts when, as textual adviser to the new Penguin Edition (1995–8), she argued the case for the importance of their earliest printed states. I am more grateful to Jim than he probably realizes for discussion over the years and for his attempts to clarify my ideas and toughen up my arguments. I hope he has saved me from some errors; if he hasn't, it isn't his fault. I have been inspired and encouraged by conversations with and timely interventions from Lyndall Gordon, Jocelyn Harris, Tom Keymer, Ann Pasternak Slater, and Peter Sabor. Geneviève Baudon Adams read more of the manuscript than a Frenchwoman, sceptical of Jane Austen's appeal, should have been required to do, and my sister Moira Wardhaugh listened in public and private and as always gave me support.

Parts of Chapters 2 and 3 were delivered as talks to the Jane Austen Society, in London and at Chawton, while the short coda to Chapter 2, on portraits of Jane Austen, began life as a paper given at the University of Magdeburg. My thanks to Brian Southam and members of the Jane Austen Society for a reception equally sympathetic and acute; and in Magdeburg to Bernd-Peter

Lange, Helgard Lange, Reini Wandel, and Hans Werner Breunig for much fun, hospitality, and comradeship. I hope I have profited from the discussions after all three occasions, not least in the proof they offered of the wide divergence in the reception lives of texts.

I am grateful to the staff of the following institutions: the Bodleian Library, Oxford; the English Faculty Library, Oxford; the Manuscript Room, the British Library; the Hampshire Record Office, Winchester; the Heinz Archive, the National Portrait Gallery; and the Pierpont Morgan Library, New York. I owe particular thanks to Tom Carpenter of the Jane Austen Memorial Trust, Chawton; to Peter Jones, Fellow and Librarian, and Rosalind Moad of the Archive Centre, King's College, Cambridge; to Tom McCullough of the Oxford University Press Archive; to Christine Nelson, Curator of Literary and Historical Manuscripts, the Pierpont Morgan Library; to Anselm Nye, Archivist, Queen Mary and Westfield College, University of London; and to David Smith, Alison Corley, and Emma Sherratt, St Anne's College Library, Oxford. For permission to quote from manuscripts I should like to thank the following: the Archive Department of the Hampshire Record Office for the Austen-Leigh Papers; the Bodleian Library, University of Oxford, and Mr David Chapman for R. W. Chapman's working notes and correspondence; the Bodleian Library, University of Oxford, for Catherine Hubback's correspondence; the Keeper of Manuscripts at the British Library for the holograph manuscript of the two chapters of *Persuasion*; the Provost and Scholars of King's College, Cambridge, for the holograph manuscript of *Sanditon*; Sir Peter Michael and Queen Mary and Westfield College, University of London, for the holograph manuscript of *The Watsons*; the National Portrait Gallery for the Chapman–Hake correspondence; Oxford University Press and Mr David Chapman for correspondence relating to the publication of Jane Austen's novels.

A version of Chapter 2, Section ii, first appeared in the Introduction to James Edward Austen-Leigh, *A Memoir of Jane Austen and Other Family Recollections* (Oxford: Oxford University Press, 2002); a shorter version of Chapter 5 appeared as 'Speaking Commas/Reading Commas: Punctuating *Mansfield Park*', in *TEXT: An Interdisciplinary Annual of Textual Studies*, 12, ed. W. Speed Hill and Edward M. Burns (Ann Arbor: University of Michigan Press, 2000). My thanks in both cases for permission to reuse material.

Hearing is the sense most favoured by attention; it holds the frontier, so to speak, at the point where seeing fails.

Paul Valéry, *Analecta*

There is Jane Austen, thumbed, scored, annotated, magnified, living almost within the memory of man, and yet as inscrutable in her small way as Shakespeare in his vast one.

Virginia Woolf, *Personalities*

Contents

List of Illustrations

Abbreviations

Austen Papers	R. A. Austen-Leigh, (ed.), *Austen Papers, 1704–1856* (London: privately printed by Spottiswoode, Ballantyne and Co., 1942)
Family Record	Deirdre Le Faye, *Jane Austen: A Family Record* (Cambridge: Cambridge University Press, 2004)
Family Record (1989)	*Jane Austen: A Family Record*, revised and enlarged by Deirdre Le Faye (London: British Library, 1989)
Gilson	David Gilson, *A Bibliography of Jane Austen* (1982; corrected edn., Winchester: St Paul's Bibliographies, 1997). Reference to individual items in Gilson's bibliography will be according to their numbered entries (eg., Gilson E150)
Jane Austen's Letters	*Jane Austen's Letters*, ed. Deirdre Le Faye, 3rd edn. (Oxford: Oxford University Press, 1995)
Life and Letters (1913)	William Austen-Leigh and Richard Arthur Austen-Leigh, *Jane Austen: Her Life and Letters. A Family Record* (London: Smith, Elder, and Co., 1913)
Memoir	*A Memoir of Jane Austen and Other Family Recollections*, ed. Kathryn Sutherland (Oxford: Oxford University Press, 2002)
Memoir (1870)	J. E. Austen-Leigh, *A Memoir of Jane Austen* (London: Richard Bentley, 1870).
Memoir (1871)	J. E. Austen-Leigh, *A Memoir of Jane Austen, to which is added Lady Susan and Fragments of Two Other Unfinished Tales by Miss Austen*, 2nd edn. (London: Richard Bentley & Son, 1871)
Minor Works	*Minor Works, The Works of Jane Austen*, Vol. 6, ed. R. W. Chapman (1954), revised by B. C. Southam (Oxford: Oxford University Press, 1969)

A Note to the Reader on Quotations

Because my concern is with textual difference I quote at different stages of my argument from different editions of Jane Austen's novels. Unless otherwise stated, where I quote from R. W. Chapman's edition it is by page from the following reprint:

The Novels of Jane Austen, ed. R. W. Chapman, 'third edition' (1932–4), revised by Mary Lascelles, 5 vols. (Oxford: Oxford University Press, 1965–6) (abbreviated as, for example, *Emma*, ed., Chapman, 235)

Finally, in the manuscript transcriptions in Chapter 3 I use the following conventions:

| denotes the end of a manuscript line;
|| denotes the end of a manuscript page;
~~strikethrough~~ denotes words or characters erased;
^ denotes insertions above the manuscript line.

1

The Making of England's Jane

'Everybody's dear Jane'

The publication in 1870 of James Edward Austen-Leigh's biographical *Memoir* of his aunt Jane Austen has long been recognized as altering her fortunes for ever—from a relatively select coterie writer, a critic's and a novelist's novelist, to a widely esteemed cultural asset, everybody's quintessential English novelist. In the space of the next two years, more periodical essays were given over to appreciations of her art than had appeared in the whole period since her death in 1817. Over the next three decades, and in the wake of Austen-Leigh's paradoxical public acclamation of one whose talents 'did not . . . in any degree pierce through the obscurity of her domestic retirement', a permanent revolution was effected in Jane Austen's reputation, the nature and consequences of which still affect us. It was led by the publisher Richard Bentley, who could make a case for his own proprietary interest having in 1832–3 acquired the copyrights of five of Austen's published novels from her brother and sister Henry and Cassandra Austen and of the remaining work, *Pride and Prejudice*, from the executors of the publisher Thomas Egerton.[1] After the posthumous appearance of *Northanger Abbey* and *Persuasion* in 1818 there had been no new English edition of any of the novels until Bentley included all six in his Standard Novels series in 1833, and he

[1] *Memoir*, 9. The copyrights of *Sense and Sensibility*, *Pride and Prejudice*, and *Mansfield Park* were for 28 years, expiring in 1839, 1841, and 1842, respectively; those of *Emma*, *Northanger Abbey*, and *Persuasion* were for 42 years, expiring in 1857 and 1860. For the publication history and critical reception of Austen's novels and for other bibliographical information, see *Jane Austen: The Critical Heritage*, ed. B. C. Southam, 2 vols. (London and New York: Routledge & Kegan Paul, 1968 and 1987), esp. ii. 58–103; and Gilson.

continued to reprint at intervals thereafter. Small cloth-bound books, these were the first single-volume editions of the novels (*Northanger Abbey* and *Persuasion* appearing together) and also the first English illustrated editions, though at this stage illustrations were confined to a modest steel-engraved frontispiece and a second title-page with engraved vignette. In 1870, almost

1. Engraved frontispiece to *Northanger Abbey* in Bentley's Standard Novels series, 1833. By kind permission of the English Faculty Library, Oxford University.

simultaneously with his publication of the Austen-Leigh *Memoir*, Bentley reissued the novels as numbers 21–5 in his 'Favourite Novels' series, to be superseded in 1882 by the deluxe Steventon Edition in six volumes. The first that might properly be called a collected edition of Jane Austen's works, the Steventon Edition included alongside the six finished novels the second, 1871 edition of the *Memoir*, which Austen-Leigh had much enlarged with previously unseen primary materials (*Lady Susan*, *The Watsons*, the cancelled chapter of *Persuasion*, and a brief summary of *Sanditon*).

The last complete edition from the Bentley house, and the first to issue the novels as a discrete set in the order of their earliest publication, the Steventon Edition is a landmark in Austen's nineteenth-century representation. It was rounded off in 1884 by the two-volume *Letters of Jane Austen*, edited by her great-nephew Edward, Lord Brabourne, son of her 'favourite' niece Fanny Knight. Apparently only waiting for his mother's death, which occurred in 1882, Brabourne had wasted no time in preparing for the press the letters he inherited from her. Brabourne marks a change in the family stewardship of Austen's reputation; what separates his edition from Austen-Leigh's pious and protective *Memoir* of only fourteen years previously is his strong sense of his great-aunt as a marketable property. The letters are an 'opportunity'; 'no one now living can, I think, have any possible just cause of annoyance at their publication, whilst, if I judge rightly, the public never took a deeper or more lively interest in all that concerns Jane Austen than at the present moment.'[2] Indicative of the 'opportunity' was the prefatory dedication to Queen Victoria. Coincidentally perhaps, but driving deeper the sense of Austen's rising commercial value, another great-nephew, Cholmeley Austen-Leigh, James Edward's son, was now a partner in Spottiswoode and Co., Bentley's printers. Of the ninety-six letters in Brabourne's collection (all but two Jane's) the bulk were from Jane Austen to her sister Cassandra, left to Fanny Knight on Cassandra's death in 1845, but which Fanny claimed to have lost when her Austen-Leigh cousin came looking for material for his *Memoir*. Inevitably, Austen-Leigh believed more family papers were lost or destroyed than turned out over the next decade to be the case.[3] Comprising censored glimpses of the juvenilia, complete and unfinished fictions, letters, personal recollections, and illustrative commentary, by 1884 Bentley's list held the substance of

[2] *Letters of Jane Austen*, ed. Edward, Lord Brabourne, 2 vols. (London: Richard Bentley & Son, 1884), i. xi–xii.

[3] *Memoir*, 132; and *Letters of Jane Austen*, ed. Brabourne, i. x. For the sense of family ownership of and rivalries over Jane Austen, see Ch. 2.

what there was to know of Jane Austen. Assembled in the Steventon Edition, biography endorsed fiction as in a mirror, both attesting to the apparent identity of an imaginary and real range, and a rootedness in a specific and known local territory—a particular segment of England. Summing up the impression left by Brabourne's *Letters*, the latest addition to the canon, the *Saturday Review* noted how their domestic preoccupations 'contain . . . the matter of the novels in solution'.[4]

It is likely that the more assiduous family and commercial marketing of Austen from the 1880s was helped by the opportune demise of the three-decker, usually placed in this decade, and the mounting appeal of the short novel. An index of her growing popularity can be found in the rash of cheap and more exclusive issues of the novels singly and in sets. As early as 1849 *Sense and Sensibility* and *Pride and Prejudice* had appeared in Routledge's Railway Library series in covers designed to imitate and usurp the Belfast publishers Simms and McIntyre's popular Parlour Library, with their distinctive green glazed boards, front board woodcut design, and brown lettering, a style later known as yellowback. Rival marketing through the later nineteenth century was to be a measure of Austen's rising fortunes, much as the competitive packaging and release of paperback tie-ins (from World's Classics, Penguin, Everyman, Broadview, etc.) has characterized her recent post-film appeal.

At the cheap end of the market Routledge's Sixpenny Novels issued *Sense and Sensibility* (1884) in double columns in buff paper covers, the front emblazoned with a lurid woodcut illustration showing Willoughby raising Marianne Dashwood from the ground; not only was each novel to be had for sixpence, they could also be traded for soap wrappers. The next year *Mansfield Park* appeared in triple columns of dense print with eight crude engravings in Volume 4 of Dicks's large format English Library of Standard Works, released in twenty-six weekly parts (*Mansfield Park* being Numbers 11–22).[5] Unlikely though it may seem, there were abridged versions and accessible summaries of already slim, accessible novels, play-text adaptations, and of course school editions. In 'condensing' the novels in 1880, Sarah Tytler

[4] *Saturday Review*, 15 November 1884, in *Critical Heritage*, ii. 41.

[5] For bibliographical details of the various cheap reprintings, see Gilson E10; E12; E13; E15–17; E23; E25; E66; E68–69. K. E. Attar, 'Jane Austen at King's College, Cambridge', *The Book Collector*, 51 (2002), 197–221, contains descriptions and illustrations of early reprints, based in part on items in Gilson's personal collection of Austen editions, now in process of finding a home at King's College. R. W. Chapman, *Jane Austen: A Critical Bibliography*, 2nd edn. (Oxford: Clarendon Press, 1955), 57, records that Routledge's Sixpenny Novels could be traded for soap wrappers.

2. *Sense and Sensibility*, 1851, a Railway Library yellowback, cover illustration. By kind permission of the Provost and Scholars of King's College, Cambridge University.

[Henrietta Keddie] sought to win 'an over-wrought, and in some respects over-read, generation of young people . . . apt to be wearied by the slightest diffuseness'; though, as she assured her febrile clientele, 'Wherever it has been possible . . . I have used the author's own words, as incomparably the best for the characters and situations.' Thus tailored, all six novels, plus biography and some critical elucidation of 'unrivalled piece[s] of art', fitted into a single volume, coming in at under 400 pages.[6]

At the lavish end of the spectrum the prettified Macmillan complete edition (Illustrated Standard Novels, Nos. 6–10, 1895–7), profusely illustrated by Hugh Thomson, the leading illustrator of the day, introduced a further popular and persistent dimension: sustained pictorial expression. This highly successful venture grew from a trade war with the publisher George Allen, who had issued *Pride and Prejudice* in 1894 in the stolen livery of Macmillan's Peacock Series, at the same time poaching Thomson for the illustrations. It is all too easy to dismiss Thomson's sentimental designs as wholly irrelevant to Austen's art; E. M. Forster called him 'the lamentable Hugh Thompson [*sic*]', whose illustrations 'illustrate nothing except the obscurity of the artist'. They are, on the contrary, an early example of the skilful visual packaging, through costume and setting, which has continued to serve so effectively in creating our easy familiarity with the details of what we take to be Austen's world. In this case, it is a whimsical, chocolate-box idyll, reflecting a nostalgia for a lost pre-industrialized society, a style which came to be known in the trade as the Cranford school of illustration, after Thomson and Macmillan's success with *Cranford* in 1891. Sneer though purists may at Thomson's coy miniatures (he was illustrating the *Pears' Christmas Annual* at the same time) and at the latitude he allowed himself—cherubs and children, conspicuously lacking from the text of Austen's narratives, peep out from initial letters; there's even a drawing in *Northanger Abbey* of a cavalry charge—they spoke to a contemporary taste as surely as do the brasher images of smouldering heroes and material girls on the make of the 1990s Austen film industry. The artful packaging of the past as amenable to our contemporary preoccupations is integral to consumer appeal in each case.

A notable feature of the major 1890s' illustrators (Thomson, the Brock brothers, and Chris [Christiana] Hammond) was their representation of the Regency period-details of the novels as part of an idealized historical time just out of reach. Recent technical innovation favoured their effects: line drawings, printed within the text, provided a form of illustration which invites plentiful and intimate visualization; and the rapid exchange of word for image, whereby illustrative vignettes interrupt the flow of the sentence, invites a competitive kind of reading, spatial rather than temporal. 'You have revivified the gently humorous Jane, and given her a new lease of life',

[6] Sarah Tytler [Henrietta Keddie], *Jane Austen and her Works* (London, Paris, and New York: Cassell, Petter, Galpin and Co., 1880), vii.

CRANFORD

Chapter I.

Our Society

IN the first place, Cranford is in possession of the Amazons; all the holders of houses, above a certain rent, are women. If a married couple come to settle in the town, somehow the gentleman disappears; he is either fairly frightened to death by being the only man in the Cranford evening parties, or he is accounted for by being with his regiment, his ship, or closely engaged in business all the week in the great neighbouring commercial town of Drumble, distant only twenty miles on a railroad.

B

3. Elizabeth Gaskell, *Cranford*, illustrated by Hugh Thomson, 1891, a style which became known as 'Cranfordization'. By kind permission of St Anne's College, Oxford University.

CHAPTER XXIV.

ISS BINGLEY'S letter arrived, and put an end to doubt. The very first sentence conveyed the assurance of their being all settled in London for the winter, and concluded with her brother's regret at not having had time to pay his respects to his friends in Hertfordshire before he left the country.

Hope was over, entirely over; and when Jane could attend to the rest of the letter, she found little, except the professed affection of the writer, that could give her any comfort. Miss Darcy's praise occupied the chief of it. Her many attractions were again dwelt on; and Caroline boasted joyfully of their increasing intimacy, and ventured to predict the accomplishment of the wishes which had been unfolded in her former letter. She wrote also with great pleasure of her brother's being an inmate of Mr. Darcy's house, and mentioned with raptures some plans of the latter with regard to new furniture.

4. *Pride and Prejudice*, with a Preface by George Saintsbury and illustrations by Hugh Thomson, 1894; the 'Cranfordized' version. By kind permission of the English Faculty Library, Oxford University.

Thomson's friend Joseph Grego assured him. In a sense, the novels were showcases for Thomson's art. As his fulsome prefatory dedications suggest, these were his books, not Austen's; and this is how they came to be known, as the 'Hugh Thomson books'. A modern equivalent might be the culture-drenched visual magnificence of the Merchant Ivory film appropriations of Forster's own novels, where period display provides an expressive indicator of 1980s and 1990s notions of heritage rather more directly than it represents Forster's socially critical vision. Compare the equally dismissive recent criticism of 'popular anglophilic adaptations of anglophobic Forster novels'.[7] To *Pride and Prejudice* alone, before he was won back to the Macmillan stable, Thomson contributed 160 line drawings (a mix of illustrations in the text, headpieces, tailpieces, ornamental initials); within a year of publication over 11,600 British copies were sold, totalling more than the lifetime sales of all Austen's novels put together.[8]

Fortuitously or not, it was in the preface to Allen and Thomson's *Pride and Prejudice* that George Saintsbury appears to have coined the term 'Janeites' to describe the quality of 'personal love' as opposed to mere conventional admiration ('loving by allowance') which now characterized the growing band of Jane Austen devotees and divided them from the sceptics. Announcing himself as writing from within 'the sect—fairly large and yet unusually choice—of Austenians or Janites' (Saintsbury's preferred spelling), he promptly declared his readiness 'to live with and to marry' Elizabeth Bennet.[9] The unconditional assent to what are agreed to be the terms of Austen's world as itself the perfection of our own sets the Janeite apart. In 1902 in her pioneering and now underrated work of Janeite critical biography, Constance

[7] For bibliographical details and the roles of Hugh Thomson and Charles Brock in the Allen and Macmillan illustrated reprintings, see Gilson E78; E82; E86; E88; E89; and M. H. Spielmann and Walter Jerrold, *Hugh Thomson: His Art, his Letters, his Humour, and his Charm* (London: A. and C. Black, 1931), 85–120. On Thomson, E. M. Forster, *Abinger Harvest* (1936; Harmondsworth, Middx.: Penguin, 1967), 164; and James N. Loehlin, on the Merchant Ivory adaptations of Forster, quoted in John Wiltshire, *Recreating Jane Austen* (Cambridge: Cambridge University Press, 2001), 134–5.

[8] A fair idea of the lifetime publication figures for Austen's novels can be estimated from those checked against publishers' records provided in Jan Fergus, *Jane Austen: A Literary Life* (Basingstoke and London: Macmillan, 1991).

[9] *Pride and Prejudice*, with a preface by George Saintsbury and illustrations by Hugh Thomson (London: George Allen, 1894), ix and xxiii; the *OED* dates the word 'Janeite' to Saintsbury's *History of Nineteenth-Century Literature* of 1896, two years later. For an overview of the cultural significance of the Janeite/anti-Janeite controversy, see B. C. Southam, 'Janeites and Anti-Janeites', in *The Jane Austen Handbook*, ed. J. David Grey (London: Athlone Press, 1986), 237–43; and Lorraine Hanaway's short lexical study, '"Janeite at 100"', *Persuasions*, 16 (1994), 28–9. For a searching and trenchant examination of the Janeite controversy and its implications for the evolution of Austen criticism in the twentieth century, see Claudia L. Johnson, 'Austen Cults and Cultures', in *The Cambridge Companion to Jane Austen*, ed. Edward Copeland and Juliet McMaster (Cambridge: Cambridge University Press, 1997), 211–26.

Hill described how Mary Russell Mitford, Austen's near-contemporary, lived during her visit to Bath 'far more in the company of Jane Austen's characters than in that of the actual celebrities of the place and found them "much the more real of the two"'.[10] '[A]rmed with pen and pencil', and with Brabourne's *Letters* and Austen-Leigh's *Memoir* as their trusted Baedekers, Constance Hill and her sister Ellen had made their way through the byways of Hampshire in search of evidence of what they called 'Austen-land'. Places, people, rural views, buildings, family connections, manuscripts, fragments of Jane's needlework were ferreted out and logged in notes or sketches; even the design Hill chose for the binding of her volume reproduced 'embroidery upon a muslin scarf worked in satin-stitch' by Austen. The Hill sisters were pilgrims, literary tourists, prepared to harangue and bully in their search for traces and relics of their favourite author; like the hay-loft above the stables of the Angel Inn in Basingstoke, which by dint of persistent enquiry they were permitted to explore and where, after experiencing 'a sudden ray of light and leading [divine guidance]', they made the discovery that here, despite bales of straw, uneven flooring, broken window-panes, and mouldering plaster, were the Assembly Rooms where Jane danced at Christmas 1798.[11]

The record the Hills published has lasting value for its extensive use of family papers and private recollections, and its documentation of places and people connected with Austen and, in 1902, soon to fade from living memory. Ellen Hill's line drawings alone contain a wealth of authentic interior and topographical detail, much of it now destroyed. At Steventon the sisters interviewed an old villager, a member of the Littlewart family, whose grandfather had served as coachman to Jane's brother James; his grandmother, they discovered, had been Jane's hairdresser and his mother was her goddaughter. The Hills themselves stand on the brink between two worlds: one the old world, Austen's world, of high hedgerows, narrow lanes, and slow communication, and the other the modern world of motor cars, aeroplanes, and radio; their own favoured method for getting about was 'a country chaise'. In voicing their preference for an English past whose locus is the ordered calm of the Austen novels, they register an appeal which a century later has lost none of its popular power. Heritage Austen sits quaintly but otherwise comfortably alongside our altogether savvier consumerist readings of her village econ-

[10] Constance Hill, *Jane Austen Her Homes and Her Friends* (1902; reissued London and New York: John Lane, 1904), 106.

[11] Ibid., 53–5; and see David Gilson's useful introduction to the recent reissue of Hill's book (Routledge/Thoemmes Press: London, 1995), v–ix.

omies, much as the four-wheel drive and the laptop computer share cultural space with Laura Ashley wallpaper and Past Times Regency-style nightgowns in the thatched cottage of many a home counties weekend retreat. At this earlier point in her reputation, Austen's greatness lay in perfected verisimilitude, in her capacity to deliver a world her readers recognized as undistorted by art yet unbetrayed by the inconstancies and brutality of life. By the kind of coincidence that simply registers timeliness, the six-volume Hampshire Edition of the same year, 1902, included for each novel a reality-to-fiction conversion index in the form of a map of the actual area in which the plot was set plus a plan of the imaginary neighbourhood. The topography of the 'real' county or town stretches across the front pastedown and end-paper of each volume, that of the particular environment of the characters fills the back pastedown and end-paper, and the novel traverses the space between.[12] In Edmund 'Clerihew' Bentley's comic summary of 1905: 'The novels of Jane Austen|Are the ones to get lost in.'[13]

In the same year, Henry James delivered his abrasive opinion that the recent Janeite enthusiasm was no spontaneous if belated tribute to neglected genius and the eventual triumph of good taste, but the cynical contrivance of a commercial publishing engine, aggressively promoting her work since 1870. Behind the phenomenon of her success, he argued, lay 'the special bookselling spirit; an eager, active, interfering force which has a great many confusions of apparent value, a great many wild and wandering estimates, to answer for'. With a high-toned assurance worthy of any latter-day cultural commentator he continued:

> For these distinctively mechanical and overdone reactions, of course, the critical spirit, even in its most relaxed mood, is not responsible. Responsible, rather, is the body of publishers, editors, illustrators, producers of the pleasant twaddle of magazines; who have found their 'dear', our dear, everybody's dear, Jane so infinitely to their material purpose, so amenable to pretty reproduction in every variety of what is called tasteful, and in what seemingly proves to be saleable, form.[14]

As patrician critic, James wished to separate the refined response, the true insight, from what he sensed to be the distorting indiscriminacy of Janeite gush and market tat. Early admirers, like George Henry Lewes in the 1850s,

[12] Gilson E98, *The Novels of Jane Austen*, maps drawn by Blanche MacManus, 6 vols. (London: R. Brimley Johnson, 1902).

[13] E. Clerihew [Edmund Clerihew Bentley], *Biography for Beginners*, illustrated by G. K. Chesterton (London: T. Werner Laurie,[1905/6]), unpaginated.

[14] Henry James, 'The Lesson of Balzac', *Atlantic Monthly* (1905), in *Critical Heritage*, ii. 230.

had with considerable assurance emphasized the exclusivity of those who appreciate her greatness: she is a writer who appeals only to the 'cultivated reader... to the small circle of cultivated minds'.[15] James in his turn is equivocal, deploring as unacceptably mediated and inauthentic the sentimental foundation of her new popularity, yet also inclined to disparage her as an artist bereft of a theory of fiction and accordingly as unconscious as her fans of the effects she achieved. For him, 'The key to Jane Austen's fortune with posterity has been in part the extraordinary grace of her facility, in part of her unconsciousness.' The fact is he finds no critical ground from which to enjoy her art because he assumes it cannot be shared ground; the widened basis of her appeal damns her. The distance between Lewes and James is crucial for registering the moment when accessibility becomes an obstacle to critical appreciation. But popularizer and 'Janite' though he was, George Saintsbury (from 1895 Professor of Rhetoric and English Literature at Edinburgh University) was no mere undiscriminating populist. To him we owe the corrective insight into Austen's Swiftian irony.[16] Other admirers included the Shakespeare critic A. C. Bradley, first occupant in 1882 of the chair of English and History at University College, Liverpool, later Professor of English at Glasgow, and in 1901 Professor of Poetry at Oxford. His 1911 English Association lecture on Jane Austen, first given at Newnham College, Cambridge, is generally considered as marking the beginnings of a serious academic criticism. Even so, it opens with the hope that his audience 'belong', as he does, 'to the faithful' and it continues with the confession (speaking again of Elizabeth Bennet) 'I was meant to fall in love with her, and I do.'[17]

It is difficult as twenty-first-century critical readers to revisit the ground of Austen's early canonization. Our own late twentieth-century defensiveness about certain kinds of evaluation, and specifically our sense that complex and competing claims *to* value must constantly adjust our aesthetic theories *of* value, has made us altogether less confident professional readers. Austen's establishment in Britain and America by mid-twentieth century as F. R. Leavis's 'inaugurator of the great tradition of the English novel' and Lionel Trilling's first to represent 'the specifically modern personality and the culture in which it had its being'[18] now appears bound up with instructional policy

[15] [George Henry Lewes] 'The Novels of Jane Austen', *Blackwood's Edinburgh Magazine* (1859), in *Critical Heritage*, i. 160.

[16] *Pride and Prejudice* (1894), xvi.

[17] A. C. Bradley, 'Jane Austen', *Essays and Studies*, 2 (1911), 28.

[18] F. R. Leavis, *The Great Tradition* (London: Chatto & Windus, 1948), 7; Lionel Trilling, *The Opposing Self: Nine Essays in Criticism* (London: Secker & Warburg, 1955), 228.

and practice which as post-1970s' academics we have found harder to defend. We hear in the early formulation of her classic status a set of rules for looking at literature and life that seem deplorably exclusive on grounds of class, race, and even gender. That status itself seems to smack of tokenism within the establishment: Austen the novelist for good girls and women-wary male scholars. The framework such rules set around text and reader alike assumes the workings of a consensus that appears partial and even offensive. The moral imagination is, we sense, more shaded; fiction itself is more intractable. Fiction is also, surely, generically more complex and impure than the constriction of its ideal scope to the operative laws of six slim novels implies. In Austen's raised status we have even detected a plot to sanitize represented female experience and the range of women's artistic experiment: it was, after all, on the feminine ground of Newnham College that Bradley equated the study of the novel with the charms of romantic love. In Austen's canonization, it would seem, too much is left out—too much literature, and too much life. But when we've argued thus far, what do we do—divest Jane Austen of her canonical status and replace her by a more intellectually restless and formally varied female contemporary (Maria Edgeworth or Joanna Baillie or Anna Barbauld?) or by a non-white, non-middle-class woman writer (presuming we can recover one)? No; we discover that, after all, her novels accommodate those readings we only seemed to miss (currently, to do with slavery, sexual deviance, and other critiques of political and family authority). That's what classics do: they license endless re-readings.[19]

Early critics like Bradley, however, appear to rise above the opportunistic and the fashionable, writing out of a secure belief in a select company of great works of literature embodying value which is directly equivalent to universal human worth. This is not a matter for abstruse investigation, the analysis of formal or structural features, of patterns of symbolism or significant textual silences, but a far simpler and harder thing: characters in books are knowable;

[19] See the thoughtful and provocative essay by Mitzi Myers, 'Shot from canons; or, Maria Edgeworth and the cultural consumption of the late eighteenth-century woman writer', in *The Consumption of Culture 1600–1800: Image, Object, Text*, ed. Ann Bermingham and John Brewer (London and New York: Routledge, 1995), 193–214. It is, however, instructive to set Myers's late-twentieth-century complaint at Edgeworth's neglect against George Henry Lewes's important 1859 reappraisal of Austen for *Blackwood's Magazine* (n. 15 above), where he contrasts Austen's relative neglect during and immediately after her lifetime with Edgeworth's high contemporary status. Drawing on Frank Kermode's earlier discussion of institutional controls on interpretation, Wendell V. Harris reminds us that a work's canonical status has little to do with the limitations imposed on its explication or 'correct' reading and much to do with the licensing of its 'interminable' re-reading ('Canonicity', *Proceedings of the Modern Language Association of America*, 106 (1991), 110–21).

and hardest of all, our pleasure in literature is intimately bound up with how we feel about them. It is in the degree to which we can get alongside fictional characters as fellow human beings that we register the merit of the work itself. These are the terms in which Bradley in his Cambridge lecture defends his choice of *Pride and Prejudice* as Austen's best novel:

> Lastly, I will ask a question: Is there anybody in *Mansfield Park* for whom we care much, not as a study, but as a person? I put this as a question, because undoubtedly there is one person, Fanny Price, for whom Jane Austen *means* us to care a great deal. 'My Fanny' she calls her, in the novel itself, and I do not think any other person in her works receives such a compliment. But—I speak for myself because I am speaking for many others—though I know, not only from this, but from the whole tone of the narrative, what I am expected to feel for Fanny, and though I try to feel it, I make but a moderate success of the business. I pity, approve, respect, and admire her, but I neither desire her company nor am greatly concerned about her destiny... In reading about Elizabeth Bennet, on the other hand, it is impossible for me to doubt either the author's intentions or my own feelings. I was meant to fall in love with her, and I do. Besides, I like her father and her elder sister better than any one in *Mansfield Park*, and I prefer both Darcy and Bingley to the Rev. Edmund Bertram. On this side, therefore, as well as on the side of humour, I must put *Pride and Prejudice* first: and this side, surely, is very important. It is a great merit, that is, in a story that, besides admiring the characters as studies, you care for some of them as persons, and care very much for at least one.[20]

Perhaps it is only in the levelling pleasure of film-text and image (not in print) that professional and popular readings again find this kind of common ground, though a nation-wide female appreciation of Colin Firth's wet-look Mr Darcy as presented in the 1995 BBC adaptation hardly matches up as a declaration of our shared human identity.

Bradley's lecture is a conspectus for a serious, systematic study. He discusses chronology and manuscript evidence, in particular emphasizing what continues to seem important to many critics, the significance for interpretation of the apparently distinct compositional phases of Austen's career—the late 1790s in Steventon and the 1810s in Chawton. And he at last moves the assessment of the individual novels to high critical ground with examinations of narrative point of view and comic design. His description of the resolution of *Emma* ('only by the benevolence of Fortune, who crowns her kindness by taking the heart of Harriet and flinging it, like a piece of putty, at her original

[20] Bradley, 'Jane Austen', 28–9.

lover') can still shock in its dismissive, cool rightness.[21] Bradley is no mere sentimentalist. The real contribution of his study, though, lies in his unevasive estimate of Austen's moral sense; it is in her genial and generous morality that we recognize Austen's greatness and the key to our own emotional response. Warming to his defence of Elizabeth Bennet against the charges of being impertinent and mercenary (how she famously alters towards Darcy only after she sees the extent of his estate), he spills over, uncharacteristically, from the main body of his text into long footnotes and finally quotation, only to break off, with the words, 'But what is the use of my quoting this? Anyone capable of seriously making the charge will take this for a confession of its truth.' His refutation is grounded in Elizabeth's very words in conversation with her sister Jane, from which he quotes: 'It has been coming on so gradually... but I believe I must date it from my first seeing his beautiful grounds at Pemberley.'[22] The choice of passage is interesting, not because it so obviously plays into the hands of the detractors, but because Bradley sees precisely that it need not. He finds in Austen what he finds in Shakespeare, a quality that M. R. Ridley, writing in the *Dictionary of National Biography*, described as Bradley's valuation of the 'supererogatory' ('Of all English critics of Shakespeare [Bradley] is the surest expositor of the "supererogatory" Shakespeare, of all that makes Shakespeare one of the supreme interpreters of the human soul').

Bradley's high valuation of literature is drawn from his adherence to the philosophy of Romantic idealism. In Austen's case, he concedes, the critic must allow for limitations: there is narrowness of range, which shows itself as a failure of sympathy towards those whom passion leads to betray the strictest social laws; he gives as example the severe treatment of Jane Fairfax's secret engagement. Bradley's charge is a serious one because it implies Austen's ultimate lack of moral courage and deep compassion. Few readers would disagree that Jane Fairfax is a missed opportunity, the kind of study in psychological complexity that Charlotte Brontë would never have passed over. But this conceded, the strength of Austen's novels, like Shakespeare's plays, is to be found, he argues, in characters who exhibit a habit of life beyond the function of the plot. Hence the conviction that there is more to Elizabeth Bennet, that her textual life is only a part of what is knowable: in evidence, he cites Austen's regular practice of extending her characters beyond the page. Though now long unfashionable as a professional protocol for

[21] Ibid., 22. [22] Ibid., 32, n.; and *Pride and Prejudice*, ed. Chapman, 373.

reading, 'knowing' or identifying with fictional characters remains highly important when it comes to explaining why we read novels for pleasure. For the generation of readers and critics after Bradley, it was through their capacity to efface all signs of their production that Austen's unself-reflexive characters and texts functioned as the highest art—the art that convinces of its prior reality and its power for stating truths. What Bradley did was to set on securer moral and aesthetic ground what James dismissed as Austen's 'unconsciousness' and popular appeal. Yet the basis of his case lies in the lecture's assumption of 'faith' in those who admire her: the faith that there is more than we see.

Janeites in the trenches

The years 1880–1914 saw the birth of the modernist movement in the arts and also the secure establishment of Jane Austen in her cult status. Although the 1914–18 war effectively marked the break between the nineteenth century and the modern world, modernism predated the break, while Austen, the novelist of traditional values, paradoxically survived it. More precisely, as the old order floundered, she, its representative, flourished. It was during these years and up to the Second World War that Austen came to represent specific qualities denoting cultural or national survival. Rejecting realism and logical exposition, modernism called into question old suppositions: the world is not a 'given' but itself depends on the kinds of assumptions we bring to its study. At a moment when art declared loudly its artefactual state, Austen's artless art was seized as evidence of a bygone integrity, when reality and the world described seemed one. It was as if Austen were motivated by a simple desire to reproduce the world visible around her, as if *her* world were *the* world, not dictated by subjective law and consciousness imposed, but based on community and with rules that could be recognized and learned. In this light, she appeared to give what modernism refused and in so doing to close the dangerously yawning gap between wishes and the reality of things. In reading Austen's novels reality appeared transformed by desire; at the same time, the naturalness of the novel form in her hands, its slightness as form, erected few barriers between the reader and its society, lost England or Austen-land.

From the far side of the 1914–18 war two interpretations, one popular and one scholarly, stand out as comments on Austen's wide curative integrity at this time, though in one only are the horrors of war openly exorcised: in

Kipling's extraordinary short story 'The Janeites', begun in 1922.[23] The other is Robert Chapman's Clarendon Press critical edition of *The Novels of Jane Austen*. Issued in 1923 in five substantial volumes, comprising text, extensive annotation, and commentary, Chapman's was the first, and remains the only, serious scholarly edition. I'll return to Chapman later. Appropriate to its subject-matter of closed societies, 'The Janeites' is a story within a story. Its frame story opens in a London Masonic Lodge in 1920 during the weekly clean and polish. In the organ-loft Brother Humberstall, a shell-shocked ex-artilleryman with 'the eyes of a bewildered retriever', is busy with wax and cloth, and as he works he slowly pieces together from his shattered recollections the story of his war-time induction into another secret society—those who read Jane Austen. Invalided out of fighting, he had returned to France and his old troop as acting mess-waiter under a private soldier named Macklin. One day on duty Humberstall and Macklin overhear a meal-time dispute among the officers as to whether Jane 'died barren' or left 'direct an' lawful prog'ny'. Macklin, who despite his non-commissioned rank, is 'a toff by birth', and in any case very drunk, loudly interrupts the discussion claiming 'She *did* leave lawful issue in the shape o' one son; an' 'is name was 'Enery James.'[24] (The bulk of the story is told through Humberstall, and Kipling puts his cockney dialect to work both as interpretative filter for his implied reading of Austen's novels and to deconstruct certain cultural assumptions about Austenian readers.) Macklin presses home his point with a short lecture, punctuated only by the noise of enemy gunfire, before collapsing dead-drunk. To Humberstall's amazement, not only is his insubordination left unpunished, Macklin is solicitously put to bed. Impressed by the licence it appears to give, Humberstall determines to be admitted into 'the Society of the Janeites' and pays Macklin to teach him. Macklin takes him through the degrees of initiation, from the First Degree (the password '*Tilniz an' trap-doors*') through the higher rite, consisting of learning by heart

[23] It was published in 1924, before being collected in a slightly different version in *Debits and Credits* (London: Macmillan, 1926), 143–76. Kipling follows his usual convention of framing the story with short lyric poems which contribute in a different, more enigmatic, register to the subject-matter expanded in the prose tale. For its appearance in *Debits and Credits* he added as conclusion the light poem, 'Jane's Marriage' (in which he speculates on Austen's ascent to Heaven and marriage to Captain Wentworth, one of her own characters) to complement the more sombre opening piece, a free translation of a Horace ode on the folly of war and the fall of civilizations. Kipling's story has not received much critical attention, yet it amply repays inspection, especially in the context of the coincident appearance of Chapman's monumental Austen edition. For an exception, see Claudia L. Johnson, 'Austen Cults and Cultures', in *The Cambridge Companion to Jane Austen*, 211–26.

[24] 'The Janeites', 153–4.

passages from *Persuasion*. In return, the mysteries of Jane bring Humberstall rewards: Turkish cigarettes, companionship ('It *was* a 'appy little Group'), and eventually his life. Wounded, 'the on'y Janeite left' after the trench is bombed, Humberstall is initially refused a stretcher place on an over-loaded hospital-train until his chance remark on the resemblance between a chattering nursing sister and the garrulous Miss Bates from *Emma* acts as a password. The matron, overhearing, questions him: ' "D'you know what you're sayin'?" she says, an' slings her bony arm round me to get me off the ground. " 'Course I do," I says, "an' if you knew Jane you'd know too." "That's enough," says she. "You're comin' on this train if I have to kill a Brigadier for you" '.[25] From the safety of the Lodge, Humberstall appears justified in his faith in Jane and in his conclusion:

> 'Well, as pore Macklin said, it's a very select Society, an' you've got to be a Janeite in your 'eart, or you won't have any success. An' yet he made *me* a Janeite! I read all her six books now for pleasure 'tween times in the shop; an' it brings it all back—down to the smell of the glue-paint on the screens. You take it from me, Brethren, there's no one to touch Jane when you're in a tight place. Gawd bless 'er, whoever she was.'[26]

In his classic study *The Great War and Modern Memory* Paul Fussell concerned himself with the literary frames within which the British experience of the First World War was first perceived and with the literary resources summoned at different stages during and after the war to register or mythologize its events as the 'crucial political, rhetorical, and artistic determinants on subsequent life'.[27] It is a starkly uninflected thesis, and if it now seems less total as an explanation of the twentieth-century imagination than it did in 1975 and the aftermath of Vietnam when it was first published, its logic remains nevertheless powerful. The general description Fussell applied to the phenomenon he explored was 'the Curious Literariness of Real Life'. The phrase is a way of suggesting the relationship between literature and life as an intersection: life is known through the symbolic structures we give it; and in 1914 those were found abundantly and most naturally in literature. In this account literature to life is a primary order equivalence rather than mere secondary explanation, and phrases like 'reading for life' assume literal significance. In particular, Fussell set the Great War in the context of a liberal faith in the moral and social powers of a national canon of Classical (Latin

[25] 'The Janeites', 172. [26] Ibid., 173.

[27] Paul Fussell, *The Great War and Modern Memory* (New York and London: Oxford University Press, 1975), ix.

and Greek) and English texts, represented on the one hand by the élite education of the old public schools and Oxbridge and on the other by the democratizing policies of the National Home Reading Union and recently introduced cheap reprint series like Oxford University Press's World's Classics and Dent's Everyman's Library. During the war, thanks to the efficiency of the Field Post Office, books were plentiful at the front, and the current issue of the *Times Literary Supplement* and *Punch*, or more bizarrely *Country Life*, might be read in the trenches. But an efficient postal service was only part of the explanation; no more than 70 miles separated the trenches from the heart of London, with its gentlemen's clubs, theatres, and restaurants. An officer might (and sometimes did) breakfast in his trench and dine at the Café Royal, while at Burwash in Sussex Kipling regularly heard the guns at Passchendaele, and Virginia Woolf recorded those heard from France in a short piece, 'Heard on the Downs', for *The Times* in August 1916. The nearness of home to the trenches was both a terrible absurdity and the real occasion for an exaggerated affectation of normality, which made the experience of soldiering in the Great War unique. Proximity gave rise to and sustained the habit of irony, amounting post-1914 to a virtual generic recalibration in the arts, that measured the short yet immense distance between these incongruous, clashing realities.

We tend to feel we recognize this irony as our own cultural response, as the voice of the modern rejecting the bankrupt orthodoxies of former values; but we all too easily misunderstand it as we look back from the far side of a different kind of exile—the exile of our diminished literacy, brought on by changes in the technologies of communication and the dramatic shift in our belief in the power of literary language as communication. Fussell paints a far different picture, in which the 'literariness of real life' is not in doubt. In the trenches it was affirmed in a variety of ways. The scholarly Geoffrey Keynes, Austen's future bibliographer, regularly received antiquarian booksellers' catalogues in his dug-out at Ypres, buying items by return of post; Herbert Read corrected proofs between raids; Vivian de Sola Pinto wrote home asking his father to send 'an indelible pencil, candles, and the works of Petronius in the Loeb edition'. The deformation and caustic revision of traditional genres and themes by trench poets Wilfred Owen, Edmund Blunden, and Edgell Rickword are better documented. Of their experiments, Fussell concludes, with forgivable exaggeration, 'the *Oxford Book of English Verse* presides over the Great War'.[28] Theirs was not a rejection of the literary *per se* nor even of a

[28] Ibid., 67 and 159; and Geoffrey Keynes Kt., *The Gates of Memory* (Oxford: Clarendon Press, 1981), 172.

national literature, but its reclamation within a less complacent context. The fertile wit of the compilers of the *Wipers Times* makes it clear that similarly vigorous counter-reading and -writing was also practised across a wide range. Corruptions and parodies pay their own tributes that enrich the national fund. A face-off between two languages, two kinds of knowing, irony was also a strange reconfiguration, a way of using the old to see the new.

In *Debits and Credits* Kipling collected several studies of war. The Masonic Lodge, 'Faith and Works No. 5837 E.C.', which figures in 'The Janeites', also provides the scene for 'A Madonna of the Trenches', 'A Friend of the Family', and the earlier wartime tale 'In the Interests of the Brethren'. To Kipling, a lifelong mason, freemasonry offered a set of social ideals based in male self-sufficiency, shared knowledge, and comradeship, where special jargon and rituals not only confer power—the power of a secret mastered and shared—but imply unity and sense, a world that makes sense, obeys rules, and protects those inside it. An Imperial War Graves Commissioner and a founder member of two lodges connected with the Commission, Kipling viewed the common soldiers as another kind of initiates, with their own peculiar loyalties, shared secrets and language, and their special bond of suffering. In 'The Janeites' he presents three closed societies, all of them homo-social; and we move from the outermost, the masons, to the most exclusive, the Janeites, by means of the intense experience of soldiering in the Great War. In the framing scene, only the (non-masonic) reader is discomforted by the lack of a shared language, but as the story shifts from talk of masonic regalia to wartime campaigns, a rift opens between the narrator and his two companions in the organ-loft, both seasoned troopers who have seen and survived action. The narrator (Kipling?), we sense from his silence, has not. Finally, the ex-gunner Humberstall alone is left to represent the most exclusive group, the happy company of Janeites.

Secret societies, whether masons, soldiers, or Janeites, share ways of making sense of the world, but they share no specific common ground; on the contrary, the exclusive particularity of the details of their mental landscapes will divide them. It is, however, the very fact that the mysteries of Jane, as Macklin communicates them, observe the laws of a known reality, beyond the esoteric dealings of army or lodge, that permits them to recover into meaning the meaninglessness of war itself. As Humberstall explains it: 'Jane wasn't so very 'ard—not the way Macklin used to put 'er... But, as I was sayin', what beat me was there was nothin' *to* 'em nor *in* 'em. Nothin' at all, believe me... I mean that 'er characters was no *use*! They was only just like people you run across any day.'[29] Unlike the defamiliarization worked by masonic or army ritual upon the everyday, Jane's power lies in her familiarity; whether recognized or not, she is already part of a wider cultural system with a common set of conventions. Assembled, therefore, within a Janeite grammar the dislocated and dislocating events of war can be made to yield meaning by bearing a family resemblance to what is known. To continue the analogy, the language of Jane is appropriately thought of as a specialized dialect but one that works only semi-autonomously within the larger linguistic scheme. Its characteristics are combinative and metonymic, ordering and making sense of the real in other parts of the shared cultural system, even (as in the example of war) at its outermost (least real, because least imaginable) limits. Its function (and the function of literature at this time) was thus to provide a language adequate to the task of imagining and reassimilating the real. The savage distortion that disturbs and redistributes the known range of literary reference in a poem by Owen or Rickword relies on the same linguistic robustness.

What characterizes the Janeites' reading of Austen and war is precisely its grounding in the facts of their lives beyond the dug-out. Like all realities, theirs is partial and skewed, and no less real for that. Theirs is a masculine world suspicious of women, sexually insecure, and vaguely homo-erotic. Among the officers, Major Hammick is a divorce-court lawyer in civilian life and Captain Mosse runs a private detective agency ('Wives watched while you wait'). Humberstall himself is an emasculated figure; a gentle giant and a virgin, he is a hairdresser in his mother's business. Invalided out he re-enlisted in his old troop in order to escape his family of women; but by the time of the story, his nerves are so damaged that he has little independence. All the Janeites are in service to negative or otherwise threatening definitions of women and domesticity. '[Jane] was the only woman I ever 'eard 'em say a good word for,' Humberstall observes.[30] Within the dug-out, despite discomfort and danger, they create as Janeites an alternative kinship group, closer to club or college fellowship than family, which they celebrate in the collegial masculine pleasures of cigarettes and port. Humberstall's chief happiness is being under the camouflage-screens with their smell of glue-paint and their 'pantomime leaves'. It is the closed community of this parody pastoral that he misses and that re-reading the novels after the war allows him to recapture. His act of chalking the names of Austen characters on the motley array of guns, 'not much more good than scrap-iron that late in the

[29] 'The Janeites', 158–9. [30] Ibid., 152.

war',[31] is a critical addition to the meaning of the novels strengthening their status as shared reality. Re-named 'Reverend Collins', 'General Tilney', and 'The Lady Catherine De Bugg' (the implications of the misspelling of 'De Bourgh' are obvious), the company's superannuated artillery seems less dangerously and more humorously inadequate; within the symbolic structure of their eccentric universe, the waste and brutality is made to make sense.

It is clear that the Janeites perform a particular style of reading which to current taste and training appears symptomatic and confined to the textual margins. Yet at the same time they are engaged in a still recognizable cultural practice. When Humberstall confesses to having named the guns, Macklin counters: 'You done nobly... You're bringin' forth abundant fruit, like a good Janeite.'[32] The story began with debate over Austen's own fruitfulness, her place in a literary tradition. What is at issue now is the role of interpretation in the production of meaning and survival of culture. The consistent illusion of life that the novels offer the Janeites is made up of period details and memorable phrases ('dances an' card-parties an' picnics, and their young blokes goin' off to London on 'orseback for 'air-cuts an' shaves'); above all, it consists in discovering resemblances—especially between fictional and real characters and situations—and piecing together a coherent social fabric from customs and sayings. Their readings are safe, empty of excitement, and totally devoid of reference to the 'war of ideas' sought by a more securely disruptive and sensational late twentieth-century taste. ''Twasn't as if there was anythin' *to* 'em... They weren't adventurous, nor smutty, nor what you'd call even interestin'.'[33] This is appropriate enough given the daily hell of their real circumstances. On the other hand, in registering the sympathy of detail between fiction and reality, the much-documented confinement of Austen's trivial vision is shown to serve a pertinent therapeutic purpose. As Humberstall's own contribution to Janeite signifying implies, the conditions of war provide an especially intense environment in which to imagine the real. It is only at the end, when the narrator, not a Janeite, blandly comments that he believes 'her books are full of match-making', that the inadequacy of his vague generalization after Humberstall's precise act of hermeneutic mastery is felt as more than the distance between two ways of reading. The experience of war has made Humberstall an expert reader of the kind Stanley Fish has described.[34] In him literature transcends the circumstances of its production

[31] 'The Janeites', 166. [32] Ibid., 162. [33] Ibid., 156–7.

[34] Most famously in *Is There a Text in this Class? The Authority of Interpretive Communities* (Cambridge, Mass.: Harvard University Press, 1980).

and addresses the psychological and affective requirements of the reader shaped by the conventions of his particular interpretative community.

R. W. Chapman restores civilization

Tastes change. In 1948 and after a second world war, C. S. Lewis pronounced 'The Janeites' 'hardly forgivable';[35] the modern reader finds it difficult to fix the story's tone. With R. W. Chapman's project for a complete, corrected edition of the novels the professionalization of Austen studies really began; with Kipling, we might wish to believe, its sentimental excesses and grosser transgressions were consigned to the arcane world of secret societies, or to amateur reading associations, far beyond the cold light of dispassionate enquiry. But the Chapman edition shares a cultural moment with Kipling's story and is not without its whiff of Janeism; looked at closely they bear the same stamp. For this reason, as long as Chapman's text remains the source of our critical readings, however contemporizing or canon exploding we think them, they will wear the contradictory mark of this legacy. In Kipling's story, Janeite practices represent a special kind of clubbable companionship to a few soldiers in a dug-out, even to the point of making the absurdities of war endurable. Chapman's edition assumes the same purpose, but on a magisterial scale.

On the outbreak of war Chapman was given a commission in the Royal Garrison Artillery and served in the Balkans, where in idle moments at his artillery position he collated the various texts of Boswell's *Journal of a Tour to the Hebrides* and Johnson's *Journey to the Western Islands of Scotland*. In the preface to his Oxford edition of 1924, he describes this wartime context, because, self-depreciatory tone notwithstanding, it is clearly important both to him and, as he sees it, to the purposes of his edition:

I had a camp behind *Smol Hill*, on the left bank of the Vardar, and a six-inch gun (Mark XI, a naval piece, on an improvised carriage; 'very rare in this state'), with which I made a demonstration in aid of the French and Greek armies, when they

[35] In 'Kipling's World', delivered to the English Association in 1948, Lewis wrote: 'Something so simple and ordinary as an enjoyment of Jane Austen's novels is turned into a pretext for one more secret society, and we have the hardly forgivable *Janeites*' (in *Literature and Life* (1948), i. 72–3). It is interesting to note that Lewis was persuaded to drop the charge from later reprintings of the essay, but only after Kipling's story had been explained to him. According to his editor, 'as Roger Lancelyn Green helped Lewis and me to see, the *point* of the story is how Jane Austen helped to save the sanity of men serving in the worst horrors of the trenches during the 1914–18 war.' (C. S. Lewis, *Selected Literary Essays*, ed. Walter Hooper (Cambridge: Cambridge University Press, 1969), 186 n. 1.)

stormed the heights beyond the river; I think in June... I had a hut made of sandbags, with a roof constructed of corrugated iron in layers, with large stones between... and here, in the long hot afternoons... a temporary gunner, in a khaki shirt and shorts, might have been found collating the three editions of the *Tour to the Hebrides*, or re-reading *A Journey to the Western Islands* in the hope of finding a corruption in the text. Ever and again, tiring of collation and emendation, of tepid tea and endless cigarettes, I would go outside to look at the stricken landscape—the parched, yellow hills and ravines, the brown coils of the big snaky river at my feet, the mountains in the blue distance; until the scorching wind, which always blew down that valley, sent me back to the Hebrides.[36]

By 1924, out of uniform and back in England, Chapman occupied his influential position of Secretary to the Delegates of the Clarendon Press, forming policy for a canon of English texts; in effect, he had the powers of a publisher. As in 'The Janeites', so in the preface to the Johnson–Boswell edition, the experience of war makes of reading a territorial act; in Chapman's case, one whose legitimacy is less provincial, bound rather to grand concepts of history and culture. It is bound to Chapman's sense, which is both geographical and psychological, that he stands at his post in Macedonia at the outermost limits of an inheritance and that the preservation of its threatened values is part of his patrol, too. In a series of essays written from Macedonia he assembled his thoughts on a range of topics, observing

There is no humaner science than grammar, and few more exciting pursuits than textual criticism... The graces of civilization and the delights of learning are far from me now. But my nomadic and semi-barbarous existence is still solaced by a few good books; and the best odes of Horace, the best things in Boswell or Elia, often awake memories of Attic nights.[37]

Without any sense of cultural or geographical confusion, Chapman makes it clear that Attic nights are Oxford nights, memories of which link him to the fellowship of Classically educated British scholars, and have nothing to do with a ravaged latter-day Balkan world. In Macedonia civilization is conjured only in moments, when he recites Horace's odes 'on long marches, or quiet nights at an observation post'.[38] In this remote region the decay of English syntax and thoughts on spelling reform assume a political resonance: 'To my

[36] *Johnson's Journey to the Western Islands of Scotland and Boswell's Journal of A Tour to the Hebrides with Samuel Johnson, LL.D.*, ed. R. W. Chapman (London: Oxford University Press, 1924), vii–viii.

[37] R. W. Chapman, 'The Portrait of a Scholar', in *The Portrait of a Scholar and Other Essays written in Macedonia 1916–1918* (London: Oxford University Press, 1920), 10 and 22.

[38] 'Reading Aloud', ibid., 45.

own ear the speech of "Eton and Christ Church", in spite of the insidious decay of its vowels, is still the most beautiful of earthly sounds . . . its cadences are instinct with breeding . . . But if phonetic spelling takes the bit in its teeth, it may hurry us to I know not what catastrophe.'[39] Chapman's grand assurance of what civilization is (and is not) is summed up in the closing words of a final confessional piece on his passion for collecting silver spoons. Plangently, and a little ridiculously, he notes: 'There are no spoons in Macedonia'.[40] As their subscripted addresses indicate, these essays are carefully located on the war-torn map of eastern Europe—written from Snevce, Mihalova, Bralo, Kalinova.

Returning to Oxford after the war, Chapman also returned to Press policy of the pre-war years. The Oxford English Texts had started life at the beginning of the century as a conscious attempt to apply the standards of the Oxford Classical Texts to the works of English authors. Ingram Bywater, the Greek scholar eulogized as mentor, friend, and last of a race of heroes in Chapman's Macedonian essay 'The Portrait of a Scholar', had died in 1914, having presided till the end over the commissioned volumes of the Classical Texts. Under his close direction the emphasis was on complete and accurate texts, replacing the nineteenth-century tradition of exam-oriented abridgements and cribs. It was now important to apply to English authors the same high standards of editorial accuracy—establishing correct texts or at least preparing exact reprints of good early editions. In this latter respect, Chapman's persistent fondness for type-facsimile editions merely continued a pre-war Oxford craze. But the aim was also for the Press to respond to a new pride in a national literature and to provide a body of edited texts in response to the growing prestige of English studies, already thanks to figures like Saintsbury and A. C. Bradley an academic discipline overtaking the Classics in provincial universities. In 1906 the English Association had been founded 'to promote the due recognition of English as an essential element in the national education'; in 1917 an English paper had been introduced into the public schools' common entrance examination; and in 1921 there appeared the report of the government committee into the teaching of English, set up by Lloyd George in the aftermath of war and chaired by Henry Newbolt. Chapman tempered his post-war despondence at the loss of civilized values, and his own preference for the life of the scholar and bibliophile, with a determination to publish in good editions virtually everything that might be

[39] 'Thoughts on Spelling Reform', ibid., 102. [40] 'Silver Spoons', ibid., 147.

regarded as English Literature, which meant everything up to some undefined point in the nineteenth century.[41]

Chapman's plans for an edition of Jane Austen's novels predated the war, but they were resituated by war.[42] Austen scholars owe an enormous debt to Chapman for his pioneering work on the text of the finished novels, the juvenilia, the unfinished fiction, and the letters. His concern to establish an accurate text, after the careless reprint history of the later nineteenth century, not only inaugurated the modern critical engagement with Austen but also the serious scholarly investigation of the English novel (of any English novel) as a literary form: Chapman's 1923 critical edition of the Austen text is the first such treatment of an English novelist. Specifically, Chapman undertook the first full collation of the novels for which we have more than one edition published in Austen's lifetime and whose revision she was known to have overseen (that is, *Sense and Sensibility* and *Mansfield Park*). In keeping with the general textual theory of his day, that final intentions, as represented by the latest authorized publication, are best, he enshrined for both *Sense and Sensibility* and *Mansfield Park* the second-edition text as the basis of all modern reading texts. Beyond that, he established the formal features of the second-edition texts as instructive for his own general practice of regularization throughout his modern edition. His promise of textual accuracy represented also a commitment to the display of Austen as a painstaking and intelligent *re*writer, a novelist capable of mature reflection. It seems likely that his model for the great English novelist was Henry James, the great American novelist (and Macklin's choice for her literary inheritor in Kipling's story); the massive and elaborately retrospective twenty-four volumes of the New York edition of *The Novels of Henry James* had been issued by Macmillan in Britain in 1909. Significantly, too, in 1923, the establishment of an authoritative Austen text was by comparison with the procedures for determining Oxford editions of the Classics and of vernacular Elizabethan and Jacobean literature. But the question remains why did Chapman believe that an apparently

[41] See Peter Sutcliffe, *The Oxford University Press: An Informal History* (Oxford: Clarendon Press, 1978), 128–32 and 196–7; and 'Constitution of the English Association', cited in C. Nowell Smith, *The Origin and History of the Association* (English Association Pamphlet, London: Oxford University Press, 1942), 5. For the post-First-World-War rise of English studies, see Chris Baldick, *The Social Mission of English Criticism 1848–1932* (Oxford: Clarendon Press, 1983), 86–108.

[42] Letters in the Oxford University Press archive (LOGE000025) dating back to 1912 make it clear that the Clarendon Press was considering at that time a complete edition of Jane Austen's works, including the manuscript writings and the letters. All that seemed to be holding it back, before war intervened, were copyright issues, the new Act of 1911 having extended protection to fifty years, thus putting the manuscript writings in Bentley's 1871 edition out of reach until 1921.

accessible body of works, the lucidity of whose style persuaded readers of their nearness to life, required or justified the kind of textual proving normally reserved by scholars for Greek and Latin authors made obscure by the ravages of time and corruption?

A Classical scholar trained at St Andrews and Oriel College, Oxford, where he won the Gaisford prize for Greek prose, Robert Chapman was appointed Assistant Secretary at the Clarendon Press in 1906, succeeding in 1920 to the Secretaryship, a post he held until illness compelled his resignation in 1942. As Secretary he shaped major Clarendon projects, not only the Oxford English Texts series but the *Oxford English Dictionary* (completed in 1928) and its *Supplement* (1933), to which as a keen lexicographer he contributed. In their context, his treatment of the Austen text assumes particular significance. It did massive ideological work, scarcely recognized within the subsequent intensive Austen criticism and publishing industry which was a feature of the second half of the twentieth century. Chapman's Austen led the post-war establishment of an OUP canon of English classics to serve as a moral and aesthetic yardstick; in the words of Desmond MacCarthy reviewing the Austen edition, such works offer 'a *refuge* from present realities'.[43] For Chapman himself, the early editions of old books are 'the title deeds of a national inheritance; and if we never saw them our minds would still repose on their existence as the source and standard of our knowledge'.[44] His work on the Austen text helped to establish the scholarly credentials of the emergent discipline of English. To this end, Chapman presented the relatively modern vernacular text of a relatively modern literary genre in an environment able to bear the scrutiny of the professional (that is, the Classically trained) scholarly gaze of his contemporaries. As A. B. Walkley, for many years a leading essayist for *The Times* and himself a recent editor of Austen, noted in the *Edinburgh Review* for January 1924, 'the Clarendon Press has published an edition ... produced with as much scholarship and research as though the work edited were a fragmentary Greek tragedian or a papyrus from the tomb of Tutankh-amen'.[45] Though extravagant, in the context of Walkley's general argument the allusion is not as ironic as it at first seems. It was also topical: the tomb of Tutankhamun was discovered in November 1922 and throughout 1923 news of further finds was reaching an England in

43 *The New Statesman*, 22 (1923), 145.

44 'Old Books and Modern Reprints', in *Portrait of a Scholar*, 51.

45 *Edinburgh Review*, 239 (Jan. 1924), 29. An Austen enthusiast, in 1923 Walkley published with an introduction the first separate printing of *The Watsons* (Gilson F4).

the grip of Egypto-mania or 'Nile-style'. Around the same time, in 1921, Sir Arthur Evans issued the first volume of his study *The Palace of Minos at Knossos* detailing his controversial reconstructions of the Cretan site, and in regular articles in *The Times* he continued to chart the course of restorations and discoveries. As well as glamorizing archaeology both projects provided great challenges to the early science of conservation. This was a moment for reconsidering the roots of Western civilization, for reassessing assumptions about the past and relationships to it.

Written a few years earlier in 1918 while on wartime service, his essay 'The Textual Criticism of English Classics' expounded Chapman's creed that 'To restore, and maintain in its integrity, the text of our great writers is a pious duty'. The essay appeared anonymously as a front-page article in the *Times Literary Supplement* for 20 March 1919. In it Chapman began setting out his claim for Austen, her name standing alongside authors with a recognized complex textual history, all of them recent candidates for Clarendon editions: Donne, Johnson, Ben Jonson, and of course Shakespeare, of whom he tellingly writes, 'The causes to which it is due that the text of Shakespeare is less certain than that of Sophocles are well known.'[46] It is with the implications of these concepts of 'restoration', 'integrity', 'greatness', and 'pious duty' for determining correctness among modern vernacular texts that Chapman and other scholars whose researches he drew on for the Austen project struggled. Their wider task, as they conceived it and as Chapman came to understand it more fully at his Macedonian outpost, was to stem the erosion of English cultural values under threat from textual corruption and eventual incomprehension: 'Those who have made it their business to reconstitute the texts of English classics know that the history of a text is the gradual accretion of error.'[47]

Like Chapman's late mentor Bywater, some were gentlemen scholars and Classicists by training, often relicts themselves of an earlier world of textual study. Others were men like Chapman, a Scottish-educated scholarship boy, who might more accurately be seen as seeking an accommodation with the English establishment by acting as mediator for figures like Samuel Johnson and Jane Austen, both authors who had attained cultural authority despite disadvantages of rank or gender. In their mix Chapman and his associates bear more than a faint resemblance to the homo-social club of Janeites, where, surprisingly, given the usual concern for social distinction in Kipling's

[46] The essay was reprinted in *Portrait of a Scholar*. See 79 and 66.

[47] 'Old Books and Modern Reprints', ibid., 49.

(and Austen's) fiction, Jane transcends class. Among them were early professors of the new discipline of English Literature, like A. W. Verrall, a brilliant and controversial editor of Aeschylus and Euripides, chosen in 1911, after A. C. Bradley turned it down, as first King Edward VII Professor of English Literature at Cambridge. Other chief collaborators included J. Arthur Platt, friend of A. E. Housman and since 1894 Professor of Greek at University College, London. Platt was an editor of Homer, and translator of Aristotle and Aeschylus. There was also Henry Bradley, the self-taught philologist and lexicographer, who graduated from clerk in a Sheffield cutlery firm to co-editor with James Murray of the *OED*, and who was from 1916 a fellow of Magdalen College, Oxford, and F. D. (Frank) MacKinnon, barrister of the Inner Temple and later a High Court judge.[48] All identified cruces in and suggested emendations to the Chapman Austen text. So, too, did the socialite Edward Marsh, civil servant, patron of the arts, and private secretary to Winston Churchill. An amateur scholar, Marsh edited the *Georgian Poetry* anthologies, was the poet Rupert Brooke's literary executor, and for a hobby undertook proof correction, a service he provided over many years for Churchill, himself a declared Janeite. In his student days at Trinity College, Cambridge, Marsh had been a pupil of Verrall's specializing in Classical textual emendation. Shortly after the appearance of Chapman's edition, he sent an article, 'Some Notes on Miss Austen's Novels', to the *London Mercury* in which he argued in close detail the case for further emendation to the text of all six novels.[49] Chapman subsequently incorporated many of these suggestions in later printings and in a pamphlet *Additions and Corrections for the Second Edition of Jane Austen's Novels*, printed in only twenty-five copies and issued privately in 1925.

Among Chapman's papers in the Bodleian Library, Oxford, are some of his working notes and correspondence for the Clarendon Austen edition. Four manilla folders contain materials relating to *Emma*, *Northanger Abbey*, *Persuasion*, and *Mansfield Park*, and some loose leaves source and describe proposed illustrations to the complete set of novels. Chapman's handwriting is a messy scrawl, not always legible, and the papers are in some disorder, but it is possible to piece together from them a fair idea of how he proceeded. Each folder contains a set of neat notes from Arthur Platt which are mainly attempts to emend the text, in the case of *Emma*, *Northanger Abbey*, and

[48] See Chapman's acknowledgements in his 'Preface' to *Sense and Sensibility*, iii–iv.

[49] E. Marsh, 'Some Notes on Miss Austen's Novels', *London Mercury*, 10 (1924), 189–93.

Persuasion from what he calls 'a rotten reprint of Routledge's' and in the case of *Mansfield Park* from a Macmillan reprint of 1908.[50] In reading his rotten Austen reprints, Platt followed what was at the time established procedure for the emendation of Classical texts. The logic of the method was based in the knowledge that for the Classics there is no equivalent to either the first or final authorized edition of modern times and no extant witness which carries the guarantee of authorially sanctioned readings. Since all textual witnesses fall short, more or less, of a lost high standard of correctness, it thus becomes the duty of the editor to recover that correctness through intuition, the expert invocation of analogy across a known body of texts, and the imposition of grammatical regularization. In these circumstances the poor reprint can serve the expert reader perfectly well for the purpose of skilled interrogation and emendation; in fact, the poorer the reprint, the greater the opportunity for honing editorial acumen. Occasionally, Platt's observations are overstretched by any standard. A phrase in *Northanger Abbey* is described as 'a beautiful Homeric idiom—επαναληψις into the nominative—e.g. Od[yssey]. i 50. . . . Daresay it is a recognized English idiom too. I've since observed two in the Ring & the Book.' Commenting on *Emma*, Volume 3, Chapter 15, he notes 'Austen's G[ree]k idiom (or muddle)' in the phrase '"*regardless of little* besides his own convenience"', adding 'Cf. *Antigone* 1–4.'[51] Marginal pencilled notes show Chapman working through Platt's suggestions and comparing them with readings from the first-edition texts.

He also had by him A. W. Verrall's annotated copies. Acclaimed by Geoffrey Keynes as the 'dawn of true Austen scholarship', Verrall's brief publications 'On the Printing of Jane Austen's Novels' and 'On Some Passages in Jane Austen's *Mansfield Park*', written in 1892–4 in the midst of editing Aeschylus, had brought rigorous textual principles to bear on the Austen text.[52] With better justification than Platt, Verrall worked from the

[50] R. W. Chapman, 'Jane Austen Files', Bodleian MS. Eng. Misc. c. 924, f. 42. The Routledge reprints used by Platt may have been Gilson E63 and 64. Chapman, *Jane Austen: A Critical Bibliography*, 57, records his ownership of A. E. Housman's copies of *Sense and Sensibility* and *Pride and Prejudice* in Routledge's Sixpenny Novels (1884) (Gilson E65–66), in which Housman corrected misprints. The Macmillan edition of *Mansfield Park* (1908) is presumably a reprint of Gilson E88 in the 'Illustrated Pocket Classics' series.

[51] Bodleian MS. Eng. Misc. c. 924, f. 107.

[52] Geoffrey Keynes, *Jane Austen: A Bibliography* (London: Nonesuch Press, 1929), xxii; A. W. Verrall, 'On the Printing of Jane Austen's Novels', *Cambridge Observer*, 1 (1892), 2–4; 'On Some Passages in Jane Austen's *Mansfield Park*', *Cambridge Review*, 15 (1893–4), 126–7 and 145–6. The edition Verrall worked from is Gilson E75. For an account of Verrall, see the 'Memoir' in his *Collected and Literary Essays, Classical and Modern*, ed. M. A. Bayfield and J. D. Duff (Cambridge: Cambridge University Press, 1913).

1892 Dent edition, in which R. Brimley Johnson attempted the first serious revision and the beginnings of a textually conscious practice. What is interesting to note is that Chapman appears to have established his text by working backwards from the Classically determined reading (and correction) of these late Victorian printings to the lifetime editions, with the Classically derived argument providing the filter for his own re-readings of the first and second editions overseen by Austen herself. In 'The Textual Criticism of English Classics' he described it as a 'useful and amusing exercise . . . to correct a reprint of a book, the most careless that can be found, and compare the emendations with a sound text', and he acknowledged the method as Verrall's.[53] An amusing scholarly game, no doubt, but it seems to modern eyes distinctly perverse when the original print witness survives; especially so because it brings with it the disturbing possibility that an editorial reading reached by this route may seem irresistibly more authentic than anything the earliest text can offer. Dead since 1912, Verrall's ghost haunts the margins of Chapman's Austen edition. As early as August 1914 Chapman was working with the 1892 Dent edition of *Mansfield Park* which had been marked up to show textual details in relation to volume arrangements in the lifetime editions, and a letter of 14 January 1915 from Edward Marsh, at the Admiralty, Whitehall, mentions having sent him Verrall's copy some time earlier. Platt's notes also appear to have been communicated between April and August 1914.[54]

Platt's close engagement with the state of the Austen text did not preclude attempts to imagine the wider world of the novels. At University College, London, he had combined the teaching of Greek with occasional lectures and papers on more modern literary topics—Cervantes, Edward Fitzgerald, 'The Relations of Poetry and Science'—some of which Housman, then Professor of Latin, collected into a volume after his death.[55] Chapman's *Emma* folder contains a sketch in Platt's hand of the relative positions of the major houses and families of the novel and their relation to the village of Highbury and the Kingston road, together with a detailed set of notes. Of the travelling arrangements to the dinner party at the Coles' in *Emma*, Volume 2, Chapter 8, Platt writes: 'Coles a little way north of central point, for Emma *follows* Knightley's carriage to them. Knightley came though from South; Emma

[53] 'The Textual Criticism of English Classics' in *Portrait of a Scholar*, 77.

[54] R. W. Chapman, Correspondence, Bodleian MSS. Eng. Letters c. 760, f. 123 and f. 74.

[55] Arthur Platt, *Nine Essays*, with a preface by A. E. Housman (Cambridge: Cambridge University Press, 1927).

fell in behind him at the κυκλος, as Thuycidides [*sic*] has it, coming from West.' It is Platt who alerts Chapman to the importance of the German Romantic play *Lovers' Vows* for understanding the wider action of *Mansfield Park*: 'If you haven't read Lovers' Vows, do so—quotations from it would be very valuable as shewing the nature of the scene between Maria and Crawford: they are perpetually in one another's arms.' Chapman later decided to publish the play, appended in full in Elizabeth Inchbald's adaptation, in the same volume with *Mansfield Park*, thereby crediting it with a unique intertextual status within his edition and determining its seeming compulsory significance for subsequent critical readings of the novel through the twentieth century. On the other hand, perhaps surfeited on pretty Victorian reprints, Platt has little time for illustrations: 'For God's sake don't have any pictures. The miscreants who illustrate Jane Austen will have a special bolgia to themselves in the next world.'[56] Several of the papers suggest the wartime context of Chapman's researches: 'Notes for a School Edition (abortive) of *Emma* (written in a troop train)'; and the pencilled notes on place and street names in the text of *Mansfield Park* written on the back of a list detailing guns and prisoners captured by the British army since July 1916.[57]

Of Chapman's other associates, Frank MacKinnon shared his near obsessive concern with charting the chronology of events in the novels. It was MacKinnon who first suggested that Austen used almanacs in fixing dates in her narratives, and together he and Chapman plotted precise fictional time-scales for the 1811–12 recasting of *Pride and Prejudice* and for *Mansfield Park*. MacKinnon read through Chapman's finalized text, supplied the printed 'Chronology' to each novel as well as many annotations (he was strong on topographical details), and he fed Chapman's passion for multiple indexes, suggesting the index of 'Literary References and Allusions': 'It would be difficult to track down the source of every one (e.g. the charades in *Emma*), but it might be done.'[58] By contrast, Henry Bradley

[56] Bodleian MS. Eng. Misc. c. 924, ff. 31–2; Bodleian MSS. Eng. Letters c. 760, f. 182. Cf. Margaret Oliphant, 'Nothing could be more easy than to make a map of [Highbury]' (in her 1870 review of the Austen-Leigh *Memoir*, in *Critical Heritage*, I. 224).

[57] Bodleian MS. Eng. Misc. c. 924, f. 7; f. 172.

[58] Bodleian MS. Eng. Misc. c. 924, ff. 120–6 (annotations and detailed chronology for *Northanger Abbey* in MacKinnon's hand); ff. 137–9 and f. 158 (notes and detailed topographical information for *Persuasion* in MacKinnon's hand); Bodleian MSS. Eng. Letters c. 760, f. 65^{r} ('Some notes on Emma enclosed in case they may be helpful'); f. 66^{v}.

represented the voice of moderation, cautioning against too easy assumptions of error and the ever-present temptation to elucidate the text. The author of popular works, *The Making of English* (1904) and *Spoken and Written Language* (1919), Bradley was associated with Chapman in the Society for Pure English (instituted in 1919 against the fear of post-war civilized collapse); but he seems to have had a finer sense of language as living, as calling for imaginative description as against narrow prescription—perhaps his non-academic origins helped here. The *Oxford English Dictionary*-style slips on which they each recorded their comments on possible difficulties in the Austen text almost invariably reveal Bradley tempering the stiltedness of Chapman's reading by an ear and eye more sympathetic to syntactic irregularity and the nuances of early nineteenth-century speech. To Chapman's complaint that the phrase 'best help' (in *Northanger Abbey*) 'strikes me as awkward and possibly corrupt. But I have nothing to suggest', Bradley replies, 'Awkward, but I see no sufficient reason for suspecting corruption'. Of various queries addressed to him concerning the text of *Emma*, he writes: 'If the text is right the expression is clumsy, but I think it quite possibly *is* right . . . the meaning so awkwardly expressed . . . fits the place better'; 'this is quite natural in unstudied speech'; 'I see no difficulty here . . . Surely the sentence has a subtle felicity of its own. Modern stylistic conventions, born of the journalistic striving after instantaneous intelligibility, render it impossible for any one to write like that nowadays; but it is a pity.'[59] Bradley probably saved the Austen text as it was prepared for the twentieth-century reader from the graver excesses of Chapman's zeal for correction.

The massive weight of learning, in the form of philological principles and expertise in textual recension and verification, which these men brought to the study of Austen's novels became itself the guarantee of their status within the forming canon of English classics. That their practices were sharpened and refined on the texts of Homer, Euripides, and Aeschylus seemed to the good because in themselves such practices were understood as the constant components of value. Activities that would constitute the prizing and appraising of modern vernacular literature needed to display this evidence of continuous operation. It is a matter of recognition: it is in these trappings, or through this lens, that we discover Austen's status as a classic. The nature

[59] Bodleian MS. Eng. Misc. c. 924, f. 109; f. 61; f. 62; f. 67.

or constancy of value in Austen, as Chapman appeared to understand it, is, accordingly, both intrinsic (for all time) and knowingly attributed. We can say that Austen's value was bound up implicitly with the functions her work was seen to serve in the then present of the 1920s, but that it also existed under certain conditions which spoke only of, and which restored her to, the pastness of the past. At one and the same time Chapman asserted Austen's availability and unavailability for certain kinds of appropriation. Her evaluation as a classic itself contributed a layer of value that rendered her appreciation a more sophisticated and a more mediated activity: after 1923, we now have to learn, or rather re-learn, how to read her. E. M. Forster seized the point in his review in the *Nation and Athenaeum*: 'And Mr R. W. Chapman's fine new edition has, among its other merits, the advantage of waking the Jane Austenite up. After reading its notes and appendixes, after a single glance at its illustrations, he will never relapse again into the primal stupor.' Until this edition, Forster argued, readers only thought they knew how to read her, with 'the mouth open and the mind closed'.[60] It is worth dwelling for a moment on this distinction between accessibility and inaccessibility as it informs the conditions of Austen's classic status, if only because as a female writer and a popular novelist she might seem to represent a threat to the (gentlemanly) established order of literature and civilization at this time. Her newly attributed inaccessibility nullified the implied danger.

At the Knossos site Evans had raised a Minoan palace from the ruins by replacing the charred and carbonized fragments of an original wooden framework, over three thousand years old by his estimation, with stone and iron girders. The reconstruction (his own preferred term) was to his mind legitimized by its appeal to the imagination. Supplied with sufficient recoverable detail, the imagination can create a picture of the past which will restore it to life: 'The result achieved by this legitimate process of reconstitution is such that it must appeal to the historic sense of the most unimaginative...We have here all the materials for the reconstruction of a brilliant picture of that remote epoch.'[61] In his review of Chapman's Austen

[60] The review appeared in the *Nation and Athenaeum*, 34 (1924), and is reprinted together with reviews of Chapman's editions of *Sanditon* (1925) and *Jane Austen's Letters* (1932) in *Abinger Harvest*, 162–79. See 162–3.

[61] Evans is reporting in *The Times*, 31 October 1905, 4.

edition, Walkley, prompted by the coincidence of further archaeological triumphs in the form of the recent Egyptian discoveries, delivered a parallel between the scholarly activities requisite for the reader's just appreciation of Austen's novels and the decipherment of ancient artefacts. As critics of Evans were keen to point out, imaginative identification carries with it a price; in Walkley's opinion all evidence of cultural distance should elicit a similarly complex response, compounded of the sympathy inspired and the real remoteness represented. The emotional intelligence manifested in weighing our own dispositions, beliefs, and sensations against those on display should not be confused with the more dubious act of 'identification'. Simulation on its own—that is, pure identificatory imagination—will yield only a partial and distorting view, and must be supplemented by an awareness of the other as existing within a rich context of difference. For Walkley, the unperceived distance of Austen's world is no less real than the perceivable distance of the Egyptian:

> And now, to crown her fame, and to pay her the tribute only rendered to authors indubitably classic, the Clarendon Press has published an edition of her six great novels, with authentic text, established by collation of the early editions, minutely annotated, illustrated by contemporary prints, fashion-plates, diagrams and maps—in short, produced with as much scholarship and research as though the work edited were a fragmentary Greek tragedian or a papyrus from the tomb of Tutankh-amen.
>
> If anyone thinks the last analogy far-fetched, let him consider that Egyptian hieroglyphics offer themselves to the decipherer as nothing but what they are, enigmas to be systematically attacked and solved; whereas the vocabulary of Jane Austen is superficially so like our own as to deceive the unwary into assuming an identity between things in fact as dissimilar as the Pyramids and the Marble Arch. The words are the same but no longer bear the same meaning.
>
> ... [Chapman's] notes ... enable us to put ourselves in her place and, in reading, to recreate her work within ourselves ... [But] We cannot obliterate the interval of time between the dead author and ourselves.[62]

After all, it seems we do not inhabit Austen-land without considerable contrivance; nor then on equal terms.

[62] *Edinburgh Review*, 239, 28–31.

Territorial acts

Chapman's restoration of the Austen novels and his rescue of them from further textual deterioration compels us to recognize their difference, their remoteness from us. As Forster has it, the reader is now wide awake, critically alert. Yet the propriety, even severity, of Chapman's editorial action in relation to the texts he sought to purify of corruption is something we encounter within an aesthetic and social space which can only be described as exuberant. In 1923 their faux-Regency presentation—old-fashioned binding with marbled paper sides, type-facsimile first-edition title-pages (extended to *Sense and Sensibility* and *Mansfield Park*, even though the text represented is that of the second edition), division of the text within each volume in accordance with the original three-volume structure—was a major selling point. So were the numerous 'illustrations from contemporary sources', showing places, costumes, and articles of furniture likely to have been encountered by Austen and her characters. Such devices represented a conscious rejection, in the interests of recovered authenticity, of the Victorian craze for sentimental interpretation and 'Cranfordization'. Regency pastiche extends into the textual space, where the visual deception provided by period typeface and page layout, complete with catchwords (catchwords were dying out by the late eighteenth century, but all the original printings have them with the exception of *Persuasion*), contributes to the broad relationship with the reader in which meaning is expressed.[63] But such reconstruction, however meticulously researched, includes its own act of temporal dislocation and is as much the work of imagination as Evans's Hall of the Colonnades at Knossos.

Chapman's immediate model, down to facsimile title-pages and catchwords, was Katharine Metcalfe's period reconstruction *Pride and Prejudice*, published by Oxford University Press in 1912. Metcalfe and Chapman married the following year, and they planned the complete Clarendon edition as a joint project at that time before war intervened. As Metcalfe originally conceived it, the edition was to involve a total immersion, designed to assist the reader in recovering the modern equivalent of what she felt would have been a Regency reading experience. A pamphlet prospectus, made up to advertise the 1923 edition sums it up thus:

[63] Cf. D. F. McKenzie's 1985 Panizzi Lectures, published as *Bibliography and the Sociology of Texts* (1986; repr. Cambridge: Cambridge University Press, 1999), 10.

THERE are many illustrated editions of Jane Austen, but none in which, as in this, every illustration is from an original which Miss Austen herself might have seen.

The text, which is based on a laborious comparison of the early editions, is free from all modernization and editorial 'improvement'.

The modest commentary, and the appendixes and indexes, are, it is hoped, equally free from any intrusion of modernity. It has been sought to explain the novels—in the relatively few places where they require explanation—from themselves, from the author's extant letters, and from books with which she was certainly or probably acquainted.

The binding of marbled boards, with cloth backs and paper labels, is likewise in the style of the Regency.

This large paper edition with illustrations in colour is limited to 1,000 sets, of which 950 are for sale. The price is five guineas net.[64]

For Metcalfe, as for Chapman, book collecting with its own special materialist illusions provided the basis for editorial excavation in a remarkably direct way. Her stimulus to edit *Pride and Prejudice* came from the apparently serendipitous acquisition of a first edition; Chapman later recalled how his own 'career as a conscious collector began when I married a lady who had bought an *Arcadia* in folio while yet a schoolgirl'. Writing to Chapman on 8 May 1923 MacKinnon remarked: 'I looked in at Sotheby's recently because they were selling a first edition of Pride & Prejudice, and also of Northanger Abbey & Persuasion. . . . N.A.& P. which lacked [half-titles] sold for 14 *shillings*!' In a world in which early editions of Austen novels are both extremely rare and prohibitively expensive it is now easy to forget the close relationship between private collecting and the development of textual studies as it existed in the first half of the twentieth century. There are several strands to this, the first of which must be the availability of texts to collate, even in Macedonia, where Chapman had with him all three lifetime editions of Boswell's *Tour to the Hebrides*. There is also the connection between a place in the literary canon and continuing sales of early editions, as witnessed in the complex intertwining of financial and literary interests in the bibliographic investigation and forgeries of Thomas J. Wise and his exposers, John Carter and Graham Pollard, two booksellers. Usually distinct from forgery, the visual likeness of facsimile reprints (an OUP fad) continued into the twentieth century to create appreciation for, and of course to

[64] A copy of the prospectus is in the Bodleian Library, 2597 d.11. The large paper edition measured 9 inches × 6 inches (8vo). By contrast, the first editions of Austen's novels were the smaller format duodecimos.

(vi)

CONTENTS

VOLUME I

VOLUME II

VOLUME III

CONTENTS vii

VOLUME IV

VOLUME V

5. Contents pages prefixed to all volumes of R. W. Chapman's edition of *The Novels of Jane Austen*, 1923, showing the array of appended information. By kind permission of Oxford University Press.

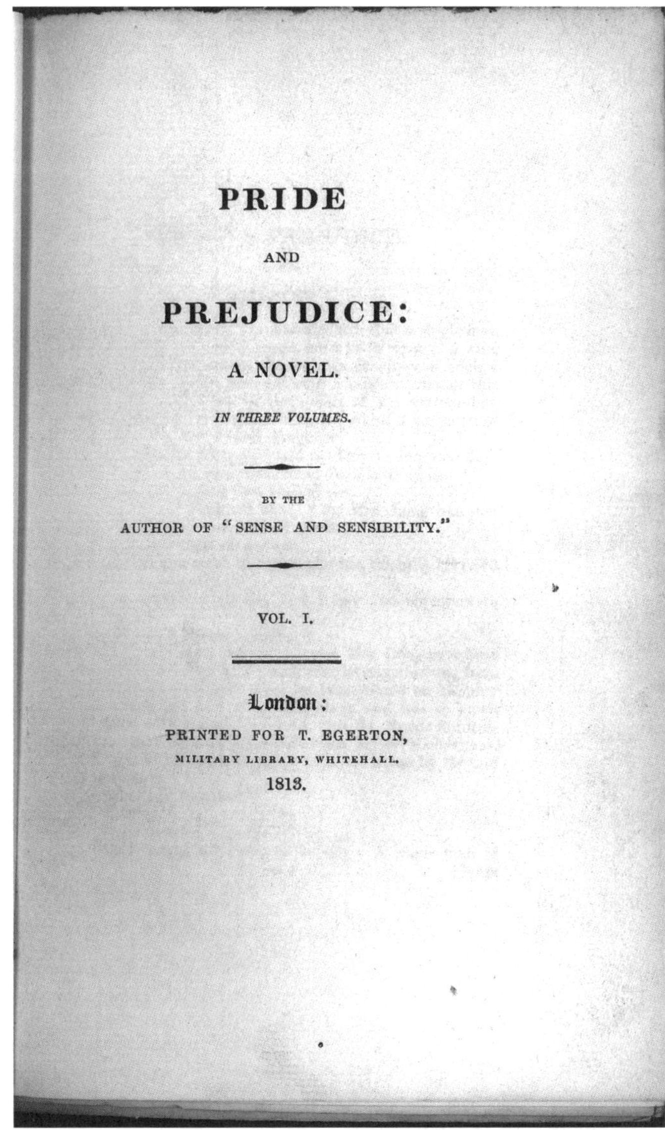

PRIDE

AND

PREJUDICE:

A NOVEL.

IN THREE VOLUMES.

BY THE

AUTHOR OF "SENSE AND SENSIBILITY."

VOL. I.

London:

PRINTED FOR T. EGERTON,

MILITARY LIBRARY, WHITEHALL.

1813.

6. Type-facsimile title-page to *Pride and Prejudice*, 1923.
By kind permission of Oxford University Press.

increase the value of, the 'real' thing. Once again, there is also a class angle, in that Chapman in the 1910s and 1920s could afford to collect Johnson and Austen, and his specialist knowledge and position within OUP would grant him admittance to the company of wealthier collectors. The easy relations in

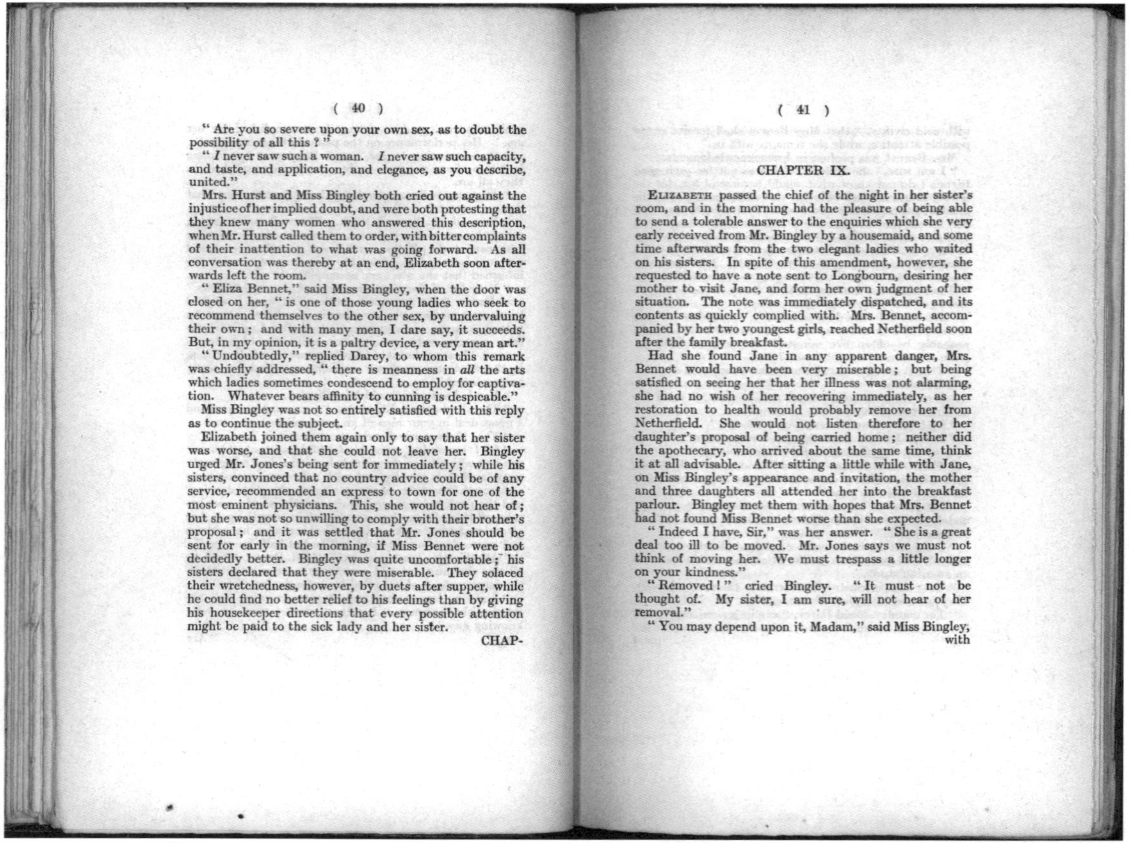

(40)

" Are you so severe upon your own sex, as to doubt the possibility of all this ? "

" *I* never saw such a woman. *I* never saw such capacity, and taste, and application, and elegance, as you describe, united."

Mrs. Hurst and Miss Bingley both cried out against the injustice of her implied doubt, and were both protesting that they knew many women who answered this description, when Mr. Hurst called them to order, with bitter complaints of their inattention to what was going forward. As all conversation was thereby at an end, Elizabeth soon afterwards left the room.

" Eliza Bennet," said Miss Bingley, when the door was closed on her, " is one of those young ladies who seek to recommend themselves to the other sex, by undervaluing their own; and with many men, I dare say, it succeeds. But, in my opinion, it is a paltry device, a very mean art."

" Undoubtedly," replied Darcy, to whom this remark was chiefly addressed, " there is meanness in *all* the arts which ladies sometimes condescend to employ for captivation. Whatever bears affinity to cunning is despicable."

Miss Bingley was not so entirely satisfied with this reply as to continue the subject.

Elizabeth joined them again only to say that her sister was worse, and that she could not leave her. Bingley urged Mr. Jones's being sent for immediately; while his sisters, convinced that no country advice could be of any service, recommended an express to town for one of the most eminent physicians. This, she would not hear of; but she was not so unwilling to comply with their brother's proposal; and it was settled that Mr. Jones should be sent for early in the morning, if Miss Bennet were not decidedly better. Bingley was quite uncomfortable; his sisters declared that they were miserable. They solaced their wretchedness, however, by duets after supper, while he could find no better relief to his feelings than by giving his housekeeper directions that every possible attention might be paid to the sick lady and her sister.

CHAP-

(41)

CHAPTER IX.

Elizabeth passed the chief of the night in her sister's room, and in the morning had the pleasure of being able to send a tolerable answer to the enquiries which she very early received from Mr. Bingley by a housemaid, and some time afterwards from the two elegant ladies who waited on his sisters. In spite of this amendment, however, she requested to have a note sent to Longbourn, desiring her mother to visit Jane, and form her own judgment of her situation. The note was immediately dispatched, and its contents as quickly complied with. Mrs. Bennet, accompanied by her two youngest girls, reached Netherfield soon after the family breakfast.

Had she found Jane in any apparent danger, Mrs. Bennet would have been very miserable; but being satisfied on seeing her that her illness was not alarming, she had no wish of her recovering immediately, as her restoration to health would probably remove her from Netherfield. She would not listen therefore to her daughter's proposal of being carried home; neither did the apothecary, who arrived about the same time, think it at all advisable. After sitting a little while with Jane, on Miss Bingley's appearance and invitation, the mother and three daughters all attended her into the breakfast parlour. Bingley met them with hopes that Mrs. Bennet had not found Miss Bennet worse than she expected.

" Indeed I have, Sir," was her answer. " She is a great deal too ill to be moved. Mr. Jones says we must not think of moving her. We must trespass a little longer on your kindness."

" Removed ! " cried Bingley. " It must not be thought of. My sister, I am sure, will not hear of her removal."

" You may depend upon it, Madam," said Miss Bingley,
with

7. Page opening from R. W. Chapman's edition of *Pride and Prejudice*, 1923, showing its faux-Regency typeface and layout. By kind permission of Oxford University Press.

8. Authenticated period illustration from R. W. Chapman's *Pride and Prejudice*, 1923. By kind permission of Oxford University Press.

the first half of the century between public institutions and rich collectors is evidenced in the role of private catalogues (Pforzheimer, Rothschild, Sadleir) as standard reference works. Finally, in the precise years Chapman was at work on the Austen text, manuscripts and other primary documents were shifting from family hands into the auction rooms, and again his specialist knowledge and position gave him access and opportunities.[65]

In the aftermath of war openness to the past was an urgent need. It informs T. S. Eliot's early essays with their concern to establish a concept of literary tradition which will make sense in the twentieth century and for English, rapidly replacing the Classics as the central humanities discipline. The progressive extinction of personality, Eliot's prerequisite for the great poet, is really a negotiation between the competing claims of the present and the past, and a plea for the recognition of the past as rescuing art from intentionalism, from a narrow relevance to now. For Eliot, the past is the common ground of difference where the individual talent discovers a shared voice. Hence, his savage dismissal of Gilbert Murray's flaccid 1906 translation of Euripides' *Medea*, with its outdated Swinburnian metres: 'We need an eye which can see the past in its place with its definite differences from the present, and yet so lively that it shall be as present to us as the present.'[66] This sounds not unlike Walkley's advice to the reader encountering the contextual richness of the Clarendon Austen. Yet as we cannot help but be aware, Eliot's redefinition of an English poetic tradition was not without the further effect of creating appreciation for his own kind of present-day poetry. 'Restoration is less about the recovery of history than it is about the production of history.'[67] The words are Joseph Grigely's in his recent study *Textualterity*, an examination of the importance of change—of unmaking, and remaking, and making over—to the understanding of art and literature. Grigely is attempting to tease out the distinction between 'restoring and preserving' texts, and the standpoints they each imply within a temporal spectrum containing both subjective (now) and objective (then) dimensions. The specific occasion of his deliberations is provided by arguments for and

[65] Some information on Metcalfe and Chapman as collectors can be found in Mary Lascelles's obituary of Chapman for the British Academy (1961), reprinted in her *Notions and Facts: Collected Criticism and Research* (Oxford: Clarendon Press, 1972), 247–57. Bodleian MSS. Eng. Lett. c. 760, ff. 68^{v}–69^{r} (MacKinnon to Chapman). T. J. Wise's creation of first-edition pamphlets of sought-after nineteenth-century authors was exposed by Carter and Pollard in *An Enquiry into the Nature of Certain Nineteenth-Century Pamphlets* (London: Constable, 1934). The catalogue of the Carl H. Pforzheimer Library was published in 1940; the Rothschild catalogue in 1954; Michael Sadleir's catalogue of his comprehensive collection of nineteenth-century fiction in 1951. All are frequently cited simply by collector's name and number. Chapman's relations with Jane Austen's collateral descendants are amply attested in his own publications and in the Bodleian Library Chapman papers.

[66] T. S. Eliot, 'Euripides and Professor Murray', in *The Sacred Wood: Essays on Poetry and Criticism* (London: Methuen and Co., 1920), 77.

[67] Joseph Grigely, *Textualterity: Art, Theory, and Textual Criticism* (Ann Arbor: University of Michigan Press, 1995), 85.

against cleaning Leonardo's *Mona Lisa*; but it could be arguments for and against the reconstruction of the Knossos site or Chapman's complexly engaged editing of Austen's novels. In order to make sense of the past we draw on a present background of beliefs and expectations, but contemporary purposes and conditions must be ready to be surprised by perceived and unperceived differences, resisting the temptation only to see then as now. As Walkley insists, textual elucidation, however thorough, can do no more than support the illusion that we can throw a bridge to the past.

After the scrupulous collation of authoritative early textual witnesses, the chief claim to importance of Chapman's edition is its annotation and commentary. A dizzying display of 'Introductory Notes', further 'Notes', 'Appendixes', Indexes of Characters', and 'General Indexes', the listing of their contents repeated across all five volumes, threatens to suck in each novel, vortex-like. Chronologies drawn from contemporary almanacs, short essays on 'The Manners of the Age', on 'Miss Austen's English', on 'Punctuation', 'Carriages and Travel', and illustrative plates of 'The Five Positions of Dancing' and 'Parisian Head Dresses' structure the act of reading and persuade of its difficulty—that it is as much a matter of initiation, of learning the right frames of reference, as it was for Kipling's Janeites, themselves no more neurasthenically fixated on 'dances an' card-parties ... 'air-cuts an' shaves' than Chapman's ideal modern reader. Again Katharine Metcalfe's 1912 *Pride and Prejudice* provided the model. She supplemented her presentation of the first-edition text of 1813 with an appendix, 'Jane Austen and her Time', being notes on contemporary life, social customs, and language. Metcalfe also included reprints of critical opinions (A. C. Bradley's being the only relatively modern one), further notes, and dates of Jane Austen's life and work. As she explains, these appended notes are there to help the reader gauge the distance between then and now. But the explanation, like the annotation, is curiously self-defeating: 'Two apparently contradictory impressions are left after reading Jane Austen's novels: a first impression of her old-fashionedness, a second of her modernness.'[68] We sense a distance tastefully if fussily packaged rather than bridged. The text of *Pride and Prejudice* as represented in Volume 2 of Chapman's 1923 edition is an exact reprinting of Metcalfe's earlier edition, only the details of annotation, though similar in range, are different. There is, too, the unexplained oddity of the Clarendon Press's near-simultaneous publication in 1923 of Chapman's

[68] *Pride and Prejudice*, ed. K. M. Metcalfe (London: Oxford University Press, 1912), 389.

complete Austen novels (November) and of Metcalfe's new edition of the single novel *Northanger Abbey* (July), as a companion volume to her 1912 *Pride and Prejudice* and with identical categories of extra-textual materials (notes on 'Travelling and Post', 'Deportment, Accomplishments and Manners', 'Social Customs', 'Games', 'Dancing', and 'Language'). Annotation differs between Chapman and Metcalfe, but the page setting of the text of *Northanger Abbey* is identical.

In the face of Chapman's public silence, it is difficult to recover the significance of Metcalfe's potentially sizeable contributions to the Clarendon Austen. Before their marriage she was an assistant English tutor at Somerville College, Oxford, and though she gave up her teaching post, as was then required, on marriage, she clearly did not abandon scholarly pursuits or the wish to be publicly recognized by them. Materials in the Chapman papers in the Bodleian Library show her working her way through the proofs of the text of her husband's edition of *Mansfield Park* and suggesting yet more notes: 'I am resolved on a very amusing note on Landscape gardening. As a subject it is *great fun*... a collection of Jane's remarks on letter writing out of her own letters & N. Abbey... Marriages in St Georges Hanover Square... might be fun. Ships of the time great fun. I want, oh so badly, to do it at once *with you*. We'd do the preface & notes together each doing bits, & the other criticising & helping!' Her enthusiasm for annotation seems to have been immense; it may be that she provided the chief energy here. Though it would seem from Chapman's working notes that he submitted the text of *Northanger Abbey* to the usual process of proving (via Platt and Verrall), her large role as collaborator should be recognized and allowed to adjust our sense of Chapman's achievement. Certainly Metcalfe's instrumentality in inaugurating and establishing the 1923 Austen edition is indisputable, while its foundation in her 1912 *Pride and Prejudice* brings into clearer focus the project's own historical gestation.[69]

[69] For Metcalfe's editions, see Gilson E133 and E151. In his 'Introductory Note' to *Pride and Prejudice* (xiii), Chapman remarks on two specific emendations which he has made to the text (at 6 and 202); but page setting in the 1912 and 1923 editions is otherwise identical. Oxford issued Metcalfe's edition of *Northanger Abbey* on 26 July 1923, and Chapman's five-volume Austen set on 1 November. Katharine Chapman's comments on the proofs of *Mansfield Park* are in Bodleian MS. Eng. Misc. c. 924, ff. 198–9. According to Mary Lascelles, Katharine Metcalfe's proposal to edit *Pride and Prejudice* from the first edition was recommended to the Delegates of the Oxford University Press by Walter Raleigh, the first holder of the Chair of English Literature at Oxford (since 1904). Like Raleigh's own approach to the novel, Metcalfe's critical judgements emphasize, Jamesian-fashion, Austen's unself-consciousness ('the simple creativeness of her mind forbade self-consciousness', *Pride and Prejudice*, ed. Metcalfe, iii). Some information on Metcalfe can be found in Mary Lascelles's obituary of Chapman, *Notions and Facts*, 248; there is

Chapman's frameworks to the Austen novels impress and disorient in equal degree. (By the time he came to edit the letters, his appetite for indexing had grown still further—as many as eight distinct levels of entry into the texts). Contextualized in these ways, Austen's texts become both more and less available: precisely lit from certain angles, but fenced inside interpretative boundaries which direct and potentially limit our responses to them. In some senses, Chapman's Austen is chiefly a vehicle for annotation, often of a startlingly redundant kind; in others, the text is enigmatically obscured by the fickleness of a patrician disdain for the kind of reader who really does need help. Obviously, something is due to distance; more than three-quarters of a century divide the twenty-first-century reader from Chapman. But the temptation to obscurity and preciousness was always there. What else explains the listing without comment of many difficult entries ('deedily', 'determinate', 'dismission', 'quiz', 'shatter-brained', etc.) in his appendix, 'Miss Austen's English', to *Sense and Sensibility*? Not only are these words (eccentric in 1923) unglossed, but the meagre reassurance offered by their listing is in most cases far removed from the volume in which they occur. As Ian Jack noted, facetiously but accurately, in an essay of 1982, it was not only the late twentieth-century reader who was likely to be puzzled by the unannotated phrase in *Emma*, she 'arranged the glasses'. He comments, 'we should surely be told that it was the windows of the carriage with which [Emma] was busying herself, not preparations for some sort of al fresco entertainment.'[70]

Chapman's explanatory notes more happily trace literary allusions—to Shakespeare, Milton, Johnson, Cowper—and his appendixes embed the novels in a wider set of social practices. The tendency to explain literary works with reference to other literary works is something we still recognize as standard. In 1923, the litany of major and minor canonical male poets declared Austen's reassuring demeanour of conformity, the known limits of her known range, and placed her individual talent within a particular (Augustan and non-novelistic) tradition; apart from a scattering of attributions to minor Gothic novels in the notes to *Northanger Abbey*, there is no suggestion that she shared literary or intellectual aspirations with a contemporary circle of female writers. Chapman's annotation, as we might expect, confines her to

also Metcalfe's short account of their collaboration and its beginnings in a letter of 25 November 1957 (OUP archive, LOGE000025); and see Gilson, 'Jane Austen's Text: A Survey of Editions', *Review of English Studies*, n.s. 53 (2002), 79–80.

[70] Ian Jack, 'Novels and those "Necessary Evils": Annotating the Brontës', *Essays in Criticism*, 32 (1982), 322. The phrase 'arranged the glasses' occurs in *Emma*, ed. Chapman, 114.

high male company (and with it, of course, to literary respectability and cultural influence), as endorsed by gentlemanly good taste around 1923. Yet it was in the 1920s and 1930s that a generation of women scholars (women like Dorothy Blakey, Joyce Horner, and J. M. S. Tompkins)[71] began to make a mark with pioneering studies of the novel and the contribution of women writers. On reflection, Chapman's enterprise might already have appeared outmoded. The twenty-first-century reader is likely to be more struck by the omission of an altogether different perspective: while Austen's relation to a particular brand of social and literary history is logged, Chapman's notes do not observe the political-historical axis around which her fictional worlds now appear to revolve. For example, references in *Mansfield Park* to Sir Thomas Bertram's 'West India Estate' and the slave trade, to the 'strange business . . . in America', and to prize money and the wartime representation of Portsmouth go unglossed, apart from the delightful throw-away comment that 'a state of war is implied throughout'.[72]

Most fascinating of all, nowhere do we find on display in this edition that admission of historical coincidence which we now sense is the unacknowledged determinant of the whole enterprise—Jane Austen the wartime novelist and Chapman her wartime editor. This is so despite the overt connection made by one correspondent, Geoffrey Callender, of the Royal Naval College, Dartmouth, to whom Chapman turned for help in locating early nineteenth-century maps. Callender replied on 7 February 1922: 'I don't think I can recommend for reproduction any old ones that I have seen. I fancy that there must have been as careful a guard over Portsmouth topography in 1814 as in 1914.'[73] But if Chapman dismissed the disruptive forces of history, he remained fascinated by the quiet details of chronology. Was it on Thursday 12 January 1809 that Edmund dined at the Parsonage? he wonders. In his rough notes for *Emma* he ponders upon the dating of December engagements: 'Now the 25th of Dec must have been earlier in the week, because the following Sunday seems some days later. 24 Dec was perhaps a Monday, which would make 18 Dec a Tuesday. Harriet's *Tuesday* . . shd be say 11 Dec. (But this is going too far?)'[74]

[71] Dorothy Blakey, *The Minerva Press, 1790–1820* (London: Printed for the Bibliographical Society at the University Press, Oxford, 1939); Joyce M. Horner, *The English Women Novelists and their Connection with the Feminist Movement (1688–1797)* (Northampton, Mass.: Smith College Studies, 1930); and J. M. S. Tompkins, *The Popular Novel in England, 1770–1800* (London: Constable, 1932).

[72] *Mansfield Park*, ed. Chapman, 557.

[73] Bodleian MSS. Eng. Letters c. 759, f. 60v.

[74] Bodleian MS. Eng. Misc. c. 924, f. 82.

It is in the act of annotation that we recover most directly the relation between value as reposing in the text and value as specific to the ideas and beliefs of a particular reading community. As critics we may make easy distinctions between text and annotation which as readers we cannot observe; in practice a body of annotation can powerfully affect the text we read. Annotation is part of its cultural space, which is its literary space, because the space in which we encounter it. Different annotations produce different texts because they make the 'same text' (only ever in illusion the same) available in different ways, to different readings.[75] There appears to be a complacency at work in Chapman's immense project of cultural connection which might be described as the faith that we can know the past; that we can enter the past and find it there; that we can place it. From his influential position within the leading Western academic publishing house of the early twentieth century, Chapman proposed an image of the past, or more precisely a body of fiction represented as an image of the past. Its buttressed completeness is a healing gesture, directed towards the Austen text but also towards the incompleteness of the war-torn modern world.

That was a verdict Reginald Farrer anticipated by several years in a landmark essay in the *Quarterly Review* for July 1917. A centenary tribute (Austen died 18 July 1817), Farrer used the occasion and the publishing context (the two great early nineteenth-century appraisals of Austen, by Walter Scott and Richard Whately, had both appeared in the *Quarterly*, owned by her publisher John Murray) to witty historical effect. A year earlier, in a facetious and zany letter to the *Times Literary Supplement*, addressed from 'The Valley of Rocks and Wolves, Tibet', Farrer, botanist and traveller, had made a double appeal to Janeites to establish in her honour a fund for the assistance of retired governesses and to support it by 'a great memorial edition' of the novels, 'sumptuous, stately, final, and as perfect as care of editors, printers, binders, and publishers can make it'; a 'Dream Edition', with prefaces 'not couched in the timid and half-apologetic vein of some editors, but inspired with the discreet and solemn rapture of the hierophant', accurate geographic etchings, and literary appendixes.[76] In 1916 that was a curiously proleptic fantasy. Now in 1917,

[75] So, for example, the argument offered by Ralph Hanna, 'Annotation as Social Practice', in *Annotation and Its Texts*, ed. Stephen A. Barney (New York: Oxford University Press, 1991), 178–84.

[76] 'A Jane Austen Celebration', *Times Literary Supplement*, 6 January 1916, 9.

Wars may be raging to their end as the background of 'Persuasion', or social miseries strike a new facet of 'Emma'; otherwise all the vast anguish of her time is non-existent to Jane Austen, when once she has got pen in hand, to make us a new kingdom of refuge from the toils and frets of life. Her kingdoms are hermetically sealed, in fact, and here lies the strength of their impregnable immortality; it is not without hope or comfort for us nowadays, to remember that 'Mansfield Park' appeared the year before Waterloo, and 'Emma' the year after.[77]

And that was how a generation of mid-century critics as diverse in their Janeite whimsicality or tough professional allegiances as E. M. Forster, F. R. Leavis, and Lionel Trilling would interpret Austen's novels: as historically defended witnesses to our shared moral lives; and so exemplary for our own historically sated present. This is why she has been enlisted with such regularity in times of peril to represent a set of values worth saving or herself to do the work of saving.

In the case of the American Trilling, it was the wars of the 1950s and 1960s—Suez, Korea, the Cold War, and Vietnam. War continued to shape Austen's twentieth-century reputation as inevitably as it suppressed full recognition of her own historical engagement as a writer of the Napoleonic Wars. Trilling's last published piece, 'Why We Read Jane Austen', was a nervous retrospect of his deeply held belief in great literature's ability to bridge historical distance and confirm our shared humanity, challenged in 1975 by the far different response of a post-Vietnam generation of American students. Their genial incomprehension drove him to troubled reflection on the possible limits of universal truths and to find some measure of salvation in the new anthropology of cultural relativism, and in particular in Clifford Geertz's essay '"From the Native's Point of View"'. Trilling's essay appeared within months of Marilyn Butler's decisively ground-shifting study *Jane Austen and the War of Ideas* (1975), where we encounter the same reflection, addressed from the other end. Here at last, in the bicentenary of her birth, was an Austen firmly embedded in her own distinct (and distinctly different) historical moment. In Trilling's essay the cultures of Iceland, Bali, and Java are enlisted as part of a half-hearted concession to the possibility of empathetic failure and a recognition of the limits of the ahistorical imagination. By contrast, in Butler's historically confident reading Austen becomes both more precisely focused and more alien, as an English anti-Jacobin writer, politically engaged like the women of Butler's own 1970s readership but in a cause they

[77] In *Critical Heritage*, ii. 249. Despite this hermetic enclosure, Farrer also observes 'how much nearer we are to-day to Anne and Fanny than to the generation immediately behind us' (257).

could scarcely grasp. Where Trilling struggled manfully to insist on the sympathy of Javan customs, Butler opened up the differences between English women across less than two hundred years.[78]

Looking back from the beginning of the twenty-first century to the 1920s, it seems that the assembly at that time of a body of universally valuable works of English literature was tied to a particularly pressing revival of a perennial need: literature as the recovery of lost community. Modern English cultural memory has long been in thrall to stories of a just vanishing or recently lost organic world, usually identified with rural England. Hardy and Lawrence wrote of it with elegiac passion; Constance and Ellen Hill went in search of it in Jane Austen's Hampshire; and Raymond Williams analysed the phenomenon with critical detachment in *The Country and the City* (1975). In 1776 Adam Smith, a Scot, was proposing 'publick diversions', by which he had in mind education in the arts ('painting, poetry, musick, dancing') as a substitute for the disappearance of country village life. 'While [a man] remains in a country village', he remarked, 'his conduct may be attended to, and he may be obliged to attend to it himself.'[79] Outside the village, patterns of behaviour and even identity itself become liable to disruption because they are ungrounded—socially, morally, and geographically.

In the opening pages of his recent book, *The Song of the Earth*, a study of literature and environmental consciousness, Jonathan Bate quotes from a passage in *Emma* in which the reader, along with Emma Woodhouse and others of the party gathered to pick strawberries, is led to survey the view from Donwell Abbey, the home of Mr Knightley:

> The considerable slope, at nearly the foot of which the Abbey stood, gradually acquired a steeper form beyond its grounds; and at half a mile distant was a bank of considerable abruptness and grandeur, well clothed with wood;—and at the bottom of this bank, favourably placed and sheltered, rose the Abbey-Mill Farm, with meadows in front, and the river making a close and handsome curve around it.
>
> It was a sweet view—sweet to the eye and the mind. English verdure, English culture, English comfort, seen under a sun bright, without being oppressive.[80]

[78] Lionel Trilling, 'Why We Read Jane Austen', *Times Literary Supplement*, 5 March 1976, 250–2. Geertz repaid the compliment in his essay 'Found in Translation: On the Social History of the Moral Imagination', in *Local Knowledge: Further Essays in Interpretive Anthropology* (1983; London: Fontana Press, 1993), 36–54; Marilyn Butler, *Jane Austen and the War of Ideas* (1975; reissued with new introduction, Oxford: Clarendon Press, 1987).

[79] Adam Smith, *An Inquiry into the Nature and Causes of the Wealth of Nations*, ed. R. H. Campbell, A. S. Skinner, and W. B. Todd, 2 vols. (Oxford: Clarendon Press, 1976), ii. 795–6.

[80] *Emma*, ed. Chapman, 360.

Bate's interest in the passage is to note, beyond the harmony of its physical and moral proportions, the clemency of site and weather, and the 'verbal euphony' of 'verdure' and 'culture', the profound association of its physical and abstract elements. At the time Austen wrote, the older and more recent senses of the word 'culture' (as cultivation of land *and* intellectual work) still coexisted, and the division, anticipated by Smith, did not yet gape between physical and mental labour. In looking out across this English landscape no disjunction is felt between its agricultural and aesthetic value. As Bate puts it: '[Austen's] ideal England is one in which social relations and the aesthetic sense—the sweetness to the eye and the mind—are a function of environmental belonging.'[81] Of course, England also witnessed at that time the intensification of agricultural enclosure and rural dispossession, and the beginnings of a nationally traumatic shift from country to city. But that's to see England through different contemporary eyes: Clare's or Cobbett's England. Some hundred years later and after the territorial disfigurements of the Great War, we sense the completion of a reversal—that in some profound way environmental belonging is now a function of aesthetic sense. The compensatory feel of projects like Chapman's Austen and the revisionary spirit of T. S. Eliot's judgements concerning a tradition of English literature propose literature itself as the route to home and identity, literature as the ground of what is known. The broken allusiveness of *The Waste Land* makes the point in negative, grimly ironic, form, where meaning depends on a sequence of textual *dis*locations. For Chapman and after him for a range of twentieth-century voices Austen encapsulated the moment before the picture and the ground shifted.

Early in the Great War Edward Thomas was commissioned by Oxford University Press to produce an anthology. *This England: An Anthology from her Writers* appeared in 1915 as part of a series designed to catch and shape the public mood alongside *Poems of War and Battle*, selected by V. H. Collins (1914) and *An Anthology of Patriotic Prose*, selected by Frederick Page (1915). Collins and Page were both in-house editors and policy-makers at OUP, Page subsequently working with Chapman on the Austen edition. The England Thomas assembled in his anthology did not reflect a set of ancient institutions or political structures, but what he described about the same time, in an essay entitled 'England', as a 'system of vast circumferences circling round the minute neighbouring points of home'.[82] Thomas's own point of home in the essay is Izaak Walton's *Compleat Angler* with its descriptions of a lush English

[81] Jonathan Bate, *The Song of the Earth* (London: Picador, 2000), 7.

[82] The essay is collected in *The Last Sheaf* (London: Jonathan Cape, 1928), 111.

countryside and a peasantry who are at one with its processes and keepers of the old ways. For them, as for the close-knit communities of Austen's fictional villages, the division has not yet been made between land and culture. In the anthology it is passages from Shakespeare, Milton, Burke, Cobbett, and many more (though not Jane Austen) which serve the same function. England is the horizon seen from a familiar place (a vantage ground of prose or verse); England is an immensity known only through a series of minute connections, literary signposts, which surround and annotate the given point (home) in a specified degree of closeness; England's knowledge is local and relative.

In Kipling's story Austen's novels provide the familiar place, the piece of English soil which the Janeites lay claim to, staking out in imagination their French dug-out as the point of home. If for Humberstall the dug-out ever afterwards remains the greatest reality, it is because re-reading Jane Austen ensures it is so. Austen's English villages, secluded behind leafy hedgerows and sheltered by gently sloping hills, are the aesthetic origin of its physical identity as home. Re-reading the novels is a means of recovering home—in this case, the faux-Austenian landscape of trench and pantomime leaves, the camouflage of the dug-out, the place of their enactment as reading, which is the place where all texts take on meaning, and where, in a profounder sense, place is itself brought into the ambit of what is known and therefore authenticated. For E. M. Forster reviewing Chapman's editions, Austen is 'part of the soil of England' and a 'country writer'. Collected in *Abinger Harvest*, named for the village of Abinger Hammer in Surrey, rich with memories of the family of the seventeenth-century diarist John Evelyn, and now part of Forster's literary and family associations, these particular Austenian observations are in their turn caught up in a wider system of aesthetic and environmental connections.[83]

'If one wanted to show a foreigner England', Forster wrote in *Howards End* (1910), 'perhaps the wisest course would be to take him to the final section of the Purbeck hills, and stand him on their summit, a few miles to the east of Corfe. Then system after system of our island would roll together under his feet.'[84] In 1913, moved by Herbert Grierson's scholarly two-volume Oxford edition *The Poems of John Donne* (1912), Rupert Brooke summarized his melancholy premonition that all good things would pass away—the beer at an inn in Royston, the sausages at another inn above Princes Risborough,

[83] *Abinger Harvest*, 166 and 177.

[84] E. M. Forster, *Howards End* (London: Edward Arnold, 1910), Ch. 19, opening paragraph.

Charing Cross Bridge by night, the dancing of Miss Ethel Levey, and the Lucretian hexameter—all, that is, except the Clarendon Press editions of the English poets: 'so the Clarendon Press books will be the only thing our evil generation may show to the cursory eyes of posterity, to prove it was not wholly bad.'[85] Already before the First World War the discovery of the endurance of Englishness was linked to a turn to literature. What war did was strengthen the discovery into a need. Less a discovery than a recovery, a means of restoration, English studies and the establishment of a canon of unambiguously representative texts became matters of urgency in the 1920s and 1930s. In the years between the Great War and the next, the agenda of professional critics and university teachers like I. A. Richards and F. R. Leavis of the moral Cambridge School asserted that the business of literature is to work on consciousness, to heal the perceived division between physical and mental realities, between land and culture, soil and language, caused by the loss of organic community. Literature, and literary criticism, fills the gap. It is worth reminding ourselves just how defensive their influential agenda was. For Leavis, Englishness was a notion to be endowed with enormous critical power (as in his verdict that 'in *Rasselas* we have something deeply English that relates Johnson and Jane Austen to Crabbe'). But its power is local and specific; it refuses cosmopolitan rootlessness (witness Leavis's dislike of Joyce's linguistic experiments). To be English is to be rooted, like Austen and like D. H. Lawrence, who 'always lived on the spot where he was. That was his genius.'[86] Hence for Leavis a great tradition must be narrow, as for Richards the act of criticism must be a close and minute engagement, the reader labouring upon the details of a specific text. His utilitarian championing of 'practical criticism' was linked to ideas of mental wholeness and psychical reconciliation, while the principles of literary criticism (in his book of that title) are 'a loom upon which it is proposed to re-weave some ravelled parts of our civilisation'.[87]

Already before the Great War Jane Austen was saving minds. Metcalfe noted somewhat donnishly that 'her limitation is the secret of her achievement' and 'her prevailing sanity' her most significant feature. In a passage

[85] From a review of Grierson's edition of Donne in *Poetry and Drama*, 1 (June 1913), reprinted in *The Prose of Rupert Brooke*, ed. Christopher Hassall (London: Sidgwick & Jackson, 1956), 92.

[86] The final sentence of 'Johnson and Augustanism', in F. R. Leavis, *The Common Pursuit* (London: Chatto & Windus, 1952), 115; F. R. Leavis, *For Continuity* (Cambridge: The Minority Press, 1933), 153, in a review of Aldous Huxley's edition of *The Letters of D. H. Lawrence*.

[87] I. A. Richards, in the preface written for the third impression (1928) of *Principles of Literary Criticism* (1924; London: Kegan Paul, Trench, Trubner & Co., 1934), 1.

from his 1911 lecture remarkable for its hinted concealment, A. C. Bradley stated approvingly that 'her novels make exceptionally peaceful reading. She troubles us neither with problems nor with painful emotions, and if there is a wound in our minds she is not likely to probe it.' Perhaps this was why a few years later the Brasenose College tutor H. F. Brett-Smith, exempt from military service but employed by hospitals to grade reading matter according to a 'fever-chart' for the war-wounded, prescribed Austen's novels for the severely shell-shocked. We are back with Humberstall again. The view continues: a recent novel, *Sleeping with Jane Austen*, by David Aitken, features a murderer confined to a mental hospital who goes to sleep with a copy of Austen under his pillow.[88] Rupert Brooke again collects the threads suggestively together, this time writing to Edward Marsh from his wartime posting in the eastern Mediterranean: 'I cannot write you any description of my life. It would need Miss Austen to make anything of it. We glide to & fro on an azure see [*sic*] & forget the war—I must go & censor my platoon's letters. My long poem is to be about the existence—& non-locality—of England.'[89] Soothing, empty of incident, anaesthetic, healing, specific, yet non-particular; the small-scale intimacy of her fictional worlds, and the equally small span of her output reassured the early twentieth-century reader, who valued literature according to its 'sanity'.

For F. R. Leavis, Lawrence is the modern writer who is 'normal, central and sane to the point of genius';[90] and if that is Lawrence, the latest representative of the great tradition that Jane Austen inaugurated, then Austen is only more so. In the sociological-cum-psychological thesis promulgated by Q. D. Leavis, Austen's sanity (the 'rational code of feeling' which is the 'source . . . of [her] strength') becomes a test, inevitably failed, by which to measure the mental robustness or moral decay of the mass reading public. The 'fiction habit', as Leavis called it, was to her mind not so different from the 'drug habit', but it was quite distinct from the experience of reading Jane Austen.[91]

[88] *Pride and Prejudice*, ed. Metcalfe, vii and xi; Bradley, 'Jane Austen', 16; and Martin Jarrett-Kerr, 'The Mission of Eng. Lit.', a letter to the *Times Literary Supplement*, 3 February 1984, 111, quoted in Christopher Kent, 'Learning History with, and from, Jane Austen', in *Jane Austen's Beginnings: The Juvenilia and 'Lady Susan'*, ed. J. David Grey (Ann Arbor, Mich. and London: UMI Research Press, 1989), 59 and 71, n. 2; David Aitken, *Sleeping with Jane Austen* (Harpenden: No Exit Press, 2000), reported in the Jane Austen Society *News Letter*, 15 (October 2000), 12.

[89] *The Letters of Rupert Brooke*, ed. Geoffrey Keynes (London: Faber & Faber, 1968), 680–1.

[90] Leavis, *For Continuity*, 152.

[91] Q. D. Leavis, *Fiction and the Reading Public* (1932; Harmondsworth, Middx.: Penguin, 1979), 110, 134, and 22. Jane Austen is the implied but curiously missing element from Alison Light's important study of Englishness between the two world wars, *Forever England: Femininity, Literature, and Conservatism*

Much as Chapman's feat of Classically propelled textual restoration recovered Austen's novels from the corruption into which they were perceived to have sunk under the Victorian reprint industry; so the professional criticism of the post-war years sought to save them from the malign popularity which so offended Henry James—indeed, and ironically given Chapman's own cultivated amateurism, from the Janeites themselves. A similar sleight rescued Austen from the taint of novelism. Chapman's extravagant and isolated scholarly respect towards the novel as Austen represented it was matched by Q. D. Leavis's discernment of a rational code of feeling linking Austen to the educated reader and separating both from the contaminations of romance and bestseller. In Leavis's thesis as in Chapman's annotations, neither Austen nor the educated reader is victim to the 'fiction habit'. Claimed for the narrow organic community of English literature and the select village of educated readers, Austen's healthy (even medicinal) cultural status was apparently assured. The smallness of her scope and its slim bulk were as much in tune with the psychic needs of the mid-twentieth century as was her guaranteed capacity to represent life as it should be. In recognizing Austen, a generation recovered itself.

between the Wars (London: Routledge, 1991). See also Deidre Lynch, 'At Home with Jane Austen', in *Cultural Institutions of the Novel*, ed. Deidre Lynch and William B. Warner (Durham and London: Duke University Press, 1996), 159–92, where Lynch argues for the crucial work done by readings of Austen's novels in the interwar years to promote a national agenda equally committed to upholding minority high literary values and promulgating new forms of down-market domestic consumption.

2

Personal Obscurity and the Biographer's Baggage

Ground rules?

Mindful of his wry title, 'One Cheer for Literary Biography', John Updike brings to a close a persistently equivocal essay by summarizing the fascination of the third-party revelations of biography as the appeal of the authentic or at least 'less artful . . . in this art-wary age'. In a description calculated to make all parties squirm, biography gives us 'the intimate underside of writers'; we enjoy it because, wary of art, 'we resent a fiction writer's manipulation of his private life, including the private lives of those around him, and rejoice when he or she loses control.' But Updike is a novelist before he is a reader (or as he fastidiously puts it, 'consumer') of biography, and from the other side of the fence, that of the consumed, things look different. What right has the biographer to intrude on private life, 'disturbing my children, quizzing my ex-wife, bugging my present wife, seeking for Judases among my friends, rummaging through yellowing old clippings, quoting *in extenso* bad reviews I would rather forget, and getting everything slightly wrong.'[1] For Updike, no party to the biographical contract escapes untainted.

In a different age, George Eliot expressed a similar revulsion when she described biography as a 'disease'. In a letter to her publisher, John Blackwood, she complained nervously of the posthumous fascination with the details of Charles Dickens's recently published 'Life':

[1] John Updike, 'One Cheer for Literary Biography', *New York Review of Books*, 4 February 1999, 5.

something should be done by dispassionate criticism towards the reform of our national habits in the matter of literary biography. Is it not odious that as soon as a man is dead his desk is raked, and every insignificant memorandum, which he never meant for the public, is printed for the gossiping amusement of people too idle to re-read his books?[2]

The year was 1874, and the ageing Eliot/Mary Ann Evans knew only too well that there was a stash of personal information filed away in Blackwood's office under the letter 'E'. John Blackwood apparently shared her reservations (exemplified in his judgement on Elizabeth Gaskell's *Life of Charlotte Brontë* (1857)—'bookmaking out of the remains of the dead'),[3] but it did not stop the firm handing over their correspondence (both by then dead), including this same letter, when her widower, John Cross, came to write her biography a few years later. In 1860 Dickens had sought to steal a march on the biographers by making a bonfire of his private papers; turning the occasion into a family party, he invited his children to roast onions 'in the ashes of the great'.[4] The act of destruction neatly encapsulates the writer's plea for an existence separate from his creations, as no integral part of their meaning. As answer to the biographer's prying art, the novelist provides onions not secrets to be raked from the ashes. But how naïve of Dickens, himself the great biographer of London, not to know that biographies will be written anyway. Despite the destruction, John Forster's life of his friend extended to three volumes and Dickens's scheme to outwit the rummagers is itself now a matter of record. Burning the evidence, it seems, is no defence against what James Joyce called the 'biografiend'.[5] This brings me to the first law of biography: biographies will be written with or without the evidence. One of the biggest miscalculations of Henry Austen's failure-filled life must surely be his pronouncement, expressed with such confidence in his 'Biographical Notice of the Author' of 1818, written only months after his sister's death: 'Short and easy will be the task of the mere biographer.'[6]

[2] *George Eliot's Life as Related in her Letters and Journals*, ed. J. W. Cross (1885; New York: AMS Press, 1965), 522.

[3] *The George Eliot Letters*, ed. Gordon Haight, 9 vols. (New Haven: Yale University Press, 1954–78), 2. 323, Blackwood to George Henry Lewes, 28 April 1857.

[4] Dickens mentions the incident in a letter to W. H. Wills, 4 September 1860: 'Yesterday I burnt, in the field at Gad's Hill, the accumulated letters and papers of twenty years. They sent up a smoke like the Genie when he got out of the casket on the seashore.' (*The Letters of Charles Dickens*, 12 vols. (Oxford: Clarendon Press, 1965–2002), 9, ed. Graham Storey (1997), 304.) Gladys Storey adds further details on the authority of Kate Perugini, Dickens's daughter, in *Dickens and Daughter* (London: F. Muller Ltd., 1939), 106–7.

[5] James Joyce, *Finnegan's Wake* (1939; London: Faber & Faber, new edn., repr. 1960), 55.

[6] *Memoir*, 137.

It is the achievement and the failure of biography as a genre to give form to a life, to make the appearance of something whole and shaped and full from whatever materials are available. Reviewing in 1930 two biographies of Christina Rossetti in her essay 'I am Christina Rossetti', Virginia Woolf had this to say about the form:

> the old illusion comes over us. Here is the past and all its inhabitants miraculously sealed as in a magic tank; all we have to do is to look and to listen and to listen and to look and soon the little figures—for they are rather under life size—will begin to move and to speak, and as they move we shall arrange them in all sorts of patterns of which they were ignorant, for they thought when they were alive that they could go where they liked; and as they speak we shall read into their sayings all kinds of meanings which never struck them, for they believed when they were alive that they said straight off whatever came into their heads. But once you are in a biography all is different.[7]

Or, as Adam Phillips neatly puts it: 'Biography gives shape to a life, but a life doesn't.'[8] Alive, Rossetti contrived to make herself fit into as small a space as possible, but a recent biography (by Jan Marsh in 1994) extends to 634 pages. The disparity between the minimalism of her life and the intensity of her poetic achievement brings into sharp focus the way biography creates meaning out of nothing—the more gaps there are, the more the biographer finds to fill them. This brings me to the second law of biography: they will be fat. Biographies are uniformly fat books, regardless of the size or shape of the lives they document: in biography, we all become obese. There are reasons for this: biography, literally life writing, has tended to assume a natural fit between its own material bulk and the life recorded; as though biography were itself a natural form and writing the outgrowth of life. Hence Terry Eagleton's remark that '[t]he structure of biography is biology.'[9] Accordingly and inexorably, lots of pages equate to lifelikeness, and this seeming natural fit disguises the extent to which the evidence is constructed. There is an element of respect, too, implied in the writing of the big biography, whose bulk straightforwardly says, 'look how important my subject is.' In Jane Austen's case, the tribute of size is regularly paid and it has little to do with whether

[7] Virginia Woolf, 'I am Christina Rossetti', *Nation and Athenaeum*, 6 December 1930, reprinted in *The Common Reader*, second series (London: Hogarth Press, 1932), 237.

[8] Adam Phillips, 'Appreciating Pater', in *Promises, Promises: Essays on Literature and Psychoanalysis* (London: Faber & Faber, 2000), 151.

[9] Terry Eagleton, 'First Class Fellow Traveller', review of Seán French, *Patrick Hamilton: A Life*, in *London Review of Books*, 2 December 1993, 12.

there is anything new to say: she is simply that important. Literary biography is bound to the twinned assumptions that a life can be written and that its writing is pre-given, that its textual traces must be 'out there' and recoverable as the chronology of thought and feeling attending a sequence of events. The lives of writers, most of all, cannot be imagined, it seems, except as written documents. The everyday ordinary events of their lives, but especially the everyday extraordinary events—love affairs, betrayals, deaths of close friends or relations—cannot be contemplated in biography except as written traces. There must be letters, diary entries, outpourings of the soul onto paper. Like Richardson's Pamela, struggling simultaneously with events and their narration, the biographee must have encountered life pen in hand. The biographical illusion works through these two devices—bulk and the naturalization of the writing process itself. We know she or he lived intensely, suffered intensely, because she/he left written evidence. The fact that this is not so as far as our own experience of life is concerned, only deepens our desire that it be so.

Even more than its close relation the novel, biography appeals to an urgent human need—to know fully and completely another person and to have access to their innermost thoughts. John Wiltshire has recently attempted to describe the complicated attraction of this 'hybrid form' with which biographers and their readers become engaged as lying somewhere between 'fact and make-believe'. Drawing on the analytic model of the paediatrician D. W. Winnicott, Wiltshire invokes the term 'transitional space' to help define biography's uneasy status. In Winnicott's thinking 'transitional space' is a 'resting place' in the normal process of illusionment and disillusionment in terms of which our post-infant selves develop. More precisely, it identifies the public as distinct from the private world of daydreaming and therefore the shared arena in which the arts exist. As Wiltshire explains it: '[t]ransitional space is that area of simultaneously psychological and social life occupied by all activities in which illusion and reality coexist, such as the arts.' But where in the arts 'fantasy and reality coexist' by agreement, in biography the relationship remains fraught and we are presented instead with a 'tug-of-war between dreaming and history'.[10] By this argument, biography as form is bound to fail, the victim of its own confused signals: caught between the unresolvable truths of dreaming and history, biography simultaneously feeds and denies our fantasies of intimacy. In the paradoxical

[10] John Wiltshire, *Recreating Jane Austen*, 17–22.

relationship between paper and life which the form enacts, the best situation of all may therefore be where we have only sufficient evidence to sanction our imagining of the textual trace but not enough to cause the shock of disappointment or guilt when fantasy departs from 'objective' reality. In such circumstances desire will be reparative of rather than in conflict with reality (since 'reality' will have so slender a claim).

By this, Cassandra Austen did biographers a profound service when she censored or destroyed her sister's private papers and correspondence. Whatever her reasons and whatever was burned, Cassandra licensed the imagining of fact, the dream of history. May not Cassandra's precise dating of her sister's last completed novels (*Emma* and *Persuasion*) point to the existence (and destruction) of a diary, Claire Tomalin speculates intelligently in her 1997 biography? and if the diary contained details of 'the starting and finishing dates' of her novels, what else might it not have contained? Extrapolating more boldly from the paucity of textual clues to the emotional crises of 1796–8, David Nokes, in his 1997 biography, despairingly asks: 'Why do we have no letters from this period? It can hardly be because Jane Austen did not write any... It can only be that Cassandra... chose to destroy them... she preferred to obliterate the memory of a period of such distress.' A favoured strategy is to reconstitute empathetically these 'destroyed' traces. Accordingly, Nokes tells us that 'Cassandra received the news [of her fiancé Tom Fowle's death] with a kind of numbness. Outwardly, she was strangely calm... Upon Jane the influence of this change in her sister's disposition was no less profound for being, at first at least, unacknowledged and unperceived.'[11] In the interests of recording the complete life, the biographer appears entitled to recover not only what must have existed and been destroyed but what only appears to be 'unacknowledged and unperceived'. In the hands of the skilful recorder, gaps and silences are even more eloquent than evidence. The form grows strangely fat on such omissions and biography's texts can seem endlessly recessive.

There is of course another, mundaner reason why biographies are fat—they are trade books whose shape and length is largely determined by commercial factors. Hence, their uniform bulk, their steady chronological march from birth to death, predictably interrupted halfway through by the inevitable motley collection of illustrations of friends and family, houses and

[11] Claire Tomalin, *Jane Austen: A Life* (Harmondsworth, Middx.: Viking, 1997), 242 and 331, n. 5; David Nokes, *Jane Austen: A Life* (London: Fourth Estate, 1997), 169–71.

favourite views, the odd manuscript page, the will, and the birth certificate—the fugitive and decomposed fragments of a life which somehow guarantee the composed consistency of the surrounding text. Biography is the interface between high culture and the mass market, and we can never have too many biographies; so biography also grows fat on its own success as a form.

Biographers, though, have been occasionally embarrassed by the identikit mould into which they must pour their precious and unique ingredients. The tenets of what became known as the 'new biography' were defined in the early twentieth century in contrast to its baggy Victorian structure. Lytton Strachey's experimentally slim study *Eminent Victorians* was published in May 1918, five months before the Armistice, and it signalled a break with the old order. His choice of subjects—Cardinal Manning, Thomas Arnold, Florence Nightingale, and General Gordon—were each in their own right heavyweights; taken together they represented the Church, Education, Public Health, and the Army, the four pillars of Victorian society. Any one of them could provide his or her bodyweight in documentary evidence, enough material to fill a multi-volume 'Life' of the old style and to sink all sense of the individual within the representative. Strachey's point is that selection, brevity, and the random detail may deliver greater insight into a human character than a historically symptomatic or comprehensive study. He writes in what was for a time a much invoked preface:

> It is not by the direct method of a scrupulous narration that the explorer of the past can hope to depict that singular epoch. If he is wise, he will adopt a subtler strategy. He will attack his subject in unexpected places; he will fall upon the flank, or the rear; he will shoot a sudden, revealing searchlight into obscure recesses, hitherto undivined. He will row out over that great ocean of material, and lower down into it, here and there, a little bucket, which will bring up to the light of day some characteristic specimen, from those far depths, to be examined with a careful curiosity.[12]

The extravagantly diffuse metaphoric range of Strachey's prose, disconcertingly at odds with its slender vehicle, sets the reader on a number of enquiries as to the true identity of the biographer—big-game hunter, marine biologist, stalker, or, given that the year is 1918, military tactician in pursuit of the enemy? But if part of his purpose is to suggest that inside every fat biography there is a thin biography trying to get out, this aspect of his experiment has not found much favour, nor can it as long as the biographer's critical sense is so closely constrained by commercial priorities.

[12] Lytton Strachey, *Eminent Victorians* (1918; repr. Harmondsworth, Middx.: Penguin, 1975), 9.

This may explain why even the most up-to-date biography can seem irritatingly or comfortingly (depending on one's point of view) old fashioned. For it is not just the novel to which biographical form is currently entailed, it is the big novel, more particularly, the nineteenth-century realist novel or *Bildungsroman*, with its illusion of the comprehensive and comprehensible life, which is the modern biographer's readiest model. This apparently endemic anxiety, coupled with a commerce-driven conservatism, leads to the conclusion that as a genre biography is more comfortable inhabiting dead forms than constructing its own; that its allegiance is doubly given to death and dark places. By this, biography is always ghost writing; it memorializes the dead twice over—as the record of a life ended (and this is the consequence of its narrative teleology whether the life recorded is indeed finished or not), and as itself the burial ground for outmoded literary practices.[13] There is, however, a proviso: as evidence of its own belatedness, modern biography borrows the contours of the nineteenth-century novel without its confident plotting; no longer secure in the use of significant pattern, the biographer more often than not substitutes detail for plot; the informative life as opposed to the shaped life. So, this is the third law of biography: biography will be the home of superannuated generic practices. In the twentieth century biography was the last home of the Victorian novel; in the nineteenth century it was the burial ground of the mixed narrative of the eighteenth-century epistolary novel—the life-and-letters form, used by J. G. Lockhart in his *Memoirs of the Life of Sir Walter Scott, Bart.* (1837–8), by Elizabeth Gaskell in her *Life of Charlotte Brontë*, and by James Edward Austen-Leigh in his *Memoir of Jane Austen* (1870).

It was the biography by Austen-Leigh, her nephew, rather than a critical revaluation or upturn in the reading of the novels which began the process that made Jane Austen into a special cultural commodity. The *Memoir* was published on 16 December 1869, the 94th anniversary of her birthday, in a relatively modest edition of a thousand copies. A year later an expanded second edition printed for the first time fragments of unfinished or early drafts of works, including the cancelled Chapter 10 of Volume 2 of *Persuasion*, the early manuscript works *Lady Susan* and *The Watsons*, and a synopsis

[13] Compare the argument offered by Leah Price, *The Anthology and the Rise of the Novel, from Richardson to George Eliot* (Cambridge: Cambridge University Press, 2000), 51–2; and Laura Marcus's comment that 'biography has always been a "haunted" form of writing', in 'The Newness of the "New Biography": Biographical Theory and Practice in the Early Twentieth Century', in *Mapping Lives: The Uses of Biography*, ed. Peter France and William St Clair (Oxford: Oxford University Press for the British Academy, 2002), 206.

of *Sanditon*, under the title of 'The Last Work'. These 'new' writings, like most of the details of the life Austen-Leigh recorded, were up to this point unknown outside the immediate family circle; after 1871 there was no further printing of Austen fiction from manuscript for the next fifty years. Almost sixty years on in 1927 Caroline Spurgeon, Shakespeare scholar and first woman professor in London University, could make the extraordinary claim that 'every scrap of information and every ray of light on Jane Austen are of national importance'.[14] Another seventy years on, and as many biographies later, Richard Cohen, writing in the *Daily Telegraph* on 20 September 1997, asked: 'How many lives of Jane Austen do we need?' Gesturing to the three titles to be published that year (by Valerie Grosvenor Myer, David Nokes, and Claire Tomalin) and a further volume then on the horizon (from Maggie McKernan), Cohen was unaware of a fifth, M. C. Hammond's *Relating to Jane* which would appear the following year and of yet another, scheduled for 2001 and at that stage no more than a gleam in Carol Shields's eye. But six biographies in fewer years is no bad record for an author about whom there is so little to know.

The primary sources for a life of Jane Austen are challengingly thin: no private diaries to suggest the existence of an inner life, a self apart; scarcely the whisper of a clue to that 'intimate underside' which causes Updike such unease; and almost nothing by way of public record even in the archives of her famously sociable publisher, John Murray—no hints of literary parties at which Miss Austen might have been a guest. Her brother Henry in his brief 1833 'Memoir' can only mention as noteworthy an invitation which from modesty she declined, a meeting with the fashionable and notorious French novelist Germaine de Staël, arranged for summer 1814. Under examination, however, this non-event collapses since the date Henry assigns for the literary encounter that never was is after de Staël's recorded departure from England. Even this little piece of wishful glamour will not stick.[15] What we know of the life of no other biographical subject is so exclusively determined through family; but the partiality of the family record (a mix of careful policing, rivalry, and absence of information) frustrates enquiry. No modern biographer can get as close as they; yet what they tell reads like myth-making rather than fact.

Simon Jarvis has suggested that some biographical subjects, Jane Austen among them, present problems 'not unlike those which face the editor of a

[14] Quoted in *Critical Heritage*, ii. 292.

[15] See *Memoir*, 150 and note.

text for which there is little manuscript or bibliographical evidence.' In both cases, the slimness of the documentary material and the closeness with which it has been scrutinized frustrate fresh enquiry; in both cases, it is difficult to dislodge a reading which has taken on authority by virtue of transmission or descent from one account to the next. Under these narrow conditions, Jarvis concludes, '[l]ife-writers promise us their subject "according to the most authentic copies", but in the event reproduce the *textus receptus* of immemorial tradition.'[16] The point seems justified in Austen's case, where the frequent rehearsal of what little there is to know effectively inhibits knowledge on other terms. But the wider thesis that biographical subjects are edited texts is worth pondering because, at least since the foundational practice in both areas of Dr Johnson, the link between the disciplines of biography and textual criticism has appeared a compelling one. If the activity of the textual critic, sifting drafts, revisions, and variant states to uncover the creative origins of and environmental impact upon the developing literary work and to establish its definitive form, seems obviously biographical, then biography on very little reflection is even more closely constrained by its textual ontology. 'In time to come Lytton Strachey's Queen Victoria will be Queen Victoria, just as Boswell's Johnson is now Dr. Johnson.'[17] Woolf's remark is more than a compliment to the compelling representations afforded by two fine biographies, it also crystallizes something far more significant: the autonomous bibliographic character of biography's authority. Biography's truth is that of bookmaking and not of life. The structure of biography is not biology but bibliography.

It is instructive to realize how late Jane Austen's biography remained a family property, and that her collateral descendants continued to exert an influence as biographers and keepers of the archive until relatively recently. Not only this, she remained the particular property of that branch of the family descended from her eldest brother, James, through the Austen-Leighs and the Lefroys. Both her niece Anna Lefroy, who had some title to consider herself Aunt Jane's literary heiress, and Anna's daughter Fanny Caroline wrote family histories, which though remaining unpublished fed anecdotes and recollections of Jane Austen into the published record, while in 1913 James Edward Austen-Leigh's grandson, Richard Arthur Austen-Leigh, published

[16] Simon Jarvis, 'Sponge Cakes or Don Juan: Irony and Morality in Jane Austen's Life and Work', *Times Literary Supplement*, 12 September 1997, 3, a review of the biographies by Nokes and Tomalin.

[17] Virginia Woolf, 'The Art of Biography', in *The Death of the Moth and Other Essays* (1942; 5th impression, London: Hogarth Press, 1947), 122.

with his uncle, William Austen-Leigh, James Edward's youngest son, an expanded biography, *Jane Austen: Her Life and Letters. A Family Record*, enlarging the 1871 *Memoir* with materials drawn from other branches of the family. Into their account they absorbed the major collection of Jane Austen letters edited in 1884 by Lord Brabourne, son of her niece Fanny Knight, as well as Jane's letters to her brother Francis (Frank) and other anecdotes about Charles and Frank published by the Hubbacks, Frank's descendants, in *Jane Austen's Sailor Brothers* (1906). At almost the same time, James Edward's daughter, Mary Augusta Austen-Leigh, published privately in 1911 a memoir of her father which added new detail about life at Steventon and Chawton in Jane Austen's day, drawn from his sister Caroline Austen's manuscript reminiscences and his niece Fanny Caroline Lefroy's manuscript history; she followed this with further family material in *Personal Aspects of Jane Austen* (1920).

Remaining the definitive Austen biography for much of the twentieth century, W. and R. A. Austen-Leigh's *Life and Letters* was, a hundred years on, surprisingly reticent, even coy, about the life it portrayed, removing names and casting a fuzzy romantic colouring over events: to the extent that popular biographies drawing upon its authority were bound to fail. It was only brought into sharper focus as recently as 1989 when Deirdre Le Faye substantially rewrote it as *A Family Record*, but still under the Austen-Leigh name and aegis. Meanwhile, in 1942, R. A. Austen-Leigh had published privately an odd assortment of family documents which in developing the background to Jane Austen's history also deepened some of its shadows; these documents were to feed into his planned revision of the 1913 life, the revision Le Faye eventually undertook. *Austen Papers, 1704–1856*, as he titled the collection, contains extracts from the correspondence of the East India surgeon-trader Tysoe Saul Hancock with his wife, Philadelphia, and daughter, Eliza, Jane's paternal aunt and cousin; other extracts are from Eliza's correspondence with her prim cousin Philadelphia Walter, by which time she is Eliza de Feuillide, wife of the faux-Comte (guillotined in 1794); and from the correspondence of another aunt, Jane Leigh-Perrot, wife of Jane's maternal uncle, during her incarceration awaiting trial on a charge of shoplifting. The details of the Hancock marriage and their domestic and business affairs in India and with Warren Hastings take on ambiguous shape in the *Austen Papers*. Here too the glamorous and teasing Eliza, brilliant counter to the more sober Austens, at last comes into focus, and something of the extraordinary fate of Mrs Leigh-Perrot is recounted in her own words. In the wrong hands these papers and the stories they sketch threatened to bury the chronicled respectability of the Austens under several cupboard-loads of family skeletons. Le Faye was engaged in the 1980s to enlarge the family biography by Mrs Joan Impey, wife of Lawrence Austen Impey, whose mother was Kathleen Austen-Leigh, James Edward's granddaughter and Jane's great-great niece. Le Faye was given access at that time to the Austen-Leigh archive and modestly describes herself in her introduction as R. A. Austen-Leigh's 'belated amanuensis'. Her accounts of the Hancocks and of Mrs Leigh-Perrot are unspeculative and respectful. Since then the Austen-Leigh family papers (among them Fanny Caroline Lefroy's 'Family History') have been deposited on open access in the Hampshire Record Office and Le Faye has again revised *A Family Record* (second edition, 2004), now under her sole name.

Le Faye's biography bears within it palimpsestically the 1870 and 1871 *Memoir* and the 1913 *Life and Letters*. By virtue of its descent, it has assumed the status of sourcebook or 'factual' biography among a teeming industry of 'interpretative' accounts. Both Tomalin in her deferential study of the writer's psychology and more curiously Nokes in his abrasive and oppositional reading of the life are content to cite evidence in the form it takes in *A Family Record* (1989), as though it represents raw data. Not only do they quote from its pages edited summaries of documents readily available to them in the Hampshire Record Office and elsewhere; on occasion they even misread Le Faye's footnotes and confuse the authorities she invokes correctly.[18] Such traffic is one-way: in keeping with its appointed status, the index to Le Faye's 2004 second edition acknowledges no debt to Tomalin or Nokes's imaginative reconstructions. That is unsurprising; but what is surprising is that a professional like Tomalin and a sceptic like Nokes should uphold the same duality and rely on the same unassailable basis of biographical knowledge: the assumption, that is, that a life can have a non-interpreted print foundation. Tomalin and Nokes both endorse the prior authority of the Austen-Leigh published recension even where it compromises, as it must in Nokes's case, the compositional authority of their overtly revisionist versions.

[18] See, for example, Tomalin, *Jane Austen: A Life*, 316 n. 1, with the added twist that Tomalin borrows the wrong reference from Le Faye. The source is not, as she suggests, 'Fanny Caroline Lefroy's notes on family history' but 'Anna Lefroy's Original Memories of Jane Austen'. Tomalin has simply copied down in error Le Faye, *Family Record* (1989), 265 n. 61 instead of n. 60. Nokes can be equally unclear about the manuscript source he draws on, conflating two different documents into one by misreading Le Faye. See Nokes, *Jane Austen: A Life*, 57 and 533 n. 4, and Le Faye, *Family Record* (1989), 18 and 258 nn. 39 and 40.

Where does the authority of a biography lie? The family record which Le Faye has so meticulously enlarged is the reasonable culmination of a particular way of telling the story, but its status as truth or as fact, like its completeness, is surely more problematic than its conferred authority suggests. Since biography, unlike the novel, implies the existence of an original, in what sense is it useful to think of the life of a person as having an original or authentic text? Jane Austen famously wrote 'seven years I suppose are enough to change every pore of one's skin, & every feeling of one's mind.'[19] The question is what is there in the text of a life to stay true to? Apart from a very few facts—date of birth, places lived, death—(and even they can be contested) how do we recognize an accurate text of a life? Specifically, can a life be distilled into one pre-eminent account? *Jane Austen, A Family Record* aims to be comprehensive, drawing upon a range of makings and remakings by branches of the family whose opinions on events and people are not and cannot be mutually consistent; and as the title implies, it ties the concept of personal history to context. Above all, the subject who emerges within and through a network of relationships will not be unitary and any attempt to sift the evidence will only risk further distorting what is already tenuous and unstable. However, there is no choice but to sift or edit, highlighting some things, diminishing others, concealing and conjecturing still others; in the process endorsing one version, silencing another, and always making critical judgements, which are at best provisional, never definitive. The danger for Jane Austen readers and biographers is that they will take any account as other than interpretative. The personal memories to which the early generations of Austens, Lefroys, and Knights gave shape remained among themselves matter of lively suspicion, speculation, and disagreement. By attributing categorical authority to one textual recension, that of the Austen-Leighs and their appointed agents, we risk mistaking preference or partiality for truth, stories for facts; eventually we risk making Jane Austen's life inaccessible to imaginative retelling.

A primary purpose of the early Austen biographies was as much to connect the novelist with a notion of Englishness as with her art. Like the systematic study of bookmaking, biography is, as Spurgeon's 1927 remark implied, an intensely nationalist activity. In neither instance is the literary function of the discipline obvious though the case is fiercely made. Among the family biographers of the second and third generation, Austen-Leigh was Jane Austen's Hampshire biographer, as Lord Brabourne was her Kentish biog-

[19] *Jane Austen's Letters*, 99.

rapher, the two of them carving up the English Home Counties between them in much the same way as they jealously presided over portions of the documentary evidence. In offering his portrait of a woman whose novels were the effortless extension of a wholesome and blameless life lived in simple, natural surroundings, Austen-Leigh was influenced by a mid-nineteenth-century ruralism, closely associated with fellow Hampshire writer Mary Russell Mitford's *Our Village* (1824–32), and with the prolific pastoral fancies of Mary and William Howitt, whose popular *Book of the Seasons* (1831) and *Wood Leighton; or, A Year in the Country* (1836) breathed, in the words of one critic, '*not* the perfumes of balls and routs, but—of violets and wild flowers; leading the mind to pure and pleasant thoughtfulness.'[20] In Mitford's village sketches, a gentle Hampshire scenery contributed to a realist idyll of true English values, to be contrasted to the immoderate passions induced by the wilder and more remote landscapes of an older regional tradition, most recently associated with Walter Scott, and into which the Brontë sisters would soon tap. Already when Elizabeth Gaskell in *North and South* (1854–5) imagined the New Forest village of Helstone as pastoral counterpart to the grim manufacturing town of Milton-Northern in Darkshire, Hampshire in particular had become quintessential England, whose gentle scenery mapped an ideal location, untouched by the upheaval, squalor, and class tension of an industrializing society. Austen-Leigh had to look no further for inspiration than the Hampshire novels in this style of his sister and niece, Anna and Fanny Caroline Lefroy.

Compressing Jane Austen's life between the engraved illustrations of the Tudor manor house at Steventon and the Norman church at Chawton, only 12 miles to the south, Austen-Leigh resisted a more complicated relationship to time and place and in the process made that life more remote, another ingredient in the pageant of old England:

> [Steventon] was the cradle of her genius. These were the first objects which inspired her young heart with a sense of the beauties of nature. In strolls along these wood-walks, thick-coming fancies rose in her mind, and gradually assumed the forms in which they came forth to the world. In that simple church she brought them all into subjection to the piety which ruled her in life, and supported her in death.[21]

[20] In the *New Monthly Magazine*, cited in S. Austin Allibone, *A Critical Dictionary of English Literature*, 3 vols. (Philadelphia and London: Childs and Peterson, and Trubner, 1859), i. 906.

[21] *Memoir*, 24–6.

He is the sentimental ruralist who mistakes for an enlightened and modern perspective on the past what is, in truth, a massive condescension and temporal distortion. In confining Jane Austen to a Victorian idyll of 'pleasant nooks and corners', 'lanes wind[ing] along in a natural curve, continually fringed with irregular borders of native turf', and hedgerows sheltering 'the earliest primroses', he sketched a mental and emotional geography whose narrow perspectives effectively cut us off from the larger contexts in which she moved, not least in their misunderstood and imposed quaintness. This is Jane Austen's world refracted through her niece's hackneyed fancy (Anna's sunny hedgerows, 'where the first sweet violets of the year were to be found, and the earliest tufts of primroses displayed their delicate blossoms . . . a scene, which, though it approached not the grand, or even the highly picturesque, was pleasing in itself, and rendered interesting . . . by a thousand associations').[22] The fact is that because of demographic and transport changes, this part of Hampshire was by 1870 more of a backwater than it had been in 1810, when Steventon 'stood almost on the Great Western Road' and Chawton was on the major stagecoach route from Southampton to Winchester and, incidentally, on one of the likely routes to be taken by an invading French army heading from the south coast for London.[23]

We might blame Mitford as much as Anna Lefroy. As Mitford suggested as early as the opening pages of her first village study, Austen's novels as much as her own 'little village' were to be her reference points: 'Of all situations for a constant residence, that which appears to me most delightful is a little village far in the country . . . nothing is so delightful as to sit down in a country village in one of Miss Austen's delicious novels.' The sleight by which a literary reference stands in for and guarantees the real ('a little village in the country . . . a country village in one of Miss Austen's delicious novels') ensures Mitford's place among the earliest purveyors of Austenian kitsch.[24] By 1870 and her article 'Miss Austen and Miss Mitford', a comparative review of the

[22] Ibid., 21–3; and [Anna Lefroy], *Mary Hamilton* (1834; London: Elkin Mathews and Marrot, 1927), 15–16. Compare the argument offered by Ralph Pite, *Hardy's Geography: Wessex and the Regional Novel* (Basingstoke: Palgrave Macmillan, 2002), 52–60. For Anna and Fanny Caroline Lefroy as writers of fiction, see Ch. 4, 'Continuations'.

[23] HRO, MS. 23M93/85/2 Fanny C. Lefroy, 'Family History', unpaginated. (Hampshire Record Office, Winchester, MS. 23M93, the Austen-Leigh papers.) Park Honan, *Jane Austen: Her Life* (New York: Fawcett Columbine, 1987), 261, succinctly describes Chawton as lying 'at a vital junction of the Winchester, London and Gosport roads only fifty miles south-west of the capital.'

[24] Mary Russell Mitford, *Our Village*, with an introduction by Margaret Lane and illustrations by Joan Hassall (Oxford: Oxford University Press, 1982), 1; and see Deidre Lynch, 'Homes and Haunts: Austen's and Mitford's English Idylls', *Proceedings of the Modern Language Association of America*, 115 (2000), 1103–8.

9. Jane Austen's first home, demolished in 1824, a wood engraving taken from a sketch drawn from memory by Anna Lefroy, in J. E. Austen-Leigh, *A Memoir of Jane Austen*, 1870. By kind permission of Oxford University Press.

Memoir and L'Estrange's *Life* of Mitford, Margaret Oliphant, prescient in this as in much else, could draw attention to what we have taken to be a twentieth-century phenomenon, the intense power of the deception, or reality-effect, implied in a reading of Austen's novels. Of *Emma* she comments, 'it is impossible to conceive a more perfect piece of village geography, a scene more absolutely real.'[25] If Austen-Leigh's narrow provincialism early determined Jane Austen's, her continuing status as English national treasure was subsequently defined in part at least by the regressive rural aesthetic of the Arts and Crafts movement of the late nineteenth century—a social description closer to the cultural yearnings of Bloomsbury in 1910 than to the condition of England in 1810. Like the exaggerated remoteness of Charlotte Brontë's Yorkshire parsonage, Jane Austen's seclusion within nature and family served a mythographic interest; in her case, the literary reconstitution

[25] [M. O. W. Oliphant], 'Miss Austen and Miss Mitford', *Blackwood's Edinburgh Magazine*, 107 (1870), 304. Cf. T. E. Kebbel, 'Jane Austen at Home', *Fortnightly Review*, 43 (1885), 269 (a review of Brabourne's *Letters of Jane Austen*): 'There is no word in the human vocabulary which lends itself so little to the purpose of imagination as "comfort". Yet in Miss Austen's stories, while we are most deeply interested and excited, we are always steeped in comfort . . . of all that could be seen from the window of a quiet English country parsonage, the whole border land in which the middle and the upper classes melt into each other, she was a perfect mistress, and such a painter as we may never see again.'

of the lost English 'village geography' we each carry in our hearts. In Constance Hill's major non-family biography of the turn of the twentieth century, *Jane Austen Her Homes and Her Friends*, the instinct to memorialize a specific location and way of life is combined with the task of the literary archivist to collect and preserve hard fact and personal recollections before it is too late. Hill's was the first Austen study published in England to combine biography with accurate topographical information. (Oscar Fay Adams's *The Story of Jane Austen's Life* had appeared in America in 1891, giving descriptions based on a series of personal visits in the summer of 1889; a second edition in 1897 included the valuable documentary evidence of photographs.) Hill was allowed access to family manuscripts and met descendants of Jane's brothers; but the two modes, of nostalgia and history or hard fact, contend bewilderingly in her account. In her opening pages she dramatizes her journey into Hampshire in search of Jane Austen as the exchange of one reality for another. Her road map fails in the disorienting confusion of country lanes emptied of helpful villagers and waymarks; the few solitary locals she encounters seem as unknowing as she, and only by circuitous means does she reach her destination, as night falls and the chapter ends. By way of tailpiece the chapter is illustrated with a signpost pointing into the clouds and inscribed 'To Austen Land'. Nowadays if you travel south from Berkshire on the M4 or one of the major 'A' roads the sign as you cross the county border reads 'Hampshire, Jane Austen's County'. In England only Warwickshire, 'Shakespeare's County', has comparable tourist-board investment in its mythopoeic identity.

Cassandra's legacies, or the family management of Jane Austen's life

There has been no serious modern critical engagement with Austen-Leigh's *Memoir of Jane Austen*.[26] It is a rag-bag affair of heavily excised fragments of letters, prosy digressions on the domestic manners of the rural gentry in Regency England, family reminiscences, and dull genealogies. But it is also

[26] An exception must be made for D. W. Harding's impatient, perfunctory, but intelligent edition, issued as an appendix to *Persuasion* (Harmondsworth, Middx.: Penguin, 1965). See, too, Roger Sales, *Jane Austen and Representations of Regency England* (London and New York: Routledge, 1994), 3–16. Sales considers Austen-Leigh's work of censorship in the *Memoir* and offers a brisk critique of the 'received biography' which he argues 'has proved remarkably resistant to the challenges offered to it by both new texts and new critical approaches' (11).

the first biography of Jane Austen of any length, and its enduring importance lies in the fact that, regardless of changes in fashion, it remains the chief authority for the subsequent tradition; for certain letters and the mock panegyric poem to Anna Austen ('In measured verse I'll now rehearse') the *Memoir* provides the only documentary witness.[27] The great problem it poses, however, as textual origin is that at the same time it is both authoritative and equivocal. The official account from the head of the family (Austen-Leigh was the only son of her eldest brother, James), it was written in a spirit of censorship as well as communication, and it is suffused with anxiety. The social anxiety surrounding its composition is evident in its engagement with genealogical minutiae and in its nervous positioning of the Austens within the pseudo-gentry. Other pressing anxieties included the fear that a non-family-derived biography might be attempted and that a younger branch of the family might publish something injudicious.

Interest in the novels, mounting gradually since the 1830s, was showing signs of taking shape in at least two ways which, in the 1860s, provided cause for family concern. Before Austen-Leigh, the public account (pieces like Mrs Elwood's saccharine study in *Memoirs of the Literary Ladies of England* (1843)) necessarily derived from the thin and pious 'Notice' of 1818 or its even thinner revision as the 1833 'Memoir', where Henry Austen, purportedly Jane's favourite brother, supplemented his brief evaluation of the life with lengthy quotation from the views of professional critics. According to Brian Southam's estimate, there were only six essays devoted exclusively to Jane Austen before 1870.[28] But from the 1840s critical heavyweights like Lord Macaulay, George Henry Lewes, and Julia Kavanagh were publicly attesting to her importance, while correspondence in 1852 between Frank Austen and the eager American autograph hunter Eliza Susan Quincy (referred to by Austen-Leigh in the *Memoir*) suggests a receptive circle of devotees as far away as Boston, Massachusetts. Kavanagh's 1863 study is impatient as well as admiring of an author whose 'fault is to have subdued life and its feelings into even more than their own tameness. The stillness of her books is not natural, and never, whilst love and death endure, will human lives flow so calmly as in her pages.'[29] Hers was a critical evaluation which threatened biographical

[27] For example, for those letters printed as nos. 111, 118, and 131, in *Jane Austen's Letters*. For the verses to Anna Austen, see *Memoir*, 75 and note.

[28] *Critical Heritage*, ii. 12.

[29] Julia Kavanagh, *English Women of Letters: Biographical Sketches*, 2 vols. (London: Hurst and Blackett, 1863), ii. 192. In private, in his journal in 1858, Macaulay noted his wish to write a short life of 'that wonderful woman' in order to raise funds for a monument to her in Winchester Cathedral (*The Life and*

challenge. Three years later, an article in *The Englishwoman's Domestic Magazine* expressed its frustration with the received hagiography more openly and humorously, and after quoting Henry's 1833 'Memoir' observed:

> We have never read of such perfection elsewhere except in epitaphs, and though we know that *de mortuis nil nisi bonum* should be uttered, we confess we wish her biographer had recorded some fault, and if not exactly a fault, a failing, a weakness, a peccadillo of the most frivolous character, such as daintiness in eating, or nervous fidgeting, for then we might have pictured her as a mortal woman, with a coalscuttle bonnet, sandalled shoes, and mittens of the period, but now we can think of her as nothing less than an angel writing novels with a quill plucked from one of her own wings, and unfortunately there is no known likeness of her to dissipate the idea.[30]

A more insidious threat lay within the family, in the fear, anxiously discussed by Austen-Leigh and his sisters, that their cousin Catherine Anne Hubback might be poised to break the family silence. Frank Austen's daughter, Hubback was not yet born when Aunt Jane died, but she had already stolen a march on the senior branch of the family by publishing in 1850 a novel, *The Younger Sister*, with a dedication 'To the Memory of her Aunt, the Late Jane Austen'. The first five chapters are based quite closely on Austen's fragment *The Watsons*; either Hubback worked from a copy or, more likely, she simply remembered the opening, from family recitation, and completed it. Writing to her brother on 8 August 1862, Anna Lefroy fears their cousin, now with several more novels to her credit, is ready to recycle the fragment known in the family as *Sanditon*: 'The Copy [of *Sanditon*] which was taken, not given, is now at the mercy of M[rs]. Hubback, & she will be pretty sure to make use of it as soon as she thinks she safely may.'[31] Not only did Anna Lefroy resent this appropriation by the lesser novelist of Aunt Jane's voice, she was now the legal owner of the autograph copy of the *Sanditon* fragment. Of all her family correspondents Anna, herself a novelist, could claim to have had the deepest fictional communing with Aunt Jane, as letters included in Austen-Leigh's *Memoir* attest. It was, after all, with Anna that Aunt Jane discussed her views on novel writing and, in any case, Catherine Hubback had never known her. Here, then, is a reason why when the *Memoir* was enlarged for a second edition it sought to place some mark on the manuscript

Letters of Lord Macaulay, ed. George Otto Trevelyan, 2 vols. (London: Longmans, Green, and Co., 1876), ii. 466).

30 *The Englishwoman's Domestic Magazine*, 2 (1866), 238.

31 HRO, MS. 23M93/86/3c. item 118.

writings as well as the life, though, as Lord Brabourne would tetchily observe some years later in his edition of the *Letters*, the holograph copy of another manuscript, *Lady Susan*, belonged to another niece, his mother, and when Austen-Leigh printed it he did so from a different copy and without his express permission.[32]

The decision to prepare a biography was taken in the late 1860s. Admiral Sir Francis Austen, Jane's last surviving sibling, had died in August 1865, aged 91. His death marked the end of her generation and therefore a moment for gathering the record in written form. In addition, those nieces and nephews who had known her in their childhoods were also now old and wished to hand on within the family some account of their distinguished relation. As early as 1864 Austen-Leigh's elder half-sister, Anna, was writing down her memories in response to his enquiries ('You have asked me to put on paper my recollections of Aunt Jane, & to do so would be both on your account & her's a labour of love').[33] His younger sister, Caroline, provided her reminiscences in 1867(subsequently published as *My Aunt Jane Austen)*:

> A Memoir of Miss Jane Austen has often been asked for, and strangers have declared themselves willing and desirous to undertake the task of writing it—and have wondered that the family should have refused to supply the necessary materials. But tho' none of her nearest relatives desired that the details of a very private and rather uneventful life should be laid before the world yet I think they would not willingly have had her memory die—and it *will* die and be lost, if no effort is made to preserve it... The generation who knew her is passing away—but those who are succeeding us must feel an interest in the personal character of their Great Aunt, who has made the family name in some small degree, illustrious.[34]

As the children of Jane's eldest brother James, Anna, James Edward, and Caroline had inhabited her natal home of Steventon, after their father took over clerical duties there on the retirement to Bath of his father, George Austen. All three were closer to her Hampshire roots (socially as well as geographically) than other branches of the family, notably the grander Knights of Godmersham, Kent, the descendants of her third brother, Edward; and of the numerous nephews and nieces (of Jane's six brothers, three, Edward, Frank, and Charles, fathered thirty children between them),

[32] *Letters of Jane Austen*, ed. Brabourne, i. x.

[33] *Memoir*, 157. Many of the letters and other written recollections that passed between James Edward, his sisters, and cousins during the writing of the *Memoir* have been transcribed in full from the Austen-Leigh archive in the Hampshire Record Office and collected in this edition.

[34] Ibid., 165–6.

they had unique personal knowledge of their aunt and were of an age to remember her.

Anna Lefroy had known her aunt from earliest childhood when she was brought aged 2 to live at Steventon after the death of her mother, James Austen's first wife, Anne Mathew. Caroline, though much younger and only 12 when her aunt died, stayed often at Jane Austen's later home at Chawton, while James Edward (known as Edward in the family) was the only one of his generation present at his aunt's funeral. Of the other nieces to have known their aunt, Cassandra Esten Austen, Charles Austen's eldest daughter, and Mary Jane Austen, Frank's eldest daughter, were both regular visitors to Chawton in their childhood. Mary Jane was now dead, but Cassy Esten was her aunt Cassandra Austen's executrix for her personal effects, and since her own father's death had inherited many papers belonging either to Jane or Cassandra. She shared information, recollections, and copies of Aunt Jane's letters with her cousin James Edward.

Anna Lefroy and Caroline Austen supplied their brother with memories of their aunt more intimate than his own. Anna's memories reached back furthest to the time when Jane Austen was barely 20, and they are touchingly quirky. Caroline, twelve years younger, remembered the daily routine later at Chawton: Aunt Jane's early morning piano playing and the stories about fairyland invented to delight her little nieces. As the daughter of James Austen's second wife, the family friend Mary Lloyd, Caroline came into possession of pocket books, in which over many years her mother had kept a brief diary of events as they occurred: Mary Austen had been at Jane's bedside when she died, having travelled to Winchester to help nurse her. Caroline thus had her mother's written and spoken recollections to draw on as well as her own. As one of the unmarried nieces, she also spent much time in later years with Aunt Cassandra. On the strength of this, Anna reminded James Edward that Caroline must have some unique knowledge: 'Caroline, though her recollections cannot go so far back even as your's, is, I know acquainted with some particulars of interest in the life of our Aunt; they relate to circumstances of which I never had any knowledge, but were communicated to her by the best of then living Authorities, Aunt Cassandra.'[35]

Austen-Leigh's *Memoir* obeys a particular impulse which distinguishes it from all later biographies. It is doubly entailed to the idea of remembrance, to

[35] Ibid., 162. For a sample of Mary Austen's terse pocket-book entries (recording Jane Austen's final days and death), see Deirdre Le Faye, '"The Business of Mothering": Two Austenian Dialogues', *The Book Collector*, 32 (1983), 313–14.

the extent that distinctions of biography and autobiography are effaced in its assimilative work of recollection. In selecting from the stream of memory to form a fitting memorial, the process and product of biography are here intimately associated, and the acts of connection by which the subject Jane Austen is revived are also inevitably acts of authorial reconnection, reuniting Austen-Leigh and his sisters with their younger selves. What binds all together is not consistency of opinion (these are emotionally charged recollections) but a living link. This poses a further anxiety: as memories their documentary status is especially fortuitous and unstable. The failures of memory and the shadow of old age as it falls across a later generation of Austens provide their own frail limit to memorializing; the note of elegy on which the *Memoir* opens contends perilously with the annihilation it is meant to stem.

Not only forgetfulness but also family rivalry compete to undermine the authority of this primary document of our later circumstantial biographizing. Another promising source both of memories and archival materials should have been Fanny Knight, now Lady Knatchbull, Edward Austen Knight's first child, who, just three months older than Anna, was Jane Austen's eldest niece. At the division of Aunt Cassandra's papers after her death in 1845, Fanny had inherited the bulk of those letters from Jane to her sister which Cassandra had chosen to preserve. But by the 1860s Fanny's memory was confused: she was senile; other family members were unable or reluctant to trace the whereabouts of the letters. Fanny's sister, Elizabeth Rice, wrote to Austen-Leigh at this time: 'it runs in [Fanny's] head that there is something she ought to do till her brain gets quite bewildered & giddiness comes on which of course is very alarming—I really do not think that it is worth your while to defer writing the memoir on the chance of getting the letters for I see *none*.'[36] Lady Knatchbull's daughter Louisa returned the same reply to requests for material, adding: 'I only wish the "Memoirs" had been written ten years ago when it would have given my Mother the *greatest* pleasure to assist, both with letters and recollections of her own.'[37]

The gap which these unforthcoming letters and recollections suggest in our retrospective understanding of Austen-Leigh's account is worth considering. Fanny Knight has been represented to posterity as the favourite niece, in

[36] NPG, RWC/HH, f. 23. (National Portrait Gallery, London, a file of correspondence between R. W. Chapman and Henry Hake, containing typescripts made from 'letters addressed to James Edward Austen-Leigh about the date of the composition & publication of the Memoir and preserved by him in an album'.)

[37] NPG, RWC/HH, f. 25.

Jane Austen's own words 'almost another Sister'.[38] It was a bond strengthened by the death of her mother when Fanny was only 15. As Anna Lefroy, another motherless niece, records: 'Owing to particular circumstances there grew up during the latter years of Aunt Jane's life a great & affectionate intimacy between herself & the eldest of her nieces; & I suppose there a [*sic*] few now living who can more fully appreciate the talent or revere the memory of Aunt Jane than Lady Knatchbull.' But in the same place Anna also writes that Fanny's family, the Knights of Godmersham, Kent, felt a general preference for Cassandra Austen and that they viewed Jane's talent with some suspicion; intellectual pursuits and a passion for scribbling did not fit with their finer family pretensions. As Anna sardonically put it: 'A little talent went a long way with the Goodneston Bridgeses [Fanny's mother's family] of that period; & *much* must have gone a long way too far.'[39] Though Jane was welcome at Godmersham, she stayed there less frequently than Cassandra, was less intimate in the family circle, and expressed some unease with its ways. Time undoubtedly dulled Fanny Knight's earlier attachment to Aunt Jane; so much so that Anna's recollections quoted above assume a wonderful inappropriateness when set against the record we do have of Fanny's opinion in 1869. Senile or not, she had energy enough to record this testament to Aunt Jane when her sister Marianne in turn raised Austen-Leigh's enquiries:

Yes my love it is very true that Aunt Jane from various circumstances was not so *refined* as she ought to have been from her *talent* & if she had lived 50 years later she would have been in many respects more suitable to *our* more refined tastes. They were not rich & the people around with whom they chiefly mixed, were not at all high bred, or in short anything more than *mediocre* & *they* of course tho' superior in *mental powers & cultivation* were on the same level as far as *refinement* goes—but I think in later life their intercourse with Mrs. Knight (who was very fond of & kind to them) improved them both & Aunt Jane was too clever not to put aside all possible signs of 'common-ness' (if such an expression is allowable) & teach herself to be more refined, at least in intercourse with people in general. Both the Aunts (Cassandra *&* Jane) were brought up in the most complete ignorance of the World & its ways (I mean as to fashion &c) & if it had not been for Papa's marriage which brought them into Kent, & the kindness of Mrs. Knight, who used often to have one or other of the sisters staying with her, they would have been, tho' not less clever & agreeable in themselves, very much below par as to good Society & its ways. If you hate all this

[38] *Jane Austen's Letters*, 144. [39] *Memoir*, 158–9.

I beg yr. pardon but I felt it at my *pen's end* & it chose to come along & speak the truth.[40]

The discrepancy between Anna Lefroy's confidence in Fanny Knight's reverence for her aunt's memory and the details of Fanny's own late outburst, both recovered across a fifty-year gap, exposes something important about biographical truth. It is not simply that Anna's sense of what Fanny will remember and hold dear is sharply at odds with what Fanny does indeed retain as significant, but that the two impressions are based on different readings of the same basic ingredients: the long visits to Godmersham, the value placed on talent and cleverness, social distinctions, and the Knights' powers of patronage within the wider Austen family.

In other words, Austen-Leigh's memoir of his aunt is not just a family production, it is the production of a particular family view of Jane Austen, and against it might be set other, different, family recollections and therefore different Aunt Janes. Here we have Jane Austen as remembered by the Steventon or Hampshire Austens, for whom she is nature loving, religious, dutifully domestic, and middle class. The Godmersham (Knight–Knatchbull) or Kentish Jane Austen was not to be made public until 1884. When in that year Lord Brabourne, Fanny's son and Jane's great-nephew, published his mother's newly recovered collection of Jane Austen letters, he attached to them a short introduction whose chief purpose appears to be to oust Austen-Leigh's biography and assert his rival claims to the more authentic portrait. Not only is Brabourne's Jane Austen located in Kent as often as in Hampshire, she is a more emotional figure, inward and passionate, and of course more gentrified, improved willy-nilly by contact with her fine relations. These letters, mainly Jane's correspondence with Cassandra, 'contain', he promises, 'the confidential outpourings of Jane Austen's soul to her beloved sister, interspersed with many family and personal details which, doubtless, she would have told to no other human being.' More pointedly, these letters 'have never been in [Mr. Austen-Leigh's] hands' and they 'afford a picture of her such as no history written by another person could give.' To settle the matter of significance, the collection is dedicated to Queen Victoria and proceeds by way of a hundred-page biographical prelude, just under half of which situates its subject in relation to Godmersham, the Knights, and other Kent associations. In case any doubt remains, Brabourne nails down the

[40] *Fanny Knight's Diaries: Jane Austen through her Niece's Eyes*, ed. Deirdre Le Faye (Alton: Jane Austen Society, 2000), 38–9.

message that: '[B]efore one can thoroughly understand and feel at home with the people of whom Jane Austen writes . . . one should know something of the history of Godmersham.'[41]

Without the Godmersham perspective, Austen-Leigh's account cannot give proportionate space to the part played by Cassandra Austen in her sister's life. But it was Cassandra herself who had done much to obscure and fragment the record. Her sister's chief heiress and executor, she was almost solely responsible for the preservation (and destruction) and subsequent distribution among brothers, nieces, and nephews of the letters, manuscripts, and memories she inherited. She decisively shaped, through stewardship of the archive, through its calculated division, and through conversation, what was available (and to whom) in the next generation. One of the mysteries we discover brother and sisters unravelling as they collect and compare their portions of knowledge is exactly what each has been given to know. The point is significant, though surely unsurprising, that, through Cassandra's management and not least through her apportioning of the inheritance, the nieces and nephews individually knew rather less than we might expect. As Caroline observed : 'I am very glad dear Edward that you have applied your-self to the settlement of the vexed question between the Austens and the Public. I am sure you will do justice to what there *is*—but I feel it must be a difficult task to dig up the *materials*, so carefully have they been buried out of our sight by the past generat-[ion].' Anna speculates: 'There may be other sources of information, if we could get at them—Letters may have been preserved', but she does not know this with any certainty. A few years later she concludes: 'The occasional correspondence between the Sisters when apart from each other would as a matter of course be destroyed by the Survivor—I can fancy what the indignation of Aunt Cass[a]. would have been at the mere idea of its' being read and commented upon by any of us, nephews and nieces, little or great—and indeed I I [*sic*] think myself she was right, in that as in most other things.' What is there to know? and from what there is to know, what might be publicly disseminated beyond the family? Confiding details of Jane's embarrassing rejection of Harris Bigg-Wither's marriage proposal, Caroline writes: 'I should not mind *telling* any body, at this distance of time—but printing and publishing seem to me very different from *talking* about the past.'[42] More anxieties.

[41] *Letters of Jane Austen*, ed. Brabourne, i. xi–xiii and 6.

[42] *Memoir*, 186–7, 162, 184, and 188.

The major ingredients of the *Memoir* as well as its reverent colouring are owed, in one way or another, to Cassandra Austen. The closeness of the relationship between Jane and Cassandra has been the subject of much speculation among modern biographers, ranging through good sense, bizarre curiosity, and wild surmise. Fanny Caroline, Anna Lefroy's daughter, sentimentally dates the closeness of the sisters' emotional bond to disappointments in romantic love, occurring at about the same time in their lives and cementing an affection of unusual intensity: 'The similarity of their fates must have endeared the two sisters to each other and made other sympathy unnecessary to each. No one was equal to Jane in Cassandra's eyes. And Jane looked up to Cassandra as one far wiser and better than herself. They were as their mother said "wedded to each other." '[43] It is undisputed that theirs was a deep and sustaining emotional bond; but it is also worth noting that Fanny Caroline is the first family biographer freed from the constraint of personal knowledge of Aunt Jane.

One thing is clear: as the guardian of her sister's reputation and material effects, Cassandra is the key to what tangibly remains. They spent weeks and months apart, often when one or other was staying at the home of another of the large Austen family, and to this regular round of visits—to Godmersham to the Edward Austen Knights, to London to Henry Austen's various fashionable addresses—we owe the majority of the surviving letters, addressed from Jane to Cassandra. The collected letters of Jane Austen, as they are now available to us, came together only in 1932, and so the reconnection of the various parts of the epistolary archive considerably postdates the *Memoir*, the publication of the largest Knatchbull cache (ninety-four letters) in 1884, and the authoritative family edition in *Life and Letters* of 1913. Of the 161 letters from Jane Austen now known to have survived, only six were addressed directly to Fanny Knight; but Cassandra left to her keeping almost all her own surviving correspondence with her sister, presumably because very many of these letters were written either to or from Fanny's childhood home of Godmersham. Without them, James Edward's memoir lacks significant information. For example, the sparseness of his record for the Southampton years and his vagueness about how long the Austens lived there (his calculation is out by about eighteen months) can be explained in part by the fact that the letters covering that period were, since Cassandra's death, with Lady Knatchbull.[44]

[43] HRO, MS. 23M93/85/2 Fanny C. Lefroy, 'Family History', unpaginated.

[44] They are nos. 49–67 in *Jane Austen's Letters*. Though only six letters to Fanny appear to have survived, according to Le Faye (p. xvii), Fanny's diaries record the receipt of forty-seven letters from Austen between 1803 and 1817.

According to Caroline, who gives the fullest account, Aunt Cassandra 'looked [the letters] over and burnt the greater part, (as she told me), 2 or 3 years before her own death—She left, or *gave* some as legacies to the Nieces—but of those that *I* have seen several had portions cut out.'[45] Between May 1801 and July 1809 Jane Austen's life was, in outward circumstances at least, at its most unsettled—various temporary homes and lodgings in Bath and Southampton, holiday visits to the seaside, new acquaintances and friendships—and for all that potentially exciting period James Edward provides only four letters. Even when the Knatchbull cache is added in, there is still a long silence between 27 May 1801 and 14 September 1804; and there are earlier hiatuses in the record: from September 1796 to April 1798, for example. These gaps coincide with important personal and family events: in the earlier years, the death of Cassandra's fiancé, Tom Fowle, James Austen's second marriage and Henry Austen's marriage to glamorous cousin Eliza, Mrs Lefroy's attempt at matchmaking during the visit of Revd Samuel Blackall to Ashe, the writing of *First Impressions* and its rejection by the London publisher Thomas Cadell; in the later years, between 1801 and 1804, almost all the romantic interest in Jane Austen's life of which we have any hints at all. We simply do not know the extent of Cassandra's careful work of destruction and whether this accounts for the unyielding nature of the evidence—in particular, the difficulty we have in recovering anything more satisfactory than a partial and unconfiding life of Jane Austen. Lord Brabourne's description of the letters he edits, as the 'confidential outpourings' of one soul to another, is from the evidence wildly inaccurate, but perfectly explicable in terms of family rivalry—his claims to marketing another Jane Austen. Equally, Caroline's account of Cassandra's pruning of the correspondence appears to suggest secrets hidden and confidences suppressed; but it is also possible that what remains is not atypical within a larger, censored record. Cassandra may have chosen to preserve and apportion with such care these letters and not others chiefly because their addressees and internal details were of particular value to one branch of the family or another. Contrary to Lord Brabourne's romantic conception of the letter form, Jane's seem to have served as news bulletins, addressed to or from a family circle, with only occasional passages in a more private voice. It might be that there never was a confiding correspondence to hold back. On the other hand, it might not. Perhaps a self-revelatory correspondence was also kept up between the sisters when apart, and this is

[45] *Memoir*, 174.

what Cassandra destroyed. Then again, we may have portions of it but not the clue, the insider's sympathy, to how to read it. '[T]o strangers,' Caroline wrote, the letters 'could be *no* transcript of her mind—they would not feel that they knew her any the better for having read them.'[46] The question is left hanging as to what the extant letters might reveal to those who did know Jane Austen.

The only 'raw' biographical data we possess, the letters continued to provoke widely divergent responses throughout the twentieth century. Mary Augusta Austen-Leigh's shrill insistence on Cassandra's work of destruction represented in 1920 the kind of triumphant dead end which the early romantic biographers inside and outside the family were drawn to celebrate in what amounted to an act of sympathetic self-annihilation. According to Mary Augusta's explanation, itself a heady cocktail of the language of pulp fiction and Biblical parable, Cassandra saved only those letters which she could be sure were utterly without interest. She writes:

> Once more let a most important fact, already referred to in a previous chapter, be stated; this being, not merely that the great mass of Jane's letters were destroyed by Cassandra, but that she kept *only* those which she considered so totally devoid of general interest that it was impossible anyone should, at any time, contemplate their publication . . . [What remains] are but a 'gleaning of grapes when the vintage is done'—when all that was precious had been safely gathered up, and garnered in Cassandra's faithful memory, and nothing had been left behind excepting that which even she deemed to be altogether negligible.[47]

In a more cynical age, Mary Favret has recently challenged the assumption that the purpose of a cull was to remove all trace of an intimate voice. Using comparative historical evidence she argues that 'Jane Austen's unyielding letters are not an isolated phenomenon'; in particular, she notices how they share an absence of personal revelation with sections of the correspondence of her, admittedly more politicized, contemporaries Helen Maria Williams and Mary Wollstonecraft. If Austen used the letter in some comparable and, for the time, conventional way to promote 'the image of a social "self"', then it may be too simplistic to assume, at least after the 1790s, that there was another highly charged emotional correspondence to purge. Favret makes a further important point when she suggests that

[46] Ibid., 173–4.

[47] Mary Augusta Austen-Leigh, *Personal Aspects of Jane Austen* (London: John Murray, 1920), 48–9; see also, 66–7.

We, who are apt to delve into the psychological depths of private letters, may find it hard to read surfaces which were so significant to Austen's contemporaries: the messages that remain unavailable in a bound volume, and on a printed page.[48]

Not only, then, do we need to concede a potential difference between our modern and earlier assumptions about the contents of private letters, but we must face the possibility that the authenticity of a letter, unlike a novel, is bound inextricably to its original material form, to such an extent that we cannot disentangle its textual from its documentary identity without imperilling its status as biographical evidence. Words alone provide an incomplete account of a form in which the manner of their disposition on paper, the handwriting and the pressure of the hand, even the paper itself, its folds, and the method of sealing, may all offer eloquent clues to the writer's identity and state of mind.

Two texts

'In constructing a story, as in building an airship, the first problem is to get something that will lift its own weight.'[49] The observation belongs to the American novelist Willa Cather, and it is as true of the biography as of the novel. The biographer's first problem is 'to get something that will lift its own weight'; and the weight of any biography is a special amalgam of author and subject. Part of the anxiety of Austen-Leigh's anxious text has to do with bodyweight—specifically, does it have enough to persuade the reader that she encounters in its pages a substantial figure? Does it have enough to get airborne? The *Memoir* is not the shaped life of the historical or psychobiographies of the twentieth century but an apparently undesigned and unprioritized assortment of textual states.[50] These range through expansive costume detail—praise for tansey-pudding, minuets, and the art of spinning, all of which in some vague way represent the world of Jane Austen—to

[48] Mary A. Favret, *Romantic Correspondence: Women, Politics, and the Fiction of Letters* (Cambridge: Cambridge University Press, 1993), 135.

[49] *The World and the Parish: Willa Cather's Articles and Reviews, 1893–1902*, ed. William M. Curtin, 2 vols. (Lincoln, Nebr.: University of Nebraska Press, 1970), ii. 728; quoted in Jane Brown, *Spirits of Place: Five Famous Lives in their English Landscape* (London: Penguin, 2001), xv.

[50] Virginia Woolf has some funny and perceptive things to say about the unshapeliness and fertile irrelevance of the memoir form in two short pieces: 'Memoirs of a Novelist' (1909), in *The Complete Shorter Fiction*, ed. Susan Dick, revised edn. (London: Hogarth Press, 1989), 69–79; and 'A Talk about Memoirs' (1920), in *The Essays of Virginia Woolf*, 3 (1919–24), ed. Andrew McNeillie (London: Hogarth Press, 1988), 180–6.

scattered references to Norse legend, standard Classical quotations, and, bizarrely, the sayings of an eleventh-century theologian, Adam von Bremen. There is a clerical desultoriness in speculation on the Welsh ancestry of the Perrot family and in the status-anxious quoting of famous readers' opinions of the novels passed on by Austen-Leigh's brother-in-law, Sir Denis Le Marchant. Through all, there is a real risk that extravagant oddments of information (more in need of annotation than the life they propose to illuminate) will sever our understanding from the vital local contexts of biographical encounter; that the biographer's baggage might sink rather than lift the ship. But two items among the motley assortment are worth further inspection.

The first is a letter, written from Constantinople in 1686 by a mother to her teenage daughter, Mary Brydges, or Poll, which Austen-Leigh introduces into Chapter 3, immediately after recording the brief personal account and physical description of Jane Austen made by Egerton Brydges, a near neighbour, bad novelist, and student of genealogy. He continues:

> One may wish that Sir Egerton had dwelt rather longer on the subject of these memoirs, instead of being drawn away by his extreme love for genealogies to her great-grandmother and ancestors. That great-grandmother however lives in the family records as Mary Brydges, a daughter of Lord Chandos, married in Westminster Abbey to Theophilus Leigh of Addlestrop in 1698. When a girl she had received a curious letter of advice and reproof, written by her mother from Constantinople.... This letter is given. Any such authentic document, two hundred years old, dealing with domestic details, must possess some interest.[51]

Having carefully prepared this moment of pure self-destruction, Austen-Leigh transcribes the letter. Long and apparently irrelevant, since he makes no attempt to integrate it into his narrative, it was not retained in later family biographies and has now disappeared from the textual record: there is no mention of it in *Life and Letters* or *Family Record*. Biographers, factual and interpretative, have forgotten the letter and its part in establishing a context for Jane Austen's life. Austen-Leigh should clearly have taken his own advice and steered clear of genealogy. Or should he? Poll, or Mary, Brydges was a common ancestor of Egerton Brydges and Jane Austen; more precisely she was Jane Austen's maternal great-grandmother. Writing to her brother as he was collecting material for the *Memoir*, Anna Lefroy drew his attention to

[51] *Memoir*, 44.

'[t]he original of Poll's letters . . . in the possession of Mrs. George Austen—it was given to her at Portsdown.'[52] Portsdown Lodge, near Portsmouth, became the late home of Jane's brother Frank, and Anna's reference here must be to the wife of Frank's third son, George. It seems that the letter was a cherished heirloom, handed down in the Leigh and Austen families; Anna's communication suggests that she at least thought it relevant to Aunt Jane. And it is. It forms part of a paper trail laid to remind the reader of Jane Austen's distant aristocratic pretensions: Mary Brydges was the daughter of James Brydges, eighth Lord of Chandos, and the sister of the first Duke of Chandos, Handel's patron. More instructively, the letter registers the periodic readjustment through history of relations between rank and trade: Mary's father was an aristocrat down on his luck, but her grandmother, with whom she lived in great splendour, was only a merchant's widow. With the injection of mercantile wealth, Mary's brother was able to live in great magnificence. In a sentence appended to the letter Austen-Leigh points the moral: 'But then, as now, it would seem, rank had the power of attracting and absorbing wealth.'

Writing of Jane Austen's fictional society, David Spring has deployed the useful term 'pseudo-gentry'[53] to describe the group comprising trade, the professions, rentiers, and clergymen whose concerns propel her narratives; a group whose membership in reality can be extended to the diversely positioned Austens themselves. The 'pseudo-gentry' are constitutionally insecure: in some cases upwardly mobile and with growing incomes and social prestige (Jane's third brother, Edward Austen Knight), and in others, in straitened and precarious circumstances (her fourth brother, Henry Austen); either way, they aspire to the lifestyle of the traditional rural gentry. Even the briefest biographical acquaintance reveals the Austen family's fascination with, and gravitation to, inheritances and the confusing but ready changes of name which accompanied upturns in their fortunes: in Jane Austen's own immediate circle Austens and Leighs become Austen-Leigh, Leigh-Perrot, and Knight. As the record of a particular historical moment of social and moral adjustment in relation to wealth, Poll's letter is significant; it becomes more complexly resonant for being naïvely documented by the later generation who treasures it. As an heirloom it throws unexpected light on the insecure worlds of patronage and opportunity, old status and new money, in

[52] *Memoir*, 184.

[53] David Spring, 'Interpreters of Jane Austen's Social World: Literary Critics and Historians', in *Jane Austen: New Perspectives*, ed. Janet Todd (New York: Holmes and Meier Publishers Inc., 1983), 53–72 (esp. 61–3). Spring adopts the term 'pseudo-gentry' from Alan Everitt.

which Austen and her family still moved and whose socio-economic relations underpin her fictions and continue to explain the consumerist investment of our modern fascination.

By contrast, Austen-Leigh's second text is securely intertextual and could not have been more topical to his first readers: the comparison he invites with Charlotte Brontë. Elizabeth Gaskell's *Life* of her friend and fellow-novelist had been published as recently as 1857. In it she set a high standard for the simultaneous memorializing and effacing of that difficult subject, the woman writer. Gaskell, we now know, aggressively manipulated the evidence, suppressing details of Charlotte's passionate feelings for, and correspondence with, Monsieur Heger and providing a misleading portrait of her father, Patrick Brontë. Both distortions were performed in the service of a domestic drama of the suffering woman, who before all else was a dutiful daughter and sister and whose 'coarse' writings were the excusable consequences of the damaging circumstances in which she lived. That the Jane Austen we encounter in Austen-Leigh's account is as inadequate to the novels we now read as is Gaskell's Brontë can be explained in terms of a similar project of containment. Austen-Leigh quotes, via Gaskell, Charlotte Brontë's now famous denunciation of Jane Austen's quiet art: 'No two writers could be more unlike each other than Jane Austen and Charlotte Brontë; so much so that the latter was unable to understand why the former was admired, and confessed that she herself "should hardly like to live with her ladies and gentlemen, in their elegant but confined houses".'[54] But by a quirk of literary history, the novelist from whose 'mild eyes' shone the unwelcome advice 'to finish more, and be more subdued' becomes liable to a biographical constraint which in part derives from Gaskell's earlier authoritative presentation of Brontë as herself the reticent and confined lady novelist. Gaskell's elevation of the ideal domestic figure, modest daughter of a country parson, not 'easily susceptible' to 'the passion of love' in which her novels abound,[55] is clearly instructive for Austen-Leigh's later presentation of an exemplary woman whose emotional and intellectual life never ranged beyond the family circle and whose brushes with sexual love were so slight as to warrant hardly a mention. Where Gaskell's Brontë walked 'shy and trembling' through the London literary scene, Austen-Leigh's Aunt Jane refused any and every public

[54] *Memoir*, 96–7 and note.

[55] E. C. Gaskell, *The Life of Charlotte Brontë*, ed. Alan Shelston (Harmondsworth, Middx.: Penguin, 1975), 443. For a pertinent metabiographical examination of the treatment of Charlotte and Emily Brontë by their biographers, see Lucasta Miller, *The Brontë Myth* (London: Jonathan Cape, 2001).

notice with an energetic determination able to transform rural Hampshire into a further retreat than Siberia, let alone the exaggeratedly remote Yorkshire parsonage. If Brontë trembled with maidenly distress (not excited longing?) at Thackeray's notice and the opportunities for social engagement provided by her kindly publisher, George Smith, then Jane Austen went one better: she lived, we are told, with calculated emphasis, 'in entire seclusion from the literary world: neither by correspondence, nor by personal intercourse was she known to any contemporary authors.'[56]

Gaskell's decision to concentrate on Brontë the woman rather than the author strikes us as strange in a sister-novelist, but it served its purpose of diverting attention from the startling sexuality of her fiction. Though Austen-Leigh had no such dilemma to address, his depiction of a woman whose first duty was to family and not to her art is clearly in line with the same codification. He uses comparable strategies to deflect enquiry from anything as intense, familially disruptive, or counter-social as writing, and disingenuously disclaims the existence of what he cannot (or will not) know about creative genius. Gaskell's eagerness to show that writing never got in the way of domestic duties led her to describe Brontë breaking off from the excitement of *Jane Eyre* to inspect the dish of potatoes which the old servant Tabby was too weak-sighted to peel: rejecting composition for housework, she would 'steal into the kitchen, and quietly carry off the bowl of vegetables, without Tabby's being aware, and breaking off in the full flow of interest and inspiration in her writing, carefully cut out the specks in the potatoes, and noiselessly carry them back to their place.'[57] When Austen-Leigh equates Jane Austen's literary creativity to her other forms of manual dexterity—her use of sealing wax, her games with cup and ball and spilikins—he delights the reader with the unaccustomed intimacy:

> Jane Austen was successful in everything that she attempted with her fingers. None of us could throw spilikins in so perfect a circle, or take them off with so steady a hand. Her performances with cup and ball were marvellous. The one used at Chawton was an easy one, and she has been known to catch it on the point above an hundred times in succession, till her hand was weary...[58]

[56] *Memoir*, 90; cf. *Life of Brontë*, 448. These early comparisons sit interestingly with the contrasted values (passion v. impersonality, high v. mass culture, good v. bad taste), evident in the writings of Woolf and Q. D. Leavis, that Austen and Charlotte Brontë would be requisitioned to serve in the first part of the twentieth century.

[57] Ibid., 306; and see Miller's reading of Gaskell's use of this domestic detail in *The Brontë Myth*, 72–3.

[58] *Memoir*, 77.

We sense that this must be true: the cup and ball are still there to be seen. But, intimate though they are, such details unsettle by their suggestion of activity carried on for social amusement to the point of personal discomfort. More disturbing, the equation signals her biographer's refusal of a deeper imaginative sympathy. Like Gaskell, Austen-Leigh conceals within, or renders a function of, domestic pastime what must also have been a profoundly self-absorbed occupation. Something unique and potentially subversive is denied: a glimpse of a woman for whom at times writing was more important than service to home and family.

Secrets and lies, or managing the family

If we look in Austen-Leigh's memoir for the kinds of encounter with the individual life which we have come to expect from literary biographies of the twentieth century we shall be disappointed. While his account remains the primary printed authority for so much of what we know, it is marked by a lack of candour which frustrates reinterpretation. There are several reasons for this, but all can be summed up by the family constraints on its construction. If not totally consensual in the 'facts' they collectively register, the family texts of Jane Austen's life are sufficiently convergent and mutually endorsing to determine the biographical space as only familial. The Austens were a family who over several generations cemented their close bonds through regular intermarriage; the *Family Record* as we now have it assumes a similarly defensive textual surface. We need to go further back if we are to unpick its tight assumptions. The modern reader, for whom the interest of a life generally increases in proportion to its inwardness, is defeated by the absence of a resistant private voice. And not only the modern reader. Margaret Oliphant, herself both novelist and biographer, reviewing the *Memoir* in *Blackwood's Edinburgh Magazine*, made it clear that she gave no credence to its idealized portrait. She pronounced the Austen family 'a kind of clan', their happy and close circle more like a prison, and Austen-Leigh's 'sweet young woman' a stifled figure, the author of books whose portrayal of human behaviour is 'cruel in its perfection'. Austen-Leigh, she suggests, had something to hide, and 'without meaning it, throws out of his dim little lantern a passing gleam of light upon the fine vein of feminine cynicism which pervades his aunt's mind.'[59] Oliphant

[59] 'Miss Austen and Miss Mitford', *Blackwood's Edinburgh Magazine*, 107 (1870), 290–1, 300, 304.

reads the *Memoir* suspiciously, against the grain, asking the psychoanalyst's question: what is the story that Austen-Leigh tells designed to prevent people thinking about Jane Austen?

As in all the best regulated families there were, of course, secrets to hide: the existence of a second brother, the handicapped but long-lived George Austen, is concealed, and Edward, Jane's third brother, is presented as the second. There is no reference to the incarceration of Mrs Leigh-Perrot on a charge of shoplifting in Bath. Neither piece of discretion is surprising; both are matters of honour and, for the time, of good taste. Austen-Leigh was his great-uncle Leigh-Perrot's heir, adding Leigh to his name on his great-aunt's death in 1837; naturally he would be discreet. But the excitement and publicity of the imprisonment and trial, occurring only a year before the Austens moved to Bath, must have continued to hang in the air and to affect the family's social standing in the city. For this reason we long to know more of Jane's impressions of life there. Furthermore, by a quirk of the laws governing textual preservation, Mrs Leigh-Perrot's trial has the doubtful distinction of being 'the only public event involving a member of the novelist's family of which significant contemporary documentation survives'.[60]

These are not the kind of insights Oliphant missed in the *Memoir*; in a later essay entitled 'The Ethics of Biography', she warned against 'that prying curiosity which loves to investigate circumstances, and thrust itself into the sanctuaries of individual feeling'.[61] Rather, she misses something to connect novels 'so calm and cold and keen' to the woman who wrote them. 'The family were half-ashamed,' she states, 'to have it known that she was not just a young lady like the others, doing her embroidery.' To carry conviction, the written life of a writer needs to expose a gap and then have the writing fill it. By this, the fiction becomes the conduit between outside and inside, telling something about the nature of artistic creation. A busy round of family visits and quiet domestic duties may include the opportunities that creativity requisitions, but in recording such a life the materials call for a plausible reconstruction—those gaps and connections—out of which interpretation can be made.

[60] David Gilson, introduction to Sir F. D. MacKinnon, *Grand Larceny, Being the Trial of Jane Leigh Perrot, Aunt of Jane Austen* (1937; repr. In *Jane Austen: Family History*, 5 vols. (London: Routledge/Thoemmes Press, 1995), vols. are unnumbered. Both family secrets were divulged in *Life and Letters* (1913), 18 and 20; and 131–40, where the charge against Mrs Leigh-Perrot is refuted and the details of her trial are explored with high indignation.

[61] M. O. W. Oliphant, 'The Ethics of Biography', *Contemporary Review*, 44 (1883), 84.

Oliphant is looking for a better, more plausible story, of which these deceptively understated critical novels will be the likely outcome.

From the start the gaps were there. David Nokes's recently expressed frustration, that '[t]racing the life of Jane Austen between June 1801 and September 1804 is like searching for a missing person', sounds a sympathetic echo to Caroline Austen's despair at evidence 'so carefully... buried out of our sight by the past generat-[ion]'.[62] In part the biographical compulsion that affects Austenites is stimulated by the challenge of their subject's persistent absence from the major events of her own life. Even where she is encountered, her presence can assume disturbingly negative proportions. Take, for example, the well-rehearsed account of when Jane Austen heard the news that she was to lose her natal home, Steventon rectory, and be uprooted to Bath. As a moment of hypothesized emotional repression it has proved irresistible to all biographers. The event on which their texts are based occurred early in December 1800, Austen-Leigh providing the first public version. He writes:

> The loss of their first home is generally a great grief to young persons of strong feeling and lively imagination; and Jane was exceedingly unhappy when she was told that her father, now seventy years of age, had determined to resign his duties to his eldest son, who was to be his successor in the Rectory of Steventon, and to remove with his wife and daughters to Bath. Jane had been absent from home when this resolution was taken; and, as her father was always rapid both in forming his resolutions and in acting on them, she had little time to reconcile herself to the change.[63]

His account is compassionate, but brisk, a little distant, and more than a little defensive: it is worth remembering that the home from which the imaginative young Jane was so swiftly ejected was also that to which Austen-Leigh (aged 2 years) was, in consequence, introduced. He hints at his subject's strength of attachment, her unhappiness, her exclusion from the decision-making process, and her powerlessness to reverse it; but he also notes that such is 'generally' the feeling of imaginative 'young persons'. After this brief paragraph he appears to leave the matter and move on to other topics. His source was his younger sister Caroline, not then born, but subsequently acquainted

[62] Nokes, *Jane Austen: A Life*, 240; and *Memoir*, 186–7. Joe Bray, 'Austen, "Enigmatic Lacunae" and the Art of Biography', in *Romantic Biography*, ed. Arthur Bradley and Alan Rawes (Aldershot, Hants: Ashgate, 2003), 58–73, considers how two recent biographers, Tomalin and Nokes, respond to the gaps in the biographical evidence.

[63] *Memoir*, 50.

with the details by their mother, Mary Austen, 'who was present'. Caroline had written to her brother, probably in April 1869:

My Aunt was very sorry to leave her native home, as I have heard my Mother relate—My Aunts had been away a little while, and were met in the Hall on their return by their Mother who told them it was all settled, and they were going to live at Bath. My Mother who was present.[*sic*] said my Aunt Jane was greatly distressed—All things were done in a hurry by Mr. Austen & of course this is *not* a *fact* to be written and printed—but you have authority for saying she *did* mind it—if you think it worth while—[64]

Caroline's disjointed, repetitive note-making assumes identity with the raw ingredients of a story smoothed out in her brother's more circumspect delivery. Its rawness revives the pain as well as the circumstantial detail ('met in the Hall on their return'), the rush and shock of the event, in a wholly convincing way. We almost hear Mrs Austen delivering her great news.

There was another version, recorded by Fanny Caroline Lefroy in her manuscript 'Family History'. She may have got it from her mother, Anna Lefroy, aged 7 at the time of the incident, and unlike her brother better able to remember the excitement and upheaval of the occasion, though whether she was present is unknown and she left no written record. In Fanny's version Jane's distress mounts even higher, and she faints at the news:

M^{r}. and M^{rs}. Austen continued to live at Steventon until 1801 when partly for the sake of the health of the latter they left it for Bath. To my two Great Aunts the removal was a great sorrow. Coming in one day from their walk, as they entered the house their mother greeted them with the intelligence 'Well girls, it is settled we have decided to leave Steventon in such a week and go to Bath.' And to Jane who had been from home and had not heard much before about the matter It was such a shock that she fainted away. The resolution to leave Steventon took all their relations by surprise and as there did not seem any sufficient reason for it in the health of either, some secret motive was suspected.[65]

This version found its way as direct quotation into Constance Hill's *Her Homes and Her Friends*.[66] Repeating the story in 1913 in *Life and Letters*, Austen-Leigh's son and grandson clarify with the aid of Jane's letters for the

[64] *Memoir*, 185; and NPG, RWC/HH, ff. 4–5.
[65] HRO, MS. 23M93/85/2 Fanny C. Lefroy, 'Family History', unpaginated.
[66] Hill, *Her Homes and Her Friends*, 91–2.

period the identity of the two aunts—Jane and Martha Lloyd, not Jane and Cassandra—and the probability that they were returning from the Lloyds' home at Ibthorpe, where Jane had been making a visit of several days, rather than from a daily walk, as Fanny Caroline implies. But though they render the immediate circumstances of the Austen parents' decision less startlingly impetuous, the later Austen-Leighs also exploit the drama and mystery of the incident as Fanny Caroline conveyed it, and they embellish it with a psychological coda—speculation on the contents of the non-extant letters. What had seemed both more whimsical in operation and less certain in effect to an earlier generation of Austens has by now hardened into Cassandra's 'rule' of destruction. This is their version:

Tradition says that when Jane returned home accompanied by Martha Lloyd, the news was abruptly announced by her mother, who thus greeted them: 'Well, girls, it is all settled; we have decided to leave Seventon in such a week, and go to Bath'; and that the shock of the intelligence was so great to Jane that she fainted away. Unfortunately, there is no further direct evidence to show how far Jane's feelings resembled those she attributed to Marianne Dashwood on leaving Norland; but we have the negative evidence arising from the fact that none of her letters are preserved between November 30, 1800, and January 3, 1801, although Cassandra was at Godmersham during the whole of the intervening month. Silence on the part of Jane to Cassandra for so long a period of absence is unheard of: and according to the rule acted on by Cassandra, destruction of her sister's letters was a proof of their emotional interest.[67]

New in 1913 is the association of Austen's behaviour with that of her hysterical heroine Marianne Dashwood (whose sorrows and joys, her narrator tells, 'could have no moderation') from the yet to be published *Sense and Sensibility*.[68] The hint was provided by Fanny Caroline, whose sentimental elaboration made the specific loss of Steventon synonymous with loss in a wide, abstract, and traumatic sense. In her telling, there is more than a trace of Brontëan melodrama, its wilder notes of wind and storm and forlorn passion softened into a seemly, wistful pastoral, recognizably the style of her own novels:

[67] *Life and Letters* (1913), 155–6.

[68] *Sense and Sensibility*, Vol. 1, Ch.1, ed. Ros Ballaster (Harmondsworth, Middx.: Penguin, 1995), 6; and see the closing paragraph of Ch. 5, Marianne's farewell to house and grounds: 'when shall I cease to regret you!—when learn to feel a home elsewhere!' (23)

But Jane loved the country and her delight in natural scenery was such that she would sometimes say she thought it must form one of the joys of heaven. It is remarkable how very little there is in her writings to indicate this taste. Some glimpses there are of it in Sense and Sensibility and Mansfield Park, but there is not what can be called a picturesque description to be found in any one of her novels. No word pictures no elaborate accounts of wind and storm of light and shade or even of the fair meadows, and the winding hedgerows and the primrose strewn coppices in which her youth was passed. Every touch she did put in was true but even here there was a remarkable reserve and reticence as to her own tastes.

The sisters had never known any other home but Steventon and the leaving it involved in a great measure the loss of their dearest friends and connections. The Miss Biggs of Manydown, M^rs^. Lefroy of the neighbouring Rectory of Ashe. The Lloyds and the Fowles, the house, and village too where they knew everyone must have been very dear to them as dear as the lanes and footpaths they had daily trod together, trod in the gaiety of early girlhood and when the hearts of both were saddened by the loss of that hope which is the sweetest charm of youth.[69]

All the family accounts imply that for Jane leaving Steventon was far more than moving house; but Fanny Caroline is the first to present the occasion as a collage of losses whose ultimate precedent is the double loss to Jane and Cassandra of romantic love. According to the emotional logic of her 'Family History' the devastation at losing Steventon is intimately connected to the death of Cassandra Austen's fiancé, Tom Fowle, and of the conjectured chief romantic interest of Jane's life—a clergyman whom she met at some Devonshire seaside resort 'before they left Steventon'. Yet Fowle had died almost three years earlier, on his way to the West Indies in February 1797, Cassandra receiving the news a few months later; and Jane's seaside romance is more plausibly dated in other family sources to some time after 1801 and the departure from Steventon.[70]

Gathering up the family traditions in 1948, with acknowledgement to the Austen-Leighs' 1913 account and more echoes of Fanny Caroline, R. W. Chapman presses the emotional 'evidence' further and in doing so gives the story a parabolic weight and shapeliness:

[69] HRO, MS. 23M93/85/2 Fanny C. Lefroy, 'Family History', unpaginated.

[70] At least two stories handed down by Cassandra Austen, probably in sketchy terms, seem to have been confused in the minds of the next generation: one was of the Revd Dr Samuel Blackall, Fellow of Emmanuel College, Cambridge, who was introduced to Jane Austen at Christmas 1797 by Mrs (Madam) Lefroy, perhaps in the hope of his replacing Tom Lefroy in her affections; the other was vaguer, involving a seaside romance, any time between summer 1801 and 1805, tragically cut short by death. Both Catherine Hubback and Fanny Caroline Lefroy confuse Blackall, whom Jane found pompous, loud, and unimpressive (*Jane Austen's Letters*, 19 and 216), with the later-met, more sympathetic seaside lover.

Jane made the best of it. . . . Jane's local attachments were of extraordinary strength; they were no small part of her genius. We cannot doubt that the loss of her native county, and of the multitude of associations which made up her girlish experience, was exquisitely painful. Her feelings cannot have been less acute than Marianne's on leaving Norland, or Anne's on leaving Kellynch. Her return to her own country, eight years later, was the long-delayed return of an exile.[71]

Austen's love of the local Hampshire countryside is intensified in Fanny Caroline's account, but Chapman takes it on himself to strengthen the relationship of equivalence between author and fictions by extending the link, fancifully made to her first heroine by later generations of Austen-Leighs, to incorporate her final heroine, Anne Elliot from *Persuasion.* It is exactly the kind of recognition a certain sort of biography delights in: the gap yawns open and the connection is smoothly traced by which sensations and the critical events of the life assume identity with the fiction. By this, fiction either offers clues back to its author or demonstrably derives directly from personal experience. In the opening chapter of the 1870 *Memoir* Austen-Leigh had been at some pains to point out that if 'Cassandra's character might indeed represent the "*sense*" of Elinor', 'Jane's had little in common with the "*sensibility*" of Marianne.'[72] But Lord Brabourne played up the romance of a more susceptible Aunt Jane, as did Austen-Leigh's descendants. Now Chapman adds the finishing touch, and Austen transforms from Marianne Dashwood into Anne Elliot, exhibiting the whole gamut of emotions from hysteria to settled romantic melancholy. Implicitly, we are told, her total achievement as a writer is to be explained in terms of the loss of Steventon, in which are implied the twinned numbing losses of the natural world and romantic love: by a happy coincidence (which of course is no coincidence) eight years, the length of Jane's 'exile' from Hampshire, also marks Anne Elliot's separation from her first and only love. Here at last is proof that the trajectory of Austen's fiction is determined by her need for reconnection with her natal environment. The suppressed letters (which if they ever did exist can only be allowed to witness to dispossession and a loss of self) and the apocryphal transformation of great distress into something greater, a temporary loss of consciousness ('she fainted away'), provide further discontinuities that the biographer can turn to some purpose. One hundred years on, in Lord David Cecil's 1978

[71] R. W. Chapman, *Jane Austen: Facts and Problems* (Oxford: Clarendon Press, 1948; repr. 1949), 47.
[72] *Memoir*, 19.

recension, Jane's response reaches its camp climax: 'Overcome by shock, Jane fainted dead away.'[73]

The faint has persisted through various shifts in twentieth-century biographical purpose as the litmus test of Austen's creative credentials. A. C. Bradley, writing in 1911, saw in it an article of faith that her art was rooted in a precise place, which in the first half of the century served an ideological purpose bringing localized notions of Englishness to bear on the foundation of university courses in English Literature. Park Honan, following Chapman, embellished its hagiologic potential when he described the relocation from Hampshire to Bath as Jane's journey into 'the Wilderness', while at the other end of the spectrum the widely available Pitkin Guide in the collectable series on 'famous people and places to visit', currently dispensed at Chawton Cottage, Bath, and other key tourist sites, gives the pleasantly intimate detail that 'she collapsed in a faint on the floor of the kitchen'. Recently David Nokes has pored over the episode, using it to jump off in a quite different direction to the robust (but unprovable) conclusion that after fainting or not fainting Jane went off to Bath to have fun; and it is because she was too busy enjoying herself that there is now a perceptible gap in the biographical record. Nokes's vision of a clubbing Jane has an appealing 1990s feel. But Carol Shields, who as a novelist looks for clues in Austen's own art and in the practices of other sympathetic women writers, protests: 'Can she really have fainted, she who in her earliest work mocked extravagant emotional responses, especially those assigned to women?' Apparently unaware of Fanny Caroline's manuscript history, Shields draws on Caroline Austen's version of the episode to write persuasively of Jane as a woman 'unarmoured . . . against change', and as a writer who, like Virginia Woolf, did 'not need stimulation, but the opposite of stimulation'. Though subtly done, her reading makes certain assumptions about a writer's pathology which, true for Woolf (and for Shields?), may not have been so for Austen.[74]

Why does this one moment appeal to biographers and why do they embellish it so enthusiastically? After all, however sudden the decision to leave Steventon, it can hardly have come as a total surprise to his children that the 70-year-old George Austen was planning his retirement and that he must,

[73] David Cecil, *A Portrait of Jane Austen* (London: Constable and Co., 1978), 90.

[74] Bradley, 'Jane Austen', 35–6; Honan, *Jane Austen: Her Life*, Part Three: 'War and the Wilderness'; *Jane Austen*, letterpress by Victor Lucas (Andover, Hants: Pitkin Unichrome Ltd., 1996), 9; Nokes, *Jane Austen: A Life*, 220–3; and Carol Shields, *Jane Austen* (London: Weidenfeld & Nicolson, 2001), 73 84, and 86.

in consequence, leave the rectory. Nor if we give it a moment's thought is the gap between great distress and fainting necessarily significant. But in a life where so much is hidden, any sign of emotion is precious. Here at last we seem to glimpse the kind of dramatic turning-point or internal revolution familiar from Romantic autobiography—Rousseau's *Confessions*, Wordsworth's *Prelude*, or De Quincey's *Confessions of an English Opium Eater*. Add to this biography's positivist relish for body parts—Byron's club foot, Shelley's incorruptible heart—and the faint/no faint can be made to carry a valuable freight. The moment matters because in a family record which consistently refuses to celebrate the exceptionality of its subject, here at last is a glimpse of a self apart, a soul inhabiting its own solitary depths. By convention, we look to detail to exhibit a special residue of personal experience. At the same time, the supreme negativity of this detail—that we glimpse a Jane apart only in the moment when consciousness is lost to intense feeling—appears also to keep faith with the paucity of the evidence and the much emphasized privacy of her character: simultaneously, we are given access to a self and no self. But what more than this does Jane's distress/faint/dead faint allow her biographers to identify? 'This reaction is unlike anything else related of her,' confides Cecil, 'and, for that reason, very revealing.' Revealing of what? Overwhelmingly the incident has been used by biographers to draw a blank, to indulge their own 'dead faint', to mark an end; specifically, an end to writing, the very activity which explains our interest in her. With almost ridiculous efficiency, the body's faint metabolizes into textual silence. The secret of, or clue to, Jane Austen's creativity lies, we are told, like DNA coding, in her original script. Though he would not recognize it presented in these terms, this is Austen-Leigh's view, and it accounts for his erasure of even the idea of struggle from his record of her writing life. Instead, what he does emphasize is that, settled in Chawton after the disruptions of the Bath and Southampton years, her habits of composition assumed identity with those he conjectures for the Steventon years, 'so that the last five years of her life produced the same number of novels with those which had been written in her early youth.'[75] To replicate, as the analyst says, is to cure.

The structure Austen-Leigh imposed in 1870 continues to have profound significance for how critics view Jane Austen's creative life. He suggested that the novels as we know them were the products of two distinct and matching

[75] *Memoir*, 81.

creative periods—roughly Austen's early twenties and her late thirties—and that these were divided by a largely fallow interlude. That he and his sisters would foreclose on their aunt's future is not surprising: in many ways the lives they lived were narrower than hers; their sympathies probably more confined. In any case, their personal contacts with her were in Hampshire and mainly during the final Chawton years.[76] A different but equally valid interpretation of the same evidence and dates, though one which has found little favour, might be that, with the exception of a version of *Northanger Abbey* (sold, under the title of 'Susan' to a London publisher in 1803), all the finished novels were the products of the mature Chawton years; that the intense burst of creativity between 1809 and 1817 was not necessarily the consequence of a return to emotional or environmental origins but the culmination of some twenty years of uninterrupted and diversely stimulated fictional experimentation. A case can be made for linking *Northanger Abbey*, possibly in a second drafting, *The Watsons*, and the revision and completion of *Lady Susan* with the disrupted Bath and Southampton years; there may also have been other drafts or revisions at this time. Distress may have transformed into something positive, not the dead faint of a soul in exile but a new if painful beginning, in which the move to Bath implies a wider social scene, with more variety and incident to fuel the aspiring novelist's imagination. This was Elizabeth Jenkins's sensible verdict in 1938 in the first serious work of interpretative biography and the only major study between Lefroy and Cecil to provide a resistant voice to the romantic reading of the 'lost' years. Jenkins disputes none of the family-derived ingredients; she simply transforms them into something closer to common experience than to trauma: yes, Jane fainted, as people of acute perceptions will; but, yes, she recovered, as people of lively interests do.[77] Given the hard critical gaze Austen turns upon domesticity and families in her fictions, can we afford to dismiss clues which suggest they are not exclusively the products of home and rootedness? In other words, what intervened between Steventon and Chawton may not have been one long swoon of unconsciousness, a syncope of around eight years, from which she only recovered when time and events conspired to restore as nearly as possible those primal scenes. Perhaps the trajectory of her career was not the doubling

[76] The point is made with some force by W. and R. L. Austen-Leigh: 'Their knowledge of their aunt was during the last portion of her life, and they knew her best of all in her last year, when her health was failing and she was living in much seclusion; and they were not likely to be the recipients of her inmost confidences on the events and sentiments of her youth.' (*Life and Letters* (1913), vi–vii.)

[77] Elizabeth Jenkins, *Jane Austen: A Biography* (London: Victor Gollancz, 1938), 110–11.

back of restoration with its rejection of opportunity but the more troublesome arc of change.

Fanny Caroline, our source for Jane's faint, was Anna Lefroy's third daughter, born in 1820, three years after her great-aunt's death. Her 'Family History', probably written not long before her own death, aged 65 in 1885, remains unpublished, dipped into by family biographers, and less frequently by others. Its ultimate authority is a tissue of stories, written and recollected, from her mother, interspersed with material from Aunt Caroline Austen's written and unwritten personal recollections and from Caroline's mother Mary Austen's pocket-book records. Its shape and range as history was provided by the life of Cassandra Leigh, Jane's mother and Fanny's great-grandmother, from the time of her marriage in 1764 to the Revd George Austen to the dispersal of the household at Chawton Cottage after her death in 1827 and Frank Austen's marriage to Martha Lloyd in the following year. But this domestic span is regularly interrupted by a more distant genealogical perspective—the histories of the Perrots, the Mathews (Anna Lefroy's mother's family), and the Leighs, extended in some instances back to medieval times. (None of Jane Austen's collateral descendants seemed able to resist the allure of obscure genealogy.) Fanny's immediate purpose is thus not the straightforward one of writing a life of her famous great aunt. Nevertheless, Jane Austen contrives to share centre-stage for much of the narrative with Fanny's mother, her niece Anna Lefroy; to a modern reader, the interest of the history lies in what this dual female focus brings into critical relief.

Specifically, Fanny Caroline offers something new in combining the lives of aunt and niece and in her willingness to speculate on romance or sexual love to account in emotional terms for Austen's genius. In her version of things, the circumstances of Cassandra's broken engagement are neatly mirrored in the tragedy of Jane's mysterious seaside lover, while Anna's troubled early history intersects and annotates other events of her aunt's life, allowing Fanny to uncover or imagine areas of equivalence in Jane. Fanny Caroline, who came to family history as a published romantic novelist, constructed a narrative in which great Aunt Jane and her namesake (Anna was Jane Anna Elizabeth Austen) are paired sentimental heroines. In Fanny's recollections, tales of Aunt Jane's lost love and of her own mother's unhappy childhood in a loveless home combine to shed a delicious melancholy; on occasion, Austen's novels even assume the status of avenging agents of Anna's unhappiness. 'It seems to me', Fanny Caroline writes with a sly glance at her more cautious elders, 'the beauty of Jane Austen's character has been marred by the too careful suppression of the romance of her life.'[78]

As Anna Austen, the unloved daughter of her stepmother, Mary, Fanny Caroline's mother had been the exile within the new Steventon household after Aunt Jane's departure for Bath. Mary Austen, Fanny Caroline writes,

> did not love her step daughter, & she slighted her; she made her of no estimation, & the last and least in her father's house. She was very far indeed from being the cruel step mother of fiction, & perhaps in truth of former times, but certainly it never entered her imagination that she was to make no difference between her and her own children.

This was not the first time Anna had found a home at Steventon. She had been brought to live at the rectory in 1795, aged 2, on her mother's sudden death, and she remained there, mothered equally by aunts Cassandra and Jane and her grandmother, until her father's second marriage in 1797. Thereafter, she maintained an intense attachment to the female household of grandmother and aunts, often returning to them for long periods during her later childhood and adolescence. 'My mother... was only between two and three at the time of her [mother's] death', Fanny Caroline records, 'but from her father she never heard even her name, not a word as to look or character or habits or of her love for her child, she had however been a very tender mother, and the poor little girl missed her so much, and kept so constantly asking and fretting for "Mama", that her father sent her away to Steventon to be taken care of and consoled by her Aunts Cassandra and Jane.' The early bond was strengthened by imaginative sympathy and a precocious talent for writing which Aunt Jane also fostered. This double debt, at once inarticulate and literary, is apparent in the fierce protectiveness Anna exhibited in old age towards Austen's manuscripts and in the story she circulated within the family that the character of Lady Susan, Austen's early experiment in female villainy, derived from Mary Austen's grandmother, 'noted for the ill usage of her daughters'. Her own unhappy childhood, as 'the prettiest and worst drest girl in the neighbourhood', also made Anna more critical than her half-brother and -sister of the much-vaunted supportiveness of the wider Austen family network. In her accounts we begin to discover the cracks that Oliphant missed from the public record: for example, her distrust of Henry Austen's easy charm and her belief that his bankruptcy in 1816 contributed to Aunt

[78] HRO, MS. 23M93/85/2 Fanny C. Lefroy, 'Family History', unpaginated. The next several quoted passages are also taken from this manuscript.

Jane's final illness. Fanny Caroline takes from her mother's manuscript history her equivocal description of Henry, by reputation Jane's favourite brother:

He was the handsomest of his family and in the opinion of his own father also the most talented. There were others who formed a different estimate and considered his abilities greater in show than in reality but for the most part he was greatly admired.

By a curious coincidence, aged 20 Anna became engaged to and soon married Ben Lefroy, a cousin of that Tom Lefroy to whom Jane had been attracted at twenty. To Fanny Caroline's romantic imagination Jane and Anna embody two divergent but related female possibilities. If in Jane the loss of love temporarily 'paralysed the faculty of invention', the habit of writing was soon re-established and thereafter stood in for romance; for Anna, on the other hand, drawn close by early emotional deprivation to her talented aunt, writing became for a time a compensation only to be overtaken by marriage and the duties of a large family—books giving place to babies.[79] One of Fanny's earliest memories was of her mother burning the manuscript novel, provisionally entitled 'Which Is the Heroine?', that Aunt Jane had encouraged her to write: 'I remember sitting on the rug and watching its destruction amused with the flame and the sparks which kept breaking out in the blackened paper. In later years when I expressed my sorrow that she had destroyed it, she said she could never have borne to finish it.' According to Austen-Leigh family tradition, in her youth Anna was 'mercurial and excitable' in character, while Austen's letters over many years evince deep concern for her troubled niece's welfare.[80] Another tradition, derived from Fanny Caroline, describes Anna as the 'unintentional' original of Emma. By Anna's own account, written in 1864, she and Aunt Jane were closest 'the two years before my marriage, & the two or three years after... when the original 17 years between us seemed to shrink to 7—or to nothing.'[81] These years, roughly 1812–17, were also Austen's most creative period. With Anna's novel burned 'in a fit of despondency' some time in the early 1820s, the best extant witnesses to their relationship are Austen's delightful mock panegyric 'In measured verse I'll now rehearse the charms of lovely Anna', which transforms into a spectacular North American geography her niece's impetuosity,

[79] See *Jane Austen's Letters*, 310: 'As I wish very much to see *your* Jemima [Anna's first child], I am sure you will like to see *my* Emma.'

[80] *Life and Letters* (1913), 241; and see *Jane Austen's Letters*, 128; 184; 231–2.

[81] *Memoir*, 159.

and the letters on novel writing from 1814. But a trail of influence and collaboration extends from the juvenilia and burlesque playlet 'Sir Charles Grandison' to Anna's late, abandoned attempt to complete the unfinished *Sanditon*.[82]

It seems inevitable that for Anna, and after her for Fanny Caroline, neither of them sophisticated professional writers, the literary and the personal would directly fuse. In comparing Jane's departure from Steventon to make way for James and Mary Austen with Marianne Dashwood's ejection from Norland by a heartless sister-in-law, Fanny Caroline suggested a plausible cause for the older generation's sudden decision to move: nasty Mary Austen had used Jane's absence to work on her parents-in-law. We do not know exactly when Fanny began her 'Family History'; soon after 1880 seems most likely. For in that year Aunt Caroline, the last of Mary Austen's children, died releasing her from simple debts of loyalty and affection. Her history with its emphatic emotional punctuation fits precisely the defence she launched at that time in the pages of Bentley's magazine *Temple Bar* against the charge that Austen's writing is limited in expressive range. She was responding to an article on the Steventon Edition of the novels, published in six volumes with Austen-Leigh's biography, in which the reviewer had noted that on the evidence of both biography and fiction:

> The passion for nature which is sometimes prompted by inward dissatisfaction or despair, was unknown to Miss Austen. Completely in harmony with the life around her, her attention was absorbed by that, and not absorbed only, but satisfied. Neither in her books, nor in her letters, do we find any trace of a heart ill at ease, of a spirit seeking rest and finding none. Such satisfaction is at once a source of strength and of weakness; it gives finish, but it necessitates limitation. . . . Had Miss Austen felt more deeply, she would have written differently.[83]

Fanny Caroline's vindication was swift and emphatic, articulating, often in identical words, the central thesis of the manuscript 'Family History', that Jane Austen wrote out of the depths of felt experience. She knew only too well the pain of lost attachment, Fanny declared; and rising to a theatrical flourish: 'does the absence of restlessness and discontent imply that no "serious attachment" has ever been felt? What if the love have ended in the grave?'[84] In just fourteen printed pages she sets out her case for an author whose emotional complexity is no less complex for being under restraint.

[82] See below Ch. 4, 'Continuations'.

[83] 'Jane Austen', *Temple Bar*, 64 (1882), 356–9.

[84] [Fanny C. Lefroy], 'Is it Just?', *Temple Bar*, 67 (1883), 275.

A sequence of intense moments from Austen's life is rapidly sketched: from lost romantic passion, through 'her great grief' at leaving Steventon, to 'the anxiety and fatigue' of nursing a brother [Henry] back from 'the very edge of the grave'. Interestingly, she prefaces it all with a eulogy to the correctness of Austen's grammar. Fanny Caroline grasps, as later Austenians will, the proximity of emotional to syntactic vulgarity and the double duty that a defence of her well-regulated prose might therefore perform.

Little more than ten years after Austen-Leigh's buttoned-up portrait of quiet spinsterhood, the challenge was now laid down to discover the depths of Jane's feeling heart. Since then, more often through indirect than direct acquaintance, Fanny Caroline's manuscript has continued to provide the romantic subtext of subsequent biographies. But Anna's side of the story, so significant to Fanny's intensification of her portrait of Aunt Jane, remains largely unaired. If Fanny's published response in *Temple Bar* was itself heartfelt, a romantic defence, Brabourne's was more calculated. Seizing the commercial opening that charge and defence supplied, he issued his collection of letters only a year later, with the published gloss that they contain 'the confidential outpourings of Jane Austen's soul' and the private explanation that 'they certainly show, as they were intended to do, the *inner life* of the woman.'[85] After her death, Augustus Austen-Leigh (James Edward's son) supplied Oscar Fay Adams with 'extracts' from Fanny Caroline's unpublished 'Family History', and Constance Hill was permitted ample use of it together with copies of Anna Lefroy's manuscript recollections for her non-family biography. Thereafter Fanny's manuscript provided much of the romantic colouring of W. and R. A. Austen-Leigh's *Life and Letters* and Mary Augusta Austen-Leigh's apologia, *Personal Aspects of Jane Austen*, the latter so wittily dismissed by Virginia Woolf in her review 'Jane Austen and the Geese'.[86] Mary Augusta, daughter of James Edward, knew and had access to the writings of Jane's nieces Caroline and Anna, and Anna's children Fanny Caroline and Louisa Bellas. But by 1920 the textual transmission had become obscured: she cites from Hill's printed version the account of Anna Lefroy's wedding, which Hill got not from Caroline Austen's original manuscript record but from Fanny Caroline's copy.[87] For another story, which members

[85] *Letters of Jane Austen*, ed. Brabourne, i. xii; letter from Lord Brabourne to Bentley, April 1885, printed in Deirdre Le Faye, 'Lord Brabourne's Edition of Jane Austen's Letters', *Review of English Studies*, n.s., 52 (2001), 101.

[86] *Times Literary Supplement*, 28 October 1920, 699.

[87] Hill, *Her Homes and Her Friends*, 225–6; Mary Augusta Austen-Leigh, *Personal Aspects*, 135–8.

of the family were anxious to deny (that Austen's *Lady Susan* was itself a work of biography based in Anna Lefroy's unkind stepmother's family), Mary Augusta went direct to Lefroy tradition. She alludes to the novella's origin in terms which are all the more sensational for being veiled: 'So far as we know, [*Lady Susan*] is the only "Study from Life" that she ever made', and she never meant publication but to exorcize her own horror at 'the story of an unnatural and brutal mother.'[88] Her relations had long found it uncomfortable to consider the seductive immorality of *Lady Susan* as a work of Austen's imagination; by resurrecting an old family grievance, itself couched in an even older tale of apparently authenticated maltreatment, Mary Augusta unwittingly enhanced the novella's provocative status, as not quite fiction, in a way which still remains difficult to dislodge.[89]

Almost a hundred years on, Constance Pilgrim's biographical novel *Dear Jane* fulfilled some of the promise implied in Fanny Caroline's manuscript by completing the story of the tragically curtailed seaside romance. 'What was the mystery in Jane Austen's life?' Pilgrim speculates, and she goes on to outline its, by now, well-rehearsed ingredients:

> Two periods of literary activity—the first in her youth, the second in her late thirties—separated by ten or more years of suppressed talent, gifts held in check, an arid period. Why? Was it the disruption of the secure country family life when their father, the Reverend George Austen, left his rectory at Steventon, handing the parish over to his eldest son, James Austen, and retiring to Bath in 1801? Or was this upheaval but an aggravation of a deeper unhappiness—the tearing apart of Jane and her elusive lover, the hero of the West Country romance?[90]

The besetting dilemma of biography appears to be set aside as Pilgrim throws historical caution to the wind and gives rein to fantasy alone. Jane's mysterious lover was, she explains, not a clergyman as supposed but an officer in the merchant navy, none other than Captain John Wordsworth, brother to the

[88] Mary Augusta Austen-Leigh, *Personal Aspects*, 100–5.

[89] While the story of cruel Mary Austen's cruel grandmother, Martha Craven, has almost disappeared from the record (but see Nokes, 151–2), it has been replaced by the assumption that Lady Susan is a portrait of Eliza de Feuillide. (Honan, *Jane Austen: Her Life*, 101–2; Tomalin, *Jane Austen: A Life*, 82.) C. L. Thomson, *Jane Austen: A Survey* (London: Horace Marshall and Son, 1929), 71–2, early backed both options, but with the reservation that Eliza provided only the acceptable aspects of Lady Susan: 'her beauty, her love of flirtation, and the fact of being a widow'. B. C. Southam, *Jane Austen's Literary Manuscripts: A Study of the Novelist's Development through the Surviving Papers*, rev. edn. (London: Athlone Press, 2001), 144–7, offers a fuller treatment of these biographical readings, though he is curiously uninterested in the Lefroy family circumstances which may explain them.

[90] Constance Pilgrim, *Dear Jane: A Biographical Study of Jane Austen* (London: William Kimber, 1971), 11.

better known William. Tragically, the lovers were doomed, and John died when his ship the *Earl of Abergavenny* went down in a terrible storm off Weymouth Sands in February 1805. Pilgrim's fantasy is both ridiculous and appealing on several counts: in forging a link between Jane Austen and William Wordsworth it satisfies our simple desire that famous people from a particular age should be known to one another (she may not have met Madame de Staël but she almost became Wordsworth's sister-in-law); it gives a kind of enhanced plausibility by association to Jane's other claim to have romance in her soul—her love of nature; and it furthers the persistent wished-for identification of Anne Elliot with her creator that Jane's mysterious lover, now a sailor, should almost be named Wentworth. There is no basis in fact for this star-crossed romance, but that matters not at all.

Through its written trace a life assumes some of the properties of a text. But in what sense is the biographer a textual critic? By training the textual critic enquires into the origin and nature of variations in a text or texts. She does so to distinguish between readings—whether accurate or erroneous, early or late, or merely multiple—to determine how they entered the text(s), and ultimately to exercise judgement: to establish the more authoritative reading, often represented as an attempt to fix the text(s) as a better text. Biographers work from comparable principles and towards similarly compromised ends: whether or not we postulate an original text for a self, the biographee becomes, in the telling, an assemblage or succession of texts, subject to the same instabilities and transformations in transmission. The aim in both cases is to provide a better text/life, but in neither case is progress unambiguous; the labour of textual critic and biographer alike is ultimately self-defeating since its outcome can only be another text and another site of authority and disorder. Sifting and weighing the relationship between information and interpretation, biography, like text editing, is also an occasional art, made that is out of the circumstances of a particular relationship, which will change with each new telling as it expresses new needs and sensibilities. Accordingly, there is with the text of a life, as with a literary edition, no easy way to set boundaries which declare where the text ends and its contexts begin. Compare Ira Nadel's defence of the multiple biographies of Dickens, Johnson, and Joyce:

> As a genre, biography continually unsettles the past, maintaining its vitality through its continual correction, revision and interpretation of individual lives. Each new version is a provocation to reassess all past lives of that subject. Versions

of a life are necessary stages in the evolution of the genre as well as in the understanding of the subject.[91]

We might think of the faint/no faint as a textual crux, the consequence of the unreliability or reserve of one contemporary eye-witness account, Mary Austen's. We might therefore think of Fanny Caroline's documentation of the incident as an act of faithful restoration of an essential element from a suppressed but authentic textual tradition; or we might think of it as a biographical equivalent to those acts of substitution by which copyists and editors throughout history have, intentionally and unintentionally, replaced difficult elements in a text by their more mundane equivalents. Fanny Caroline's romantic imagination, in this latter case, would be guilty of the kind of accessible banality that makes too ready sense of a textual hiatus. But accurate or not as emendation, the detail liberated the narrative potential of a particular moment, making it readable for several generations of biographers, and by extension making emotional and artistic sense of the life and the novels.

There are perhaps four chief strategies, four ways of shaping the text of the life, favoured by the modern Austen biographer. There are, firstly, the few events or stories which have some primary documentary status, which relate directly to Jane Austen, and which must be dutifully recorded and re-recorded—the well-rehearsed account of her leaving Steventon, passed on by at least one eye-witness, Mary Austen, is one such; the Harris Bigg-Wither marriage proposal, perhaps related by Cassandra to her niece Caroline and certainly passed on by Caroline's mother, Mary Austen, is another.[92] Events or stories of this kind constitute essential pieces of the received text, handed down from one biographer to another. If we think of a life as a text, then these are the original stories we must keep telling. The reader expects to find them in the index of each new biography, and the biographer must arrange them as she can.

Secondly, there are those ingredients, equally essential to the picture, in which the emphasis is less on eventfulness than interpretation. Here we are

[91] Ira Bruce Nadel, *Biography: Fiction, Fact and Form* (London and Basingstoke: Macmillan, 1984), 103.

[92] Caroline described the circumstances of the proposal, which can be dated precisely to 2–3 December 1802, in a letter to her niece, James Edward Austen-Leigh's daughter Amy (Emma) in 1870. For a transcription, see Joan Austen-Leigh, 'New Light on JA's Refusal of Harris Bigg-Wither', *Persuasions*, 8 (1986), 34–6. The incident formed part of one of the major revisions to the second edition of Austen-Leigh's *Memoir* (29 and note), but in so veiled a form as to provide no names or details and presumably no offence. The account published by the family remained highly elliptical long into the twentieth century, despite the fact that Hill had named Bigg-Wither in 1902.

looking not for the facts but for the truths of the situation (not that she left Steventon but how she felt as she left); again, the reader will come to the latest biography with a checklist. These are curious ingredients because, in obedience with some law of biographical physics, they transmit a positive and a negative charge. Of this kind are the following: Jane Austen's relationship with her mother; her experience of Bath; her attitude to her rich brother Edward. Jane Austen's mother was uncaring towards her children when they were small and a selfish hypochondriac in later years; alternatively, her mother provided practically and lovingly for her small children, and Jane held her in great respect. Jane hated Bath; in more recent interpretation, Jane loved Bath. Jane resented Godmersham and Edward's good fortune and did not think he shared it sufficiently with his mother and sisters; Jane relished Godmersham and found in Edward a loving and considerate brother.[93] It is worth noting that bi-polar readings of the evidence are not a modern development but can be traced to the rival early accounts of Austen-Leigh and Lord Brabourne.

Thirdly, there are the contrasting characters, all female so far, against whom Jane's own personality can be discovered and projected. For well over a century her sister Cassandra was the only one to fill this space. In Austen-Leigh's influential account, coloured by the more intimate recollections of his sisters,

> [t]hey were not exactly alike. Cassandra's was the colder and calmer disposition; she was always prudent and well judging, but with less outward demonstration of feeling and less sunniness of temper than Jane possessed. It was remarked in her family that 'Cassandra had the *merit* of having her temper always under command, but that Jane had the *happiness* of a temper that never required to be commanded.'[94]

[93] John Halperin, *The Life of Jane Austen* (1984; 3rd printing, Baltimore: Johns Hopkins University Press, 1996), 63–4, 144–5, 229–30, 338–9, weaves through his controversial text surmises as to the difficult relationship between Jane and her mother; Alison Sulloway, *Jane Austen and the Province of Womanhood* (Philadelphia: University of Pennsylvania Press, 1989), 92–3, reaches the odd conclusion that despite general family support for Austen's writing, her mother and sister were distinctly unhelpful; Tomalin, *Jane Austen: A Life*, 6–7, describes Jane as emotionally traumatized by early weaning and an associated withdrawal of maternal emotion. Nokes, *Jane Austen: A Life*, 222, offers the rare suggestion that Jane may have enjoyed life in Bath. Anna Lefroy, more critical in this than her half-sister Caroline, 'thought Edward should have done more for his mother and sisters', *Family Record*, 175; Tomalin, 192, embellishes this view: 'his sisters may well have asked themselves how much of Edward's luck was passed on to them when even the idea of providing a permanent home for them and their mother did not occur to him at the time of his father's death.' Irene B. McDonald, 'Contemporary Biography: Some Problems', *Persuasions*, 20 (1998), 61–8, writes amusingly of the changing fashions in Austen biography.

[94] *Memoir*, 19.

Anna Lefroy preserved into old age a childhood memory of 'two Aunts' known apart only by their bonnets.[95] Two women distinguishable from their bonnets and sunniness of outlook—these are the slight material and psychological origins of biographical rehearsal. Cassandra, the elder by almost three years, was simply protective; theirs was a mutually sustaining emotional pact, which in Fanny Caroline's account is made even deeper through their shared sorrow in love. Alternatively, Cassandra hampered and restricted Jane's emotional development. In some late twentieth-century recensions of the life-text, this pairing or doubling has taken on Gothic proportions: Cassandra as the villainous, anxious partner enforcing Jane's emotional deprivation, and with lurid speculations about incestuous lesbianism.[96] However refashioned, the structural significance of the dualism Austen-Leigh established has remained crucial in excavating a personality for Jane. Either she is what Cassandra is not or events in Cassandra's life anticipate and determine, usually in negative terms, the course of Jane's.

More recently, two or perhaps three other female figures have come into contention as alter egos or simply contrasting personalities to domestic Jane. Her older cousin, Eliza Hancock, later Eliza de Feuillide, and later still Eliza Austen, born in India and brought up in England and France, is beginning to be seen as Jane's adventurous, cosmopolitan, and 'outlandish' other. If anyone can help us recover Jane the urbanite, as counterweight to the Hampshire frump, it is probably Eliza. Family recollections acknowledge Eliza as a significant influence on Jane's teenage years; once married to her brother Henry and moving in smart London circles, she provided rich cultural opportunities. Reviewing Deirdre Le Faye's recent compilation of Eliza's *Life and Letters*, Michael Shelden went so far as to describe Jane within Eliza's ambit as 'this Regency party animal' and Eliza herself as 'worthy of a

[95] *Memoir*, 157.

[96] Tomalin suggests that owing to the early severance of the maternal bond there may have been something infantalizing in Cassandra's influence, and that their relationship was not unlike that of many couples: 'sisters can become couples' (211); Terry Castle's sensationalized review of Le Faye's 1995 revised edition of the *Letters* proclaimed 'the primitive adhesiveness—and underlying eros—of the sister–sister bond' (*London Review of Books*, 3 August 1995, 3), provoking in the *LRB*'s letters column much heated discussion and rejection of the dual charges of incest and lesbianism. With no apparent evidence, Honan, *Jane Austen: Her Life*, remarks that Jane enjoyed watching Martha Lloyd and that 'there was no more than a slight trace of guilt in her joy over Martha's person' before concluding that '[o]bservers from a harder age might see lesbianism in Jane Austen's delight in her friend' (251). Deborah Kaplan makes the interesting suggestion, obviously influenced by post-1970s feminism, that Jane and Cassandra may have made a pact to enter middle age prematurely in order to exploit 'contemporary stereotypes about spinsters' and 'to reserve more private time to spend with... intimate female friends' (*Jane Austen Among Women* (Baltimore and London: Johns Hopkins University Press, 1992), 122).

Hollywood epic'.[97] Where Cassandra has served to confine Jane, Eliza offers a fully sexualized counter-image. Further speculation on the extent and nature of her relationship with her early mentor, (Madam) Anne Lefroy, seems set to cast an interesting light on the young Jane Austen's intellectual aspirations, on her early love life, and on her reputed unsatisfactory relationship with her mother;[98] while potentially more sensational than the role created for Eliza de Feuillide is the mounting interest in a third figure, Jane's Aunt Jane Leigh-Perrot. Accused of shoplifting a card of white lace and charged not with petty theft but grand larceny, a crime punishable by death, Aunt Leigh-Perrot spent seven months incarcerated, awaiting trial. Mrs Austen even offered to send one or both of her daughters to stay with her in the Somerset County Gaol at Ilchester. Biographers have regularly noted with relish the details of the case, and especially the equivocal nature of the evidence: Jane Leigh-Perrot was acquitted, but was she innocent? The challenge to make the incident connect with and illuminate Austen's own life is considerable, but it has so far proved elusive. In a recent study, William Galperin draws on Mrs Leigh-Perrot's letters in the *Austen Papers* to argue that what he calls 'the inscrutable density of Aunt Perrot's historical reality' can and should contribute to our understanding of the kinds of fictional histories Austen wrote.[99] He proposes that where the biographical record preserves Jane's silence over the trial, a personal response and even 'collaboration' can be found in the complementary trajectory of trial, defence, and acquittal which many of her narratives enact.

[97] The reinterpretation stimulated by Le Faye's book (*Jane Austen's 'Outlandish Cousin': The Life and Letters of Eliza de Feuillide* (London: British Library, 2002) is in sharp contrast to earlier verdicts on Eliza's character. See, for example, Sidney Ives's description of her as the original for Mary Crawford (from *Mansfield Park*), 'the vilest woman in English fiction', *Persuasions*, 2 (1980), 26. The connection with Mary Crawford was made in criticism of the novel as early as C. L. Thomson, *Jane Austen: A Survey*, 148, on the basis of Hubback family tradition: 'Mary Crawford . . . was suggested by Eliza de Feuillide, who, according to a family tradition, refused James Austen, in his short widowhood . . . because she could not bear to be the wife of a clergyman.' Deborah Kaplan, *Jane Austen Among Women*, 77, argues that the edited version of Eliza's letters in the *Austen Papers* is responsible for the distorted view that she was 'primarily interested in herself'. George Holbert Tucker, *A History of Jane Austen's Family*, rev. edn. (Stroud, Glos.: Sutton Publishing Ltd, 1998), 107, points to the family origin in Mary Austen of stories disparaging Eliza. Tucker also notes (141–2) the cultural enrichment to Jane of visits to Eliza's London addresses. Anna Lefroy, Mary's step-daughter, recollected Eliza's 'valuable assistance' to Jane and Cassandra in teaching them French and perhaps Italian. She was, writes Anna, 'an extremely accomplished woman, not only for that day, but for any day.' (*Memoir*, 183.)

[98] According to Honan, *Jane Austen: Her Life*, Mrs Lefroy 'saw in Jane Austen a kindred spirit', while Jane found with her an outlet for sensibilities 'stifled at Steventon' (40–1); Tomalin, *Jane Austen: A Life*, describes her as 'the ideal parent to be preferred to the everyday one' (38); Nokes, *Jane Austen: A Life*, on the other hand, senses Jane resented her interference in the Tom Lefroy affair and concludes that she 'deprived' Jane of 'the solace of wedded love' (345).

[99] William H. Galperin, *The Historical Austen* (Philadelphia: University of Pennsylvania Press, 2003), 36.

Galperin's reading is more involuted than this summary suggests. It is also strained and unconvincing; especially so (to risk a naïve comment) in view of the biographical evidence, in the form of letters, declaring Austen's settled lack of sympathy with her aunt. But now that the relationship has been formulated in these terms it may not be long before someone connects the two Janes in a way that will strike us as plausible.

Galperin writes in the first instance for an American audience. It is from North America and Australia that the boldest, least reverent critical revaluations of the novels are currently emerging. How long, then, will it be before we can no longer comfortably assume that the texts of Jane Austen's life will continue to respect the agreed contours of their reticent British manufacture? This brings me to the fourth biographical strategy—context or secondary colour. The primary sources for a life may be desperately thin but the secondary colour is rich. Jane Austen never left the south of England but her aunt Philadelphia Austen travelled to India in 1752 in search of a husband, soon marrying there Tysoe Saul Hancock. As Mrs Hancock she was intimate with Warren Hastings, the future Governor-General of Bengal and official godfather of her daughter Eliza. But was Eliza in fact Hastings's child?[100] Sensation and speculation continued to surround Eliza during her life and in family memory long after her death. Her first husband, a spurious French count, was guillotined in the aftermath of the Revolution. According to one unreliable tradition she barely escaped to England with her life; according to another, her husband was the real Comte de Feuillide's valet, who had murdered his master and taken both title and property; but by another, this deception was itself considered a trick to disinherit Eliza and her family.[101] More far-flung drama is provided by Austen's two brothers, Frank and Charles, who saw active service as sailors through the long wars with France. There were shady dealings between Frank Austen and the directors of the East India Company, involving shipments of silver, described in detail by one recent biographer.[102] Frank, one of Nelson's band of brothers, just missed

[100] Tucker approaches the matter cautiously but seems eventually to be persuaded that Hastings was Eliza's father (*Jane Austen's Family*, 39–45); Nokes, *Jane Austen: A Life*, 31–3, and 48–50, is sensationalist and unequivocal; but Le Faye remains sceptical: 'not the slightest hint in Hastings's diaries and other private papers that would corroborate such a claim' (*Jane Austen's 'Outlandish Cousin'*, 20).

[101] On the authority of Henry Austen's second wife, Eleanor Jackson, Fanny Caroline Lefroy records the story that Eliza's first husband was only the Comte's valet and also the suspicion that this may have been a further fabrication by a later generation of Feuillides, in HRO, MS. 23M93/85/2 'Family History', unpaginated.

[102] See Honan, *Jane Austen: Her Life*, 68–9, and 242–3, drawing upon unpublished records of the East India Company.

action at Trafalgar, but he saw service in the Peninsular campaign and Charles chased enemy warships in the Mediterranean in the summer of Waterloo. Such secondary colour affords no direct evidence for Jane Austen's life and contributes nothing to the contestable concept of personality, but it offers a choice of frames, and it gestures to the wider horizon. It provides a sense of a surrounding world whose interests may have chimed with, contrasted with, or thwarted her aspirations; a context which may place her but may just as effectively displace her, as Margaret Oliphant suggested was the case when she dismissed Austen-Leigh's charming but constricting idyll of rural Hampshire. Context thus performs the same intrusive function as textual annotation, though in Austen's case we must think of her biographies as texts fully textualized only through annotation. Put another way, if a life is a text, then almost all we can know of hers takes the form of conjectural commentary or repair.

Jane Austen biography has reached an interesting moment in its development; it may be about to shed some of its most cherished assumptions. As the interface between high culture and mass culture, biography as a genre has taken for granted a particular agenda. Whatever else they are, biographies have so far tended to be national portraits, hemmed in by national cultural assumptions—not just the texts of specific lives but texts which contribute from inside to a sense of the history of particular societies—*our own* famous men and women. A penumbra of emotional, aesthetic, and ideological resonances cluster around figures whose stories are regularly told; literary lives, in particular, speak to and of shared communities of knowledge. In a seminal essay Thomas Carlyle, Jane Austen's near contemporary, considered why we want biography: 'every mortal has a Problem of Existence set before him . . . to a certain extent *original*, unlike every other; and yet, at the same time, so *like* every other; like our own, therefore; instructive, moreover, since we also are indentured to *live*.' But he saw how what can be generalized also translates into something particular:

> Define to thyself, judicious Reader, the real significance of these phenomena, named Gossip, Egoism, Personal Narrative (miraculous or not), Scandal, Raillery, Slander, and such like; the sum total of which (with some fractional addition of a better ingredient, generally too small to be noticeable) constitutes that other grand phenomenon still called 'Conversation.' Do they not mean wholly: *Biography* and *Autobiography*?[103]

[103] Thomas Carlyle, 'Biography' (1832), *The Collected Works of Thomas Carlyle*, 16 vols. (London: Chapman and Hall, 1858), iv. 36–7.

The association of biography with gossip, with the confidential aside, with the easy and familiar, encloses the form generically, making it inevitable that the earliest expounders of the text of a life will be insiders, friends, enemies, family, those with local knowledge. Furthermore, the same compact with local knowledge will be made by the reader. Jane Austen has shed her family biographers more reluctantly than any other much-biographized figure. This means she has shed more slowly verification by gossip, confidential insight, and familial anecdote. Though her life in recent years has been written by many outside the ambit of family, it is only beginning to be redescribed in other terms. Part of the power of the familial text in her case has been its exact fit with an equally powerful and seductive myth of Englishness. How far can the familiar features of the text which we take to be the life be submitted to redescription without turning into a text we no longer recognize? And since most of the life-text we have for Jane Austen is context, can we re-imagine her life—for example, from the perspective of the kind of post-colonial reading we might now believe that context requires? How shall we receive the first Indian biography of Jane Austen—one written, that is, from a non-English perspective on the evidence?

Coda: portraits

One useful way of thinking about biography is through thinking about its near relation, the portrait. In a nineteenth-century context the connection seems irresistible; for though biography and the portrait have longer formal histories, both received institutional recognition at that time. From the late eighteenth century biography's investment shifted to encompass the mind, character, and domestic life of the famous, not just their deeds: by 1809 Coleridge was inveighing against 'this AGE OF PERSONALITY';[104] while the National Portrait Gallery was founded in 1856 by the particular efforts of three biographers, Carlyle, Macaulay, and Stanhope. Like biography, portraits, more directly than other art forms, 'confront the issue of truthfulness of representation'.[105] But it is a truth which depends less on descriptive accur-

[104] Samuel Taylor Coleridge, *The Friend*, ed. Barbara E. Rooke, 2 vols. (London: Routledge & Kegan Paul, 1969), ii. 138.

[105] Richard Brilliant, *Portraiture* (London: Reaktion Books Ltd., 1991), 13; for David Piper, the evidence of portraits is always 'loaded', offering the 'record of a dialogue between sitter and artist' and subsequently extending to the 'beholder' (*Personality and the Portrait* (London: BBC Publications, 1973), 2).

acy—did Jane Austen really look like this or like this—than on the coincidence of the perceptions shared by portraitist and viewer, neither of whom is innocent. Both genres denote an agreement between the artist or biographer and the viewer or reader in which the subject can end up occupying third place.

While the events of her life have been minimally recorded, her appearance curiously has not. We might think that where so many eye-witness accounts have come down to us we would have some chance of a consistent portrait of Jane Austen. But, as Claire Tomalin notes, their discrepancies portray her as somewhere between a doll and a poker. So, for example, one observer remembers that she was 'fair and handsome', and another that she had 'a clear brown complexion' with 'darkish brown' hair; a third writes that she was a 'light brunette', with 'mottled skin, not fair... hair, neither light nor dark'; while a fourth gives her 'large dark eyes and a brilliant complexion, and long, long black hair down to her knees'. Yet another observer, who knew her from childhood, says she had 'a good deal of colour in her face—like a doll... very lively & full of humour'; to a neighbour, later in life, she was 'a tall thin *spare* person, with very high cheek bones great colour—sparkling Eyes not large but joyous & intelligent'. Looking back in old age, and with help from his sisters, her nephew writes in the *Memoir* that she had 'full round cheeks, with mouth and nose small and well formed, bright hazel eyes, and brown hair forming natural curls close round her face', but 'not so regularly handsome as her sister'. To Mary Mitford we owe the acerbic diptych of the young Jane as 'the prettiest, silliest, most affected, husband-hunting butterfly', and the older Jane as 'the most perpendicular, precise, taciturn piece of "single blessedness" that ever existed... no more regarded in society than a poker or a fire-screen, or any other thin upright piece of wood.' Neither was from firsthand observation, but Mitford adds a nice touch of her own, to the effect that once the authorship of *Pride and Prejudice* was acknowledged, Austen became 'a poker of whom everyone is afraid'.[106]

Austen-Leigh issued the first public portrait more than fifty years after his aunt's death; he commissioned a professional portraitist, James Andrews of Maidenhead, to execute a reconstruction based on a simple sketch by Cassandra dating from approximately 1810, when Jane was 35 years old. This reconstruction was the model for the engraved plate used as frontispiece to

[106] Contemporary descriptions, cited in Tomalin, *Jane Austen: A Life*, 108–9; for Mitford's catty secondhand impressions, see *Memoir*, 133 and note; and ibid., 70 for James Edward's memories of his aunt's appearance.

the first edition of the *Memoir.* The difference between the engraving, for public circulation, and Cassandra's private sketch is evident to the most cursory glance. Her crude likeness is sharp-featured, pursed-lipped, unsmiling, and withdrawn. In its Victorian refashioning, the face is softer, its expression pliant, and the eyes only pensively averted. Cassy Esten, daughter of Jane's brother Charles, and by then the owner of Cassandra's original sketch, expressed some relief at how the commissioned picture had turned out:

I think the portrait is very much superior to any thing that could have been expected from the sketch it was taken from.—It is a very pleasing, sweet face,—tho', I confess to not thinking it *much* like the original;— but *that,* the public will not be able to detect.

Austen-Leigh's sister Caroline recorded a similar impression, telling her brother,

there is a *look* which I recognise as *hers*—and though the general resemblance is *not* strong, yet as it represents a pleasant countenance it is *so* far a truth—& I am not dissatisfied with it.

To her sister-in-law, Emma Austen-Leigh, she confessed her agreement with their cousin Elizabeth Rice, who had written 'I think it very like only the eyes are too large, not for beauty but for likeness.' Caroline added: 'She is right about the *eyes*—they *are* larger than the *truth,* that is, rounder, & more open.'[107]

The portrait sent into public circulation in 1870 remained the chief authorized image of the adult Jane Austen until 1948, when Cassandra's original sketch was purchased at auction by the National Portrait Gallery. The commission's authority is both complex and compromised. Endorsed as the official likeness by the family who lived intimately with her, it is described by the same witnesses as looking not much like her and as representing 'a truth'; witnesses, moreover, who imply a willingness to pass off a confected image if not a wish directly to mislead the public. What are we to make of this? Madame Tussaud's original head moulds of Louis XVI and Marie Antoinette are among the most authentic representations we have from the

[107] NPG, RWC/HH, f. 15, later typescript of part of a letter from Cassandra E. Austen to James Edward Austen-Leigh, 18 December 1869; ff. 16–17, later typescript of part of a letter from Caroline Austen to Austen-Leigh (in *Memoir,* 192); f. 20, later typescript of part of a letter from Elizabeth Rice to Austen-Leigh, 10 January 1870; HRO, MS. 23M93/ 87/3/164, from Caroline Austen to Emma Austen-Leigh, early in 1870.

10. Cassandra Austen's pencil and watercolour sketch of Jane Austen, *c.* 1810. By kind permission of the National Portrait Gallery, London.

period; similarly, the life and death masks of Jane Austen's contemporaries, Keats, Wordsworth, and Coleridge, attest to a form of representation, common throughout the nineteenth century, whose intentions are quite different from those of portraiture. Masks have illusionist designs upon the viewer; they are attempts to replicate an original, from which portraits evidently depart. Between masks and portraits lies the distinction between the replicable and the referential. For the art critic Maurice Grosser portraiture is 'almost a conversation';[108] a life mask, on the other hand, implies no such communion, but

[108] Maurice Grosser, *The Painter's Eye* (1951), quoted in Brilliant, 72; and Pamela M. Pilbeam, *Madame Tussaud and the History of Waxworks* (London: Hambledon, 2003).

11. Engraving after Cassandra Austen, from a portrait commissioned by J. E. Austen-Leigh as a frontispiece to the *Memoir*, 1870. By kind permission of Oxford University Press.

thereby retains its own integrity. If portraits, regardless of their skilful execution as art, express a social relationship as part of their primary meaning, then it follows that they become in the viewing a visual predicate.

This is powerfully so with the 1870 Austen portrait which in its function as frontispiece to her nephew Austen-Leigh's biography defined what it is to be Jane Austen. Austen-Leigh assembled a hagiographic account of a blameless life in which the duties of selfless spinster aunt, grateful sister, and uncomplaining daughter take precedence on every page over the life of the novelist. To be Jane Austen, according to Austen-Leigh, was to enact a set of family assumptions for which his prefatory engraving provided a highly structured iconic representation. The complacent, sweet image gives no hint of the edgy, satiric novelist whose vision of human nature appeared to Margaret Oliphant 'cruel in its perfection'. For this we must return to Cassandra's sketch. Where

12. Medallion portraits of Elizabeth I and Mary Queen of Scots by Cassandra Austen in 'The History of England', *Volume the Second* (Add. MS. 59874). By kind permission of the British Library, London.

the engraved portrait offers a public identification, the sketch is resolutely private. Its amateurish lack of finish is not in doubt; but critics have been oddly reluctant to consider the coincidence of its execution (a matter of style not chronology) with that of Cassandra's humorous cartoons illustrating the teenage spoof 'History of England... By a partial, prejudiced, & ignorant Historian'. We have been readier to assume that the sketch is just bad rather than that it is also calculated in what it reveals of a 'partial and prejudiced' social satirist. The double portrait of sketch and commission inevitably unsettle each other, forcing a recognition of the limits of any impersonation.[109] Not being 'like', as the family recognized in the case of the engraved commission, functions as a form of protection at the same time as it offers an image which can live outside and thus comfortably escape control.

Portraits rarely lose their contentiousness (or, rather, when they do they cease to interest us at all): none more so than the few we have of Jane Austen. Among the generation of nieces and nephews, the agreed favourite likeness was a back view, little more than a bonnet and buttocks; more recently, the undetermined authenticity of the Rice portrait (a romantically posed pubescent girl) has precipitated a flood of highly charged and partisan claims which threaten to reawaken the inter-family disputes of the nineteenth

[109] See the argument offered by Margaret Kirkham in 'The Austen Portraits and the Received Biography', in *Jane Austen: New Perspectives*, ed. Todd, 29–38.

century. For a long time (roughly the 1880s to the 1940s) known and accepted in Austen circles as the Zoffany portrait, the Rice portrait made its appearance opportunely as Lord Brabourne was preparing his Kentish Jane, the vibrant and soulful counterpart of Austen-Leigh's domesticated spinster; but since the middle of the twentieth century it has been surrounded by controversy. In this case, debate has nothing to do with whether the portrait might look like Jane Austen and everything to do with whether it is Jane Austen. It will not help clarify the muddy waters of this controversy that critical and commercial revaluations of the juvenile fiction are now making it highly desirable that we have a visual representation of a teenage Jane to identify with their voice.[110]

Would we identify someone in the street from a portrait? Perhaps we might, but unlike the passport photograph, that is not the portrait's purpose. Portraits evidently depart from an original, and in the twentieth century this was compounded by the realization that the self is either non-existent or multiple (compare Woolf's statement that 'a biography is considered complete if it merely accounts for six or seven selves, whereas a person may well have as many thousand').[111] If portraits appear to invite us to understand them as a kind of visual biography, the very concentration of their scope and symbolic codes of representation permits us to see more clearly how representational practices do their work. Like biography, portraiture neither implies nor intends an innocent relation to reality; but, unlike biography, the medium draws attention more directly to its own artfulness. It is therefore all the more bizarre that in December 2002 the Jane Austen Centre in Bath unveiled a newly commis-

[110] The history of Jane Austen's portraits is surprisingly vexed. For its development in the twentieth century, see *Life and Letters* (1913), 62–3; Chapman, *Jane Austen: Facts and Problems*, 212–14; Committee of the Jane Austen Society, 'The Zoffany Portrait', in 'Report for the Year, 1973', Constance Pilgrim, 'The Zoffany Portrait: A Re-appraisal', in 'Report for the Year, 1974', both in *Jane Austen Society Collected Reports, 1966–75* (1977; reissued Alton, Hants: Jane Austen Society, 1999), 197–200, and 220–5; Madeleine Marsh, 'Ozias Humphrey and the Austens of Sevenoaks' and 'The Portrait', in 'Report for the Year, 1985', in *Jane Austen Society Collected Reports, 1976–85* (Alton, Hants: Jane Austen Society, 1989), 350–7; Pauline Elliott, 'The Zoffany Portrait', in 'Report for the Year, 1991', in *Jane Austen Society Collected Reports, 1986–95* (Alton, Hants: Jane Austen Society, 1997), 215–17; Richard James Wheeler, *The Rice Portrait of Jane Austen: The Ill-Conceived Controversy* (Westerham, Kent: Codex Publications, 1996); Deirdre Le Faye, 'A Literary Portrait Re-examined: Jane Austen and Mary Anne Campion', *The Book Collector*, 45 (1996), 508–24; Wheeler and Margaret Campbell Hammond, *The Rice Portrait of Jane Austen: A Summary of Conclusive Evidence* (Sevenoaks: Codex Publications, 1997); Claudia L. Johnson, 'Fair Maid of Kent? The Arguments For (and Against) the Rice Portrait of Jane Austen', *Times Literary Supplement*, 13 March 1998, 14–15; and replies in *TLS*, 20 and 27 March, and 3 and 17 April 1998. There have been calls (see Margaret Anne Doody, *TLS*, 27 March, 17) for an independent committee to investigate the painting's authenticity. For later rumblings of the same controversy in the letters columns of the *TLS*, see Jacob Simon, 18 December 1998, 15; Brian Southam, 15 October 1999, 19; Jonathan Roberts, 3 May 2002, 17; Claudia L. Johnson, 2 August 2002, 15.

[111] Virginia Woolf, *Orlando: A Biography* (1928; London: Hogarth Press, 7th impression, 1954), 278.

sioned portrait or rather counter-portrait. No ordinary representation, it was announced with wide national media coverage as *the* definitive portrait of Jane Austen. Its authority rests on the credentials of the painter, Melissa Dring, who has a degree in the psychology of facial identification and training from the FBI, Washington, as a police forensic artist. Dring, described with odd complacency as working 'for police forces throughout Britain', based her portrait on a variety of evidence: letters, eyewitness accounts, and images of other members of the Austen family; she is adamant that it represents the real Jane Austen.[112] Exploiting for painting a naïve interpretation of how photography works, Dring implies for her picture a relation to reality that most photographers would not dare claim. She died in 1817 at the early age of 41, but Austen might reasonably have lived as did her brothers into the age of photography. Indeed, the photograph is all that is missing from the reality effect or promotion of kitsch, in which she was from early on enlisted. Repairing the relationship, Austen-Leigh in 1870 described her writing as 'a genuine home-made article' and 'like photographs . . . the unadorned reflection of the natural object' whose value 'must increase as time gradually works more and more changes in the face of society itself.'[113] Like photographs, Austen's novels were early prized for their apparent capacity to recycle events and images, giving renewed access to what we believe we have lost—our own previous experience, whether real or desired. Little wonder, then, that anything which threatens to unsettle this pleasant fixity should meet with howls of protest. The innocence and loss implied in fixity are contrived and patronizing, yet they denote a counter-representational impulse to which Austen biography too has persistently and loudly laid claim. Of Jane Austen's textual lives her biography has been among the least susceptible of reinterpretation. Perhaps the only question now worth asking is not who was Jane Austen; but how did the archive evolve from which she has been fashioned with such a mixture of circumspection and apparent ingenuousness? The kinds of truths biographies and portraits deal in are not the replicable truths to be found in head moulds, death masks, or photographs but the truths of conversation, changing with its participants. Biographies, Jane Austen's included, are 'statements about the world', not 'pieces of it.'[114]

[112] Dalya Alberge, 'Put aside Pride and Prejudice, This is the Real Jane Austen', *The Times*, 11 December 2002, 13.

[113] *Memoir*, 90 and 116.

[114] I here recycle Susan Sontag, *On Photography* (Harmondsworth, Middx.: Penguin, 1979), 4: 'Photographed images do not seem to be statements about the world so much as pieces of it.'

3

Manuscripts and the Acts of Writing

Dead ends and false starts

There is something more than usually poignant about the evidence provided by Jane Austen's manuscripts. Their survival could hardly have been better planned. They stand for bold, facetious experiment, for failure or dead ends, and eventually for death itself. In the case of the juvenilia and the novella *Lady Susan*, a bookmaker's pride enhances their faircopy status as confidential documents.[1] These are her exuberant beginnings as a writer, the make-believe or vanity publications for family circulation of a literary apprentice. In appearance they are far different from her mature and frustrated beginnings, given much later the titles *The Watsons* and *Sanditon* (also of course her dead end), and from the discarded first ending to *Persuasion*, all working manuscripts with shared physical characteristics. This distinction between apprenticeship and workaday experiment that the fair and foul papers graphically enact is maintained with surprising neatness. Though she treasured for more than a decade the aborted family study *The Watsons*, there is no evidence that she made a faircopy; nor is there evidence that she kept early drafts ('Elinor and Marianne' as novel-in-letters, for example) beyond their recasting into

[1] I draw here and elsewhere on the distinctions outlined by Donald Reiman in the subtitle of his book *The Study of Modern Manuscripts: Public, Confidential, and Private* (Baltimore and London: Johns Hopkins University Press, 1993). According to Reiman's argument, an author's intention for a manuscript to be private, confidential, or public is essential in determining how to take what it says, though such knowledge is often part of a manuscript's unwritten aspects, its contexts of generation and reception. Confidential manuscripts are 'addressed to a specific group of individuals all of whom either are personally known to the writer or belong to some predefined group that the writer has reason to believe share communal values with him or her.' (39)

new forms. But whether faircopies or working drafts, the manuscripts have this in common: they constitute the extremes of a writing career without the middle ground. With the tiny exception of one chapter of *Persuasion*, the six finished novels are known only through their public texts; their private performance was long ago silenced in print. It is by no means inevitable that unfinished and lifetime unpublished writings should cast an author in a new light; it is least expected where, as with Austen, the published corpus has by tradition been considered to form so impregnable a unity. But Austen's manuscripts matter for several reasons: they are so few; and being available only for those works which did not see print in her lifetime they increase the canon and extend her range as a writer. In the case of the post-juvenile or working manuscripts, there is the further possibility that they will give access to a creative process—the process of writing and revision—otherwise denied us.[2]

If lifetime unpublished writings need not change what we know about a writer, autograph manuscripts will and do alter our angle of vision. Autograph manuscripts, like paintings and unlike printed books, are highly individual, unique documentary witnesses, and where they are working drafts as opposed to faircopies, as is the case with the opening scenes of *The Watsons*, the cancelled chapters of *Persuasion*, and the *Sanditon* fragment, the hand's trace upon the paper of the movements of the mind embodies another uniqueness. Pierre Macherey wrote of the 'specific' labour which constitutes a literary work as the special process which guarantees its autonomy and wrests it from the everyday materials of its production, 'the usual ways of speaking and writing'.[3] Working drafts provide the somatic clues to this unusual specificity—the wayward spellings, irregular dashes, and erasures—the signs of the hand's performance of the mind's bidding, which are effaced by print. But by the same rule, even as they bring some features into greater relief, manuscripts might also be said to distort in other ways our critical understanding of what constitutes a literary work: in studying autograph

[2] This point should perhaps be qualified by the evidence of revision available in those second lifetime editions known to have been overseen by Austen—that is, the second editions of *Sense and Sensibility* and *Mansfield Park*.

[3] Pierre Macherey, *A Theory of Literary Production* (*Pour une théorie de la production littéraire* (1966)), trans. by Geoffrey Wall (London, Henley, and Boston, Mass.: Routledge & Kegan Paul, 1978): 'The specificity of a work is also its autonomy... It is the product of a specific labour, and consequently cannot be achieved by a process of a different nature. [It] has its beginning in a break from the usual ways of speaking and writing.' (52)

manuscripts we can easily confuse two kinds of uniqueness, two forms of evidence.[4]

The point may be obvious but because we value the draft pages of modern manuscripts as dynamic sites of creation, giving us imagined access through erasures and substitutions to the artistic process itself, we have tended to confuse this knowledge, born of the particularities of writing, with the uniqueness of the work itself. It is tempting to think of the disorder of each holograph manuscript as a genetic thumbprint of the writer's mind and of the work's deep identity. But except in special circumstances, modern manuscripts, unlike medieval manuscripts, are private documents, meant for the eyes of the author only or at most for an intimate circle. Where they also function as printer's copy, this confidentiality is still scarcely breached; only in rare cases does an author assume that the printer will translate what he reads exactly as it stands into public text. The printer is in a special relation to the work: he recognizes and makes allowances for the confidentiality of the manuscript as document; and he distinguishes this from its public aspect as message or content. The particulars of printing, a labour distinct from that of the writer, replace her performance of the text with another which, though non-authorial, is in most cases an authorized part of the text's meaning and grows over time, in further printings and reprintings, while the hand's performance of the decisive break from 'the usual ways of speaking and writing', necessarily is stilled. The distinction, as far as the work of writing and printing is concerned, could not be greater: the writer discovering meaning by invention and discontinuity, the printer by repetition and conformity; the writer aiming to extend the capacities of language, the printer to regularize and normalize it. We could look at the issue another way and ask whether we consider the vast majority of works of the early modern period, for which we do not have manuscript evidence, as less expressive because their existence is confined to print or whether we would wish to attribute greater emphatic power to those works which, like Pepys's diaries or Leonardo Da Vinci's notebooks or Charlotte Brontë's juvenilia, take privacy of expression furthest in their graphic forms.

Anxious to narrow the disruptive distance between fiction-making and, to his Victorian sensibilities, more orthodox feminine domestic pastimes (he

[4] Cf. the warnings against overvaluing the disorders of the draft page in Daniel Ferrer, 'The Open Space of the Draft Page: James Joyce and Modern Manuscripts', in *The Iconic Page in Manuscript, Print, and Digital Culture*, ed. George Bornstein and Theresa Tinkle (Ann Arbor: University of Michigan Press, 1998), 249–67.

On reading in the Newspaper, the Marriage of "Mr. Gell of Eastbourne to Miss Gill." —

Of Eastbourne Mr Gell
From being perfectly well
Became dreadfully ill
For the love of Miss Gill.

So he said with some sighs
"I'm the slave of your eyes.
Oh! restore if you please
By accepting my ease."

J. A.

13. Lithograph facsimile of Jane Austen's manuscript verses included in J. E. Austen-Leigh, *A Memoir of Jane Austen*, 1870. By kind permission of Oxford University Press.

mentions her skill at satin-stitch and the game of spilikins), Austen's nephew and early biographer, James Edward Austen-Leigh, provided a lithographic facsimile of his aunt's 'clear strong handwriting', declaring '[h]appy would the compositors for the press be if they had always so legible a manuscript to work from.'[5] It is a calculatedly innocuous calligraphic sample, a party-piece (the manuscript of the verses on Mr Gell and Miss Gill now in the Pump Room, Bath), and as such quite unrepresentative. Where the faircopied juvenilia are reflexively encoded documents with conspicuous artefactual status, with the working manuscripts we face a series of frustrations rather than revelations. The same familiar irregularities in spelling, the same free use of dashes and initial capitals occur across their range. These are the performative signs, clues to the harmonizing of hand and brain or reflections of fashions in handwriting and punctuation, that we would expect print to erase. As evidence they are insufficient to generate a set of probable creative

[5] *Memoir*, 77–8.

procedures by which Austen may have worked from novel to novel. However, the physical particulars of writing, the care she took in preparing its material surface, and the presentation of her working copy may indicate more than we have realized about her practice in readying manuscripts for the press, and more than is often the case with writers for whose published works complete manuscript states exist.

Manuscripts surviving from the early nineteenth century, like the holograph manuscripts of Walter Scott's novels or Shelley's faircopies of private lyrics later known as the Trelawny manuscripts, often do so because, despite appearances and later uses, they were not the direct origin of a contemporary printed text. Scott's novels were routinely set from allograph copies made by an amanuensis; Shelley's lyrics were not intended for the press; in some other cases, we can assume that Mary Shelley or Claire Clairmont wrote out the lost press copies.[6] The stark absence of such evidence for Austen's lifetime publications, by contrast, suggests that her manuscripts were straightforwardly transitional documents that led lives of narrow and thrifty expediency, serving first her expressive needs, then providing copy for the press, before ending up as printing-house wastepaper. The confidential status of the juvenile faircopies, on the other hand—their status, that is, as domestic publications—guaranteed their survival in much the same way as it did the multiple customized copies of Coleridge's *Christabel*.[7] What ensured the survival of the working drafts of the adult fragments was their interrupted journey towards print and a wider public.

In thinking about the form in which Austen's manuscripts went to press we are faced with a series of non-verifiable choices (non-verifiable since no trace seems to have survived from any of the novels of the actual manuscript copy used to set type). We can either extrapolate a possible set of procedures from the admittedly sparse evidence that survives; or, building on what survives, we can conjecturally create what does not (but might reasonably be expected to have existed). Austen presents a tantalizing case in that we have, across the range of her writing, examples of several textual states—from rough draft to faircopy to print—but no single work exists authoritatively in more than one

[6] For Shelley's manuscripts, see Reiman, *The Study of Modern Manuscripts*, 95–7. For the status of Scott's surviving holograph manuscripts and their relationship to the destroyed scribal copies used in the printing house, see my 'Made in Scotland: The Edinburgh Edition of the Waverley Novels', *TEXT*, 14 (2002), 305–23.

[7] Jack Stillinger lists 'nine manuscript versions (or partial versions)' for *Christabel*, mainly transcriptions made by friends, before the first printed text of 1816 (*Coleridge and Textual Instability: The Multiple Versions of the Major Poems* (New York and Oxford: Oxford University Press, 1994), 79).

state, with the small exception of one chapter of *Persuasion*, where we have both working draft and print; and the reasons for this suggest it is something of a special case. By contrast, the disciplined accessibility of a faircopy manuscript of an adult work like *Lady Susan* poses a different kind of special case or problem, threatening to blur the distinction between a manuscript prepared for private circulation and printer's copy: the one a finished work, the other transitional; but would they have looked comparable? Did compositors in the early nineteenth-century printing house expect to receive clean copy or were they able and prepared to set type from messy drafts, scarred by erasures, interlinear insertions, and loose additional sheets? And supposing they expected clean copy, how clean was clean? In an age when electronic text storage makes the production of a stream of handsomely formatted drafts seductively necessary, it is only too easy for us to imagine unrealistically high standards for manuscript copy. Did compositors ever take responsibility for punctuation, expansion of abbreviations, and even for paragraphing an author's copy? And if in some cases they did set type from messy drafts and did consider themselves at liberty or better fitted to style a manuscript than the author, did they therefore do so for Austen?

It is at this point that the *Persuasion* fragment assumes significance. The only manuscript evidence we have from a novel completed for publication, it seems to have survived because at a late stage in composition it was extracted from its surrounding text and replaced by a revision. Deirdre Le Faye has informally made the pleasing suggestion that Cassandra may have been regularly employed as her sister's amanuensis, executing clean printer's copies from her sister's drafts, in the manner of Dorothy or Mary Wordsworth. In support, we know Cassandra made a copy of *Sanditon* for brother Frank, but this was for private circulation and she did not subsequently destroy the original. Nor if she made a clean press copy of *Persuasion* is she likely to have destroyed the bulk of the working draft, retaining only the unrevised fragment. If it was normal practice to make a faircopy from a finished novel, then the working draft would surely have been routinely kept until after the novel appeared in print. In the case of *Persuasion*, seen through the press by Henry Austen and perhaps Cassandra herself, it would have been even more vital to preserve the original, its author now dead, for comparative purposes. Would Cassandra subsequently have destroyed this precious relic as routinely as in earlier days; and if so, why would she keep as memento a section only parts of which represent a distinctly separate version? Furthermore, the attested habit of Cassandra and other family members making copies of the various manuscript writings does not fit easily with wholesale destruction of surviving holograph copies.

Though unprovable, it seems more likely that the *Persuasion* fragment is all that remains from a working manuscript which went to the printing house in a comparable state: that is, complete with erasures, insertions, and the other signs of Austen's composing hand; and that the fragment as we have it was removed and the revised section inserted in its place. What I am suggesting is that there may not have been extensive faircopying of the finished novels once a full draft had taken shape and that this unique draft may routinely have been sent to press. It is clearly not only possible, but likely, that those novels on the stocks from the mid-1790s would have gone through several drafts; but once she settled to habits of tighter conception, execution, and publication there may well have been only a single complete draft. Certainly, a printer could have set copy from manuscript of the quality of the *Persuasion* fragment. I shall return to this in '*Persuasion:* from manuscript to print', later in this chapter.

Sense and Sensibility and *Pride and Prejudice* must each have taken shape, wholly or partly, in more than one draft, between 1795–8 and 1810–12, by which time the former had been recast from a novel-in-letters and the latter, in Jane Austen's own words, 'lop't and crop't', and according to Cassandra's later memory altered and contracted.[8] *Mansfield Park* has a recorded gestation and composition period of some three years, from February 1811 to mid-1813, which if correct means that for some months in 1811 she had three novels on the go: she was recasting *Pride and Prejudice* (Chapman pointed out that its action fitted in general terms the calendars for 1811–12),[9] drafting *Mansfield Park*, and for one busy month, April 1811, also correcting proofs of *Sense and Sensibility.* Apart from proof correction, we do not know what form or forms creative activity took at any particular moment during this intense period—whether planning new material in more or less detail, revising old drafts, or full-scale composition. By January 1813 references in letters suggest *Mansfield Park* was more than half written, but that is two years after Cassandra's vague recollection that it was 'begun sometime about Feby 1811'.[10] On 27 January 1813 Austen received her first copy of *Pride and Prejudice* ('I have got my own

[8] *Jane Austen's Letters*, 202; Cassandra Austen's 'Note of the Date of Composition of her Sister's Novels', in *Minor Works*, facing p. 242. Much of the evidence for dating in this paragraph relies on Cassandra's Memorandum.

[9] 'Chronology of *Pride and Prejudice*', in *Pride and Prejudice*, ed. Chapman, 401.

[10] *Jane Austen's Letters*, 198 and 202; Cassandra Austen, 'Note of . . . Composition'.

darling Child from London'), and the novel was advertised the next day in the London *Morning Chronicle* for 18 shillings. Writing to Cassandra on 29 January, she apologizes for the unforeseen delay in getting a copy sent to Steventon, where her sister was then on a visit to James and Mary Austen. (*Pride and Prejudice* was, in a special sense, a Steventon novel as James's daughter Anna Lefroy would later recall.) Then, her exuberance breaking through the polite family formalities, she bursts out: '*18*^s—He [Henry or perhaps her publisher?] shall ask £1–1– for my two next, & £1–8– for my stupidest of all.'[11] The very particularity of 'my stupidest of all' suggests this is no vague projection or insubstantial boast but that there are three further novels on the stocks.

Mansfield Park was well in hand, though Henry Austen was only introduced to the manuscript in its finished state, complete with volume divisions, on the journey to London more than a year later in March 1814 to have it published.[12] Again by Cassandra's late account, *Emma* was 'begun Jany 21st 1814, finishd March 29th 1815', which means that in the early stages she was working on the new novel, *Emma*, and seeing *Mansfield Park* through the press: not an easy division of concentration. But had she already begun to think of *Emma* a year earlier, by January 1813 (is this the implication of 'my next two'), and what about 'my stupidest of all'? Is this a reference to the novel written, by Cassandra's estimate, 'about the years 98 & 99' and brought up to date if not more fully revised before being bought in 1803 by the publishers Crosby and Co. under the title 'Susan'? Austen had asked at least once (in April 1809) to have the unpublished manuscript returned to her, but according to Austen-Leigh, it would not be bought back until 1816, after the publication of *Emma*.[13] However, if her 1809 reference to a second copy of the manuscript was more than a facetious threat, she may at any time after August 1809 have been revising 'Susan' in this second copy for publication as 'Catherine'.

Then again, if it is possible to conjecture some overlap in the writing of *Mansfield Park* and *Emma*, the same is true for *Persuasion* and the revised 'Catherine', especially if there was only one manuscript copy and not two. *Persuasion* was begun on 8 August 1815 and the first draft completed on 18 July

[11] *Jane Austen's Letters*, 201; for Anna Lefroy's childhood memory of hearing read aloud at Steventon or nearby Deane parsonage an early version of what became *Pride and Prejudice*, see her 'Recollections of Aunt Jane' (1864), in *Memoir*, 158.

[12] *Jane Austen's Letters*, 255. See my argument at pp. 227–8 below.

[13] *Jane Austen's Letters*, 174; and *Memoir*, 106.

1816. In the surviving correspondence it is not until 13 March 1817, in a letter to her eldest niece, Fanny Knight, that Austen mentions both *Persuasion* (though not by a title) and 'Catherine'. At this point she thinks of them together because they are short, about the same length.[14] Presumably Henry Austen's involvement in the repurchase of the manuscript made it difficult to keep progress on the revision of 'Catherine' a secret from the wider family. But only five days after this letter Austen dated the last words of the *Sanditon* manuscript, '18 March 1817'. *Persuasion*, 'Catherine', and *Sanditon* share the years 1816–17, as *Sense and Sensibility*, *Pride and Prejudice*, and *Mansfield Park* share 1811–12, as 'First Impressions' (a draft of *Pride and Prejudice*), 'Elinor and Marianne'/*Sense and Sensibility*, and 'Susan' share 1795–9, and as *Mansfield Park* and *Emma* may share 1813.

The precise dates Cassandra fixed for the writing of the novels in her memorandum may derive from pocket-book entries, subsequently lost or destroyed, which Austen made at the time; they are also supported by her habit of dating her manuscripts at several points as she wrote. But against the certainties afforded by the implied particularity of the moment when pen touched paper, there needs to be set the vaguer and more associative kind of dating by which the novels provide hinterlands or contexts for one another. I am not suggesting anything so calculated as a grand plan nor so philosophically conceived as Balzac's *Comédie humaine*. However, the overlapping implies something more than the routine expectation that novels by one author will share ingredients, themes, and narrative treatment in common; rather it suggests a settled and characteristic habit of composition, with associated gestation and even allocation of materials within a broader framework than the individual work. It explains our sense as readers that the novels enact a process of expansion and repetition, retracing the old ground and discovering it as new ground. *Mansfield Park* and *Emma* belong together as mirrored studies of social repression and ennui and of the relationship between human behaviour and environment, the psychology of setting. This new interest in setting marks them off from *Pride and Prejudice* and *Sense and Sensibility*, while according to family tradition, the Heywoods in *Sanditon* were to occupy the same role as the Morlands in *Northanger Abbey*.[15] Incidents and themes from the aborted fragment *The Watsons* are transposed or recycled in *Mansfield Park* and *Emma*, while critics have detected links

[14] *Jane Austen's Letters*, 333.

[15] Anna Lefroy in a letter to James Edward Austen-Leigh, 8 August 1862, HRO, MS. 23M93/86/3c–118(ii): 'but you are not just to the Heywoods. They stand in the place of the Morlands.'

between *The Watsons* and *Pride and Prejudice* and even 'Catharine; or, The Bower' from *Volume the Third.*

The textual critic Louis Hay has argued that regardless of period or nationality or language all writers follow one of two practices when they write: either they write programmatically or immanently. In the former case, they plan structure, scenes, and narrative evolution in some written detail in advance; in the latter, writing is more spontaneous, and even though it may evolve in a fragmentary fashion these fragments are more fully textualized from the outset.[16] In Austen's case we simply do not have the evidence to know whether she followed a general practice in writing and what it might have been. Long periods of gestation and of critical reflection post-composition are mentioned within the immediate family and can be adduced from the record of dates; it was not just 'Miss Catherine' that she 'put upon the Shelve for the present'.[17] The accident of posthumous publication coupling together two such apparently different works as *Northanger Abbey* and *Persuasion* can on reflection be seen as the inevitable consequence of a chronology of writing which included alongside new ventures the mining over time of manuscript fragments and the revision of earlier completed writings, a pattern which leaves us with *Sanditon*, her final work, as the sequel to *Northanger Abbey*, one of her earliest. At the same time, the evidence of the abandoned ending to *Persuasion* suggests forcefully that in this instance at least she wrote with no overall structure mapped in advance. And this way of working is confirmed by those few occasions when documentation of technical details in plot or setting appears to be collected in the late stages of composition or not until revision for a second edition.[18] The unique evidence of the working drafts suggests writing without much prior material preparation and the almost immediate emergence of fully textualized prose in which grammatical structures and stylistic elaboration are already well developed, even though the phrasing may be adjusted and revisited on several subsequent occasions—the procedures, in other words, of an immanent writer. This is confirmed by Henry Austen's statement that 'in composition she was equally

[16] Louis Hay, 'Die dritte Dimension der Literatur: Notizen zu einer "critique génétique"', *Poetica*, 16 (1984), 311–14.

[17] *Jane Austen's Letters*, 333.

[18] *Mansfield Park* affords several examples of the late or fortuitous researching of details (eg., *Jane Austen's Letters*, 198, the alteration of 'Government House' to 'Commissioner's'); and, in the case of the second-edition revisions to Vol. 3 Ch. 7 (Ch. 38, where volume division is lost), of the post-publication refinement of nautical details.

rapid and correct'.[19] But (and it is a very big but) all we have by way of evidence to substantiate these speculations are false starts and dead ends.

The case for Jane Austen as an immanent writer can be made from the evidence of the working drafts; it can be strengthened by obvious similarities to her habits as a letter writer. At the same time, there is testimony in the revisiting and permutation of a common range of narrative elements for a degree of general planning best described as preoccupation. Austen was a novelist whose instinct, as she tells us herself, was to concentrate. The range of her subject-matter and story patterns is restricted; on the other hand, the play of tone and moral imagination (the ethical compass in which her characters live, act, and react) is wide, far wider than that of her contemporary novelists. The activity of critical reading disciplined her scope as a writer, from her beginnings in the fertile intertextual parodies of the juvenilia. Subsequently all her full-length novels imply a critical perspective on fiction writing and fiction reading. In her novels the novel itself is assumed as the common ground or shared locus of illusion on which all readers can draw. Not the least aspect of this textual reflexiveness is the dialogue over years her novels enter into with one another.

The Watsons: *Jane Austen's other Bath novel*

The fragment of what reads like a substantial beginning to a novel, about 17,500 words, was given the descriptive title *The Watsons* by James Edward Austen-Leigh, 'for the sake of having a title by which to designate it', when he first presented it to the public in 1871.[20] It is the earliest dated evidence we have of a narrative by Austen thoroughly grounded in social realism; its documentation of the economic, emotional, and moral bleakness that attend a family reduced to the very limit of genteel poverty is stark and uncomfortable. According to Austen-Leigh, it is 'probable, that it was composed at Bath, before she ceased to reside there in 1805.'[21] In terms of the chronology of the early drafting of the full-length novels, and setting aside *Lady Susan*, this would make *The Watsons* her fourth novel and would place its composition after the unrevised but fully drafted 'First Impressions' (*Pride and Prejudice*), *Sense and Sensibility*, and 'Susan' (later titled 'Catherine', and later still,

[19] Henry Austen, 'Biographical Notice of the Author' (1818), in *Memoir*, 138.

[20] *Memoir* (1871), 295.

[21] Ibid., 295.

probably by Henry or Cassandra Austen, *Northanger Abbey*) and before *Mansfield Park*. Versions of what were subsequently published as *Sense and Sensibility*, *Pride and Prejudice*, and *Northanger Abbey* were all written by 1799 before the Austen family's removal to Bath. In this early form *Pride and Prejudice* and *Northanger Abbey* had been offered to publishers, in November 1797 and early 1803, respectively. Despite a shared anxious attention to the gradations of wealth and social standing and plots whose resolution hinges on the surmounting of such distinctions, none of these early studies in its final form allows the constrictions of circumstantial reality to win out over romance and comedy. *The Watsons* seems set to reverse these priorities and to test the survival of romance and comedy in the person of Emma Watson, imported in its opening pages into the meanest degree of gentrified provincial life.

Unlike her practice later with the manuscript of *Sanditon* and the various attempts at a conclusion to *Persuasion*, the surviving fragment suggests that Austen did not date her writing of *The Watsons*. Austen-Leigh considered that the 'internal evidence of the style' offered no clues to when it was written, and he based his dating on the evidence of watermarks; he mentions dates of 1803 and 1804 in the paper, though in my recent examination I have discovered the watermark date 1803 only. A more precise dating of the writing, albeit at a distance of eighty years, is provided by Fanny Caroline, daughter of Anna Lefroy, the niece with whom we know Austen on occasion discussed her work. According to Fanny Caroline, 'Somewhere in 1804 [Austen] began "The Watsons", but her father died early in 1805, and it was never finished.'[22] Cassandra Austen bequeathed the manuscript to Anna's half-sister, Caroline, in whose possession it was when first published by her brother in 1871. In his account, Cassandra shared with her nieces 'something of the intended story':

> Mr. Watson was soon to die; and Emma to become dependent for a home on her narrow-minded sister-in-law and brother. She was to decline an offer of marriage from Lord Osborne, and much of the interest of the tale was to arise from Lady Osborne's love for Mr. Howard, and his counter affection for Emma, whom he was finally to marry.[23]

Why was the story abandoned? Could Austen have been discouraged by the failure of a second novel, 'Susan', in the hands of a publisher for over a year, to appear in print? There is evidence from the Chawton period that publication

[22] [Fanny C. Lefroy] 'Is It Just?', 277.

[23] *Memoir* (1871), 364.

was a vital stimulant to new writing; now it seemed that two novels had been rejected. In Austen-Leigh's opinion the failure was artistic; though there is vigour in the character sketches and especially in the development of relationships through conversation, it is probable that

> the author became aware of the evil of having placed her heroine too low, in such a position of poverty and obscurity as, though not necessarily connected with vulgarity, has a sad tendency to degenerate into it; and therefore, like a singer who has begun on too low a note, she discontinued the strain. It was an error of which she was likely to become more sensible, as she grew older, and saw more of society; certainly she never repeated it by placing the heroine of any subsequent work under circumstances likely to be unfavourable to the refinement of a lady.

As a critical judgement, this is hopelessly snobbish and inept. It has no wider family authority, but it conforms with Austen-Leigh's own mid-Victorian social anxieties and is therefore, in its way, further confirmation of the uncomfortable and uncompromising study in manners Austen was prepared to embark on at this time.

The conjectured 1804 dating is the clue to a new realism, strengthened by the unusual similarity between the domestic situation of the Watsons and Austen's own reduced household at this time. In the story there are four Watson sisters, all unmarried and all with little money in the present or security for the future. Their precarious grasp on respectability is further threatened by an invalid father, a poorly beneficed clergyman, whose death will deprive them of their home. The three elder sisters know that their only hope of escaping destitution or dependence on unwilling relations lies in marriage; their several ways of coping with the dwindling prospects of a husband emphasize the ugliness of their lot and of the people circumstances have made them. *The Watsons* is set to be an unswerving study in the harsh realities of dependent women's lives without the romantic illusions which in *Sense and Sensibility* and *Pride and Prejudice* sweeten life's evils for some as they cast the behaviour of others, outside the charmed circle, in a crueller light. Here, by contrast, the searchlight of criticism shines more evenly.

Despite Austen-Leigh's attempts to cover it up, it is likely that life in Bath opened Austen's eyes to a wider range of social behaviour and a keener sense of the precariousness of economic well-being than she had known before. If at 28 or 29 she herself was about the age of Elizabeth, the eldest Watson sister, Cassandra was three years older and their almost-sister and domestic companion, Martha Lloyd, was 39. Cassandra and Martha both had disappointed plans for marriage behind them and Jane had the awkward episode of 2 December 1802 when in the space of twenty-four hours she had accepted and rejected the security offered by Harris Bigg-Wither's marriage proposal.[24] Behind all, the loss of their Steventon home and the auctioning of precious possessions on their father's retirement to Bath in 1801 had meant a reduction in domestic comfort for the Austens; it had left a general impression on Jane that '[t]he whole World is in a conspiracy to enrich one part of our family at the expence of another.'[25] On George Austen's death and the full reversion of the livings of Steventon and Deane to his son James, his wife and daughters knew they would be almost completely reliant on the younger Austen males for necessary financial assistance.[26]

Before she had brought the new novel to the domestic crisis to be caused by Mr Watson's death, real events overtook fiction: George Austen died suddenly after a short illness on 21 January 1805. Within two months the Austen women had given up their house in Green Park Buildings, Bath, and moved into modest lodgings in Gay Street. Martha Lloyd's mother dying only weeks later, she firmed up plans to join the Austen household on a permanent basis. For the next four years they would all live relatively unsettled lives in temporary accommodation—more lodgings in Bath, long visits to stay with relations at Steventon and Godmersham, Adlestrop, and Stoneleigh Abbey, a long trip to Worthing, and eventually lodgings in Southampton, for a time shared with and subsidized by Jane's newly married brother, Frank. The four women would eventually settle permanently in 1809 at Chawton, in a cottage owned by Jane's third brother, the prosperous landowner, Edward. Thereafter they remained lifelong beneficiaries of his good fortune. This was in the future, but in 1804–5 a new novel based in the real harsh circumstances of women's material existence came unexpectedly closer to the events of her own life than Austen was perhaps able to bear.

We are accustomed to think of Austen's sources as literary, yet recent biographers have been drawn to the autobiographical resonance of *The Watsons* as setting it apart from her other writings and explaining its

[24] Biographical details for the relevant period, including the fiasco of Harris Bigg-Wither's marriage proposal, are taken from *Family Record*, 135–59.

[25] *Jane Austen's Letters*, 88.

[26] In 1805 the widowed Mrs Austen and Cassandra each had a small personal income, producing together about £210 annually. If Henry Austen's calculations at this time were acted upon, this was made up to £450 per annum by Mrs Austen's sons, still a modest sum for the three women to live on. Jane had no independent income of any kind at this stage. See *Austen Papers*, 234–5, and 264, where Mrs Austen reviews her income in 1820; and *Family Record*, 147.

fragmentary state—as though its rawness is not simply attributable to an unrevised draft but represents a closer convergence of life and art either than she attempts elsewhere or than she could sustain.[27] There is some late family authority for this. Though Caroline Austen inherited the manuscript, it was among Frank Austen's descendants that it retained a living currency into the twentieth century. This was appropriate: not only had Frank come to the rescue of his mother and sisters when he provided them with a home in Southampton, but much later, in 1828, he married Martha Lloyd as his second wife. Growing up under the formidable tutelage of Martha and Cassandra, Frank's children received an intensely interactive exposure to the range of their dead aunt's writings. First Frank's daughter Catherine Hubback published a three-decker novel, *The Younger Sister* (1850), the opening five chapters of which are based closely on Austen's fragment. Then, in 1928, a year after Chapman's Clarendon Press transcription of the manuscript, Catherine's granddaughter Edith Brown published with her husband Francis a modest completion grafted onto her own verbatim transcript, paragraphed and punctuated in modern style, of the original.

Edith Brown's novel *The Watsons* divides Austen's fragment into ten chapters and develops it in a further seventeen. Unlike her grandmother's extravagantly romantic refashioning, Brown's aim was to do no more than expand what seemed implicit in the original. In a preface, she attempted to explain the novel's genesis and abandonment, and naturally enough she identified its circumstances with her own branch of the Austens. She dates its writing not to 1804 but 1807, when Austen was living in Southampton with Frank and his new wife, Mary Gibson, and she suggests that it was set aside because it replicated too closely this later stage in her depressed economic circumstances:

Why then was the novel left unfinished? I believe the reason was this. Jane was deeply devoted to her family, and quite aware that family life is a fine art. Her heroine, Emma Watson, was to lose her father and go to live with her brother and sister-in-law. But Jane had lost her father and gone to live with her brother and sister-in-law. Was it wise to write on that subject at that time? Think of the feelings involved! Again, was it possible?[28]

[27] Shields, *Jane Austen*, 93, even makes the instructive mistake of misnaming its heroine Emma Austen. Fergus, *Jane Austen: A Literary Life*, 114, makes a succinct case for the fragment's origin in Austen's confrontation of the prospect of 'dispossession, poverty, and marginality' in her own life.

[28] Edith and Francis Brown, *The Watsons* (London: Elkin Mathews and Marrot Ltd., 1928), 7.

We can extract a useful insight from this explanation while admitting the likelihood of its distorting partiality: one aspect of what Margaret Oliphant shrewdly dubbed the clannishness of the Austen family was their persistent annexation of the writings to their own agendas. The date of 1807 suits the active part played by Frank Austen in his sister's history (and therefore it suits his descendant Edith Brown's sense of *her* family history) rather better than it fits Austen's real circumstances. Though her domestic situation was still unsettled in 1807 there is no evidence to suggest that personal events could not by then be held under imaginative restraint within a fictional setting. In 1804–5, however, her confidence to distinguish fiction from reality must have been dangerously imperilled by the unexpected convergence of art and life. In 1805 *The Watsons* would have been a narrative haunted by affiliation rather than, as it might have been in 1807, capable of exorcising it.

The bleak critical eye Austen trains upon the surface of small town society in *The Watsons* affords no concealment for characters or narrator—no softening social sympathy and no self-protective irony. The few letters to survive from the Bath years register in similar angular tones the lack of privacy, the discomfort, dreariness, and petty aggravations of life in lodgings on a limited income, and the alliances of convenience which pass for friendship in a transient society. From Lyme Regis on 14 September 1804 Jane writes to Cassandra of 'the general Dirtiness of the House & furniture, & all it's Inhabitants'.[29] With her father and mother she is holidaying by the sea having recently vacated their Sydney Place address in Bath, their home for three years. With some pique, she remarks that its new tenants, the Coles, 'have got their infamous plate upon our door'. The Austens are between permanent homes and will not move into Green Park Buildings until the following month. In the meantime, though their personal servants James and Jenny are more than satisfactory, there is a general unsuitability about their accommodation. Among the 'bold, queerlooking people, just fit to be Quality at Lyme', Jane dances with 'a new, odd looking Man who had been eyeing me for some time'. She walks on the Cobb for an hour with 'my dear friend Miss Armstrong', who 'is very conversable in a common way', though '[s]he seems to like people rather too easily', and '[l]ike other young Ladies she is considerably genteeler than her Parents': a reference to Mrs Armstrong who 'sat darning a p^{r} of Stockings the whole of my visit—.'

29 *Jane Austen's Letters*, 93.

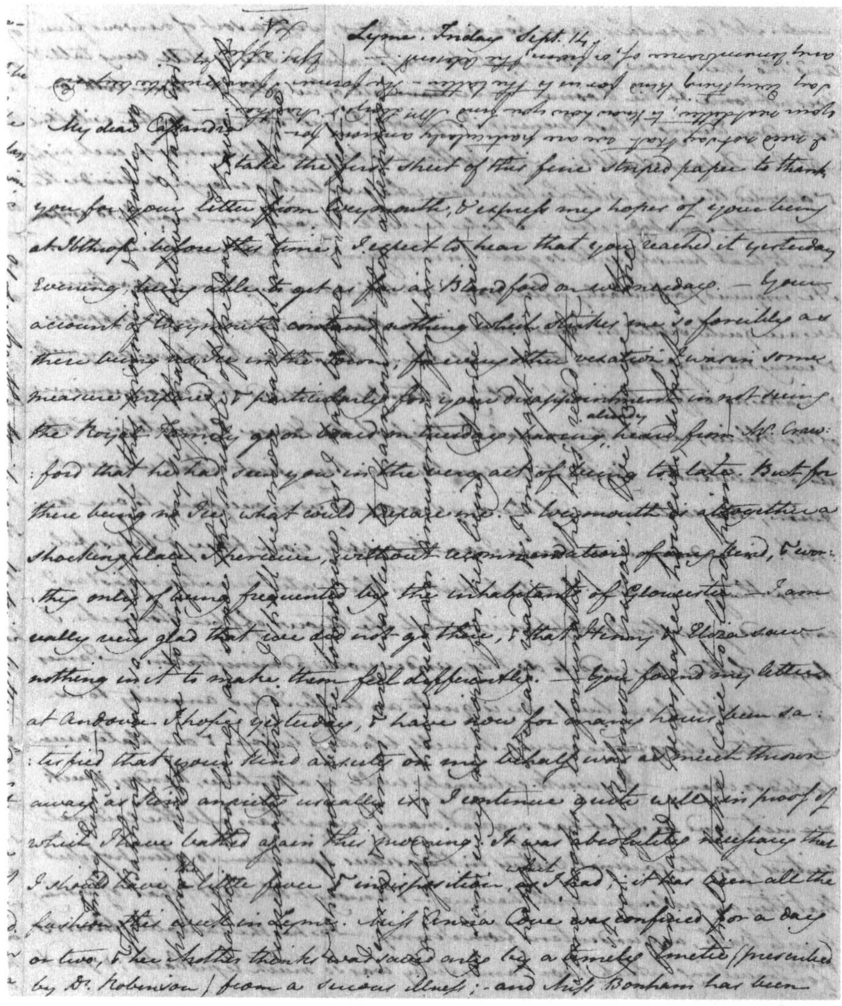

Lyme. Friday Sept. 14

My dear Cassandra

I take the first sheet of this fine striped paper to thank
you for your letter from Weymouth, & express my hopes of your being
at Ibthrop before this time. I expect to hear that you reached it yesterday
Evening, being able to get as far as Blandford on Wednesday. — Your
account of Weymouth contains nothing which strikes me so forcibly as
there being no Ice in the Town; for every other vexation I was in some
measure prepared, & particularly for your disappointment in not seeing
the Royal Family go on board on Tuesday, having already heard from Mr. Craw:
:ford that he had seen you in the very act of being too late. But for
there being no Ice, what could prepare me. — Weymouth is altogether a
shocking place I perceive, without recommendation of any kind, & wor:
:thy only of being frequented by the inhabitants of Gloucester. — I am
really very glad that we did not go there, & that Henry & Eliza saw
nothing in it to make them feel differently. — You found my letter
at Andover I hope yesterday, & have now for many hours been sa:
:tisfied that your kind anxiety on my behalf was as much thrown
away as kind anxiety usually is. I continue quite well, in proof of
which I have bathed again this morning. It was absolutely necessary that
I should have a little fever & indisposition, which I had; — it has been all the
fashion this week in Lyme. Miss Anna Cove was confined for a day
or two, & her Mother thinks was saved only by a timely Emetic (prescribed
by Dr. Robinson) from a serious illness; — and Miss Bonham has been

14. Holograph manuscript of the first page of a letter from Jane Austen to Cassandra Austen, 14 September 1804 (MS. MA 2911). By kind permission of the Pierpont Morgan Library, New York.

The following Spring, in the more stratified society of Bath, Miss Armstrong, now hard to shake off, will seem a less desirable companion. Jane writes ruefully to Cassandra at that later time and in consequence of the renewed acquaintance of her resolution to 'endeavour as much as possible to keep my Intimacies in their proper place, & prevent their clashing.'[30] The

[30] *Jane Austen's Letters*, 104.

whole of this long letter from Bath, written over three days (from 21–3 April 1805), reads like a lesson in the precarious and difficult art of keeping (that is, knowing and defending) one's social place. A few lines earlier we heard of attempts to ward off the unwelcome attentions of Aunt Leigh-Perrot, a permanent Bath resident and once again, with more charges of theft rumoured, apparently something of an embarrassment to her relations.[31] But Jane knows that in refusing to join her aunt on various outings she simply restricts her own social freedom, putting it 'out of my power to go at all, whatever may occur to make it desirable.' Then towards the end of the letter, and in a lapse of critical reflection, she records a little personal social triumph—a visit to 'a Countess'. Jane and her mother have called that morning on Lord and Lady Leven, whose son is serving in the navy alongside Charles Austen. But the Austen women's evident intention to promote Charles's interests almost backfires when Lord Leven employs the polite fiction that his wife is not at home to receive them: Austens too, it seems, like Armstrongs, can overstep the mark. Finally, the letter returns to the vexed subject of 'My Uncle & Aunt', to describe how the Leigh-Perrots drank tea with Jane and her mother, Uncle Leigh-Perrot's sister, 'last night' (Monday 22 April):

> I have not much more to add. My Uncle & Aunt drank tea with us last night, & in spite of my resolution to the contrary, I could not help putting forward to invite them again this Evening. I thought it was of the first consequence to avoid anything that might seem a slight to them. I shall be glad when it is over, & hope to have no necessity for having so many dear friends at once again.[32]

What does she mean by 'it' being 'over'? The specific anxiety of her aunt's situation? The repeated tea-drinking with the embarrassing relations who must nevertheless not be shunned? Or something more general—the shallow complexities and constrictions of Bath society? The Austen women would not leave Bath permanently for Southampton until October 1806, another eighteen months away. But in June 1805 they made an extended visit to Godmersham and may not have returned to Bath until the following March.

[31] Mrs Leigh-Perrot, a long-standing Bath resident, was charged with shoplifting and committed to gaol awaiting trial in 1799. Her case was a local sensation and she was acquitted in 1800 only months before the Austens moved to Bath. It seems that more rumours were in circulation by late 1804, this time of stealing plants. See Sarah Markham, 'A Gardener's Question for Mrs Leigh Perrot', *Jane Austen Society Collected Reports, 1986–95*, 213–14. Such rumours can only have added to Aunt Leigh-Perrot's unpopularity with her niece.

[32] *Jane Austen's Letters*, 106.

Mary Lascelles, one of the keenest interpreters of Austen's style, made the connection between *The Watsons* and an 'irritability' settling on Austen even before she left Steventon. The same critical sensitivity and impatience that finds vent in the Bath letters in the sharp observation and denunciation of her own and others' behaviour infuses the prose of *The Watsons*. Lascelles described it thus: 'Jane Austen seems to be struggling with a peculiar oppression, a stiffness and heaviness that threaten her style'.[33] More recently, for David Nokes, 'something about the hard, cynical tone of the piece deterred her from ever returning to it.'[34] Another explanation may be that, unlike in the finished novels, Austen could not find in *The Watsons* a structure adequate to restrain the play of domestic particulars; rather, it is the case that a structural atomization in perception reflects a deeper personal anomie. As in her letters, detail proliferates, contradictorily and uncomfortably, and takes on a local life of its own. To borrow a phrase from Deborah Kaplan, describing the letters, in the *Watsons* fragment we are presented with 'pre-ideological' or unresolved writing.[35] Because I believe Austen was instinctively an immanent writer, I think it would have been impossible for her ever to resolve writing once articulated in this form.

From the outset, the expository functionality of its narrative and dialogue and its cold, peculiar angularity of vision make reading *The Watsons* an uneasy experience. Such exposition and angularity equate stylistically to the shallowness and open calculation which determine relationships in its small-town society. The Osbornes, we are told, are expected to honour the first assembly of the winter season to be held on Tuesday 13 October, in the town of D. in Surrey. The Edwardses, with their own carriage and a house in town, never miss these occasions, and are in the habit of extending an invitation to the Watson girls, who living in a village 3 miles away are poor and carriageless. Of all Austen's famously brisk and informative openings, this is the briskest. In few words, the pecking order is in place. We might calculate that revision would have smoothed out, softened, or deepened the effect, but this does not diminish the impact of the critical energy under which the novel begins nor does it fit with the effect of rewriting elsewhere in the draft. Of the four Watson girls, all unmarried, only the eldest, Elizabeth, and the youngest, Emma, are at home, and since their invalid father requires company, one

[33] Mary Lascelles, *Jane Austen and Her Art* (Oxford: Clarendon Press, 1939), 99–100.

[34] Nokes, *Jane Austen: A Life*, 253.

[35] See Deborah Kaplan, 'Representing Two Cultures: Jane Austen's Letters', in *The Private Self: Theory and Practice of Women's Autobiographical Writings*, ed. Shari Benstock (London: Routledge, 1988), 211–29.

must stay behind. Emma, newly returned to her family having spent the last fourteen years in the guardianship of an aunt and uncle in Shropshire, takes up the invitation.

On their short drive into town, Elizabeth fills in some of the blanks in Emma's knowledge of her two other sisters, Penelope and Margaret. Some years before, Penelope destroyed Elizabeth's prospects of marriage to

of the name of Purvis

'a young man — ~~a neighbour~~'. 'Do not trust her with any secrets | of your own, take warning by me, do not trust her;' Elizabeth advises; 'she has her good | qualities, but she has no Faith, no Honour, no Scruples, if she can pro: |:mote her own advantage.'[36] Penelope is currently staying in Chichester with a married friend whose rich, elderly, and sickly uncle she is attempting to trap into marriage. Margaret's character survives examination little better:

is a little

'she | is all gentleness & mildness when anybody | is by.—But she ~~has a good~~

fretful & perverse

~~deal of spirit~~ a: | :mong ourselves.'[37] All three sisters have in the past attracted and been grateful for the meaningless attentions of Tom Musgrave, a local lounge-lizard and hanger-on of the grander Osbornes. Emma, too, Elizabeth suggests, will be lucky if she draws his attention. There is something both distasteful and perfectly fitting in Elizabeth's way of thinking and talking. She has found a way of coping with the world by making her ethical expectations even of those nearest (and who should be dearest) to her commensurate with its limited opportunities. Emma, who has recently suffered the kind of reversal of material fortunes that precipitated Fanny Burney's Cecilia into the world, is not yet (and as putative heroine presumably never can be) in tune with this commensurability; for Emma and the reader, unconfined by such pragmatism, mean thoughts in mean circumstances jar.

There is a particular energy at work in the fragment by which spaces, objects, physical things are given precision in order to confine the ideas they house, to check thought within material limits. Such writing proposes a kind of figurative constraint, inimical to the usual enlivening function of literary language, and profoundly disturbing in effect. On the contrary, there seems to be a conscious effort to restrict expression and thus to starve the capacity

[36] In each case my readings are drawn from the holograph manuscript, but for ease of reference I also include in brackets directions to the relevant page in Chapman's transcription, *The Watsons: A Fragment* (Oxford: Clarendon Press, 1927). *The Watsons*, PML MS. MA1034, Leaf 2^{r}–2^{v} (5–7).

[37] Ibid., Quire 1, 2^{v} (11).

15. Holograph manuscript page from *The Watsons*. By kind permission of Sir Peter Michael and Queen Mary and Westfield College, University of London.

for imagining, leaving it equally narrow and mean. An examination of the manuscript shows Austen repeatedly using revision to pare down her writing—literally, to make it meaner. In this spirit, the early description of Mr Edwards's townhouse is drained of colour and reduced to the barest socially denotative features:

was higher than most of its neighbours with ~~two~~ windows on each side
M^{r}. E.s | House ~~was of a dull brick~~ ^ ~~colour, & an high~~ | ~~Elevation, a flight of stone steps~~
the door, ~~&~~ ~~five~~ the windows guarded by ~~a chain & green~~ posts & chain the door
~~to the Door~~, | ~~& two windows flight of stone steps with~~ | ~~white posts, & a chain~~,
approached
^ ~~divided~~ by a flight of | stone steps.[38]

In more charged situations, like the early scenes at the assembly, the exceptional precision in the attention to detail generates the tension it describes:

while she attended with
M^{rs}. Edwards carefully guarding her own dress, | ~~& watching over the~~ yet greater Solicitude to | the proper security of her young Charges' shoulders | & Throats, led the way up the wide staircase, | while no sound of a Ball but the first, ~~tuning~~ | Scrape of one violin, blessed the ears of her fol: |:lowers

The party passed on—M^{rs}. E's sattin gown swept | along the clean floor of the Ball-
to the fire place at the upper end, where while were
room ^ ~~where~~ | ^ one party only were formally seated, ~~& a~~ | three or four Officers ^
together, ~~backwards & forwards~~
lounging ~~about, &~~ | passing in & out from the adjoining card- | -room.[39]

Little by little, by the smallest increments, the anxiety of the scene is wrought to a distinctive pitch—care for the 'security' of shoulders and throats, the 'scrape' of the violin, the sound of satin on the clean floor, the long walk through the cold empty room to the fireplace at the upper end, the women's consciousness of the presence of the self-consciously unconscious officers. Hypersensitivity (whose?) to the occasion is conveyed by a perfectionist. There is nothing quite like this unmediated attention to detail elsewhere in Austen's fiction. (But compare it with a passage from a letter of 9 December 1808, describing a Southampton ball where 'the melancholy part was to see so many dozen young Women standing by without partners, & each of them with two ugly naked shoulders!')[40]

[38] *The Watsons*, QMW MS. Quire 2, f. 2^{r} (19–20).
[39] Ibid., Quire 3, ff. 2^{v} and 3^{r} (32–4).
[40] *Jane Austen's Letters*, 156–7.

Virginia Woolf used the opportunity provided by her brief and percipient discussion of *The Watsons* to conjecture Austen's writing practice in general, arguing that 'the stiffness and the bareness of the first chapters prove that she was one of those writers who lay their facts out rather baldly in the first version and then go back and back and back and cover them with flesh and atmosphere.' The evidence of the draft manuscripts supports this kind of incremental adjustment, but only if we allow that repeated revisiting and minor change also worked in an exactly contrary fashion—to remove the flesh and on occasion expose the bones. We shall see the same paring back in revisions to *Sanditon*, and indeed Austen recommended its practice (she calls it 'scratching out') to her novel-writing niece Anna in a letter of 1814.[41]

Later, at home in the village rectory with their widowed father, the Watson girls are defined and confined by domestic details—the dish of fried beef that Emma and Elizabeth share, 'the Tray & the Knife-case' which

a foot larger each way than the other

announce the unfashionable three o'clock dinner, and 'the best parlour ^',

little

the 'usual ^ sitting room'.[42] Girls of slender means, their poverty licences a careless disregard, even insolence, in their guests: in the staring Lord Osborne (as 'odd looking' and as given to staring as Jane's dancing partner at Lyme), whose conversational gambit settles too precipitately and with too much particularity on neat female ankles and half-boots—'nankin galoshed with

looks well

black ~~have~~| ~~a~~ very ~~good air~~.—Do not you like Half-boots?'[43] Even brother Robert, the smug attorney made comfortable by marriage to his master's bitchy daughter, is described in greeting Emma as 'more in: |:tent on . . . pondering over a doubtful halfcrown, than | on welcoming a Sister, who was no longer likely | to have any property for him to get the di:|:rection of.'[44] There is something unavoidably judgemental in this style of writing. Unlike the Portsmouth scenes in *Mansfield Park*, where again Austen tackles domestic meanness, there is no room here for displacement. 'Novels', Martin Amis wrote, 'are all about not going out of the house.' Fanny Price may prove this with unusual literalness, but the obsessiveness with which she clings in

[41] Virginia Woolf, 'Jane Austen', *The Common Reader*, 1st ser. (London: Hogarth Press, 1925), 173; Q. D. Leavis was of the same opinion, arguing that 'her novels are geological structures . . . with subsequent accretions', 'A Critical Theory of Jane Austen's Writings', repr. in *Collected Essays*, 1, *The Englishness of the English Novel*, ed. G. Singh (Cambridge: Cambridge University Press, 1983), 64; *Jane Austen's Letters*, 276.

[42] *The Watsons*, QMW MS. Quire 6, f. 3^{v} (67); Quire 7, f. 2^{v} (75); Quire 9, f. 3^{v} (102–3).

[43] Ibid., Quire 7, f. 3^{v} (78).

[44] Ibid., Quire 8, f. 3^{r} (88).

imagination to one particular house while inhabiting another, offers the possibility that in Portsmouth, as at Mansfield Park, things may be otherwise than they seem to her. Fanny's capacity for disassociation from the space she inhabits (her longing for Portsmouth at Mansfield and Mansfield at Portsmouth) allows the reader imaginative space too. In what we have of *The Watsons*, however, there is no such saving or distorting distance; the consequence is a kind of claustrophobia, which is both a material and an ethical constriction.

Mary Waldron has recently suggested the possibility that 'much of *The Watsons* was incorporated into the eventual revision of "First Impressions" that became *Pride and Prejudice*.'[45] There is a general similarity in the economic pressures upon the Watson and Bennet girls to insert themselves into satisfactory marriages as well as a family likeness between Lord Osborne and Mr Darcy, while the stiff position-taking which informs the discussion between Elizabeth and Emma Watson of marrying for mere security appears to be amplified and dramatically fictionalized in Mrs Bennet's vulgar manœuvrings and Charlotte Lucas's pragmatism. Granted the kinship, it is, however, difficult to imagine that these elements, fundamental to its design, were not already in place in the earlier novel. But if it is the case that in revising *Pride and Prejudice* Austen absorbed and enlivened aspects of the subject-matter of *The Watsons*, it is even more apparent that in general colouring and in its depiction of physical and emotional constraint—of sheer frustration—the fragment is far closer to *Mansfield Park* and *Emma*.

The Watsons enacts with special intensity the moment when a new and tough realism took centre stage in Austen's art and in doing so changed decisively many of its elements. In *Sense and Sensibility* and *Pride and Prejudice* place functioned as little more than a series of theatrical sets. Now in *The Watsons* we see her working out a role for place and setting as something more than backdrop, as an informing environment with power to determine who we are and the opportunities we have. Linked to this is the significance of small objects. The emotional freight of the few personal possessions (what the narrator calls her 'nest of comforts') which Fanny Price assembles around her in the east room at Mansfield Park, the

[45] Mary Waldron, *Jane Austen and the Fiction of Her Time* (Cambridge: Cambridge University Press, 1999), 26; her view is shared by Southam, *Jane Austen's Literary Manuscripts*, 152, who challenges Q. D. Leavis's case for the wholesale absorption of *The Watsons* into *Emma* ('A Critical Theory', 76–81). More intriguing is Jan Fergus's suggestion that '*The Watsons* may have developed from Austen's earliest attempt at a novel, "Catharine, or the Bower"', *Jane Austen: A Literary Life*, 115.

disturbing triumph associated with her purchase of a silver penknife for Betsey, and the poignancy of Harriet Smith's dull collection of 'most precious treasures'—'a small piece of court plaister' and 'the end of an old pencil'—all take their origin in the psychological study of banality that *The Watsons* inaugurates.[46] The cramped assembly rooms at the White Hart Inn, where 'The Tearoom was a small room within the Cardroom', which was itself 'straightened by Tables' that 'hemmed in' Mrs Edwards's party, look forward to the discussion in *Emma* of the suitability of the room at the Crown Inn as a space for dancing. In both cases, the decision appears in the end to be subjective as to whether a space is confining or accommodating.

always
'It was ^ the pleasure of the | company ~~always~~ to have a little bustle & | croud' the narrator observes in *The Watsons*.[47] Yet this is only true in a simple sense; it is an aspect of what has been called Austen's 'domestic pathology'[48] that her characters will, whether heroically like Emma Woodhouse or foolishly and tragically like Maria Bertram, wrest opportunity from confinement. All Emma will look for in dancing is 'space to turn in'.

The bleakness of its social vision, the queer Dickensian humour of Tom Musgrave and Lord Osborne, and the uncertainty as to how the heroine might be developed explain the difficulty in connecting *The Watsons* to the finished novels despite some powerful passages of conversation and description. But there are at least two moments which appear to be recycled in *Mansfield Park*. The first is Mr Watson's encomium on Mr Howard's gifts as a preacher, more specifically his talent for reading aloud, 'without any Theatrical grimace or violence'. Mr Watson, returned from a clerical visitation, is full of the occasion and especially struck by Mr Howard:

> own I do not like ~~I cannot~~
> "I ~~have an abhor:~~ | ~~:rence of~~ much action in the pulpit— ~~& of the~~ ||
> I do not like ~~endure~~ the ||
>
> artificial
> studied air & ^ inflexions of voice, which your | very popular & most
> admired Preachers generally | have.—A simple delivery is much better calcu : |

[46] *Mansfield Park*, ed. Kathryn Sutherland (Harmondsworth, Middx.: Penguin, 1996), 127; for the incident of the penknife, see pp. 320–1 and 329; *Emma*, ed. Fiona Stafford (Harmondsworth, Middx.: Penguin, 1996), 280–1.

[47] *The Watsons*, QMW MS. Quire 4, f. 3^{r} (44); *Emma*, ed. Stafford, 206–11.

[48] Bharat Tandon, *Jane Austen and the Morality of Conversation* (London: Anthem Press, 2003), 191.

:lated to inspire Devotion, & shews a much | better Taste.—M^{r}. H. read like a scholar & a | gentleman."[49]

Later in *Mansfield Park* the topic is enlivened by Henry Crawford's reading from *Henry VIII* and through debate with the newly ordained Edmund Bertram; in all this Fanny Price is their attentive listener. In the fragment this little drama is merely reported intelligence, a hint, perhaps, of the heroic significance Mr Howard's character was to assume, but in the meantime inert information.

The second moment occurs almost at the end of the fragment where we are told Emma prefers sharing the retirement of her father's sick room to the family party downstairs, made painful to her by her sister Margaret's 'perverseness' and the vulgarity of her brother and sister-in-law. The passage is a chance for the narrator to convey something of Emma's emotional history and to excavate an inner, counter-social space suggestive of the self she has become in the fourteen years since she left her natural family, the self who is assaulted by the return home. The narrator observes:

mortifications
In his chamber, Emma was at peace from the | dreadful ‸ ~~Evils~~ of
unequal Society, & family | Discord – from the immediate endurance of | Hard-
low-minded Conceit ~~and a~~ folly, engrafted
hearted prosperity, ~~mean-spirited~~ ‸ ~~self-suffi:~~ | ~~:ciency,~~ & wrong-headed ‸ ~~ill~~
still in the
~~disposed~~ on an un: | :toward Disposition.—She ‸ suffered from them | ~~only in~~
Contemplation ceased
of their existence; in memory & in pros: | :pect, but for the moment, she ~~had~~
to be effects. was
~~a pause~~ | tortured by their ‸ ~~effusions~~—She ~~could~~ at leisure, | she could read & think . . .[50]

Emma Watson promises to be a different kind of heroine (different from Elinor and Marianne Dashwood and Elizabeth Bennet, that is) whose translation from one habitation to another will be the ground of her identity, as it will be for Fanny Price and Anne Elliot. But the work of describing what this might mean—how it might play out in terms of personality and plot—has scarcely yet begun. We know little more than that

[49] *The Watsons*, QMW MS. Quire 7, ff. 1^{v}–2^{r} (73–4); *Mansfield Park*, ed. Sutherland, 278–82.

[50] *The Watsons*, QMW MS. Quire 10, f. 4^{r} (117–18).

for
'It was | well for her that she was naturally chearful;— | the Change had been
might
such as ~~to~~ ∧ have plunged | ~~as it was a change which~~ weak spirits ~~must~~ | ~~have~~
~~gloom~~ in
~~into~~ ∧ ~~wretchedness~~ ∧ Despondence.—' In Fanny Price the study in translation is developed, but it is also complicated in a way which would not have been possible in *The Watsons*, through the diffidence of Fanny's personality and the deeper structural resonances in *Mansfield Park* of translation as narrative and thematic device. Introduced as a timid child rather than a cheerful young woman, Fanny is given emotional and psychological depth in her search for belonging; by the same procedure the narrator is afforded critical distance. Emma Watson's 'air of healthy vigour', her 'open Countenance', and sanguine disposition are far more of a challenge to narrator and narrative. The life of the novel lies outside her, as it lies outside Fanny, but Emma, already a shrewd observer of human worth, and with no hint of an interesting pathology to explore, appears to require no inner growth to redress the balance. It is accordingly difficult to see how the heroine, and therefore the novel, might have developed. By contrast, the assault Portsmouth offers to Fanny's emotional defences is profounder than we sense is the impact of her family's social meanness on Emma Watson. But it is worth asking whether Austen could have reached *Mansfield Park* without the experimental social study of *The Watsons*. It is also worth asking what *The Watsons* owes specifically to Austen's Bath years and whether Bath, contrary to received biographical tradition, challenged and deepened her scope as a novelist.

R. W. Chapman made the first and only close scholarly examination of the holograph manuscript in its entirety in 1924, by which time it had already been divided into two portions: *The Watsons* appears to be Austen's only work of fiction surviving in manuscript to have suffered in this way. It passed intact from Caroline Austen to her nephew William Austen-Leigh, and he presented the first 6 leaves (a quire of 2 leaves and a quire of 4 leaves) to a charity sale in aid of the Red Cross in April 1915. When Chapman examined these 6 leaves, they were in the possession of Alice, Lady Ludlow. But soon afterwards they were with the London dealer C. J. Sawyer, who, after unsuccessfully trying to purchase the larger part of the manuscript from its then owners (the nephew and nieces of William Austen-Leigh), offered the fragment of the fragment for sale. It was acquired for the Pierpont Morgan Library in 1926, where it remains. The larger portion of the manuscript was in family ownership (though much of the time on deposit in the British Museum) until 1978. Since 1988 it has been the property of Sir Peter Michael and is now on deposit at Queen Mary and Westfield College, where Sir Peter was once a student and is now an honorary fellow.[51] This larger portion consists of ten quires, numbered 2 to 11 on the recto of each first leaf. Quires 2 to 10 consist each of 4 leaves and the final quire, 11, consists of 2 leaves, the second of which is blank. There are in total 44 leaves (6 of which are in the Pierpont Morgan). After the first 2, which are slightly larger, each leaf measures approximately 19 × 12 cm (7.5 × 4.75 inches). Chapman detected the watermark date of 1803 in quires 8, 9, and 10, and the watermark WS in 5, 6, and 7. What he did not notice, however, is that each quire from 2 to 10 is formed from a half sheet of paper, measuring 38 × 24 cm (15 × 9.5 inches), which has again been cut in half and one half folded inside the other to form a booklet of 4 leaves or 8 pages. One whole sheet measuring approximately 38 × 48 cm (15 × 19 inches), thus provided paper for two quires or booklets. In some cases the cutting of the sheets has made it more difficult to see the watermark, but examined closely every sheet is watermarked, by the date 1803 and the initials or countermark WS. The manuscript thus provides a small clue as to how Austen prepared her writing surface. Though an intriguing idea, there is no evidence to suggest it was in Bath, where privacy was harder to come by than at Steventon, that she began the habit of composing her drafts in such small homemade booklets. But the booklets of the *Watsons* fragment do provide a surface to be repeated in the identically sized, though thicker, booklets made to hold *Sanditon*, which suggests that at least by 1804 Austen had established the practice whereby her writing surface physically instantiates in miniature, booklet by homemade booklet, the appearance of an emerging novel.

In presentation, too, the holograph manuscript of *The Watsons* is similar to the *Sanditon* manuscript of fourteen years later, again suggesting habits of working which may have remained much the same across the mature novels. In both manuscripts the pages are filled in a neat, even hand with signs of concurrent writing, erasure, and revision, interrupted by occasional passages of heavy interlinear correction. There is no pagination, no clear or regular paragraphing, and no separation of speaking parts one from another. (Over a third of the *Watsons* fragment is cast in direct speech.) Unlike the *Sanditon* manuscript, *The Watsons* is without chapter divisions, though not without

[51] Information drawn from Chapman's 'Preface', *The Watsons* (1927); Gilson F10; and QMW Archive.

informal division by wider spacing and ruled lines. These obvious similarities aside, the fragment offers a special kind of evidence for joining Jane Austen's life to her art in the method she here adopted for inserting large revisions into her pages.

Unlike many of her contemporaries (Walter Scott and William Godwin, for example), she left no space within her manuscripts for large-scale rewriting; the pages of all her working drafts are full, suggesting that she did not anticipate a protracted process of redrafting. By contrast, both Scott and Godwin adopted the common practice of writing out full text on the recto, reserving the facing blank verso for corrections and additions. With no calculated blank spaces and no obvious way of incorporating large revision or expansion Austen had to find other strategies. The reopening of the ending to *Persuasion* will later provide one kind of artistic and physical solution to the problem, but in *The Watsons* she literally applied patches to the manuscript—attaching with straight pins small pieces of paper, each of which was filled closely and neatly with the new material, to the precise spot where erased material was to be covered or where an insertion was required to expand the text. There are three such patches in the fragment, inserted into quires or booklets 7, 9, and 10. The first patch, replacing a heavily erased section, represents a significant redistribution of authority in a conversation between Emma and Lord Osborne and, on second thoughts, a chastening of his insolence. The second patch is an insertion filling out a conversation between Emma and her brother Robert with useful background details on Emma's recently dead uncle and her unwelcome return to her family. The third, in which Emma questions Tom Musgrave about 'the Parsonage family', allows Austen to broaden the hint that her heroine is interested in Mr Howard. All three significantly expand or complicate the action; all three show Austen projecting her story into the future and laying down the foundations for a full-length novel.

All three patches are carefully cut to the shape of their written texts and, unlike the quired leaves, are materially tailored to fit narrative need: in the patches to quires 9 and 10 the only indication of where they are to be placed is provided by the pin holes. The best clue we have that they represent a later stage of creation rather than immediate second thoughts is that all three are written on paper which, though common to themselves, is not used for the bulk of the manuscript. The patches are on thicker paper with distinct chainlines; they may even come from the same sheet and represent a single concerted act of revision.[52] The method of their insertion displays a particular feminine frugality in her craft as a writer, Austen appearing to have returned to her manuscript on one particular occasion and patched or mended it in much the same way as she might patch a smock or darn a stocking.

The fragment of *The Watsons* offers a precious and unexpected material clue to what we know by less tangible means was Austen's practice as social commentator: her preference, that is, for crossing, recrossing, and crossing back again over her small plot of fictional ground. The kind of retracing which weaves together details of character, incident, and plot across the novels (the reader's sense of a generic village community) has long seemed to find its unravelling in *The Watsons*, in whose unfinished state critics have regularly detected a series of patches subsequently recycled through or applied to the published novels.[53] This is supported by the evidence of the manuscript where we see physically manifest a correlative more pertinent than her famed skill 'at overcast and satin stitch'[54] of the frugal arena of her imagination. In her letter from Lyme Regis on 14 September 1804 Austen had complained of the ungenteel Mrs Armstrong darning stockings throughout her visit. It is a pleasing thought that the hand which recorded Mrs Armstrong's darning may soon have been attending to a little patching of her own.

[52] There is of course one patch pasted into the *Persuasion* manuscript (described in Gilson F8), suggesting that this remained Austen's preferred method of correction where there was no space for extensive rewriting. With allowance for rubbing at the edges, the paper of the bulk of the *Watsons* manuscript, Quires 2–10, corresponds in its uncut size to 'post' writing paper (38.5 × 48 cm / 15.25 × 19 inches) and is wove (that is, without chainlines). The patches are inserted at Quire 7, f. 4^{r} (79–80); Quire 9, f. 1^{v} (94–6); Quire 10, f. 2^{r} (110–12). The patch in Quire 10 appears to bear the watermark MJL. Quire 11, comprising the final two leaves (the second blank) of the manuscript, is also from a different batch of paper, with the watermark Curteis & Son, and like the paper used for patching, it is laid and has prominent chainlines, but it is not so thick and the chainlines are closer together. In the paper used for patching the distance between chainlines is 26 mm; in Quire 11 it is 24 mm. The Curteises were well-known good-quality papermakers in Carshalton, Surrey (D. C. Coleman, *The British Paper Industry, 1495–1860* (Oxford, 1958; repr. Westport, Conn.: Greenwood Press, 1975), 156).

[53] In addition to Fergus, Q. D. Leavis, Southam, and Waldron (n. 45 above), see the interesting essay by Joseph Wiesenfarth, '*The Watsons* as Pretext', *Persuasions*, 8 (1986), 101–11. Wiesenfarth helpfully reprises other critical views (up to the mid-1980s) on the recycling of the fragment.

[54] *Memoir*, 171. The detail, remembered by Caroline Austen, of her aunt's proficiency at needlework seems to lie behind several early critical estimates of Austen's method of composition. For example, Chapman, *Facts and Problems*: 'her creative imagination worked most freely within a framework fixed for her by small points of contact with reality.' (122)

Persuasion*: from manuscript to print*

> 'for no compositor can know the writer's meaning so well as his pen does'
>
> (Richard Blackmore, 1864)[55]

The two manuscript chapters of *Persuasion* possess unique status in being the only surviving holograph pages of a novel which Austen planned and completed for publication. They have survived in part because in their extant form they did not see print in the posthumous first edition of 1818, being withdrawn and replaced at a late stage in writing. They were intended as the concluding chapters (10 and 11 in the second and final volume) of the novel, and we have an unusual amount of detail about the circumstances of their writing and substitution. We know from Cassandra Austen's notes that the novel was written in almost exactly a year, between 8 August 1815 and 6 August 1816. The manuscript fragment, a single gathering of sixteen unnumbered leaves, is dated 'July 8' at the top right-hand corner of the first leaf, immediately above 'Chap. 10', and at the bottom right-hand corner of what would be page 27 (f. 14^{r}), 'July 16. 1816'. The word 'Finis' inscribed below the text at this point marks the first attempt at an ending. As it has come down to us, subsequently revised, it reads:

She | had but two friends in the world, | ~~independent of himself, whom | she~~ to add
to his List, Lady R. | & M^{rs}. Smith.—~~Lady R.~~ To those | however, he was very well-
disposed | to attach himself. Lady R—in: | :spite of all her former transgressions, | he
could now value from his | heart;—while he was not obliged | to say that he beleived
been originally almost
her to ~~be~~have | ^ right in ^ dividing them, he was | ready to say ^ anything else in her |
favour;—& as for M^{rs}. Smith, | she had ~~agreableness~~ claims of | various kinds to
recommend her | quickly & permanently.—Her recent | good offices by Anne had
their marriage in: her
been || enough in themselves—and ~~in:~~ | :stead of ~~being~~ depriv~~ed~~ing ^ of one | friend
~~the~~
~~by Anne's marriage, it~~ | ~~gained her another~~ secured her two. | ~~When they had any home,~~
~~she~~ | ~~was frequently w~~ She was one of | their first visitors in their settled | Life—and
her Husband's
Capt. Wentworth, by | putting her in the way of reco: | :vering ~~the~~ ^ property in the

[55] In *Letters to Macmillan*, ed. Simon Nowell-Smith (London: Macmillan, 1967), quoted in Allan C. Dooley, *Author and Printer in Victorian England* (Charlottesville and London: University Press of Virginia, 1992), 13.

W. Indies, | by ~~giving her the~~ writing for her, & | acting for her, & seeing her through | all the petty Difficulties of the case, | with the activity & exertion of a | fearless ~~friend~~ Man, & a determined | friend, ~~convinced her of his~~ | ~~being much nearer Perfection~~ | ~~than her~~

ever
~~intercourse with the~~ | ~~world had~~ fully requited the | services she had rendered or had ^ |

~~And having received~~
meant to render ~~her friend~~, to his | wife.~~—and could not fail of~~ | ~~establishing his And~~
~~such a benefit from~~ ~~him, not~~[?] ~~even his wife could~~ ~~M^{rs}. Smith's estimate of his Perfection~~
~~could having done~~ | ~~so much for her, scarcely could~~ | ~~his wife even think him nearer~~ |
~~be surpassed only by that Wife's.~~
~~perfection~~,

~~Finis.~~

~~July 16.~~
~~1816~~.[56]

It is impossible to untangle with certainty the pre- and post-16 July erasures. But in its first settled form, the ending was something like: 'Capt. Wentworth . . . fully requited the services she had rendered or had ever meant to render to his wife. And having received such a benefit from him, M^{rs}. Smith's estimate of his Perfection could be surpassed only by that Wife's.'

It is not difficult to see why Austen might have had second thoughts almost immediately; why she would wish to throw more emphasis in the final lines on the reunited lovers rather than on Mrs Smith. Accordingly, the last sentence was erased and over the page a further 26 lines of text were written, followed again by 'Finis' and the date, two days later, 'July 18. 1816'. Written out with little of the hesitation that accompanied the first ending, this second passage, along with what was left of the first ending, survived subsequent major revision to the final chapters and, with minor changes, it formed the novel's closing paragraph in the printed text of 1818. In manuscript it reads:

with
M^{rs}. Smith's enjoyments were not spoiled | by this improvement of Income, ^ some | improvement of health, & the acquisition of | such friends to be often with, for her | chearfulness & mental Activity did not | fail her, & while those prime supplies of | Good remained, she might have bid de: | :fiance even to greater accessions of | worldly Prosperity. She might have been | absolutely rich & perfectly healthy, & yet | be happy.—Her spring of Felicity was in | the glow of her spirits—as her friend | Anne's

[56] *Persuasion*, BL MS. Egerton 3038, ff. 13^{v}–14^{r} (37–8). In each case my readings are drawn from the holograph manuscript, but for ease of reference I also include in brackets the relevant page in Chapman's transcription, *The Manuscript Chapters of Persuasion* (*Two Chapters of Persuasion* (1926); repr. London: Athlone Press, 1985).

was in the warmth of her | Heart.—Anne~~'s~~ was Tenderness itself;—and | she had ~~all~~
full
the ^ worth of it in Captn. | Wentworth's affection. His Profession | was all that could ever make her friends | wish <u>that</u> Tenderness less; the dread of a | future War, all
dim
that could ~~overspread~~ | her Sunshine.—She gloried in being a | Sailor's wife, but she must pay the | tax of quick alarm, for belonging to | that Profession which is ~~not more~~
in it's   in it's
~~distinguished~~ —if possible—more | distinguished ~~for~~ Domestic Virtues, | than ~~for~~
Importance.
National ~~Renown.—~~

Finis

July 18. 1816.[57]

After this second ending, a further three full pages of text follow in the manuscript (beginning 'He was very eager & very de:|:lightful in the description of |
at the Concert.—
what he had felt ~~the Even^{g}. before.—~~' and ending '["]Since that moment, I have
been   decided
~~waited~~ | ~~only for its confirmation determined~~ | what to do—and had it been
This ~~day~~ should have been my <u>last day</u> in Bath."'
con:|:firmed, ~~I should have left Bath~~ | ~~tomorrow.)~~ presumably written about the same time or soon afterwards. This passage is keyed by a large X to f. 8^{v}, where it was to be inserted towards the close of Chapter 10. This original Chapter 10, with its swift resolution of the love story and the comic stage-business provided by Admiral and Mrs Croft, was subsequently almost wholly rejected in favour of a broader and deeper study of restored love, the ending that found its way into print, written some time between 18 July and 6 August. But the three-page addition found a place, virtually word for word, in this substituted printed text.[58] This is hardly surprising—the latest written of the surviving holograph fragment, it at last allows the lovers to speak openly about issues of *Persuasion* and *Duty* (in the manuscript the abstract nouns are given the strong rhetorical emphasis of capitalization and underlining) which drove them apart eight years before. The rights and wrongs of giving advice and of bending to the advice of others gather throughout the novel, but it is the one particular act, by which

[57] BL MS. Egerton 3038, f. 14^{v} (38–9).

[58] BL MS. Egerton 3038, ff. 15^{r}–16^{v} (22–5; where Chapman inserts the passage in the body of his transcription of Ch. 10). For the passage as it appears in print in Vol. 2, Ch. 11 (Ch. 23) of a modern edition, see *Persuasion*, ed. Gillian Beer (Harmondsworth, Middx.: Penguin, 1998): 'That evening seemed to be made up of exquisite moments . . . and I felt that I had still a motive for remaining here.' (214–15)

under pressure Anne Elliot gave up Captain Wentworth, whose ethical and emotional implications suffuse the narrative and which has needed to be revisited. We sense that the novel was always feeling its way towards this point, though it might be interesting to consider whether our certainty would be quite so strong if Henry or Cassandra Austen had not chosen the title *Persuasion* in preference to Austen's apparent working title of 'The Elliots'.[59]

Austen-Leigh first mentioned the existence of the manuscript fragment in his *Memoir*, where he derived his circumstantial account from family recollections:

> The book had been brought to an end in July; and the re-engagement of the hero and heroine effected in a totally different manner in a scene laid at Admiral Croft's lodgings. But her performance did not satisfy her. She thought it tame and flat, and was desirous of producing something better. This weighed upon her mind, the more so probably on account of the weak state of her health; so that one night she retired to rest in very low spirits. But such depression was little in accordance with her nature, and was soon shaken off. The next morning she awoke to more cheerful views and brighter inspirations: the sense of power revived; and imagination resumed its course. She cancelled the condemned chapter, and wrote two others, entirely different, in its stead. The result is that we possess the visit of the Musgrove party to Bath; the crowded and animated scenes at the White Hart Hotel; and the charming conversation between Capt. Harville and Anne Elliot, overheard by Capt. Wentworth, by which the two faithful lovers were at last led to understand each other's feelings. The tenth and eleventh chapters of 'Persuasion' then, rather than the actual winding-up of the story, contain the latest of her printed compositions, her last contribution to the entertainment of the public.... The cancelled chapter exists in manuscript. It is certainly inferior to the two which were substituted for it: but it was such as some writers and some readers might have been contented with; and it contained touches which scarcely any other hand could have given, the suppression of which may be almost a matter of regret.[60]

This description compresses at least two different stages and kinds of revision: the longer and later stage, which ran, by Cassandra's reckoning, into the first week in August and produced two substitute chapters; and the immediate period of dissatisfaction, between 16 and 18 July, resulting in the patched rewriting and new final paragraph to the original Chapter 11 and possibly also

[59] According to family tradition 'The Elliots' was Austen's preference among several working titles. See *Family Record*, 238.

[60] *Memoir*, 124–5.

the late insertion into Chapter 10. Nor is it quite accurate to describe the substituted chapters as 'entirely different', since they incorporate several large sections from the old, 'condemned' Chapter 10, among them the late three-page addition. What found its way into print in the posthumous edition of 1818 was a wholly new Chapter 10, a partly new Chapter 11, incorporating sections from the old Chapter 10 in its first and second draftings amounting to more than a quarter of the original, and the old Chapter 11, incorporating its redrafted ending, now renumbered Chapter 12. Thus only parts of the original Chapter 10 were 'cancelled', and, contrary to Austen-Leigh's implication, the manuscript fragment is not totally distinct from the printed text. Rather, it is unique among Austen's manuscripts for two reasons: it represents drafts of the same material at several stages of composition; and it includes a complete chapter for which we also have print copy. This chapter (Volume 2, Chapter 11 in manuscript and Volume 2, Chapter 12 or 24 in print, where the two-volume division is lost) is unique among Austen's extant works in providing our only opportunity to compare directly manuscript and print and thus draw some idea of how her novels were transformed from private into public texts.

The final chapters of *Persuasion*, then, would appear to form a conspectus of Austen's texts in the making, allowing on a modest scale the kind of survey of the stages of literary creation, available to textual critics of Wordsworth, Shelley, Keats, and other Romantic writers. For these few chapters we possess, uniquely, a drafted ending with revisions, but known to have been set aside; a later drafting, known only from its printed text, providing a more radical rejection and reworking of the earlier materials and their selective incorporation with new materials into a second ending; and a portion of text surviving in manuscript and print (though significantly not in the manuscript copy used in the printing house). The unusual gap in the evidence is the author herself, who died before the novel was brought to publication. Her brother Henry saw *Persuasion* and *Northanger Abbey* through the press and probably read them in proof. Some of the changes between manuscript and print would be authorial, at the redrafting stage, others suggest the usual interventions of printing-house or even publishing-house practices, which would have gone on with or without the author's blessing; but in some instances the work of regularization is taken so far that it blunts the rhetorical force of the manuscript reading. In these cases, we might assume the author would have objected.

In presenting, in the second edition of his *Memoir*, the cancelled Chapter 10, Austen-Leigh acted 'in compliance with wishes both publicly and privately expressed'.[61] The manuscript fragment was then in the possession of his half-sister Anna Lefroy; Austen-Leigh probably worked from a copy, which he subsequently tidied with the help of the 1818 printed text, rather than from the original.[62] He inserted paragraphing, expanded contractions, regularized Austen's gestural and performative punctuation to conform to syntactic rules, and altered or added the occasional word to 'improve' her sense or clarify her grammar. The *Memoir* text is thus far from being a faithful transcript. For example, where the manuscript reads 'Anne was sitting | down, but now she arose again—| to entreat him not to interrupt M^{rs}. C——', the *Memoir* text has 'Anne *was* sitting down, but now she arose, again to entreat him not to interrupt Mrs. Croft'. In one instance, a sentence is missed in transcription: 'This was spoken, as with | a fortitude which seemed to meet the | message.' It was probably passed over because in the manuscript it occupies a space across three lines, the first and last of which begin with the same word, 'message'. Elsewhere, the manuscript reading '"I could not derive benefit || from the later Knowledge of | your Character which I had ac:|:quired"' is rendered in the grammatically less awkward form, '"I could not derive benefit from the late knowledge I had acquired of your character."' Since this also represents the reading in the printed text of 1818, where the passage has been worked into Chapter 11, it appears that Austen-Leigh occasionally spliced his transcription with readings from the published novel. In some few cases, his departure from both manuscript and printed text introduces a third reading. For example, the manuscript reading '& only at Lyme that he | had begun to understand his own | sensations' became in the reworked passage of 1818 'and only at Lyme had he begun to understand himself'. But in the *Memoir* text it appears as 'and only at Lyme that he had begun to understand his own feelings'.[63] Most of these small changes display a fastidiousness which recalls the biographical pedantries of the elderly Austen-Leigh.

[61] *Memoir* (1871), p. v.

[62] HRO, MS. 23M93/64/4/2, a volume containing transcriptions in several unidentified hands of letters, poems, and short stories by Austen, includes a copy of the cancelled Ch. 10 of *Persuasion*. It is unparagraphed and preserves the contractions of the holograph but is otherwise a clean faircopy. It seems likely that the volume was a sourcebook or repository for pieces used in the *Memoir*.

[63] BL MS. Egerton 3038, f. 3^{r} (8), *Memoir* (1871), 170; the missing sentence is at Egerton 3038, f. 5^{v} (14–15); Egerton 3038, ff. 15^{v}–16^{r} (24), *Memoir* (1871), 178, and *Persuasion* (London: John Murray, 1818), ii. 291. See, too, the manuscript reading 'Was || not it enough to make the fool | of ‸^{me} which my behaviour expressed?' Egerton 3038, f. 15^{r-v}(23), which becomes in the reworked 1818 text (ii. 290) and in the 1871 transcript (178), 'Was it not enough to make the fool of me which I appeared?' For Austen-Leigh's departure from manuscript and printed 1818 text, see Egerton 3038, f. 6^{v} (18), *Persuasion* (1818), ii. 283, and *Memoir* (1871), 175.

Both manuscript chapters were transcribed for the first time in Chapman's *Two Chapters of Persuasion* of 1926. However, here Chapman only reproduced Austen's final discarded version, relegating her first, second, and in some cases third thoughts without comment or speculation to a back-of-volume list. Furthermore, this transcription did not replace Austen-Leigh's hybrid *Memoir* text, which continued to be included as an appendix to the regularly reissued 1923 Oxford text of *Persuasion* until 1969. Oxford's reluctance to reset any part of the Chapman text of the novels, even as late as the revisions to the annotations undertaken by Mary Lascelles in 1964–6, served to discourage reflection upon the precise nature and method of the textual changes to the ending of *Persuasion* and thus obscured a vital critical dimension of the novel, unless the reader knew to invest in two Oxford volumes rather than one.[64]

It is difficult to account for the existence of the holograph fragment at all. We have no such fragment of any other of the six published novels. From this it seems reasonable to infer that, regardless of what she hinted to the contrary to Crosby and Co., it may not have been Jane Austen's habit to make duplicate copies of her works, and that the one fully drafted copy for each of the novels normally became printer's copy, which, once set in type, would be routinely destroyed in the printing house. Chapman suggests that the reason this was not the fate of the final chapter of *Persuasion* (holograph Chapter 11, which became in print Chapter 12), the only portion of the manuscript fragment to be reproduced in print more or less exactly, is because it 'was so embedded that it could not without some loss of tidiness have been removed' from its surrounding manuscript.[65] Since Chapter 11 in the holograph begins on the verso of f. 9 and continues to f. 14 verso, the division of the manuscript would not in fact have been difficult at this point; but it is reasonable to assume that, though identical with the preserved portion, its further transcription was necessary to the physical and intellectual process of keying the new section to its surrounding text.

More interesting are the questions the holograph's survival stimulates us to ask about the condition and appearance of the copy Austen might have submitted for printing. Would it have looked different from these small,

[64] There is an extensive correspondence in the Oxford University Press archive from Mary Lascelles (22 February 1964–27 February 1966), during the time she was marking up corrections for the latest reprint of the 1923 edition, arguing forcefully for the replacement of Austen-Leigh's '*bad* text'... 'It will be censured, and rightly.' (OUP archive, LOGE000025).

[65] In his 'Preface' to *The Manuscript Chapters of Persuasion.*

closely written sheets, with their erasures, interlinear substitutions, and insertions? Would it have been a clean faircopy on larger paper, divided into paragraphs, and with contractions expanded as is the case with *Lady Susan*? or would it have retained something of the appearance of a working draft? Is the very craftedness of the *Lady Susan* manuscript (what Mary Lascelles called its 'discretion')[66] a sign that it was not at that stage considered by its author as printer's copy, that it had already achieved the status of precious object? We cannot know for certain; but the total absence of manuscript copy for any other of the printed works suggests that, unlike Walter Scott in her own age or George Eliot later in the century, Austen did not regard the manuscript stage as something to be safeguarded or restored intact once set in print. In particular, the fact that the rejected draft chapters for this one section of *Persuasion* are all that remains of a novel sent posthumously to the press suggests that the bulk of the manuscript would not have been faircopied and that it may have been sent to her publisher, Murray, with minimal tidying. It may, in other words, have looked much like this fragment. Even the small size of the paper (at 15.5 × 9 cm or 6.12 × 3.5 inches it is smaller even than that used for *The Watsons* and *Sanditon*) need not imply there was a later transcription onto large paper for the printer. Shelley had his poetry copied onto very small slips to reduce postage from Italy to his publisher, Charles Ollier; and we can assume that compositors were used in other cases to handling small, crowded copy.[67]

Only in the course of the nineteenth century did writers begin regularly to present clean copy free from messy corrections, written on one side of the paper, and in sheets of uniform size. This seems to have been part of the bargain by which they in their turn gained control over matters of punctuation. Before that, and certainly in Austen's time, there was little expectation on the side of author or printer that manuscript layout or punctuation would transmit into print.[68] It is therefore highly unlikely that, supposing she did

[66] Lascelles, *Jane Austen and Her Art*: 'Among the manuscripts, *Lady Susan* alone is a discreet, unrevealing, fair copy.' (88)

[67] Reiman, *Modern Manuscripts*, 96, mentions the small size of many of Shelley's press copies.

[68] Bruce Redford examines the challenging physical state of the unfinished and heavily revised manuscript of the biography of Samuel Johnson that Boswell provided for the compositor in his *Designing the Life of Johnson* (Oxford: Oxford University Press, 2002). Printers' manuals of the late eighteenth and early nineteenth centuries regularly carry warnings and complaints about the messiness and poor (ungrammatical, that is) punctuation of author's copy and assert the printer's authority in this area. Caleb Stower, *The Printer's Grammar* (London: B. Crosby and Co., 1808): 'the duty of punctuation is often made to devolve on the [printing-house] corrector; and what has been disregarded as a matter of little consequence, by the author, becomes an important part of the corrector's business. Let him discharge

make faircopies of her manuscripts for the press, she would in the process of transcription have adopted a less performative and more grammatical style of punctuation. Printers also expected at this time to take responsibility for expanding common contractions and substituting the full forms of characters' names in those instances where the author provided only initials. The copy of *Persuasion* sent for publication may have retained such shorthand forms as 'Lady R.——'and 'Capt. W.——', which mark the surviving fragment. It is worth noting that such contractions are not a consistent feature of the holograph fragment but interspersed fairly regularly with their full forms; a press corrector might not have to look far to check a name. On the other hand, the printer's commitment to normalize incomplete copy would also explain why unusual manuscript forms such as 'Lady Russel' and 'Captain Benwicke' become in the printed text 'Lady Russell' and 'Captain Benwick'. Caleb Stower's *Printer's Grammar* of 1808, a standard and much-invoked authority throughout the early nineteenth century, argues that it is the duty of the printer's corrector to cleanse author's copy of eccentricities:

> If therefore a corrector suspects copy to want revising, he is not to postpone it, but to make his emendations in the manuscript before it is wanted by the compositor, that he may not be hindered in the pursuit of his business, or prejudiced by alterations in the proof, especially if they are of no real signification; such as far-fetched spelling of words, changing and thrusting in points, capitals, or any thing else that has nothing but fancy and humour for its authority and foundation.[69]

There is some evidence that at least from 1815, when she began to be published by the prestigious house of John Murray in Albemarle Street, a professional reader, either William Gifford, editor of the house periodical the *Quarterly Review*, or an associate, intervened in the presentation or marking up of Austen's manuscript. We know that Gifford undertook to provide this service (promising even to 'amend' 'expressions') for the manuscript of

this duty with propriety and uniformity.' (391) Other standard works, Philip Luckombe, *The History and Art of Printing* (London: J. Johnson, 1771), 377, and T. C. Hansard, *Typographia* (London: Baldwin, Cradock, and Joy, 1825), 741–2, make a similar point. Dooley, *Author and Printer in Victorian England*, draws most of his examples from the period post-1830, but he outlines in general terms some of the practices and shifts in control occurring across the century as a whole. Precisely relevant are what he has to say about the status of printer's manuscript copy, author's piecemeal correction of proofs without recourse to copy, and how these practices affected a writer's ability to control her texts at production stage (7–22).

[69] Stower, *The Printer's Grammar*, 213.

Emma, Austen's first novel to be submitted to Murray. He may also have been responsible for the more decisive shift towards grammatical (as distinct from rhetorical) punctuation in the second edition of *Mansfield Park*, published by Murray in 1816; it is even more likely that the posthumous novels will bear the marks of Murray's reader.[70] But whether by Albemarle Street or the printing-house corrector, Austen's submitted manuscripts would have been normalized in various ways in preparation for setting in type. A rough estimate of the length of the book (based on format and type size) and division into volumes would be made as part of the usual process known as 'casting off', undertaken by printer or publisher before work could begin. A further and unusual complication was that Austen's manuscripts were also regularly submitted to a prior division by volume among several printing houses. Though as literary critics we are trained to discover design in volume division, it is by no means clear that Austen composed all her novels in the actual volume-format in which they appeared. Certainly by the time of *Mansfield Park*, when she is already a published author with some practical experience of the industry, there is evidence to suggest she may have measured out the volumes carefully and been responsible for marking the original divisions.

But in whatever state they were submitted, once they arrived at the printing house her manuscripts were regarded as printer's copy, which means that if they were folded and formed into little booklets they might be cut up into individual leaves and distributed in portions or 'takes' among several compositors. A take could be large or small, though in the early part of the century it was usually not less than a half-sheet or forme (in the case of one of Austen's novels this would be 12 pages). When each compositor had finished setting his take in type, he would receive another portion, which would not be consecutive with his first take but would represent a later section of the manuscript.[71] Individual compositors worked in an orderly

[70] Samuel Smiles, *A Publisher and His Friends: Memoir and Correspondence of the late John Murray*, 2 vols., 2nd edn. (London: John Murray, 1891), i. 282; and see Ch. 5, 303–4 below.

[71] For the division of author's manuscript into takes in the period, see Philip Gaskell, *A New Introduction to Bibliography* (Oxford: Clarendon Press, 1972), 191–3;–and also Luckombe, *History and Art of Printing*, 452–6. Peter Garside's comprehensive study of novels published in Britain in the early nineteenth century suggests that no more than 5–10 per cent show from the evidence of their colophons more than one printer involved in their production; further, that it seems to have been the practice with the works of better known authors (Edgeworth's *Belinda* (1801)) or where competing translations of high-profile foreign titles (for example, de Staël's novels) would indicate that speed of publication was an important factor. But in Austen's case, *Pride and Prejudice*, *Mansfield Park* (first and second editions), and *Emma* all show the same multiple printer pattern. (Information supplied from chronological listings in

and systematic way but neither continuously nor sequentially on a single manuscript, and once the manuscript had been divided for setting in type there was no provision in the process for reconnecting its parts. Typesetting small sections, printing, proofing in batches of one, two, or three sheets at a time (with a printed sheet for a novel containing between 16 and 24 pages, depending on format), in-house revising, breaking-up of type, and the setting of further sections of text all went on concurrently. Whether or not more than one house was engaged in printing, both author and compositor would by this stage see copy as non-sequential chunks, and there was no convention until after the middle of the nineteenth century of sending back the relevant portion of manuscript with the proof sheets for author's correction.[72] Eventually, at any one of several stages in the process, the divided portions of manuscript would be lost sight of, recycled as wastepaper, or destroyed. Even supposing Austen had by her an earlier draft for use in proofing she would not at this late stage be comparing like with like.

The fact of its survival tells us that between the holograph manuscript of Chapter 11 and the printed text in the first edition of 1818 there intervened a further draft of the conclusion which became printer's copy and eventually wastepaper. That this further draft was not a simple transcription is borne out by the introduction of several new phrases into the printed text. In every case they polish the sense, and though this is not in itself proof that Austen made the changes, we can assume they were mainly authorial: an author, as distinct from an amanuensis, rarely attempts a literal, word-by-word copy of her own work. The description of Sir Walter Elliot's satisfaction with the physical appearance of Captain Wentworth contracts and then expands, on third thought, between manuscript and print: 'On the contrary | when he saw more of Capt. W.—— ~~saw~~ | ~~him by daylight~~ & eyed him well' becoming 'On the contrary, when he saw more of Captain Wentworth, saw him repeatedly by daylight and eyed him

The English Novel 1770–1829: A Bibliographical Survey of Prose Fiction Published in the British Isles, 2 vols. (Oxford: Oxford University Press, 2000), Vol. 2: 1800–1829, ed. Peter Garside, and from Professor Garside's database.) When Henry Austen is reading *Mansfield Park* in manuscript in March 1814 it is already divided into volumes, though these may not be identical with the printed divisions. See *Jane Austen's Letters*, 258. Marilyn Butler throws suspicion on authorial volume division in a fascinating essay, 'Disregarding Designs: Jane Austen's Sense of the Volume', *Jane Austen Society Collected Reports, 1976–85*, 99–114.

[72] This seems to be the case, as Dooley concludes (*Author and Printer in Victorian England*, 38–40) from his examination of Stower and Hansard's manuals. Gaskell, *A New Introduction to Bibliography*, 352, reaches the same conclusion.

well'.[73] Mary Musgrove's complacency at her sister Anne's forthcoming marriage appears in manuscript as 'It was cre:|:ditable to have a Sister

and she

married, | she might flatter herself that ~~it had~~ | ~~been at her house, that it~~

the connection staying

had | been greatly instrumental to ~~it~~ ^ by | having Anne ~~to stay~~ with her in | the Autumn'. In print this becomes 'It was creditable to have a sister married, and she might flatter herself with having been greatly instrumental to the connexion, by keeping Anne with her in the autumn'.[74] (It is possible that this second example represents the kind of grammatical smoothing that a reader at Murray's might make.)

But the majority of the changes do not suggest authorial polish; rather, they indicate the routine readying of manuscript for publication by an external hand. Between holograph and print the text has been paragraphed—fairly mechanically, at those points where a new topic is introduced or a shift of perspective. Austen's characteristic capitalization of initial letters of proper and abstract nouns and her rhetorical dashes and emphases have also been stripped systematically. Eccentric spellings have been regularized—'beleive' becomes 'believe'—and other forms are house-styled—'connection' becomes 'connexion' and 'Good-will' becomes 'good-will'. Contractions are expanded—'&', 'c^{d}', 'tho'', 'M^{r}. E.——'—and considerable care is taken over repunctuation. For example,

holograph manuscript (erasures and line breaks are not reproduced)	printed text (1818)
M^{rs}. Clay's affections had overpowered her Interest, & she had sacrificed for the Young Man's sake, the possibility of scheming longer for Sir Walter;—she has Abilities however as well as Affections, and it is now a doubtful point whether his cunning or hers may finally carry the day, whether, after preventing her from being the wife of Sir Walter, he may not be wheedled & caressed at last into making her the wife of Sir William.—	Mrs. Clay's affections had overpowered her interest, and she had sacrificed, for the young man's sake, the possibility of scheming longer for Sir Walter. She has abilities, however, as well as affections; and it is now a doubtful point whether his cunning, or hers, may finally carry the day; whether, after preventing her from being the wife of Sir Walter, he may not be wheedled and caressed at last into making her the wife of Sir William.

[73] Egerton 3038, f. 10^{r} (30–1), and *Persuasion* (1818), ii. 299–300. In manuscript, the passage is part of the patch, fourteen lines long, pasted onto the lower part of f. 10^{r} and cancelling what was written underneath.

[74] Egerton 3038, f. 11^{v} (33), and *Persuasion* (1818), ii. 302.

She might have been absolutely rich & perfectly healthy, & yet be happy.——Her spring of Felicity was in the glow of her spirits—as her friend Anne's was in the warmth of her Heart.—Anne was Tenderness itself;—and she had the full worth of it in Captn. Wentworth's affection. His Profession was all that could ever make her friends wish that Tenderness less; the dread of a future War, all that could dim her Sunshine.——She gloried in being a Sailor's wife, but she must pay the tax of quick alarm, for belonging to that Profession which is—if possible—more distinguished in it's Domestic Virtues, than in it's National Importance.——

She might have been absolutely rich and perfectly healthy, and yet be happy. Her spring of felicity was in the glow of her spirits, as her friend Anne's was in the warmth of her heart. Anne was tenderness itself, and she had the full worth of it in Captain Wentworth's affection. His profession was all that could ever make her friends wish that tenderness less; the dread of a future war all that could dim her sunshine. She gloried in being a sailor's wife, but she must pay the tax of quick alarm for belonging to that profession which is, if possible, more distinguished in its domestic virtues than in its national importance.

These individually small but cumulatively significant changes mark a decisive shift in the ownership of the text. The supplementary dashes of the holograph manuscript after commas, semi-colons, and full stops are performative gestures which contribute to the reader's sense of the mental processes of the writer still struggling to retain control of the written words. As they cluster, disperse, and regroup these dashes, much like the shorthand contractions Austen also uses, give body to the text and contribute a visual and aural component to its meaning. The same is true of her irregular capitalization and her marked use of underlining (to denote italics), especially in the closing revelation and reconciliation between Anne and Wentworth (see Illustrations 16 and 17). In preparing the text for print these aural and visual indicators are silenced, to be replaced by a less substantive and more discreet syntactic emphasis. This is utterly routine, but it is not something Austen herself is likely to have done. She could no more have silenced her own text in this way than she could have reformed, between drafts, her eccentric spellings or taught herself a new style of punctuation.

In particular, the loss of underlining (italicization) between manuscript and print demonstrates nothing more than print's conventional suppression of rhetorical features, but in this instance, as Chapman also suggested, there is cause for regret.[75] The novel's closing scenes enact an intense drama of pose, speech, and gesture. It is difficult to believe Austen would not have wished the emotional clues of accentuation and emphasis marking the holograph manuscript to be retained. But only someone as acutely aware as the author of the dynamic process by which her words became text is likely to have caught and queried their loss at proof stage. Whether Henry Austen or some other authorial representative read proofs of *Persuasion*, it would have been in small batches, perhaps non-sequentially,[76] most certainly against the clock, and without aid of the marked-up manuscript used at the press. Neither an author nor her representative would attempt at this stage to make type-set sheets conform to manuscript. Either they would work from memory or, more likely, they would take the printed sheets on their own terms and simply correct obvious errors, address printer's questions written in the margins of the text, and query layout. Then as now, they would be discouraged from extensive (and expensive) revision; but unlike now, there would be no chance to see the work as a complete printed unit before publication. A substantial printing house would work on several jobs concurrently; no firm, large or small, would tie up its precious stock of a whole fount of type in composing an entire book at once. As Edward Bull pointed out as late as 1842, in his *Hints and Directions for Authors*:

> It is the custom of printers to send out only two or three sheets at a time to the author, and not to send more until these are corrected and worked off.... In some of the largest printing-offices, there is indeed no difficulty in getting up six, or twelve, or even more sheets set up at a time; but, in the general run of establishments, the type employed for the first three or four sheets, is often wanted for the second three, and is taken to pieces and reset, or recomposed, as soon as the author's final corrections have been attended to.[77]

The general points to note are that by proof stage there were several agents apart from the author or her representative with a vested interest in and right to determine the text; and the receipt of proofs piecemeal inevitably limited an author's control over revision and over the appearance of the printed text.

75 Chapman, 'Preface' to *The Manuscript Chapters of Persuasion*, where he writes that 'the italics of the manuscript... in the print of 1818 may have been suppressed beyond the author's intention.'

76 Though only one house was involved in each case in setting the two volumes of *Northanger Abbey* (C. Roworth) and *Persuasion* (T. Davison) this would still not ensure receipt of sequential copy.

77 Edward Bull, *Hints and Directions for Authors* (1842), 17, quoted in Dooley, *Author and Printer in Victorian England*, 16.

16. Holograph manuscript pages of *Persuasion* (MS. Egerton 3038), part of the passage added at the end of the fragment and keyed for insertion towards the close of the subsequently discarded Volume 2, Chapter 10. By kind permission of the British Library, London.

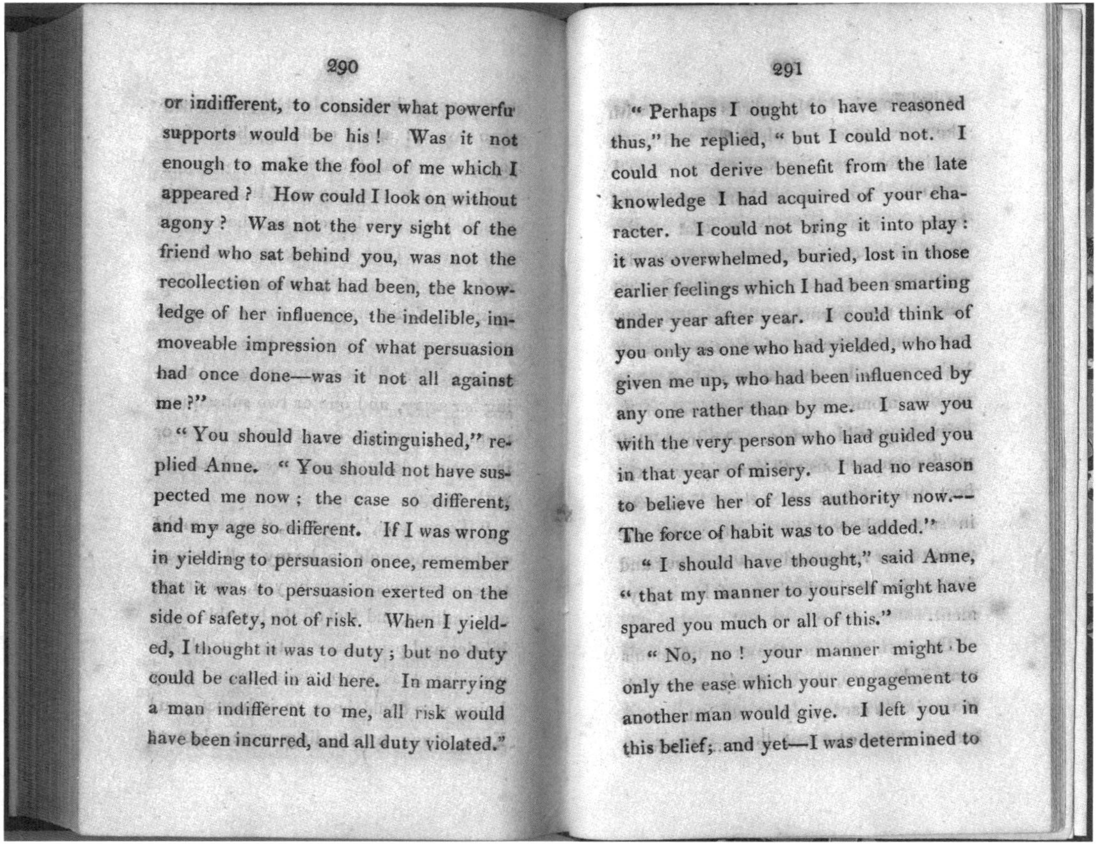

290

or indifferent, to consider what powerfu supports would be his! Was it not enough to make the fool of me which I appeared? How could I look on without agony? Was not the very sight of the friend who sat behind you, was not the recollection of what had been, the knowledge of her influence, the indelible, immoveable impression of what persuasion had once done—was it not all against me?"

"You should have distinguished," replied Anne. "You should not have suspected me now; the case so different, and my age so different. If I was wrong in yielding to persuasion once, remember that it was to persuasion exerted on the side of safety, not of risk. When I yielded, I thought it was to duty; but no duty could be called in aid here. In marrying a man indifferent to me, all risk would have been incurred, and all duty violated."

291

"Perhaps I ought to have reasoned thus," he replied, "but I could not. I could not derive benefit from the late knowledge I had acquired of your character. I could not bring it into play: it was overwhelmed, buried, lost in those earlier feelings which I had been smarting under year after year. I could think of you only as one who had yielded, who had given me up, who had been influenced by any one rather than by me. I saw you with the very person who had guided you in that year of misery. I had no reason to believe her of less authority now.— The force of habit was to be added."

"I should have thought," said Anne, "that my manner to yourself might have spared you much or all of this."

"No, no! your manner might be only the ease which your engagement to another man would give. I left you in this belief; and yet—I was determined to

17. The same passage as it appeared in print in the substituted text of *Persuasion*, 1818, Volume 2, Chapter 11. By kind permission of the English Faculty Library, Oxford University.

In the case of those novels she did see through the press, Austen's first comprehensive reading in print would only be when copies arrived on publication. This explains why some things in the appearance of the printed text struck her as odd or unsatisfactory only at this late stage. There are her comments in her letter of 29 January 1813 to Cassandra on the newly arrived *Pride and Prejudice*: 'There are a few Typical [typographical] errors—& a "said he" or a "said she" would sometimes make the Dialogue more immediately clear . . . The 2^{d} vol. is shorter than I c^{d} wish—but the difference is not so much in reality as in look, there being a larger proportion of Narrative in that part.'[78] It may also explain why she did not catch the inconsistent spelling of the names of certain characters: for example, the butler in *Mansfield Park*, who is Baddeley at Volume 2, Chapter 1 and Volume 3, Chapter 1, but Baddely at Volume 3, Chapter 3. We know from her description of reading *Emma* in proof that the printing house of Charles Roworth, responsible for setting Volumes 1 and 2 in type, sent three sheets for correction on 24 November 1815, and that in the evening of the same day she received a further sheet. Since the novel was published in duodecimo, each sheet was presumably composed of 24 printed pages. At this stage she was proofing sheets from all three volumes concurrently, informing Cassandra that '1st & 3^{d} vol. are now at 144.—2^{d} at 48.' (That is, she has seen six sheets of Volumes 1 and 3 and two sheets of Volume 2.) Volume 3 was being printed by John Moyes, and two days later, the printers continuing 'to supply me very well', she responded to a query in the margin of one of Moyes's sheets, on her idiomatic spelling '*arra*-root'. It is clear from the letter of 24 November that after she corrected the sheets they were not returned direct to the two printing houses but to Murray's for further inspection.[79] We have no information to suggest she saw author's revises—that is, a second set of corrected proofs. She would presumably take it on trust that her corrections would be made.

With printing distributed between two houses, as was the case with the first editions of *Pride and Prejudice*, *Mansfield Park*, and *Emma*, a three-volume novel could be set in type and published in as little as eight weeks from receipt of manuscript. In the case of the second edition of *Mansfield Park*, each of the three volumes went to a different house for printing, but here it was an easier task for printers working from a marked up copy of the first edition and not from manuscript. The interval between the arrival of a manuscript in the printing house and author's receipt of the first batch of proofs might be as

[78] *Jane Austen's Letters*, 201–2. [79] Ibid., 298–300.

little as a few days; and after that sheets could be expected on a daily basis, with considerable pressure to return them at the same pace. This timescale seems to fit with Austen's habit of staying in London during a great part of the production process.[80]

Persuasion is Austen's *Winter's Tale*, an impossible romance of dead love revived, of second chances against all the odds. Though not probable in substance, it must in the emotional resolution feel utterly satisfactory. The first attempt at an ending gathers up the action in the prompt dispatch of stage comedy, traces of which remain in the printed text. The sly comment in the final chapter 'and if they could but keep Captain Wentworth from being made a baronet' appeared in the holograph manuscript as 'and if they could | but keep Capt. W—— from being | ~~Knighted~~ made a Baronet', and shows how early established and calculated was the comic threat to discomfort Sir Walter. But in general the broad farce of the first ending is removed. In that earlier version the pace was swift and the action spare: a small cast of characters assuming stock stage roles—Admiral and Mrs Croft as the old married couple, Anne and Captain Wentworth as the young lovers—some off-stage business with a mantuamaker and an errand to the post office, some loud whispers behind a door, a misunderstanding over an engagement to marry and a property lease, the lovers left alone, a little hesitation, a few nervous words, a penetrating glance, the blood coming and going in Wentworth's face, a rapid unravelling of the mistake, and the present falls away, the past is restored.

[80] For conventions of proofing, see Stower, *The Printer's Grammar*, 395–6; and Hansard, *Typographia*, 747. Both emphasize the need for speed and minimal correction on the author's part. From some time in March to May 1811 Austen was in London correcting proofs of *Sense and Sensibility* (advertised for publication on 30 October); in a letter of 25 April 1811 to Cassandra, she describes having received 'two sheets to correct' (*Jane Austen's Letters*, 182). From 1 March to some time in April 1814 she was again in London seeing *Mansfield Park* through the press (published 9 May); from early October to mid-December 1815 she was nursing her brother Henry and seeing *Emma* (published 16 December) and a revised edition of *Mansfield Park* (published February 1816) through the press. It would not have been difficult to get 1,250 copies (the estimated run of the first edition of *Mansfield Park*) of a three-volume novel printed and ready for publication in two months, especially divided between two printers. Walter Scott's *Guy Mannering* (1815) was written and published within an eight-week period in an edition of 2,000 copies. Of course, James Ballantyne, Scott's printer, had an unusually large number of presses and Scott's second novel was a high priority; but the record for that period shows that Ballantyne was also turning out other materials and that *Guy Mannering* was effectively squeezed in. (For information, see *Guy Mannering*, ed. Peter Garside (Edinburgh: Edinburgh University Press, 1999), 357 ff.) The unusual delay in publishing *Sense and Sensibility* after setting in print might be explained by the fact that it just missed the end of the spring season, the summer being generally considered the dead period for sales of fiction.

He was a moment | silent.—She turned her eyes towards him | for the first time since his re-entering | the room. His colour was varying—| & he was looking at her
Power
with all the | ~~brilliancy~~ & Keenness, which she be: | :leived no other eyes than his ~~could~~ |
possessed
~~command~~.—"No Truth in any such | report!—he repeated.—No Truth in | any part of
enjoying releif
it?"—"None."—He had | been standing by a chair—~~feeling~~ the | ~~comfort~~ of leaning
or &
on it— ^ of playing | with it;—he now sat down—drew it | a little nearer to her— ^ looked, with an | expression which had something more | than penetration in it, something | softer;—Her Countenance did not || discourage.—It was a silent, but a very | powerful Dialogue;—on his side, Suppli: | :cation, on her's acceptance.—Still, a | little nearer—and a hand taken and | pressed—and "Anne, my own dear | Anne!"—bursting forth in the fullness | of exquisite feeling—and all ~~was~~ | Suspense & Indecision were over —. | They were re-united. They were restored | to all that had been lost. They were | carried back to the past, with only an | increase of attachment & confidence, & | only such a flutter of present Delight | as made them little fit for the | interruption of M^{rs}. Croft, when she | joined them not long afterwards.—[81]

The scene is tightly structured and well directed. The mute and spoken dialogue are accomplished and in their way satisfying, a way that draws deftly upon the stage use of gestures and props for the facial expressions of the lovers and the business with the chair. It makes a creditable piece of theatre. But though this earlier ending answers the needs of the narrative at this point, it does not resolve the novel thematically nor accord with its deeper logic. In particular, it does not address or begin to match, in its sudden emotional reversal, the deep undertow of feeling which has been building through the work. To achieve this more complicated and satisfying thematic resolution something more diffused was needed. This issue of structural repair gives the fragment a different status as discarded draft from the unfinished manuscripts of *The Watsons* or *Sanditon*.

The substituted Chapters 10 and 11 are also dramatically crafted, but theirs is a drama of indirection. A wider cast of characters extends by parallel and echo or by contrast the rediscovered love of Anne and Wentworth until that love encompasses a more general study of the whole nature of love between men and women. Revision gives two chapters for one and at their kernel, now transposed to Chapter 11, the passage arrived at in the third attempt to resolve

[81] Egerton 3038, f. 5^v–6^r (15–16).

the old Chapter 10.[82] It is attractive to think that this passage, in which Anne and Wentworth do more than recover old love, was the prompt to unlock the new ending. In reviewing the rights and wrongs of *Persuasion* and *Duty* the fictional future is born from the past by a process which is psychologically and morally satisfying. To discover a new ending that resonates so well with the novel's larger structure, did Austen work forwards and back from this particular piece of rewriting? We cannot know, but it is noteworthy how much of the satisfaction of the printed ending, and notably its restored elegiac strain, derives from its thematic concentration on revision—literally seeing again. It is peculiarly the case in this intense novel that the kinds of anticipation and retrospection that mark all acts of writing and rewriting also drive through and determine the narrative's emotional logic. It also explains why Wentworth's act of writing, the dropped pen, and the device of the letter hidden beneath the scattered paper work so well.[83] In these devices we sense a linked thematic and somatic recovery of rhythm that accounts for the almost unbearable tension of the printed ending.

The curtain-call of characters who turn up at the White Hart—the Musgroves and Captain Harville, and even Sir Walter and Elizabeth Elliot—relocates to Bath a whole set of Anne's acquaintance, though curiously Admiral Croft, the linchpin of the earlier ending, disappears totally, and there is no attempt to bring off the difficult encounter between Wentworth and Lady Russell. As the narrator herself observes of the new setting, 'A large party in an hotel ensured a quick-changing, unsettled scene.'[84] External bustle, kept off-stage in the earlier ending, now assumes centre stage and becomes the cover under which emotional revelations can unfold at a more varied pace. More particularly, the unsettled scene of the White Hart reintroduces several characters whose minor stories reprise the relationship of Anne and Wentworth. The projected marriage of Henrietta Musgrove to Charles Hayter anticipates a different resolution to the dilemma of young, penniless love; Wentworth's commission to have the miniature of Captain Benwick reset rehearses the subject of old and new love and in leading Anne and Captain Harville to speak of the relative constancy of men's and women's feelings tests the strength of the narrative's oldest love. In contrast to the open declaration of the draft ending, it is a feature of the printed ending that the restoration of love to Anne and Wentworth is underpinned by this layered indirection.

[82] See n. 58 above. [83] *Persuasion*, ed. Beer, 208. [84] Ibid., 194.

But here we come up against a huge puzzle in understanding how Jane Austen worked. How could such an integrated, deeply satisfying ending as the revised and printed conclusion have been arrived at by chance? How is it that it was not, in idea though not in detail, part of the plan for the novel from the start? Surely the shift in tone between the two endings from broad comedy to elegy suggests a deep, if temporary, loss of command over the material? In a novel where so much hangs upon returning, remembering, and seeing again, it is extraordinary to realize that careful structural planning was not part of the novelist's programme and that she reached the revised ending apparently by accident. The fragment of *Persuasion* may offer the surest proof that Austen was a supremely and recklessly immanent writer whose intuitive grasp in this instance briefly but massively failed her; or it may be unrepresentative and already marked by the illness soon to overwhelm her. Even with the closer-grained printed ending, there is still something rushed and unsatisfactory about this truncated novel—a feeling that the plot has been unravelled too hurriedly and characters in consequence short-changed. We sense this in the way Mrs Smith is hustled into prominence: for at least two days, before the writing of the second draft ending, Mrs Smith even upstages Anne Wentworth in the novel's final lines. The crudeness of Mr Elliot's motives in wishing to marry Anne in order to keep Sir Walter single remains a more lasting blemish. There is something at fault here more than Austen's usual impatience with the business of winding up her story. Are these structural defects signs of the exhaustion which would leave the *Sanditon* fragment a brilliant but largely directionless study?

Sanditon

By the simple fact of its existence as working copy for a substantial and evolving narrative, *Sanditon* is set apart from the six printed novels; unlike the abandoned draft of *The Watsons*, all that seems to have interrupted its progress were preparations for death. The holograph manuscript is contained in three small bundles of ordinary writing paper, cut down and folded to form three booklets, the third being smaller in size but also thicker than the first and second, which are roughly similar. All three were given stout paper fascicled bindings and newly stitched through the centrefold in the late twentieth century, but when Chapman inspected them in the mid-1920s only the first and second seem to have shown signs of original sewing.

Their appearance now of three home-made paper pamphlets provides a thin material echo of the three handsome, commercially manufactured volumes which contain the juvenilia.

Booklets 1 and 2 are of wove paper, with the watermark Kent 1812, and measure the same as the booklets in which *The Watsons* is written, approximately 19 × 12 cm (7.5 × 4.75 inches), suggesting that they were made in much the same way by cutting down sheets of 'post' writing paper, 38.5 × 48 cm (15.25 × 19 inches), to form quires or basic units of up to 8 leaves (16 pages) which could then be assembled inside one another to make fatter booklets. Booklet 3 measures 16.2 × 10 cm (6.4 × 4 inches) (again approximately) and is of laid paper, watermarked Joseph Coles 1815. Booklet 1 consists of 16 leaves or 32 pages of closely written text, and comprises Chapters 1 to 3. Booklet 2 contains 24 leaves or 48 pages, again closely written, comprising Chapters 4 to 8 and the opening pages of Chapter 9. Booklet 3 is considerably fatter, containing 40 leaves or 80 pages, and consists of the bulk of Chapter 9, Chapters 10, 11, and the incomplete Chapter 12 with which the fragment ends. Although some contrivance is used to make Booklet 1 contain the first three chapters (the last few words of Chapter 3—'~~she was become~~ that Loveliness was | complete.—' being inserted at the foot of page 1), Booklet 2 ends mid-sentence, with a half-line of writing and room to spare ('She desired | her best Love, [Booklet 2 ends] [Booklet 3 begins] with a thousand regrets at ~~her~~ being so | poor a Creature'). Booklet 3 ends with one completed line of writing at the top of f. 20^{v}, exactly mid-way through, and the remaining 40 pages are blank.

All three booklets are unpaginated, in keeping with *The Watsons* and the draft of *Persuasion*, and all three are closely written in a clear, neat, and controlled hand with no sign of the physical deterioration that James Edward Austen-Leigh detected in the fragment's abrupt cessation. If anything, the hand is tighter in Booklet 3 and the letters more carefully formed, which is probably simply explained by the effort of writing on even smaller sheets. All the paper is small and fits the evidence of *The Watsons* and *Persuasion* as well as family tradition that small sheets were used because more easily secreted ('put away, or covered with a piece of blotting paper') from prying eyes. As with the manuscript of *The Watsons*, modest size also suggests portability, bundles of paper folded and stitched into booklets implying a self-sustaining work surface to be written on at desk or table or elsewhere. Above all, these are highly focused sites of composition, already novelistic in physical form, and intimating a disciplined and thrifty use of drafting with only limited expectation of or scope for rewriting—in other words, the surface of a confidently immanent writer. It is tempting to see in these densely written booklets the physical correlatives for Austen's village portraits, 'the little bit (two Inches wide) of Ivory on which I work with so fine a Brush, as produces little effect after much labour'.[85]

Austen's hand dates the writing of the draft at three points: in the top left-hand corner of the first page of Booklet 1 is written 'Jan. 27.—1817'; Booklet 3 is similarly inscribed on its opening page 'March 1st'; while f. 20v has written below its one line of text 'March 18'. No date marks the beginning of Booklet 2, while the significance of the dating of 1 and 3 seems to be enforced by a bold 1, surrounded by a semi-circle above the first line of writing in Booklet 1 and a similarly placed 2 in Booklet 3. Curiously out by one day, Austen-Leigh casts a melodramatic light over this chronology, writing: 'March 17th is the last date to be found in the manuscript on which she was engaged; and as the watch of the drowned man indicates the time of his death, so does this final date seem to fix the period when her mind could no longer pursue its accustomed course.' His affecting description of the 'latter pages', some of which 'seem to have been first traced in pencil, probably when she was too weak to sit long at a desk, and written over in ink afterwards' is not, however, borne out by the evidence.[86] Only parts of f. 19 in Booklet 2 (amounting to no more than 31 lines) were first written in pencil, to be traced over subsequently in ink (the effort of tracing causing a slight shake in the hand at that point). This represents a short passage in Chapter 7 (from 'cried Lady D—| And if we cd. but get a young Heiress to S! | But Heiresses are monstrous scarce!' to '["]I have Miss Clara with me now, which | makes a great difference." She spoke this | so seriously that Charlotte'); both its position in relation to the rest of the manuscript and its brevity suggest nothing more than that it was perhaps inconvenient at that

[85] The holograph manuscript of *Sanditon* is in the possession of King's College, Cambridge. Although its division into three booklets is original, at some later stage the booklets were stitched into paper bindings. King's College has no record of conservation work on the manuscript earlier than 1993 when minor changes were made to the outer covers to correct the misnumbering of the booklets. (Information from Melvin Jefferson, Senior Conservator, Cambridge College Libraries Conservation Consortium.) Further information is taken from R. W. Chapman, 'Preface', *Fragment of a Novel written by Jane Austen, January–March 1817* (Oxford: Clarendon Press, 1925); from Gilson F6; and from K. E. Attar, 'Jane Austen at King's College, Cambridge', 197–221. The family tradition that Austen used small sheets of paper in order to hide her work from the eyes of visitors is recorded by her nephew in *Memoir*, 81; see too Park Honan, *Jane Austen: Her Life*, 352, for a sensitive assessment of the physical evidence of the manuscript. Austen's own famous description of her work as a miniaturist on ivory is in a letter to the young Austen-Leigh, *Jane Austen's Letters*, 323.

[86] *Memoir*, 127; and *Memoir* (1871), 181.

moment to use a pen.[87] The manuscript continues thereafter in ink and in a steady hand for a further 50 pages. In all it totals 120 pages, with between 20 and 28 lines per page, depending on the size and openness of the hand—about 24,000 words, and perhaps one-fifth of a completed novel.

When Chapman transcribed the manuscript it was still in family ownership. In the division at Cassandra's death, it had passed to Austen's niece Anna Lefroy. Either Austen-Leigh, her half-brother, worked directly with the autograph copy when he provided quotations from and a précis of 'the last work', as he portentously called it, in the second edition of his *Memoir* (1871), or Anna, more expert as to its contents, supplied an account. This was the first public mention of the unfinished novel. The manuscript itself is untitled, and 'Sanditon' was an unofficial title in use within the family at least from the mid-nineteenth century. From Anna Lefroy it passed down through the Lefroys to Mary Isabella Lefroy, daughter of George Benjamin Lefroy and Anna's granddaughter, and so Jane's great-great niece. She presented it to King's College, Cambridge, in October 1930, in memory, as she told Chapman at the time, 'of my sister, & brother in law she the gt gt niece of "Jane" & he the gt nephew, & the most popular Provost, & Provostess "Kings" has ever had.'[88] Isabel, as she was known, refers here to her sister Florence Emma and Florence's husband Augustus Austen-Leigh, Provost of the College, 1889–1905, and a son of James Edward, the biographer. Despite this reconnection in marriage of the Austen-Leighs and Lefroys, Augustus's brother and nephew do not seem to have consulted the manuscript for their expanded family biography of 1913, which repeats the *Memoir*'s brief description along with its errors. Another copy of the manuscript, made by Cassandra, had a different descent, passing down through Jane's brother Frank's family—to Janet Austen, later Sanders, eldest daughter of Frank's fifth son, Edward Thomas Austen. It was from her father that Mrs Sanders got the information, which she communicated to Chapman in February 1925 after the publication of his transcription, that Austen's intended title was 'The Brothers'. Cassandra's copy of the manuscript, also untitled, is now in Jane Austen's House, Chawton.[89]

[87] In Chapman's transcription, *Fragment of a Novel* (1925), the passage occurs at 99–101. There is a paginated facsimile of the manuscript, *Sanditon: An Unfinished Novel*, with an introduction by Brian Southam (Oxford: Clarendon Press, London: Scolar Press, 1975). It is possible (just) to see the pencilled outlines, at 69–70.

[88] In a letter of 28 October [1930], kept with the *Sanditon* MS. in King's College, Cambridge. For Anna Lefroy's close familiarity with the *Sanditon* manuscript and her attempt to finish it, see Ch. 4, 'Continuations'.

[89] In a letter of 8 February 1925, kept with the *Sanditon* MS. in King's College, Cambridge. Janet Sanders published this family tradition in 'Sanditon', *Times Literary Supplement*, 19 February 1925, 120. For Cassandra Austen's copy, see Ch. 4, 'Continuations'.

The holograph manuscript is a working draft, in which long passages of smooth flowing, uncorrected or minimally corrected prose are interspersed with more densely worked and reworked sections. In appearance it shares many features with the holograph manuscripts of *The Watsons* and *Persuasion*, suggesting that Austen's habits in composition remained fairly constant over the period 1804–17. There are no white margins and none of the regular blank spaces which characterize the working manuscripts of some writers; every page is filled, implying that no large-scale revision of the draft in this form was contemplated. While the alteration of a single word or phrase may provide no insight into a wider method, the relation of revised to unrevised sections and the kinds of changes made nevertheless offer important clues to how Austen worked in this her last novel. In terms of modern conventions of preparing a manuscript for other eyes, it may seem far from finished; the absence of paragraphing and the frequent recourse to abbreviation ('B^{r}' for Brother, 'c^{d}' for could, 'S' for Sandition) reveal how far this is from a faircopy in the style of *Lady Susan*. But in presentation the *Sanditon* holograph is not dissimilar to the unrevised chapters of *Persuasion*, which were probably extracted at a late stage from a manuscript ready for the press.

Yet in its unmediated state as manuscript, or as the printed transcription of manuscript (which is the form in which we most often encounter it), the *Sanditon* fragment reads quite differently from a classic Jane Austen novel; and in view of its poignant history it is tempting to interpret every aspect of this difference as particular rather than as evidence of a routine stage of writing. The concision and impetus that verbal expansion and paragraphing, the print stage, properly thwart meet no resistance from *Sanditon*'s unbroken manuscript surface. The narrative is delivered as a raw, uninterrupted sequence with its own special energy. The effect on the reader of this unpunctured momentum is much the same as can be achieved in painting by the loss of foregrounding and background. Without perspective, there is no assumption of a centre or single point for which the visual field is arranged. In narrative time, as opposed to pictorial space, the consequence is experience conveyed in impressionistic and abstract rather than defined and psychological form. In the case of the *Sanditon* fragment, not only is this a direct consequence of those scholarly protocols which demand that our print encounter with manuscript be constrained by as little editorial normalizing as possible—print which is not print but the imitative trace of script—it is also a further development of the emotional and asyndetic compression that characterized *Persuasion*. The challenge posed therefore by the accidental identity of the *Sanditon* text with its manuscript state is to distinguish usual physical disorder from those other elements that point to a new expressive energy and stylistic difference. In short, and somewhat confusingly, *Sanditon* is both more like and less like the classic printed novels than we might initially think.

The experiment was already taking shape in *Persuasion* by which fully textualized passages are exchanged for others marked by heavy ellipsis to deliver events in a rhythm mimetically suited to the rush of emotion and change of perception they both depict and induce. The single paragraph outlining the terrible event on the Cobb works in this way:

> There was too much wind to make the high part of the new Cobb pleasant for the ladies, and they agreed to get down the steps to the lower, and all were contented to pass quietly and carefully down the steep flight, excepting Louisa; she must be jumped down them by Captain Wentworth. In all their walks, he had had to jump her from the stiles; the sensation was delightful to her. The hardness of the pavement for her feet, made him less willing upon the present occasion; he did it, however; she was safely down, and instantly, to shew her enjoyment, ran up the steps to be jumped down again. He advised her against it, thought the jar too great; but no, he reasoned and talked in vain; she smiled and said, "I am determined I will:" he put out his hands; she was too precipitate by half a second, she fell on the pavement on the Lower Cobb, and was taken up lifeless![90]

The paratactic looseness of the passage reads like a sequence of notes for a scene before the imposition of subordination. It provides a structure in which changes in tempo can be dizzyingly swift (the fateful movement of verb tenses from 'he had had to' to 'I am determined I will'), the shortened clause structure and the abandoned conjunction registering palpably and immediately the mounting, bewildering pace and change of events and the breathless shock of their outcome. The effect is a syntactic and emotional pile-up, raw, unfinished, and energetic, as befits a crisis too dreadful to be easily assimilated. It is also the dissolution of style, its decomposition into the jottings and memoranda that precede writing. That, of course, is the problem and the puzzle that the late writing sets us.

The conventional reading of Austen's progress as novelist and social commentator records how she discarded the monologizing epistolary and dramatic modes of her early writings and moved towards perfecting a form in which language's implied contract of commitment and affinity between

[90] *Persuasion*, ed. Beer, 98.

people is seemingly strengthened and subtly probed. The hybrid idiom of free indirect discourse, her particular contribution to the development of the English novel, allowed her to write at the same time from within and from without a character, and to merge characters, often to disconcerting effect in the consequent parodic or slightly surreal encounter of simultaneous animation and commentary—of speaking and being seen to speak. In the mature novels such conversability becomes a shrewd statement on the gravitational pull towards consensus within language and on the ways in which we comply with and evade it. An older criticism figured this in moral and disciplinary terms, as the interdependence of self-understanding and social knowledge in the maturing heroine; Austen's early readers frequently claimed to recognize known acquaintances in her characters. At the other extreme, in the late twentieth century, computational analysis (the Oxford Concordance Package at work on machine-readable texts) allowed John Burrows to quantify precisely the far greater part played by free indirect discourse in the later novels as a proportion of the whole narrative and in relation to spoken dialogue. Burrows's term for free indirect discourse is 'character narrative', and he lays stress on its ever more sophisticated deployment as a language of interiorization, whose concealments imply a withdrawal from social consensus and an oppositional trajectory of individual development. If, as it has been argued, the literary explosion of the period 1780–1830 needs to be understood in terms of writing's overwhelming encroachment at this time on the powers of speech—in particular, writing's capacity to reproduce conversation—then Austen's novels, an ongoing experiment to test conversation's limits, are the most subtle manifestation of this intrusion.[91]

After the close accommodation between pure narrative and character narrative that marks *Persuasion*, *Sanditon*'s change of direction comes as a shock. Among the family and early critics it was assumed that the fragment was no more than a rudimentary first draft, largely on the grounds that it did not continue the steady work of interiorization of the other mature novels. On Burrows's reckoning, *Sanditon* 'includes only 1211 words of character narrative'; disconcertingly for the reader who comes from reading *Mansfield*

[91] The emphasis on Austen's moral vision informs much major twentieth-century criticism, from that of F. R. Leavis (*The Great Tradition* (1948)) and Lionel Trilling (*The Opposing Self* (1955)) to Jan Fergus (*Jane Austen and the Didactic Novel* (1983)) and philosophical studies like Alasdair MacIntyre's (*After Virtue: A Study in Moral Theory* (1981)). J. F. Burrows, *Computation into Criticism: A Study of Jane Austen's Novels and an Experiment in Method* (Oxford: Clarendon Press, 1987), 165–7. On the importance of the conversational element in literature in the period, see Clifford Siskin, *The Work of Writing: Literature and Social Change in Britain, 1700–1830* (Baltimore and London: Johns Hopkins University Press, 1998), 165.

Park or *Emma*, there is no comparable merging of the narrator's voice with that of a central female character.[92] Those who assume that *Sanditon*'s Charlotte Heywood would have developed into a familiar kind of mature Austen heroine should consider the almost equal division of the narrative's small use of free indirect discourse between Charlotte and Mr Parker, one of its leading eccentrics. Austen-Leigh's solution to how to represent the fragment to the wider public in 1871 was to turn the bulk, apart from a few chosen extracts, into a form of editorially adduced indirect discourse, while Chapman, one of the few to study the manuscript closely, felt sure (following a hint from Anna Lefroy) that Austen would have toned down the caricatures of Mr Parker, his sister Diana, Lady Denham, and Sir Edward: 'she would have smoothed these coarse strokes, so strikingly different from the mellow pencillings of *Persuasion*.'[93]

The reluctance of an earlier age at witnessing the dying novelist in an undecorous state of stylistic undress ('[*Sanditon*] contains some promising sketches; but it would be useless, if not impertinent, to pass an opinion on a work so obviously incomplete') has recently been repackaged as high camp titillation and a celebration of Austen's liminal art of the erotic. By this reading *Sanditon* becomes a full-blown seaside gothic extravaganza, in which Lady Denham, land speculator and elderly widowed proprietor of Sanditon House, figures as 'Austen's prototypical[*sic*] rich lesbian vampire'. No discreet critical silence here. Occupying neither the extreme of gallantry nor of sensationalism, Tony Tanner's remarkable critical reading of the mid-1980s described a work whose partial state gestures to a radically changed social vision. 'This is not mere burlesque', Tanner wrote; 'She is writing herself out of the world she is writing about.'[94] This range of interpretation—greater than for any of the finished novels—is testimony to the imaginative power of fragments, writings severed or released from context, and suggests

[92] Burrows, *Computation into Criticism*, 169. A contrary view is expressed in Southam, *Jane Austen's Literary Manuscripts*, where he describes Charlotte Heywood's 'as the point of view through which much of the action is observed' (112); in Southam's reading both Mr Parker and Charlotte Heywood assume greater authorial complicity, in the adaptation of reported speech to the 'living voice' (128–9). Perhaps the most interesting point to be drawn from this discrepancy is that Austen's subtly attenuated prose can bear such different apportioning of its effects between character and narrative voices.

[93] Chapman, *Facts and Problems*, 208; Anna Lefroy had written of the eccentrics to Austen-Leigh on 8 August 1862, when publication was first mooted, 'I think those parts ought to be a good deal trimmed, & softened down' (HRO, MS. 23M93/86/3c, item 118).

[94] The various interpretations of *Sanditon* are provided by Francis Warre Cornish, *Jane Austen*, 'English Men of Letters' series (London: Macmillan, 1913), 231; Clara Tuite, *Romantic Austen: Sexual Politics and the Literary Canon* (Cambridge: Cambridge University Press, 2002), 174; and Tony Tanner, *Jane Austen* (Basingstoke and London: Macmillan, 1986), 284.

that Austen's final enigmatic fragment should be up there with other famously unfinished Romantic works—Coleridge's 'Kubla Khan' and Keats's two 'Hyperion' poems.

Among the mature novels *Sanditon* travels a reverse trajectory which troubled its early readers and still manages to startle and disquiet. A study, by a dying woman, of people who imagine they are ill, and of restless activity (Austen used and erased the phrase 'the disease of activity' in Chapter 10) by one who, on her own admission, could scarcely get about unaided during its composition, it challenges both the course of her life and the usual course of her fictions—towards probability and verisimilitude. Instead, this unfinished fragment seems to recall the spirit of the early, finished fragments of juvenile burlesque. Once again, Jane Austen is engaged in imagining not how we are but how we imagine how we are: she is imagining imagining. Where the mature novels have won appreciation for their naturalism, *Sanditon* defies nature. Yet, in the same spirit by which we say that death is the great event of life, it has been all too tempting to tighten the biographical constraints around a work which seems flatly to deny that it is written from life. As somatic witness, the manuscript has a special part to play in this.

The disposition on paper of first and second (occasionally third) attempts at a word, phrase, or longer passage and the tendency where revision is heaviest for second or third thoughts to lead directly into passages of uncorrected text—into first thoughts—suggests that most of the reworking was continuous with, or barely divisible from, first writing, with no evidence of particular portions of the manuscript being set aside and reworked at a later stage. A good example of Austen's general method can be found in Chapter 10, in a passage which introduces Charlotte Heywood to Arthur Parker:

some removals to look
—When they | were all finally seated, after ~~looking~~ ^ | ^ at the Sea & the Hotel, Charlotte's
next
place | was by Arthur, who was sitting close | to the Fire with a degree of Enjoyment |
civility in wishing her to take his
which gave a good deal of merit to | his ~~polite civil offer offering her his own~~ | Chair.—
There was nothing dubious in || her manner of declining it, & he sat down | again with
much his Person as
~~great~~ satisfaction. She | drew back her Chair to have all the ad: | :vantage of ~~him for~~ ^ a
Screen, & was | very thankful for every inch of Back & | Shoulders beyond her pre-
Arthur was heavy in Eye as well as figure, but by no means
conceived idea. | ~~He had in every respect a heavy Look.—~~ | ~~Yet was not~~ indisposed to

cheifly he
talk;—and | while the other 4 were ~~very much~~ | engaged together, ^ evidently felt it no |
~~well good agreable~~ — a fine young Woman
penance to have ^ ~~a good-looking Girl~~ | ^ next to him, requiring in common | Politeness
~~gr~~ decided
some attention—as his B^r^., | ~~observed with much pleasure~~ who felt | the ~~great~~ want of
Powerful object him
some motive for action, | ~~of~~ some~~thing source~~ of animation for ~~Arthur~~, | observed with ~~no~~
~~in~~considerable pleasure.—| Such was the influence of Youth & Bloom | that he
began even to make
^ ~~made~~ a sort of apology for having | a Fire.[95]

The pattern of erasures and substitutions suggests speed, instinct, and economy, by which the half-formed 'polite' becomes 'civil offer', to be replaced by the fully formed phrase 'offering her his own Chair', while the finished phrase, inserted above the line, 'civility in wishing her to take his [Chair]', leaves only the word 'Chair' uncorrected but at the same time recycles earlier ingredients. The substituted 'Arthur was heavy in Eye as well as figure' is a less spontaneous reworking but one that tightens the play of meaning through the passage in its consciously metaphoric extension of Arthur's broad physical frame; it was clearly fully fashioned before it reached paper. The evolution of the phrase 'a good-looking Girl' into 'a fine young Woman' is likewise more calculated in its transference of emphasis from Charlotte's physical attractiveness to a set of qualities which indicate a wider range of well-being. Other alterations show an initial statement becoming more complexly subordinated in the process of writing, as when 'his B^r^. observed with much pleasure' is written and immediately erased and qualified by the explanatory 'who felt the great want of some motive for action . . . observed'.

Elsewhere, rewriting is heaviest in those passages offered in the narrative voice, while the speaking voices of the various characters flow in most cases more freely—something which may point to a general characteristic of Austen's method of composition. Some passages of intense reworking occur where we would expect to find them: the opening section of the narrative with its precise attention to scene-setting culminating in the overturning of the carriage; and the late description of the approach to Sanditon House in Chapter 12, a passage reworked with keen attention to the placing of natural, architectural, and human phenomena.

[95] *Sanditon*, Booklet 3, f. 8^r^–8^v^ (136–7). Reference is to the holograph manuscript followed, in brackets, by the appropriate pages in Chapman's transcription, *Fragment of a Novel* (1925).

Evidence of heavier revision in those passages which anticipate the entrance of Sidney Parker, and in those few scenes in which the narrative voice converges with Charlotte Heywood's, is less expected, suggests some anxiety about how to use these two characters, and is therefore of particular interest in speculating on how the story might have developed. Belonging more to her usual method of character development, Charlotte and Sidney submit the narrative to probability tests which often restrain its freer development. This may account for the higher levels of revision associated with their portrayal. For example, the passage in Chapter 4 in which Mr Parker first draws the outline of his brother Sidney's character is considerably reworked, and the disposition of deletions, substitutions, and new material shows the dynamic interrelation of processes of correction and creation. In the following transcription I try to disentangle these processes, suggesting an order in which the writing evolved, as stages 1, 2, and 3, in what was a single act of writing:

1. ["]There—now the old House | is quite ~~out of~~ left behind.—What is it, your | Brother

1. Sidney says about its' being a Hospital?" | "Oh! my dear Mary, merely a Joke of his. |

[later addition] He pretends to advise me to make a Hospital of it. |

He pretends to laugh at my Improvements. |

1. Sidney says any thing you know. He has | always said what he chose ~~of his eldest~~ |

2. Most Families have such a member among

1. B^{r}~~. & to his Eldest~~ B^{r} ~~&~~ of & to us, all. | ~~A young Man of Abilities & Address, &~~ |

3. privileged by superior abilities or spirits

2. them I beleive Miss Heywood.—There is a | 2. someone in most families ~~who is privileged~~ |

1. ~~general ease of manner Miss H.—who says~~ | ~~anything~~ ^

3. In ours, it is Sidney; who is a and with great powers of pleasing.—

2. to say anything.— ~~Sidney is~~ ^ very clever | young Man,— ^ ~~very lively, very pleasant~~ |

3. He lives too to be settled; that is his only fault. ~~I wish we may~~

2. ~~living very~~ much in the World ~~& liked~~ | ~~by every body. I should~~ |

3. He is here & there & every where. I wish we may | | get him to Sanditon.["][96]

A passage of intense reworking in Chapter 7 finds Charlotte struggling to extricate her new understanding of Lady Denham's calculated meanness from her earlier more favourable impressions and from her continuing good opinion of Mr Parker, whose capacity for indiscriminate activity, optimism, and psychological obtuseness now presents itself to her in a starker critical light. Though it cuts a clear path through the moral maze, Charlotte's dogmatic assertion reads like copybook moralism and, at this stage in the narrative, seems too apposite in its determination. One senses that her clarity

[96] *Sanditon*, Booklet 2, f. 3^{r}–3^{v} (49–50).

is a consequence of the loss of subtle conspiracy between heroine and narrator; that they do not inhabit the same sphere of reflection:

but
She could not carry her | forbearance farther; ~~&~~ without attempting to |
& only conscious that Lady D. was still talking
listen longer, ~~while Lady D. still talked~~ on in | the same way, allowed her Thoughts to
thoroughly mean.
form || themselves into such a meditation as | this.—"She is ~~much worse than I~~
I had not expected any thing so bad.
~~expected~~ —| ~~meaner—a great deal meaner. She is~~ | ~~very mean~~.—M^{r}. P. spoke too
mildly of | her.~~—His own kind Disposition makes him~~ | ~~judge too well of others.~~ His
~~always~~
Judgement is | evidently not ^ to be trusted. ~~in his opinion of~~ | ~~others~~.—His own

Goodnature misleads him ~~in~~ | ~~judging of others~~. He is too kind hearted to see | clearly.—I must judge for myself.——[97]

Uncertainty in the deployment of Charlotte Heywood is the biggest hint that, as with the ending of *Persuasion*, Austen did not have the narrative and thematic structure of her new novel under control. In *Sanditon* there is the added problem that the workaday plot of girl meets boy, in which Charlotte and Sidney Parker must figure credibly, has become almost completely detached from the engrossing thematic issues of hypochondria and the ill-founded fortunes of Sanditon itself.[98]

Austen now seems to have little energy for characters who require some probable development and whose non-eccentric idiolects do not immediately determine their sphere of action. Instead, revision draws attention to her near exclusive reliance on conversation for character delineation and the advancement of the narrative, and the extent to which this is conversation only in the most limited sense. In a novel which promises to lean heavily on distinctions between the speech patterns, verbal idiosyncrasies, and obsessions of a range of bizarre figures, special care is taken to distinguish voice from voice. 'I never eat for | about a week after a Journey', announces Diana Parker in characteristic defiance of the laws of nature, adding that brother Arthur, 'is much more likely to | eat too much than too little'. This conveys the necessary information,

[97] *Sanditon*, Booklet 2, f. 20^{r}–20^{v} (103).

[98] Cf. the argument offered by Alistair M. Duckworth, *The Improvement of the Estate: A Study of Jane Austen's Novels* (1971; Baltimore and London: Johns Hopkins University Press, 1994): 'This is a world, it would seem, so far removed from traditional grounds of moral action that its retrieval through former fictional means is no longer possible, a world in which the heroine, though she remains a fundamentally moral figure, can no longer be an agent of social renewal.' (221)

but in a slack and non-idiomatic form; on second thoughts it is erased and the shorter phrase 'eats enormously' substituted. This, too, is crossed through and the brilliantly inflected comment inserted—Arthur 'is only too much disposed for Food'.[99] Sir Edward Denham's turn for nonsensical, Edward-Lear-style hyperbole is heightened in revision; and in a single speech in Chapter 8, in which he explains his taste in novels, 'unconquerable Decision' becomes the strangely expressed 'indomptible Decision', 'his Rival' becomes 'any opposing Character', and 'the most sagacious Man' becomes 'the most anti-puerile Man'.[100] A nice example of Austen catching just the right tone comes in Chapter 5, in a short passage given to the usually silent Mrs Parker. She nervously agrees with Charlotte's hinted reservation at the Parker sisters' 'habit of self-doctoring', and adds by way of conciliating her husband, 'You often think they | w^{d}. be better, if they w^{d}. leave themselves | more alone—& especially ~~p~~ Arthur.'[101] The erased 'p' suggests that Austen was about to write 'poor Arthur', giving him the epithet by which he is consistently described by his brother and sisters. Instead she allows Mrs Parker to draw back from this family conspiracy, in a barely perceptible moment of critical detachment.

What the refinement of idiolects tends to show is second thoughts restraining rather than embellishing first. Time and again, revision clears the text of information and works to counter the temptation of first thoughts to over-direct the reader's response and anticipate evaluation. Thus Charlotte's commonsensical revulsion on hearing of Susan Parker's 'Three Teeth | drawn at once!' is purged of redundant overemphasis: 'Three Teeth | drawn at once!—
more
~~It is really~~ frightful!— | . . . ~~most~~ distressing ~~to one's imagination~~ than | all the rest.—'[102] Mr Parker's comment on Arthur's fancied sickness is also censored to read 'It <u>is</u> bad;—it <u>is</u> bad that he should | be fancying himself too sickly for any | Profession—& sit down at 1 & 20, ~~idle &~~ | ~~indolent,~~ on the interest of his own little | Fortune, without any idea of attempting to | improve it,
the slightest plan
or ~~any prospect~~ of engaging in || any occupation that may be of use to | himself or others.'[103] Such revision is usually in the direction of fewer rather than more words. Paradoxically, too, revision draws attention to a kind of disengagement in the dwindled significance of the narrative voice, its slender treaty of trust with the central female character, and the mounting

[99] *Sanditon*, Booklet 3, f. 5^{r} (127).
[100] Ibid., Booklet 2, f. 21^{v} (107–8).
[101] Ibid., Booklet 2, f. 8^{v} (66).
[102] Ibid., Booklet 2, f. 8^{r}–8^{v} (65).
[103] Ibid., Booklet 2, f. 8^{v}–9^{r} (66–7).

sense of perceptual alienation as, in turn, the strongly drawn eccentrics take central stage and speak.

The composition of the draft seems from the evidence of the hand to have been for the most part smooth. There is little general display of hesitation and uncertainty as to how to proceed. We can deduce from this one of two possibilities: either that this is not in all cases a first draft and that some preliminary sketching of scenes and speeches was subsequently destroyed or lost; or that by the time she came to setting it down on paper much of what Austen wanted to express had already taken substantial shape in her mind, in line with the immanent method that marks the endings to *Persuasion*. The letter in Chapter 5 which first brings Diana Parker into play, in effect a dramatic monologue or reported monodrama, is a bizarre self-declaration, setting before us in one unrestrained sweep her personal hypochondria and social meddling, and the neurotic, frustrated energy which fuels both and makes her character tick. The strength of the portrait lies in the assurance with which the voice is caught and in the seamless and strange congruity of its private and public fantasies. This seamlessness is mirrored in its uninterrupted graphic presentation. In the 89 manuscript lines which the letter occupies there are only 13 corrections, most of them slight:

at

He read.—"My dear Tom, We were all | much greived ~~by~~ your accident, & if | you had not described yourself as fallen | into such very good hands, I sh^{d}. have | been with you at all hazards the day | after the rec^{pt}. of your Letter, though | it found me ~~hardly able to~~

~~my~~ suffering

~~crawl from~~ | ~~the Bed to the Sofa~~ ^ under a more | severe attack than usual of my old |

& hardly able to crawl from my Bed to the Sofa·

greivance, Spasmodic Bile^.—But how | were you treated?—Send me more Particu: | :lars in your next.—If indeed a simple | Sprain, as you denominate it, nothing | w^{d}. have been so judicious as Friction, | Friction by the hand alone, supposing | it could be applied <u>instantly</u>.—Two | years ago I happened to be calling on M^{rs}. | Sheldon when her Coachman sprained | his foot as he was cleaning the Carriage | & c^{d}. hardly limp into

use steadily

the House—but | by the immediate ~~application~~ of Friction | alone, ~~well~~ persevered in,

six

(& I rubbed | his Ancle with my own hand for ~~4~~ | Hours without Intermission)—he was | well in three days.—Many Thanks my || dear Tom, for the kindness with respect | to us, which had so large a share in | bringing on your accident—But pray | never run into Peril again, in looking | for an Apothecary on our account, for | had you the most experienced Man in his | Line settled at Sanditon, it w^{d}. be no | recommendation to us. We have entirely | done with the whole Medical Tribe. | We have consulted Physician after Phy^{n}. | in vain, till we are quite convinced | that they can do nothing for us & that we | must trust to our own knowledge of our | own wasted Constitutions for any releif. ~~to~~ | ~~be obtained~~.—|But if you think it ad: | :visable for the interest of the Place, to | get a Medical Man there, I will un: | :dertake the commission with pleasure, | & have no doubt of succeeding.—I ~~know~~ | ~~where to apply~~ could soon put the ne: | :cessary Irons in the fire.—As for getting | to Sanditon myself, it is quite an Im: | :possibility. I greive to say that I dare | not attempt it, but my feelings tell | me too plainly that in my present | state, the Sea air w^{d}. probably be the | death of me.—and neither of my dear | Companions will leave me, or I w^{d}. || promote their going down to you for a | fortnight. But in truth, I doubt whether | Susan's nerves w^{d}. be equal to the effort. | She has been suffering much from the | Headache and Six

10 days together so

Leaches a day for ~~the~~ | ~~last week have~~ releived her ~~a~~ ^ little | that ~~I~~we thought it right to change our | measures—and being convinced on exa: | :mination that much of the Evil

accordingly

lay | in her Gum, I persuaded her to attack | the disorder there. She has ^ had 3 Teeth | drawn ~~accordingly~~, & is decidedly better, | but her Nerves are a good deal deranged. |

trying to

She can only speak in a whisper—and | fainted away twice this morning | on poor suppress ~~coughing~~ a cough.

Arthurs ~~sneezing~~ ^ He, I am | happy to say is tolerably well—tho' | more languid than I like—& I fear | for his Liver.—I have heard nothing | of Sidney since your being together in Town, |but conclude his scheme to the I. of Wight | has not taken place, or we should have | seen him in his way.—Most sincerely | do we wish you a good Season at Sandi: | :ton, & though we cannot contribute to | your Beau Monde in person, we are | doing our utmost to send you Company | worth having;–&– think we may | safely

one

reckon on securing you two || large Families, ~~that of~~ a rich West Indian | from Surry,

Girls

the other, a most respectable ^ | Boarding School, or Academy, from Camber: | :well.—I will not tell you how many | People I have employed in the business |—wheel within

But

wheel.— ^ Success more than | repays.—Yours most affec^{ly}— &c"[104]

Though few, such revisions as there are adjust the text at different moments in starkly different directions—a change of word ('at' for 'by', 'use' for 'applica-

[104] *Sanditon.*, Booklet 2, ff. 6^{v}–8^{r} (60–4).

tion', 'steadily' for 'well', the deft repositioning of 'accordingly') brings the voice subtly closer to the idiom of ordinary conversation; elsewhere, slight verbal revision jerks the text into ever more extravagant specificity ('six' for '4', '10 days together' for 'the last week'). One of the largest of these small changes converts written language into a colloquialism which is also a miniature word-portrait of overbearing interference—'I know where to apply' becoming 'I could soon put the necessary Irons in the fire'. The tiny increments by which the following passage was rebalanced, 'She . . . fainted away twice this morning on poor Arthurs sneezing', which then becomes 'on poor Arthurs coughing', and finally 'on poor Arthurs trying to suppress a cough', brilliantly heighten the absurdity of this small family drama. Revision enhances the collusion between brother and sisters to support and stimulate one another's symptoms. But what is remarkable in the letter as it is inscribed in the manuscript is the readily achieved strangeness of its effects. It is almost instantly and completely textualized, most tellingly in its grammatical development. Any adjustments are slight to what takes shape on paper at once as a finished study of 'the amazing behaviour of the hypochondriacal body'.[105]

The fact that revision introduces nothing new but only enforces or tactically moderates, in the interests of a subtler improbability, the eccentricities of the original suggests that Diana Parker, a character constituted largely as speech idiolect, assumed identity during a prior period of mental drafting. Character and manuscript provide at this point apt substantiation for the testimony of two nieces, Marianne and Louisa Knight, who, probably remembering her visit to Godmersham in 1813, recorded much later their memories of unexpectedly seeing Aunt Jane at work:

> Aunt Jane would sit quietly working [sewing] beside the fire in the library, saying nothing for a good while, and then would suddenly burst out laughing, jump up and run across the room to a table where pens and paper were lying, write something down, and then come back to the fire and go on quietly working as before.
>
> She was very absent indeed. She would sit silent awhile, then rub her hands, laugh to herself and run up to her room.[106]

These memories suggest the mental absorption, assimilation, and final projection onto paper of characters as fully dramatized beings. It is a method

[105] The phrase is John Wiltshire's in his impressive study, *Jane Austen and the Body: 'The Picture of Health'* (Cambridge: Cambridge University Press, 1992), 214.

[106] Marianne Knight's memories of her aunt were first published, from the account of a younger cousin to whom she told them, in Hill, *Her Homes and Her Friends*, 202. Both are included in *Family Record*, 206.

which if habitual would yield an insignificant amount of documentation in the form of draft notes and other written schema. Contrary to Austen-Leigh's defensive observation of the effect of illness on the appearance of the manuscript, it is a notable feature that the energy which animates its extraordinary range of eccentrics does not correlate with graphic disorder. If anything, the writing hand is less confident in establishing the range of normal behaviour and in discovering the boundary between the sympathetic and the absurd. If what Marianne and Louisa Knight remembered seeing was a favoured, even instinctive mode of working, it also explains why in early 1817, the fully realized eccentrics threaten to upstage the workaday elements of plot and probable characterization, all of which (like the ending of *Persuasion*) would require a greater effort of planning and greater stamina in execution than now may have been within Austen's capacity.

Two scenes—the adventure of the overturned carriage with which the narrative opens and Charlotte Heywood's glimpse of the 'stolen Interveiw' between Clara Brereton and Sir Edward Denham, at the close of the fragment—display in the flux and continuum of erased and substituted words an unusual striving after roughness of effect. They are both key moments of architectonic or narrative organization. They also share patterns of revision, and in particular a heightened attention to external circumstance and to fixing more precisely the accidental or peripheral detail. In each case, rewriting exaggerates the effect it works to create—of perceptual concentration and disorientation—making of both highly reflexive moments in which the achieved textual surface mimics its subject. Roughness of finish, perceptual opacity, and the levelling of relevant and non-relevant information are in both cases the purposefully achieved effects of textual amplification. Passages of close observation about close observation, they distort as they call into question what we take for granted in Austen's polished narratives: that detail is relevant; that it is bolted in beneath the surface. Now instead we are confronted with the disturbing possibility of redundant, factitious, or otherwise disconnected perception. It could be argued that passages like these merely display Austen's loss of control, representing the kind of extraneous verbiage we should expect in an unfinished fragment, and that such redundancies would have been pruned from the finished novel. But this argument does not hold for two reasons: the pattern of revision in each case is towards heightening rather than removing such signs; and, though few, such passages recur throughout the narrative.

In transcription, with erasures and rewordings recorded, the opening page of the manuscript looks like this:

A Gentleman & Lady travelling from Tun | bridge towards that part of the Sussex |
being induced by Business to quit
coast which lies between Hastings & | E. Bourne, ~~were on quitting~~ the high | road, &
~~toil~~ attempt a very rough Lane were
~~toiling up a very long steep hill~~ | ~~through a rough Lane~~, overturned in | toiling up its'
half rock, half sand.
long ascent ‸. The accident | happened just beyond the only Gentleman's | House near
a first take direction
the Lane—~~the~~ House, which | their Driver on being ‸ required to ~~turn~~ that | ~~way~~, had
conceived to be necessarily their | object, & had with most unwilling Looks | been
by—. He had grumbled & shaken his shoulders
constrained to pass ~~two minutes~~ | ~~before grumbling~~ so much indeed, ~~& looking~~ | ~~so~~
and pitied & cut sharply
~~black, & pitying & cutting~~ his Horses so | ~~much~~, that he might have been open to | the
not his Masters
suspicion of overturning them on pur: | :pose (especially as the Carriage was ~~not~~ | the
had considerably
Gentleman's own) if the road ‸ not | indisputably ~~& evidently~~ become ~~much~~ | worse
expressing
than before, as soon as the | premises of the said House were | ~~passed~~ left behind—~~as~~
~~saying~~ with a most intelligent ~~and seeming~~ countenance
portentous
~~Bad as it had~~ | ~~been before the~~ ‸ ~~Change seemed to say~~ | ‸ that beyond it no wheels but
could safely proceed.
cart | wheels ~~had ever thought of proceeding~~. ||

While it is not possible to say how far apart each change was made—whether they represent the shifting thoughts and purposes of different moments in a single session or whether some represent alterations made at a later re-reading (how much later—that evening, the next day, after a week?)—we can nevertheless infer some sense of a method of working. The winding opening sentence, apart from the further qualification 'half rock, half sand', which could have been added at any time, did not find its circuitous way towards a main clause until its major integral revisions were in place. Its final form must therefore be the work of a single session and it clearly took some labour to achieve. The corrections, in particular the testing of verb tenses ('~~were on quitting~~ > being induced . . . to quit', '~~toiling up~~ > attempt'), reveal a protracted struggle to find the right rhythm and temporal dimension in which to record the events described, while the discarded and repositioned 'toiling up' ('~~toiling up~~, ~~toil~~, attempt . . . toiling up') was only possible once a

18. Opening page of the holograph manuscript of *Sanditon*. By kind permission of the Provost and Scholars of King's College, Cambridge University.

satisfactory version of the earlier part of the sentence was in place. The drawn out, circuitous phrasing followed by jerky, staccato monosyllables suggest in motion, rhythm, and length the slow, arduous, and finally disrupted progress of the carriage. The irregular stress patterns throw into doubt matters of perspective and distance and the position of the carriage and its occupants in the visual field—now distant, now close. The effect is phanopoeic rather than onomatopoeic, visual as well as aural.

Such evidence of the struggle of rewriting is not so insistently marked elsewhere in the passage, where it is possible to read the erased first thoughts as a continuous draft with no disturbance to grammatical sense. In the later portion of the opening section (everything after the first sentence), changes represent attempts to render the sense more precise, to prune away slack phrasing, and to vary the tempo of the narrative. For example, in the first rush of writing, there was a tendency to overuse the adverb 'much'; of its three appearances, the second two are removed in revision ('so much indeed', 'his Horses so ~~much~~ > sharply', 'become ~~much~~ > considerably worse'). Other slack phrasing is tightened, on second thought: 'to turn that way' becomes 'to take that direction'; '& looking so black', coming so soon after 'most unwilling Looks' is erased; 'indisputably & evidently' becomes simply 'indisputably'. More instructive, because more idiosyncratic, are two other kinds of revision: the initial reliance for constructing the scene on verbal participles is subsequently reconsidered and pruned; and the complex subordination of the second sentence is cut through and a new sentence begun with 'He had grumbled & shaken his shoulders'. The effect of the second revision is to vary the rhythm of the wider passage by resisting the desire to replicate, and so risk diluting, the surprise impact of the sinuous turns and uneven phrasing of the opening sentence. The verbal participles which litter the uncorrected text and which revision brings under effective control—'quitting', 'toiling', 'grumbling', 'looking', 'pitying', 'cutting', 'expressing', 'saying', 'proceeding' —suggest how fundamental to the work's conception was the heightened degree of movement or restlessness that critics have commented on as a prime characteristic of its overall design. By contrast with the first sentence, the much rewritten third sentence made a complete sense unit in its unrevised form. It would seem likely therefore that sentences two and three were separated as they were being written. But it is not impossible that they were initially penned as a single sprawling sequence of detail and observation before being divided, rewritten, and given clearer temporal definition. There is evidence of haste or carelessness in rewriting, as for instance where the correction 'not his Masters' has been written above the erased 'not' of the phrase it replaces ('not the Gentleman's own'), while the rest of the phrase, occupying the first half of the next line, has been left. This is merely a slip; other changes display mounting confidence in pruning away excessive description or explanation and enhancing the atmosphere of alienation in the opening scene. Particularly vivid is the revision which compresses the prosaically informative '~~as Bad as it had~~ | ~~been before the Change seemed to say~~ | . . . ~~had ever thought of proceeding~~' into something altogether stranger—'expressing with a | most intelligent portentous | countenance . . . could safely proceed'. Combined with the change by which the driver's black look ('~~looking so black~~') is erased, the road's 'portentous countenance', personified and animated in revision to convey 'intelligent' information, brilliantly enhances the quirky angle of perception and oddly non-human investment of the scene. Of the potential actors encountered so far, only the road and the coach driver, neither of which will figure again in the narrative, have a face.

If the consequence of the opening page is an overturned carriage it is also an overturning of our preconceptions of how a novel by Jane Austen will begin. Until now, her beginnings had been remarkably similar in style: biographical, descriptive, and static—a snapshot with relevant commentary or a dramatized tableau introducing a named family or member of a family at a particular moment in its history. Not only does the manuscript's fifth word, the active participle 'travelling', inject an unusual degree of movement and implied action into the opening sentence, biographical detail is noticeably and teasingly withheld in the repeated use of common rather than proper nouns—'A Gentleman & Lady', 'their Driver', 'the said House'—the effect of which is to simulate something like the detached evidentiary tones provided by a police report of an incident. The narrative voice has so far, and unusually, declared no clear sympathy with the human drama of the scene. The tone of reportage is never entirely abandoned: Mr Parker remains 'the Travellor' until the end of the tenth page of the manuscript, and Charlotte Heywood is curiously labelled 'the visiting Young Lady' in Chapter 3. In the opening pages, the effect Austen achieves is not dissimilar to the impersonal and brooding cinematic beginning to a novel to be written half a century later, Dickens's *Our Mutual Friend* (1864). Indeed, one of the oddest features of *Sanditon* is its ready cinematic style—its metonymic close-ups, more easily interpreted by cinema-goer than novel-reader; and its other elliptical devices of fragmented vision, temporal discontinuity, and a pervasive flirtatious play of surfaces.

Critics have regularly noted the 'air of mystery' in the opening scene as a contrived effect independent of the manuscript's abandoned state.[107] The deployment of Charlotte Heywood, first introduced at the end of Chapter 2, occasions a more sustained cognitive disturbance. Anna Lefroy, who inherited and attempted to complete the fragment, had much earlier, in 1814, begun her own novel, tentatively entitled 'Which is the Heroine?' Commenting on drafts of Anna's unfinished novel led Austen between July and September of that year to formulate her art of the novel. The strong commitment she made at that time to verisimilitude and psychological and narrative probability now seems to be set aside as she approaches something closer in spirit to the implied uncertainties of Anna's title, and a new kind of writing.[108] The contents of Mrs Whitby's circulating library introduce the subject of holiday reading, which is further elaborated in the freewheeling fantasies of Sir Edward Denham's overstuffed imagination. But in Charlotte too the narrator explores the permeable boundary between fiction and reality. Where Catherine Morland or Emma Woodhouse, tutoring Harriet Smith, must learn to distinguish life from novels, in *Sanditon* that boundary is deliberately blurred, and the fictional foundation of actions and identities is teasingly implied.[109] In Mrs Whitby's library, Charlotte looks over the pretty and useless objects on sale and reflects, rather too self-consciously, on the duties of a young woman to regulate her purse and her pleasures. She is thinking herself into the predicament of the contemporary novel heroine and the narrator helps her along by placing a useful prop on the counter, a volume of Fanny Burney's *Camilla*. An odd choice, we might think, since Camilla is not 'two & Twenty' (Charlotte's age) but only nine years old when her adventures begin. The shift halfway through writing, that recasts the passage from passive to active voice and makes Charlotte take up the volume rather than let it lie, is also a shift by which she is made to submit her everyday actions to a prior fictional authority. A slight change, but it contributes to the disturbing sense which

[107] Southam, *Jane Austen's Literary Manuscripts*, extends the comment, perceptively remarking: 'As the opening section of a full-scale work, this fragment is strikingly different from the equivalent parts of the other novels . . . it breeds an air of mystery.' (111–12)

[108] See *Jane Austen's Letters*, 267–9, and 274–8; and Ch. 4, 'Continuations'.

[109] Though Southam seeks to exempt Charlotte Heywood from the general blurring of illusion and reality which infects the actions of the other characters, he rightly notes that 'in *Sanditon* the state of fictional illusion is deliberately and continually violated' (*Jane Austen's Literary Manuscripts*, 122). Cf. Tanner's conclusion that unlike *Northanger Abbey*, the implication in *Sanditon* is that '*everybody* is likely to live a para-fictional life to some extent. The texture of everyday life now *includes* the texture of the fictions it produces' (*Jane Austen*, 279).

runs throughout the fragment that life is being lived at a critical distance, as a second-order reality:

She took up a Book; it happened to be a
A vol: of Camilla. ~~happened~~ | ~~to lie on the Counter~~. She had not
so, she turned from the
Camilla's | Youth, & had no intention of having her |Distress,— ~~The Gl~~ Drawers of rings & Broches | ~~must be resisted~~ repressed farther solici: | :tation & paid for what she bought.—[110]

Is Charlotte to be the heroine? Leaving the library on her first evening in Sanditon, she immediately meets Lady Denham and her young companion Clara Brereton, in whom she could see

whatever Heroine might
only the most perfect re: | :presentation of ~~all the most beautiful~~ | ~~& bewitching Heroines~~ be most beautiful | & bewitching, in all the numerous vol:^{s} | they had left
on
behind them ~~in~~ M^{rs}. Whitby's | Shelves.—Perhaps it ~~was from~~ might be partly || oweing to her having first issued from | a Circulating Library—but she c^{d}. not | separate the idea of a complete Heroine | from Clara Brereton.[111]

In Lady Denham's cynical money-spinning scheme, the West Indian heiress Miss Lambe is set to figure as heroine or victim. 'She was about 17, half | mulatto, chilly & tender, had a maid | of her own, was to have the best room | in the Lodgings, & was always of the | first consequence in every plan of M^{rs}. | G.—' With this extraordinary and succinct description Miss Lambe is added to the narrator's list of eccentrics, but who is to say where the line would have been drawn between the plausible and implausible in her characterization? Basking in the comfort of their private romantic illusion, the 'two Miss Beauforts' have also arrived in Sanditon with their harp and drawing paper 'meaning | to be the most stylish Girls in the | Place'.[112] Their self-enchantment is logged and added to the fragment's critical anthology of heroinism.

The distance between Charlotte and the world she encounters and attempts to analyse is rarely bridged. Like Alice in Wonderland she experiences the loss of peripheral vision that inhabiting a strange world entails. For much of the fragment she is our eyes and ears on events, yet if she stands outside what she witnesses she also shares less of the narrator's confidence to understand than any other mediator since Catherine Morland. By this double

110 *Sanditon*, Booklet 2, f. 10^{r} (72).
111 Ibid., Booklet 2, f. 11^{r}–11^{v} (75).
112 Ibid., Booklet 3, f. 13^{v} (152); Booklet 3, f. 14^{v} (154).

estrangement we sense further that Austen is setting at a distance the implied contract of sympathy with her readers. *Sanditon* reads like an experiment in testing the social basis of perception. Because in this village of eccentrics consensual reality cannot be assumed, sensory perceptions are both more acute channels of communication and also more fallible. Charlotte's eyes and ears are assailed by the new and the unexpected in a narrative which lays particular stress on seeing and hearing as means of enquiry. Vision promises to link us directly with a world of objects—with real solid things—but just as those solid things can and do exhibit a resistance to connection, so vision is peculiarly liable to illusion. The underlying grammar of resemblances—a kind of conversation of the senses—on which we depend for the organization and intelligible processing of the sights and sounds we encounter, is here called into question. Events repeatedly test Charlotte's capacity to trust her eyes and ears, culminating in the scene in Chapter 12 on the road to Sanditon House:

road ~~by~~
The ~~approach~~ to Sanditon |H. was ~~at first only~~ ^ a broad, hand: |
~~about a q^{r}. of a miles length~~, & conducting
approach at the end of a q^{r}. of a mile,
:some planted ~~road~~ ^ between fields, ~~of~~ | ~~but ending in about a q^{r}. of a mile~~ |
through second Gates not
^ into the Grounds, which though ^ extensive || ~~were~~ had all the Beauty
These Entrance Gates were so much
& Respectability | which an abundance of very fine Timber | could give.— ~~They were so~~
in a corner of the Grounds or Paddock, so near one of its Boundaries
an
~~narrow at~~ | ~~the Entrance~~, that one ^ outside fence | was at first almost pressing on
here there threw to
the | road—till an angle ~~in one~~, & a curve | ~~in the other gave~~ them ^ a better distance. |
clusters ~~rows~~ of fine
The Fence was a proper, Park paling in | excellent condition; with ^ ~~vigorous~~ Elms, |
rows of line
or ^ old Thorns ~~& Hollies~~ following its ~~course~~ | almost every where.—Almost must be |
stipulated—for there were ~~intervals~~ vacant | spaces—& through one of these, Charlotte |
over the pales
as soon as they entered the Enclosure, | caught a glimpse ^ of something White & |
Womanish ~~over the pales~~, in the field | on the other side;—it was a something | which
immediately brought Miss B. into | her head—& stepping to the pales, she | saw indeed
decidedly in spite of the Mist,
—& very ~~distinctly, though~~ | ~~at some distance before her~~ Miss B—| seated, not far
before her, at the foot of | the ~~sloping~~ bank which sloped down | from the outside of

Path
the Paling & ~~at~~ | which a narrow ~~track~~ ^ seemed to | skirt along:—Miss Brereton seated | apparently very composedly—& Sir || E. D. by her side.—[113]

Rewriting here achieves a contrived particularity in disposing the solid objects of entrance gates, fence, and trees which one moment conceal from view and another frame and enhance the view. Chapman noted the effect of this calculated itemization as something 'as clearly deliberate as it is certainly novel'.[114] Yet the angle of the fence, directing the line of vision, even the structure and condition of the fence, and the species of trees that follow its limit, further instructing the eye, are given a marked, even exaggerated, attention that is far from clarifying. It is 'a close, misty morn[g]', atmospheric conditions contribute to the by now socially endemic loss of peripheral vision; but the confusion effected by the proliferating detail creates its own semantic mist. Objects magnified beyond their common proportions, the geometric lines of the fence, its relation to road, path, and field, confuse our sense of the wider landscape and of who stands where in relation to which enclosed space. Revisions in the manuscript show that the effect—at once mesmerizing and disorienting—was achieved with considerable effort.

Unusually, two lines of rewriting rather than one have been squeezed in at the beginning of the passage, the original reading going through at least two distinct revisions. In my transcription, passages in square brackets could have been revised at either the first or second revision stage or subsequently:

1. The approach to Sanditon H. was at first only a broad, handsome planted road between fields, but ending in about a q[r]. of a mile in the Grounds
2. The [approach] road to Sanditon H. was [at first only] by a broad, handsome planted [road] approach between fields, ~~but ending in about a qr. of a mile~~ of about a q[r]. of a miles length and conducting [through second Gates] into the Grounds
3. The [approach] road to Sanditon H. was [at first only] ~~by~~ a broad, handsome planted [road] approach between fields, ~~of about a q[r]. of a miles length~~, & conducting at the end of a q[r]. of a mile through second Gates into the Grounds[115]

The introduction of a second set of gates and the particular attention to the phrase, first adverbial, then adjectival, and then adverbial again, which

[113] *Sanditon*, Booklet 3, ff. 18[v]–19[v] (166–8).
[114] Chapman, *Facts and Problems*, 209.
[115] It is possible to read the passage's opening lines in the following way, The road ~~approach~~ to Sanditon | H. was ~~at first only~~ by ^ a broad, hand: | :some planted ~~road~~ approach ^ between fields, ~~of~~ | ~~about a q[r]. of a miles length~~, & conducting | ~~but ending in about a q[r]. of a mile~~ | at the end of a q[r]. of a mile through second Gates ^ into the Grounds, which though not ^ extensive ||

establishes the distance between outer and inner gates, signal a heightened spatial awareness, which is continued in the reworking of the vaguer 'They were so narrow at | the Entrance', which becomes 'These Entrance Gates were so much in a corner | of the Grounds or Paddock, so near one of its Boundaries'. With the phrase 'Grounds or Paddock' the mounting specificity of the scene begins to assume a strangely equivocal design. Revision sharpens the initially vague phrasing of 'an angle ~~in one~~ here & a curve | ~~in the other gave~~ there threw them to a better distance', but does not dispel the perceptual anxiety that detail itself is becoming a problem. Why are we told that the fence is 'a proper, Park paling' and that it is 'in | excellent condition'? Why do 'rows of vigorous Elms' become 'clusters of fine Elms'? Why are there at one moment elms, old thorns, and hollies, and at the next only elms and thorns? Why are we told that the 'something White & | Womanish' is 'over the pales', 'in the field', *and* 'on the other side'? The excess is worked carefully into the text, creating what Tanner has well described as 'a new kind of phenomenological complexity', in which '[I]dentification is deferred, vision itself is becoming narrativised'.[116]

Criticism has periodically enjoined an appreciation of Austen's art of surfaces. Barbara Hardy has perceptively noted how she was 'moved less by a symbolic urge than by a sense of appropriateness' and that her world is accordingly 'full of small objects... and they are often arbitrary and accidental'. The complex business of surfaces which are neither overtly symbolic nor merely superficial gives the lie to Charlotte Brontë's famous dismissal of a writer whose 'business is not half so much with the human heart as with the human eyes, mouth, hands, and feet'.[117] The social and pathological resonances of this particularity are experimented with in the draft of *The Watsons*. What seems different and disturbing in *Sanditon* is less the fact that objects

But such a reading requires us to assume that on a first writing Austen narrowed uncharacteristically the spacing between the lines at the foot of what is in other respects an evenly spaced page. If instead we accept that the uncorrected manuscript page retains an even consistency throughout, then we see that two lines of rewriting rather than one have been squeezed in and that the original reading went through at least two distinct revisions.

[116] Tanner, *Jane Austen*, 282. D. A. Miller, *Jane Austen, or The Secret of Style* (Princeton and Oxford: Princeton University Press, 2003), suggests facetiously and plausibly that the hollies disappear because of their proximity in the manuscript to Charlotte's late reference to 'Poor Mr. Hollis!' Avoiding the 'inadvertent and... ridiculous affinit[y]' Austen rescues her text from the kind of 'undisciplined... associationism' that left to stand 'ludicrously flattens the imaginary depth of representation into the literal surface of a linguistic performance.' (85–7) Miller works this small point hard, but his insight rings true.

[117] Barbara Hardy, 'Properties and Possessions in Jane Austen's Novels', in *Jane Austen's Achievement*, ed. Juliet McMaster (London and Basingstoke: Macmillan, 1976), 104; Brontë made her remark in a letter to her publisher's reader, W. S. Williams, in 1850. The passage is extracted in *Critical Heritage*, i. 128.

have their solid existence apart from our possessive purposes as the frequency with which they resist all active enquiry. Where objects go, people follow. The unusual range of strongly drawn characters who occupy the foreground, serially and in so short a space—Mr Parker, Diana Parker, Sir Edward Denham, Lady Denham, Arthur Parker—each one adrift in their own language-loop, deny by their robust self-absorption an underlying principle of consensus. There is none.

If the social scene is also widening beyond the middle-class group, there is no suggestion that it is deepening; rather the opposite. The paradox is that the rapid sketching in of a more extensive social context than has appeared before in Austen's village studies—the settled inhabitants and the changing, drifting visitors to the new resort—denies as it amplifies the capacity to make connection. Old Stringer and son market gardeners, Jebb the milliner, William Heeley shoemaker, Miss Whitby at the subscription library, 'with all her | glossy Curls & smart Trinkets', and 'old Sam' uncording the trunks at the hotel, each has their moment of attention. It can be an intensely focused moment, as the care taken over names and other details reveals. 'Old Stringer' was first 'old Salmon'; 'old Sam' was 'old Hannah'; 'Mr Woodcock' was 'young Woodcock'; Miss Whitby's 'smart Trinkets' were originally 'ornamented Combs'; 'William Heeley' was 'old Heeley' and the passage in which he appears first read 'Look at old Heeley's windows.—Blue | Shoes, & nankin Boots!—Who w^{d}. have | expected such a sight in old Sanditon!' Almost two whole lines of additions are unusually squeezed in between the lines of otherwise uncorrected text, suggesting that the wares in the shop window, in whose panes Mr Parker's character is also reflected, were embellished as an afterthought and purely for the delight of it:

William
"Look at ~~old~~ Heeley's windows.—Blue | Shoes, & nankin Boots!—Who w^{d}. have |
at a Shoemaker's
expected such a sight ^ in old Sanditon!—|This is new within the month. There was no blue Shoe when | we passed this way a month ago."|[118]

Particular attention is given to the names recorded in the List of Subscribers to Mrs Whitby's library. 'The List of | Subscribers was but commonplace', the narrator observes; accordingly, 'D^{r}. & M^{rs}. Henderson' is altered to 'D^{r}. & M^{rs}. Brown', joining the proliferous Mathews family ('M^{rs}. Mathews—| Miss Mathews, Miss E. Mathews, Miss H. | Mathews'), 'Lieut: Smith R.N.', 'Miss

[118] *Sanditon*, Booklet 2, f. 4^{r} (53).

Fisher' and 'Miss Scroggs', in a list which socially descends, or rather dissolves, through the undistinguished and commonplace to the slightly zanily named.[119] The relation of the lady living 'almost next door to' Mrs Charles Dupuis, through whose circuitous good offices the promise comes of a holiday rent from a girls' seminary in Camberwell first 'attends some of the girls of the | Seminary, to give them lessons in | Botany & Belles Lettres' but this is revised even before the sentence is finished, to read

> M^{rs}. Charles Dupuis lives almost | next door to a Lady, who has a || relation lately
> who actually attends the Seminary   and gives lessons on Eloquence
> settled at Clapham, | ~~& attends some of the girls of the~~ | ~~Seminary, to give them lessons~~
> and
> ~~in~~ | ~~Botany &~~ Belles Lettres to some of the | Girls.[120]

Revisions of this minute and purely local kind have a special interest beyond the significance attributed to those structural changes made to strengthen fundamental aspects of character or tighten the logic of cause and effect. In the detail whose meaning remains local we glimpse a freer creativity. An effect of imagination which makes more luminous its own little world of meaning would appear to give the lie to E. M. Forster's judgement on the *Sanditon* fragment, that 'the numerous alterations in the MS. are never in the direction of vitality', and that it 'gives the effect of weakness, if only because it is reminiscent from first to last.'[121] What these solid little globes of detail, unentailed to the teleologies of plot or characterization, announce is a creativity in debt to nothing beyond the space of writing that it occupies.

This lack of entailment of course points to the enigma of *Sanditon*. Where the revised, printed ending to *Persuasion* substitutes a thematically satisfying conclusion for the expeditious plot resolution of its earlier drafting, *Sanditon* seems from the outset to abandon plot in favour of local embellishment and thematic obsessions. Do we deduce from this that already in *Persuasion*, overtaken by illness, Austen is losing control of the technical management of her materials? Is the perceptual experimentation of the *Sanditon* fragment evidence of a radical adjustment in the relations between her familiar, even hackneyed plot and an increasingly divergent thematic development, or a further undeniable sign of a loss of structural stamina? Is the asyndetic

119 Ibid., Booklet 2, f. 9^{v} (70).

120 Ibid., Booklet 3, f. 5^{r}–5^{v} (127–8).

121 Highly influential on the subsequent critical reading of *Sanditon* and much quoted, Forster's comments appeared in the *Nation*, 21 (March 1925), in a review of Chapman's transcription of the fragment. The review is reprinted in *Abinger Harvest*, 167–8.

sentence that emerges in *Persuasion* harbinger of a new stylistic tautness or of an exhausted dissociation? Tanner made playful comment on the homonymic affinity of Sanditon and Asyndeton to argue that 'Sanditon is built on—and by—careless and eroding grammar'; but his argument assumes that the disease is largely contained within Austen's characters.[122] By the evidence of *Persuasion* this is not the case. The energy and immediacy generated by the omissions and compressions which mark asyndeton may be misleading. It brings Austen's fictional narrative closer to the kinds of writing conventions encouraged in her personal correspondence, where, with the erosion of grammar, sense often chases after the more dominant effects of sound and rhythm. In familiar letters the risk of miscommunication is small; but in literature ellipsis, like the loss of peripheral vision, can denote an attentive disorientation, either the consequence of over-intense concentration or loss of consensual reality. Part of the peculiar energy of *Sanditon* derives from our strong feeling that the author too is in a strange place, seeing the world anew.

In her haunting essay 'On Being Ill', Virginia Woolf, one of Austen's acutest readers, described the cultural omission by which illness 'has not taken its place with love, battle, and jealousy among the prime themes of literature'. A bravura performance whose metaphoric free association contrives to seem more than usually extempore, the essay enacts what the imagination and the senses can do when, in illness and in Woolf's words, 'the police', our intelligence, are 'off duty'.[123] Keats would probably agree. '[I]llness', he wrote, 'as far as I can judge in so short a time has relieved my Mind of a load of deceptive thoughts and images and makes me perceive things in a truer light... shapes and coulours as are [*for* are as] new to me as if I had just created them with a superhuman fancy';[124] while according to Novalis, another fragmentary writer, only sickness is really interesting, because sickness 'belongs to individualizing'.[125] There seem to be here the sufficiently diverse makings for a defence of the imaginative potential of illness. But if Keats and Novalis are strange company for Austen, our interpretation of the textual disconnection, however brilliant in improvisation, that characterizes the fragment ought likewise to be remote from our appreciation of her

[122] Tanner, *Jane Austen*, 260.

[123] Virginia Woolf, 'On Being Ill' (1926), in *The Essays of Virginia Woolf*, 4 (1925–8), ed. Andrew McNeillie (London: Hogarth Press, 1994), 317 and 324.

[124] *The Letters of John Keats*, ed. Hyder Edward Rollins, 2 vols. (Cambridge, Mass.: Harvard University Press, 1958), i. 260, to James Rice, 14–16 February 1820.

[125] In a fragment from 1799–1800, quoted in Susan Sontag, *Illness as Metaphor* (1978; Harmondsworth, Middx.: Penguin, 1983), 35.

polished art. In closing the distance between the fragment's status as authentic trace—the immediate site of composition/the imprint of a peculiar imagination—and the public articulations of the finished novels—in particular, in naïvely celebrating its fragmentariness as experiment or new departure—we risk mistaking composition for the more painful but no less revelatory labour of decomposition. What seems and is new in *Sanditon* may be the vivid emergence of imagination and perception from the decay of form, which is, if we think about it, an odd cause for celebration.

4

Textual Identities: Part 1

'Print settles it'

The emphasis in criticism, almost regardless of fashion or theoretic inflection, is by convention on the private status of the literary work, on its symbolic representation of or substitution for inwardness, and its equivalence to human isolation, subjectivity, intimacy, and individualism. Seen from this perspective, literature's impact on mentalities is a private affair: writer, work, reader inhabit unique space. Consider Maurice Blanchot's linked statements in *The Space of Literature*:

In the solitude of the work—the work of art, the literary work—we discover a more essential solitude... The work is solitary: this does not mean that it remains uncommunicable, that it has no reader. But whoever reads it enters into the affirmation of the work's solitude, just as he who writes it belongs to the risk of this solitude.[1]

Blanchot's meditation appeared in French in 1955. Throughout the twentieth century criticism maximized its strategies for representing literature as private pleasure, albeit through predictable, common, and uniform acts of isolation. Typically under these conditions, as Blanchot's English translator notes, terms like 'space' (in 'l'espace littéraire'/'the space of literature') denote 'the site of... withdrawal' and the withdrawal itself 'of what is ordinarily meant by

[1] Maurice Blanchot, *The Space of Literature*, trans. by Ann Smock (Lincoln and London: University of Nebraska Press, 1982), 21–2. The view is a commonplace of twentieth-century literary criticism of all persuasions. Cf. Forster, *Aspects of the Novel* (1927; Harmondsworth, Middx.: Penguin, 1962), 21: 'The reader must sit down alone and struggle with the writer'.

"place" '[2]—literature as the place of no place. The space of literature is accordingly an absence of place, which is both a negation and a purification of the conditions under which non-literary space functions, as Humberstall intuits in Kipling's 'The Janeites', a story of the afterlives of Austen's novels in the trenches of the First World War. But if we approach the literary work through its documentary forms—that is, from the material structures of its representation (as opposed to the semantic structures of its affectation)—it can appear to make loud and precisely located statements. Such statements not only draw attention to the dispersed authority of the literary work's construction, they situate the reader: now every act of solitary interpretation is also conducted within social space. The American poet Susan Howe explains it like this: 'Messages must be seen to be heard to say.'[3] For Howe the literary space is a noisy space, not withdrawn but contested. A painter in words, her concern is with recovering the space of print on the page—'the space of the paper itself'—and the material embeddedness of text in the vehicle which conveys it. As she makes abundantly clear, hers is a conjoined bibliographic and political agenda to unsettle European perspectives on literature and print by connecting the marginal status of American literary history with challenges to typographic convention or 'settlement' and the 'look' of the printed page. But in muted form Howe's challenge is more generally to modern conventions of reading. She suggests one way of recovering the sociability of some literary forms, their resistance to regularization or, as is the case I shall argue for Austen's novels, their preservation as an aspect of textual substance of the differences between writing and speaking, seeing and listening.

In a characteristically provocative passage Austen's contemporary Charles Lamb examined his professed aversion to the sight of an author's manuscript—in this case, the manuscript of Milton's 'Lycidas' preserved in Trinity College, Cambridge. For Lamb, manuscripts testify to the messiness of human presence and thereby destroy the desired illusion of literature as a withdrawal from space. He writes:

> There is something to me repugnant at any time in written hand. The text never seems determinate. Print settles it. I had thought of the Lycidas as of a full-grown

[2] *The Space of Literature*, 10. Again, compare Forster's image of the circular room in which the English novelists write as a space without context, outside of time (*Aspects of the Novel*, 16).

[3] Susan Howe, *The Birth-Mark: Unsettling the Wilderness in American Literary History* (Hanover and London: University Press of New England, 1993), 157. Howe is discussing the poetry of Emily Dickinson and its editorial treatment.

beauty—as springing up with all its parts absolute—till, in an evil hour, I was shown the original written copy of it, together with the other minor poems of its author, in the Library of Trinity, kept like some treasure to be proud of. I wish they had thrown them in the Cam, or sent them after the latter cantos of Spenser into the Irish Channel. How it staggered me to see the fine things in thin ore! interlined, corrected! as if their words were mortal, alterable, displaceable, at pleasure! as if they might have been otherwise and just as good! As if inspiration were made up of parts, and those fluctuating, successive, indifferent! I will never go into the workshop of any great artist again, nor desire a sight of his picture till it is fairly off the easel. No, not if Raphael were to be alive again, and painting another Galatea.[4]

The distinction in the life and aspect of text that Lamb laments in self-mocking earnest is an important one for what it tells us about the cultural authority of printed books. Despite the cultural and technological impact of the computer and our new intellectual assent to instability, from the point of view of the majority of readers, who continue to encounter literary texts in the illusory singleness and fixity of printed books, 'print settles it'. This is true even though most of us would credit the autograph manuscript of a Milton poem or a Charlotte Brontë novel or a Lamb essay with intrinsic and particular interest, as the site of a special kind of activity and agency, and even though every year thousands of tourists visit the manuscripts of Shelley's 'Ode to the West Wind' and Austen's discarded fragment of *Persuasion* in their exhibition cases in the British Library.

For Lamb is surely right that the very completeness of the illusion of print undermines the idea of its constructedness just as it obliterates the failures and lapses of artistic purpose which lie behind it. He is also right to imply that from the perspective of the print reader, the authorial manuscript is the text's decomposition over whose unarticulated parts (of which the 'repugnant', dismembered hand marking the paper is the emblem) there lingers an air of decay and ruin. Autograph and allograph manuscript copies are as much literary remains as origins, and their fascination is as relics, trophies of the famous. Objects of a national heritage, like mouldering castles, they are also available for the more intimate private pleasures of voyeurism and fetishization, as the scissored and scattered record of Austen's letters witnesses,

[4] 'Fragments of Criticism', No. 12, in *The Works of Charles Lamb*, ed. William Macdonald, 12 vols. (London: Dent, 1903), iii. 277. There seems to be some doubt as to attribution as the passage is not included as Lamb's in all collected editions of his works. But compare Lamb's injunction to Coleridge over the printing of some verses in a letter of 1796, 'The Fragments I now send you I want printed to get rid of 'em'. (*The Letters of Charles and Mary Lamb*, ed. Edwin W. Marrs, Jr, 3 vols. (Ithaca and London: Cornell University Press, 1975), i. 59.)

divided and subdivided to appease autograph hunters. Around Lamb's exaggerated rejection of the great artist's 'workshop' there even lies the stench of Frankenstein's 'workshop of filthy creation', bringing forth in secrecy a monstrous birth, misshapen by ink blots and errors. Far different from the work of ideal creation which the printing press appears to deliver whole and intact, the manuscript is the private, mutating other, the contradiction of the stability and health of the public print text. In its extremity, Lamb's rejection of the evidence of Milton's writing hand ('I wish they had thrown them in the Cam') curiously mimics the poem's declared occasion (the drowning of Edward King) and its development through a sequence of watery graves via the dismemberment and aquatic burial of the arch-poet Orpheus. It is as though for Lamb print not only exonerates manuscript of its textual burden, it also appropriates its creative charge.

In practical terms this is quite consistent with routine printing-house procedure. The reason we have no manuscript evidence for her six completed novels, all lifetime and immediately posthumous publications, apart that is from the discarded (unpublished) final section of *Persuasion*, is that Austen's were only ever working drafts and valued as such by author, publisher, and printer alike. Sent to the printing shop, they were in all probability destroyed in due course once their text was set in type.[5] Yet there are at least two good reasons why in Austen's case we cannot simply dismiss this stage: one is the testimony provided by the variety of manuscript states in which the works unpublished in her lifetime have come down to us, making it hard to ignore the kinds of evidence of preparation, revision, and attention to textual presentation they contain; and the other is the coincidence of Austen's career with the Romantic revaluation (despite Lamb) of manuscript as something more than print's pre-text.[6] By the simple fact of their survival in quantity from the early nineteenth century onwards, when from previous periods such evidence is much sparser, pre-print states (autograph and allograph drafts, faircopies, proofs) make us think differently about the nature of text and the labour of literary production; and they do so precisely at the time that, thanks to advances in mechanization (for example, the commercial use of stereotyping which rendered the appearance of print more uniform), the printed text

[5] For an idea of the normal routines of the nineteenth-century printing house in treating manuscript as printer's copy, proof sheets, etc., see Ch. 3, 155–65.

[6] The term 'pre-text' was suggested by Jean Bellemin-Noël in his *Le Texte et l'avant-texte* (Paris: Larousse, 1972), 15, to describe the drafts, manuscripts, proofs, and variants as seen from the perspective of what precedes a work as a 'text'.

appears to lose the potentially rich variability of early printed versions. In other words, manuscripts become interesting as or because 'print settles it'.

But what is it that print settles? Chapman appears to have identified sufficiently with Lamb's embarrassment at the author's scripted disarray to wish such evidence had not always been preserved for Austen. In the preface to his printed transcription of *Volume the First*, one of the three surviving manuscript notebooks in which she collected together her juvenile compositions, he put on record a remarkable confession:

> It will always be disputed whether such effusions as these ought to be published; and it may be that we have enough already of Jane Austen's early scraps. The author of the MEMOIR thought a very brief specimen sufficient. But perhaps the question is hardly worth discussion. For if such manuscripts find their way into great libraries, their publication can hardly be prevented. The only sure way to prevent it is the way of destruction, which no one dare take.[7]

Only months before writing the preface he had contrived the manuscript's purchase by a 'great library', and he anticipated the general disappointment publication would bring. *Volume the First* was the last of the three Austen notebooks to come to Chapman's attention, though he was not allowed sight of the actual manuscript *Volume the Second* until 1951 nor permission to publish *Volume the Third* (which he had inspected years before) until 1949.[8] He had long suspected *Volume the First* to be the source of the one slight item the family had selected to publish from the early writings in 1871; but he had not been able to trace it when preparing his own edition of Austen-Leigh's *Memoir* in the mid-1920s. At that time he knew of the volume's contents only from the hazy description in the later Austen-Leighs' *Life and Letters* and from extracts copied and circulated in manuscript form by different generations of the family. One such manuscript collection, of letters, poems, and short stories by Austen, transcribed in several hands, is in the Austen-Leigh archive in the Hampshire Record Office. Since it contains copies of

[7] Jane Austen, *Volume the First*, ed. R. W. C[hapman] (Oxford: Clarendon Press, 1933), ix.

[8] Letters in the Oxford University Press archive show that Chapman was negotiating, unsuccessfully, from 1924 to obtain sight of *Volume the Second* (*Love and Freindship*, as he calls it after the collection published in 1922, with a preface by G. K. Chesterton). Its then owner, Janet Sanders, was adamant in refusing him permission to see it, and he came to the conclusion that she was the editor of the 1922 edition and anxious to preserve her own interests as well as to avoid scrutiny of her text. Chapman had more success with its later owner, Mrs Mowll, though the correspondence hardly does him credit. (OUP archive, LOGE000025 'Jane Austen's Novels'; and PBED013422, 'The Works of Jane Austen Volume 6'.) It is clear from the archive that the separate edition of *Volume the Third* (1951) was undertaken as preparation for *Minor Works* (1954) and that Chapman never developed an appreciation of the juvenile works.

'The Mystery' and the cancelled Chapter 10 of Volume 2 of *Persuasion*, as well as several letters recorded in the *Memoir*, it is likely that this was a sourcebook or repository for James Edward Austen-Leigh; while the presence in it of copies of two further items from *Volume the First*—'Memoirs of Mr Clifford: an unfinished tale' and 'The Adventures of Mr Harley'—suggests these short pieces too were at some point under consideration for inclusion in the *Memoir*. Inherited by Jane's brother Charles, the autograph *Volume the First* had passed to his eldest daughter Cassandra (Cassy) Esten and then to the daughters of his son Charles John. Three of these daughters, by then hard up, sold various Austen manuscripts in the 1920s, *Volume the First* among them.[9] In November 1932 Chapman located it and arranged for its purchase by the Friends of the Bodleian Library, Oxford; in the following year he issued his transcription.

All three notebooks (the other two are now in the British Library) contain mainly autograph copies, with some later additions and revisions, of early compositions which do not survive in original drafts. As a three-volume set they constitute a collected (though significantly incomplete) manuscript edition of Austen's earliest writings.[10] Probably as early as 1787, when she was not yet 12, she began writing short stories, dramatic sketches, a parody history of England, and other miscellaneous items. She transcribed twenty-seven of these pieces, approximately 90,000 words, into the notebooks, giving them the archly comic designation 'Volume the First', 'Volume the Second', and 'Volume the Third', in imitation of the popular format of a contemporary published novel. The large, round, childish hand of the earliest entries in *Volume the First* (the first eleven items) suggests they were probably written and copied first, though the earliest dated entry in any of the notebooks is 'Love and Freindship' (13 June 1790) in *Volume the Second*; and it is clear from evidence of hand, dating, and style that entries were made in both other notebooks before *Volume the First* was completed (according to internal dating on 3 June 1793 when she was aged 17). There is further

[9] *Volume the First*, v–vi; and *Life and Letters* (1913), 55–7. HRO, MS. 23M93/64/4/2, a volume containing miscellaneous manuscript copies of letters, poems, and short stories by Austen, in several hands. R. Brimley Johnson, *Jane Austen: Her Life, Her Work, Her Family, and Her Critics* (London and Toronto: J. M. Dent and Sons, 1930), 270–1, describes another such composite manuscript of Jane Austen writings, copied out by Mary Austen-Leigh, James Edward's daughter. R. W. Chapman, 'A Jane Austen Collection', *Times Literary Supplement*, 14 January 1926, 27.

[10] Southam, *Jane Austen's Literary Manuscripts*, 19, notes that twelve leaves are missing from *Volume the Second*, and that 'two little plays and some early "novels" [prose sketches] may not have been entered in the notebooks.'

evidence that she altered or added detail over a longer period—as late as 1811; and that later still hands other than her own inserted new material.[11]

Of the Austen manuscripts to survive in seemingly entire form, the bulk—that is, the three notebooks, the recently attributed play 'Sir Charles Grandison', and possibly *Lady Susan*—are of early works. But in view of the long gestation, rejection, or subsequent rewriting of compositions which in later versions became *Pride and Prejudice*, *Sense and Sensibility*, and *Northanger Abbey*, any concept of 'early' must in Austen's case be treated with extreme caution and allowed an elastic longevity. The first drafts of these novels, which we know only by their titles 'First Impressions', 'Elinor and Marianne', and 'Susan', were subsequently buried or destroyed in rewriting, and cannot easily be separated in time from work done on stories in the three manuscript volumes. Conversely, if the origins of the earliest novels lie alongside the juvenilia, critics have been eager to extend the life and influence of the three notebooks into the period of mature publication. Not only may their status as faircopies constitute them as durable and semi-public collections to be read and re-read, as a kind of family theatre, but Austen may have recycled their ingredients over a considerable period: that is, they may have served as a workshop or storehouse of ideas for later fictions or as an evolving work in progress, a dramatic counter to the disciplined project of psychological realism which her later and published writings would lead her to develop.[12] The suggestion attributes to these manuscripts a near-Wordsworthian status to record the growth, setbacks, and compromises of the novelist's mind.

When Chapman turned to *Volume the First* in 1933 it was ten years after his conservative and holistic treatment of the printed works. He had in the

[11] B. C. Southam, 'The Manuscript of Jane Austen's *Volume the First*', *The Library*, 5th ser., 17 (1962), 232–4. For later additions to the notebooks, see pp. 225, 247–8 and n. 46 below.

[12] See 'The Manuscript of Jane Austen's *Volume the First*', 234: 'At first, it was something of a show-piece', only later 'a handy collection of stories to read aloud to the family'; Mary Gaither Marshall, 'Jane Austen's Manuscripts of the Juvenilia and *Lady Susan*: A History and Description', in *Jane Austen's Beginnings*, 115, suggests that at a later stage, represented by revisions to the manuscript, 'Jane was using the volume as a repository for future ideas or perhaps as a working manuscript for future publication rather than as a source for family entertainment.' This is a point with which a recent editor of the manuscript notebooks appears to concur, see *Catharine and Other Writings*, ed. Margaret Anne Doody and Douglas Murray (Oxford: Oxford University Press, 1993), where Doody concludes: 'Certainly these early works were important companions to [Austen] during the rest of her writing career' (xx). These views are in marked contrast to the major critical trend of the first half of the twentieth century, whose tendency was to see the juvenilia as apprentice works to be outgrown rather than recycled. See, for example, Virginia Woolf, 'Jane Austen Practising' (1922), in *The Essays of Virginia Woolf*, iii. 334; and Q. D. Leavis's influential 'A Critical Theory of Jane Austen's Writings', in *Collected Essays*, i. 61–146.

interval prepared a uniform edition of the later manuscript writings—*Lady Susan* and *Sanditon* in 1925, *Plan of a Novel... and other documents* and *Two Chapters of Persuasion* in 1926, and *The Watsons* in 1927.[13] More radically than these later pieces, many of which can accurately be described as print's pre-textual drafts, the early manuscript books dispute an identity settled in and through print. This is one explanation for the reticence felt by the family, and by Chapman as their respectful agent, when it came to making them public; even as late as 1989 Joan Austen-Leigh, James Edward's great-granddaughter, can be heard expressing regret at 'many of the earliest scraps' seeing 'the light of day'.[14] In the first edition of the *Memoir* Austen-Leigh had been content simply to remark: 'There is extant an old copy-book containing several tales, some of which seem to have been composed while she was quite a girl'; he gave no extracts and argued 'it would be as unfair to expose this preliminary process to the world, as it would be to display all that goes on behind the curtain of the theatre before it is drawn up.' But a year later, in revisions to the second edition, the single old copybook has multiplied ('There are copy books extant...'), and he includes 'a specimen', to exemplify 'the kind of transitory amusement which Jane was continually supplying to the family party'. The item selected is the dramatic sketch or playlet entitled 'The Mystery. An Unfinished Comedy.'[15] Dedicated 'To the Rev.[d] George Austen', Jane's father, it may have been written for a family theatrical as early as 1788;[16] and if so it is one of the earliest pieces to survive, its inspiration possibly being Sheridan's burlesque play *The Critic* (1779).

[13] For bibliographical details of Chapman's 'uniform edition' of the post-juvenile manuscript writings, see Gilson F5–F10.

[14] Joan Austen-Leigh, 'The Juvenilia: A Family "Veiw"', in *Jane Austen's Beginnings*, 177.

[15] For details, see *Memoir*, 39–42 and notes 217–19. *Volume the First* was presumably at this time in the possession of Jane's niece Cassy Esten. Southam, 'The Manuscript of Jane Austen's *Volume the First*', 231, has assumed that Austen-Leigh did not see *Volume the First* but worked instead from a copied extract. But this is by no means clear from what Austen-Leigh actually says. His detached style of reference ('There are copy books extant...') is more likely adopted as a means of protecting Austen's reputation as a writer of mature novels, which might suffer with wide publication of early pieces meant only for family eyes. Since Cassy Esten was willing to help with other materials (letters and Cassandra's sketch of Jane) it is hardly likely she would have withheld *Volume the First*. *Volume the Second* was a different matter—owned since Frank Austen's death by Fanny Sophia, who was reluctant for letters in her possession to be made available to the public. Indeed, it seems clear from differences in the texts of the two editions of the *Memoir* that in the year which intervened between them, Austen-Leigh gained more information about and personal familiarity with the manuscript notebooks, their number, and their contents. A more interesting question is why Austen-Leigh did not print extracts from his own inherited manuscript, *Volume the Third*.

[16] Le Faye, *Family Record*, 66.

'The Mystery' barely fills two printed pages; cryptic as to structure and content, it has an interrupted plot and is composed of incomplete snatches of dialogue, spoken in whispers. Formally an episode or fragment, its subject is a secret or mystery, shared among the characters but out of hearing of the reader or listener. Its effect is both contrived and indeterminate. It seems likely Austen-Leigh chose it on the grounds that it was one of the shortest pieces and least offensive to his Victorian sensibilities—not a trace here of the drunkenness, female brawling, sexual misdemeanour, and murder which run riot across the pages of many of the other tales; that far from revelling in its pre-print potential he wished to limit any connection between the juvenile writer and the public novelist. In this he was successful, since 'The Mystery' remained the only one of the notebook writings to reach print for the next fifty years; not until 1922 did a transcription of the hitherto unknown *Volume the Second* appear under the title *Love & Freindship and Other Early Works*, with an important preface by G. K. Chesterton.[17]

If he meant by this to stifle interest in the child-writer, the unintended consequences of Austen-Leigh's decision are also worth considering; for his choice of this brief dramatic sketch, one of only three such pieces in the juvenilia, accidentally brings into sharper relief a vitally diffused ingredient of the early writing—ellipsis. Where ellipsis conventionally signals incoherence or disintegration—a breakdown of communication—within a close community its effect is precisely the opposite, and the listener or audience can be relied upon to fill in the gaps. Essentially what transforms ellipsis into something communicable is not the visual code of inked dashes but the delivered pace of speaking or reading aloud, which triggers association and stimulates speaker and listener to collaborate in expanding the text. A great deal of what we define as parody works in this way, requiring for its success a 'peculiar combination of sophistication and provinciality... the former for obvious reasons, the latter because the audience must be homogeneous enough to get the point.'[18]

[17] 'The Mystery' was given an extended life in reprints of the *Memoir* through the late nineteenth century. It was also reprinted in two early works of biographical criticism: S. F. Malden, *Jane Austen* (Eminent Women Series) (London: W. H. Allen and Co., 1889); and Oscar Fay Adams, *The Story of Jane Austen's Life* (Chicago: A. C. McClurg and Co., 1891). As late as 1913, in *Life and Letters*, it was still the only piece the family was prepared to publish from the juvenilia. See David J. Gilson and J. David Grey, 'Jane Austen's Juvenilia and *Lady Susan*: An Annotated Bibliography', in *Jane Austen's Beginnings*, 243–62.

[18] Dwight Macdonald, quoted in Linda Hutcheon, *A Theory of Parody: The Teachings of Twentieth-Century Art Forms* (1985; repr. New York and London: Routledge, 1991), 27.

Austen's early writings are 'provincial' in just this sense (which is not at all identical with the 'village ethos' of her published novels); by a variety of means they co-opt the reader/recipient into the textual space. Within it the conventions of confidentiality apply: formal codes are recycled and creative boundaries are blurred as a means to draw close to literary models and discuss shared reading. As literary apprenticeship, the method is communal and performative. It is all the more interesting, then, that Austen's niece Caroline, who as a child had shared in the family-based storytelling, should in later life have considered its processes to be distinct from the creativity which fuelled the published novels. Writing to her brother in 1869, as he collected materials for the *Memoir*, she observed: 'I have always thought it remarkable that the early workings of her mind should have been in burlesque and comic exaggeration, setting at nought all rules of probable and possible—when of all her finished and later writings, the exact contrary is the characteristic.'[19]

Not only are the early writings traversed by different voices, those voices are discontinuous, interruptive, given to surprise and reversal rather than completion. They challenge one another and multiply with cheerful disregard for the proprieties of the larger frame. If it is the nature of printed texts to produce local and occasional variants, then these manuscript books are continuously, constitutionally variant: in generic range, but also in matters of orthography and formal presentation. The early manuscripts, *Lady Susan* included, have something to say about the importance of appearance to the relationship with the reader within which writings achieve their effects. The juvenilia parody calligraphically the conventions of book-making—in paratextual features such as tables of contents, dedications, titles and chapter divisions, and in the heavy use of 'printers' rules'—to create something like, but ultimately very unlike, a printed book. *Lady Susan*, too, is a faircopy, almost free from corrections or erasures, and laid out with scrupulous attention to paragraphing and speech demarcation, quite unlike Austen's habit in her working manuscripts. Presentation enhances the work's dramatic arrangement—something Chapman chose oddly to diminish by providing a print transcription in which speeches are collapsed together, curbing the visual expression of the work's energetic virtuosity in favour of the composure of the reporting voice. This is, after all, an epistolary novel; so its speeches should properly express the partialities of those who write (not those who

[19] *Memoir*, 186.

101

I could have wished in my Daughter, or had I
even known her to possess so much as she does,
I should not have been anxious for the match."

"It is odd that you alone should be ignorant
of your Daughter's Sense."

"Frederica never does justice to herself; — her
manners are shy & childish. She is besides afraid
of me; she scarcely loves me. — During her poor
Father's life she was a spoilt child; the severity
which it has since been necessary for me to
shew, has entirely alienated her affection; neither
has she any of that Brilliancy of Intellect, that
Genius, or vigour of Mind which will force it:
:self forward."

"Say rather that she has been unfortunate in
her Education."

"Heaven knows my dearest Mrs Vernon, how
fully I am aware of that; but I would wish to

19. Page from the holograph faircopy manuscript of *Lady Susan*. (MS. MA 1226). By kind permission of the Pierpont Morgan Library, New York.

speak). But the effect of Chapman's editorial redirection of the manuscript text is to dull the edge of the characters' accomplished mimicry and to mute its rhetorical force as textual performance. In this case, and to redirect Lamb's phrase, 'print ruins it'.[20]

[20] *Jane Austen's Lady Susan: A Facsimile of the Manuscript in the Pierpont Morgan Library and the 1925 Printed Edition*, preface by A. Walton Litz (New York and London: Garland Publishing, Inc., 1989).

(111)

regretting it, my dear Sister, said she; on the contrary, I am grateful for so favourable a sign of my Daughter's sense. Sir James is certainly under par—(his boyish manners make him appear the worse)—and had Frederica possessed the penetration, the abilities, which I could have wished in my daughter, or had I even known her to possess so much as she does, I should not have been anxious for the match." "It is odd that you alone should be ignorant of your Daughter's sense." "Frederica never does justice to herself; her manners are shy & childish. She is besides afraid of me; she scarcely loves me. During her poor Father's life she was a spoilt child; the severity which it has since been necessary for me to shew, has entirely alienated her affection; neither has she any of that Brilliancy of Intellect, that Genius, or Vigour of

Mind

(112)

Mind which will force itself forward." "Say rather that she has been unfortunate in her Education." "Heaven knows my dearest Mrs Vernon, how fully I am aware of *that*; but I would wish to forget every circumstance that might throw blame on the memory of one, whose name is sacred with me."

Here she pretended to cry. I was out of patience with her. "But what, said I, was your Ladyship going to tell me about your disagreement with my Brother?" "It originated in an action of my Daughter's, which equally marks her want of Judgement, and the unfortunate Dread of me I have been mentioning. She wrote to M^{r} De Courcy." "I know she did. You had forbidden her speaking to Mr Vernon or to me on the cause of her distress; what could she do therefore but apply to my Brother?" "Good God!—she

exclaimed

20. R. W. Chapman's transcription of the same passage in *Lady Susan*, 1925. By kind permission of Oxford University Press.

Chapman's experience of Austen, as a writer constituted through print, did not equip him to appreciate the broad scribal relationship with the reader and the diversity of effects that print sets about effacing; nor did his general editorial stance sit easily with the self-consciously experimental decompositions, performative flourishes, and bibliographic jokes of the manuscript hand. His embarrassment is not at the look of blotted and revised pages (for these are not first drafts) but at a deeper exposure—of the substantive anarchy of a fertile, even heartless imagination beyond the schooling of a subsequently acquired moral and print conformity. As if taking Gérard Genette's thesis on the function and effects of paratexts (title-pages, prefaces, running heads, etc.) to heart, many of the pieces in the juvenile notebooks are more paratextual than textual, their creative energy lodged (and discharged) in the borderlands which mediate between work, author, and reader.[21] Disproportionate dedicatory outgrowths barely fettered to the convention of content, they gesture extravagantly and crudely towards their amputated texts which merely serve as the ostensible pretexts for their far more substantial pre-textual existence. Such exhibitionism marks the literary space as only sociable:

To Charles John Austen Esqre

Sir,

Your generous patronage of the | unfinished tale, I have already taken the | Liberty of dedicating to you, encourages | me to dedicate to you a second, as unfinish:|:ed as the first.

I am Sir with every expression
of regard for you and yr noble
Family, your most obed:^{t}
&c. &c. . . .
The Author

Compare, for example, the facsimile manuscript and transcription in the following instances: f. 92 (p. 101); f. 96 (p. 105); f. 97 (p. 107); ff. 99–102 (pp. 109–12); and ff. 110–12 (pp. 121–2). Whether Chapman himself or some other agent in the production process was responsible for 'correcting' manuscripts in transcription (and such regularization is a feature of others of the printed transcriptions), he as editor must take responsibility.

[21] Gérard Genette, *Paratexts: Thresholds of Interpretation* (in French as *Seuils* (1987)), trans. by Jane E. Lewin and Richard Macksey (Cambridge: Cambridge University Press, 1997).

Memoirs of Mr Clifford
an unfinished tale—

Of Chapman's contemporaries, only G. K. Chesterton seemed at home with what he called the controlled and directed 'exuberance', the 'passion', and 'joyous scorn' of the early manuscript writings.[22] But his was a lone voice, and until the feminist revaluation of the 1970s, the juvenilia would be pressed to serve an ideal of the artist's development closely modelled on an anthropological concept of primitive versus civilized culture, in which the 'raw', anarchic energy of youthful manuscript publication embarrasses or disturbs the polished, 'cooked' conformities of mature print.[23]

In Austen's case the usual routines of the early nineteenth-century printing house have caused an unusual division. She is the only major writer of the period for whom we have a body of manuscript writings and a body of printed texts which are almost exactly disjunct. In her case, there is a near precise correlation between the loss of the writing hand and the appearance of print, between the expressiveness of writing and the absence of print. We have in other words, the two major traces of textual activity in the period, writing and print, but they never form the two parts of the same whole. The Austen we are most of us familiar with, the writer of six classic novels, exists and is recoverable only within a print tradition. It is left to the written remains to unsettle the represented idea of the unitary author by which Chapman sought to regulate further the printed works, just as it is the printed tradition's evolving purpose to defend and normalize its exclusion of an unacceptable range of variation. But the demonstrable energy of the one textual form and the imputed conservatism of the other both miss their mark. It is worth noting that neither Chapman nor subsequent print editors of the early manuscript notebooks attempt to regulate them for publication to such a degree as to suggest that their proper textual state is print. The peculiar layout and look of the manuscript volumes—their calligraphic gestures towards bookmaking, for example—are routinely considered worth preserving, even though an appearance in print neutralizes such exaggerated signs of

[22] Bodleian MS. Don. e. 7. pp. 111–12; *Love & Freindship and Other Early Works, now first printed from the original ms. by Jane Austen*, with a preface by G. K. Chesterton (London: Chatto & Windus, 1922), xv.

[23] This older critical view is exemplified by Q. D. Leavis (see n. 12 above) and by A. Walton Litz, *Jane Austen: A Study of Her Artistic Development* (New York: Oxford University Press, 1965). The turning-point comes with Sandra M. Gilbert and Susan Gubar, *The Madwoman in the Attic: The Woman Writer and the Nineteenth-Century Literary Imagination* (New Haven: Yale University Press, 1979).

113

The beautifull Cassandra

a novel in twelve Chapters.

dedicated by permission to Miss Austen.

Dedication.

Madam

You are a Phoenix. Your taste is refined, your Sentiments are noble, & your Virtues innumerable. Your Person is lovely your Figure, elegant, & your Form, magestic. Your Manners, are polished, your Conversation is rational & your appearance singular. If therefore the following Tale will afford one moments amusement to you, every wish will be gratified of

your most obedient
humble servant
The Author

116

The beautifull Cassandra.

a novel, in twelve Chapters.

Chapter the first

Cassandra was the Daughter and the only Daughter of a celebrated Millener in Bond Street. Her father was of noble Birth, being the near relation of the Dutchess of —'s Butler.

Chapter the 2d

When Cassandra had attained her 16th year, she was lovely & amiable & chancing to fall in love with an elegant Bonnett, her Mother had just compleated bespoke by the Countess of — she placed it on her gentle Head & walked from her Mothers shop to make her Fortune.

Chapter the 3d

The first person she met, was the Viscount

21. ‘The Beautifull Cassandra’, *Volume the First* (MS. Don. E. 7). By kind permission of the Bodleian Library, Oxford University.

determination. Nor do editors of the print novels, faced with a crux in the print text, conjecturally restore the lost trace of the writing hand.

The simplest recourse for the editor of the manuscript works is to publish a photo-facsimile; and one stage beyond that is an exact printed transcription of the manuscript version, recording erasures and corrections, and preserving contractions and other orthographic idiosyncrasies which we know were ironed out in most cases in the early printed texts of the published works. Chapman employs both these methods, and while the result is a conservative text of considerable scholarly value, there are few, if any, concessions to the reader wishing to connect the parts of Austen's literary life into a typographic and creative whole. The division is starkest and least justifiable when it comes to the post-juvenile manuscript writings, which proceed in terms of no anti-bibliographic purpose. The drafts of *The Watsons* and *Sanditon*, for which we have only the unparagraphed pages, full of insertions, erasures, and abbreviations, undoubtedly represent Austen's regular practice in adult composition. It is difficult therefore to defend in their case the kind of non-interventionist[*sic*] editing that refuses to employ the normalizations of print—paragraphing, expansion of contractions, etc. Recently a new wave of editors has made a closer compromise between Austen's adult manuscript and print works by distinguishing some aspects presumed to be characteristic only of manuscript style and altering them, either to accord with the evidence of the printed works or the assumed needs of the modern (easily bewildered) reader. However, this editorial traffic is limited, cautious, and all in one direction, with little corresponding unsettling of the print tradition. For the time being, we continue to have two Austens, each bibliographically and largely critically distinct.[24]

One example—that of Mrs Elton's 'caro sposo'—must suffice for now to suggest how critically instructive an unsettling of the print history might be. In *Emma* Mrs Elton, the *arriviste* interloper into the well-bred drawing-rooms of Highbury, refers three times to her new husband as her 'caro sposo'. But that is in Chapman's edition and subsequent reprintings derived therefrom. In the first-edition text of 1816 the phrase appears each time

[24] Chapman's edition of the *Minor Works* (1954), as a belated Vol. 6 in his *Novels of Jane Austen*, is characterized by a concern to preserve manuscript features in print which accords with the 'minor' status to which he relegates these writings. In several subtle but instructive ways the volume is not made to conform to the rest of the collection. A more holistic but still tentative intention is outlined by John Davie in his 'Note on the Text' of *Lady Susan, The Watsons*, and *Sanditon* as issued by World's Classics (*Northanger Abbey, Lady Susan, The Watsons, and Sanditon*, ed. John Davie (Oxford: Oxford University Press, 1980), xxxiv–xxxv).

printed differently, as 'cara sposo', 'cara sposa', and only finally 'caro sposo'. Bentley's text, issued in 1833 and reprinted throughout the nineteenth century, retained the irregularity but with the nice correction to 'caro sposo' (from 'cara sposo') after the first occasion, when Emma mimics Mrs Elton's usage of the phrase ('"insufferable woman!" was [Emma's] immediate exclamation..."...A little upstart, vulgar being, with her Mr. E., and her *cara sposo*..."', 1816). Austen's heroine might be presumed to make the correct agreement between adjective and noun (hence the Bentley emendation), though I think this is to lose the vital point of Emma's mimicry—emphasized in the first-edition text by the phrase on this occasion only being set in italic type. When William and Richard Arthur Austen-Leigh, sharp readers of their ancestor's prose, published what was the first survey of the textual history of all six novels as an appendix to *Life and Letters* (1913), they made no comment on the irregularity of the three spellings, comfortable with the implied joke. Chapman, however, emends all three to the grammatically correct 'caro sposo'. Surely (as a reading of the anarchic orthography of the juvenile manuscripts, complete with wacky Italian, would confirm)[25] there is a good chance that Chapman's zeal has effaced what was for the narrator and her heroine yet another symptom of Mrs Elton's appalling vulgarity; and that in her case the outmoded slang of the phrase is compounded by a further solecism. Among modern editions, only Stephen Parrish's Norton Critical Edition of 1972 and Fiona Stafford's 1996 Penguin text restore the irregularity, and with it the added comic edge.[26]

[25] Cf. 'Lesley Castle' in *Volume the Second*: 'I had for many years constantly hollowed whenever she played, *Bravo, Bravissimo, Encora, Da Capo, allegretto, con expressione*, and *Poco presto*' (*Minor Works*, 130).

[26] The phrase 'caro sposo' has received a good deal of recent critical attention, particularly from Pat Rogers, '"Caro Sposo": Mrs Elton, Burneys, Thrales, and Noels', *Review of English Studies*, n.s., 45 (1994), 70–5; and 'Sposi in Surrey', *Times Literary Supplement*, 23 August 1996, 14–15, where Rogers observes of the 1816 first-edition text, 'Only on its final appearance does the reading appear as "caro sposo". These variants suggest trouble in the printing-house; but it would be in keeping for the imperfectly educated Mrs Elton to use an ungrammatical form' (15). The Bentley text (1833) was reprinted from the same stereotype plates until 1866 and reset in 1870, with further reprints in 1878–9 and 1882. No further alterations were made to regularize Mrs Elton's Italian. For Chapman's 'correction' of the phrase, see *Emma*, ed. Chapman, 278, 279, 302, 356. For the restored first-edition readings, see *Emma*, ed. Stephen M. Parrish (New York: W. W. Norton and Co., 1972), 189 and note ('it may have been Mrs. Elton, not Jane Austen, who fractured her Italian'); and *Emma*, ed. Stafford, 229, 248, 294. It is worth noting that Edward Marsh questioned Chapman's correction of the phrase in a letter of 24 February 1941. He writes: 'You will remember my raising the question of Mrs Elton's reference to Mr E., sometimes as her *cara sposo*, sometimes I think as *cara sposa*, & only once as *caro sposo* (I forget the details). Did you notice the first footnote on p. 262 of the delightful book on Mrs Thrale that you have just brought out, in which the *Morning Herald* is quoted as calling Piozzi her *cara sposa*? It looks as if it might have been a common mistake.' (Bodleain MSS. Eng. Letters c. 760, f. 76.) If, as Anna Lefroy suggests, Jane Austen knew some Italian (*Memoir*, 183), mimicry of the 'common mistake' could also have been part of her joke against those who spatter their conversation with Italian for fashion's sake, but do not know the basic rules of agreement.

Professional writer: Jane Austen's other identity. A digression

The hagiographic critics of the mid-twentieth century did not care to notice how shrewdly Austen intercepted critical and market trends in launching her novels on the public stage; and how remarkable was her contemporary success in view of her reluctance to abandon anonymity. Some facts: Austen's lifetime coincided with the first systematic attempt to calibrate a British national character according to literature's agency; reading became during these years (roughly 1780–1830) a significant social and individual indicator and people participated in public culture by virtue of what and how they read. At the same time, the foundations were laid for the professionalization of the activities of writer and critic, and literature was increasingly subject to modes of marketing and consumption which helped consolidate its functions, whether for entertainment or instruction, within a domestic space.

As recently as 1774, the year before Austen's birth, the House of Lords decision in *Donaldson* v. *Beckett* signalled the end of exclusive privilege in books. By breaking the English booksellers' right of perpetual copyright in texts, the publishing industry was changed for ever, opening the way for brisker competition between firms and creating a climate in which profits must be turned quickly. In the short term, the price of books fell and, in the longer term, the boost given to a competitive reprint trade in out-of-copyright works inaugurated a canon of English 'classics' which accrued mounting national and literary significance throughout the period. (Copyright was at this time and throughout Austen's life a maximum of twenty-eight years from first publication.) What began as a trade dispute served to define a concept of literature as a set of significant works from the past which would gain cultural value (and extend booksellers' profits) by their freer circulation. This is important to how we view Austen's relation to her chosen medium because in reprint series the reader was confronted not just with drama, poetry, or novels, but with the beginnings of an implied genealogy and classifying features of literary forms. Late eighteenth-century reprint series like Bell's *British Theatre* and *The Poets of Great Britain Complete from Chaucer to Churchill*, and Harrison's *Novelists' Magazine* consolidated readerly interest in distinct genres and encouraged in their textual associations a concentration on their native evolution—the British drama, the English poets, the British novelists.[27] This is a trend Austen consciously confronted and sought to exploit in her regionally located English novels.

Other institutional practices proposed further ways to group, diversify, and cheapen new literature at this time. The proliferation of varied methods of access, through circulating libraries, subscription libraries, and reading clubs contributed to blur distinctions between the public-political and private-unpoliticized space of reading, between kinds of literature, and specifically between 'high' and 'low' genres and the tastes and capacities of socially and economically diverse audiences. Like the periodical press, which exploded into activity in the early nineteenth century, the circulating library branded readers as group-identified, sociable consumers and made literature accessible when the cost of new works as distinct from reprints remained prohibitively high and purchasing power beyond all but the very wealthy. Inevitably the profit of such libraries lay in mass appeal, with romances and novels forming the bulk of their purchases. In his pamphlet *The Use of Circulating Libraries Considered; with Instructions for Opening and Conducting a Library, either upon a Large or Small Plan* (1797), Thomas Wilson, bookseller and stationer of Bromley, Kent, provides advice on account-keeping, terms of subscription, uniform binding of books, and the kinds of businesses most suited to combine with a lending library. He also makes recommendations for proportionate purchasing of stock across the various literary categories. Imprecise though such divisions were, they point to the ascendancy of the novel within popular culture at the end of the eighteenth century. By Wilson's calculation, a modest library in a small provincial town should consist of 'fifteen hundred volumes, which should be well chosen from different subjects, in the following proportion: 60 volumes of History; 60——of Divinity; 30——of Lives; 20——of Voyages; 20——of Travels; 30——of Poetry; 20——of Plays; 1050——of Novels; 130——of Romances; 10——of Anecdotes; 40——of Tales; 30——of Arts and Sciences.' Almost twenty years later, A. K. Newman's *Catalogue* (1814, with supplements to 1819) of the hugely powerful Minerva Library in Leadenhall Street, London, lists about 40 per cent of its holdings under the unwieldy heading 'Novels, Romances, Imaginary Histories, Lives, and Adventures'. Catalogues from comparable commercial

[27] Richard D. Altick, *The English Common Reader: A Social History of the Mass Reading Public, 1800–1900* (1957; 2nd edn., Columbus, OH: Ohio State University Press, 1998); Kathryn Sutherland, '"Events ... have made us a World of Readers": Reader Relations 1780–1830', in *The Romantic Period*, ed. David B. Pirie (Penguin History of Literature, 5), (Harmondsworth, Middx.: Penguin, 1994), 1–48.

circulating libraries in other towns suggest similar high proportions (usually between 40 and 70 per cent) of fiction in their stock.[28]

At the same time, the space which now opened for the delineation of a common literature became in many ways more uncertain and more contested, reflecting the variety, complexity, and sheer imprecision in the concept as formulated by the different interest groups of publishers, writers, readers, and critics. Efforts to align literature with the practices from which it was becoming increasingly distinct (specifically the authority of speech and intimate conversation among the likeminded) witness to an anxiety about print's capacity to communicate in the right way and inscribe a paradoxical bibliographic unease into publications, particularly those associated with high Romantic writers, most famously Wordsworth and Coleridge. The implied situatedness of much Romantic literature—as table talk, autobiography, and anecdote—attempts to reinstate within the passive encounter with the printed text the aura of exchange as the living dialectic of speech and the power of personality to stimulate response. A similarly ethical parochialism informs Austen's contribution to the novel as situated conversation within a small community. Where questions of authentic and inauthentic communication also surface as questions of genre (with poetry occupying the high ground and the novel relegated to a lesser space shaped by the low and sensational expectations of its mass readership), it is important to notice how cleverly Austen positioned her incursion into the lesser form. Her novels were immediately understood to be counter-novelistic, and as contributing to an authentic localism endangered by the mass centralized production of literary responses as of other commodities. Hence Walter Scott's curiously ambiguous commendation of their failure to seduce as fictions and of their 'pleasure nearly allied with the experience of [one's] own social habits'. As reviewers and ordinary readers regularly observed, Austen's novels dealt in probable reality and the kinds of people one felt one already knew.[29]

[28] [T. Wilson], *The Use of Circulating Libraries Considered; with Instructions for Opening and Conducting a Library, either upon a Large or Small Plan* (London and Bromley, Kent: J. Hamilton and T. Wilson, 1797), 26–7; A. K. Newman, *Catalogue of A. K. Newman and Co.'s Circulating Library... Consisting of a General Selection of Books in Every Department of Literature, and Particularly Embracing the Whole of the Modern Publications*, 7 parts (London: Minerva Press, 1814–[19]); Peter Garside *et al.*, *The English Novel 1770–1829*, ii. 18–19.

[29] Scott's review, the first major notice of Austen's novels, appeared anonymously in the *Quarterly Review*, 14 (1815), 188–201. Dated 1815, it was, in fact, written later and published March 1816, at John Murray's instigation. Extracted in *Critical Heritage*, i. 68. For the opinion of one ordinary reader, Lady Gordon, on the everyday reality Austen's fictions appeared to reproduce, see 'Opinions of *Mansfield Park*', in *Minor Works*, 435: 'there is scarcely an Incident or conversation, or a person that you are not inclined to imagine you have at one time or other in your Life been a witness to, born a part in, & been acquainted with.'

The debate over the status of the novel in the period has only recently moved beyond the anecdotal and the single-author study, methods which did much to perpetuate the familiar high Romantic dismissal of the form and of hack women writers as among its chief exponents. Thanks to new research, some revisions to these older views are now matters of fact. There was a statistical rise in the number of new novels from the 1780s which ensured that, despite occasional troughs in output (most interestingly in the middle years of the 1810s, when both Austen and Scott began publishing), by the end of the 1820s it was the dominant literary form; and it remained so for the rest of the nineteenth century.[30] There is also evidence throughout the period for the talking up of a genre which could be as mobile in its categorization as the fortunes of the heroes and heroines charted in its pages. Godwin, in his essay 'Of History and Romance' (1798), appeared to argue that works of fiction alone release for the examination and profit of writer and reader the complexities of social and psychological behaviour as exhibited by the individual. Coming hard on the Treason Trials and attempts at censorship of the mid-1790s, his faith in the recording powers of fiction over history carried political conviction. It follows that if the novel at this time acquired new significance as the record of 'the very web and texture of society, as it really exists',[31] so too did the critical debate over its significance. The period saw not just a statistical rise in the output of novels, but also serious attempts to account for its contemporary value and to place the form in historical context, most notably in John Dunlop's *The History of Fiction* (1814) and Anna Laetitia Barbauld's *British Novelists* (1810).

Issued in fifty volumes, *British Novelists* went further than any other collection in the period in its comprehensive attention to the generic integrity of modern fiction, in its presentation of the novel in nationalist terms, cleansed of the European excesses levelled against Gothic (the year was 1810 and Britain was at war with France), and in its positive critical observations on women as writers and consumers. The seriousness of the project was signalled by the 37 booksellers who underwrote its initial print run of 1,000 copies and whose names alone form a conspectus of the trade in the early nineteenth century. Barbauld, too, was by 1810 a highly regarded editor and

[30] Garside *et al.*, *The English Novel 1770–1829*, i. 26–8 and ii. 38–40.

[31] William Godwin, 'Of History and Romance', *Political and Philosophical Writings*, general editor Mark Philp, 7 vols. (London: William Pickering, 1993), v. 300–1; William Hazlitt, 'Standard Novels and Romances' (*Edinburgh Review*, February 1815), in *Complete Works*, ed. P. P. Howe, 21 vols. (London and Toronto: Dent, 1930–4), xvi. 5.

cultural commentator, with editions to her credit of the poetry of Collins (1794) and Akenside (1797) as well as Richardson's *Correspondence* (1804) and *Selections from the Spectator, Tatler, Guardian, and Freeholder* (1805). As a sign of her stature and the confidence felt in this new enterprise she was paid the considerable sum of £300 for her editorship of *The British Novelists*. In the collection, the chosen works of each novelist are prefaced by a biographical and critical introduction and the whole is fronted by an essay 'On the Origin and Progress of Novel-Writing'.

Barbauld's essay followed a characteristic Enlightenment trajectory, where 'progress' is discernible as a shedding of non-native (typically oriental and European) superstition and improbability, in a steady march towards a superior native manufacture. According to this thesis, the novel emerged from eastern origins, through medieval European romance, to its highest evolution as a British work of moral instruction, in which 'the interest, even of the generality of readers, is most strongly excited when some serious end is kept in view'.[32] Even Barbauld's unapologetic insistence on the epithets 'novel' and 'novelist' constituted a bold defence at a time when respected writers like Fanny Burney and Maria Edgeworth approached the term nervously. 'The following work is offered to the Public as a Moral Tale—the author not wishing to acknowledge a Novel', Edgeworth wrote in her 'Author's Advertisement' to *Belinda* (1801), a title chosen for inclusion in the collection. Barbauld has no time for such equivocation. On the contrary, she argues, the modern female novelist is unsurpassed in establishing the novel as a substantial ethical vehicle. Of the twenty-one British novelists represented in her collection, eight are women. Importantly, too, several (Burney, Edgeworth, Inchbald, Radcliffe) were still alive in 1810. If the convention to date in reprint collections had been to exclude contemporary writers, Barbauld and her bookseller-collaborators actively promoted the concept of a living tradition for a form whose moral and literary significance they shrewdly conflated with its popularity.

Published on the eve of her professional career, *British Novelists* provides a history and textual authority for the kind of fiction Austen writes: novels in which seriousness and standards of truth to life are promoted (witness the Barbauld-like panegyric to the female novel in *Northanger Abbey*, Chapter 5). Following Barbauld's critical instruction, every one of Austen's lifetime title-pages has beneath the work's title and printed in large capitals the simple,

[32] [Anna Laetitia] Mrs. Barbauld, 'On the Origin and Progress of Novel-Writing', *The British Novelists*, 50 vols. (new edn., London: F. C. and J. Rivington *et al.*, 1820), i. 57.

unqualified description A NOVEL. Austen positioned herself with canniness and ambition in relation to the contemporary fiction market, and this too conforms with Barbauld's thesis. On the one hand, she openly enthuses as reader over the indiscriminate range on offer in the circulating libraries; on the other, she shows from the outset a twin determination to enter the market as writer at the élite end and to garner as much prestige and money from the business as she can.

Walter Scott's example has undoubtedly skewed our sense of the fortunes to be made from novel writing in the early part of the century. Peter Garside has recently provided details for 2,256 fiction titles first published in Britain between 1800 and 1829, showing peaks in output in the first years of the new century, a clear trough coinciding with the economic depression of the 1810s, when Austen entered the market, and a steady rise in the 1820s. Annual production of new titles averaged over the period between 60 and 80 (still only a small percentage of book production overall), and, contrary to some critical claims, there appears to be no uninterrupted upward trend, 1808 and 1824 standing out as high points (over 100 new titles in 1808, 99 in 1824).[33] Throughout, impression numbers for first and subsequent editions were modest, with a run of 500–750 copies remaining a norm, only increasing to 1,500–2,000 for established authors by the 1820s. Scott was the exception: 6,000 copies of his third novel *The Antiquary* (1816) disposed of in a few weeks, and first impressions of 12,000 copies of subsequent novels by the early 1820s. Against this, *Emma* (1816), Jane Austen's first novel to be published by John Murray, ran to a healthy first impression of 2,000 copies, some 750 copies more than the first run of her previous novel, *Mansfield Park*, printed in 1814 for the less distinguished firm of Thomas Egerton.[34]

Where Scott's annual novel profits were estimated in 1818 at a colossal £10,000, Fanny Burney's excellent deal (up to £3,000) with the firm of Longman, Hurst, Rees, Orme, and Brown for the manuscript of *The Wanderer* (1814) gambled on the novel going through several editions. Burney, who in 1776 sold her first novel for only £20, to which her publisher Lowndes subsequently added £10 more, was by now a big name and this much-delayed new work was eagerly awaited. But Longman's plan to market an initial print run of 6,000 as a first edition of 3,000, dividing the remainder into three subsequent editions (a common enough ploy), collapsed when in the event, *The Wanderer* was a critical failure, and copies were later

[33] Garside *et al.*, *The English Novel 1770–1829*, ii. 38–40.

[34] Gilson, 49 and 69.

pulped.[35] From a very respectable £300 given for *Belinda* (1801), Maria Edgeworth could command an impressive £1,050 for the second series of *Tales of Fashionable Life* (1812), followed by £2,100 for *Patronage* (1814).[36] Without the same fame, Austen failed to make more than small profits, though she managed with some skill the game of 'on commission' publishing, and there is no evidence that any publisher egregiously cheated her.[37] With Cassandra Austen's sale for £210 of the five remaining copyrights to Richard Bentley in 1832 (only the copyright of *Pride and Prejudice*, which turned out to be her most commercially successful novel, was sold during the author's lifetime), the overall earnings from her novels can be estimated at around £1,625, most of which was received after her death.[38] It is worth comparing these modest profits with the general situation at the end of the eighteenth century, when the price for the average novel manuscript ranged from £5 to £20.[39] This was around the time that Austen sold 'Susan' (a version of *Northanger Abbey*) for £10 to Crosby and Co. When we take into account the significant but by no means proportionate hike in the retail price for a three-volume work, which tripled from 10*s.* 6*d.* in 1800 to 31*s.* 6*d.* in the later 1820s, we discover a clear signal of the greater economic respect in which the profession of novel writer was held post-1800. In general terms, though, the period is best viewed as one of moderate financial rewards for a small proportion of writers and of consolidation and cautious expansion in the trade rather than innovation and risk-taking.

In context, we can see that Austen received in her lifetime considerable literary if only modest financial success. *Emma* issued in three volumes for a guinea in 1816 with the esteemed and fashionable imprint of John Murray and a dedication to the Prince Regent was quite a different article from the kind of pulp fiction Crosby produced. We have not paid sufficient attention to the shift in late 1815 from Egerton's publishing house to Murray and what this suggested for Austen's contemporary critical reputation. Murray was not a noted novel publisher; his list was mainly poetry and travel writings. We do not know why he took an interest in Austen: perhaps Henry Austen, ever the

[35] Garside *et al.*, *The English Novel 1770–1829*, ii. 45.

[36] Marilyn Butler, *Maria Edgeworh: A Literary Biography*, (Oxford: Clarendon Press, 1972), 490–3.

[37] For methods of publication in the period and Austen's preferred arrangement of publication on commission or by the author, see Jan Fergus, *Jane Austen: A Literary Life*, 9–14; and Garside *et al.*, *The English Novel 1770–1829*, ii. 80–2.

[38] Fergus, *Jane Austen: A Literary Life*, 171 and 193; Edward Copeland, *Women Writing About Money: Women's Fiction in England, 1790–1820* (Cambridge: Cambridge University Press, 1995), 191–201.

[39] Blakey, *The Minerva Press, 1790–1820*, 73.

opportunist, approached him; perhaps William Gifford, his editor and reader for the press, alerted Murray to her potential; certainly he greatly admired *Pride and Prejudice*. Whatever the factors involved, it is clear that Gifford was engaged in late summer 1815 to read *Pride and Prejudice* closely and critically, paying attention to the quality of its production, and to report back to Murray; only after this do we hear that a bargain has been struck for publishing *Emma*.[40]

Murray's initial plan was to buy the copyrights of all three available novels, *Sense and Sensibility*, *Mansfield Park*, and *Emma*; it is also possible he may have had designs on the attractive copyright of *Pride and Prejudice*, owned by Egerton. He offered the reasonable (though not generous) sum of £450 for all three; and if Austen had been willing to sell, she would have been effectively incorporated from that moment as a writer of serious fiction into his stable of establishment and experimental talents alongside such contemporary luminaries as Scott, Southey, and Byron. She preferred instead to continue to bear the cost of production herself and to retain copyright, an option which was both riskier for the author and less of an incentive to the publisher. Nevertheless the move to Murray meant a larger print run, a more handsome and prestigious material product, and her first major review.

Like the big houses of Constable and Blackwood in Edinburgh, Murray in London established his formidable publishing network around his own critical periodical. Among the evolving institutional relations of the modern literary market, the periodical represented the chance to control both the fortunes of particular books, by arranging for favourable reviews, and the opinions of readers, to whom it served up a digest of views on a variety of issues and across a range of genres. With massive print runs and readerships of 50,000 and more a periodical could become the mainstay of a publishing firm; and a favourable review in Constable's *Edinburgh Review*, *Blackwood's Edinburgh Magazine*, or Murray's *Quarterly Review* signalled serious critical acclaim. In commissioning Walter Scott to review *Emma* for the *Quarterly* Murray was promoting his own imprint, a fact that gives more point to Scott's concern to distinguish the new novel from the common run of circulating library fiction ('far superior to . . . the ephemeral productions which supply the regular demand of watering-places and circulating libraries').[41] But he was doing something more than this: in contrast to the late eighteenth-century periodicals, these new heavyweight journals gave little

[40] Smiles, *A Publisher and His Friends*, i. 282; *Jane Austen's Letters*, 291–4.

[41] In Southam, *Critical Heritage*, i. 59.

space to fiction reviewing; so an essay of this length and discrimination (Scott introduced his critique with an excursion into the history of fiction) was also giving in loud terms the establishment seal of approval to a serious new talent. When she moved to Murray only four years after her début as a published author, Jane Austen had arrived.

'The Steventon Edition'

Writing to Martha Lloyd from Chawton on 29 November 1812 Austen inserts the following information, between talk of Mr Digweed shooting rabbits on Tuesday at Steventon and news that *Pride and Prejudice* has been sold to Egerton for £110: 'The 4 lines on Miss W. which I sent you were all my own, but James afterwards suggested what I thought a great improvement & as it stands in the Steventon Edition.'[42] The reference is to a four-line quatrain written in anticipation of the marriage of the middle-aged and, to Austen's comic mind, desperate Urania Wallop and the elderly Revd Henry Wake. Like others of her comic verses, the joke hangs upon the punning associations of the victims' names, 'having in vain danced at many a ball, | [Maria] Is now happy to *jump at a Wake*.' The text as reproduced by Chapman and more recently by Margaret Doody comes from Austen-Leigh's *Memoir*, and presumably is the version improved by James Austen, Austen-Leigh's father, and handed down in the family. James Austen, Jane's eldest brother and ten years her senior, had been settled at the Steventon rectory since his father's departure in 1801, and this perhaps explains the joking reference to the 'Steventon Edition'. More particularly, Jane and her mother had been staying at Steventon as recently as June; since then and back at Chawton she had been entertaining herself and her Steventon nieces, Anna and Caroline, with verses and stories. No surviving manuscript of the Wallop–Wake lines is known at present, either of the version sent to Martha Lloyd or of its Steventon recension; but a variant text preserved in the diary of Stephen Terry, father-in-law to Anna Lefroy's fourth daughter, Georgiana, confirms that two versions were circulated in the family.[43]

[42] *Jane Austen's Letters*, 196–7.

[43] The text derives from the *Memoir* (1870), 116. It is reprinted in *Minor Works*, 444; and in *Catharine and Other Writings*, ed. Doody and Murray, 244. Austen-Leigh gives the verses the title, almost as long as the piece itself (and all in capitals) 'On the marriage of a middle-aged Flirt with a Mr Wake, whom, it was supposed, she would scarcely have accepted in her youth', and Chapman repeats it.

It is not necessary to imagine the material existence of a larger 'Steventon Edition' of Austen's manuscript works, though the speculation is an intriguing one, not least because we cannot know if such an 'Edition' existed and is now lost or whether the surviving three juvenile *Volumes*, with their clear evidence of family collaboration and shared purpose, might form a significant part of it. The published works were in their final form all the products of the Chawton period (post-1809 when Jane, Cassandra, their mother, and Martha Lloyd moved in to Chawton Cottage), and so can be said to form the 'Chawton Edition'; but the years at Steventon rectory (up to 1801) were also prolific (drafts of three full-length novels among other writings). That does not explain why, eleven years after leaving Steventon, Austen might still describe her compositions as contributing to the 'Steventon Edition'. What might explain it is Steventon's status as the most complete of Austen's family homes (the home in which most of her immediate family lived together over a period of years), and the role that family members continued to play in the gestation, composition, and revision of her writings. Charles was the last brother to leave home, in 1791, and Jane began writing in earnest about 1787. In the summer of 1812 she appears to be reinvoking the comic absurdities of her early Steventon sketches when she encourages Anna, James's 19-year-old daughter, in writing a Gothic romp 'The Car of Falkenstein'. Remembering her aunt more than fifty years later, Anna recorded how during that summer 'the original 17 years between us seemed to shrink to 7—or to nothing' as they spent their time laughing over and parodying the improbable contents of the volumes provided by the fiction list of the local Alton circulating library: 'Greatly we both enjoyed it, one piece of absurdity leading to another, till Aunt Cassan[dr][a] fatigued with her own share of laughter w[d]. exclaim "How *can* you both be so foolish?" & beg us to leave off—'.[44] During the same months Austen was also in the late stages of revising 'First Impressions' for publication as *Pride and Prejudice* and enjoying with Cassandra the joke of concealing from Anna her authorship of the published *Sense and Sensibility*.[45]

For the Terry version and the name changes (from Camilla to Maria, perhaps at James's instigation) to conceal identity, see David Gilson, 'Jane Austen's Verses' (1984), reprinted in *Jane Austen: Collected Articles and Introductions* (privately printed, 1998), 47–8; and *Jane Austen's Letters*, 409 n. 7.

[44] Anna Lefroy, 'Recollections of Aunt Jane' (1864), in *Memoir*, 159. For 'The Car of Falkenstein', a nonsensical name for the local Alton coach, see ibid., 160 and note.

[45] HRO, MS. 23M93/85/2 Fanny C. Lefroy, 'Family History', unpaginated: 'It was in searching this Library [Alton circulating library] that my Mother came across a copy of Sense & Sensibility which she threw aside with careless contempt, little imagining who had written it, exclaiming to the great amusement of her Aunts who stood by "Oh that must be rubbish I am sure from the title."'

What we know of Austen's working methods as writer is slight, a matter of occasional remarks scattered thinly across her surviving letters, of deduction from the examination of manuscript copies preserved in different states of completeness, and of family anecdotes remembered or constructed across a considerable stretch of time. As evidence it is at best partial and local, providing little that can be extrapolated as a set of general procedures for how she usually went about her writing business. There are indications, for example, that she refined her fictions consensually within the circle of family and close friends: that is, that her view of authorship was consistent with the social dynamic developed in her novels, where individual identity is held within a fabric of communal approval and assent. In support of this, hands other than her own are present in the manuscript book known as *Volume the Third*, where separate leaves loosely inserted and initialled by Anna Austen, in her married name Lefroy (they are initialled 'JAEL' [Jane Anna Elizabeth Lefroy]), provide a four-page continuation to 'Evelyn'. Since Anna did not marry Benjamin Lefroy until 1814 this means that the addition was made at least twenty-two years after Austen began the story in 1792. Other additions to *Volume the Third* and an allusive reference, in a letter of August 1814 from Jane to Cassandra, to a passage from 'Love and Freindship' (written twenty-four years earlier and recorded in *Volume the Second*), suggest that these collections retained long currency within the family circle from regular re-reading. During the 1810s, when her Steventon niece and nephew were testing their skills as novel writers, the old notebooks may even have served a pedagogic function. Elsewhere, specific evidence in the form of updating of internal details points to Austen's possible rediscovery of the manuscript notebooks after July 1809 when the family belongings were unpacked at Chawton.[46] If so, we might link renewed enjoyment and even collaborative editing of their contents with the exact period when the novels drafted in early form at Steventon, and first among them *Sense and Sensibility*, were being refashioned for publication.

[46] *Jane Austen's Letters*, 270 and 435 n. 3 ('It put me in mind of my own Coach between Edinburgh & Sterling'). For details of alterations and updating over time and the presence of other hands in the notebooks, see Southam, *Jane Austen's Literary Manuscripts*, 17–18; supplemented by Southam, 'Interpolations to Jane Austen's *Volume the Third*', *Notes and Queries*, 207 (1962), 185–7; *Catharine and Other Writings*, ed. Doody and Murray, xix–xx, 266, and 271–2; and 'Note on the Text' in *Jane Austen's Evelyn*, ed. Peter Sabor *et al.* (Edmonton, Alberta: Juvenilia Press, 1999), xvi–xx. From a comparative study of Austen family handwriting, Sabor makes the interesting suggestion that other attempts to continue 'Catharine' and 'Evelyn' in *Volume the Third* were the work of James Edward Austen, not as a child but as late as 1829.

Family recollections supply insights into the pre-print lives of two of the novels. A version of *Sense and Sensibility*, in the form of a novel in letters, was read aloud at Steventon as early as 1795 when Austen was not yet 20; while Anna Lefroy recalled a reading a year later in the family circle from one of the earliest versions of what would become *Pride and Prejudice* and the caution then expressed that she, a child, might unwittingly divulge its story—unnecessarily, as it turned out, because she admits to no memory of the novel from that period (she was $3\frac{1}{2}$), only of later talk about it.[47] But it is an interesting anecdote because it chimes both with Austen's early habit of family 'publication' of her work—all but one of the juvenilia ('Edgar and Emma') has its dedication to a family member or friend, broadcasting its semi-public status—and with her anxiety about licensing too widely what she also hopes to publish by more conventional means. (According to Austen-Leigh, though with no hard evidence, the novel rejected sight unseen by the publisher Cadell in November 1797 was 'First Impressions', a draft of *Pride and Prejudice*.)

Two letters to Cassandra, one in January 1799 and the second in June of that year, give some insight into Austen's half-comical (but only half) sense of herself as an author poised between frankness and secrecy, vanity and fear: 'I do not wonder at your wanting to read *first impressions* again, so seldom as you have gone through it, & that so long ago'; 'I would not let Martha [Lloyd] read First Impressions again upon any account, & am very glad that I did not leave it in your power.—She is very cunning, but I see through her design;—she means to publish it from Memory, & one more perusal must enable her to do it.'[48] Writing twelve years later and at last on the verge of publication, she admits to a settled dread associated with the business of going into print and the inevitable risk of comparison: 'I . . . am always half afraid of finding a clever novel *too clever*—& of finding my own story & my own people all forestalled'.[49] It is April 1811 and she is in Sloane Street, London, staying at her brother Henry's, and despairing at the slow progress of *Sense and Sensibility* at the printer's. The 'clever' novel is Mary Brunton's *Self-Control*, published in 1810, a copy of which she has been unsuccessful in procuring. The extraordinary contemporary success of Brunton's improbable moral tales of independent heroines would continue to irk Austen through

47 *Family Record*, 89; and Anna Lefroy, in *Memoir*, 158.
48 *Jane Austen's Letters*, 35 and 44.
49 Ibid., 186.

the 1810s and in her mind at least invite unwanted association with her own all too probable compositions.[50]

From *Mansfield Park*, the first of the novels to be conceived as well as executed and published in maturity, we sense a change. When Henry, who by this stage is fully settled in the routines of unofficial literary agent, is given the completed manuscript to read at the beginning of March 1814 he and Austen are already travelling by carriage to London to see it through the press. But literary agent though he is, *Mansfield Park* clearly comes as something of a surprise to him. From comments in her letters to Cassandra on his progress through the narrative and his opinions of the characters, it is clear that Henry is discovering most if not all of what he reads for the first time: 'We did not begin reading till Bentley Green. Henry's approbation hitherto is even equal to my wishes; he says it is very different from the other two, but does not appear to think it at all inferior . . . He took to Lady B. & Mrs N. most kindly, & gives great praise to the drawing of the Characters. He understands them all, likes Fanny & I think foresees how it will all be.' 'Henry has this moment said that he likes my M.P. better & better;—he is in the 3^{d} vol. —I beleive *now* he has changed his mind as to foreseeing the end;—he said yesterday at least, that he defied anybody to say whether H.C. would be reformed, or would forget Fanny in a fortnight.' By 9 March 'Henry has finished Mansfield Park, & his approbation has not lessened. He found the last half of the last volume *extremely interesting*.'[51] A fragment from the same period, dated 21 March and probably to her brother Frank, contains a postscript, 'Perhaps before the end of April, *Mansfield Park* by the author of S & S.—P.&P. may be in the World.—Keep the *name* to yourself. I sh^{d} not like to have it known beforehand.'[52] The caution is, of course, a pointed

[50] See my 'Jane Austen and the Invention of the Serious Modern Novel', in *The Cambridge Companion to English Literature, 1740–1830*, ed. Thomas Keymer and Jon Mee (Cambridge: Cambridge University Press, 2004), 256–8.

[51] *Jane Austen's Letters*, 255, 258, and 261. Partly because of the reference to volume divisions, Deirdre Le Faye assumes (ibid., 428–9 n. 2), wrongly I think, that Henry Austen is reading *Mansfield Park* in proof and that Austen must have arranged printing when she was in London in November 1813. But not only is it unlikely Henry would encounter the novel for the first time during proofing, we also know (for example, from what Austen tells us about correcting the sheets of *Emma*, ibid., 298) that proofs were sent piecemeal, offering no possibility of continuous reading. This was especially the case when more than one printing house was involved in the production, as with *Mansfield Park*. Chapman, who assumes the manuscript is being read, points out that Austen herself would at this stage as an experienced novelist be writing in her own volume divisions. See *Jane Austen's Letters*, ed. R. W. Chapman (2nd edn., London: Oxford University Press, 1952), note to Letter 92. In the 1810s a novel could be set in print from manuscript in as little as two months. See Ch. 3, 164–5 and n. 80.

[52] *Jane Austen's Letters*, 262. A novel entitled *First Impressions* appeared in 1801 from Margaret Holford, published by the Minerva Press. See Garside *et al.*, *The English Novel 1770–1829*, ii. 135–6. Garside here adjusts the date of 1800, previously given by Blakey (*The Minerva Press, 1790–1820*, 193).

reference to Austen's fear of being anticipated, as she was in her favoured title *First Impressions* for *Pride and Prejudice*; but it also signals a more general reticence. The novel was advertised in the newspapers as published on 9 May 1814, and Henry's intimacy with it at this point appears to be no more than two months old; yet by Cassandra's later estimation it had been on the stocks since February 1811. A letter of January 1813 to Cassandra not only suggests that it is already about half written but that Cassandra at least is closely acquainted with its smallest details.[53]

I think what this tells us is that the size and function of the family audience as a site or trial ground for publication shrank as Austen's public textual life grew. Of course something must be put down to the dispersal of the large family group after the Steventon days; but that accounts for only part of the change. The Austens remained a closely knit family whose ties as they extended to a growing band of scribbling nieces and nephews became arguably more, not less, complexly literary. And once settled at Chawton, on brother Edward's Hampshire estate, Austen was no more than 12 miles from the Steventon family whose visits were almost daily. Something also must be allowed for the huge gaps and silences in the record as we have it—the lost or destroyed letters which may, if they existed, tell a different story; and something more again must be credited to the compressed timescale during which the mature novels were conceived and executed, in intense creative bursts, though this does not seem to apply to *Mansfield Park*, which represents possibly the longest continually sustained creative effort of all. Nevertheless, it is tempting to connect the emergence of a new reticence with a particular stylistic and tonal change that *Mansfield Park* inaugurated, and to see this change as itself the working out of an adjusted understanding of authorship as self-control, as keeping one's own counsel. Such a reading of the Chawton period does not fit with the account Austen-Leigh presented in the *Memoir*, and that subsequent biographers and critics have tended to accept, where the return to composition is described as a picking up of the old Steventon habits; but the evidence tells a different story.[54]

Austen's mature Regency writings have long appeared to critics to strike a constrained note, sardonic rather than witty, cautioning retirement and the

[53] *Jane Austen's Letters*, 198–9, where Austen refers to incidents in *Mansfield Park*, Vol. 2, Chs. 6 and 7 (Chs. 24 and 25).

[54] According to Austen-Leigh, at Chawton 'she resumed the habits of composition which had been formed in her first [home], and continued them to the end of her life' (*Memoir*, 81); and see Ch. 2, 95–7 above.

wisdom of second thoughts. In *Mansfield Park* and in Fanny Price Austen begins to develop the inner voice as a 'second idiolect', resembling the heroine's distinctive forms of speech but adapting and extending them to express what is private or concealed from open utterance. It is noticeable that from *Mansfield Park* onwards the central characters 'think' as much as or more than they 'speak'.[55] The change marks a new kind of self-regard in the novel heroine who increasingly comes to inhabit a psychological as much as a physical space, a space more deeply interiorized than it is openly expressive. It is a change consistent with an adjusted relationship between inner and outer realities as they affect the practices of composition, too, representing a recalibration Austen probably had to make if she was to acquire depth as a writer. Commenting shrewdly on the juvenilia her most recent biographer, the novelist Carol Shields, points to the absence of 'secrecy and confessional desperation' which is a usual part of young girls' writings; she remarks: 'Instead, all of the work appears to have been shared openly with family and friends. The erasure of the private self from Jane Austen's early work suggests a confusion concerning that self or else a want of permission from those around her.' Half way through writing *Mansfield Park* Austen's own verdict on the newly published *Pride and Prejudice* was that 'it wants shade'.[56] As *First Impressions* it had received considerable exposure: it was read by Cassandra, Martha Lloyd, and George Austen, Jane's father, before he offered it to Cadell; it was read aloud at the parsonage at Deane where James then lived. All Austen's novels explore the mis-match between the heroine and her immediate family, but in *Mansfield Park* we see how crucially this mis-match functions as motor and context for the heroine's inner liberation and growth—for her ability to test out who she is and who she must become. The withdrawal of family encouragement and approval may well be the dark counter to openness in terms of which a private self is discovered—the private self of the novelist as of the heroine. What exists as a routine (if dysfunctional) condition within the fiction may have been engineered congenially or less dramatically acquired by other means in reality. However achieved, by

[55] The term 'second idiolect' to describe the inner voicing of thought in Austen's mature novels ('the expression of ideas too private or, as frequently in Emma's case, too outrageous for open utterance') is used in J. F. Burrows, *Computation into Criticism*, 166. Burrows also points out the higher proportion of inner voicing in the later novels: 'from less than 5 per cent in *Sense and Sensibility* and 10 per cent in *Pride and Prejudice* to almost a third in *Mansfield Park* and *Emma*'. He notes, too, that 'In both *Mansfield Park* and *Persuasion*, the character narratives of the heroines are considerably larger than their spoken parts' (166). For Burrows 'character narrative' describes those occasions when the narrator 'renders the thoughts of the characters, especially the heroines'.

[56] Shields, *Jane Austen*, 31; *Jane Austen's Letters*, 203.

knowing or unknowing conspiracy, it marked a departure from the performative practices of confidential publication in which the early writings had been nurtured.

Two letters from 1817 to her niece Fanny Knight of Godmersham (much later to become Lady Knatchbull and the repository of the bulk of Austen's correspondence with Cassandra) seem to confirm the contracted sphere in which the later novels were incubated. With Fanny as she grew to womanhood Austen shared a degree of intimacy—'You are inimitable, irresistable. You are the delight of my Life. Such Letters, such entertaining Letters as you have lately sent! . . . Such a lovely display of what Imagination does' is how she opens her letter of 20 February 1817 to her niece. Yet Fanny clearly writes in some uncertainty of receiving information about the progress of her aunt's latest writings. Austen replies on 13 March: 'I *will* answer your kind questions more than you expect.—Miss Catherine [*Northanger Abbey*] is put upon the Shelve for the present, and I do not know that she will ever come out;—but I have a something ready for Publication, which may perhaps appear about a twelvemonth hence. It is short, about the length of Catherine.—This is for yourself alone.' Ten days later, she writes again to Fanny that Henry has asked whether she has anything ready for publication, and 'I could not say No when he asked me, but he knows nothing more of it.'[57] The reference is to the novel published posthumously with *Northanger Abbey* as *Persuasion*,which Cassandra tells us was finished as long before as August 1816. The delay in soliciting publication for a completed work at this stage in her career may be explained by the persistence of old habits, according to which she laid finished work aside to settle, but also by the listlessness which marked her final illness. Nevertheless, Austen found energy enough to write twelve chapters of a new novel (the fragment *Sanditon*) between January and March 1817. What is clear is that Henry was less conversant than ever with the progress of her writing, even though he had recently recovered the manuscript of 'Susan' or 'Catherine' from Crosby and Co.; and even though he was now living more closely within the Steventon and Chawton households.

Declared bankrupt in March 1816, Henry left his fashionable London life and took clerical orders; by early 1817 he held a curacy at Chawton. Four years her senior, sanguine and unreasonably optimistic, he was the least successful and reportedly Jane's favourite among the Austen men. By turns a captain in the militia, a banker, a receiver of taxes, and a clergyman, he incurred

[57] *Jane Austen's Letters*, 328, 333, and 335.

throughout his varied careers severe financial losses to several members of his family. These reverses may also have played a significant part in holding Austen back during the latter half of 1816 from the financial risk of immediate publication at her own expense (as was her norm) of her latest work. Perhaps she was awaiting profits from the recently published *Emma* to cover the costs of a new venture; since any gains from *Emma* were also needed to defray costs of the failed second edition of *Mansfield Park*, money might well be tight. Nevertheless, there is nothing to suggest that she now doubted Henry's critical judgement. Rather, the evidence points towards a settled confinement and concentration of her perspectives consistent with the deepening shade of her mature fictional vision and a continued experimentation with an inward, only obliquely locatable, fictional voice.

The comic 'Plan of a Novel, according to hints from various quarters' was probably written in early 1816, immediately after the fuss over the royal patronage of *Emma* and the encounter with James Stanier Clarke, the Prince Regent's ridiculously self-preening librarian. A bravura pastiche, it revives the hybridity and ellipses of the juvenilia, drawing in voices as diverse as those of William Gifford, editor and reader for John Murray, and Mary Cooke, Austen's second cousin. As an exercise it belongs with the stories about Chawton neighbours, recollected half a century later by Caroline Austen, in which '[t]he laugh she occasionally raised was by imagining for her neighbours impossible contingencies . . . that *could* deceive nobody'.[58] In manuscript it bristles with marginal notes, acknowledging the human sources of its bizarre twists of plot and characterization; and it provides clear evidence that habits of confidential collaborative writing and circulation persisted throughout Austen's career even after conventional print publication became her dominant method. But whatever literary opinions and creative amusements continued to be aired in the semi-public context of the wider family group, the novels for print publication followed an increasingly divergent evolution.

The all-female Chawton household (Cassandra, their mother, and Martha Lloyd) was probably the vital nurturing and trial ground for the later novelistic idiolect.[59] With roots in the interruptions and discontinuities of familiar conversation, the rhythms of this later style seek out and trace the

[58] 'Plan of a Novel', in *Minor Works*, 428–30; the correspondence with the Revd James Stanier Clarke began over the royal dedication and continued with his attempts to interest her in his ideas for romantic novels; 'Plan of a Novel' was its outcome. See *Jane Austen's Letters*, 296–7, 305–7, and 312. Caroline Austen, 'My Aunt Jane Austen' (1867) in *Memoir*, 172.

[59] Cf. Kaplan, *Jane Austen Among Women*, 100–8.

patterns of thought of a mind confident in its powers to dominate (to record and disregard) its own immediate models and surroundings. The style Austen is more or less credited with inventing for the English novel (free indirect style) diverges from the dramatic delivery of the juvenilia in its transposition of their assumptions to the uses of performance at even closer quarters. So close that what functions in the early work to collapse the boundary between storyteller and audience, inviting them to conspire in imagining and rioting within a shared textual space, becomes in the indirect style of the mature fiction a device for dissolving the perspectives of narrator/narration and character. Where the juvenilia perform their effects loudly and rhetorically, Austen's mature indirect style is a self-regulating instrument of quiet devastation and subtle, internal parodic collapse.

Austen preferred the fact of her authorship to remain a secret known only within the family. When Henry's indiscretion and pride in his sister's achievements made this impossible her resignation hints at some personal pain at the invasion of her privacy, but it does not suggest that, as was the case with her contemporary Walter Scott, secrecy was a vital post-publication game that must be played out. She replies to Frank's warning that the use in *Mansfield Park* of the names of his old ships risks betraying the secret of her authorship:

> I was previously aware of what I sh^{d} be laying myself open to—but the truth is that the Secret has spread so far as to be scarcely the Shadow of a secret now—& that I beleive whenever the 3^{d} appears, I shall not even attempt to tell Lies about it.—I shall rather try to make all the Money than all the Mystery I can of it.—People shall pay for their Knowledge if I can make them.[60]

Though her name was withheld from the title-pages of all lifetime editions, she appears to have been proud of the mutual identification of her novels and even jealous for their reputations when they were not recognized as forming an accumulating and interdependent fictional stock. Only the title-page of her first publication, *Sense and Sensibility* (1811), includes the ascription BY A LADY; thereafter they admit only textual alliances, each new novel invoking the assistance of its predecessors. Such assistance is strictly inconsistent with absolute anonymity; on the contrary, her title-pages map a knowable fictional space or estate: 'MANSFIELD PARK: A NOVEL. IN THREE VOLUMES. BY THE AUTHOR OF "SENSE AND SENSIBILITY," AND "PRIDE AND PREJUDICE."' Precisely like the signature, there to ensure that texts will not be misprised, the inventory

[60] *Jane Austen's Letters*, 231.

of titles establishes a chain of possession by setting up a 'structure of resummons'.[61] The simplest explanation for Walter Scott's disappointing failure to mention *Mansfield Park* in his review of *Emma* for the *Quarterly* in 1816 is that this textual resummons temporarily broke down: *Emma*'s title-page merely records it as a novel 'BY THE AUTHOR OF "PRIDE AND PREJUDICE," *&c. &c.*'[62]

Cassandra, the executrix and chief beneficiary of Austen's will, may have made her important list of the composition dates of the six major novels soon after her sister's death, as an aid to memory, and perhaps to assist Henry in editing the final works for the press and compiling his brief biography.[63] This is confirmed by the fact that she refers to the two posthumously published novels not by their working titles of 'Catherine' and 'The Elliots' but by those credited to Henry. By Cassandra's account, it was her sister's habit to adopt a provisional title and then to write her way towards a preferred title at a late stage. It was also her habit at that stage to pass on to the family circle of nieces and nephews news of the activities of her characters beyond the limits of their novels—part of the performative afterlife of her texts which harks back to the early, semi-public, modes of composition at Steventon and the importance at that time of text as occasion. 'In this traditionary way', writes Austen-Leigh,

> we learned that Miss Steele never succeeded in catching the Doctor; that Kitty Bennet was satisfactorily married to a clergyman near Pemberley... that the 'considerable sum' given by Mrs. Norris to William Price was one pound; that Mr. Woodhouse survived his daughter's marriage, and kept her and Mr. Knightley from settling at Donwell, about two years; and that the letters placed by Frank Churchill before Jane Fairfax, which she swept away unread, contained the word 'pardon'.[64]

For the second edition of his biography Austen-Leigh, prompted by his sister Caroline, eked out a little further the detail of his aunt's method of

[61] The phrase belongs to Seán Burke, 'The Ethics of Signature' in *Authorship: From Plato to the Postmodern*, ed. Seán Burke (Edinburgh: Edinburgh University Press, 1995), 289.

[62] For her disappointment, see *Jane Austen's Letters*, 313.

[63] *Family Record*, 259. Cassandra's notes are produced as a plate in *Minor Works*, facing p. 242. There are extant two manuscript memoranda recording the dates of composition of the novels, both now in the Pierpont Morgan Library. Until recently it was thought that one, unsigned, was in the hand of Jane Austen, and it is reproduced as such by Chapman in *Plan of a Novel, etc.* (1926). It now seems likely, however, that both memoranda are in Cassandra's hand. The two hands are difficult to distinguish, but in any case there is further confirmation in the fact that the unsigned memorandum mentions *Persuasion* by name, and we have no other record of Austen referring to her last completed novel by this title. See Park Honan, *Jane Austen: Her Life*, 324; and David Gilson, 'Jane Austen's Text: A Survey of Editions', *Review of English Studies*, n.s., 53 (2002), 62.

[64] *Family Record*, 238; *Memoir*, 119.

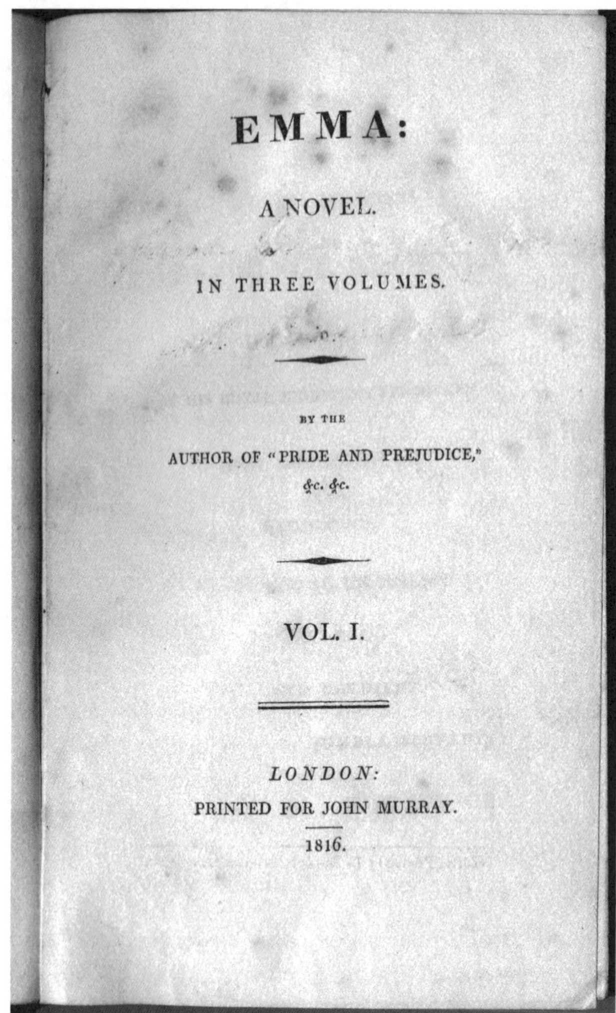

22. Title-page of *Emma* (1816). By kind permission of the English Faculty Library, Oxford University.

working at Chawton. Between them they memorialized the compelling devices by which the family sitting-room functioned simultaneously as public space and cocoon for Austen's private imaginings. (At Steventon she had known more privacy, in the form of a dressing-room shared with Cassandra.) We learn now of the 'small sheets of paper which could easily be put away, or covered with a piece of blotting paper', of the 'swing door which creaked' but was never oiled because it gave notice of anyone approaching, and of the pen 'busy at the little mahogany writing-desk'.[65] The mahogany writing-desk may have been a nineteenth-birthday present from her father; it remained a working tool, and on Cassandra's death Caroline inherited it.[66]

Henry, who wrote his 'Biographical Notice of the Author' some time in the second half of 1817 (in printed form it is dated 13 December) as a preface to Volume 1 of *Northanger Abbey*, there describes his sister as an inveterate re-reader though not rewriter: 'For though in composition she was equally rapid and correct, yet an invincible distrust of her own judgement induced her to withhold her works from the public, till time and many perusals had satisfied her that the charm of recent composition was dissolved.'[67] Something must be allowed for his consistently eulogistic presentation of his sister as a near-saintly figure in her modest retirement, as it must for his defensive endorsement of the reservation implied in Austen's own 'Advertisement' to *Northanger Abbey*—a work that the 'public are entreated to bear in mind' was finished thirteen years before and begun even longer ago. Nevertheless, the three manuscript note-books attest to habits of revision over many years; while we know from her own account that she 'lop't and crop't' the text of *Pride and Prejudice* at a late stage in readiness for publication.[68] There is also the suggestion, again with reference to a version of what later became *Northanger Abbey*, that Austen may have made second copies of her novels. Writing to Crosby and Co. on 5 April 1809 to complain that the 'MS. Novel in 2 vol. entitled Susan' sold to them six years previously has not yet appeared in print, she offers to supply 'another Copy' should the first now be lost.[69] This reads like a facetious threat; but it is not improbable that the long composition histories of *Northanger Abbey*, *Sense and Sensibility*, and *Pride and Prejudice* might have left a semi-durable paper trail in the form of early drafts.[70]

The last of her novels Austen saw through the press was the second edition of *Mansfield Park*, which appeared in February 1816, two months after *Emma*. Thereafter her publication history and her reputation lay in family hands, where in some significant ways they remained at least for the rest of the nineteenth century. Henry Austen began the repossession within months of

[65] *Memoir*, 81–2.

[66] *Family Record*, 89 and 271. The desk descended in the Austen-Leigh family. It can now be seen in the British Library.

[67] *Northanger Abbey and Persuasion*, 4 vols. (London: John Murray, 1818), i. vii, in *Memoir*, 138.

[68] *Jane Austen's Letters*, 202.

[69] Ibid., 174.

[70] For consideration of whether Austen may have made faircopies of her novels, see Ch. 3, 123–4 and 154–6.

his sister's death when in the 'Biographical Notice of the Author' he called attention to the nature of an authority 'open to remark, and submissive to criticism', and its real location '[I]n the bosom of her own family'.[71] His comments position Austen's authority as a novelist so as to flatter family sensibilities (not least his own), in the process rejecting, or at the very least diminishing, strong evidence of a contrary trajectory taking her towards ever greater independence of creative judgement. We should not read this as a sinister move on Henry's part: his sister was dead; love, and a brotherly duty increasingly tinged by his own religious conformity, were sufficient motives for the constrained shaping of her literary life. It is nevertheless ironic that if while she was alive his pride made it impossible for him to preserve her anonymity, after her death there was little he was prepared to divulge publicly by way of personal detail; in the 'Biographical Notice', he drew attention to the emptiness of circumstance in which his sister's life was lived and contented himself with generalities. The 'Memoir of Miss Austen', a reworking of the 1818 piece, which subsequently he provided to accompany the edition of *Sense and Sensibility* issued in 1833 in Bentley's Standard Novels series, eked out its meagre contents not with more family memories but with extracts from critical appraisals already in the public domain. In place of personal recollections, Henry fitted his sister to a set of social expectations (rather as Chapman would later fit out her text to a set of critical expectations). His is a defensive construction in which domestic propriety, social retirement, and orthodox Christian principles, the parameters of generalized, respectable female life in the nineteenth century, are seen to dominate. Why if not to diminish the purposeful and individual artistry of her fiction, with its potential to distract from the everyday duties of woman, did Henry feel it necessary to quote in 1817 and 1833 carefully censored extracts from his sister's letters, accompanied by the not wholly accurate observation that '[t]he style of her familiar correspondence was in all respects the same as that of her novels'?[72]

The direct effect of Henry Austen's emptying of the biographical space of individual traits was the consolidation of Austen's art on the side of the homely and familiar / familial. This in turn had large consequences for the texts of the novels as Chapman sought to understand and present them and as they have come down to us. For example, Chapman looked for evidence to

[71] 'Biographical Notice' (1818), in *Memoir*, 140.

[72] Ibid., 141; and 'Memoir of Miss Austen' (1833), ibid., 150.

strengthen the family view, propounded by Henry and later by his nephew Austen-Leigh, that Austen circumscribed her art to her brothers' talents, each brother taking a significant share in forming her abilities. According to Austen-Leigh, 'She was always very careful not to meddle with matters which she did not thoroughly understand... But with ships and sailors she felt herself at home, or at least could always trust to a brotherly critic to keep her right.' Chapman embellished a further hint when he concluded that Jane's eldest brother, James, Austen-Leigh's father, 'directed Jane's reading and formed her taste, much as Edmund Bertram did Fanny's'.[73] The assumption in each case is that the brothers must have done this, for how else would Jane have known, not only about ships, but also and more generally about matters of literary judgement (James being an occasional and mediocre poet). The contrary evidence afforded by Austen's increasingly confident independent acts of literary negotiation, as for example with the Prince Regent's librarian and John Murray, carries little weight here.

By the early twentieth century such traditions had hardened into something more tangible and were even represented as textually provable. Taking instruction from Austen-Leigh, there had grown up a belief that the major substantive changes between the first and second editions of *Sense and Sensibility* and *Mansfield Park*, the two novels for which we have more than one authorially sanctioned edition (in the one case, changes having to do with legal detail and, in the other, with nautical terminology) were made under the influence of Austen's technically expert brothers, Henry the failed banker and her literary agent, and Charles and Frank the sailors.[74] For Chapman, looking to absorb this family inheritance, the normative textual authority of second and last thoughts carried in Austen's case the added weight of a legitimate (because familial) intervention. More particularly, the assumption of an authorized level of 'expert' correction, evident specifically in the changes to the second editions of *Sense and Sensibility* and *Mansfield Park*, appeared to sanction his own ameliorating treatment of the Austen corpus, and in

[73] Ibid., 18 and 16; and Chapman, *Facts and Problems*, 8.

[74] In the alterations to legal details between the first and second editions of *Sense and Sensibility* (changes to do with women's access to the inheritance of property), Chapman sees Henry Austen's hand, arguing that Henry, who was dealing with the printer, probably advised his sister, before the appearance of the first edition, that some changes were necessary. (*Sense and Sensibility*, ed. Chapman, 383.) Chapman's note to *Mansfield Park*, Vol. 3, Ch. 7 (ed. Chapman, 380), where the changes in nautical terminology are made between the first and second editions, reads: 'Mr Geoffrey Callender has very kindly enlightened me on these changes in nautical terms, which he tells me only a sailor could have found necessary. Miss Austen was no doubt indebted to her brother Frank' (549). See also Geoffrey Keynes, 'The Text of *Mansfield Park*', *Times Literary Supplement*, 30 August 1923, 572.

particular, his characteristic expert interventions to regularize and adjust what he deemed to be the woman author's faulty grammar or infelicitous phraseology. In Chapman's Austen text we find the completion of Henry's domestic apologia, as matters of female propriety shade into issues of stylistic and linguistic fitness. Once it has reached this point, the tradition has done powerful work indeed, questions of language and linguistic precision being at the heart of Austen's critical estimation throughout the twentieth century.[75]

Chapman's editing marks the end of the direct family stewardship of Austen's novel texts; but at the very least it is an ambivalent ending, best seen as the point at which family censorship shades into the associated confinements of scholarly surveillance. Cassandra Austen had died in 1845 and by her will her sister's surviving effects were divided among the various branches of the family. Of the juvenile writings, *Volume the First* went to their brother Charles ('I think I recollect that a few of the trifles in this Vol: were written expressly for his amusement'), *Volume the Second* to brother Frank, and *Volume the Third* to James's son James Edward (Austen-Leigh). Of the adult works, Fanny, Lady Knatchbull, inherited *Lady Susan*, *The Watsons* went to Caroline Austen, and to Anna Lefroy the cancelled chapters of *Persuasion* and the *Sanditon* fragment.[76] There is no evidence to suggest that this decisive apportioning of the literary inheritance reflected any other judgement than Cassandra's own.

When in the mid-1860s Austen-Leigh and his sisters Anna and Caroline consulted together over their memories of their aunt they did so in an attempt to retain family control of the biographical record after the death in 1865 of Frank, Jane's last surviving sibling. Between 1870, when the first edition of the *Memoir* appeared, and 1884, when Lord Brabourne published the *Letters of Jane Austen*, the final living links were severed. Anna Lefroy died in 1872, Austen-Leigh in 1874, Caroline Austen in 1880, and Fanny, Lady Knatchbull, Brabourne's mother, in 1882. These were the last family members to have known Austen. Between them they had guarded, sifted, and eventually released into public knowledge the printed versions of the letters, manuscript fictions, and personal recollections that effectively launched the Austen mania

[75] As, for example, in the following judgements: Austen's 'realms are language and its power' (Laura Mooneyham, *Romance, Language, and Education in Jane Austen's Novels* (New York: St Martin's Press, 1988), ix); and 'the world of a Jane Austen novel is radically linguistic' (George Steiner, *After Babel* (Oxford: Oxford University Press, 1992), 9).

[76] Cassandra's manuscript note in *Volume the First*, quoted in *Family Record*, 271; ibid., 270, from an unpublished letter from Cassandra to her brother Charles Austen, 9 May 1843.

of the last twenty years of the century. For this generation textual authority was bound up with appeals to textual property and the right of ownership and therefore censorship. Brabourne, who had never known his great-aunt, died in 1893, at which time the bulk of the letters in his possession were auctioned. But as early as 1891 he had been willing to offer ten of the letters for sale at Sotheby's, suggesting he held her autograph effects in little sentimental esteem. The occasion marked a significant point in the family's loss of control of the material remains, only a little more than a decade after the loss of the intangible trace of living memory.[77]

In particular for the family generations who knew Jane Austen, the space of her texts was a fertile intersection of manuscript, print, and memories, as Anna Lefroy testified. Her tale of hearing an early version of *Pride and Prejudice* read aloud when no one thought she was listening hinges on a double anxiety of the adults then present: that she might talk of the novel beyond the family circle, and that it might not be recognized as a fiction. As she informed her half-brother in 1864, 'Listen however I did, with so much interest, & with so much talk afterwards about "Jane & Elizabeth"'.[78] Austen's habit of using family names for her characters, like her concentration on 'pictures of domestic Life in Country Villages',[79] reassured early generations of critics that her art was appropriately womanly; but it also raises questions of how to demarcate textual space and determine its limits. It is the other side of Henry's anxiety: this time the fear that the literary work may not appear artful enough. By their pruning, editorial remaking, and selective release of the textual record, the family showed their keenness to control its artful as well as its biographical space. Henry Austen was the earliest gatekeeper, his congenital dilatoriness proving an unexpected asset when it came to reducing the biographical record: apart, that is, from one major embarrassing gaff—his airy reference to his sister's composition on her deathbed of comic verses 'replete with fancy and vigour'.[80]

[77] David Gilson, 'Introduction' to *Letters of Jane Austen*, ed. Lord Brabourne (London: Routledge/Thoemmes Press, 1994), repr. in *Collected Articles and Introductions*, 60–8, offers the best summary of auction details.

[78] Anna Lefroy, 'Recollections of Aunt Jane', in *Memoir*, 158.

[79] *Jane Austen's Letters*, 312.

[80] Henry Austen's 1818 reference to the comic verses 'When Winchester races first took their beginning', written by Austen in the last days of her life, caused the next and primmer generation of the family much discomfort. This may explain why the reference was excised from his 'Memoir' of 1833. Caroline Austen wrote to her brother in July 1871 of the lines 'to which unluckily Uncle Henry alluded more than half a Century ago—Nobody felt any curiosity about them *then*—but see what it is to have a growing posthumous reputation! we cannot keep any thing to ourselves *now*, it seems' (in *Memoir*, 190). The verses were not published until 1906. See ibid., 131 and note.

Pre-eminently among the next generation Austen-Leigh was responsible for the earliest culling and dissemination of texts of the manuscript writings; appropriately enough, since to him Austen wrote the famously modest letter describing her method of composition ('the little bit (two Inches wide) of Ivory on which I work with so fine a Brush, as produces little effect after much labour') from which Henry had twice been happy publicly to quote.[81] For Austen-Leigh, memories and the protection of memory (an inevitable part of the construction of author as family member) constituted elements in determining the authenticity of certain pieces and the authority to excise others. An old man when he began his biography, he and his sisters built upon hints in Henry's hagiographic account to enhance an image of their aunt which accorded with their own mid-Victorian domestic sensibilities and with the perceptible shift in morals and manners between 1817 and 1870. Brabourne, too, played his part, in the make-over, the more easily for not having known his great-aunt. His mother had let it be known that to her mind and standards as a daughter of Godmersham Park the Austens of the early nineteenth century were not as refined as one might wish. Fanny's son took the hint. In re-addressing his great-aunt's letters to Queen Victoria his dedicatory preface made discreet reference to the textual adjustment (sanitization) necessary to project the right contemporary image: 'These letters are printed, with the exception of a very few omissions which appeared obviously desirable, just as they were written'. The 'obviously desirable' omissions included: 'I was as civil to them as their bad breath would allow me', from a letter of 20 November 1800, which in Brabourne's edition became: I was as civil to them as circumstances would allow me'; and the removal of details of the ailing Henry Austen's physical symptoms ('Stomach . . . disordered . . . no Indigestions!'), from a letter of 26 November 1815.[82]

Even after the living connection was broken, the understanding of textual space as family space continued to lend authority to the contributions of,

[81] *Jane Austen's Letters*, 323. In his 'Biographical Notice' Henry Austen either misquotes the letter or quotes from a slightly different copy. 'How could I possibly join them on to a little bit of ivory, two inches wide, on which I work with a brush so fine as to produce little effect after much labour?' (*Memoir*, 142).

[82] *Letters of Jane Austen*, ed. Lord Brabourne, i. v, i. 243, and ii. 257 (cf. *Jane Austen's Letters*, 61 and 301–2). Austen-Leigh similarly censored letters reproduced in the *Memoir*. On 14 September 1804, Austen had written to Cassandra of the family housekeeping on holiday at Lyme Regis: '[I] give the Cook physic, which she throws off her Stomach. I forget whether she used to do this, under your administration', which Austen-Leigh prints as: '[I] keep everything as it was under your administration' (*Memoir*, 59–60 and note). Deirdre Le Faye has recently questioned whether Brabourne as editor or Bentley as publisher might take the greater responsibility for sanitizing the letters, 'Lord Brabourne's Edition of Jane Austen's Letters', *Review of English Studies*, n.s., 52 (2001), 91–102.

among others, John Henry Hubback and his daughter Edith Charlotte (the grandson and great-granddaughter of Austen's brother Frank), whose *Jane Austen's Sailor Brothers* appeared in 1906. Under her married name of Mrs Francis Brown, Edith Hubback later wrote continuations and completions of Austen's works, like *The Watsons*, 'by Jane Austen, completed in accordance with her intentions by Edith (her great grand-niece) and Francis Brown' (1928).[83] In this Edith was perpetuating a family tradition, her grandmother, Frank Austen's daughter Catherine Anne, having issued a reworking of *The Watsons* in 1850 under the title of *The Younger Sister.* Frank's daughters, who acquired the 63-year-old Martha Lloyd as step-mother in 1828, grew up listening to stories of their dead Aunt Jane and hearing her novels and manuscripts read aloud whenever Aunt Cassandra paid her long visits. These recitals followed the fashion established by the older generation in their youth, by which ingredients—verbatim quotation, details, and style—from published literature were appropriated to new situations, which is itself a kind of text-editing.

We would be wrong to suppose that the criteria laid out by scholarly editors do not also establish text proprietorially as a selected space, one censored and ventriloquized according to a further range of subjectively and socially determined legitimations. We have been used to placing confidence in scholarly editions as faithful representations, as defining (if not definitive) loci of meaning which in some mysterious way carry within their pages authorial approval—implicit proof of completion 'in accordance with [the author's] intentions'. But we might as justifiably think of these too as residues, as what is left after the record has been 'lop't and crop't' according to other criteria. In both, as in every case, the textual space of the literary work is established only by recourse to a further fiction. The trick is in knowing the rules by which each textual space operates. By a not unlikely coincidence, the first collected edition proper of Austen's novels was issued from the house of Bentley in 1882 to conform with the second edition of Austen-Leigh's *Memoir.* It was marketed as the Steventon Edition.

[83] As Mrs Francis Brown, she subsequently wrote *Margaret Dashwood; or, Interference* (London: John Lane, the Bodley Head, 1929), a continuation of *Sense and Sensibility*; and *Susan Price; or, Resolution* (London: John Lane, the Bodley Head, 1930), a sequel to *Mansfield Park.*

Continuations: Anna Lefroy's Sanditon *and Catherine Hubback's* The Younger Sister[84]

In Jane Austen's house at Chawton is preserved a copy in Cassandra Austen's hand of the final, unfinished novel *Sanditon.* According to tradition, Cassandra made it for her brother Frank at some unspecified time after their sister's death. Transcribed into three small (19.5 × 16 cm; 7.7 × 6.4 inches), commercially manufactured exercise books, each containing twenty leaves of faintly ruled paper, the copy does not simulate with any exactness the three small, homemade booklets into which the holograph draft was composed. But the similarities are sufficient to be significant, suggesting it was copied thus and treasured as much for its ability to invoke the material object of the original as for its precious contents. Inside there is no attempt to reproduce the look of the original manuscript with its passages of heavy revision, erasure, and interlinear insertions, the signs of struggle between first and second thoughts, and its typical contractions of proper names and absence of paragraphing. In Cassandra's copy the text flows smoothly, contractions are expanded, and speeches are carefully apportioned: significantly, the whole is confidently paragraphed. But if in formal terms its subdued and tidied appearance gives no clue to the dynamic evolution of the original, as to substance this is as literal a copy as is humanly possible. Where the original is a working draft, this is a faircopy, interpreted or edited for family publication.

In the next generation, neither Austen-Leigh nor his family associates were overly concerned to reproduce with the nicest attention to accuracy the documents they quoted from or transcribed. In some cases, Austen-Leigh may have been supplied with an abbreviated, inaccurate, or censored copy of a letter; in others, he could not resist improving the grammar or sentence structure of his original, as is the case with his transcription for publication of the cancelled Chapter 10 of *Persuasion.*[85] Among the family there was much circulation of copies and making of further copies of Jane Austen's letters and manuscripts. The practice gained sanction from Cassandra's habit of visiting her brothers' families with copies (her own transcriptions or the originals) of

[84] There is a growing interest in and bibliography for completions, continuations, and sequels to Austen's novels. See Gilson J1–14; Brimley Johnson, *Her Life, Her Work, Her Family, and Her Critics,* 230–47; David Hopkinson, 'Completions', in *The Jane Austen Handbook*, ed. Grey, pp.72–6; Andrew Wright, 'Jane Austen Adapted', *Nineteenth-Century Fiction,* 30 (1975–6), 421–53 (includes stage, screen, radio adaptations); and proliferating internet bibliographies: for example: those listed at www.pemberley.com/janeinfo

[85] For Austen-Leigh's editing of the *Persuasion* manuscript fragment, see Ch. 3, 152–3.

her sister's writings which then contributed to the social occasion. Writing of the division of the holograph manuscripts after Cassandra's death, Lord Brabourne, unhappy at the publication by Austen-Leigh of *Lady Susan* from an allograph copy, had this to say: 'It seems that the autograph copy of another unpublished tale, "The Watsons", had been given to Mr. Austen-Leigh's half-sister, Mrs. Lefroy, and that each recipient took a copy of what was given to the other, by which means Mr. Austen-Leigh became acquainted with the existence and contents of "Lady Susan".'[86] Brabourne, who by now had inherited the holograph of *Lady Susan* from his mother, felt cheated of an opportunity; but his observation opens up the possibility of multiple derived copies of all the writings published for the first time in the second, 1871, edition of the *Memoir* (the cancelled chapter of *Persuasion*, *Lady Susan*, *The Watsons*, and *Sanditon*, the latter mainly in paraphrased form and still under the title of 'The Last Work') as well as the occasional verses and three volumes of juvenile writings. Where are these copies now?

We do not know when Cassandra made her copy of *Sanditon* or when she gave it to Frank, but it is tempting to associate its memorial function with the event which marked the final break up of the Chawton household, his marriage to Martha Lloyd only one year after old Mrs Austen's death. Cassandra lived on in the cottage with the occasional company of one of the numerous nieces and nephews—in particular, two unmarried nieces Caroline, James's daughter, and Cassy Esten, Charles's daughter, stayed with her for long periods and became vital sources of information in the next generation. Her own visits to Frank and Martha at Portsdown Lodge, near Portsmouth, inevitably became occasions for recovering the past, which with the assistance of the manuscript writings, turned into hybrid extensions of the novels, a renewed traffic between text and society. Frank's family was large and relatively young; two of his daughters then at home—Catherine Anne and Fanny Sophia—became so habituated to Austen's writings as a continuation of family conversation that they could articulate 'some question or answer, expressed quite naturally in terms of the novels; sometimes even a conversation would be carried on entirely appropriate to the matter under discussion, but the actual phrases were "Aunt Jane's".'[87]

[86] *Letters of Jane Austen*, i. ix–x. Brabourne was misinformed: Caroline Austen not Anna Lefroy inherited *The Watsons.*

[87] J. H. and Edith C. Hubback, *Jane Austen's Sailor Brothers: Being the Adventures of Sir Francis Austen, G.C.B., Admiral of the Fleet, and Rear-Admiral Charles Austen* (London: John Lane, 1906), viii; and *Family Record*, 268.

It is doubtful whether Catherine Anne launched her subsequent career as novelist on the basis of further material copies of *Sanditon* and *The Watsons*, as Anna Lefroy jealously suspected;[88] or whether, as is more likely, she came to inhabit her aunt's narrative space and style by listening, memory, and the improvisation or ventriloquism recorded by the Hubbacks in the next generation—through habits of family performance, that is, rather than transcription. (One is reminded of Austen's half-serious anxiety that Martha Lloyd might have memorized an early draft of *Pride and Prejudice*.) Anna, who had lived intimately with her aunt and served a more direct literary apprenticeship to her, was outraged by what she considered an unlawful requisitioning of Austen's text by the niece who had never known her. If, after 1845, a proprietary interest belonged to anyone, she considered it was hers, as inheritor of the holograph manuscript of *Sanditon*, and Caroline's, as owner of *The Watsons*. By the terms of Cassandra's will, their prior emotional claim to their aunt received a sanction which seemed to them to extend, morally at least, beyond the physical object (Jane Austen's autograph document) to the right to imagine and control its afterlife, including copies made or otherwise retained (even in memory) prior to their inheritance. In Anna's mind ownership of *Sanditon* not only confirmed her special relationship to her aunt but also the artistic strength of her position, making the difference between an authorized and an unauthorized continuation.

The family crucible of Austen's talent, so influential in the biographical recension, continued to endorse Anna's claim well into the twentieth century, and long after her own writings were forgotten. In Rosemary Anne Sisson's *The Young Jane Austen*, a 1962 fictionalization of the life for children, derived largely from Elizabeth Jenkins, Constance Hill, and the Austen-Leighs, Anna, Cassandra, and Jane form a secret pact to the exclusion of every other family member:

> 'Who can that gentleman be?' said Mrs Austen, 'who has just ridden past the gate? I thought for a moment it was Mr Holder, but it was too tall for him.'
>
> 'Perhaps it was Mr Darcy, Grandmama,' said little Anna.
>
> 'Mr Darcy?' exclaimed Mrs Austen. 'Who can the child mean? I am sure we do not know anyone of that name.'
>
> 'Was it not James Digweed, Mama?' said Cassandra, hastily, while Jane, convulsed with laughter, dropped her scissors, and pretended to search for them on the floor.

[88] See Ch. 2, 72–81, for a discussion of family rivalries in the later nineteenth century over ownership of Austen manuscripts and memorabilia.

A moment afterwards, Mrs Austen went out of the room, and Jane took Anna upon her lap.

'Anna, my love,' she said, 'you know what a secret is.'

'Oh yes, Aunt Jane. A secret is something special which no one else knows about.'

'Well,' said Jane, 'just for the moment, Mr Darcy is a secret between you and me and Aunt Cassy.'

Anna looked very solemn.

'Is Elizabeth a secret too?' she asked, 'and Mr Collins?'

'Oh yes,' replied Jane, glancing with a smile at Cassandra, 'certainly Mr Collins. In fact, all the people in that story are a secret, so I would be obliged if you would not mention them outside our own private room.'

'Very well, Aunt Jane,' said Anna. 'But I would like you to keep *my* stories a secret, too.'

Anna's role is clearly to enlist the sympathy of the 1960s child for Austen's novels; with her own special reading audience in mind, Sisson even carries things so far as to suggest that little Anna's writings might occasionally upstage Aunt Jane's. The point of course is not a literary one, but further evidence of Austen as a woman before she is an artist. Even in 1962, it seems, the Victorian legacy of genius at the service of domesticity must be rehearsed:

. . . Jane . . . was at the writing desk getting ready to begin the next chapter [of *Pride and Prejudice*] on one of her little folded sheets of paper. 'And I have made up a story, Aunt Jane. Will you write it down for me?'

'Let me write it, Anna,' said Cassandra. 'Aunt Jane wishes to write her own story now.'

Anna's lip began to tremble, and her eyes filled with tears.

'Aunt Jane always writes my stories,' she said. '*You* draw the pictures.'

'You are quite right, Anna,' cried Jane. 'We writers must defend ourselves against the encroachment of the artists. Come and tell me your story and I will write it down.'[89]

With their author dead, the kinds of performance implied in copying or family re-reading lose vitality and move closer to acts of remembrance unless referenced (as in the Steventon parodies) to a new set of literary and social codes. It is a shift which involves some contradictions: on the one hand, the loss of the enlivening authorial voice and the dynamic autographic environment of inkblots and erasures; on the other, the re-experiencing of the eventfulness and shared occasion in which the juvenile manuscripts at least

[89] Rosemary Anne Sisson, *The Young Jane Austen* (London: Max Parrish, 1962), 123–6.

were nurtured. But in the case of the later, unfinished writings, this Victorian reinstating of the circumstances of confidential publication also suppresses the far different conditions in which they originated—their privacy *from* family. The practices of continuation in which the female family members engaged imply a reversion, as continuation does—in this case to the habits of closed circulation and performance which preceded Austen's print life. There is of course evidence to suggest that, though crucially redirected at the later, professional stage, such confidential habits never entirely deserted her: informing her talent for reading aloud, as Henry Austen recorded immediately after her death ('Her own works, probably, were never heard to so much advantage as from her own mouth'); for dramatic improvisations, as Caroline Austen remembered ('She amused us in various ways—once I remember in giving a conversation as between myself and my two cousins, supposed to be grown up, the day after a Ball'); and for extending the lives of her characters beyond the end of their novels, as Austen-Leigh reported. But there is a crucial difference; in attempting continuations of *The Watsons* and *Sanditon* Catherine Hubback and Anna Lefroy do not inherit Austen's authority (as Lefroy at least implies she does) so much as presume its equivalence with their own reiterative practices. Unlike the authorized collaboration of print in the case of novels authorially prepared for publication, their collaborations reconstitute the text only as the product of its reception, as posthumous reversions to the lifelong ephemera of the 'Steventon Edition'.

Anna Lefroy was just 6 weeks old when her name was first associated with Austen's writings, as the unwitting dedicatee of two miniature mock-didactic stories, entitled 'Miscellanious Morsels' in *Volume the First*: 'My Dear Neice, Though you are at this period not many degrees removed from Infancy, Yet trusting that you will in time be older, and that through the care of your excellent Parents, You will one day or another be able to read written hand, I dedicate to You the following Miscellanious Morsels'.[90] Anna is known to have collaborated with Austen on at least four specific occasions. In conjectured order of composition they are: the playlet 'Sir Charles Grandison', a 53-page manuscript in Austen's hand whose critical attribution, in some quarters at least, has interestingly shifted over the years from niece to aunt; a 'mock heroic story' or Gothic romp, no trace of which seems to remain; the unfinished continuation to 'Evelyn', which she signed with the initials of her married name JAEL; and the continuation to *Sanditon*, also unfinished. The

[90] *Minor Works*, 71.

'Grandison' collaboration (if such it was) was dated improbably but emphatically in family history to Anna's early childhood by her daughter Fanny Caroline's account: 'I have still in my possession in Aunt Jane's writing a drama my mother dictated to her founded on Sir Charles Grandison a book with which she [Anna] was familiar at seven years old.'[91] This would indeed make hers a precocious talent! According to Fanny Caroline, ultimate source for Sisson's fanciful little sketch, 'To my mother she [Aunt Jane] was especially kind writing for her the stories she invented for herself long ere she could write and telling her others of endless adventure and fun which were carried on from day to day or from visit to visit.' Habits of hybrid oral and written composition, beginning before Anna was 5 (before she could write) were still evident in summer 1812 when she was 19 and when their reading of the Gothic romances in the local Alton circulating library resulted in the jointly credited spoof romance featuring the Alton coach or 'Car of Falkenstein'.[92]

In late 1814, at the earliest, Anna added four pages to 'Evelyn', in an attempt to resolve the narrative dilemma which may have caused the 16-year-old Austen to abandon it twenty-two years before. Together 'Evelyn' and 'Catharine, or the Bower' make up the contents of *Volume the Third*. Much the shorter of the two, 'Evelyn' was abandoned after little more than twenty pages. But Austen left the next nine pages blank before beginning 'Catharine' (ff. 30–127, and also unfinished). At some later stage these blanks were filled, and 'Evelyn' was completed in seven pages in a hand which closely resembles that of the mature James Edward Austen-Leigh, Anna's brother. Anna's own aborted continuation is, appropriately, on paper loosely inserted into the notebook.[93] A narcissistic tale in which characters are propelled by insane acts of benevolence to satisfy the scarcely formulated desires of the protagonist,

[91] HRO, MS. 23M93/85/2 Fanny C. Lefroy, 'Family History', unpaginated. The claim was first made public in 1902 by Hill, *Her Homes and Her Friends*, 240. Brian Southam's examination of the manuscript, which only came to public notice in 1977 (see Gilson K17), dates the bulk of the dramatization from evidence of watermarks to the later 1790s. He argues for Anna's minimal involvement, 'offering suggestions . . . inserting a word or two here and there, changing a phrase, bringing a character on stage'. Other Austen scholars, loathe to abandon family tradition, believe Southam underestimates Anna's contribution and redate the collaboration to Anna's late teens or early twenties, arguing for Anna's primary role. (*Jane Austen's 'Sir Charles Grandison'*, ed. Brian Southam (Oxford: Clarendon Press, 1981), 11; Park Honan, review of Southam's edition, *Notes and Queries*, 228 (1983), 173–4; and Tucker, *A History of Jane Austen's Family*, 196 ff.)

[92] Caroline Austen, in her recollections of 1867, writes of 'a few chapters which I overheard of a mock heroic story, written between herself and one of her nieces . . . it had no other foundation than their having previously seen a neighbour passing on the coach . . .' (*Memoir*, 172). See Anna Lefroy's recollections of 1864, ibid., 159–60.

[93] See Gilson F14 and n. 46 above.

Frederick Gower, 'Evelyn' is, as David Nokes neatly puts it, 'an *Arabian Nights* fantasy transposed to the Sussex countryside'; in Caroline Austen's view, it was 'clever nonsense' but worth the risk of publishing in 1870.[94] It appears only to leave off because the fantasy breaks down and darker elements intrude; but neither Anna nor Austen-Leigh found a convincing way forward. Austen-Leigh's conclusion is a competent pastiche of his aunt's style, but it merely retreats from the problem, rescuing desire from disillusionment by regressive comedy. Anna launches out more boldly, grasping the fact that a new developmental stage and a new tone are required. In her continuation the creaking machinery of comedy Gothic gives substance to the hysterical symptoms of the protagonist's mounting unease; but her sudden abandonment four pages in suggests an inability to grapple with the large moral dimension opening up as she wrote.[95] If Anna's effort dates from late 1814, soon after her marriage and about the time she was corresponding with Austen about her own novel-in-progress, then this may explain her grandmother's solicitous reference in her Christmas Day letter of that year, where she writes: 'Surely My dear, your head must be quite bewildered by composing two works at the same time.'[96]

Jane Austen was deeply immersed in the contemporary novel and followed its fads critically and anxiously. Together with the hilarious 'Plan of a Novel', the short sequence of five letters, written between July and November 1814, in which she shared her views on novel writing with the 21-year-old Anna, constitute her 'art of fiction'. Writing at a stage in her own publishing career when she can express with some confidence what she believes the novel should do, she here sets in ludicrous light many of the devices of contemporary commercial fiction. The occasion for the letters is Anna's sending drafts of her novel, tentatively entitled 'Which is the Heroine?', for her aunt's inspection. From its description (the novel was never finished) it appears to be a sprawling romance of fashionable life, possibly parodic in the style of *Northanger Abbey* and peopled by improbably named characters—St Julian, Devereux Forester, and Lady Clanmurray—whose adventures are to take

[94] Nokes, *Jane Austen: A Life*, 129 ; and Caroline Austen, in *Memoir*, 186.

[95] Anna Lefroy's continuation is in *Minor Works*, 240–2.

[96] Mrs Austen's letter is one of a collection addressed to Anna now held in Princeton University Library. It is transcribed in Deirdre Le Faye, 'Anna Lefroy and Her Austen Family Letters', *Princeton University Library Chronicle*, 62 (2001), 532. A copy is also preserved in Fanny C. Lefroy, 'Family History'. It seems most likely that, as Peter Sabor suggests ('James Edward Austen, Anna Lefroy, and the Interpolations to Jane Austen's "Volume the Third" ', *Notes and Queries*, 245 (2000), 304–6), Anna attempted her continuation of 'Evelyn' soon after her marriage (in late 1814 or in 1815) rather than at a later date when, as her own writings show, she would have had far less sympathy with Gothic indulgence.

them from London's Berkeley Square to Ireland. As the sections of manuscript arrived by post Austen read them aloud to Cassandra and their mother, sending the ensuing comments in her letters back to Anna. This was a method that worked for her own early drafts, which were, during the Steventon years, routinely tested by ear on a family audience.

What dominates Austen's reading of Anna's manuscript is the emphasis she places on particular features of style and psychological and narrative enlargement, which taken together stress the importance of verisimilitude. She insists on consistency ('Remember she [your heroine] is very prudent;—you must not let her act inconsistently');[97] on naturalness ('I do not like a Lover's speaking in the 3^{d} person;—it is too much like the formal part of Lord Orville [in Burney's *Evelina*]'); on conciseness ('we have thought the sense might be expressed in fewer words'); on writing from experience ('we think you had better not leave England. Let the Portmans go to Ireland, but as you know nothing of the Manners there, you had better not go with them . . . Stick to Bath . . . There you will be quite at home').[98] While Aunt Cassandra 'does not like desultory novels, & is rather fearful yours will be too much so', she, on the other hand, can 'allow much more Latitude . . . & think Nature & Spirit cover many sins of a wandering story'. In any case, 'People in general do not care so much about it.'[99] Nevertheless, she advises against overwriting—'your descriptions are often more minute than will be liked. You give too many particulars of right hand & left'—and argues the advantages of extensively editing the manuscript at a late stage—'I hope when you have written a great deal more you will be equal to scratching out some of the past.'[100] But her chief criticism is reserved for 'thorough novel slang': 'Devereux Forester's being ruined by his Vanity is extremely good; but I wish you would not let him plunge into a "vortex of Dissipation". I do not object to the Thing, but I cannot bear the expression;—it is such thorough novel slang—and so old, that I dare say Adam met with it in the first novel he opened.'[101] Finally, she commends the concentrated study of social relations over the 'wandering' style she earlier excused: 'You are now collecting your People delightfully, getting them exactly into such a spot as is the delight of my life;—3 or 4 Families in a Country Village is the very thing to work on.'[102] She was at the time engaged on *Emma*.

Fanny Caroline subsequently transcribed the letters into her 'Family History', where she noted that her mother's novel and the interest it roused

[97] *Jane Austen's Letters*, 275. [98] Ibid., 267, 268, 269. [99] Ibid., 269.
[100] Ibid., 275, 276. [101] Ibid., 277. [102] Ibid., 275.

at Chawton in 1814 'became a source of great amusement and delight'. Without the manuscript (burned in the early 1820s) it is impossible to do more than conjecture the novel's progress from Austen's critical commentary. Anna is encouraged to draw on her aunt's experiences and travels ('I am not sensible of any Blunders about Dawlish. The Library was particularly pitiful & wretched 12 years ago')[103] and on her superior knowledge of the intricacies and gradations of social position or rank. Indeed, the emphasis of Austen's commentary on teasing out relative social standing to the finest degree and its implications for meetings and the niceties of etiquette reveals how far an alertness to such codes and conventions renders social reality in her own novels. She protests, for example, at the impropriety of a surgeon being introduced to a peer and Anna's botching of the form of introduction used for the peer's brother ('I have also scratched out the Introduction between Lord P. & his Brother, & Mr Griffin . . .'). While 'Lesley *is* a noble name', '[t]here is no such Title as Desborough—either among the Dukes, Marquisses, Earls, Viscounts or Barons.'[104] The creation, in the interval between letters, of a new character Lady Kenrick is praised as removing 'the greatest fault in the work', which appears to be that of 'Mrs F.'s settling herself as Tenant & near Neighbour to such a Man as Sir T. H. without having some other inducement to go there . . . some friend living thereabouts to tempt her.'[105] But if she appears to approve of Anna moving into the same fictional space as herself, she warns against too close imitation: 'I *do* think you had better omit Lady Helena's postscript;—to those who are acquainted with P.&P it will seem an Imitation'; 'we do not thoroughly like the *Play*; perhaps from having had too much of Plays in that way lately.'[106] (*Mansfield Park* had been published in May 1814.) Most instructive of all is Austen's reaction to the news that Anna is also showing sections of her novel to her fiancé, Ben Lefroy, to which she responds: 'I did very much like to know Ben's opinion . . . but I cannot flatter him with there being much Incident.'[107]

Despite warm interest and encouragement, the particulars of Austen's annotation of Anna's draft imply a story and characters evolving according to the diffuse and sensational inheritance of contemporary circulating library fiction rather than within a space discovered by her example. And rather than reflections upon novel-writing in general, Austen's insistence on naturalness and probability overwhelmingly argues the superior example of her own work, in which plot and romance are subject to continual surveillance and

103 *Jane Austen's Letters*, 267. 104 Ibid., 268, 275. 105 Ibid., 274–5, 277.
106 Ibid., 268, 269. 107 Ibid., 277.

trimming. In paring down incident, in 'scratching out' rather than supplementing, in suppressing specific knowledge in such a way as to stimulate us, in Woolf's phrase, 'to supply what is not there', Austen would appear in retrospect a novelist without genealogy, forerunner of the modernist experiment in fiction.[108]

Though she was still working on *Which is the Heroine?* in 1818, we cannot know whether Anna's novel could have survived to completion the strictures imposed by her aunt's advice. As it happened, babies and domestic routines got in the way. But we have a later residue of their conversations about writing, another fragment, in the continuation to *Sanditon* which Anna probably undertook soon after 1845 when the manuscript came into her possession. In any event, a letter of 8 August 1862 from Anna to James Edward, raising the possibility of publishing the original fragment, makes it clear that her own aborted continuation is by now a matter of old news. What exercised brother and sister at this time was the fear that Catherine Hubback, her fictional seam running low, might soon find opportunity to absorb into one of her prolix three-deckers Cassandra's Portsdown Lodge copy. Anna makes it clear, both here and in a brief note probably written two years later to accompany her biographical 'recollections of Aunt Jane', that her own authority to speak for *Sanditon* is chiefly by virtue of legal possession locally modified by inside knowledge of Aunt Jane's specific intentions for the novel. Her letter voices a confidence, critical as much as proprietorial, to speak for the original, which, it is implied, her addressee sanctions:

> I agree with you that the M.S. as it stands is very inferior to the published works—and *perhaps* by no corrections could be worked up to an equality with any other 12 opening Chapters: for *that* I think the fairest sort of comparison. If publishing the M.S. can only gratify curiosity at the expense of the Authoresse's [*sic*] fame of course under ordinary circumstances it ought not to be attempted—but then comes the question of how entirely to prevent it. The Copy which was taken, not given, is now at the mercy of M^{rs}. Hubback, & she will be pretty sure to make use of it as soon as she thinks she safely may.
>
> Now let us look at the matter the other way; the publishing way. One ought to do in this case what the Authoress would certainly have done for herself—slightly alter, & very carefully correct—& though I should be sorry in such a business to trust solely to my own small knowledge of composition, it certainly might be done.
>
> Now for the characters, so far as they are sketched—premising that I give up Sir Edwd. Denham—& don't mean to say a word for him—but you are not just to the

[108] Virginia Woolf, 'Jane Austen', *The Common Reader* (London: Hogarth Press,1925), 174.

Heywoods. They stand in the place of the Morlands. In the last named family the Wife is the more prominent character—the *talker* in short; in Sanditon it is the Husband, & I think M^{r}. Heywood talks as much to the purpose as M^{rs}. Morland. Perhaps we were to have seen very little more of the Heywoods; in which case they are made enough of—On the other hand, in Northhanger [*sic*] Abbey M^{rs}. Allen stands out before her Husband but in Sanditon the Lady is kept back. I do not mean to deny M^{rs}. Allen's being more cleverly imagined than M^{r}. Parker—at least it may be so—but I think she would have been much the most tiresome in real life. The truth is, I am getting fond of M^{r}. Parker. The other members of the Parker family (except of course Sidney) were certainly suggested by conversations which passed between Aunt Jane & me during the time that she was writing this story—their vagaries do by no means exceed the facts from which they were taken—but are too broadly stated for fiction—I think those parts ought to be a good deal trimmed, & softened down. Lady Denham in the Authoresse's [*sic*] hands would have been delightful—I do not feel as if I c^{d}. ever do her justice—I am also partial to the Miss Beauforts—one must bear in mind that no story can be made up of first rate, & front stage performers—the back ground must be provided with its D^{r}. & M^{rs}. Grants & such like—but its time to finish, so I will only add, that in nothing do I so entirely disagree with you all as in the comparison of my own addition with the original. There seems to be just the same difference as between real Lace, & Imitation.[109]

I have in my possession a few pages of M.S. the last effort of my dear Aunt's pen . . . the story was too little advanced to enable one to form any idea of the plot . . . [110]

[This second passage seems to be a note prepared for the outline or synopsis that Austen-Leigh will present under the title 'The Last Work' in the second edition of the *Memoir*.]

Anna's continuation of *Sanditon* was forged in the circumstances of a special relationship to both author and original by which its writing in 1817

[109] Anna to Austen-Leigh, 8 August 1862. HRO, MS. 23M93/86/3c. item 118. Deirdre le Faye, '*Sanditon*: Jane Austen's Manuscript and her Niece's Continuation', *Review of English Studies*, n.s., 38 (1987), 56–61, also provides a transcript of Anna's letter.

[110] Included in *Jane Austen's Sanditon: A Continuation by her Niece, together with 'Reminiscences of Aunt Jane', by Anna Austen Lefroy*, transcribed and edited by Mary Gaither Marshall (Chicago: Chiron Press, 1983), 153. Anna's draft notes for her recollections of Jane Austen and her manuscript continuation of *Sanditon* were sold in December 1977 to James Borg, bookseller and publisher (Chiron Press) of Lake Forest, Illinois. Marshall describes Lefroy's manuscript in 'Jane Austen's Legacy: Anna Austen Lefroy's Manuscript of *Sanditon*', *Persuasions*, 19 (1997), 226–8. Marshall's transcription and edition, unfortunately, are not reliable; nor is there any reason to accept her conjectures (*Sanditon: A Continuation*, xvi, xxiv–xxvi, xxxv) that Austen discussed the plot of *Sanditon* in any detail with Lefroy or that Lefroy's continuation 'is of literary and historical significance as an indication of Jane Austen's own plans for the completion of her last work' (xliii). Lefroy herself makes it clear that this is not so. There has been little critical attention paid to Lefroy's continuation, but see Peter Sabor and Kathleen James-Cavan, 'Anna Lefroy's Continuation of *Sanditon*: Point and Counterpoint', *Persuasions*, 19 (1997), 229–43, for a lively and perceptive exception.

and post-1845 registers, albeit unequally, the traces of a shared conversation. But by what criteria do we judge its continuation or completion?—as if a work by Jane Austen? or as a work in the manner of Jane Austen? or as a work by another? And what of the uncertain status of that other, writing neither as herself nor as the authority she both impersonates and partly invents? Which author, then, summons the text to account? She who writes it or she in whose style it declares itself to be written? The questions are significant because the most salient characteristic of Lefroy's continuation is its refusal of the kind of emancipation or re-referencing that impelled Austen's own juvenile textual appropriations. An act of mimicry rather than an attempt to redirect or supersede, Lefroy's continuation is an imitation or pastiche rather than a parody. By contrast, Hubback's 'trans-contextualization' of the *Watsons* fragment within an exuberant Victorian canvas of borrowings is a form of sustained, if imperfectly articulated quotation, which in its new setting is nearer to parody.[III] For all its imitative proximity and decorous restraint, Lefroy's continuation is the lesser incorporation: roughly the same length as Austen's text, about 20,000 words, it was also left unfinished and, unlike her attempt to continue 'Evelyn', has been kept, at least since 1930 when the *Sanditon* manuscript went to King's College, Cambridge, physically separate from its original.

From the outset Lefroy takes firm control of her materials, showing a painstaking attentiveness to the contours and voice of the original. Her confidence in the geography of Sanditon is sufficiently secure to extend Austen's relatively innovative presentation of figures within the wide perspective of the Sussex Downs. Like Austen, she deploys the full canvas of sky and sea and open countryside; like Austen she visualizes and enters its spaces. She enlarges the indigenous local community around the fishing cove of old Sanditon, where the addition of a humble public house, the Hollis Arms, precursor of the modern hotel on the higher, fashionable ground, nicely underscores the tension already established in Austen's mapping of old and new social arrangements. In particular, the act of imagination by which Hollis land and Hollis money provide the means for conjuring the new developments of Denham Place, Denham Villas, and Denham Gardens, as explained in Lefroy's opening sentences, appears to flow effortlessly from the closing words of Austen's fragment: 'Poor Mr Hollis!—It was impossible not to feel

[III] I am here invoking parody in the broad or 'neutral' sense favoured by Linda Hutcheon, as 'imitation with critical difference' rather than in its more restricted, and ironically inflected, usage. See Hutcheon, *A Theory of Parody*, 36–41.

him hardly used; to be obliged to stand back in his own House & see the best place by the fire constantly occupied by Sir H. D.' The same goes for the details Lefroy invents to develop the potential of the seaside resort: from the Hollis Arms the landlord's two boys are to be dragooned into Mr Parker's latest scheme of providing donkey rides 'for... invalid Ladies, or children, as one sees them at all other Watering Places'. This is a project which eventually gets Lady Denham's vote: 'the truth being, that she rather approved of an experiment, which if it failed could bring no loss to herself: & if successful might the next season open a more advantageous course of life for her two milch Asses'. The Steadman boys, the donkeys' minders, being naturally more inclined to beach life than Sunday School even become the means of bringing out Diana Parker's wholly probable Tractarian zeal: 'as to the Boys if they were supplied with interesting books or tracts to read at leisure moments... it might be the positive saving of them!'[112]

It is impossible to fault such details; as the conscientious extension of their textual precedent, they appear to grow from within the original, to involve no act of re-imagination but strictly to extend what we already know of Mr Parker, Diana Parker, Lady Denham, and even the asses. Such additions are not double voiced but formally and structurally congruent with Austen's text. Much the same can be said for the development of the shallow and showy Beaumont girls, who in Austen's fragment 'w^{d} have been nothing at Brighton, [but] could not move here without notice'. True to her declared partiality for them, Lefroy has expanded Austen's hint that their object is husband-hunting ('to captivate some Man of much better fortune than their own') and combines this with their previous detectable impression on Arthur Parker's coddled senses ('though little disposed for supernumerary exertion [he]... quitted the Terrace... for the sake of a glimpse of the Miss Bs—') to form the basis for a miniature courtship comedy in which Miss Letitia Beaufort's wiles and flounces receive the appropriate tribute of Arthur's sluggish stirrings.[113]

Lefroy appreciates the fine absurdities of Austen's comic technique; she can also catch the exact rhythms of an Austen sentence. This is skilfully done in a recognizable Austenian moment where narrative voice and the conventions of indirect speech are overlaid; that is, where narrative voice merges relationally with the ear and judgement of Charlotte Heywood, the nominal outsider, apparently attending to Mr Parker speaking: 'no sands, nor even Beach, to be

[112] *Sanditon: A Continuation*, 15, 46, and 26–7.

[113] *Fragment of a Novel*, 153 and 156–7; *Sanditon: A Continuation*, 22, 25, and 27–8.

sure, worth mentioning the character of the ground on that side preventing it; but to make more than amends these houses would have, on their own level, & directly in front of them, the Denham gardens—beautiful to the eye, & the greatest possible advantage in many ways, especially to Invalids—So Mr. Parker talked.'[114] Elsewhere, and with equal success, the cool tones of the narrative voice alone are to be inferred: 'Before the end of the week there came a melancholy change of weather, & two stormy days & nights of cold continuous rain. Such is always a trying season for the pleasure-seekers of a bathing place, whose first object, after securing their Lodgings is to be as little with inside them as possible.'[115]

But it is the departures from Austen's text which offer the greatest critical insight into both original and continuation, since according to the degree of Lefroy's declared fidelity, they represent failures to follow the model rather than bold improvisations upon it. In suggesting the limits of mimicry, they are also clues to what is most particular in Austen's handling of her subject. Some simple differences first: in Lefroy's continuation, the apparently submissive (but in fact quietly sceptical) Mrs Parker finds her voice and it is disappointingly commonplace and sensible—one sign that, as Lefroy stated in her 1862 letter to Austen-Leigh, the eccentrics wearied her and she believed they should be 'softened down'; at the same time Charlotte Heywood's point of view becomes more straightforwardly complicit with the narrator's than it is in Austen's version, ultimately to be lost in the omniscient perspective. If such changes suggest a faltering of imaginative sympathy, most telling of all are the introduction of Mr Tracy, Sidney Parker's holiday companion, and the reappraisal of the characters of Sir Edward Denham and Clara Brereton. Both represent departures from the original which by contrast flag up something peculiar in Austen's treatment of the novel in general and of the *Sanditon* fragment in particular—her dependency on dialogue (or, in the case of *Sanditon*, overheard monologue) to advance the action and reveal character, her spare use of particulars, and above all her suppression of plot.

Austen rarely deals in villains or plot, by which I mean she shuns a declared system of formal conventions, distinct from the contingent workings of everyday reality, which saturate the narrative of the generality of nineteenth-century novels with loudly expressive devices. At the level of style this is apparent in her avoidance of metaphorical language and cultivation of

[114] Ibid., 33.

[115] Ibid., 49–50. The phrase 'with inside' [*sic*] is used by Austen in *Emma*: 'Harriet, she found, had never in her life been within side the Vicarage' (ed. Stafford, 72).

a seeming neutrality of expression. Of course, her novels are plotted, but the private lives of her characters define a textual space in which action converts into conversation, visits, dances, games of whist, and other social assemblies, the patterned but seemingly plotless events of ordinary life. Only when the pattern has been played out do we see the mark or stain that plot leaves. Though charm and even decency can (and do) cast in retrospect a shadow across all Austen's subdued local dramas, their actions no more than ruffle a surface dedicated to affirming the efficacy of prudence and gentility, and doing very little.

Here is the problem: for Lefroy 'the story was too little advanced to enable one to form any idea of the plot'; and, she avers, no other first twelve chapters provide so little by way of clues to development. By contrast, the end of Chapter 12 marked the close of the first volume (that is, 50 per cent) of *Persuasion*. Lefroy's structural solution is unAustenian: to throw some very heavy grit into the machine. Accordingly, she introduces the sinister Mr Tracy, a man of mysterious circumstances and origins, urbane and rootless, and a 'very useful political agent'. Without occupation, income, or debts, he gambles occasionally and successfully, and some years before has been of service in rescuing the young Mr Edward Denham from a fleecing during his short European tour. Tracy is a foil to Sidney Parker and a less well-intentioned outside observer than Charlotte Heywood. He has the power and the will to expose both Sir Edward Denham and Clara Brereton. Clara, the beautiful damsel-in-distress of Charlotte's imagining, is set, somewhat surprisingly, to become a scheming fortune hunter in Lefroy's continuation, less the victim of Lady Denham's meanness and Sir Edward's extravagant fantasy (in Austen's fragment he intends to seduce her or carry her off to Timbuctoo) than the architect of her own plan to relieve Lady Denham of her money. A substantial second section of Lefroy's continuation is given to excavating a background and a motive for Clara's transformation into a Dickensian minx, made 'cold, calculating, & selfish' by destitution and the squalid intrigues of her Whitechapel relations.[116] By contrast, Austen had maintained the moral neutrality of Clara's poverty. Sir Edward, drawn in less exaggerated lines but now with the suspicion of a secret past, is set to become Clara's victim, an unexpected variation on Austen's instruction that 'Clara saw through him, & had not the least intention of being seduced'.[117] Mr Tracy in particular is a kind of character Austen avoids, whose mysterious history, observations, and

[116] *Sanditon: A Continuation*, 34–8; and 81.

[117] *Fragment of a Novel*, 111.

actions solidify into something menacing and palpable; in so doing his portrait reduces the subtle moral comedy at play in Austen's characterization in favour of a simpler division of characters into good versus bad. Hints that Mr Parker is already in financial difficulty suggest that Tracy may become in some way implicated in his fate. In particular, Charlotte and Sidney Parker, whose entrance seemed to promise so much by way of subtly comic criticism when anticipated in Austen's fragment, are at risk of becoming merely good characters. Mr Tracy, by contrast, is that most unAustenian thing a plotter, keeping, in a further unAustenian gesture, a private journal in which he jots for his and our benefit his observations on events so far.

Lefroy's nerve failed her and she abandoned the story at the point where, all the signposts in place, the plot had to (but could not) deliver. It seems fair to say that she was stymied by her own conformism; that too conscious of her original, she could not measure herself against it in any terms that would give creative authority to her own continuation. With the leading characters assembled for an evening's entertainment at Trafalgar House, an unexpected visit is announced from Mr Woodcock of the Sanditon Hotel. Sidney Parker leaves the room to attend him, and the final words provide a cliff-hanger in the best traditions of melodrama: 'Charlotte felt a little nervous—What *could* have happened—.'[118] Since at this point Lefroy turned to the second section of her manuscript, her account of the life of Clara Brereton, it would seem that she too could not answer Charlotte's question. Unpublished until 1983, her continuation nevertheless forms the first critical appreciation of Austen's fragment, which in its similarities and differences offers a valuable insight into the delicate and difficult art of the plotless novel.

Part of the problem lay in the fact that by the time she came to write it Lefroy was a published author in a quite different genre from her aunt's. By an inevitable irony, impulsive, unsteady Anna, whose giddiness pulled her despite Austen's best efforts towards improbable romance, had become a writer of books for young people, in the style made successful by Harriett Mozley, John Henry Newman's sister and wife of a keen Tractarian. Unlike the Evangelical school whose excesses Austen had ridiculed, the Tractarian novelists deplored showy religiosity; Mozley's own tales (*The Fairy Bower* (1841), *The Lost Brooch* (1842)) are low-key studies of psychology and relationship within small family groups, explorations of everyday social behaviour. In her concentration on ordinary events and realistic settings Mozley in fact bore

[118] *Sanditon: A Continuation*, 78.

comparison with Austen, whom she much admired.[119] Both Anna Lefroy and subsequently her more prolific novelist daughter, Fanny Caroline, worked towards the romantic end of this kind of Church–Party fiction.

Anna Lefroy appears to have launched her career as a published writer with the novella *Mary Hamilton* in Alaric A. Watts's *Literary Souvenir* (1834). Narrated in maturity by two first-person narrators, Sir Henry Tracey and a female servant, old Hannah, it is the story of Tracey's early attachment to a particular place, Knightswood, and its inhabitants, and his banishment ('for making love to my cousin Julia') and return after sixteen years to marry not Julia but another childhood companion, the orphaned and neglected Mary Hamilton. It is a humourless and insipid tale, told with little skill. Mary Hamilton remains insubstantial, though her history (in particular, her sitting room at Beauchamps and her irregular education by and attachment to her cousin Mark) is heavily indebted to Fanny Price's situation in *Mansfield Park*.[120] In other respects the novella's narrator resembles Scott's Guy Mannering, stripped of mystery and angst, but supplied with a good dose of Christian morality. (He seems to have nothing in common with Lefroy's other Mr Tracy, of the *Sanditon* continuation.) It is tempting to link the tale's publication and advertisement, as 'By a Niece of the Late Miss Austen', with the issue only the previous year of Bentley's Standard Novels set of Austen's fiction and the reawakening of interest that caused. A similar sleight of marketing no doubt explains its rescue from obscurity and reissue by Elkin Mathews and Marrot in 1927 to coincide with the tail-end of Chapman's fan-fared, scholarly publication of the novels and manuscript writings. A preface to this reissue, given over to misty-eyed Austenian recollection rather than to Lefroy's novella, describes *Mary Hamilton* with misplaced enthusiasm as 'a kind of miniature *Persuasion* enlivened by occasional sallies obviously derived from *Northanger Abbey*... a conspectus of Jane Austen's earliest and latest manners.'[121] Even the most fervently uncritical Janeite might feel cheated by the purchase.

[119] Kathleen Tillotson, *Novels of the Eighteen-Forties* (1954; London: Oxford University Press, 1961), 132–6. For Mozley's appreciation of Austen, including a reference to 'Mrs Ben Le Froye' (who 'seems to have inherited all her Aunts charms'), see Tillotson, *Times Literary Supplement*, 17 September 1954, 591.

[120] For editions of *Mary Hamilton*, see Gilson L4–5. *Mary Hamilton* (1927), 26–7 and 39–40, draw on *Mansfield Park*. For Anna Lefroy's writings, see Brimley Johnson, *Her Life, Her Work, Her Family, and Her Critics*, 224–8; David Gilson, 'Anna Lefroy and "Mary Hamilton"' (1977), repr. in *Collected Articles and Introductions*, 132–4; and Gilson M56. The Bodleian Library copy of *The Winter's Tale* (London: James Burns, 1841) contains a handwritten correspondence between Tillotson and Chapman, including a transcript of a letter from Harriett Mozley to Jemima Mozley, 18 December 1841, establishing Anna Lefroy's authorship.

[121] *Mary Hamilton* (1927), 9.

With James Burns, a well-known Tractarian publisher who handled books by Mozley and Newman, Lefroy issued two further works, both anonymously: *The Winter's Tale* (1841), a tale of Christian children in Roman Britain; and a second children's story, *Springtide* (1842). By contrast, Fanny Caroline Lefroy's novels (five between 1856 and 1861) are more diffusely moralized and sentimental. Some assume the perspective of the decent labouring poor, and the impression left by their confusion of Christian morality and unbridled romance is of Hannah More grafted onto Barbara Cartland. *'Long, Long Ago': An Autobiography* (1856), issued by the publisher-branch of the Mozley family, purports to be 'a true picture of a country home, such as it might have been nearly sixty years ago'. The setting is an Austenian past (opening in 1800 when the narrator, Mary Lisle, is 5) and an Austenian country rectory, like Steventon 'about a mile distant from the great western road... in a pretty woody meadow'.[122] The rectory children enjoy private family theatricals and even perform Sheridan's *The Rivals*, part of the Steventon repertoire; but the story of Mary's happy family life in idyllic rural surroundings, her romantic attachment to a Willoughby-like fortune hunter, and her eventual marriage ('from duty') to an older man, is told in a sub-Brontëan style bearing no resemblance to Jane Austen's.

If the fiction of the Lefroys, mother and daughter, quickly sank without trace, the novels of Catherine Anne Hubback floated for a while in the broad shallow waters of the Victorian fiction market. She even has a brief entry in Allibone's 1859 *Critical Dictionary of English Literature*, the kind of anthologized tribute that eluded Jane Austen in her lifetime. Here we encounter: 'Hubback, Mrs., a niece of Jane Austen, the authoress... also known as a successful novelist', with at this stage five listed works to her credit, though she had doubled that number by 1863, when her last was issued.[123] Her entry immediately precedes that of John Hubback, memorialized for 'an able work' on 'the Evidence of Succession to Property and Peerages' (1844). This was her

[122] [Mary Lisle], *'Long, Long Ago': An Autobiography* (London: J. and C. Mozley, 1856), 2. Other titles by F. C. Lefroy, some published anonymously, are *Hannah Lavender; or, Ladyhall* (London: Society for Promoting Christian Knowledge, 1857); *My Three Aunts; or, Lowminster* (London: J. and C. Mozley, 1858); *'Straight forward': and Patience Hart; or, The Dissembler* (London: J. and C. Mozley, 1860); and *The Force of Habit; or, The Story of Widow Monger* (London: Joseph Masters, 1861).

[123] S. Austin Allibone, *A Critical Dictionary of English Literature, and British and American Authors, Living and Deceased*, 3 vols. (Philadelphia and London: Childs and Peterson, and Trubner, 1859), Vol. 1. Among Austen scholars, Hubback has attracted even less attention than Lefroy; but see a recent series of short internet essays by Tamara Wagner, 'Mrs Hubback's *The Younger Sister*: The Victorian Austen and the Phenomenon of the Austen Sequel', *The Victorian Web* (October 2003) and further instalments at http://www.victorianweb.org/victorian/authors/hubback/

husband, a barrister who after a promising start to his career suffered a devastating mental breakdown from which he never recovered. By 1850 his alarming symptoms left Catherine no choice but to have him confined to an asylum, she and her three small sons returning to live with her father, Frank Austen, at Portsdown Lodge, near Portsmouth. Anna Lefroy had returned to fiction in her early widowhood; for Catherine in her almost-widowhood novels became a source of income and distraction.[124] Her first, *The Younger Sister*, was written during a long stay in Wales, where she had taken her husband in hopes of finding a cure. A completion of Austen's nameless and unfinished fragment, only entitled *The Watsons* in 1870 by Austen-Leigh, it was published in three volumes in 1850 by Newby of Cavendish Square, who had also issued the first novels of Trollope and Emily and Anne Brontë.

The family tradition that Catherine did not work from a copy of the manuscript but was instead familiar with it from hearing it read aloud and discussed by Cassandra Austen and her stepmother, Martha Austen, is substantiated in the opening chapters, which bear a remarkable yet strangely distorted relationship to the original. The mounting sense, as one reads, is of Austen's fragment lying as a palimpsest beneath the more circumstantial prose of its Victorian refashioning. Catherine's son, John Hubback, described his mother's method in a late account written when he was over 90:

> My mother had studied this manuscript with her Aunt Cassandra so effectively that when she began to publish on her own account she was able to reproduce from memory the text of this manuscript almost word for word, despite the seven years' interval since she had seen it. She developed the story partly in accordance with traditions of Jane's own intentions of continuing it, and gave it a conclusion in the current Victorian three-volume style; her own ideas were modified in the third volume by those of her publisher... I should like to make it clear that 'The Younger Sister' begins with a supreme effort of memory, and she often told me that neither she nor the publisher saw any reason for refraining from giving it all to the public.[125]

Even in 1935 Hubback's tone is defensive; it is also confused. His implication, that the huge effort of memory involved exonerates his mother from the charge of plagiarism or illegal occupancy of expressions and phrases not her own, defies both law and the actual evidence of the text, which is mostly a paraphrase of Austen's fragment and not a verbatim reconstruction. He

[124] See Maggie Lane, *Jane Austen's Family Through Five Generations* (London: Robert Hale, 1984), 231–42; and David Hopkinson, 'A Niece of Jane Austen', *Notes and Queries*, 229 (1984), 470–1.

[125] John H. Hubback, *Cross Currents in a Long Life* (privately printed, 1935), 5.

defends his mother's right to memorize and narrate another's work when it could equally be argued that this is precisely what she failed to do.

The events of Austen's manuscript are roughly coextensive with the first five chapters of Hubback's first volume, and a comparison of parallel passages describing the same incidents reveals the close assimilation not only of details but actual words and turns of phrase within a broad frame which from the outset neither recalls nor suggests Austen's style. The result is familiar and disconcerting in equal measure, an unstable compound of free adaptation, memory or plagiarism, and displacement. (Unaccountably, too, while Hubback recalls complete phrases from the manuscript she forgets the names of major characters: Austen's Mrs Blake becomes first Mrs Wells and later Mrs Willis; Tom Musgrave more explicably becomes Musgrove.) For example, the early exchange between Emma Watson, introduced to us as a disappointed heiress, and her elder sister, Elizabeth, over the perils of the impoverished unmarried state is presented thus in Austen:

'To be so bent on Marriage—to pursue a Man merely for the sake of situation—is a sort of thing that shocks me; I cannot understand it. Poverty is a great Evil, but to a woman of Education & feeling it ought not, it cannot be the greatest.—I would rather be Teacher at a school (and I can think of nothing worse) than marry a Man I did not like.'—'I would rather do any thing than be Teacher at a school—said her sister. *I* have been at school, Emma, & know what a Life they lead; *you* never have.—I should not like marrying a disagreable Man any more than yourself,—but I do not think there *are* very many disagreable Men;—I think I could like any good humoured Man with a comfortable Income.—I suppose my Aunt brought you up to be rather refined.'

Hubback rewrites the passage as:

'I would rather do anything than marry for money,' observed Emma, 'it is so shocking. I would rather be teacher at a boarding school.'

'I have been at school, Emma, which you have not, and know what a school teacher is—such a life—I would rather do anything than that!'

'But to marry without love—that must surely be worse,' persisted Emma.

'Oh, I would not marry without love, exactly; but I think I could easily love any tolerably good-tempered man, who could give me a comfortable home. I am sure I would make any body a good wife; unless they were very cross. But your idea of *loving* is just another of your refinements, Emma; and only does for rich people who can afford such luxuries.'[126]

[126] *The Watsons, A Fragment*, 9–10; Mrs Hubback, *The Younger Sister. A Novel*, 3 vols. (London: Thomas Cautley Newby, 1850), i. 17–18.

Seeking to inhabit Austen's words, she produces from the pitiful coupling of spiritual and economic meanness that marks the original something that sounds merely smug and lower middle class.

Hubback's second chapter opens with the Edwards family, Emma in tow, entering the assembly room where preparations for the ball are in hand. Austen's spare prose had captured as a series of dissociated sense impressions the awkwardness, the physical and social chill, of their unfashionably early appearance:

> Mrs Edwards... led the way up the wide staircase, while no sound of a Ball but the first Scrape of one violin, blessed the ears of her followers... Mrs E's sattin gown swept along the clean floor of the Ball-room, to the fireplace at the upper end, where one party only were formally seated, while three or four Officers were lounging together, passing in & out from the adjoining card-room.—A very stiff meeting between these near neighbours ensued...

In Hubback's loose rendering of the same scene its most powerful effects—friction, physical discomfort, anxiety—are smoothed out despite the retention of specific detail:

> They entered the ball-room; it looked very cold and very dull; the candles as yet hardly lighted, and the fires yielding far more smoke than heat. Over one of these several officers were lounging; Mrs. Edwards directed her steps to the other, and seated herself on the warmest side; her two companions found chairs near her, Mr. Edwards having left them at the door of the ball-room, to seek out his old associates at the whist-tables.[127]

Though the effort of memory behind Hubback's early chapters evinces a particular and conscientious attachment to her aunt's text, the general effect is annotative or explanatory rather than ventriloquial or revivifying.

But before Austen-Leigh published the original fragment of *The Watsons* in 1871, as an appendix to his *Memoir of Jane Austen*, the reader had no clue either to the fact or the circumstances of Hubback's belatedness. Shorn of the fragment, her novel would merely have been another contribution to a style in vogue from the 1840s, the tale of private life set in the past, the kind of tale from which obvious historical incident is absent, though a hazily sentimental pastness is implied.[128] Thackeray, the Brontës, and Gaskell were all writing novels whose narratives were set at a comfortable forty-sixty years distance;

[127] *The Watsons*, 32–4; *The Younger Sister*, i. 28.

[128] See Tillotson, *Novels of the Eighteen-Forties*, 91–115.

like Fanny Caroline Lefroy's *'Long, Long Ago'* and Austen-Leigh's *Memoir*, Hubback's novel is set 'sixty years ago'. In describing the town ball at which Emma has her first taste of the provincial society in which her family moves, Hubback indulges in an unAustenian digression on dance through the ages, from the 'stately pavin' to the 'merry country-dance and cotillon', which closely anticipates in substance and tone a similar period detail developed twenty years later by Austen-Leigh to pad out his review of manners and customs of Jane Austen's youth. As he there explains, 'in most of [Austen's] works, a ball or a private dance is mentioned'.[129] Hubback advances the narrative of her continuation by means of two further balls; while at least since Metcalfe and Chapman, it has seemed necessary to Austen annotators and adapters to anatomize the dance in their quest to replenish her texts and resist their estrangement. As film adaptations prove, such detail (card games offer another) continues to function metonymically as a system of recall in the afterlife of Austen's novels.

In light of its continuation, Hubback's curious feat of memory in the opening chapters of *The Younger Sister* appears to have been a means to kick-start her own fictional motor. She gave no public hint of the borrowed characters or plot, and the affectionate dedication—'To the Memory of her Aunt, the Late Jane Austen . . . though too young to have known her personally . . . from childhood taught to esteem her virtues, and admire her talents'—serves less to acknowledge a debt than to solicit further favour. From the failure of memory there emerged a compensatory hybrid style. The tale Hubback develops reads like a transitional stage between Austen and Gaskell's provincial studies, with the occasional wobble towards Brontëan melodrama. If the incident in Volume 1, used by Hubback and later by her granddaughter Edith Brown, of Emma Watson being snowed up at Mr Howard's sister's, was indeed a 'genuine Jane incident' passed on by Cassandra,[130] then the events of Volume 3 belong to an altogether more highly coloured narrative whose shape and momentum are dictated by the recent publishing sensation, *Jane Eyre*. Here Emma's trials assume sensational proportions: she is rejected as a nursery governess on the grounds of alleged sexual impropriety (a detail that interestingly reappears in Anna Lefroy's history of Clara Brereton); she encounters a gipsy who rises up by a fairy fountain to predict tragic news; and there is the news itself, preceded by a

[129] Cf. *The Younger Sister*, i. 30–1 and *Memoir*, 32.

[130] According to Edith Brown, and as recorded by R. Brimley Johnson, *Her Life, Her Work, Her Family, and Her Critics*, 83.

dreadful night-time scream cutting through the jollifications of yet another ball to announce that Mr Howard, Emma's lover, has been killed by a fall from his horse.[131] Howard's apparently fatal adventure takes place in Wales, where Hubback was writing. In his subsequent 'resurrection' and return to marry Emma there can be glimpsed the kind of miracle she herself needed to restore her deranged husband. Such heightened effects may appear to contest the genre of probable fiction, Austen's special arena, from within. But Hubback was a sensationalist, writing in a far different register from her aunt; *The Younger Sister* represents the reabsorption of Austen's material into the kind of circulating library fiction from which she had worked hard to distance her own art. Though Hubback did not again borrow directly from her aunt, she was happy to publish later novels as 'Mrs. Hubback, niece of Miss Austen', while one reviewer eventually took the hint and described her eighth novel, *The Rival Suitors* (1857), as proof that she was 'as nearly allied by genius as she is by blood to the first of English female novelists, Miss Austen.'[132]

In 1870, at the age of 52, Catherine Anne Hubback set sail to make a new life in California, settling in Oakland with her second son Edward. The letters she sent back to her eldest son John and his wife in Liverpool contain some of her liveliest writing. The privations and indulgences of the American way of life provoked her wit and her prejudice and the keen political sense we glimpse on occasion in her novels. She planned a series of short stories based on her Californian impressions, and she decided on a new 'nom-de-plume':

> My story has come out in the Oct. overland [*The Overland Monthly*], but I have not received any money yet. I am anxious to know how much they will pay—I have two more ready, but I don't write for nothing—by & bye they can be all put in a vol. & published again—I mean in future to have my name printed M^{rs}. C. Austen Hubback & make believe the A. stands for that—I never have written it *at length*—so nobody knows—and Austen is a good nom-de-plume. Have you seen or heard of E. A. Leigh's vol—Lady Susan—I think he is mean not to send it to me—very mean & real ugly, & I feel quite bad about it—& shall not have a good time till I get it—I am real mad—(not that I am a bit—but those are Californian expressions—) He has not said the first thing about sending it—I have to keep my Californiania aired, for use in in [*sic*] my stories, so I practice it on you.[133]

131 *The Younger Sister*, iii. 51; and 273 ff.

132 Cited in Hopkinson, 'A Niece of Jane Austen', 471.

133 Bodleian MS. Eng. lett. e. 150, f. 6, Catherine Hubback to her son John in Liverpool, 24 September 1871. Hubback refers to the publication of the second edition of Austen-Leigh's *Memoir* (1871), enlarged by *Lady Susan* and other Austen manuscripts.

It is in these letters, where a familiar Austenian register delivers impressions of America, that Hubback's inheritance seems most secure, a legitimate rather than a ventriloquial power. If Lefroy's anxious fidelity assured her silence, Hubback's expansive textual liberties led eventually to the discovery of an authentic Californian-Austenian voice:

> [American women] are all educated & turned out above domestic labour—they play *piannies*, & learn french (I have not met one who can speak it, except the Kirkhams)—and study geometry and philosophy—& of course they can't go to service, but they have to take to dress making, or clerkship or suchlike—& they marry early, & turn into domestic drudges, making their own bread & dresses, and being their own servants, and working hard, & growing old early, and disappearing out of the world—and their children roll about in the streets & steal their neighbours plums . . .[134]

But the Californian novel was never written; Hubback died of pneumonia in February 1877 in Virginia, where she had moved in 1876 to live with her youngest son, Charles. Her letters home were funny, caustic, and tough minded to the end. Writing on 28 August 1876 to John whose business was in trouble, she passed on this advice:

> For nearly 30 years now I have had so much of change of disappointment & uncertainty in every thing, mixed up with so much of good and so many helps and blessings, that I always feel when things are going well or ill that it will probably not last . . .[135]

[134] Ibid., f. 25^{v}, 21 July 1872. [135] Ibid., f. 100^{v}.

5

Speaking Commas

'A total inattention to stops, and a very frequent ignorance of grammar'[1]

For much of the twentieth century debates about textual authority operated according to the unexamined claim that authorial practice and textual corruption shared a common identity when the author was female. Put bluntly, it was assumed that the texts of works by female authors were likely to display more errors, more fundamentally, and in more places. Such assumptions had much to do with the ideological gendering of the act of writing and of textual critical practices as they served to form and defend a literary canon, first of Classical and in more recent centuries of vernacular works. Underlying textual criticism in its Classical, Johnsonian, and, in the twentieth century, its New Bibliographical guises was the belief that all material manifestations of a literary work (all the documents or vessels which transmit the work) in some significant way falsify its essence—that what conveys betrays—and that the work's authentic state lies beyond expression. This is the spirit/matter dichotomy according to which the text is encountered as a physical body, usually diseased or deformed, and requiring the editor's healing or cleansing intervention to restore its original health. In the terms of this explanation, the editor is both surgeon and priest, attending to the body in order to give relief to the soul of the text and restore it to a state of grace.

[1] *Northanger Abbey*, ed. Marilyn Butler (Harmondsworth, Middx.: Penguin, 1995), 25, Henry Tilney's pronouncement on the female art of letter-writing.

The traditional rhetoric of textual criticism since humanist times organized itself around this familiar binary, where the soul or spirit of the text was guaranteed or recovered by the periodic inspection and cleansing (or chastisement) of the textual body. Predictably in the body/spirit dynamic, the body (or matter of the text) tended to be gendered female and the spirit male, with the corruption or unchastity of the female text, and the correction it required, providing useful legitimation of the activity of the (usually male) editor whose task it was to represent the interests of the betrayed authorial intention.[2] When, rarely, the author was herself female (and text inevitably under the sign of a double contamination, as matter twice over) a further refinement was usually deemed necessary to discriminate authority from intention as, for instance, in the widespread invocation of a male family member (Percy Shelley or Henry Austen) to underwrite her productions. Interestingly, anonymous or traditional literature, never accorded the canonical respect of authored works, provided editors with a similar dilemma which they figured in similarly gendered terms. As the Victorian editors of Thomas Percy's influential collection of British balladry and song *Reliques of Ancient English Poetry* (1765) imply, in such cases the editor carries heavy parental responsibilities for the untutored text: 'As to the text, [Percy] looked on it as a young woman from the country with unkempt locks, whom he had to fit for fashionable society.'[3] This is to see text as some rustic Eliza Doolittle and the editor in the dubious role of Professor Higgins's mentor-lover, a relationship Austen early attempted to refresh in the comic education of Catherine Morland by Henry Tilney in *Northanger Abbey*, a novel whose complex literary cross-references draw attention to the unexpected sophistication of untutored, female-authored texts.

Where material suspicion (a distrust of matter) might seem a plausible or at least a convenient excuse for editorial intervention when the early record of a work's production and transmission is lost in the mists of time or provably falsified, it appears less so when, as is the case with much modern vernacular

[2] Stephanie H. Jed, *Chaste Thinking: The Rape of Lucretia and the Birth of Humanism* (Bloomington and Indianapolis: Indiana University Press, 1989), proposes a wide feminist argument about the transmission of texts and the gendered ideological grounding of Classical textual critical practices. See, too, Valerie Wayne, 'The Sexual Politics of Textual Transmission', in *Textual Formations and Reformations*, ed. Laurie E. Maguire and Thomas L. Berger (Newark: University of Delaware Press, 1998), 179–210; and Andrew Murphy, '"To Ferret Out Any Hidden Corruption": Shakespearean Editorial Metaphors', *TEXT*, 10 (1997), 202–19. The *locus classicus* for the trope of the text as gendered and/or diseased body is Samuel Johnson, 'Preface to Shakespeare' (1765).

[3] *Bishop Percy's Folio Manuscript*, ed. John W. Hales and Frederick J. Furnivall, 4 vols. (London: N. Trubner and Co., 1867–8), i. xvi.

literature, the history is fuller. But in fact precisely as the textual record began to groan under the weight of preserved drafts, revisions, early and late versions, and authorized printings, the distrust of textual matter found reinforcement from the Romantic poet's anxious vindication of his wordy aspirations as 'far hidden from the reach of words', wordless in their unambiguated expression; beyond, too, it is implied, the material forms which broadcast them. In Wordsworth's case, those forms are books, whose very processes, regardless of accuracy or error in their operation, constitute a record of disauthentication, of deterioration and betrayal, relieved only by the author's periodic re-appropriation of his text, in the act of revision and re-inscription. As he writes in *The Prelude*, the poem left appropriately untitled and unpublished at his death, 'deeply did I feel | How we mislead each other, above all | How books mislead us . . . | Effeminately level down the truth | To certain general notions for the sake | Of being understood at once'.[4] Here, it seems, the old argument against the corruptions attendant on transmission is given a new twist, in the interests of a knowledge estranged from the (over-) systematized structures of a trade in books. The conventions of bookmaking, and not least the assumption of a commonly agreed correspondence between meaning and words, deceive us into seeking cultural homogeneity where it does not exist. The language of Wordsworth's manuscript poem, unfettered by anticipations of print, is noticeably masculinist in its gesturing to a familiar trope of neo-Classical Republican aesthetics: the independent and manly virtue of writing as against the feminizing or over-refining tendency of print is just another rehearsal of the old body/spirit opposition. In this understanding, books and the art of printing also constitute a false conformity to be distinguished from true textual authenticity.[5]

We have no more than a discarded scrap of manuscript evidence for the six printed books that chiefly make up Austen's literary reputation. In Wordsworth's terms, hers is a reputation founded on conformity. Nowhere is this more evident than in the critical attention paid throughout the twentieth century to the surface texture of her novels, to their finished achievement as a

[4] *Prelude*, 3 (1805), 185; and 12 (1805), 205–13.

[5] Compare the Republican-influenced rhetoric of the Scottish Enlightenment thinker Adam Ferguson opposing the book as an instrument of knowledge to the activity of understanding: 'The knowledge of books', he claims, shackles the intellectual energy in a commercial society and inhibits the freedom of 'the inquisitive or animated spirit', which impels writing (*An Essay on the History of Civil Society* (1767), ed. Fania Oz-Salzberger (Cambridge: Cambridge University Press, 1995), 206). See, too, William Godwin's related argument on the distinction between reading a book and hearing a man speak (in *Thoughts on Man, His Nature, Productions, and Discoveries. Interspersed with some particulars respecting the author*, in *Political and Philosophical Writings*, vi. 176).

matter of style. The precision attributed to Austen's English—the propriety and effectiveness of her linguistic mastery—announced the place her works were expected to fill in a particular kind of literary academy—that associated with Empson, the Leavises, and the New Criticism. According to Q. D. Leavis, along with Richardson, Scott, and the late eighteenth-century novelists, Austen drew upon 'an idiom for common standards of taste and conduct', an accessible and 'urbane shorthand' which represented a generally held stock of values made current in Addisonian polite discourse.[6] But what had been 'common' in the eighteenth century was lost in the course of the nineteenth, subsequently becoming the utopian aspiration of the educated twentieth-century reader dissatisfied by the syntactic and emotive looseness of the modern novelist's vocabulary.

By Leavis's argument, far from confounding meaning in conformity, the textual evidence Austen's novels provide for this shared linguistic currency both restores a vanished civilization and enriches contemporary culture. There is of course little real opposition between Wordsworth's and Leavis's élitist critiques of mass culture; what is different is the cultural work they each discover in the same period of literature and the same technological moment. For both, present-day technologies (notably the publishing institutions of their own time) detract from the contemporary writer's ability to provide a text unavailable to misreading. In each case, unambiguous value lies in a past idealistically skewed and shorn of material circumstance. Only under these conditions does Austen's printed œuvre escape its gendered predetermination and attain its high place in the literary canon in the twentieth century.

By the terms of the close verbal analysis the Leavises proposed as a method of critical reading, every aspect of a text must bear witness to an authorial intention. Where each word or mark of punctuation can and will give rise to a critical insight there must be no unintended (non-authorial) interference, no betrayal of textual spirit by body. We might well ask why a kind of critical exegesis perfected on the closed interplay of form and meaning associated with the confined economy of the sonnet or short lyric poem should have

[6] Q. D. Leavis, *Fiction and the Reading Public*, 106–7. For a late elaboration of the same thesis, see Stuart M. Tave, *Some Words of Jane Austen* (Chicago and London: University of Chicago Press, 1973), a critical study of the intertwined moral and lexical register of a few words in the novels. Tave's opening observation that Jane Austen was fond of dancing provides a leitmotiv to invoke the regularity, order, and desirable limitations of society. As it is in the dance, so is it in prescriptive grammar, and so too in the Austenian world: 'There is a continuum of words in which the passage from one to another is a passage from one moral state to another; a notation is available to name the steps and the critical moment the misstep is made' (28). Bharat Tandon, *Jane Austen and the Morality of Conversation*, offers a reassessment of this line of thinking.

been thought transferable to the novel, where issues of scale are likely to defeat the most resourceful intentionalist. Austen's miniaturist art sets her novels apart from the common run of nineteenth-century fiction. The self-declared smallness of her scope (that 'little bit (two Inches wide) of Ivory on which I work with so fine a Brush'),[7] the famed steadiness and narrowness of her gaze, seemed to reduce the role of contingency in her text to nothing. 'Whatever she produced', declared James Edward Austen-Leigh in a far-resounding formulation, was a 'genuine home-made article'.[8] Which of itself appears to deny those acts of collaboration—linguistic, intellectual, cultural, and historical—that shape literary works and their texts at every stage of realization. Such denial was for much of the twentieth century the most significant aspect of the critical reproduction of Austen's novels as hermetically sealed objects of study. It played a far larger part in the estimation of her work than of that of earlier or later novelists, whose value was accordingly diminished to the extent that they were shown to engage with other discourses and the institutional practices surrounding them—Scott's and Dickens's notoriously commercial art being cases in point.

Scott declared his imagination to be as far as possible from the home-centred, something more like a factory. In the fictitious prefaces which introduce several of his tales he considered the divisible structures of the novelist's art as the dispersed and interdependent components of industrialized production, ingeniously establishing through his metaphor the high cost of commercial manufacture as the real representation of his value as an author, and at the same time justifying the hike his fame gave to the price of new novels and the fortune he was busy making.[9] The first bestseller and the first novelist consciously to address a mass audience, he exploited that craving for 'novel' experiences and new products which lies at the heart of consumerism and which contributed decisively to the contemporary success of the genre. Austen's novels, on the contrary, until relatively recently have

[7] *Jane Austen's Letters*, 323.

[8] *Memoir*, 90.

[9] Scott and his publishers drove up the price of new fiction to previously unimagined heights (setting a standard with *Kenilworth*, at 31*s*. 6*d*. or 10*s*. 6*d*. per volume, in 1821). Prefaced to his late novel *The Betrothed* (1825) is an account of a meeting of the characters and pseudonymous narrators involved in the production of the Waverley Novels which provides a description of his art as a network of subdivided labour. Scott habitually used the fictional preface to conflate the artistic process with the production process, equating the labour investment of the imagination with the economic value of the produced commodity. In *The Betrothed* the analogy concludes with a proposal, from the fictional characters, to go it alone and form a joint-stock company to turn out future fiction without an author and by machinery. See my 'Fictional Economies: Adam Smith, Walter Scott, and the Nineteenth-Century Novel', *English Literary History*, 54 (1987), 97–127.

been praised for dealing only in the familiar, for reaching the reader untainted by novelty and large commercial success. The modest success of her second publication, *Pride and Prejudice*, undoubtedly made her greedy for more and seems to have alerted her to the value to be found in digression, as narrative padding and to promote the importance and earning power of the author. But her hints, rueful, comic, and knowing, on how to enlarge the internal economy and commercial appeal of the home-spun domestic tale with 'an Essay on Writing, a critique on Walter Scott, or the history of Buonaparte' remained just that, evidence that she understood the market but meant to play it on different terms.[10] Reviewing in March 1818 the posthumously published *Northanger Abbey* and *Persuasion*, the *British Critic* commented, 'she seems to have no other object in view, than simply to paint some of those scenes which she has herself seen, and which every one, indeed, may witness daily.'[11] Austen's is an art uncontaminated by expansion. It is difficult to overestimate the value of her apparently anti-novelistic (because anti-materialist) confinement to the social and moral critics of the mid-twentieth century for whom she represented what her fellow novelists could not achieve—untainted cultural capital.[12]

For Norman Page in 1972, 'Jane Austen's greatness lay in exploiting the distinctive strengths of the English language as she found it, and in resisting some of the influences which were at work to change it even as she wrote.'[13] Page's study of Austen's language is intelligent and particularly attuned to its conversational rhythms; but like that of K. C. Phillipps written a few years

[10] *Jane Austen's Letters*, 203; and see Ch. 4, 'Professional writer'.

[11] *British Critic*, n.s., 9 (1818), in *Critical Heritage*, i. 80. In the same year the *British Review* commented on Scott's latest novel, *The Heart of Midlothian*, that it had been spun out into four volumes much as a cloth manufacturer spins cloth, to make more money: 'if he had not been compelled by his mercantile engagement to spin out the thread of his story, with or without materials, so as to make out a *fourth* volume, and by that means secure the *fourth* thousand pounds, he would have scorned to introduce any part of the trash, of which he has composed the latter part of his work.' (*British Review*, 12 (1818), 404.)

[12] I would here take issue with the uncomplicated equation of economic and cultural capital implied in Gary Kelly's otherwise richly informative and briskly fashioned essay, 'Jane Austen's Real Business: The Novel, Literature, and Cultural Capital', in *Jane Austen's Business: Her World and Her Profession*, ed. Juliet McMaster and Bruce Stovel (Basingstoke and London: Macmillan, 1996), 154–67. In arguing for Austen's importance in transforming the novel into Literature and therefore cultural capital he makes a too easy elision between the symbolic use to which Literature as cultural capital is put by those bent on acquiring or already in possession of material and social capital and what he wishes to see as Austen's own material advantage from publication. As Q. D. Leavis's unabashedly snobbish argument suggests, the distribution of material to cultural capital is more ambiguous than this, the long-term symbolic value of Austen's work being bound up with its failure to achieve adequate commercial conversion in the short term. Accordingly, her classic status stands guarantee for the cultural success of a professional class of readers who themselves would hardly wish to inhabit the paradoxical economy that guarantees her art as art.

[13] Norman Page, *The Language of Jane Austen* (Oxford: Basil Blackwell, 1972), 9.

previously, it emphasized, Leavis-like, the defensive link between moral and linguistic probity, between cultural stability and Englishness itself that her fictional usage could be made to represent. Examining the frequency of the auxiliaries 'may', 'must', and 'used to', Phillipps concluded, '[i]t is remarkable, as it is also thoroughly characteristic, how frequently such expressions of compulsion and disposition occur. Like Fanny Price at Portsmouth, Jane Austen often seems to be pining, at least subconsciously, for a more ordered world.' Accordingly, there is a 'grammar of conduct' as of linguistic usage, and '[t]o be blatantly ungrammatical in the novels is to be ungenteel', like Nancy and Lucy Steele in *Sense and Sensibility* or Mrs Elton in *Emma*; such characters threaten something more widely disruptive than solecism.[14] Where linguistic acts are so finely judged, it is interesting to note that Austen's own linguistic freedoms (like her occasional use of nouns as verbs) are vindicated by reference to the law-giving dispensation of Shakespeare's usage, which effectively annuls her transgressive daring.[15]

Until late in the twentieth century, the conservative bounds for the operation of Austen's linguistic variety seemed overwhelmingly to declare her willing pupillage to the master linguist Samuel Johnson. Early critics, like A. C. Bradley, Mary Lascelles, and C. S. Lewis, even constituted the relationship as ventriloquy: Johnson speaking through Austen.[16] For Chapman, who permitted himself to doubt whether she 'was conscious of having a style of her own',[17] so entailed did her vision seem to a Johnsonian standard, the idea of identity between the two voices was a powerfully seductive one, clearly influencing his editorial judgements in detecting error or artistic lapses in the pupil where there was not perfect harmonization. In recent criticism, however, the domestic agenda of much eighteenth- and nineteenth-century English fiction has been reassessed and discovered to anticipate a more general and major restructuring of social and institutional relations in the modern world; in particular, shifting linguistic authority from male lexicog-

[14] K. C. Phillipps, *Jane Austen's English* (London: André Deutsch, 1970), 123 and 145. The phrase 'grammar of conduct' is C. S. Lewis's, 'A Note on Jane Austen' (1954), reprinted in *Selected Literary Essays*, 185.

[15] Phillipps, *Jane Austen's English*, 200: 'Jane Austen shows great freedom, and even daring, in her conversion and use of almost any part of speech as any other part of speech. Shakespeare was the precursor to whom she might look in this; Shakespeare whose writings, in the words of Henry Crawford . . . are "part of an Englishman's constitution".'

[16] The point is made by Janet Sorensen, *The Grammar of Empire in Eighteenth-Century British Writing* (Cambridge: Cambridge University Press, 2000), 215, where she describes the twentieth-century estimation of Austen as a writer indebted to Johnson and the Augustans, 'a talented imitator of a dominant world view and its language'.

[17] Chapman, *Jane Austen, Facts and Problems*, 209.

rapher to female novelist. According to Nancy Armstrong's influential Foucauldian study, *Desire and Domestic Fiction: A Political History of the Novel* (1987), novels and non-fictional conduct books written by and for women in this period helped inaugurate the modern subject. Austen is the heroine of Armstrong's argument, the steadiness of her domestic preoccupations witnessing to and promoting the relocation of a 'common' language away from the public world to a private and feminized system of cultural values. More recently still, the accommodation that such wide-scale social 'feminization' implies has itself been subjected to scrutiny as critics have begun to address the expressive potential of Austen's irony as a device for linguistic defamiliarization—for disturbing as opposed to authorizing the power invested in the domestic environment.[18] What these various critical adjustments review in Austen's practice is the relation of a moral or civil grammar to an English language grammar, and particularly the function of community and interpersonal relations as matters of linguistic consensus, as made or unmade in language—and above all, in speech. But what remains a constant through all the critical shifts, from conservative to radically disruptive, is Austen's exemplary status in portraying the relationship between grammar and usage within community.

Austen is credited with being a pioneer in establishing conversation as the mode of social authority and knowledge in fiction. With both prescriptiveness and challenge haunting the margins of her domestic text she discovers in conversation a space which is neither tractable nor openly interrogative. This space is best imagined as filled with sound—an intricate pattern of *sotto voce* conversations which her characters have with themselves, which the ideal (and misunderstanding reader) has with the re-read text, and which, as a consequence of her comically antithetical syntax, the text has with itself and with generic expectations for the novel. Imagining her novels as conversations is to recover their language as performance, as pitch, tone, and voice, as personally invested and opaque—above all, as studies in what Johnson, defending the descriptive failings of his *Dictionary*, called 'living information'

[18] In Nancy Armstrong's reinterpretation of the rise of the novel as instrumental in the restructuring of modern middle-class institutions, Austen's traditional exemplary status within definitions of Englishness is linked specifically to her domestic and feminine transformation of a public-political language of cultural reproduction. The peculiar capability of Austen's communities 'to be both permeable and restrictive' is the key to their resilience. In linguistic terms it is 'the power of usage to modify grammar or the rules governing usage'. See *Desire and Domestic Fiction: A Political History of the Novel* (New York: Oxford University Press, 1987), 134–60 (esp. 156–9). The critical potential of Austen's linguistic defamiliarization is the subject of recent studies by Inger Sigrun Thomsen, 'Words "Half-Dethroned": Jane Austen's Art of the Unspoken', in *Jane Austen's Business*, ed. McMaster and Stovel, 95–106; and Sorensen, *Grammar of Empire*, 212 ff.

subject to 'local convenience', which includes the convenience of exercising deception and of being misunderstood.[19]

The exchange of conversation, whether as dialogue or reported speech, or in its most urgent form as the interiorized discourse of the self with the self, unspoken and heard only in the mind's ear, is Austen's major resource as a writer as it is her characters' chief life skill. Recognizing the power of conversation, her novels imply, is what everything comes down to, in art and in life. By extension, Austen's mastery (accommodated or subversive) of a common style and her identification with or departure from a Johnsonian norm are recognizable as the strategies of familiarization and defamiliarization which establish Austenian critical acts as themselves shifting conversations within and across generations of scholars. Yet this healthy critical commerce is something the printed textual history of Austen's novels has attempted to resist rendering it in some sense against the grain, against authorial intention as editorially articulated.

R. W. Chapman's five-volume Clarendon text of 1923, *The Novels of Jane Austen*, was the first edition to consider systematically the full textual record of the novels; it has remained the standard authority ever since. It is the basis for all later British editions, including the Penguin English Library edition issued in the 1960s, Mary Lascelles's revisions for the 1963 Dent / Everyman edition, and James Kinsley's Oxford English Novels edition of 1970–1, currently issued as the World's Classics edition. Chapman, Lascelles, and Kinsley were the three chief exponents of the Austen text in the twentieth century, though it is worth noting that Chapman's authority went largely unchallenged by any and all scholars revisiting his editorial decisions in the 1960s and 1970s. Chapman's edition is also the basis for modern American editions, including the Norton critical editions, the most recent of which are Claudia Johnson's *Mansfield Park* (1998) and *Sense and Sensibility* (2002), both reconsidered reprints of Chapman's copy-text. The chief distinctions between Kinsley's editorial work and Chapman's (and the auxiliary work of Mary Lascelles in her revision of Chapman's text for the so-called 'third' Clarendon edition of 1965–6) is that Kinsley inserts into the text of the Oxford English Novels certain of the emendations Chapman proposed but was content to leave within the Notes to his edition. These emendations remain in the text as it continues to be reissued in World's Classics format and represent some slight but significant distinctions between the revised

[19] Samuel Johnson, 'Preface' to *A Dictionary of the English Language* (1755), in *Samuel Johnson: A Critical Edition of the Major Works*, ed. Donald Greene (Oxford: Oxford University Press, 1984), 323.

Clarendon and English Novels texts: in effect, there are two current Oxford texts of Jane Austen, both deriving ultimately from Chapman's evaluation of the early textual record. Put simply, there is no modern issue of Austen's complete works (Dent / Everyman, Oxford, Penguin, and Norton) which does not bear the mark of Chapman's editorial interpretation. A partial exception to this should be made in the case of the newly revised Penguin edition of the late 1990s, which, in an attempt to bypass Oxford's proprietary interest, returned for its texts to the first editions of all six novels. The forthcoming Cambridge Edition, under the general editorship of Janet Todd, promises a thoroughly re-edited text, but like the recent Norton editions it endorses Chapman's, and indeed the once traditional viewpoint that the second-edition texts of *Sense and Sensibility* and *Mansfield Park* must necessarily be the preferred copy-texts for a new edition.[20]

There are major reasons for reconsidering Chapman's editorial rationale after a lapse of some seventy-five years, and for giving the textual surface of his edition the kind of scrutiny that literary critics have regularly and uncritically assumed it has the authority to bear. Since Chapman's day the emphasis in editing has shifted several times; questions of gender are now addressed in different terms; while the diffused but enhanced authority of production contexts as sites of legitimate meaning has highlighted the role of the editor as the agent of a potentially illegitimate textual idealization, modernization, or regularization. Such matters bear upon the work of Chapman in mediating the Austen text and upon the kinds of critical readings we can draw from his presentation of it.

[20] All six Austen novels appeared in a small-type edition, in Richard Bentley's cheap Standard Novels series (6*s*. a volume, one novel to a volume, except for *Northanger Abbey* and *Persuasion*, which were bound together) in 1833, with reprints until 1866, and a reset edition in 1870, with reprints in 1878–9 and 1882 (the Steventon Edition). In the case of *Sense and Sensibility* and *Mansfield Park*, the second-edition text is reprinted. J. M. Dent published a ten-volume edition in September 1892, with a second impression in November of the same year. The volumes were edited and introduced by Reginald Brimley Johnson and contain the beginnings of a textually conscious practice, with Brimley Johnson privileging the 'B' text (the authorized second-edition text) where it exists but drawing readings from the first edition where he suspected error. This is the ancestor of the Everyman edition, revised by Mary Lascelles in 1963. It is also the model for Chapman's more thorough collation of the two texts and for his enshrinement of the second edition as authoritative. For more detailed information on publishing history, see Gilson, 'Jane Austen's Text: A Survey of Editions', 61–85, which extends and updates material in his magisterial *Bibliography* and traces the fate of the Austen text more or less chronologically up to the 1990s. The new Penguin texts of *Sense and Sensibility*, ed. Ballaster (1995) and *Mansfield Park*, ed. Sutherland (1996) are the most instructive, being based, against Chapman's authority, on the first-edition texts of 1811 and 1814, respectively. The Cambridge Edition of the Works of Jane Austen, General Editor Janet Todd, is scheduled to appear in 2005 / 6.

From a modern standpoint Chapman's editorial policy appears intrusive. He is predisposed to the detection of error in the early printed Austen text—particularly, where they exist, in the unrevised first-edition texts which are most likely to represent Austen's uncounselled (or least counselled) judgements. As a consequence, his edition of the novels is flavoured by a censorious response to what he sees as Austen's lexical, grammatical, or stylistic lapses. At the same time, and paradoxically, Chapman is a remarkably reticent emendator. Reluctant to tamper, he frequently asserts the impossibility of a reading only to leave the text as it is and to include his proposed emendation in the form of a back-of-text note. Effectively, the practice sets up a tension, between his respectful sense of the text's autonomy and his critical sense of its faultiness, which can place text and its commentary in a contradictory relation, occasionally to the undermining of the former and the elevation of the superior, though tactfully withheld, editorial judgement. Such is the effect of his note to *Emma*, Volume 3, Chapter 8, pointing out the error in the text at that point, where Miss Bates refers to Jane Fairfax's readiness to see the advantages of 'Mrs. Suckling's situation' and to accept the post as governess to her children. As is perfectly clear from the context, 'Mrs. Suckling's situation' is a mistake for 'Mrs. Smallridge's situation'. The error is a trivial one and had in fact been corrected in Brimley Johnson's Dent edition of 1892. But Chapman (and under his intimidating influence almost every other modern editor) restores the mistake. His note explains, '*Mrs. Suckling's situation* was of course Mrs. Smallridge's; but the mistake, if there is one, should not be ascribed to the printer. Printers do not make mistakes of this kind.'[21] Of course it is a mistake, and Chapman's half-hearted attempt to foist it onto Miss Bates, as an indication of her confusion over names, does not convince. The effect is to cast doubt on textual and/or authorial reliability and to enhance the interpretative power of the editor.

In other instances, after the fashion of editing Greek and Latin texts, the purpose of speculating upon but withholding emendation appears to be to derive from its paratextual editorial supplement a sense of the text's augmented significance. For example, a note on a passage in Volume 3, Chapter 3 of *Mansfield Park* comments, 'It has occurred to me that *scene* should perhaps be *screen*. I find the same suggestion in Dr. Verrall's copy.' The passage in both

[21] *Emma*, ed. Chapman, 381 and 493 (Chapman's note). James Kinsley in his revision of Chapman's text for the 1971 Oxford English Novels edition corrects to 'Mrs. Smallridge's situation', but neither Stephen Parrish, editing *Emma* for the Norton edition (1972; 3rd edn., 2000), nor Fiona Stafford, editing for Penguin (1996), even notes the error.

lifetime editions (the texts of 1814 and 1816) reads 'at that moment she thought that, but for the occupation and the scene which the tea things afforded, she must have betrayed her emotion in some unpardonable excess.'[22] Not only is there in this instance absolutely no reason to prefer Chapman's choice of word (suggested, one presumes, to sharpen the phrase in its immediate context), but in the larger context of the chapter's careful intertextual deployment of readings from Shakespeare's *Henry VIII*, the authorized reading *scene* carries a highly pertinent and comic theatrical resonance, as we discover a few pages later when the *scene* of 'the tea things' is again enacted to Fanny Price's relief, and now with overtly borrowed theatrical ceremony. ('The solemn procession, headed by Baddely, of tea-board, urn, and cake-bearers, made its appearance, and delivered her from a grievous imprisonment of body and mind. Mr. Crawford was obliged to move. She was at liberty, she was busy, she was protected.')

There is a discernible nineteenth-century history to Chapman's Classically derived method of emendatory commentary which converges in Austen's case with his uncritical endorsement of the family tradition, hardened into fact in Austen-Leigh's *Memoir*, that changes between authorized lifetime editions of novels (between the first and second editions of *Sense and Sensibility* and *Mansfield Park*) were made at the suggestion of her brothers. Austen-Leigh had also assumed the male family privilege of correcting the unpublished texts he first presented in 1871, and his example, though clumsy, may well have encouraged her more professional editors. In the case of *Sense and Sensibility* and *Mansfield Park* changes attributed to family members imply for Chapman both improvement and superior authority, and though in substantive terms they are few and local (a matter of some adjustments to legal details in the former and to nautical information in the latter) they effectively determine his general editorial policy on the more insidious matter of the styling (notably the punctuation) of his own edition.

This is why the revisions to the passage in *Mansfield Park* (at Volume 3, Chapter 7) in which Mr Price reports the departure of his son's ship, the *Thrush*, from Portsmouth harbour to berth in the deeper waters at Spithead require Chapman's closest attention. A great deal hangs for him on whether the changes between first and second editions indicate a sharpening of the technical vocabulary at this point. Do they declare a greater confidence in

22 *Mansfield Park*, ed. Chapman, 548 and 335. Compare this with the similarly redundant emendation, this time inserted into the text, which Chapman felt compelled to make in *Persuasion* (described in n. 36, below).

handling the known facts of Portsmouth's situation as a military port (with its inner harbour too shallow for anchorage)? What exactly might Mr Price have been able to see and report, and from which vantage point? In answering these questions, the passage and its revision provide Chapman with a general test in authorial competence. It is amusing therefore to note the ponderous consultations he had with Geoffrey Callender, Honorary Secretary and Treasurer of the Society for Nautical Research, Royal Naval College, Dartmouth. Callender explains, with sketched illustrations for the presumably nautically ignorant Chapman, the difference in the phrases 'under weigh' (1814) and 'slipped moorings' (1816), plots the probable route of the *Thrush* in joining the other vessels at Spithead, and shows the positions of the dockyard, Portsmouth Point, and the battery, relative to Mr Price on Broad Street. He concludes, 'Jane's corrections are mostly obvious, though none but a naval officer of the period would have spotted such specks.' The only real problem is Austen's revision of the vague 'I have been to Turner's [a naval suppliers] about your things' (1814) to 'I have been to Turner's about your mess' (1816). Callender writes, 'It [mess] is really the most interesting word of the lot.' Obviously, a brother suggested it, but its precise meaning is misapplied in context, since 'mess' properly refers only to a captain's supplies, and certainly would not be appropriate for those of Lieutenant William Price. Callender concludes by imagining a conversation in which Austen enquired of her sailor brothers which word she should use, they of course provided her with the correct term, but she then mistakenly transferred it to the wrong rank. Chapman's subsequent annotations to the passage rely heavily on Callender's information. Callender's detailed correspondence and the might of the Dartmouth naval archives are brought to bear on the revised text, proving to Chapman's satisfaction its family origin and, by extension, the general wisdom of Austen's tutored second thoughts, her sharing of authority.[23]

[23] See Ch. 4, n. 74. Geoffrey Callender's researches for the revisions to the passage are in the Chapman Correspondence, Bodleian MSS. Eng. Letters c. 759, ff. 57–63. Recently, and in defiance of a changed climate of opinion favouring textual primitivism and the autonomy of the female author, Zacharay Leader has defended Mary Shelley's authority in soliciting and accepting Percy Shelley's revisions of *Frankenstein* (in *Revision and Romantic Authorship* (Oxford: Clarendon Press, 1996), 167–205). Her relegation of autonomy does not necessarily suppose constraint, argues Leader, but may suggest the 'social' and 'humane' (205) conditions under which revision takes place. My point is not so much that Austen loses (or even gains) authority in relation to 'expert' revisions made to the second-edition text of *Mansfield Park*, but rather that these revisions (from whatever source) represent a drive to improvement which ultimately distorts the internal relationship between parts of the text. Informed by a feminist critique, my argument rests upon the value we can ascribe to internal textual evidence rather than the text's availability for socialized revision.

In the case of *Mansfield Park*, it is because the first-edition 1814 text is closer to an uncounselled authorial practice that its readings, even when retained in the revised 1816 text, are subject to Chapman's censure. This is particularly evident in his failure to appreciate the relationship between sentence structure, punctuation, and meaning. Such an interpretation is irresistible in the light of a persistent tendency in his practice to conflate authorial immanence with textual error. 'Of all the editions of the novels, the first edition of *Mansfield Park* is by far the worst printed', he writes in his 'Introductory Note'. He continues, '[i]t is very ill punctuated, and there are a good many verbal errors'; adding a few lines later, '[t]he spelling... [of] the first is more likely to reflect the author's practice.'[24] In the absence of manuscript evidence, the yoked statements on poor printing, verbal error, and a more accurate reflection of authorial practice, provide some insight into the uncertainty of distinction between authorial intention and the corrupt indications of the material text when the author is female and herself under the sign of a debasing contingency. Chapman's 'Notes', the site of his commentary, reveal his characteristic response to the dilemma. Correcting the phrase 'in *propria persona*', where the preposition 'in' is presented in both 1814 and 1816 editions in roman typeface, without the conventional italicization of foreign phrasing, he observes, 'Miss Austen may have been unaware that *in* is part of the Latin.'[25] He apparently rules out the likelihood (surely very high) of compositor's error—even in this 'the worst printed' text—when (female) authorial ignorance can supply the explanation.

In recent years, work towards a feminist textual criticism has drawn upon a mixture of deconstructive and historicist approaches in an attempt to refigure the authority/intention dilemma for the female author by dissociating intention from the metaphysical privilege ascribed to the ideal text by many traditional textual theorists and practitioners. This is not done with the purpose of questioning the priority of intention (as something in a writer's head) but rather of rejecting its editorial co-option in delivering a true text. Intention, as I have suggested, seems always to have served women authors less satisfactorily than male. Acting on this knowledge, recent editors of women's writings have proposed to recast intention as compounded in their case of more than the usual range of purposive and non-purposive intentions which accompany all intended acts. Accordingly, female intention is to be examined in the light of a further range of authorizing or inhibiting circum-

[24] *Mansfield Park*, ed. Chapman, xi–xii. [25] Ibid., 550.

stances (gender and the gendered conditions of social production and reception among them).

Hence, for example, arguments for a palimpsestic reading of Virginia Woolf's revisions which maintain (against the conventional dictum that authors aim to improve their work by revision) that the discarded drafts of her works represent the intended text and thus constitute the repressed 'textual unconscious' of the accommodated (though authorized) published text. Or, in a well-aired recent editorial debate, arguments against translating and appropriating through the inadequate equivalence of print the unique 'domestic technologies' which determine Emily Dickinson's artefactual poetry. In Dickinson's case, the suppression of the material significance (its meaning as textual matter) of her highly personal technological choices has led to the diminution of her work by generations of paternalistic editors. Dickinson represents in extreme form the case for text as resistant feminized matter, where there is no accommodation possible between the authority of the version and the concept of the work as a whole.[26] What the different examples of Woolf and Dickinson both point to is the degree of institutional coercion implied in a purified and standardized understanding of intention, and the possibility that a cleansing and conformant editorial practice may close down interpretation of authors and individual texts. It is worth reminding ourselves at this point that all editorial acts are about reception, about how we constitute texts for present needs.[27] This is no less the case when we invoke intentionality or attempt to restore an original integrity since perceived to have been lost in the process of transmission. What is always at issue are the boundaries we set for texts that they might accommodate our own present cultural preoccupations; in which case we might more honestly see the author and her text as always the agents of a shifting social will, a changing readerly intention.

[26] I refer here to the work of Susan Stanford Friedman, 'The Return of the Repressed in Women's Narrative', *Journal of Narrative Technique*, 19 (1989), 144–5; and Brenda R. Silver, 'Textual Criticism as Feminist Practice; or, Who's Afraid of Virginia Woolf, Part II', in *Representing Modernist Texts: Editing as Interpretation*, ed. George Bornstein (Ann Arbor: University of Michigan Press, 1991), 193–222. For a revisionist editorial approach to Emily Dickinson's poetry, see Jeanne Holland, 'Scraps, Stamps, and Cutouts: Emily Dickinson's Domestic Technologies of Publication', in *Cultural Artifacts and the Production of Meaning: The Page, the Image, and the Body*, ed. Margaret J. M. Ezell and Katherine O'Brien O'Keeffe (Ann Arbor: University of Michigan Press, 1994), 139–81; and Marta L. Werner, *Emily Dickinson's Open Folios: Scenes of Reading, Surfaces of Writing* (Ann Arbor: University of Michigan Press, 1995).

[27] Compare the argument in Morris Eaves, '"Why Don't They Leave It Alone?" Speculations on the Authority of the Audience in Editorial Theory', in *Cultural Artifacts and the Production of Meaning*, ed. Ezell and O'Keeffe, 85–99.

In the case of texts of works by women writers, however, shifts in social will may require a more fundamental adjustment to accommodate the notion of female authorship, itself traditionally held on different terms from those defining male authorship. Take the question of the formal features of printed texts (their spelling and punctuation, and the general look of the text on the page). Arguments in favour of respecting and perpetuating in new editions such features of early authorized editions currently dominate approaches to editing and are founded in the appeal to a text as historical detail regardless of whether its own identity as 'detail in history' is the only existence possible to a text or not. Consequently, original and old-style spellings and conventions of punctuation have tended to replace in recent editions of canonical writers an earlier twentieth-century preference for modernizing as a way of emphasizing cultural familiarity or the timeless status of classic texts.[28] It is a divergence of presentational views which in some ways (though not all) mirrors the debate among musicologists and performers over the opposed merits of modern and 'authentic' performance practice. But when the same policy is applied to new editions of works by non-canonical, newly recovered, or female authors, the effect is differently understood. Recent editors of women's writings have suggested that by refusing to modernize their appearance women's works are too narrowly confined to a formal (as opposed to a substantive) existence, that is, to *mere* bodily presence. In their case, the life of the text can appear perilously fragile—not so much anchored in history as relegated to it.[29] More worrying still, 'the author's meaning or the essence of his [*sic*] expression',

[28] Compare the arguments for and against modernization offered by two recent editors of Romantic-period texts. In his four-text *Prelude* Jonathan Wordsworth continues to justify modernization in traditional terms: 'To preserve original spelling in *1799* and *1805* is to preserve the choices and idiosyncracies of [Wordsworth's] helpers . . . As a poet Wordsworth wished above all to reach out, and was above all sensitive to the tendency of language to create barriers . . . He would have had no sympathy for preserving old spellings/forms when their unfamiliarity might be the cause of uncertainty, or give his poetry an antiquated air. His writing, he tells us in the Preface to *Lyrical Ballads*, is designed "to interest mankind permanently". He sought a permanent language to embody what seemed to him abiding human values.' (*The Prelude: The Four Texts (1798, 1799, 1805, 1850)*, ed. Jonathan Wordsworth (Harmondsworth, Middx.: Penguin, 1995), liii–liv.) Set against this the historically situated view of Jerome McGann: 'Conventions of punctuation have not changed so drastically during the past two hundred years as to present any serious difficulties of reading. Besides, the modern historical sense of "period" began to develop strongly in the romantic age, and many romantic poems positively solicit the slight sense of historical distancing that an "old-fashioned" textual appearance can give.' (*The New Oxford Book of Romantic Period Verse*, ed. Jerome J. McGann (Oxford: Oxford University Press, 1993), xxvi.)

[29] See, for example, the argument offered by Julia Flanders, 'The Body Encoded: Questions of Gender and the Electronic Text', in *Electronic Text: Investigations in Method and Theory*, ed. Kathryn Sutherland (Oxford: Clarendon Press, 1997): 'The process of modernization is a way of minimizing the text's difference, making it seem to speak a familiar language . . . As a technique of scholarship it underpins a view of literary writing which has helped, I think, to produce our current misconceptions about the role of women in the history of our literate culture.' (137)

which in the classic formulation of the great bibliographer Walter W. Greg defined the substantive aspect (the words) of texts, may be said to fall under particular threat when its formal fashioning, its 'general texture' or 'accidentals', as he called punctuation and spelling, is derived from a notoriously uninformed source, the grammatically ill-equipped female writer.[30] Akin to the strategy of defamiliarization that critics have recently been keen to detect in Austen's linguistic usage, a concentration on formal irregularities as constitutive of meaning in her texts risks compromising her high cultural status.

In dividing texts for editorial purposes into these two kinds of features, substantives and accidentals, Greg not only announced what he considered to be a constitutive distinction in their nature but attempted to explain the unarticulated principle of practice adopted by compositors in translating manuscript into print. Accidentals (punctuation, spelling, capitalization, italicization, contraction) witness to the historical contingency of texts. They are the unstable components of texts in transmission, not because they are less significant to meaning but because the conditions of transmission make them so (the liberty that compositors and editors have traditionally allowed themselves to house style or improve these formal features). At the same time, accidentals provide the articulatory framework on which is borne the lexical freight of meaning (the text's substance). They represent those features that Malcolm Parkes has referred to as 'the "pragmatics" of the written medium'.[31] Punctuation, in particular, gives voice to the unvoiced text of print and in so doing conditions readers in habits of narrative attention and exerts control over meaning.

What interests me in the textual history of Austen's novels is the value of apparently 'bad' (grammatically incorrect) punctuation as the formal expression of an early textual integrity which resists the incorporation of subsequent editorial correction. What justifies the interest in general terms is the possibility punctuation offers for reconfiguring the traditional misalliance of female author/material text/intended meaning. In the case of Austen, a canonical female author known through a distinguished modern editorial tradition, the argument may seem unnecessary and a touch perverse. But questions of authority and intention, of textual form and content, are particularly pertinent in determining the status of the first-edition, 1814 text of *Mansfield Park*, which Chapman declared to be Austen's 'worst printed'

[30] W. W. Greg, 'The Rationale of Copy-Text', *Studies in Bibliography*, 3 (1950–1), 21.

[31] M. B. Parkes, *Pause and Effect: An Introduction to the History of Punctuation in the West* (London: Scolar Press, 1992), 2.

work and which, as I suggested in the last chapter, was her first largely uncounselled production. Against Chapman, I am proposing the significance of *Mansfield Park* 1814 to the recovery of Austen's vital ungrammaticality, her stylistic defamiliarization. My argument is a textual one, but it is one in which issues of textual recovery draw significance from what they imply for wider critical practices—in particular, for a twenty-first-century critical reading of Austen. Influential on what I propose are the aural (heard and spoken) trace within the printed text; and bibliographic detail as a category of literary meaning.

'To an editor nothing is a trifle by which his authour is obscured'[32]

Chapman's chief authority in the practice of textual criticism from the margins, Samuel Johnson, is uncommonly frank about the limited value of the kind of critical reading that engages the editor. As he acknowledges in his 'Preface' to Shakespeare, 'It is not very grateful to consider how little the succession of editors has added to this authour's power of pleasing. He was read, admired, studied, and imitated, while he was yet deformed with all the improprieties which ignorance and neglect could accumulate upon him; while the reading was yet not rectified, nor his allusions understood.'[33] For Johnson there is normally a disjunction between the enjoyment of reading and the anxiety which characterizes the possessive and protective regard of the elucidating critic; and as he points out time and again, the editor's textual reverence is not without its element of coercion towards both author and reader. Shakespeare's terrifying carelessness ('So careless was this great poet of future fame, that . . . he made no collection of his works') is matched only by the carelessness of the late-coming reader who, without benefit of annotation, reads 'without any other reason than the desire of pleasure'.[34]

In this candid description of how we read, where 'the mind is refrigerated' by the interruption that annotation occasions, the critic, and especially the textual critic, is presented as managing and continuing a tradition of commentary and preservation which is at one and the same time instructive,

[32] 'Preface' (1765), in *Johnson on Shakespeare*, ed. Arthur Sherbo, Yale Edition of the Works of Samuel Johnson, Vol. 7 (New Haven and London: Yale University Press, 1968), 104.

[33] Ibid., 111.

[34] Ibid., 92 and 61.

redundant, and antithetical to pleasure: it is literally mind-numbing! The textual critic's acknowledged labour is, as Johnson is at pains to show, precisely marginal to the encounter of reader with work:

As I practised conjecture more, I learned to trust it less; and after I had printed a few plays, resolved to insert none of my own readings in the text. Upon this caution I now congratulate myself, for every day encreases my doubt of my emendations.

Since I have confined my imagination to the margin, it must not be considered as very reprehensible, if I have suffered it to play some freaks in its own dominion. There is no danger in conjecture, if it be proposed as conjecture; and while the text remains uninjured, those changes may be safely offered, which are not considered even by him that offers them as necessary or safe.[35]

There is a strong ethical sense at work throughout the 'Preface', nowhere clearer than in Johnson's confrontation of the problem that because literature and its criticisms inhabit the same medium—language and print—all criticism, but especially textual criticism, threatens to confuse itself with its object of study, absorbing and recycling it to its own purposes. Maintaining the spatial distinction between text and commentary is both an ethical choice not to identify the two and a caution against stabilizing that element which is bound to change—interpretation. Operating within his properly marginal realm, the textual critic can risk all his imaginative potential in dialogue with the text uninhibited by demands of exactness and untainted by the charge of imposture.

But in distinguishing the enjoyment of the careless text from the anxious instruction of its careful other, Johnson was also honest enough to recognize the convergence of the two kinds of reading in the risky business of emendation. Emendation is a dangerous pleasure because the rewards are puny and the risks immense. The scholar hazards his reputation for what can always be proved worthless, and that is precisely why, to a profession congenitally cautious and pedantic, the practice is, in Johnson's admission, irresistible. Emendation threatens to erase the critic's superiority to the careless reader, to humiliate and abase the expert. The sexual thrill is barely concealed: 'His chance of errour is renewed at every attempt... sufficient to make him not only fail, but fail ridiculously... It is an unhappy state, in which danger is hid under pleasure. The allurements of emendation are scarcely resistible.'[36] For

[35] 'Preface' (1765), in *Johnson on Shakespeare*, ed. Sherbo, 108.

[36] Ibid., 109. Compare Chapman, 'The Textual Criticism of English Classics', *The Portrait of a Scholar*, 76: 'The practice of conjecture is pleasant, but like other pleasant things is dangerous'; and *Persuasion*, ed. Chapman, 240, line 30, and note at 273. Chapman has adopted into his text A. C. Bradley's suggested

Johnson there is no possibility of submitting such risk to science, of operating according to a calculus of variants, as Walter Greg later would propose.[37] There is only danger and pleasure.

Jane Austen early acquired heavyweight readers who, with the exaggerated attention of solicitous lovers, pored over her wording and punctuation, anxious to detect and root out minor blemishes. The historian Thomas Babington Macaulay, unkindly described by Henry James as her 'first slightly ponderous amoroso',[38] is presented by his biographer, his nephew George Otto Trevelyan, as 'never for a moment waver[ing] in his allegiance to Miss Austen'. Ten years before Austen-Leigh, he was contemplating writing a short life as well as raising a monument to her in Winchester Cathedral. In particular, 'he prided himself on a correction of his own in the first page of Persuasion, which he maintained to be worthy of Bentley'. Macaulay's emendation has been generally adopted as a good one and is included in Chapman's text. It was simply effected by removing a full stop from the first, posthumous edition of 1818 and substituting a comma (*contempt. As he turned over*... 1818; *contempt, as he turned over*... Macaulay),[39] thereby liberating the rhythmic sweep, dependent on phrasal repetition, of Austen's long paratactic sentence. As it stands after correction, the sentence fills the whole first paragraph of the novel, announcing in its fluidity and the mounting crescendo of its repetitions what will be the mood and leitmotiv of the narrative as a whole—repetition and return, where lives like sentences revisit, reinhabit, their earlier shapes.

Yet the invocation of Richard Bentley as editorial authority should set alarm bells ringing. The eighteenth-century scholarly editor of Horace, Bentley controversially brought assumptions about the corruption of ancient documentary witnesses to bear on his editing of Milton's *Paradise Lost*, a poem at the time of his 1732 edition with a publication history of only sixty-five years. As Marcus Walsh has recently argued, of the '800 conjectural emendations, and around 70 conjectural deletions' proposed by Bentley to

emendation replacing *it for* (1818) with *for it*. Chapman writes: 'This elegant correction is perhaps not absolutely certain, but I have not been able to resist it.' He would have done well to attend to his own warning. The change is wholly unwarranted, constricting the expressive potential implied in the unexpectedness of the original construction. As D. W. Harding sharply counters in restoring the original reading in his Penguin edition, 'this is more like Bradley's elegance than Jane Austen's' (*Persuasion*, ed. Harding, 395).

[37] W. W. Greg, *The Calculus of Variants: An Essay on Textual Criticism* (Oxford: Clarendon Press, 1927).

[38] Henry James, in 'The Lesson of Balzac' (1905), in *Critical Heritage*, ii. 230.

[39] The story of the emendation which gave Macaulay such pleasure is told in Trevelyan, *The Life and Letters of Lord Macaulay*, ii. 466–7.

the text of *Paradise Lost*, 'just two, both of them apparently errors of the press, have proved convincing to later editors.' Walsh concludes that in some instances at least, 'the criterion of authorial meaning is under pressure from the criterion of significance to the editor, Miltonic sense giving way to the Bentleian.'[40]

It is undoubtedly the case that the Austenian text was threatened with the same kind of editorial improvement by its Classically trained late-nineteenth-century emendators, for all of whom the recensions of Aeschylus, Euripides, and Catullus were more of a living reality than habits of modern authorial composition and printing-house practice of only three-quarters of a century before. Arthur Verrall, for most of his career Classics fellow at Trinity College, Cambridge, and briefly the first King Edward VII Professor of English, provides the most important case in point because his suggestions, even where unadopted, were so influential upon Chapman's general thinking about the obscurity and possible attrition of the Austen text. Through his influence not only on Chapman but on Geoffrey Keynes, Edward Marsh, E. M. Forster, and a generation of Oxbridge-trained readers Verrall was a key figure in extracting Austen from the general into the specialist domain, and in making her 'difficult', the prerequisite of her classic status. As late as 1941 Chapman was still lamenting the 'rudimentary' state of editorial method as applied to English texts and maintaining the usefulness of the techniques of Classical scholarship in elucidating modern authors.[41]

But it was in rejecting rather than inserting emendations that Verrall displayed the full extent of his ingenuity. In arguing the removal of two apparently simple typographical corrections, both established in the Victorian reprint history of *Mansfield Park* (*Mrs Grant* for the non-existent *Miss Grant* and *his cousin* for *her cousin*, both in Volume 1, Chapter 8), Verrall

[40] Marcus Walsh, *Shakespeare, Milton, and Eighteenth-Century Literary Editing: The Beginnings of Interpretative Scholarship* (Cambridge: Cambridge University Press, 1997), 67–71.

[41] R. W. Chapman, 'A Problem in Editorial Method', *Essays and Studies By Members of the English Association*, 27 (1941), 43. In response to Chapman's edition, Edward Marsh, a former pupil of Verrall's, went into print with 'Some Notes on Miss Austen's Novels', *London Mercury*, 10 (1924), 189–93, suggesting further emendations to the texts of all six novels. Chapman incorporated some of Marsh's conjectures in the notes of subsequent printings of the novels. For example, *Persuasion*, ed. Chapman (1926 and 1933), 92, line 23, and note at 271. Of the reading at this point in the first-edition text ('I wish Frederick would . . . bring us home one of these young ladies to Kellynch. Then, there would always be company for them.') Marsh observed (192–3), 'This remark of the Admiral's seems quite meaningless . . . All would be well if we could read "company for us," *i.e.*, for himself and Mrs. Croft, who were alone at Kellynch; and the words "bring *us* home" seem to make this correction almost certain.' James Kinsley incorporated Marsh's emendation into his 1971 Oxford text. The Norton (1995) and new Penguin (1998) editions retain 'for them'.

decisively proclaimed Austen's unavailability for anything other than the most strained kind of editorial decompression. According to his argument, put forward in two brief notes published in 1893, the text as it stands in the unemended lifetime editions is in both cases correct, though in each case its meaning would be clearer from the insertion of inverted commas or the use of italics ('Miss' Grant, *her* cousin). If Austen is to be found at fault here, he claimed, it is in her lack of 'professional skill' in marking up her text for those specific formal features, like italics, which would highlight the full complexity of her stylistic concision. According to Verrall, the non-existent Miss Grant, invited by Mrs Rushworth to visit Sotherton, is to be read as a piece of authorial witticism at Mrs Rushworth's confusion; on similar grounds Edmund Bertram's reference to Miss Price as *her* cousin (and not *his* cousin) is evidence that Mrs Rushworth believes Fanny to have another cousin also known as Miss Price. Rather than see the text as incorrect at these points (easily attributable to the compositor's misreading of the manuscript or a minor authorial slip), as all modern editors, including Chapman, have done, Verrall preferred to read the author as 'fastidious', 'scarcely allow[ing] herself words enough for her meaning'. By this way of arguing, neither text nor author is at fault; what was mistakenly thought to be an error is presented as a vital aspect of the portrayal of the fictional character of Mrs Rushworth, a woman now revealed to be as muddle-headed as her son. (Here, presumably, is the precedent for Chapman's own equally implausible claim that Miss Bates, and not the author or compositor, may be the source of the Mrs Suckling/Mrs Smallridge error in *Emma*.) The fact that the text in each case had been corrected so persistently over the years was itself sufficient proof to Verrall of a Rushworthian dimness in previous readers.

For Verrall, less generous than Johnson, corrections such as these are 'among many frequent proofs, how little activity of the mind may go to the amusement which we dignify by the name of reading'. Verrall's own style as editor has been described as imaginative and intuitive. His purpose in textual reconstruction seems to have been to discover meaning from within, by simulating the workings of an author's mind, whether Euripides at work on *Medea* or Jane Austen writing *Mansfield Park*. But practised with such over-refinement, it is hard to distinguish its results from imposture. Why Verrall's display of scholarly pretension is at the same time so perverse and so instructive in these examples from *Mansfield Park* is because it proposes no change; but in restoring the uncorrected text to the reader it chastises her with her incompetence to probe its authoritative inaccessibility. Verrall removes emendation and thereby makes the text unavailable for non-specialist reading.[42]

Between Verrall and Chapman there stands the sixteen-page textual survey of the publication history to date of all six novels that William and Richard Arthur Austen-Leigh appended to their authoritative *Life and Letters* of 1913. The son and grandson of James Edward, author of the *Memoir*, the Austen-Leighs provide something important—a charting of textual authority and degeneration in the context of the fullest record to date of the family circumstances of Austen's artistic personality. It is surprising, given the use he obviously made of their insights, that Chapman expresses no debt to their textual researches and no acknowledgement of the timeliness of their critical intervention into the spate of reprints. While editions and reprints from Bentley, who had bought the Austen copyrights in the 1830s, dominated the market for most of the nineteenth century, they had sporadic competition from Routledge and a few other firms. But in 1892 Dent issued a ten-volume set edited by Reginald Brimley Johnson, whose attention to differences between the original and early editions provided the first attempt at a serious consideration of the text. It was in response to Brimley Johnson that Verrall took up the textual challenge and, in Geoffrey Keynes's opinion, inaugurated 'true Austen scholarship'.[43] The Austen-Leighs in their turn provided a conspectus of the first hundred years of Austenian textual history, incorporating into their study points of difference between the original editions, the various Bentley editions, the Dent, and the subsequent 'Hampshire' and 'Winchester' editions; and in the process they efficiently dispatched Verrall's suggestions.

What they offer is a series of sympathetic and intelligent amateur interventions into the Austen text based on a proprietary intimacy with it. They declare familiarity with its grain and with what they sense is its proper intonation, its capacity for performance, features which persistently charac-

[42] For an appreciation of Verrall's intuitive scholarship, see the 'Memoir', in his *Collected and Literary Essays, Classical and Modern*, ed. Bayfield and Duff, xx–xxii; and for his 'remarkable power of reconstructing for himself [Austen's] mind', see the proposed emendation at *Mansfield Park*, Vol. 2, Ch. 6 (Ch. 24), of *derelict* to replace *his direct*, in the phrase 'his direct holidays', referring to William Price's navy leave (xcii). Verrall elucidates the two passages from *Mansfield Park* in 'On Some Passages in Jane Austen's *Mansfield Park*', *Cambridge Review*, 15 (1893–4), 126–7 and 145–6. I quote from both short pieces.

[43] 'The Text of Jane Austen's Novels', in *Life and Letters* (1913), 405–20. Verrall addressed the Brimley Johnson Dent edition in his short article 'On the Printing of Jane Austen's Novels', *Cambridge Observer*, 1 (1892), 2–4; Geoffrey Keynes delivered his verdict on Verrall's Austenian scholarship in his *Jane Austen: A Bibliography*, xxii. See n. 20 above for further details of Austen's nineteenth-century textual history.

terize the Victorian family inheritance. They range comfortably among the various nineteenth-century editions and reprints, picking readings with a confident eclecticism; and they contribute to the mounting sense that the Austen text as reprinted through the nineteenth century is not correct, and that getting it correct matters. Unfortunately, their own careless presentation of passages, into which they introduce plenty of fresh typos, does not help their case. But on the positive side, they resist the unexamined rule that Brimley Johnson had already adopted and that Chapman would soon adopt, that the latest lifetime edition overseen by the author is likely to be more correct than the earliest. On the contrary, they boldly reject the second (and by then standard) edition of *Mansfield Park* as containing 'more misprints than any of the other novels, including one or two that do not appear in the first edition', their criticisms of its textual history often hanging on what they perceive to be the author's own carelessness over proofing. They are sensitive to punctuation, to the difference that a transposed comma and semi-colon can make to meaning, and to the importance in *Pride and Prejudice*, a novel in which even intimate conversation has so much the appearance of public declamation, of attributing speeches correctly to their distinct speakers. Such distinctions are not only more difficult but also less desirable in the later novels. In the case of *Pride and Prejudice*, to whose texts they pay most attention, they noticeably attach no greater authority, in matters of variant readings, to the first edition than to either of the two other unauthorized lifetime editions; on two occasions, they prefer Bentley's adopted readings over the lifetime editions and over Brimley Johnson's systematic reconsideration of the text.[44]

In several places it seems likely that the Austen-Leighs are the conduit for an emendation which finds its way into the Chapman text. In *Emma*, for example, at Volume 2, Chapter 7, we discover Emma modifying her opinion of Frank Churchill as a consequence of his going to London, as she believes, 'merely to have his hair cut'. In the first edition (the only lifetime edition and therefore Chapman's copy-text) the passage in question reads:

> Vanity, extravagance, love of change, restlessness of temper, which must be doing something, good or bad; heedlessness as to the pleasure of his father and Mrs. Weston, indifferent as to how his conduct might appear in general; he became liable to all these changes.

[44] 'The Text of Jane Austen's Novels', esp. 405 and 408–11.

In the Bentley editions 'indifferent' is replaced by the grammatically consonant 'indifference', while in Brimley Johnson's Dent edition and in the Winchester edition (1898) 'indifferent' is retained but 'changes' is corrected to 'charges' (which makes better sense and perhaps corrects what was a manuscript or compositorial slip caused by the eye recollecting 'change' a few lines earlier). The Hampshire edition is alone in emending in both cases to 'indifference' and 'charges'. And it is the reading of the Hampshire edition, published but not edited by Brimley Johnson in 1902, that receives approval from the Austen-Leighs. Recording none of this history, Chapman simply takes over the Hampshire emendations inserting them into his text as if his own.[45] Similarly, at Volume 2, Chapter 10 of *Persuasion*, Anne Elliot is described in the first, posthumously printed edition of 1818, as so exhausted by her recent mental and emotional exertions that 'at present she felt unequal to move, and fit only for home'. The Bentley editions retain 'move' but the Hampshire and Winchester editions read 'more' ('at present she felt unequal to more'), which the Austen-Leighs approve. Again, Chapman takes over the correction as his own.[46]

Chapman's declared editorial stance was conservative—mainly a matter of restoration. And a good case might be made for arguing that restoration remained the agreed Oxford policy for all aspects of Clarendon editions, not just their texts, throughout the twentieth century. As late as 1982, Ian Jack, considering the Clarendon edition of the Brontë novels, defined the duty of an annotator in terms precisely applicable to Chapman annotating Austen sixty years earlier. According to Jack, this duty is 'to attempt to enable his contemporaries to read a book as its original audience read it.'[47] By the same rule, of course, the editorial labour involved will grow (as will the quantity of editorial matter) as the distance between a work's historical point of origin and its readership itself grows greater. At some stage, if only for the sake of manageability (not to mention Johnsonian pleasure), the definition will need to be reconsidered. The contemporary reviewers of Chapman's edition took its textual (and implied authorial) assessments at face value, quick to agree

45 'The Text of Jane Austen's Novels', 415; and *Emma*, ed. Chapman, 205 and 491 (Chapman's note on the emendation). Other modern editors have been divided in endorsing these emendations. James Kinsley's reconsidered Oxford text keeps both, but Stephen Parrish for the Norton edition and Fiona Stafford for Penguin both restore the first edition reading 'indifferent' and retain the emendation 'charges', the effect being to restore, against grammatical propriety, the irregular processes of Emma's inward, reflective voice.

46 'The Text of Jane Austen's Novels', 420; and *Persuasion*, ed. Chapman, 227 and 273 (Chapman's note on the emendation).

47 Ian Jack, 'Novels and those "Necessary Evils" ', 323. In passing, Jack makes some useful comments on Chapman's 'quirky' style of annotation.

that, though only a hundred years old, Austen's text was undoubtedly in need of urgent scholarly recovery. The *Times Literary Supplement* of 1 November 1923 commented, '[t]he real importance of the edition is its treatment of the text, which matters in Jane Austen for two reasons: first because the condensed precision of her style requires the *ipsissima verba*, and secondly because for most of their existence her novels have been current in a "vulgate" which deformed the originals.' The *London Mercury* in December 1923 praised 'Mr Chapman's labours' as 'immense', 'even if one ignores the work in the text of an author whose text has been considerably corrupted.'[48]

In the case of *Mansfield Park*, Chapman claimed to present 'in the main' a 'reprint' of the second, 1816, edition, the text which he knew had the benefit of Austen's second thoughts, which she herself had declared 'as ready for a 2[d] Edit:' as she could make it, and which he also felt sure showed evidence of expert brotherly intervention.[49] His statement repays attention since the edition he produced in 1923 is both overtly and covertly more eclectic than this implies. He picked over the first edition, the 1814 text, for preferred substitutions—of words, spellings, and punctuation—even when a reading in the 1816 text might stand; and he did not feel required to acknowledge these substitutions in all cases, especially in matters of punctuation and spelling. Sometimes his method can be inferred, but not always. For example, he noted that the form 'teize' in the 1814 text is 'certainly Miss Austen's own', as against 'tease' in the 1816 text, but he properly refrained from the amendment; yet 'cloathe' (1814) is silently substituted for 'clothe' (1816).[50] In justification, one might turn to Chapman's own distinction, in his 'Introductory Note', between changes in the second edition which are 'due to accident or design', where designed change is change having its likely origin in the author, whether advised by others or not, and where the changes though generally 'slight' by 'their very slightness [show] some "particularity" of revision'.[51] As the measure of authorial intention, however, designed slight change is problematic, taking insufficient account of the advertent and customary

[48] *Times Literary Supplement*, 1 November 1923, 725; and *London Mercury*, 9 (December 1923), 223.

[49] *Mansfield Park*, ed. Chapman, 541; *Jane Austen's Letters*, 305.

[50] *Mansfield Park*, ed. Chapman, xii. The spelling 'teize' occurs in the 1814 text at Vol. 1, Chs. 1 and 16, and Vol. 3, Ch. 9 (Ch. 40). In the 1816 text all three appear as 'tease', which is reproduced in Chapman's edition at 10, 157, and 394. A further spelling 'teaze' occurs in both 1814 and 1816 texts at Vol. 3, Ch. 5 (Ch. 36), and Chapman retains this (362). The spelling 'cloathe' occurs in the 1814 text at Vol. 3, Ch. 17 (Ch. 48), and is silently substituted by Chapman at 471 against the authority of 'clothe' in the 1816 text.

[51] Ibid., xii.

interventions of printers to regularize the text, particularly in matters of spelling and punctuation. There is also a potential contradiction in an editorial method which chastises the irregularities and rawness of the uncounselled 1814 text as possible authorial blemishes yet distinguishes subsequent surface changes as 'too good for the printer'.[52]

But what the contradiction also signals is something of the prescriptiveness of Chapman's own method in arriving at the Austen text of 1923 by means of a law of harmonization deduced from what he believed to be the author's own best practice. It is a law under which he operates tactfully and, on occasion, brilliantly. Nevertheless, the cumulative effect of acknowledged and unacknowledged substitutions from the 1814 into the 1923 text is to further the work of grammatical and syntactic regularization which is a feature not of 1814 but of 1816, and to continue this in his own silent repunctuation of the 1923 text. In this sense, Chapman appears to regard the repudiated 1814 text as the fitful and irregular representation of a work more continuously (but still not fully) manifested in the 1816 text. Discreetly implied in his practice is the intended status of his own 1923 text. He does not question the then prevailing wisdom that an author's second thoughts or final intentions are to be preferred, that they are in some sense indicative of a general maturing and improvement of the whole work, in which all the changed particulars of the later version are in some way authorially sanctioned. This view has recently been labelled the Whig interpretation of textual variants, whereby 'versions of a work are organically or teleologically related . . . [and] the work . . . is always aiming at the final version'.[53] It is a seductively optimistic view of texts as of life, which ignores the practical issue that changes are not necessarily planned with the larger structure in mind, but are usually made locally (by author, printer, publisher's corrector) without recourse to the whole composition and on occasion to the detriment of its earlier coherence. As often as not in these circumstances, change represents not an organic growth but a change in direction that the surrounding text does not support. Evidently, too, the law of textual improvement is at odds with a commitment to recovery and restoration, the basis of Chapman's declared policy. On the other hand, the

[52] *Mansfield Park*, ed. Chapman, 543, referring to a change at Vol. 1, Ch. 8 ('civility, especially' 1814; 'civility especially,' 1816). Chapman remarks of the altered position of the comma, 'This is one of the improvements in punctuation by *B* [1816] that seems too good for the printer.'

[53] James McLaverty, 'Issues of Identity and Utterance: An Intentionalist Response to "Textual Instability"', in *Devils and Angels: Textual Editing and Literary Theory*, ed. Philip Cohen (Charlottesville and London: University of Virginia Press, 1991), 146. Compare the argument offered by Stephen Parrish, 'The Whig Interpretation of Literature', *TEXT*, 4 (1988), 343–50.

Whig interpretation does give honourable and seemingly legitimate place to the editor as he continues the author's work of amelioration—something impossible to ignore in explaining its attractiveness.

The following examples of the shift to syntactic punctuation through the texts from 1814 to 1816 to 1923 suggest something of Chapman's Whiggish method and his authority for it. In each case I have keyed the passage to its page appearance in Chapman's edition:

It is felt that distinctness and energy, may have weight in recommending the most solid truths; (1814)
It is felt that distinctness and energy may have weight in recommending the most solid truths; (1816, 1923), 340.

though Mansfield Park, might have some pains, Portsmouth could have no pleasures. (1814)
though Mansfield Park might have some pains, Portsmouth could have no pleasures. (1816, 1923), 392.

He was going—and if not voluntarily going, voluntarily intending to stay away, for excepting what might be due to his uncle, his engagements were all self-imposed. (1814)
He was going—and if not voluntarily going, voluntarily intending to stay away; for, excepting what might be due to his uncle, his engagements were all self-imposed. (1816, 1923), 193.

Mrs. Norris being not at all inclined to question its sufficiency, began (1814, 1923), 305 [a silent substitution from 1814 into Chapman's text].
Mrs. Norris, being not at all inclined to question its sufficiency, began (1816)

Edmund was in town, had been in town he understood, a few days, (1814)
Edmund was in town, had been in town, he understood, a few days; (1816)
Edmund was in town, had been in town he understood, a few days; (1923), 401 [a silent substitution from 1814 into Chapman's text].

I... earnestly hoped that she might... not owe the most valuable knowledge we could any of us acquire—the knowledge of ourselves and of our duty to the lessons of affliction—and immediately left the room. (1814, 1816)
I... earnestly hoped that she might... not owe the most valuable knowledge we could any of us acquire—the knowledge of ourselves and of our duty, to the lessons of affliction—and immediately left the room. (1923) 459 [Chapman's acknowledged emendation deduced from Austen's 'normal punctuation of a parenthesis' using a dash followed by a comma (note at 551); and see the appendix on 'Punctuation' attached to *Emma*, 518].

Miss Crawford knew Mrs. Norris too well to think of gratifying *her* by commendation of Fanny; to her it was as the occasion offered,—"Ah! Ma'am . . . " (1814, 1816)
Miss Crawford knew Mrs. Norris too well to think of gratifying *her* by commendation of Fanny; to her it was, as the occasion offered,—"Ah! Ma'am . . . " (1923), 277 [Chapman's acknowledged emendation].

But I have long thought Mr. Bertram one of the worst subjects to work on, in any little manoeuvre against common sense that a woman could be plagued with. (1814, 1816)
But I have long thought Mr. Bertram one of the worst subjects to work on, in any little manoeuvre against common sense, that a woman could be plagued with. (1923), 212 [Chapman's acknowledged emendation].

I have laboured this point because punctuation holds a key to *Mansfield Park*, and I think Chapman both understood this and wholly missed its implications. The appendix 'Miss Austen's English', in *Sense and Sensibility*, is the longest of his many appendixes but is taken up mainly with matters of lexis. A separate and far briefer piece on punctuation (three pages as against thirty-four) is merely a defensive listing of a few 'irregular' and 'illogical' uses with little attempt to discover what they contribute to meaning.[54] The working notes and correspondence for the Austen edition in the Bodleian Library reveal a general concern to respect early punctuation which was evidently severely tested by the particular challenges of *Mansfield Park*. In an early draft for the 'Introductory Note', Chapman wrote that the 'most serious fault' in the presentation of the 1814 edition is 'its meagre punctuation; but it abounds in such minor evils as unnecessary capitals, misplaced or omitted quotation-marks, misplaced apostrophes, and faulty paragraphing. There are a good many obvious verbal errors' and, he repeats, 'It is under-punctuated.' He concludes, 'All modern editions that we have seen are based upon the second; and there can be no doubt of its superiority over the first.'[55]

[54] The appendix 'Miss Austen's English' appears at the end of *Sense and Sensibility*, Vol. 1 of Chapman's collected edition, while that on 'Punctuation' is appended to *Emma*, Vol. 4. In noting the 'illogical use of semi-colon and comma' in *Mansfield Park*, where the heavier pause of the semicolon precedes the lighter break of the comma in a series of three clauses, Chapman observes that this 'may represent correctly the natural pauses of the voice'. But he does not follow up this crucial insight or appear to act on it in his own elucidation of counter-grammatical passages in the text. (*Emma*, ed. Chapman, 518.)

[55] R. W. Chapman, 'Jane Austen Files', Bodleian MS. Eng. Misc. c. 924, f. 252. ff. 257–61 list and comment on spelling and punctuation changes between 1814 and 1816. A set of notes in Frank MacKinnon's hand begins, 'I gather you aim at reproducing J. A.'s punctuation. *Query* if in all cases she really intended some of it? I should prefer to treat many instances as eccentricities of compositors left uncorrected' (f. 187).

Working from Brimley Johnson's edition, Verrall had earlier summed up the punctuation of *Mansfield Park* as 'always irregular, frequently embarrassing, sometimes grotesque', and capable of destroying the meaning 'as effectively as a wrong word'.[56] But the charge of under-punctuation was partly challenged by Henry Bradley, to whom Chapman regularly turned for linguistic advice and who as regularly cautioned against correcting what only appeared faulty to the modern eye. To Chapman's query about how he should repunctuate the phrase 'a quick looking girl' (describing Susan Price, Volume 3, Chapter 10), Bradley replied that he should leave it alone:

> I should be inclined to follow the early edition (i.e. to insert *neither* comma nor hyphen), and leave the reader to interpret. A century ago people used to write 'a tall handsome woman', and their printers allowed them to do so. The printer of today, I believe, usually insists on putting a comma after 'tall'. Your alternatives of comma and hyphen imply different constructions, and I am not quite sure which is right, or whether the author may not have felt the collocation as something between the two . . . is it not possible that if we demand that it *must* be either comma or hyphen, we shall be insisting on a precision of grammatical analysis which punctuation has rendered instructive to readers of today, but which *c* 1800 only a grammarian would be capable of?[57]

It would be difficult to overestimate the importance of Bradley's good sense and the intelligence of his warning against fixing too rigidly the text and its play of meaning. He was of course largely ignored: by Chapman and afterwards inevitably by the critical reader of Chapman's texts. Guided by Bradley, Chapman did allow the phrase to stand, here and in other similar instances (for example, where Mary Crawford is described as 'a talking pretty young woman', in Volume 1, Chapter 5); but he resisted the wider implications of the advice against insisting on punctuation as a guide to grammatical precision. In so doing it is not inappropriate to argue that he prepared a text which actively and misguidedly promoted Austen's twentieth-century reputation as a conformant and prim stylistician.

Because his principled concern 'To restore, and maintain [textual] integrity'[58] is entailed to a Classically derived model of the corrupt material witness, the emphasis of Chapman's textual intervention, on discovering and restoring meaning through syntactical punctuation, is continually at odds with the

[56] A. W. Verrall, 'On the Printing of Jane Austen's Novels', 3.

[57] Bodleian MSS. Eng. Letters c. 759, f. 44, a communication dated 14 February 1922.

[58] Chapman, *The Portrait of a Scholar*, 79.

non-grammatical punctuation which dominates the 1814, the rawer, first-edition text, and which retains more than a vestigial presence in his 1816 copy-text. The distinction is not mere scholarly preference for one form of pointing over another; for it is the older punctuation which, as it turns out, represents the essential and meaningful trace of the text's origins. Against this, Chapman's editorial consciousness was determined according to specific assumptions (a mixture of Johnsonian and late-nineteenth century preferences) about linguistic and grammatical propriety. The cultural freight (the perfection of a bygone era) which the deduced elegance of the authoritative Austen text must carry for Chapman eventually demanded its verbal emendation as a consequence of its grammatical recovery, its recovery into syntactically confined meaning, that is. It is at this point that his editorial method begins to look seriously flawed.

'For this book is the talking voice that runs on'[59]

What is compelling about Austen's ungrammaticality is its significance for her work as a whole. The questions really worth asking about the punctuation of the 1814 text of *Mansfield Park* are what does it contribute to meaning? how does it invite us to interpret this novel? and, by extension, what does it tell us about Austen's evolving narrative method? Returning to the unregularized text of 1814 means returning to spelling variants ('teize', 'independance', 'harden'd'), to colloquialisms ('you was' for 'you were'), to a rash of initially capitalized proper nouns, and, most importantly, to a lighter system of punctuation, to rhythmical punctuation, all of which are banished from the 1816 text. Where the denser punctuation in the second edition of 1816, the basis for Chapman's reprint, accords with still current standard usage in marking off grammatical units, the cursory rhythmical punctuation of the 1814 text marks emphasis and balance which often run counter to grammatical sense but which can be closer to the inflections of language as spoken and heard. Where *Mansfield Park* 1816 and 1923 are marked by a punctuation of semicolons and colons denoting lexical and grammatical units, *Mansfield Park* 1814 is distinguished by an overwhelming reliance on commas, full stops, and long dashes, the only marks normally used in the transcription of spoken discourse, and which, rather than delimiting syntactic boundaries,

[59] Stevie Smith, *Novel on Yellow Paper, or Work it out for Yourself* (1936; London: Virago Press, 1980), 39.

represent the more uncertain thresholds within speech.[60] In the following examples I have keyed the passage to its page appearance in the 1996 Penguin edition based on the 1814 text:[61]

To know him in bits and scraps, is common enough, to know him pretty thoroughly, is perhaps, not uncommon, but to read him well aloud, is no everyday talent. (1814, 1996), 279.
To know him in bits and scraps, is common enough; to know him pretty thoroughly, is, perhaps, not uncommon; but to read him well aloud, is no every-day talent. (1816, 1923)

Fanny felt the advantage, and drawing back from the toils of civility would have been again most happy, could she have kept her eyes from wandering between Edmund and Mary Crawford. (1814, 1996), 226.
Fanny felt the advantage; and, drawing back from the toils of civility, would have been again most happy, could she have kept her eyes from wandering between Edmund and Mary Crawford. (1816, 1923)

We tend not to recognize the aural trace of the written text when that text (as here, a novel) is unproblematic in its status as silent written form (as distinct from the written text which overtly appropriates oral genres). However, the restoration of its heard (as opposed to seen and read) conversational and counter-grammatical rhythms dissolves one of the most commented-upon textual cruces of *Mansfield Park* and in doing so asserts the authority of the 1814 text and the redundancy of Chapman's proposals for emendation here and elsewhere. In Volume 3, Chapter 2, Fanny Price, the heroine, is discovered brooding over Henry Crawford's selfishness in persisting against her will as her lover. The texts of 1814 and 1816 both read at this point:

Here was again a want of delicacy and regard for others which had formerly so struck and disgusted her. Here was again a something of the same Mr. Crawford whom she had so reprobated before. How evidently was there a gross want of feeling and humanity where his own pleasure was concerned—And, alas! how always known no principle to supply as a duty what the heart was deficient in. (1814, 1816, 1923, 1996), 271.

Chapman was sure that the phrase 'And, alas! how always known no' was 'certainly corrupt' and proposed (though he confined it to his 'Notes') the

[60] I draw here on the distinction between the uses of punctuation to transcribe intonational boundaries and to represent written-language structures as outlined in Geoffrey Nunberg, *The Linguistics of Punctuation* (Stanford, Calif.: Center for the Study of Language and Information, 1990), 10–14.
[61] *Mansfield Park*, ed. Sutherland.

emendation 'And, alas! now all was known, no'. This suggestion alone worked so powerfully on E. M. Forster that he remarked on it in his review of the 1923 edition in *The Nation and Athenaeum* as initiating the Austenite into a new level of critical admiration and comprehension: 'And so . . . with the shapeless sentence from *Mansfield Park*. Here we emend "how always known" into "now all was known"; and the sentence not only makes sense but illuminates its surroundings.' But according to Mary Lascelles, who prepared revisions in 1966, Chapman became dissatisfied with his suggestion, and she offered the correction, 'And, alas! now as always no known'. Other suggestions came in a series of notes to the *Times Literary Supplement* between 1960 and 1962, from Warren Derry, J. D. K. Lloyd, and B. C. Southam. James Kinsley, in his reconsideration of Chapman's emendations for his 1970 Oxford English Novels edition, accepted from among these Lloyd's simple transposition of 'known no' to 'no known', rendering the sense 'And, alas! how always no known'. This he inserted into the text currently issued under the World's Classics imprint. The only dissenting voice was Southam's when he hinted in 1962 that perhaps the passage as it appears in 1814 and 1816 might stand.[62]

In defending the unemended 1814 reading it is necessary to recognize its stylistic compression rather than corruption. To read the passage aright we must listen to Fanny Price's inner monologue (her free indirect thought) whose irregularly yet insistently repeated structures, *heard* rather than merely seen and read, shape her thoughts and clarify the text: 'Here was again a want . . . Here was again a something . . . How evidently was there a gross want . . . how always known no principle . . . '. There is no call here to disambiguate female author from material text since neither, it turns out, was in quite such a state of unpreparedness or error, verbal or syntactic, as editorial tradition had determined. If Chapman's misreading of formally endorsed punctuation (punctuation signalling graphically the text's aural dimensions) led him in several similar cases into the presumption of textual corruption, it was largely owing to the imposition, onto the 1816 text and continued in his own further schooling of that text, of a syntactic structure whose tendency is to suppress the acoustic trace which the earlier, rhythmic punctuation serves. One consequence is the inability to read (because it is an inability

[62] *Mansfield Park*, ed. Chapman, 548; and see the updated note by Mary Lascelles in her 1966 revision (again, 548) of Chapman's text. Forster's review is extracted in *Critical Heritage*, ii. 280. For the history of this textual crux, see a series of notes in the *Times Literary Supplement*: Warren Derry, 'Jane Austen', 29 December 1961, 929; and replies by B. C. Southam, 19 January 1962, 41; by J. D. K. Lloyd, 2 February 1962, 73; and by Mary Lascelles, 21 October 1965, 946. See, too, *Mansfield Park*, ed. James Kinsley (London: Oxford University Press, 1970), 297 and 'Textual Notes', 436.

to hear) particular local passages which retain the acoustic trace or resist its reinstruction.

Other examples support such an interpretation of Chapman's proposals for emendation. At Volume 3, Chapter 7, Fanny Price returns to her Portsmouth family after eight years away. Her renewed acquaintance with her young brothers Tom and Charles is recorded by the narrator thus:

Both were kissed very tenderly, but Tom she wanted to keep by her, to try to trace the features of the baby she had loved, and talked to, of his infant preference of herself. (1814, 1816, 1996), 316.

Both were kissed very tenderly, but Tom she wanted to keep by her, to try to trace the features of the baby she had loved, and talk to him of his infant preference of herself. (1923)

In establishing and this time confidently inserting the emendation 'and talk to him', Chapman asserts the sheer impossibility of the unemended reading. He observes: 'The reading has not so far as I know been challenged, but it seems impossible. Fanny could not have talked to Tom of his infant preference of herself, before she left Portsmouth, for he was then a mere infant.'[63] But 'and talked to' is not only a possible, it is clearly a correct reading. Where Chapman teases out the compression into syntactic and consecutive sense, the passage needs to be heard as a looser, unbalanced, paratactic construction: 'Tom she wanted to keep by her . . . and [Tom she] talked to . . . '.

Though less dependent on a grammatically consequential (and therefore mistaken) reading, Chapman's unhappiness a few chapters later with Mary Crawford's phrase 'You have politics', in her letter to Fanny at Volume 3, Chapter 12, is the result of a similar failure to *hear* the balanced construction of the passage. In conjecturing 'You hate politics' he overcomes his own unease that Mary 'should give reasons for not retailing' the political news. This, he argues, 'seems unlikely'. He continues: 'The correction *hate*, which occurred to me years ago, has been made independently by Mr. MacKinnon, and was approved by Dr. Bradley.'[64] But the point is that Mary is distinguishing between two kinds of news, neither of which she proposes to relate to Fanny: the one, political, Fanny has access to through the newspapers; the other, social ('the names of people and parties, that fill up my time'), she

[63] *Mansfield Park*, ed. Chapman, 381, line 19, and note at 549.

[64] Ibid., 415, line 31, and note at 550. Chapman refrains here from inserting the emendation into the text.

assumes Fanny would either be bored by or envy. Again, and insistently, the larger passage directly invites the reader to avoid misunderstanding by *hearing* and *listening to* the speaker:

> My dear, dear Fanny, if I had you here, how I would talk to you!—You should listen to me till you were tired, and advise me till you were tired still more; but it is impossible to put an hundredth part of my great mind on paper, so I will abstain altogether, and leave you to guess what you like. I have no news for you. You have politics of course; and it would be too bad to plague you with the names of people and parties, that fill up my time. (1814, 1816, 1923, 1996), 343.

What these occasions for mistaken editorial conjecture hold in common is a quality characteristic of Austen's mature narrative style which can be described as vocal encroachment. It is most famously present in those passages in which a central fictional consciousness (usually female, often the heroine's) is absorbed into the omniscient narrator's voice, a fusion of first- and third-person narrative, usually designated 'free indirect discourse'. The skill of such a method lies in its compression, and in particular in the overlaying of one voice by another. It is at just such moments, when the text is most richly and at the same time least precisely voiced, that it betrays the logic of the reading eye and denies its visual confinement. That these textual moments carry a peculiarly feminine charge can be argued both in terms of the gendered paradigms of traditional textual criticism (the resistance of apparently messy textual matter to 'necessary' editorial castigation, grammatical correction, or reconstruction) and of the co-opted aural interiority of the Romantic text.

A recurrent Romantic motif involves the private and feminine aural text intruded upon, refashioned, or otherwise overcome by the public and masculine written or printed text. Walter Scott, for example, deploys such textual occlusion (usually in the form of a female-communicated folk song set aside in favour of a male-derived prose explanation of events) as a marker of the ambiguous nature of historical progress in several novels, while Wordsworth's poet-cum-textual critic reflects upon one such occasion in 'The Solitary Reaper'. In Austen's case, there is the intriguing possibility that in their construction for the ear such passages indicate a vital aspect of her composing method (rooted in overheard conversation); further, that in their vigorous resistance to syntactic reinstruction (to the extent that substantive emendation becomes necessary in order to restore sense after grammatical regularization) they might be described as access points to the text's deep structure.[65] There is ample evidence not only of the importance to Austen of the spoken performance of her finished compositions, but also of her reliance in creation on voicing and the transcription of heard (whether overheard or mentally constructed) conversation.[66]

We do not know whether the systematic syntactic repunctuation of *Mansfield Park* for the second edition represents authorial revision—Austen's best, or counselled, or at least her second thoughts—or whether (far more likely) it marks the publisher's or corrector's decision implemented at the printing house. That Austen had an intention and that this represented a union of form and content would seem to go without saying, though the amused tolerance she showed towards printers' attempts to standardize her idiosyncratic spelling suggests a willingness to defer to others and a readiness to inhabit their version of textual space which might prove on occasion problematic. In a letter of 26 November 1815 to Cassandra she mentions that she is correcting proofs of Volume 3 of *Emma*: 'The Printers continue to supply me very well, I am advanced in vol.3. to my *arra*-root, upon which peculiar style of spelling, there is a modest *qu:*[ry]*?* in the Margin.—I will not forget Anna's arrow-root.' The printed text's correction to 'arrow-root' represents gain and loss—the regularized spelling and so immediate intelligibility, but the loss (now that we know it) of a rare clue to Austen's own pronunciation.[67] It is

[65] For a comparable argument against the male editor's visual instruction of the irregular female text, see Janine Barchas, 'Sarah Fielding's Dashing Style and Eighteenth-Century Print Culture', *English Literary History*, 63 (1996), 633–56. Barchas calls for the reconsideration of the interpretative function of accidentals and links this to the early censorship (begun by her brother Henry) of Fielding's apparently eccentric graphic figuring of her novel *The Adventures of David Simple* (1744). Barchas draws particular attention to the eradication of a non-verbal signifier (the dash) which functions for the female author as an eloquent print equivalent of an enforced female silence. The dashes removed, such silence is doubly silenced. Though both Barchas and I position our arguments within a feminist criticism, such an interpretation of the evidence does not disallow the fact that in the writings of male authors, too, punctuation and other stylistic features have regularly been normalized, sometimes to their detriment, by compositors and editors. One might point to the editorial treatment of Hardy and Thackeray or to the visual instruction of marginalized writers, like James Joyce and John Clare, whose works, on various counts, have been deemed to require regularization. See, for example, the eloquent case made for the importance of Hardy's manuscript punctuation to meaning by Juliet Grindle, in 'Some Features of the Manuscript Punctuation', in *Tess of the d'Urbervilles*, ed. Juliet Grindle and Simon Gatrell (Oxford: Clarendon Press, 1983), 88–99. See also James C. McKusick, 'John Clare and the Tyranny of Grammar', *Studies in Romanticism*, 33 (1994), 255–77.

[66] See, for example, Austen's letter of 4 February 1813 to Cassandra, in which she expresses dissatisfaction at their mother's way of reading aloud from *Pride and Prejudice*: 'tho' she perfectly understands the Characters herself, she cannot speak as they ought' (*Jane Austen's Letters*, 203). Caroline Austen recalled her aunt reading aloud from Burney's *Evelina*, 'I thought it was like a play' (*Memoir*, 174). Constance Hill recorded a family story which strongly suggests the source of Austen's composition in mental voicing. (See Ch. 3, n. 106.) The family preserved several distinct memories of the quality of Austen's voice in speaking and reading, including Henry Austen's interesting observation, in his 'Biographical Notice' of 1818, that she excelled 'in conversation as much as in composition' (*Memoir*, 139). There is also Austen's advice to her niece Anna on the importance of conversation in the development of a narrative (*Jane Austen's Letters*, 276).

[67] Ibid., 300; cf., 235, again to Cassandra, 'Have you any Tomatas?'

important to resist the assumption, however, that she was a consistent misspeller; some of her seemingly idiosyncratic forms were in fact permissible eighteenth-century variants. As for my argument for restoring the unnormalized punctuation of the first edition, that derives primarily from respect for neither authorial intention nor the delegated social intention of the contemporary production process, but from the value there may be in observing the internal relationship between the parts of a text (its formal and substantial expression) as a simultaneous evolution.

We do not know whether Austen had particular views on how a printed page from her manuscript should look. But we do know that in the case of both editions of *Mansfield Park* she was following her preferred practice of publishing on commission and therefore defraying costs herself; so economy was of vital interest to her, presumably affecting her attitude to the costly business (then as now) of proof correction and revision in the late stages of production. We know that two printers, Charles Roworth (Volume 2) and Gabriel Sidney (Volumes 1 and 3), were employed on *Mansfield Park* 1814 and three printers, James Moyes (Volume 1), Roworth again (Volume 2), and Thomas Davison (Volume 3), on the second edition of 1816. The first edition was published by Thomas Egerton and the second by John Murray, Roworth printing, as was perfectly common at the time, for both publishers. Moyes, Davison, and Roworth were among Murray's most regular printers, Davison working closely with Murray on Byron editions and Roworth on the *Quarterly Review.* Roworth had printed a total of sixteen volumes of Austen's work by 1818, more than any other printer, and seems to have been on good terms with her. His compositors would be used to deciphering her script and fitting it to the conventions of print.[68]

Egerton produced the 1814 edition of *Mansfield Park* very cheaply (on thinner paper than his first edition of *Pride and Prejudice* and with two more lines of print per page), providing Austen with the largest lifetime profit she ever received for any novel; and though he had bought the copyright for *Pride and Prejudice*, Austen retained those for all other novels. It is tempting therefore to see the economies of the first edition of *Mansfield Park* as a

[68] Nicholas Barker, 'A Note on the Typographical Identifications', in Gilson, xi–xii; William B. Todd, *A Directory of Printers and Others in Allied Trades, London and Vicinity, 1800–1840* (London: Printing Historical Society, 1972); and Peter Isaac, 'Byron's Publisher and His "Spy": Constancy and Change among John Murray II's Printers, 1812–1831', *The Library*, 6th ser. 19 (1997), 1–24. See, too, *Jane Austen's Letters*, 298, a letter of 24 November 1815, during the printing and proofing of *Emma*, referring to Austen's cordial relations with Murray and Roworth.

sign of her control over printing, for which she knew she would have to pay the bill. Murray, on the other hand, produced her books more expensively, but his imprint carried far more prestige. His second edition of *Mansfield Park* lost money, its cost being set against the profits from his edition of *Emma*.[69] In setting Volume 2 of *Mansfield Park* in 1814 and 1816 Roworth used different punctuation conventions and house styles, most probably under the instruction of the publishing house, and in neither 1814 nor 1816 do the three volumes achieve a consistent internal practice over spelling, capitalization, hyphenation, or the separation of compounds. A standard manual of the time advises authors to 'leave the pointing entirely to the printers, as from their constant practice they must have acquired a uniform mode of punctuation.'[70] Yet by using several different printers and treating each volume as a separate job, it is clear that it was not considered necessary, even by a publisher with as high standards as Murray, to achieve either typographical match or formal consistency across a three-volume novel. The layout of the second edition shows that it was set from a corrected copy of the first edition and not from a revised manuscript. When Austen described the novel in a note to Murray as being 'as ready for a 2^{d} Edit: I beleive, as I can make it', it seems certain that she was sending a marked up copy of the first edition.[71]

It is possible that book copy for the second edition was corrected not only by Austen herself but also by William Gifford, editor of Murray's *Quarterly Review*, who may have imposed his standard of punctuation on the seemingly wayward text. Gifford, notoriously pedantic, acted as reader and reviser of the manuscript of *Emma* and was highly critical of Egerton's printing and punctuation of *Pride and Prejudice*, which he described, with affected exaggeration, as 'wretchedly printed, and so pointed as to be almost unintelligible'.[72] Most of the punctuation changes to *Mansfield Park* 1816 are just the kind we would expect from a practised editor like Gifford. We also know from the production of *Emma* that after Austen corrected proofs they were

[69] Fergus, *Jane Austen: A Literary Life*, 144–5 and n. 47 (190–2); and 157–9.

[70] Stower, *The Printer's Grammar*, 80. Stower also points out the inadvisability and expense of authorial alterations at proof stage: 'Authors are very apt to make alterations, and to correct and amend the style or arguments of their works when they first see them in print. This is certainly the worst time for this labour, as it is necessarily attended with an expense which in large works will imperceptibly swell to a serious sum' (396). The earliest advice manual specifically addressed to authors that I have come across is *Hints to Authors in preparing Copy, with practical Directions for correcting Proof Sheets for the Press* (8 pp., n.d., but watermarked 1813).

[71] *Jane Austen's Letters*, 305.

[72] Samuel Smiles, *A Publisher and His Friends*, i., 282.

sent back to the printing house via Murray's office: in other words, that hers was not the final examination of the text. We have no hard information that Austen checked proofs of either the first or the second editions of *Mansfield Park*; but since this was her practice with other novels, it is highly unlikely that she did not. However, it is important to remember the conditions under which she would have read proofs: against the clock and her own purse and with the printer's boy at the door; without sight of the marked up copy of her manuscript (still in use in the print shop); and in batches of only a few sheets (two or three at a time); that is, with no opportunity to assess changes other than in their local textual environment. Add to this several print shops regularly dividing a novel between them, and we also find the author working sporadically and concurrently on proofs for all three volumes. Under these circumstances, the idea that proof stage might represent a serious opportunity to reconsider the overall shape of the novel or systematically to control its formal features is highly improbable. What all this suggests is that the punctuation and formal presentation of the second edition of *Mansfield Park* is likely to have moved well beyond authorial control, as it is undoubtedly further from representing the pointing of the manuscript than the first edition or of registering an intimate and sustained connection with its lexical evolution.[73]

While no critical reader has doubted that an author's words matter, punctuation, spelling, and such formal features as paragraphing and speech indentations have attracted divergent opinions. In Austen's case, we acknowledge a consummate linguistic artistry, and increasingly we recognize her mature style as instinct with the emphases and rhythms of the spoken as opposed to the written sentence. But because we have no way of knowing whether Austen considered how the look of the printed page might capture the presentational features of her few extant mature manuscripts (which rarely indent for paragraphs and often run conversations together), we have no real sense of how important those features might be. From a similar ignorance, we have tended, too, to set aside the formal irregularities of the earliest printings in favour of the enhanced uniformity of second editions where they exist.

[73] On 25 April 1811, Austen recorded 'two sheets to correct' of the proofs of *Sense and Sensibility*, and on 24 November 1815, 'three sheets' of *Emma* are come from Roworth, and a few hours later the addition 'A *Sheet* come in this moment. 1st & 3[d] vol. are now at 144.—2[d] at 48.' (*Jane Austen's Letters*, 182, 298–9, where it is mentioned that sheets are returned not to the printer but to Murray.) The format of Austen's lifetime editions was duodecimo, which means that a single proof sheet would have held twelve leaves (twenty-four pages). For further details of production process, see Ch. 3, 155–65.

The progress of printing as of editing during the course of the nineteenth and twentieth centuries is a Whiggish narrative of refinement and standardization—of improvement. In printing, the goal was to achieve a uniformity of look by banishing typographic irregularities. It was a procedure which emphasized print as a visual and silent record and its technology as transparent, a non-interfering medium whose own physicality should not impinge—visual but not too visible. We can trace a similar development in the respectful submission of editorial intervention to a notional authorial intention. In each case ways have been devised to limit the difference that print/editing appears to make and, by extension, to suggest that the printed book/the edited text is a natural growth. It is also importantly noiseless. There is ample evidence that texts from earlier periods of print were altogether noisier things, and that this noise was both ambient (a consequence of their non-standardized printing) and integral: the poorly or non-uniformly executed printing communicating in its typographic disruption something that gives voice to the text.[74]

There is a world of difference between the ephemeral political pamphlets of the seventeenth century, which use print as if it were a form of public speaking, and the late eighteenth- and early nineteenth-century novel's more muted representation of the social space of dialogue. But even the print history of the novel poses questions of whether and how texts can be said to speak at all, and whether and how we silence them, and at what cost. When Walter Scott came to revise his early novel *Guy Mannering* (1815) for republication in 1829, 'the most prominent single feature' was the insertion of 'no fewer than 320 dialogic signposts identifying speakers'. These signposts varied from simple pointers, such as 'said Brown', to fuller indications of how a speech should be read—'awkwardly', or 'his laugh sinking into a hysterical giggle'. But the overall incremental effect was to unravel previously unmediated dialogue carefully attributing its separate components to individual speakers and reducing the acoustic play of the text to something comprehended rather than heard. Peter Garside, *Guy Mannering*'s most recent editor, concludes that the revision is 'explainable in terms of a shift in the conventions of presenting fiction in the 1820s and/or the anticipation of a readership

[74] Work has been done on this aspect of seventeenth-century printed texts. See, for example, D. F. McKenzie, 'Speech-Manuscript-Print', in *New Directions in Textual Studies*, ed. Dave Oliphant and Robin Bradford (Harry Ransom Humanities Research Center: University of Texas at Austin, 1990), 86–109; and Antony Hammond, 'The Noisy Comma: Searching for the Signal in Renaissance Dramatic Texts', in *Crisis in Editing: Texts of the English Renaissance*, ed. Randall McLeod (New York: AMS Press, 1994), 203–49.

less adept at negotiating the kind of polyphonic diversity found in the original text.'[75] It was, in other words, part of the progressive silencing and more rigid classification of text.

It has recently been suggested that gossip, a conventionally trivialized form of feminine conversation, more accurately identifies both the social register of Austen's fictional community and the novelistic technique of free indirect discourse which she perfected. In free indirect discourse, as in gossip, authority is unlocatable—nowhere and everywhere—its presence multiple and its source ultimately secret. A compulsion to gossip characterizes the intra-group relations of Austen's small societies and a narrative style which works by 'disseminating [authority] among the characters' so that it is neither precisely internalized nor merely external.[76] In the mode of reporting which characterizes Austen's mature novels, narrative voice, dialogue, and the conventions of indirect speech converge. As in gossip, utterances are imitatively replicated and diffused to the point where voices and characters are reinvested in a comically disturbing vocal equivalent of enantiomorphy, unsettling and dramatizing a set of relationships rather than disclosing a permanent truth.

Free indirect discourse operates much as Bakhtin described 'double-voiced discourse' as operating. That is, it is 'discourse with an orientation toward someone else's discourse', where 'in one discourse, two semantic intentions appear, two voices'. Double voicing can function in a variety of ways, affirming or parodying another's discourse, combining the voice and perspective of one speaker with those of other characters and/or the author-narrator.[77] Often in such passages of technical experimentation the purposive and highly controlled fluidity, by which we cannot (and are not expected to) extract one voice from another, is marked by a corresponding typographic and syntactic indeterminacy.

A good example of this appears in *Emma* at Volume 3, Chapter 6, during the strawberry-picking party to Mr Knightley's estate at Donwell Abbey. In one long paragraph we follow the reporting voice of the narrator into the 'thought-idiolect' of her heroine, the narrator providing a commentary on what goes through Emma's mind as she looks about her at the scene and the

[75] *Guy Mannering*, ed. P. D. Garside, 406.

[76] Casey Finch and Peter Bowen, ' "The Tittle-Tattle of Highbury": Gossip and the Free Indirect Style in *Emma*', *Representations*, 31 (1990), 3.

[77] Mikhail Bakhtin, *Problems of Dostoevsky's Poetics*, ed. and trans. by Caryl Emerson (Manchester: Manchester University Press, 1984), 189–99.

company.[78] In turn, this reported internal commentary is invaded by the voice of Mrs Elton discoursing to the company at large on the topic of strawberries. Though Mrs Elton's words are supplied within quotation marks, they are not separated off into a distinct speech paragraph of their own; they are offered only as fragments from speech, and they mix features of spoken and reported style. Importantly, there is no narrative or formal pressure to distinguish the three voices. Rather, the passage typographically binds them together in textual space. The punctuation of long dashes which segmented the shifting topics of Emma's narratorially reported thoughts is intensified, signalling dramatically the shift in tempo of Mrs Elton's truncated observations, but also marking their syntactic continuity with what has gone before. But the three voices (narrator-author, narrator-agent-heroine, narrator-agent-antagonist) are interwoven in a controlled interplay that is also unsettling. For it is by no means clear whose voice and which perspective has priority in modifying which other. What we appear to hear is Mrs Elton's voice unmediated. But her speech is edited in such a way as at least to suggest that it comes to the reader only in snatches. As the surrounding paragraph shows, it also comes to our ears by way of Emma's, and it is by no means certain that what we overhear is not after all Emma's selective mimicry of Mrs Elton. Then again, Mrs Elton's speech in praise of the English strawberry also plays a parodic variation upon Emma's meditative pride in the English scene before her with which the paragraph opened and which has insidiously transformed into arrant smugness at her own 'untainted' connections before it is hijacked by Mrs Elton's mad eulogy; and the narrating voice has laid one upon the other for the reader to experience as a visually unsettled equivalent of their play of sound:

> She felt all the honest pride and complacency which her alliance with the present and future proprietor could fairly warrant, as she viewed the respectable size and style of the building, its suitable, becoming characteristic situation, low and sheltered—its ample gardens stretching down to meadows washed by a stream, of which the Abbey, with all the old neglect of prospect, had scarcely a sight—and its abundance of timber in rows and avenues, which neither fashion nor extravagance had rooted up.—The house was larger than Hartfield, and totally unlike it, covering a good deal of ground, rambling and irregular, with many comfortable and one or two handsome rooms.—It was just what it ought to be, and it looked what it was—and Emma felt an increasing respect for it, as the residence of a family of such true gentility,

[78] I borrow the phrase 'thought-idiolect' from J. F. Burrows, *Computation Into Criticism*, 173–5.

untainted in blood and understanding.—Some faults of temper John Knightley had; but Isabella had connected herself unexceptionally. She had given them neither men, nor names, nor places, that could raise a blush. These were pleasant feelings, and she walked about and indulged them till it was necessary to do as the others did, and collect round the strawberry beds.—The whole party were assembled, excepting Frank Churchill, who was expected every moment from Richmond; and Mrs. Elton, in all her apparatus of happiness, her large bonnet and her basket, was very ready to lead the way in gathering, accepting, or talking—strawberries, and only strawberries, could now be thought or spoken of.—"The best fruit in England—every body's favourite—always wholesome.—These the finest beds and finest sorts.—Delightful to gather for one's self—the only way of really enjoying them.—Morning decidedly the best time—never tired—every sort good—hautboy infinitely superior—no comparison—the others hardly eatable—hautboys very scarce—Chili preferred—white wood finest flavour of all—price of strawberries in London—abundance about Bristol—Maple Grove—cultivation—beds when to be renewed—gardeners thinking exactly different—no general rule—gardeners never to be put out of their way—delicious fruit—only too rich to be eaten much of—inferior to cherries—currants more refreshing—only objection of gathering strawberries the stooping—glaring sun—tired to death—could bear it no longer—must go and sit in the shade."[79]

Claude Rawson has well described the effect of such fluid indeterminacy where it occurs in the later *Persuasion* as conveying 'not confusion, but consensual interplay'.[80] In the passage from *Emma* consensus is not assured and the interplay is a contrived tampering or distortion by the controlling narrator, much as a sound engineer might overlay for varying effects voices or instruments one upon the other. In a letter written soon after its publication Austen complained that the faulty punctuation of the printer had made two speeches into one in *Pride and Prejudice*. It is, she confided to Cassandra, the 'greatest blunder in the Printing that I have met with'.[81] On the brightly lit stage of the early novel conversation is as formal an affair as dancing, with the various players taking their turn with a considerable degree of ceremony and choreographed direction. With *Mansfield Park* we sense a shift, a loss of witty exchange and epigrammatism and a corresponding increase in the mixing of speech and narratorial agency and the overlaying of voice upon voice.

[79] *Emma*, ed. Stafford, 295–6.

[80] Claude Rawson, in his introduction to *Persuasion*, ed. John Davie (Oxford: Oxford University Press, 1990), xiii.

[81] *Jane Austen's Letters*, 203. The speeches are at Vol. 2, Ch. 15, and were correctly printed in the third edition of 1817. But since Austen had sold the copyright to Egerton, she had nothing to do with the correction.

In *Mansfield Park* it is more difficult to decide in all instances whether conversation should be formally indented for each new speaker or run together as a continuous paragraph in which the visible blending of the various speeches might suggest something of the experimentation in vocal interplay that characterizes the later novels. There are several occasions on which the 1814 text fails to distinguish shifts in speaker by a paragraph break, preferring instead to run the conversation together. However we interpret these moments—as compositor's error or as rare traces of Austen's compositional style, which have survived the printer's standardization—the difference in presentation functions as changes in a musical score, affecting how we hear the relationships between the various parts.

For example, in Volume 1, Chapter 3, on two occasions the conversational exchange between Lady Bertram and her sister, Mrs Norris, is run together. There is no likelihood that the reader will confuse the voices, but in *seeing* their proximity I think we *hear* their conversation as a more humorously nuanced affair. Later in Chapter 6, when Edmund Bertram, Mary Crawford, and Fanny Price are discussing the merits of the old house on Mr Rushworth's Sotherton estate, the 1814 text collapses into one paragraph what are three speeches, with the middle, unattributed speech possibly belonging to Fanny. In the printing of 1816, this is divided into two speech paragraphs and the unattributed speech is absorbed into Mary's, making into a dialogue what may have been a three-way conversation, and reducing Fanny to silence. Later still, in the closing scene of Chapter 11, both the 1814 and 1816 texts fail to apportion correctly all the short speeches within a longer dialogue between Edmund and Fanny. Their subject is star-gazing. Carefully differentiated, as they subsequently are in all modern editions, the conversation assumes a more exaggeratedly staccato performance. In each case, the effect is to reduce our capacity to hear conversation as vocal interchange in the interests of a more orderly visual presentation of the printed page.

It is tempting to invoke at this point the evidence of the extant manuscripts, where paragraphing is far more fluid than print conventions normally allow. But the manuscripts are not reliable as an indicator of Austen's print intention since, as in the cancelled fragment of *Persuasion*, for example, there is no paragraphing of any kind throughout a whole chapter. What I think the collapsing of voices and speeches together in manuscript tells us is something vital about Austen's mature compositional method which even she may not have realized would continue to remain important in the translation into print. Evidence of reset paragraphing between printed editions also reinforces the idea that Austen may not have attended to this aspect of her text with great care even at the late stage of preparing her manuscripts for the press. It may be that what now exists as a vital visual guide to comprehension for the reader was never more than an afterthought to Austen, even a delegated duty, and one which on occasion betrays the more complex structuring effects of the compositional process.[82]

Changes to formal presentation and particularly to punctuation between *Mansfield Park* 1814 and 1816, from whatever source (whether, as seems unlikely, from Austen's hand or simply accepted by her as part of the process of refinement which accompanied a second edition from the house of Murray), undoubtedly represent a drive to improvement. But it is an improvement which ultimately distorts the internal relationship between parts of the text. This relationship depends for its fullest expression on the rhetorical, tonal, and emotive voice indicators which are more fully sounded in the noisier punctuation of the 1814 text and muted in the repunctuation of 1816. Considered in this way, the typographic irregularities which Chapman complained of as marring the appearance of the first-edition text (inconsistencies in spelling and capitalization) also signal the text's inception as an aural sociable space. Such indicators suggest the text's original narrative trace and enact at the surface level that vocal encroachment which characterizes Austen's mature narratives in general, and which is driven deep into the thematic structures of *Mansfield Park*. The case for restoring the punctuation of the 1814 text derives, then, from internal evidence, from a recognition of the way in which all its textual parts punctuate (interrupt and connect to) one another. The fact that the repunctuation of 1816 appears to require lexical change to sustain it is itself a telling indication of how substantive accidentals can be to the constitution of text and, of course, how integral idiosyncratic punctuation can be to meaning. In an important sense, Austen's wayward accidentals can be described accurately as super-substantive, for they are the primary agents of a particular structural dynamic underlying her mature novels, the dynamic of conversation and heard discourse.[83]

82 One of the clearest examples of the way the 1816 text imposes inappropriate visual correction occurs in Vol. 1, Ch. 17, where Mary Crawford's quotation from Hawkins Browne's 'Address to Tobacco' is set off from her normal speech to the diminishment of its aural effect. In the merged form of the 1814 text we *heard* her quotation and parody; now we merely *see* them. Cf. *Mansfield Park*, ed. Chapman, 161; and ed. Sutherland, 134.

83 Fredson Bowers makes the point forcefully when he states that '[i]n modern texts the effect on meaning of the different forms of accidentals varies considerably... Punctuation as it illuminates the

What is finally at issue is the amenability of *Mansfield Park* to a syntactic as opposed to a rhetorical punctuation. Chapman, who carried with him into war-torn Macedonia the memory of 'a series of summer evenings in Perthshire, when a lady read *Persuasion* to admiration', affirmed, in his 1918 essay of that title, the civilizing skills of reading aloud.[84] The charge of 'ill' punctuation subsequently levelled at the 1814 text of *Mansfield Park* is bound up, I believe, with its apparent resistance to some of the features of text which adapt it to the specialized spoken genre called 'reading aloud'. Lest this seem to contradict my argument for an aurally informed 1814 text, I want to invoke by way of explanation a distinction, hinted at earlier, from the linguistics of punctuation, between the transcripted text and the transdicted text.[85] In the former, the transcripted text, text is the written or printed expression of a previous oral function, and punctuation and other formal features are used to textualize the voice. By convention such punctuation is minimal (a matter of commas, dashes, and full stops) and aims to replicate or mark off intonational boundaries rather than syntactic units. In the latter, the transdicted text, punctuation voices the text: it voices the text according to a previous written or printed function, and its marks are by convention more varied (colons, semicolons, quotation marks). The difference is one of direction or derivation, and signals the prior existence of either voice or print: voice become print (transcription); print become voice (transdiction). Reading aloud (transdiction) is a function of print and tends to replicate the features of written

contextual modification of word, phrase, or clause, may sometimes be as vital to the meaning as the substantives, the words themselves ... Normally, punctuation when not setting off syntactical boundaries in the interest of clarity enables the author to direct the flow of his style as if he were reading aloud, with the pauses and emphases that he felt when writing and that he wants to transmit to the reader. It is not by chance that Nathaniel Hawthorne, for example, utilizes a heavy parenthetical punctuation whereas Stephen Crane, with an entirely different purpose, omits some of what are usually considered to be normal punctuation divisions.' ('Regularization and Normalization in Modern Critical Texts', *Studies in Bibliography*, 42 (1989), 98, n. 2.)

[84] In Chapman, *The Portrait of a Scholar*, 48.

[85] See Nunberg, *The Linguistics of Punctuation*, 12–14: 'In a number of cases, to be sure, there is some correspondence between the use of punctuation marks and intonational boundaries of various sorts, notably as regards commas, periods and dashes (the only marks, I should note, that are ordinarily used in the transcription of spoken discourse.) ... the intonational correlates of marks like the semicolon, quotation mark or parenthesis do in fact exist in the specialized spoken genre used for reading aloud, which is used in what we might call the "transdiction" of written texts'; and David R. Olson, *The World On Paper: The Conceptual and Cognitive Implications of Writing and Reading* (Cambridge: Cambridge University Press, 1994), where writing systems are described as originating the representable structures of speech and hence as determining our awareness of how linguistic structures work, to the detriment of spoken systems—so much so that the 'history of reading' can be seen as 'a series of attempts to recognize and to cope with what is *not* represented in a script' (93).

discourse—to discipline the representable structures of speech to a set of grammatical and visually orthodox rules.

The shift whereby punctuation as the visible trace of the acoustic image which inaugurates the text is replaced by punctuation as the expression of a written function is relatively routine. Editors, both commercial and scholarly, have conventionally imposed syntactic punctuation upon the looser paratactic structures of 'careless' authors, male and female; as teachers we perform similar corrections on student essays. What a close attention to the texts of *Mansfield Park* suggests, however, is the limited usefulness of such a procedure, especially when what is written or printed retains a high dependence upon the aural trace. It is worth considering in this respect how far our renewed acquaintance with the non-print forms of texts—through audio-cassette, television, and film versions, as well as the livelier typographic presentation of the electronic screen and of e-mail—may help us recover aspects of text which have tended to be silenced within the print tradition as it has been perfected. Unsettling the imposed regularities of print is in Austen's case a step towards recovering the vital defamiliarity of her style. *Mansfield Park*, and I think the same argument might be extended to the other mature novels, resists visual correction, and this can be demonstrated through the necessity of the uncorrected, transcripted text to its meaningful communication. Interestingly, too, the novel reinforces such textual resistance at the thematic level. In the implied irregularity of acting *Lover's Vows*, in the crucial distinction between acting on stage and in social situations, in the novel's scrutiny of public and private speech, but above all in the tension between the foregrounded motif of reading aloud and the urgent interiorized speech of the central character with which it contends, the narrative thematically refigures what is contested at the level of syntactic and paratactic structures, ultimately to the moral and effective disadvantage of Henry Crawford, the consummate actor and skilful public reader.[86]

Re-editing *Mansfield Park* in 1996, I was chiefly concerned to 'unschool' the edited text, by rejecting the imposed and suggested emendations of previous editors. An exercise in unemending, the intention was to re-establish the authority of its uncorrected form, based on a recognition of the harmony which exists in the 1814 text between its parts—in particular between punctuation (paratactic phrasing) and thematic development. This meant attend-

[86] In *Mansfield Park*, Vol. 3, Ch. 3 (Ch. 34) (the chapter immediately following that in which Fanny's inner meditation caused Chapman so much confusion), the art of reading aloud is discussed at some length and Henry Crawford's talent for it is displayed.

ing to the emphasis placed throughout the novel on listening, especially in the figure of Fanny Price, the good listener and herself the model for the novel's preferred narrative voicing. By this means, the restored detail of the overheard (rather than read) inner dialogue of the heroine endorses the aural formulation of the 1814 text, the text by tradition assigned a more feminine status among Austen scholars. It realigns the corrupt detail to the corrupt whole in a work whose legitimating marks are the spots or stains of its illiterate signature, its feminine grammatical resistance. Chapman's error of emendation, on the contrary, established the culturally endorsed necessity for a subsequent visual instruction, and with it, of course, *Mansfield Park*'s translation into an English classic.

6

Textual Identities: Part 2

'The grammar of literary investigation': or, a brief history of textual criticism in the twentieth century

The certainties that the Chapman Austen edition evinced and the uncertainties it stood to deflect now strike us quite differently. Chapman's self-dedication to the Austen œuvre was a heroic labour: after the novels he went on to publish the juvenilia and later manuscript writings, the letters, and a supplement to the family-derived biographical record. But the immersion therapy proposed through the recreation of a Regency world and reading experience now seems both quaint and partial. Archly knowing—in the matter of the rules for the game of speculation or the carriage design of the barouche landau—such information now appears wholly inadequate in its assumptions about what we need to know to get our novelistic bearings. Like Miss Bates in possession of a secret, it is hopelessly beside the point, intrusive rather than illuminating. In his preface to *Sense and Sensibility*, Chapman had defended his habit of annotation by reference to Dr Johnson's pronouncement that 'all works which describe manners, require notes in sixty or seventy years'. By this reckoning it is time to revisit his elucidations of 1923. This is no new thought: the history of twentieth-century editing in its commercially successful guise is the history of annotation and commentary. By these criteria, the literary classic is recognized in the extent of its supplementary textualization, which usually sits behind the work insisting surreptitiously on its own importance in uncovering its buried elements and inadequately expressed representation of other works. Without annotation,

annotation seems to say, the literary work will scarcely be comprehensible; annotation adapts or realizes its potential.

What is the identity of a literary work of art? Whose labours constitute it? When is it finished? Can we know it apart from a document or a text that embodies it? And just how different can its different documents or texts be from one another and still represent the work? Do we recognize it in all guises as the same work, or can we know it only in some shapes and not in others? As editors and critics, we are less and less willing to believe in the singularity of the work, its status as object; as consumers, seduced or bewildered by its multiple presences as paperback, audio-cassette, televised serial, feature film, or electronic hypertext, we are more and more persuaded by the real conditions of variance. We are fascinated by processes and transformations, origins and traces, prequels and sequels, revamps and make-overs, and creative re-(can they ever be (mis-)?) appropriations. Can we say we know *Hamlet* or *Emma* or *Trainspotting* apart from a medium and a context of interpretation, apart from the space in which we encounter it? And since with literature, as with music, we are dealing from the outset of its public life with a disseminated and not a uniquely identified art form, can't we simply forget ideas of authenticity? After all, with a very few eccentric exceptions the literary work of art is not a single or even a limited-edition object. Literary works exist not as things or work-of-art particulars, so the standard explanation goes, but as tokens (representations of representations); as a consequence we do not hold a notion of their uniqueness, as in some sense we do of a painting. This being so, we need to distinguish not between authentic states but authoritative states—a sufficiently vexed issue in itself, as the crude but effective question 'whose authority?' indicates.[1]

[1] The distinction in either case may only be one of essence, having little or nothing to do with how we experience paintings or literary works, where the essential difference is masked by the conditions of reproduction which define our everyday encounters with both. For example, the deluxe, limited edition of the literary work fosters the illusion that it is an object, while artists' own replicas and mass reproduction as postcards or colour slides or tee-shirt images dissolve in distribution and consumption the unique thingness in our encounters with paintings. Nevertheless, it remains that in thinking critically about the intrinsic identities of paint works and literary works terms like 'original' and 'copy' carry different significances. Whatever else we say by way of qualification, we cannot say that the literary work *per se* is an object, though our way of perceiving it and our modes of cultural validation may and often do dress it as such. For debate on this issue, see James McLaverty, 'The Mode of Existence of Literary Works of Art: The Case of the *Dunciad Variorum*', *Studies in Bibliography*, 37 (1986), 82–105; and Joseph Grigely, *Textualterity*, 137–40. Grigely is inclined to dismiss the issue of intrinsic, fundamental difference as a merely nominalist issue, as against what he sees as the more significant levelling of difference through dissemination and contextualization—that is, through our social encounters with both literary and art works. While sympathizing with this important qualification, I would not want to diminish the complexity of what is essential difference.

In the course of the twentieth century photography in the form of film and television came to inhabit much of the authority of the verbal text which had itself become more narrowly visual in the course of the nineteenth. As I write, we are reconceiving the authoritative state of both print and image as electronic impulse, a shift which among its many other consequences delivers analogue states, the stuff of our visual impressions, by means of digital storage and processing. Specifically, the electronic medium is reconfiguring author–publisher–printer–reader relations in new ways, as Stephen King's recent attempt at a web-written and web-distributed novel in instalments aimed to test, and as websites like Eastgate.com's Storyspace demonstrate. But this is only to restate a general condition of text—that any and every medium of transmission, whether it be manuscript, print, film, recorded sound, disc or website, is a rich complex of expressive signs which operate upon and beyond the text they express. Like e-text or film, the printed book, which for the moment continues to dominate our thinking about literary texts, does not merely reproduce a prior intention, it confers a new mode of existence. It is an intentional refashioning which adds its own intended and unintended meaning.

Granted the non-neutrality of forms, can we nevertheless say that some of those forms are more true than others—that *Emma* in this form is more truly *Emma* than *Emma* in that form? Leaving aside for the moment the matter of the different editorial interpretations or makings of text, we cannot doubt Austen's intention to be printed. But it *is* extremely doubtful that she had much if any control over the expressive features of her lifetime printed books (obviously she would have none later), none of which is merely inert. Typeface, ink, page layout, decoration, binding, even volume divisions, which appear to indicate formally a fidelity to the inner economy of the work, are all disputable areas of authority at the same time as they contribute to the relationship with the reader within which literary effects function. Even if we concede that the book abolishes many of the expressive features of the written manuscript, rendering them (and the authoring hand) effectively pre-textual, we might argue nevertheless that such a transformation was within the terms of the contract the author held with her society, and therefore part of her intention for the work. However, there is still the matter of the uses printed books are put to, which also shape and reshape texts even after they are fixed in print. Looking no further than Austen's own practice, we discover the persistent interaction in her understanding of text between its spoken and silent functions. In her case, and in a family and society which experienced reading as a shared voicing of text as much as its private internalization, even the apparent fixity of print on paper must submit to the relativities of place, time, and local intonation, all of which imply that text's objectivity, its singularity, is an illusion.[2]

There is nothing new in these qualifications. In their wider implications they throw up questions to do with the conditions for meaning, with how meaning is attributed, and by whom; they are also issues of reproduction and reception—of how we read, see, take possession of, and otherwise experience literary works. As such they are matters for cultural history and maybe philosophy. But in their recent concern to re-evaluate the function of edited literary works, textual critics, by inclination and training a fairly conservative breed, have begun to address them too. In the last twenty years theorists have submitted the practicalities of editorial procedure to a vigorous reassessment, among the effects of which has been a questioning of the relationship of text to author as an identifiable totality, and of editor to author as simply honest broker, carrying out what once were seen as the duties of an executor.[3]

The legal analogy is not inappropriate, nor is it unfamiliar: editors often have been literary executors appointed by authors or their representatives. In the modern period and as a consequence of copyright laws, the solemnity of the editorial role, long figured as that of foster parent to the orphaned or abandoned text, has regularly been strengthened by direct family inheritance of legal property in literary works. In such cases, the alliance of textual authority and textual property has appeared unassailable, as Chapman found to his irritation when in the 1920s he tried and failed to get sight of *Volume the Second.* In the nineteenth and twentieth centuries, many of the earliest editors of an author's literary remains were family members, as they were in the Romantic period for Wollstonecraft, Percy Shelley, Coleridge, and Jane Austen. Even when that is not the case, editors nevertheless have accrued to their activities the moral weightiness of directly delegated authority. Editors, it is implied, are privy to the dearest wishes of the author whose continuing interests they serve in relation to the text. If texts have spirits, and we tend to talk as though we believe they do, then we think of this as something connecting to the author (the text's spirit as a kind of authorial

[2] I have discussed Austen's aural/vocal composition and performance of text at various points in this book (see especially Chs. 3 and 5). For a wider examination of the uses of female oral culture, see Patricia Howell Michaelson, *Speaking Volumes: Women, Reading, and Speech in the Age of Austen* (Stanford, Calif.: Stanford University Press, 2002).

[3] The field is wide and growing; but see, for example, the essays collected in *Devils and Angels: Textual Editing and Literary Theory*, ed. Philip Cohen.

trace), and something we have by convention entrusted to the safekeeping of the editor.

It is not that we now know editors to be dishonest or unreliable stewards; it is rather that we have reconsidered both their situation and the situation of the text. We now recognize editors as partial and interested readers, just like the rest of us, and we no longer see the text–author alignment as the sole or even the most meaningful relationship for investigation. Texts, like editors, may be explained in other ways. This seems a good thing: for the editor whose labours, through their very incompleteness or partiality, at last become visible; for the critic who, recovering the different states of a work as the ground for enquiry, recognizes more forcibly its existence only in and as interpretation; for text, whose real conditions of circulation and reception are as much a part of its identity as the moment of conception and creation; and for the reader/consumer, thereby guaranteed an endlessly renewable supply of pleasure. Put simply, we now see that texts of works are not the basis of critical thought but its products. It is their nature to be changeful and multiply attributable.

But this wasn't always so. The prior factual nature of texts was for a long time a confident assumption of a scholarly and a reading community. The reliable, stable, and author-attributed text was not only the goal of most twentieth-century editorial labour, it was also taken for granted that it was the origin of critical discourse, the thing which guaranteed the discourse's validity both in point of detail and in general terms: the fixed existence of the text-object ratified the critical activity done upon it. In this understanding the accurate text possesses of itself the authority to adjudicate between good (true) and bad (false) readings—interpretation being submitted to the text rather than the text to interpretation. This was especially the case with the early Clarendon Press editions, where the declared policy was to make available the most authoritative texts based on the most scientific methods, and in uniform or at least mutually recognizable volumes. Before 1930 the Clarendon list was dominated by editions of the seventeenth-century poets, those writers who would become the staple of the New Criticism's critical practices. Herbert Grierson's two-volume Oxford Edition *The Poems of John Donne* (1912), L. C. Martin's *Works of Henry Vaughan* (1914), and his *Poems English, Latin, and Greek of Richard Crashaw* (1927) provide the publishing context for Chapman's Austen, together with Ernest de Selincourt's monumental edition of Wordsworth's *Prelude* (1926); Herford and Simpson's great edition of Ben Jonson was also at last beginning to appear (Volume 1 in 1925).

Though not all edited according to the same criteria nor at this stage uniformly identifiable in dark-blue 'Oxford' bindings, these works nevertheless form the basis for a body of texts determined and recognizable in certain shared and specific ways. They are a canon of relatively modern works for which a concept of authorial intention was seen as the best measure of authenticity. As L. C. Martin wrote in his introduction to Crashaw's *Poems*, the text should 'not only supply the most accurate possible record of what the poet wrote, but by its convenient disposition serve as a mirror to his growing and changing nature as thinker and as artist'.[4] The biographical function of editor and text was still uppermost in the 1920s, with the edition as the textual precipitate of a life narrative, to be measured as such against a chronology of thought and feeling. Just as we would now insist on a reconsideration of the exclusive literary existence of dramatic texts, so different bodies of literature (from different cultures and periods) would also dispute what in the 1920s and in a relatively narrow company of works appeared to be common problems and solutions.

The early Clarendon editions have come down to us as cultural objects in their own right; but also as objects which enshrine other objects as museum cases hold precious artefacts. In the Clarendons, the encased artefact is usually a valuable but defective early edition from the age of hand printing (roughly 1550 to 1830) which has been deemed to need judicious repair to recover its integrity. Because such artefacts have been rescued from the unreliability of their early physical states, and because it is an intellectual or ideational integrity rather than a previous physical wholeness that requires attention and recovery, their materiality is something they share only with one another. Under these circumstances, the characteristic Oxford regard to period detail in the physical appearance of its volumes—old-style type-founts and page layout which imitate seventeenth- and eighteenth-century print conventions—was a strategy for *dis*placing the text, a faux-historical guise situating it in some temporal limbo, neither the past nor the present. Shorn of the contexts of their first production and cleansed from the caprices of historical transmission, such texts inhabit an ideal material state, whose corporate bibliographical form harmonized with contemporary literary critical valuations, like E. M. Forster's visualization of the English novelists, 'seated together in a room, a circular room, a sort of British Museum

[4] *The Poems English, Latin, and Greek of Richard Crashaw*, ed. L. C. Martin (Oxford: Clarendon Press, 1927), vii.

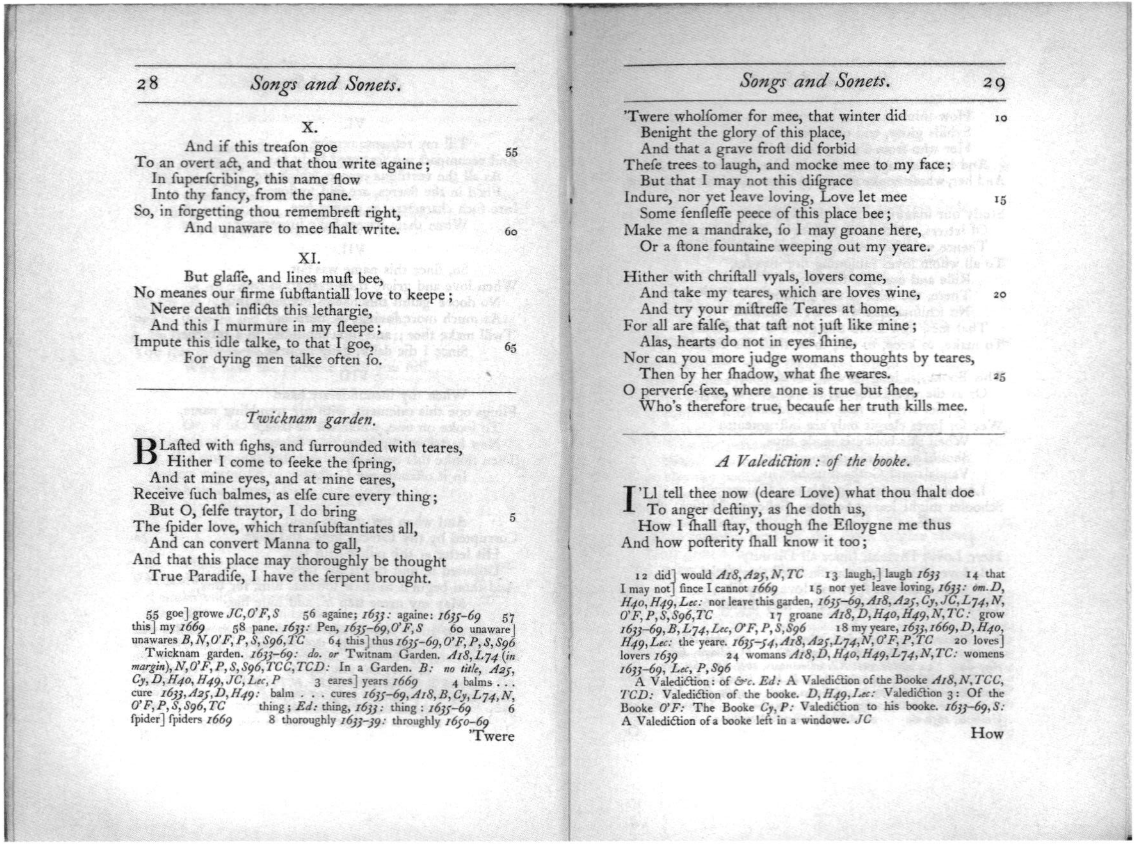

28 *Songs and Sonets.*

X.

And if this treaſon goe
To an overt act, and that thou write againe;
In ſuperſcribing, this name flow
Into thy fancy, from the pane.
So, in forgetting thou remembreſt right,
And unaware to mee ſhalt write.

XI.

But glaſſe, and lines muſt bee,
No meanes our firme ſubſtantiall love to keepe;
Neere death inflicts this lethargie,
And this I murmure in my ſleepe;
Impute this idle talke, to that I goe,
For dying men talke often ſo.

Twicknam garden.

BLaſted with ſighs, and ſurrounded with teares,
Hither I come to ſeeke the ſpring,
And at mine eyes, and at mine eares,
Receive ſuch balmes, as elſe cure every thing;
But O, ſelfe traytor, I do bring
The ſpider love, which tranſubſtantiates all,
And can convert Manna to gall,
And that this place may thoroughly be thought
True Paradiſe, I have the ſerpent brought.

55 goe] growe *JC, O'F, S* 56 againe; *1633*: againe: *1635–69* 57 this] my *1669* 58 pane. *1633*: Pen, *1635–69, O'F, S* 60 unaware] unawares *B, N, O'F, P, S, S96, TC* 64 this] thus *1635–69, O'F, P, S, S96*
Twicknam garden. *1633–69*: *do. or* Twitnam Garden. *A18, L74* (*in margin*), *N, O'F, P, S, S96, TCC, TCD*: In a Garden. *B*: *no title*, *A25, Cy, D, H40, H49, JC, Lec, P* 3 eares] years *1669* 4 balms . . . cure *1633, A25, D, H49*: balm . . . cures *1635–69, A18, B, Cy, L74, N, O'F, P, S, S96, TC* 6 thing; *Ed*: thing, *1633*: thing: *1635–69* 6 ſpider] ſpiders *1669* 8 thoroughly *1633–39*: throughly *1650–69*

'Twere

Songs and Sonets. 29

'Twere wholſomer for mee, that winter did
Benight the glory of this place,
And that a grave froſt did forbid
Theſe trees to laugh, and mocke mee to my face;
But that I may not this diſgrace
Indure, nor yet leave loving, Love let mee
Some ſenſleſſe peece of this place bee;
Make me a mandrake, ſo I may groane here,
Or a ſtone fountaine weeping out my yeare.

Hither with chriſtall vyals, lovers come,
And take my teares, which are loves wine,
And try your miſtreſſe Teares at home,
For all are falſe, that taſt not juſt like mine;
Alas, hearts do not in eyes ſhine,
Nor can you more judge womans thoughts by teares,
Then by her ſhadow, what ſhe weares.
O perverſe ſexe, where none is true but ſhee,
Who's therefore true, becauſe her truth kills mee.

A Valediction: of the booke.

I'Ll tell thee now (deare Love) what thou ſhalt doe
To anger deſtiny, as ſhe doth us,
How I ſhall ſtay, though ſhe Eſloygne me thus
And how poſterity ſhall know it too;

12 did] would *A18, A25, N, TC* 13 laugh,] laugh *1633* 14 that I may not] ſince I cannot *1669* 15 nor yet leave loving, *1633*: *om. D, H40, H49, Lec*: nor leave this garden, *1635–69, A18, A25, Cy, JC, L74, N, O'F, P, S, S96, TC* 17 groane *A18, D, H40, H49, N, TC*: grow *1633–69, B, L74, Lec, O'F, P, S, S96* 18 my yeare, *1633, 1669, D, H40, H49, Lec*: the yeare. *1635–54, A18, A25, L74, N, O'F, P, TC* 20 loves] lovers *1639* 24 womans *A18, D, H40, H49, L74, N, TC*: womens *1633–69, Lec, P, S96*
A Valediction: of *&c. Ed*: A Valediction of the Booke *A18, N, TCC, TCD*: Valediction of the booke. *D, H49, Lec*: Valediction 3: Of the Booke *O'F*: The Booke *Cy, P*: Valediction to his booke. *1633–69, S*: A Valediction of a booke left in a windowe. *JC*

How

23. Page opening from *The Poems of John Donne*, edited by Herbert Grierson, Clarendon Press, 1912. By kind permission of Oxford University Press.

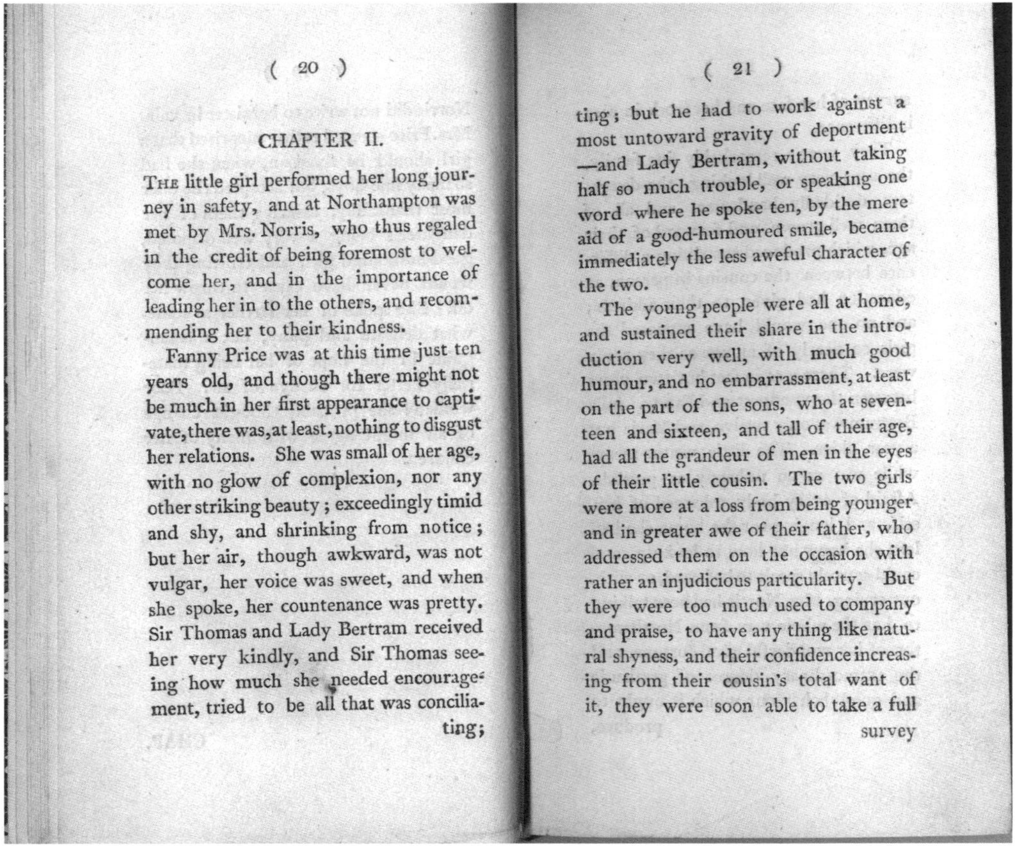

(20)

CHAPTER II.

THE little girl performed her long journey in safety, and at Northampton was met by Mrs. Norris, who thus regaled in the credit of being foremost to welcome her, and in the importance of leading her in to the others, and recommending her to their kindness.

Fanny Price was at this time just ten years old, and though there might not be much in her first appearance to captivate, there was, at least, nothing to disgust her relations. She was small of her age, with no glow of complexion, nor any other striking beauty; exceedingly timid and shy, and shrinking from notice; but her air, though awkward, was not vulgar, her voice was sweet, and when she spoke, her countenance was pretty. Sir Thomas and Lady Bertram received her very kindly, and Sir Thomas seeing how much she needed encouragement, tried to be all that was concilia-

ting;

(21)

ting; but he had to work against a most untoward gravity of deportment —and Lady Bertram, without taking half so much trouble, or speaking one word where he spoke ten, by the mere aid of a good-humoured smile, became immediately the less aweful character of the two.

The young people were all at home, and sustained their share in the introduction very well, with much good humour, and no embarrassment, at least on the part of the sons, who at seventeen and sixteen, and tall of their age, had all the grandeur of men in the eyes of their little cousin. The two girls were more at a loss from being younger and in greater awe of their father, who addressed them on the occasion with rather an injudicious particularity. But they were too much used to company and praise, to have any thing like natural shyness, and their confidence increasing from their cousin's total want of it, they were soon able to take a full

survey

24. Page opening from *Mansfield Park*, 1814. By kind permission of the English Faculty Library, Oxford University.

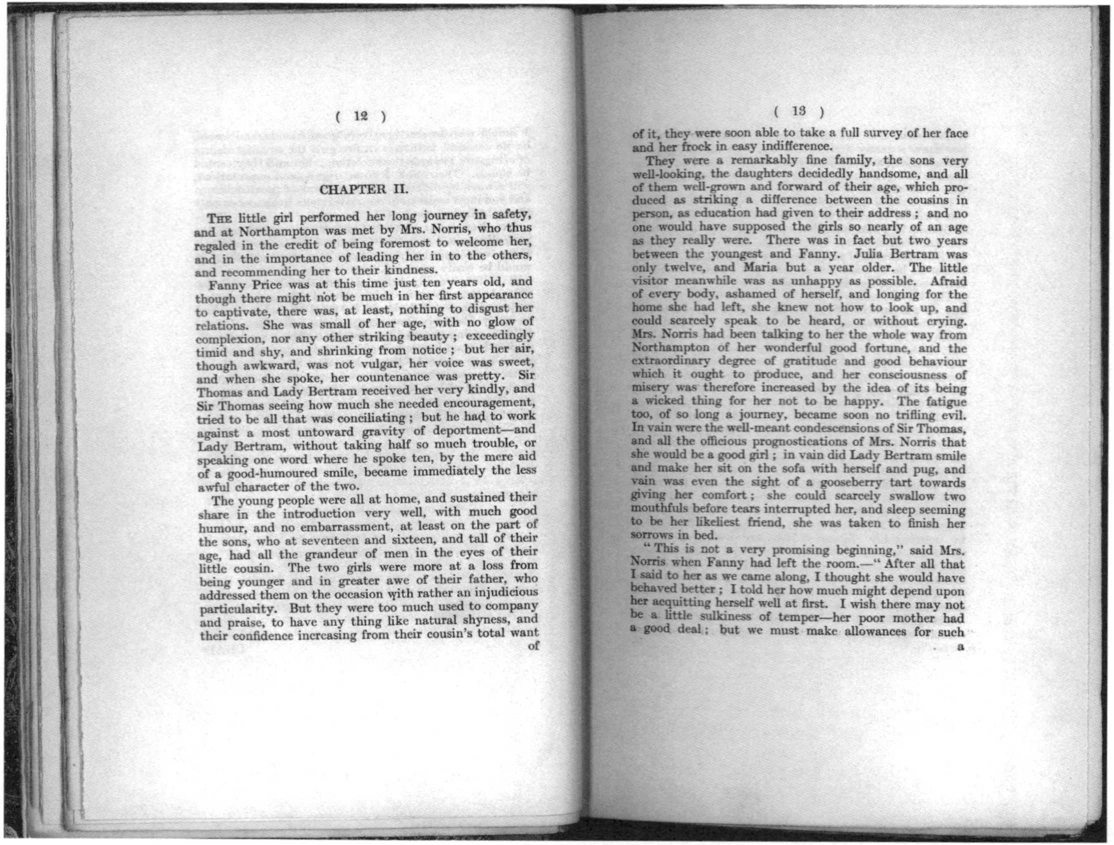

(12)

CHAPTER II.

The little girl performed her long journey in safety, and at Northampton was met by Mrs. Norris, who thus regaled in the credit of being foremost to welcome her, and in the importance of leading her in to the others, and recommending her to their kindness.

Fanny Price was at this time just ten years old, and though there might not be much in her first appearance to captivate, there was, at least, nothing to disgust her relations. She was small of her age, with no glow of complexion, nor any other striking beauty; exceedingly timid and shy, and shrinking from notice; but her air, though awkward, was not vulgar, her voice was sweet, and when she spoke, her countenance was pretty. Sir Thomas and Lady Bertram received her very kindly, and Sir Thomas seeing how much she needed encouragement, tried to be all that was conciliating; but he had to work against a most untoward gravity of deportment—and Lady Bertram, without taking half so much trouble, or speaking one word where he spoke ten, by the mere aid of a good-humoured smile, became immediately the less awful character of the two.

The young people were all at home, and sustained their share in the introduction very well, with much good humour, and no embarrassment, at least on the part of the sons, who at seventeen and sixteen, and tall of their age, had all the grandeur of men in the eyes of their little cousin. The two girls were more at a loss from being younger and in greater awe of their father, who addressed them on the occasion with rather an injudicious particularity. But they were too much used to company and praise, to have any thing like natural shyness, and their confidence increasing from their cousin's total want

of

(13)

of it, they were soon able to take a full survey of her face and her frock in easy indifference.

They were a remarkably fine family, the sons very well-looking, the daughters decidedly handsome, and all of them well-grown and forward of their age, which produced as striking a difference between the cousins in person, as education had given to their address; and no one would have supposed the girls so nearly of an age as they really were. There was in fact but two years between the youngest and Fanny. Julia Bertram was only twelve, and Maria but a year older. The little visitor meanwhile was as unhappy as possible. Afraid of every body, ashamed of herself, and longing for the home she had left, she knew not how to look up, and could scarcely speak to be heard, or without crying. Mrs. Norris had been talking to her the whole way from Northampton of her wonderful good fortune, and the extraordinary degree of gratitude and good behaviour which it ought to produce, and her consciousness of misery was therefore increased by the idea of its being a wicked thing for her not to be happy. The fatigue too, of so long a journey, became soon no trifling evil. In vain were the well-meant condescensions of Sir Thomas, and all the officious prognostications of Mrs. Norris that she would be a good girl; in vain did Lady Bertram smile and make her sit on the sofa with herself and pug, and vain was even the sight of a gooseberry tart towards giving her comfort; she could scarcely swallow two mouthfuls before tears interrupted her, and sleep seeming to be her likeliest friend, she was taken to finish her sorrows in bed.

"This is not a very promising beginning," said Mrs. Norris when Fanny had left the room.—"After all that I said to her as we came along, I thought she would have behaved better; I told her how much might depend upon her acquitting herself well at first. I wish there may not be a little sulkiness of temper—her poor mother had a good deal; but we must make allowances for such

a

25. Page opening from *Mansfield Park*, 1923. By kind permission of Oxford University Press.

reading-room—all writing their novels simultaneously'.[5] For Forster, great writers are 'approximated by the act of creation', and the old British Museum reading-room is a place outside time; but we might also accurately describe this canonical transcendence as approximated by the act of textual reproduction, by an imposed bibliographical identity, for which the Clarendon packaging provided typographic indicators, the manufactured signs of cultural timelessness.

For Walter W. Greg, associated from the beginning of the century with OUP through his general editorship of the Malone Society publications, an interest in the printed text (as distinct from early, usually Classical, manuscripts) as the subject of bibliographical investigation was 'mainly a development of the twentieth century, largely even of the post-war years'.[6] He delivered this view in 1933, and it is worth considering how far war—its remembrance and in the 1930s its growing anticipation—conditioned the brand of textual ideology (now known as New Bibliography) with which the names of Greg, A. W. Pollard, and R. B. McKerrow, the great British textual ctitics of the first half of the twentieth century, became associated. Not only was this the case in the 1920s in the aftermath of the Great War, but even more so in the years following the Second World War, when Greg's American disciple Fredson Bowers was establishing in Charlottesville, Virginia, the influential periodical *Studies in Bibliography*, dedicated to serving the interests of the pure text. If the textual theorist Louis Hay is right, that 'editing has always embodied the main ideological and cultural concerns of its day',[7] then the atemporal text championed by Bowers can be seen to link the New Bibliography as it was refined by mid-century to some of the major essentializing strategies of the contemporary modernist movement in literature, criticism, and other arts.

In particular and as regularly noted, the aims of New Bibliography and New Criticism were sufficiently similar to constitute a shared enquiry into the nature of text. Both promote the autotelic status of the artistic work and its disengagement from attention to origin or effects or continuous development, except as they explain and assist in the eradication of error; and in New Bibliography, as in other parts of the modernist experiment, the self-referential nature of literary works establishes a coherence of meaning out of

[5] Forster, *Aspects of the Novel*, 16.

[6] W. W. Greg, 'The Function of Bibliography in Literary Criticism Illustrated in a Study of the Text of *King Lear*', repr. in *Collected Papers*, ed. J. C. Maxwell (Oxford: Clarendon Press, 1966), 274.

[7] Louis Hay, 'Genetic Editing, Past and Future: A Few Reflections by a User', *TEXT*, 3 (1987), 117.

its own fragmentary forms. In the case of New Bibliography, a commitment to the recovery and preservation of authorially intended texts from the past necessitated a measure of intervention to remove what was obviously erroneous or corrupt. The history of textual criticism in the twentieth century was a history of progressive eclecticism born of an increasing distrust of (or, perhaps, an increasing confidence to reverse) the conditions under which texts are transmitted. To the New Bibliographer all textual carriers are inherently corrupt and suspect (witness the French medievalist Eugène Vinaver's description of textual criticism as founded upon a 'mistrust of texts', which David Greetham recently glossed as a 'hermeneutics of suspicion').[8] Under these circumstances, the mid-century identification by Bowers of a notional pure text is to be seen as a compensatory resource, a justifiable abstraction, locating authority in some permanent self-identical presence always and everywhere the same—the one text, deducible from but fully expressed in none of its many documentary forms. It is this ideal textual presence which, we are to believe, takes on hypostatized reality in the eclectic edition, usually under the imprint of a top British or American university press—Oxford, Cambridge, Princeton, or Yale. Only here and under these conditions can text be trusted, because only here is its historical life sifted and repaired. By the 1940s, the dark-blue 'Oxford' binding was the standard uniform for all Clarendon texts conferring, surely intentionally, the appearance of a set of family bibles.

But for Greg and McKerrow and the first generation of British New Bibliographers textual eclecticism was not the aim so much as the inevitable and sorry consequence of weighing dispassionately the effects and failures of history. Greg's concern for the evidentiary importance of print technology and the disseminative details of textual transmission, and his sensitivity to the cultural significance of material forms, grants to all textual witnesses, however imperfect, a degree of authority and meaning. His 1932 pronouncement that a text is 'a living organism which in its descent through the ages, while it departs more and more from the form impressed upon it by its original author, exerts, through its imperfections as much as through its perfections, its own influence upon its surroundings' vindicates the bibliographer's clinical analysis of every stage of textual descent and every aspect of book production.[9] If history is not by this the enemy but the maker of meaning, its processes are nevertheless

[8] Eugène Vinaver, 'Principles of Textual Emendation', in *Studies in French Language and Medieval Literature presented to Professor M. K. Pope* (Manchester: Manchester University Press, 1939), 352; D. C. Greetham, *Textual Scholarship: An Introduction* (New York and London: Garland Publishing, 1994), 296.

[9] W. W. Greg, 'Bibliography—an Apologia', in *Collected Papers*, 259.

detectable as errors and irregularities in transmission which it is the work of the critical bibliographer (not the intuitive literary critic) to interpret and regulate. Only late in his career, in a famous essay, 'The Rationale of Copy-Text', did Greg bow to the inevitable and in suggesting a divided authority in copy-text endorse eclectic editing. But this is an eclecticism derived from the apparently counter-intuitive (that is, scientific) evidence of printing-house practices with regard to the non-authorial treatment of the spelling, punctuation, and other surface features of authorial texts.

In weighing the price of history to the preservation and transmission of literary texts, early twentieth-century scholars not surprisingly registered also the burden of their own historical moment; in Greg's case, an understanding of Elizabethan printing-house practices was itself historically conditioned. It is not too extravagant to argue that the shadow of the Great War loomed over a generation of bibliographers, and that heroic (if unglamorous) projects like A. W. Pollard and G. R. Redgrave's *Short-Title Catalogue* (STC) were impelled by an urgency, equivalent to that of the modernist poets, to shore up fragments against our ruin. In the case of the STC, published in 1926, what is assembled is a check-list of books 'printed in England, Scotland, and Ireland, and of English books printed abroad, 1475–1640'. A preface contextualized the project as it finally took shape after 1918 and the 'ransacking' of the Printed Books Department of the British Museum 'for rarities to be conveyed to the place of safety from air-attacks'.[10] An author list, with group headings for anonymous works, of books held in certain British libraries, and, if rare, elsewhere, the STC is itself a 'place of safety', a virtual repository or grand archive for what exists in reality only in scattered and partial (and in times of war increasingly perishable) form. Every entry in the STC is numbered, and these numbers, preceded by the letters STC, came to be used in catalogues to locate and identify the disparate elements of the ideal library. The STC undoubtedly embodies eclecticism. A bibliographic equivalent to the collage texts of Ezra Pound or T. S. Eliot, it was produced by a comparable, conscious reaction to the hazards of material existence, a defensive act of cultural stewardship, and in this case of 'Englishness', in the face of imminent historical collapse.[11]

[10] *A Short-Title Catalogue of Books Printed in England, Scotland, and Ireland, and of English Books printed abroad, 1475–1640*, compiled by A. W. Pollard and G. R. Redgrave (London: Bibliographical Society, 1926), v.

[11] Compare the recent cultural positioning of New Bibliography, with regard to technological and legal developments and the defence of Englishness within an expanding transatlantic market in books, by Joseph F. Loewenstein, 'Authentic Reproductions: The Material Origins of the New Bibliography', in *Textual Formations and Reformations*, ed. Laurie E. Maguire and Thomas L. Berger (Newark: University of Delaware Press, 1998), 23–44.

Later, in America and after the Second World War, Bowers's important study *Principles of Bibliographical Description* (1949), which he dedicated to Greg, signalled the decisive dehistoricizing shift in the status of historical evidence by establishing the authoritative notion of the 'ideal copy', the control for determining the physical make-up of the book as it was intended as distinct from realized in the act of printing.[12] In Bowers's transference to the editing of nineteenth-century American works of those disciplinary procedures established by McKerrow and Greg for correcting the texts of sixteenth- and seventeenth-century literature, there can be detected a prescriptive cultural agenda. The function Bowers set for textual criticism, the 'recovery of the initial purity of an author's text... and the preservation of this purity', procedures which he argued lie 'at the base of all intellectual endeavor in our cultural heritage', was subsequently instituted and monitored in the case of American editions through the sanitizing agency of the Center for Editions of American Authors (set up in 1962–3).[13] There is a link between canon formation and other forms of cultural regulation: to define a nation in terms of its writings is always a selective act (these writings and in these versions by these authors; but not those writings in those versions by those authors) which we have long recognized as bound up with issues of territorial mapping and demarcation and the obliteration of the interests, rights, and cultural identity of some. More fundamentally, from the eighteenth century onwards, in North America, in Australia and New Zealand, and, nearer to home, in the Scottish Highlands, for example, indigenous cultures were the

[12] 'A bibliographer is not concerned with accidental combinations resulting from binding; his business is to describe the ideal copy as the printer intended it to leave his hands... Only by reference to this ideal formula... could the owner of a particular variant understand the makeup of his copy.' Fredson Bowers, *Principles of Bibliographical Description* (Princeton: Princeton University Press, 1949), 8.

[13] Fredson Bowers, 'Textual Criticism', in *The Aims and Methods of Scholarship in Modern Languages and Literatures*, ed. James Thorpe (New York: Modern Language Association of America, 1963), 24. Grigely, *Textualterity*, 23–7, has recently argued a shocking connection between the language and cultural presuppositions of Bowers-style eclectic textual bibliography and politically driven mid-century eugenics movements. It is difficult to read extensively in any work by Bowers without becoming aware of the moral framework within which his theory and treatment of text is situated. For example, 'One can no more permit "just a little corruption" to pass unheeded than "just a little sin" was possible in Eden.' (*Textual and Literary Criticism* (Cambridge: Cambridge University Press, 1966), 8.) Even the examination of narrowly physical evidence can, in Bowers's understanding, be fraught with opportunities for 'sin' for the uninitiated, as when probing the distinction between an individual and an ideal copy: 'By this principle one avoids the sin of offering a description only of an imperfect state of a copy' (*Principles of Bibliographical Description*, 113 n. 48). But this language of corruption is inherited from a long Classical tradition of textual criticism, and is shared (for example, with Paul Maas, who fled Nazi Germany) in ways that complicate any simple political analogy. It is at least as pertinent to observe the 'eugenic' analogy provided by Bowers's early interest in breeding pedigree dogs.

more easily unperceived and deterritorialized by their Anglo-Saxon conquerors because they took no obvious written and printable form.[14]

More unequivocally than Greg, Bowers was in the business of textual reconstruction. But his ideal text or copy was never merely imagined; it was constructed on the basis of evidence and the consultation of several material copies, and specifically from an understanding of the processes of production, presented to the reader in the form of a critical apparatus acknowledging the documents from which the pure text of the 'definitive' edition was distilled. The American Editions policy of tidying away such apparatus at the back of the volume represented an important departure from standard British editorial practice, where foot-of-page variants provide both a more historically compromised and a more Classical look. In Grierson's Donne, as in the later Clarendon Dickens, Eliot, and Charlotte Brontë, the evidence of the text's history (its life in history) is always before the reader; in Bowers's 'clean-page', neutral or modern typeface American editions history is visually suppressed or relegated. Chapman's decision to hide his apparatus away is therefore initially surprising but combined with the artful, faux-Regency look of the Oxford Austen text it in fact represents an alternative engagement with (or dressing up as) history.

For most of the twentieth century the Greg–Bowers tradition dominated Anglo-American textual thinking, justifying its procedures according to a scientific model implying impartiality and rigorous method. From the beginning there was the declared faith that what was new in the New Bibliography was its 'analysis of the physical details of books for evidence that could solve textual cruxes without the use of literary judgment'.[15] In 1912, addressing the Bibliographical Society in London, Greg described the province of the editor as 'critical bibliography', which he further defined as 'the grammar of literary investigation', in its own right worthy to be considered as a science: 'Critical bibliography is the science of the material transmission of literary texts' which 'aims at the construction of a calculus for the determination of textual problems.'[16] In 1930, and now speaking as President of the Bibliographical Society, he reiterated many of the same points. In the intervening

[14] Arguments for the relation of nationhood to print identity are now commonplace. For a defining statement, see Benedict Anderson, *Imagined Communities: Reflections on the Origin and Spread of Nationalism* (1983; London and New York: Verso, 1991), 37–46.

[15] This is how G. Thomas Tanselle describes it in 'Editing without a Copy-Text', *Studies in Bibliography*, 47 (1994), 2. As a textual bibliographer Tanselle is himself in direct line of inheritance via Bowers from Greg.

[16] W. W. Greg, 'What is Bibliography?' in *Collected Papers*, 83.

twenty years he had successfully argued the case for bibliography to the post-war British government committee on the Teaching of English in England as that aspect of literary studies which underpins the subject's claims to be 'research'. According to Greg, bibliography came of age about 1920, when it began to be 'self-conscious' and 'to discover its own significance' in reflecting critically on the stuff that constitutes English Studies. Grounding its own critical acts in a textual consciousness which enquires into and challenges the instability of textual states, bibliography can claim to be the stable basis for all critical enquiry because it conducts its own enquiries at a profounder level. It is 'the organon of research into the transmission of literary and historical documents' and as such a system of knowledge, or in Greg's words, 'a mature science'.[17] Three years earlier, in 1927, in his *Calculus of Variants*, he had attempted to expand on the suggestion that mathematics might provide a model for weighing with greater certainty the material evidence of change or variance in literary texts, and for generating some kind of predictive scheme for calculating levels of textual deviance from an ideal norm (and thereby redressing it). A combination of intensive empiricism, drawn from the 'facts' and observation of text- and bookmaking through the ages, and of rigorous abstraction, critical bibliography would anchor the lighter-weight, subjective and impressionistic, activities of the literary critic.

As Austen editor and textual scholar Chapman was influenced by the first wave of the London–Oxford based New Bibliography, with its emphasis on the analysis of physical details of books and, at this early stage, its tentative eclecticism. Its chief vehicles were the scholarly editions the Clarendon Press was busy commissioning and publishing under his direction. His own concern for the recovery and presentation of an emended documentary Austen text owed much to McKerrow's restrictive understanding of the nature of 'copy-text' editing, while his imposition of a prescriptive cultural grammar on the Austen reader can be seen as extending Greg's claim for the scientific function of textual scholarship.[18] Like McKerrow and like Greg until very late in his career, Chapman was not openly won over by the idea that a critical text emerges from active editorial choices among variant readings. (I say not openly, for his enjoyment of the game of correcting

[17] W. W. Greg, 'The Present Position of Bibliography', in *Collected Papers*, 212 and 222.

[18] The classic statement of McKerrow's position on copy-text is to be found in his edition of *The Works of Thomas Nashe*, 5 vols. (London: A. H. Bullen and Sidgwick and Jackson, 1904–10), i. xi, where he modestly describes his procedure and the term he has coined thus: 'the copy-text, by which, here and throughout the book, I mean the text used in each particular case as the basis of mine . . . followed exactly except as regards evident misprints.'

careless reprints licensed his occasional silent intrusive 'improvement' of the Austen text.) Rather, he worked by one rule, the rule of the latest lifetime edition likely to have been overseen by the author. This formed his copy-text, to be adhered to in the main and altered only at obviously erroneous places. It was far from his view, as it was from McKerrow's or Greg's in the early decades of the twentieth century, that editing is textually constructive as opposed to emendatory. He was confirmed in this by the precept of his great master, Samuel Johnson, whose instruction to caution ('As I practised conjecture more, I learned to trust it less')[19] led him into some curious double thinking when it came to establishing the Austen text.

Writing Chapman's *DNB* entry soon after his death, another Johnson scholar L. F. Powell reminds us of the basis for authority of this Austen text: 'All the persons and events of her novels were present to him with such distinctness and precision that he could detect the small misprints which had long passed muster, and the bigger blunders which had been dismissed or ignored as beyond cure.'[20] The language is both eighteenth century (Johnsonian) in its medical-moralism and New Bibliographic in the implied exhaustiveness and objectivity of an enquiry which purports to obliterate the subjective element under the sheer volume of 'precise' knowledge. It is easy to overlook that what is being described in such weighty, forensic terms is Chapman's familiarity with fictional characters and situations—impressive maybe, but still impressionistic; and that the editorial practice here defended is subjective and in reality untrammelled by empirical data (largely unavailable in Austen's case). As a method it may nevertheless sound reasonable enough, except that Chapman was clearly unhappy with many of the readings his non-interventionism required him to retain. But any other course would have meant succumbing to acknowledged personal preference (critical judgement). As a consequence, his editorial approach is characterized by ambivalence, his respect for documentary authority often winning out over a strongly held belief that an early reading is flawed. In these circumstances he used textual commentary to relieve frustration over the limits for choice (between what he saw as good and bad readings as distinct from 'corruptions') within his own rule. It is this commentary which now provides the twenty-first century reader with an insight into Chapman's critical editing and its underlying cultural assumptions.

[19] 'Preface' (1765), in *Johnson on Shakespeare*, ed. Arthur Sherbo, 108.

[20] *The Dictionary of National Biography, 1951–1960*, ed. E. T. Williams and Helen M. Palmer (London: Oxford University Press, 1971), 208. Powell is quoting an earlier authority on Chapman.

As a means of establishing text the New Bibliographic model was only seriously challenged from the 1980s and (not coincidentally) around the time when technology in the guise of the computer appeared to offer the opportunity to simulate the newly recognized contingency and hybridity of all textual forms. Only now, and with the computer as the declared repository of bulk and tool of plurality, do we appear to be in a position to reclaim literary works by other than synoptic and eclectic means. As the varying textual histories of their multiply contextualized forms, literary works can now seem as dauntingly uncontained as previously they were 'defined'. In some senses this is to do no more than turn the old method inside out—a scaled-up- or macro-eclecticism which owes its existence to celebrating the conditions of history rather than defying them. Thus far, it might be said, technology and ideology remain complicit.

In fact, another way of thinking about the motivation for the New Bibliographer's thinking about the nature and condition of text is to invoke print technology itself. The concept of the perfected, ideal text, like that of the text as a mirror in which we find the image of the author, is a Romantic notion and was born of the kind of uniformity in print only mechanically possible after the eighteenth century. Up to the end of the hand-press period (around 1830), it was generally difficult if not impossible to guarantee the identity of printed copies—variation (usually minute) rather than a disease or imperfection or corruption of print text was its normal condition and a function of the technology that transmitted it. In the course of the nineteenth century the commercial use of stereotyping made it easier to reduce the play of typographic variation between copies and between impressions and to render the appearance of the printed page uniform and seemingly neutral. This material change in the appearance of text, it could be argued, informed a concept of text at the immaterial level and legitimated (because it now appeared to be attainable) an intellectual turn to perfection and purity. If we think of the variation in the printing of words and symbols in the hand-press book as like the play of form and meaning in language itself, it makes it not in the least inappropriate to consider New Bibliography, as Greg does, as a prescriptive literary grammar, or as providing in print the equivalent to standard or received pronunciation in spoken language. In this understanding, improvements through the nineteenth and for much of the twentieth century in the technology of printing maximized print's socio-political function, which at that time was to reduce linguistic diversity and create a unified field of communciation, and by extension a literary canon.[21] Only in recent years and as a consequence of electronic technology have we recovered a linguistic plurality and expressive freedom currently situtated somewhere between written/printed and spoken conventions.

Yet despite, or paradoxically because of, its foundationalist purposes, there is a real problem in recognizing the powerful critical work of the so-called definitive printed edition. The problem lies in its very determinacy, which can make it seem unengaged in the distinct and irreconcilable interpretations that the texts it presents provoke. This is why it is difficult to endorse without qualification the verdict of Donald Reiman, a distinguished apologist for the textual critic, when he claims that 'Much of the best [textual criticism]—including the research and editing . . . of R. W. Chapman on Jane Austen's texts—was carried out in defiance of the critical fashions of the day, and literary theorists updated their own work over the years as they absorbed and made use of the editorial discoveries.'[22] Anyone who has tried to interest an academic publisher in an edition of an author or a work for which there is not already a significant body of current critical interest knows that editorial endeavour does not lead the market but follows it. Entailed to older models of Classical editing, Chapman's principles and methods harmonized perfectly with the moral and psychic priorities for literature of his leading critical contemporaries—of the Leavises and I. A. Richards; his edition was greeted with enthusiasm, as marking a change in Austen's fortunes. But the implication that edited texts contain messages which work slowly on the critical imagination, that editorial discoveries are reprocessed as 'new' critical insights at a later stage, is surely right. In this sense, editions and editors can work quiet revolutions in the history of taste.

This is as true of Chapman's editorial work as of that of any and every editor whose edition provides the space in which the authored text is encountered. For the literary critical act is always circumscribed by, and therefore written within, the prior textual critical act of the editor; our encounters with print are not innocent of meaning until we imbue them with it. Just as print itself is not value-neutral, not a transparent window onto text which somehow lies in authentic state behind it; so our encounters with edited texts are in significant ways forestalled. Before the critical reader activates the text into meaning, there has been a previous reader, more usually a series of previous readers (compositors or typesetters, page designers, a whole commercial production team, as well as literary editors), who have

[21] Cf. Benedict Anderson, *Imagined Communities*, 43–4.

[22] Donald H. Reiman, *The Study of Modern Manuscripts*, 140.

staged the occasion, set the lighting, the mood, and engineered our expectations. Such engineering is often subtly effected through typography and layout: the choice of period fount and catchwords for the Clarendon Austen; or the subliminal message, working beneath the threshold of consciousness because in the space of the physical book literally *beneath* or beyond the threshold of the text, in the use foot-of-page variants and back-of-text apparatus. Offered in schematic, highly condensed form, amputated from the textual body, such information is only slowly reconnected; yet it may contain profound insights into how the text is arrived at and how its semantic range is constructed. Those editorial acts which enter the text as emendations work a different change, too fine even when acknowledged to be discriminated from the general attribution of the text to a single authorial consciousness.

New Bibliography's prescriptiveness is, then, both a function of technological change and of the limits or regulation on thinking about text imposed by that change. In the same way, the recent renewed interest in variability and the non-identity of text to text and text to work, what we might call critical bibliography's claim to be a *de*scriptive literary grammar, is desirable and intellectually persuasive now that the computer makes it technically more achievable. The expanded (though still limited) capacity of the computer as a text-repository appears to license deregulation and the storage of text as an archive of variant forms, the non-standard idiolects of utterance rather than the internally regulated system of print. It would be a bold editor who at the dawn of the twenty-first century announced his text as 'definitive', as in the 1960s and 1970s during the heyday of the Greg–Bowers school. Where once the ideally constructed, composite text, freed from the mishaps of transmission, delivered what could be defended as the author's intended appearance before a readership, now the dependency of the transmission process itself determines the course of most discussions, including how we think about authors.

Where the prescriptive practices of New Bibliography grew out of the consolidative Anglo-Saxon nationalism of the Great War, one measure of which was the urgent establishment of a hermeneutically stable canon of literary texts for all English speakers, the diversity that post-print technology makes it possible to represent coincides with the late twentieth-century emergence of devolutionary challenges in the form of smaller nation states demanding their own distinct 'voices': within Britain, Scottish, Irish, and Welsh idiolects. Throughout the twentieth century the Oxford Clarendon imprint signalled something important about the classic status of its recipients: we have no Clarendon Edgeworth or Wollstonecraft or Scott. Regardless of fashion and of whether we read such editions or not, the marginal status within a particular definition of literature of Austen's formally diverse and, in their own time, more famous contemporaries remained generally accepted: canonical literary authors, it seemed, should be English rather than British, non-polemical, and, for preference, mono-generic in their output. It is worth speculating whether the devolved environment of electronic reproduction is yet revising or will revise our canonical assumptions.

Looking back at the history of textual criticism in the twentieth century it does seem that some long time after we abandoned unitary critical readings of texts we still held on to the idea of the unitary text, being reluctant to investigate its varying conditions of existence. Recent moves among editors and theorists have been in two directions: towards text-based theories grounded in the literary work's collaborative status as a socially constructed product; and towards a reconsideration of authorial intention itself, not as a determinable principle leading the neutral and 'scientific' editor towards a final, correct, or best manifestation of the work, but as the promoter of unstable versions. The former, social model, with its roots in reception theory (or at least in American varieties of reader-response criticism) is associated with the theoretical writings of Jerome McGann; the latter, with its directly opposed presentation of text as an act (or acts) of writing (not reading), is represented in English-speaking textual circles by the European-based 'genetic' theory and practice of Hans Walter Gabler, best, or infamously, known for his edition of James Joyce's *Ulysses* (1984).[23] In both reconceptions, what is in question are the nature and limits of intention. Whose intentions matter in regard to a literary work? In what sense can we say that authorial intention establishes a literary work? Which embodiments and aspects of the work: the

[23] For early summary statements of the positions they each represent, see Jerome J. McGann, *A Critique of Modern Textual Criticism* (Chicago: University of Chicago Press, 1983); and Hans Walter Gabler, 'The Synchrony and Diachrony of Texts: Practice and Theory of the Critical Edition of James Joyce's *Ulysses*', *TEXT*, 1 (1984 for 1981), 305–26. McGann here rejects what he sees as the traditionalist editor's 'hypnotic fascination with the isolated author' which 'has served to foster an underdetermined concept of literary work' (122). He argues instead that the 'concept of literary work' we now require is 'a socialized concept of authorship and textual authority' (8). See, too, Jerome McGann, 'What Is Critical Editing?' and T. H. Howard-Hill's critical response, 'Theory and Praxis in the Social Approach to Editing', *TEXT*, 5 (1991), 15–29 and 31–46 (and McGann's response to the response, 47–8). Working from a theoretical foundation in structuralism, Gabler also dismisses a narrow intentionalist rationale, proposing a temporal model of text which refuses the selection or creation of a single best version. Against the concept of the 'synchronous' or 'static' text, he sets what he calls 'a natural condition of the literary work', which is its existence in time, as a succession of states whose totality is 'a kinetic system of signification whose dynamics revolve on the variant' (306 and 309). Both McGann and Gabler have refined and further argued their positions over the last two decades; both have provoked considerable debate.

holograph manuscript only? or the printed text also? and what about the readerly text? Then again, what is an authorial intention?—an intention to mean or to do? How fixable is intention?—do authors intend singly, serially, multiply? What such questions and their variously inflected answers undoubtedly establish is the status of editorial theory and practice as culturally embedded critical endeavours. As such, they are no longer exercises in dealing definitively with text but interpretatively, subjectively, and, of course, temporarily.

It is most probably the deconstructive challenge it directed at old-style editorial activity, together with its implication of failure for the editorial project in general, which explains the invigorating and particular appeal for literary critics in the 1980s and 1990s of McGann's approach to text. His suggestion that works only exist under the sign of change and that such change is what signifies has been used to bring the bibliographical methods of textual criticism to bear more widely on what previously seemed exclusively matters of literary interpretation. The mixed method has yielded rich local insights into how particular texts (usually poetry texts and usually post-1800 poetry texts) manifest their histories. Arguing against the false distinction between the extrinsic labour of the textual scholar and the intrinsic activity of the literary critic, McGann has done much to reformulate editorial activity itself as distributed and provisional, a matter of the informed selection of particular readings for particular purposes—that is, as a contingent critical act. But if by this we are all now textualists, where does that leave the peculiar textual activity of the editor (neither intending author nor openly participating critical reader), whose work traditionally lies in distinguishing among and reassembling documentary forms? By what criteria do we now measure a 'good' edition or recognize the value of its contribution—to the life of the literary work, to the community of readers, to the wider culture into which it inserts itself? Despite much recent talking up of its discipline from within the textual camp, little has been achieved in repairing the academic status of the editor or in recognizing the critical functioning of textual criticism as editing, in decline throughout the second half of the twentieth century.

When it comes to the practical business of text-editing and its wider reception within and outside the academy, despite lip-service to certain vaguely held standards which the critical edition is seen to embody, things have usually looked bleak. Much, if not most, editing is done piecemeal, with little reference to the theoretic dimensions of the task. Explanatory annotation, often dismissed by serious editors as an optional extra to the more important work of critical editing—the establishment of the text, its variants, and transmission history—is at the same time the kind of editing most in favour with literary critics, general readers, and commercially minded publishers, to all of whom it is perceived as adding value. Moreover, literary criticism, which for most of the twentieth century flourished as a distinct and more highly regarded (and rewarded) academic discipline than textual criticism, has persistently represented textual criticism/editing as the merely mechanical imposition of certain technical procedures—a form of drudgery as distinct from its own imaginative engagement with texts. Yet textual criticism has usually been practised only upon works of high cultural status—theological works and their literary equivalents, upon what have succinctly been termed our national scriptures. Perhaps that is why literary critics, when confronted with a textual critic, often react as though they are meeting the assistant who cleans the glass case in which the museum exhibit stands: they see the value of the exhibit but not the work that mediates it. The exceptions to this critical law are editions of Shakespeare, whose plays we never weary of re-editing, and whose editors we appear to esteem (if academic promotions are anything to go by); and readings of certain Romantic poets, whose own loudly declared purposes of revision—of writing and rewriting as a form of self-renewal or self-deferment—compel the literary scholar, willy-nilly, into the morass of textual consciousness, effectively blurring the distinction between the two levels of critical activity.

As a genre, the novel in particular has appeared less in need of editorial instruction than of literary critical elucidation and annotation: in part, this is a function of its bulk, which persuades us it is a less scrupulous form; in part, too, of its accessibility and robustness—its capacity to survive meaningfully in poor reprints of inexact texts. It is worth reminding ourselves that the biggest upturn in Jane Austen's critical reputation, at the end of the nineteenth century, was tied in to the large-scale marketing of textually unconsidered and even careless reprints of her novels. Clearly, Chapman thought an accurate novel text was both important and achievable, but he remains a member of an exclusive club, even among professional academics. The kind of labour he expended on the text of Austen's novels has been spent on very few others. His edition of 1923 may have initiated the serious critical and textual engagement with the novel in English, but since then there has been no full-scale reassessment of his editorial principles; no other single critical interpretation of Austen has gone so long unchallenged. It was not until the 1970s that other major nineteenth-century novelists, George Eliot and Charlotte and Emily Brontë, were paid the honour of a Clarendon edition; and the Clarendon edition of Dickens's novels, begun in 1966, remains, for a variety of reasons, unfinished. In neither Austen's nor Dickens's case have literary critics registered a disadvantage, nor has the cultural currency of their works among general readers appeared to suffer, either from the unsanctioned state of the Dickens text or the specific and out-dated determination of Austen's.

It is worth reminding ourselves of the expected shelf-life of the edited text of a literary work—far longer than that of any other critical study or opinion—because this fact alone threatens to distort any changes in critical practice. What has been slowest to shift in the market-place if not in the classroom is the assumption that at some fundamental level the textual vehicle which conducts the literary work can be freed of those fluctuations, biases, and manipulations which condition every other cultural engagement—that it can function as a permanent object of analysis. The self-identical text may now be an exploded theoretical commitment, but the economics of publishing tell a different story. As literary and cultural critics, after Barthes, Derrida, and the computer, we entertain ourselves with the fluid, dispersive, and 'textile' identity of text; but it remains that the texts we examine are largely fashioned according to text's other etymology, 'textus receptus', the received text of authority, with its implied identity to the tablets hewn from Mount Sinai.[24] OUP continue to repackage Chapman's 1923 Austen text, which fact of itself, and after more than three-quarters of a century, gives it a kind of lapidary authority. As Jo Modert shrewdly observed of the negotiations around 1990 for overhauling Chapman's 1932 edition of *Jane Austen's Letters*, 'the question whether the "expensive plates" should be replaced was once more raised—and this after more than fifty-five years of lucrative use!' 'Once more' because when Chapman himself had the opportunity to correct his own text, as he did from time to time as originals of some of the letters turned up, few corrections were made in the published texts because of expense. As Modert points out, Chapman's roles as Austen editor and Secretary to the Delegates at the Press were inevitably in conflict here.[25]

[24] As recent commentators are keen to point out, both textual and literary criticism since the second half of the twentieth century have drawn on theories which depend on variations in these two oppositional meanings of 'text' (one fixing and the other unfixing its range of reference), both of them dating from the word's appearance in English in the fourteenth century. For an extended discussion of this point, see D. C. Greetham, *Theories of the Text* (Oxford: Oxford University Press, 1999), 48 and 61–3.

[25] *Jane Austen's Manuscript Letters in Facsimile*, ed. Jo Modert (Carbondale and Edwardsville: Southern Illinois University Press, 1990), xxix.

A similar case can be made with regard to the text of the novels, where the so-called 'Second' and 'Third' editions of 1926 and 1933–4 are no more than new printings from the same first-edition plates, with additional notes and textual deliberations inserted at the end of each volume. Not until the 'Third revised edition' of 1965–6 were the variously accumulated addenda properly incorporated into the revised notes by Mary Lascelles, together with a few new notes of her own, but still the text proper is to all purposes unchanged from the first edition of 1923.[26] The appearance of a refreshed text, as the reset title-pages artfully declare, is a good marketing ploy. But, looked at another way, its very sameness from impression to impression is a strength, a sign of its permanence and universality as a source of reference and a cultural measure—of its institutional rather than its textual status. Chapman's is *the* Austen text. It is through the conjunction of economics and technology that Chapman's text gained its authority—our perception of this being in proportion to its stability, which it turns out is not quite the same with its accuracy or its validity in the light of changing critical valuations, his own included.

Post-structuralism responded early to the perceived danger of uniformity in interpretation by recognizing the constitutive agency of the reader: reading renews the life of reception by which the text circulates and lives; through reading, the text comes into full existence. By this, the text-as-reception habilitates variation, locating it apart from documentary forms in the performative acts of changeful readers within specific interpretative communities. No longer situated in some ideal space, text is to be thought of as phenomenological or eventful and socially constructed out of its readerly features. More recently, some materialist criticisms have argued for the reconnection of a broadly bibliographical approach to text and its critical interpretation. By this, the physical features of texts are not after all dispensable but compelling indicators of their editorial constructedness and paratextual variability—a valuable linking of production and reception.[27] Textual

[26] See the bibliographical information provided in Gilson E150, especially 299, where reference is made to 'memoranda in the Oxford University Press files dated September 1949' which show that there was then a plan for re-setting, 'but that it was thought "better to produce a photolitho edition from a good copy of the first edition rather than to re-set".'

[27] See, for example, recent debate around the issue of the materialist Shakespeare, in Margreta de Grazia and Peter Stallybrass, 'The Materiality of the Shakespearean Text', *Shakespeare Quarterly*, 44 (1993), 255–83. For de Grazia's earlier work on similar lines, see her 'The Essential Author and the Material Book', *Textual Practice*, 2 (1988), 69–86, and *Shakespeare Verbatim: The Reproduction of Authenticity and the 1790 Apparatus* (Oxford: Clarendon Press, 1991). De Grazia and Stallybrass's definition of materialism is contested in Graham Holderness, Bryan Loughrey, and Andrew Murphy, '"What's the Matter?": Shakespeare and

critics, too, have recovered and mapped a similar material ground in reconsidering the social and ontological value of the 'document', the body or medium of transmission which in any given instance carries the text of a work. The document witnesses to the (physical) constructedness of each instantiation of a text, the varying material conditions of its existence and transmission, and despite the term's revised currency in the virtual space of the electronic environment, it remains narrowly evidentiary in its range.[28] Under these renewed critical and bibliographical conditions it may be possible to reconceptualize documentary editing freed from the charges of hermeneutic censorship and élitism levelled with some justification against the New Bibliography—in particular, against its mistaken identification of cultural and temporal specificity with permanence. As textual and literary critics open up further the play of difference among the terms work, text, and document, rather than thinking of them as monolithic substitutions one for another, we shall uncover new ways of thinking about literary texts as environmentally sensitive semantic spaces whose normal condition is change. At the same time we may begin again to see the critical work of editing as Chapman and his colleagues did, as fundamental to the production and reading of literature.

Film as textual future

Irvine Welsh articulated one of the central dilemmas of the relationship between books and films when he suggested that 'you can't have a faithful interpretation of something; you can maybe have it in spirit, but it's going to change as it moves into a different medium.'[29] Welsh was addressing the distance between his 1993 novel *Trainspotting* and the 1996 film version, directed by Danny Boyle and scripted by John Hodge; specifically, he was

Textual Theory', *Textual Practice*, 9 (1995), 93–119; and from a different, less sympathetic perspective in Edward Pechter, 'Making Love to our Employment; Or, the Immateriality of Arguments about the Materiality of the Shakespearean Text', *Textual Practice*, 11 (1997), 51–67. Pechter's objection—that de Grazia and Stallybrass 'demonstrate merely that Shakespeare's texts *may* be studied as an aspect of the history of printing' (54)—suggests how fundamental (and contested) the shift is from author-intentional literary studies to a criticism grounded in the non-identity of literature's constructed forms.

[28] For an acute analysis of the category 'document' and its material and literary aspects, see Paul Eggert, 'The Work Unravelled', *TEXT*, 11 (1998), 41–60. Eggert lays the groundwork in an earlier piece, 'Document and Text: the "Life" of the Literary Work and the Capacities of Editing', *TEXT*, 7 (1994), 1–24.

[29] From an interview with Irvine Welsh, in John Hodge, *Trainspotting & Shallow Grave* (London: Faber & Faber, 1996), 118.

addressing the changes (in some cases from the bleakest realism to fantasy) entailed in the transference from word to screen of life from the heroin user's point of view. Both novel and film deal in relentless and complex detail with drugs, unemployment, poverty, and hopelessness in modern (1980s) Edinburgh; as the title of one chapter in the novel puts it 'Scotland Takes Drugs In Psychic Defence'. Fidelity of film to novel as of both to life in Thatcherite, post-industrial, northern Britain is a matter of finding equivalence in difference. Because the shock of language and the shock of image happen at different speeds, and because film leans ineluctably towards the specific, the cinematic equivalent of Welsh's near unbearable realism must on occasion be surrealism or fantasy.

For example, the film employs a recurrent tropical motif of escape, first used in the scene in the bookie's toilet where Renton goes to shit and then plunges into the pan to recover his suppositories. In the novel the nauseating detail is built up slowly and relentlessly as he lowers his arm into the brown, scummy water to find the suppositories and then anally reinsert them. But in transferring the scene to screen Renton's whole body dives through the filthy toilet bowl to emerge into a sunlit lagoon from the floor of which he picks up the suppositories 'which glow like luminous pearls'. The change is faithful because it registers, through transformation (the transformation of one medium into another) the vitality and defiance of the character, *his* capacity for resilience or transformation in the face of environmental despair.[30] Being true means doing it different.

A little reading in the right places—reports in film magazines and newspapers of interviews given by scriptwriters, producers, even novelists—uncovers the same reply, in almost the same phrases to the inevitable and tiresome question of authenticity. Tiresome because, one senses, purists in neither camp will be fooled by talk of faithful, disembodied spirits. So the producer Andrew Eaton, on *Jude* (Revolution Films, 1996), the film version of Hardy's novel *Jude the Obscure*, dubbed by the outraged Thomas Hardy Society 'Jude the Obscene' on account of its unauthorized explicit sex scenes. Eaton's defence was: 'There comes a point when being true to the spirit of the book is more important than reproducing the details exactly.'[31]

[30] Cf. Irvine Welsh, *Trainspotting* (1993; London: Vintage, 1999), 24–7; and Hodge, *Trainspotting*, 12–13. Welsh praised the film's use of fantasy as an equivalent to the novel's 'non-judgemental' portrayal of life and its refusal to see the characters simply as social victims (in his interview in Hodge, *Trainspotting*, 118–19).

[31] Interviewed by Peter Stanford, 'True to the Word or the Spirit?' *Sunday Times*, 22 September 1996, Review Section, 5.

In light of the battles of the twentieth century over the status of the edited literary text this filmic distinction between spirit and detail assumes particular significance; in both cases, being true involves scrutinizing the text in order to uncover the essence. The textual critic anatomizes text according to a Classical procedure by which its body disassembles into a mass of potentially wayward or misleading details each capable of betraying the spirit or essence of the work. Film adaptation as a topic of study or defence, and as the activity engaging screenplay writer and director, appears to require us to revive and then suppress the same binary opposition: first the transference of novel to film involves a distinction between form (expendable) and content (essential); then it requires the affirmation of filmic form as true to content. To some extent it is a question of finding material and technical correspondences between the two media; but it is also more profoundly to do with asserting film as an artful object in its own right, embodying an equivalent intention.

Whether practised by film-makers or text editors, as its defensive phrasing suggests, there is something residually anomalous about fidelity criticism, with its awareness of a set of limitations to representation (in the existence of a prior model) and its potentially incompatible belief in the possibility of separating an original from its representation. In film there is the further anomaly that since the only real measure of faithfulness is subjective (does this audio-visualization of the novel coincide with my conceptual image of it as a reader?), the same adaptation can appear both faithful and unfaithful. As Brian McFarlane has argued from the diverse critical reception of Peter Bogdanovich's 1974 film of Henry James's *Daisy Miller* (1878): 'The fact that one writer finds "boringly faithful" a film which another sees as having only "a tenuous relation" to the original while yet another finds it "too faithful" suggests that there is no clear consensus about what "faithful" means in this discourse. Faithful to what?' And he concludes that fidelity 'cannot profitably be used as an evaluative criterion; it can be no more than a descriptive term to designate loosely a certain kind of adaptation.'[32] Though McFarlane does not take the discussion in this direction, it also seems reasonable to infer from the kinds of production values regularly invoked in adducing fidelity (among which are authentic period detail and use of the

[32] Brian McFarlane, *Novel To Film: An Introduction to the Theory of Adaptation* (Oxford: Clarendon Press, 1996), 165–6. Though fidelity may be a tired concept, adaptation has long been a key issue in cinema studies. See, for example, George Bluestone, *Novels into Film* (1957; Baltimore and London: Johns Hopkins University Press, 2003); Dudley Andrew, *Concepts in Film Theory* (Oxford and New York: Oxford University Press, 1984); and Kamilla Elliott, *Rethinking the Novel/Film Debate* (Cambridge: Cambridge University Press, 2003).

words of the original text) that, as with editorial apparatus and publisher's packaging, indicators of print text's classic credentials, film too can compete for institutional status and that this is bound up with its capacity to rise above simple mass appeal. The artful literary adaptation adds cultural and even national value to cinema. As Erica Sheen suggests, 'Fidelity criticism is perhaps most appropriately seen as a rhetoric of possession.'[33]

How is a film unlike a novel; more particularly, how is a film unlike a Jane Austen novel? In moving from novel to film how is an equivalent story told by means of non-equivalent codes? And, given their different codes, how can film, respecting the novel's difference, also occupy the same space in its own structural terms? Austen's novels are largely plotless (and film relishes action); Austen's text displays a weak dependence on metaphor and figurative language (and film's power lies in the manipulation of image and imagery); Austen's mature art (and, risky word, her 'essence') is a sophisticated aural figuration in which, through free indirect discourse, voice is laid on voice to produce critical (specifically, ironic) connotative effects, and the blurring of character with character and narrator, which are almost impossible to achieve in film whose aural effects, however sophisticated, are subordinated to an immense visual rhetoric. The camera's ability to operate between subjective viewpoint and distance can achieve something, as can other devices of juxtaposition or ironic editing (jump cuts and montage) and voice-over; but the reliance of Douglas McGrath's feature film *Emma* (Columbia/Miramax, 1996) on the heroine apparently addressing herself in a mirror, or writing in her very un-Austenian diary (used also in Patricia Rozema's feature film *Mansfield Park* (BBC/Miramax, 1999)), and elsewhere the conversion of indirect discourse into direct conversation (between Emma and Mrs Weston), appear clumsily reductive or inapposite by comparison with the novel's subtler ambiguities of voicing. Part of the problem is that the effects we see are always more specific than those we hear and, on occasion, only half hear. The screen absorbs the viewer into an artfully homogenized representation in which meaning is delivered as spectacle more swiftly than words absorb the reader into the illusion of a total environment—though words, especially heightened, literary words, can do this too, but at a slower pace.

On the other side of the argument, the side that considers how a novel is like a film, Paula Byrne has noted how '[t]he building bricks of Austen's novels were also dramatic scenes. This is one reason why they adapt so well to

[33] 'Introduction', *The Classic Novel: From Page to Screen*, ed. Robert Giddings and Erica Sheen (Manchester: Manchester University Press, 2000), 3.

film representation.' Byrne applauds the 'fine propriety' by which 'a new generation has been brought to Austen via the screen', arguing that her novels 'have returned full circle to their origins.'[34] The obvious dramatic qualities of Austen's art have ensured her regular adaptation from the late nineteenth century:[35] encounters and incidents structured as scenes in a play (the opening of *Pride and Prejudice*, the action in the grounds of Sotherton in *Mansfield Park*), brisk dialogue, strong characterization (including excellent comic cameos), a reliance on dramatic entrances and exits (Sir Thomas Bertram's return from Antigua), her fine use of stage business (Frank Churchill fiddling with Mrs Bates's spectacles). It is interesting to note that almost all these devices were employed in the first, discarded ending to *Persuasion*, and that Nick Dear adapts some of Austen's abandoned detail in his 1995 screenplay for the BBC/WGBH telefilm: for example, the awkward conversation between Anne Elliot and Captain Wentworth (transposed on film to an anteroom to the public Pump Room, Bath), in which is communicated Admiral Croft's offer to relinquish his lease on Kellynch Hall in the event of a marriage between Anne and Mr Elliot.[36]

Given the differences between word and image, one might reasonably assume that in the truthfulness business fidelity to detail is more achievable than fidelity to spirit, and that finding equivalents in film for the emotional relationships which form the core of a novel will involve a more momentous transformation than getting right period niceties like costume, hairdos, or modes of transport, all of which the camera dwells on with loving attention. But detail can prove unexpectedly faithless. For James Edward Austen-Leigh, Austen's early biographer, looking back from his mid-Victorian plenty, his aunt's era seemed embarrassingly empty of consumer comforts; so much so that he felt he must apologize for the meanness of her domestic life, its absence of detail:

> At that time the dinner-table presented a far less splendid appearance than it does now... silver forks had not come into general use: while the broad rounded end of the knives indicated the substitute generally used instead of them... a still greater difference would be found in the furniture of the rooms, which would appear to us lamentably scanty. There was a general deficiency of carpeting in sitting-rooms,

[34] Paula Byrne, *Jane Austen and the Theatre* (London and New York: Hambledon, 2002), xii–xiii.

[35] Gilson, Section H, lists dramatic adaptations of the novels of which a published text survives from 1895.

[36] *The Manuscript Chapters of Persuasion*, 12–14; and Nick Dear, *Persuasion by Jane Austen, a Screenplay* (London: Methuen, 1996), 80–1. Dear incorporates phrases as well as the general sense from the conversation in Austen's discarded ending.

bedrooms, and passages ... There would often be but one sofa in the house, and that a stiff, angular, uncomfortable article ... But perhaps we should be most struck with the total absence of those elegant little articles which now embellish and encumber our drawing-room tables ...[37]

By contrast MGM's 1940 feature film of *Pride and Prejudice* (screenplay by Aldous Huxley and Jane Murfin) notoriously robed the Bennet girls (Greer Garson's Elizabeth Bennet and Maureen O'Sullivan's Jane Bennet) in antebellum crinolines and enclosed the production within a series of consciously artificial sets (stuffed drawing rooms and lush gardens), while the visual excess which characterizes many of the 1990s adaptations transforms the novels into embodiments of the Prince Regent's well-documented exuberant materialism. In both cases, the filmic need to make a visually comprehensible psychology renders settings enhanced carriers of meaning in which detail seduces as it proliferates.

The heritage movie genre, in particular, within which classic novels tend to find their filmic accommodation, produces sumptuous affairs drenched with material significance: not just glamorous costumes but grand sets crammed indoors with priceless art objects and antique furniture, and out-of-doors painstaking period-styled tableaux. One might see this visual packaging as equivalent to the absorption or branding of literary texts as high cultural objects, through annotation and inclusion in 'classic series' (Oxford English Texts, Penguin Classics), the value added by editors and publishing houses, different only in the film text's tighter coherence of meaning and vision: the heritage film is overtly entering the cultural space occupied previously by the up-market packaging of the literary text. In her preliminary notes to the screenplay of *Sense and Sensibility* Emma Thompson parades what Robert Giddings and Keith Selby have labelled the tradition in Jane Austen adaptations 'of Quality Street-National Trust village-Empire line'. She enthuses indiscriminately over the general cultural prestige of the heritage properties and houses used on set: 'two of them ... belong to the National Trust, and in another, the World War II Normandy invasion ... was planned.'[38] Given the early importance of literary adaptation to cinema, and the positioning of the literary classic within the heritage market, it is a nice coincidence that

[37] *Memoir*, 30–1.

[38] Robert Giddings and Keith Selby, *The Classic Serial on Television and Radio* (Basingstoke and New York: Palgrave, 2001), 102; Emma Thompson is cited in Jocelyn Harris, '"Such a transformation!": Translation, Imitation, and Intertextuality in Jane Austen on Screen', in *Jane Austen On Screen*, ed. Gina Macdonald and Andrew F. Macdonald (Cambridge: Cambridge University Press, 2003), 46.

the National Trust and the first public film screenings both celebrated their centenary in 1995, the year the Thompson/Ang Lee (Columbia/Mirage) feature film *Sense and Sensibility* was released.[39]

If MGM's sentimental vision of an English Victorian family appears to owe something to the novel's 'Cranfordization' by late nineteenth-century illustrators (and even more to mid-century America's middle-class expectations of feminine comfort and domesticity), the high production values of 1990s adaptations equated the Austen novel's classic status with other heritage-themed consumer make-overs of our late capitalist fantasy. Accordingly, settings became more spectacular: balls grew grander, dinner tables groaned, houses became more stately. The exterior of the house used as Hartfield in background shots of McGrath's *Emma* is huge, scarcely conceivable as the novel's 'comfortable home' which 'in spite of its separate lawn and shrubberies and name, did really belong [to the village of Highbury]'; while the wretched family of villagers to whom Emma and Harriet administer soup are tastefully bedecked in colour-coordinated designer 'rags'. A narrative statement in *Pride and Prejudice* makes it clear that Pemberley is not to be equated with Chatsworth; nevertheless, a British film version currently in production will use Chatsworth, ancestral home of the Dukes of Devonshire, for Mr Darcy's estate; but we have yet to see an Austen heroine authentically eating peas from her knife in a meagrely furnished room in accordance with Austen-Leigh's memory of how things were among the lesser gentry at the start of the nineteenth century.

The point is that period magnificence is a scarcely contestable assumption of the conjoined heritage discourse and visual tyranny which now shape classic film adaptations as they once shaped classic literary texts. Thanks to the meticulous labours of archival researchers and designers, even period squalor exhibits a lavish material excess. Authentic detail in costume, furnishing, setting is thus saturated in general consumerist/voyeurist significance rather than expressing any specific act of faithfulness. As Erica Sheen wittily put it in considering the mid-1990s' spate of Austen adaptations, 'the material resources of one representational system [film] can offer, as Darcy can offer Lizzy, to support a text in more than the style to which it has been accus-

[39] Andrew Higson, 'The Heritage Film and British Cinema', in *Dissolving Views: Key Writings on British Cinema*, ed. Andrew Higson (London and New York: Cassell, 1996), 236, notes the connection between cinema and the National Trust as well as cinema's early co-option into the heritage business. The film of *Trainspotting*, released within weeks of *Sense and Sensibility*, plays out the dark implications of the same turn-of-the-century fascination with heritage, as at least one reviewer noted at the time. See Martin Wroe, 'Hard Drugs and Heroine Addiction', *Observer*, 10 March 1996, 13.

tomed'; that is to say, film adaptation absorbs the novel-text into 'a semiotic system with a higher disposable income'.[40]

As in the discipline of editing, so in film, detail thus can sometimes carry a greater freight of significance than 'spirit' or 'essence'. A visual checklist, assembled like Chapman's researches into period archives for appropriate plates—'Oxford Street from Stratford Place. From a print in the Crace Collection (British Museum)' (facing page 1 of *Sense and Sensibility*); 'Ball Dress. From Ackermann's *Repository of Arts*, October 1816' (frontispiece to *Emma*)—detail in film delivers authenticity, not so much to the author as to the age in which she lived and which it is presumed she recorded with equal meticulousness. Rather like book illustration, which throughout the nineteenth century fulfilled the function later usurped by textual annotation, period detail in film prioritizes or amplifies some elements over others, and directs us towards the significance we discover in the work as a whole.[41] But more hazardously than this, like annotation run riot, visual detail risks literalizing and pre-empting effects which in the novel take much longer to unfold or are more subtly nuanced for not being seen or fully textualized. The early scene in McGrath's *Emma* where Emma and Mr Knightley practise their archery on a splendid lawn by a lake is not so much troublesome because it does not occur in the novel: as authentic period detail it is as contextually appropriate as Chapman's illustrative plates; while its embodiment of a visual allusion to a similar scene in the 1940 MGM *Pride and Prejudice* gives it enhanced film-textual authority. The problem is rather that its visual knowingness delivers too quickly and simply (in an arrow's flight) what it takes a reading of the whole novel, with its twists and turns, to know with the same certainty, that cupid's match is between these two contestants. Visually, it is both splendid and crude.

By contrast, the invention of a detail in the Dear/Michell *Persuasion* has the opposite effect of disclosing Anne Elliot's suppressed inner life by alternative, visual means. In a film scene which has no original in the novel, Anne is

[40] Erica Sheen, 'Where the Garment Gapes': Faithfulness and Promiscuity in the 1995 BBC *Pride and Prejudice*', in *The Classic Novel: From Page to Screen*, ed. Giddings and Sheen, 17; Sam Leith, 'Modern Men Make the Search for Mr Darcy a Struggle', *Daily Telegraph*, 12 June 2004, points out that the British company Working Title, in production with a film of *Pride and Prejudice*, will use Chatsworth for Pemberley. It could be argued that the inflation of heritage values in film adaptations of the classics is not dissimilar in intention to the editorial packaging by R. W. Chapman of the Clarendon Austen text; the difference lies in the visual intensity of film as a medium. For a defence of 'heritage' see Raphael Samuel, 'Heritage-baiting', *Theatres of Memory*, Vol. 1 (London: Verso, 1994), 259–73.

[41] The link between nineteenth-century book illustration and film is explored in Kamilla Elliott, *Rethinking the Novel/Film Debate*, 31–76.

26. Emma (Gwyneth Paltrow) watches as Mr Knightley (Jeremy Northam) engages in target practice with bow and arrow, in Douglas McGrath's *Emma*, a 1996 Miramax Films release.
EMMO19AC MATCHMAKER/MIRAMAX/THE KOBAL COLLECTION

discovered walking by daylight through the rooms of Kellynch Hall as servants around her cover the furniture in white dustsheets in preparation for the closing of the house. In the screenplay, the direction reads: 'The linen billows around Anne. It's a sad picture, as if the deceased house is being wrapped in a shroud. On and on it goes: an ocean of white linen.' In the next scene, now lit by candle-light, Anne is in a store-room packing up her few personal possessions. She comes across an eight-year-old copy of the *Navy List* and in its pages 'a letter folded up into a paper boat', which she quickly tucks out of sight. Not only are these scenes and details invented, a literal-minded reader might argue that since the house is to be immediately inhabited by Sir Walter's tenants, the Crofts, such shrouding of furniture is unnecessary. But, transferred to film as a sequence of silent images, the billowing linen, Anne also dressed (shrouded?) in white, and the letter-boat, hidden inside the *Navy List*, are potent associative testimony to what the narrative divulges more slowly, by inner voicing and the agony of private recall. These scenes effectively sketch a visual shorthand which is also a structural equivalent for the narrative's temporal unfolding of the personal sorrow of Anne's inner life.

27. Elizabeth Bennet (Greer Garson) shows her skill at archery, assisted by Mr Darcy (Laurence Olivier) and watched by Miss Bingley (Frieda Inescort) in *Pride and Prejudice*, MGM, 1940. PRIOO6AP MGM / THE KOBAL COLLECTION.

As Anne conceals the letter-boat, a close-up shows her face looking out of the shot, and the voice of Lady Russell, articulating what Anne cannot, provides a lead-in to the next sequence: 'For eight years you have been too little from home, too little seen. And your spirits have never been high since your... disappointment.' When in a later scene in Anne's presence Admiral Croft makes a paper boat to entertain the Musgrove boys the detail revives our understanding that Anne has an unresolved past. These visual effects work because they manage to be both eloquent and reticent: eloquent of sorrow and life suspended; yet reticent as to its specific cause. As such they amplify the inner life by external means rather than using a strong visual trope to obliterate its necessity.[42]

[42] Dear, *Persuasion... a Screenplay*, 10–11 and 23; and see Wiltshire, *Recreating Jane Austen*, 91–6, for a more sustained reading of the same scenes.

Perhaps the most obviously problematic ingredient in the transference of Austen novel to film is the visualization of the leading romantic males, because in this is buried the rich novelistic ambivalence over their ultimate significance (teasingly located somewhere between mere detail and essential ingredient) in the heroine's maturation and the wider depiction of her relations with society. By contrast, the film versions consistently invert the novels' assumptions, and in doing so they jettison a whole classificatory system of complex and, on occasion, manipulative social relations between women and of gender imbalances between potential lovers: young woman/older man; male pedagogue/female pupil; controlled, even repressed male/wayward female.[43] In place of emotional and physical restraint, the consequences of the polite domestic boundaries within which their novelistic characters are drawn, the films endow their male protagonists with both physical and emotional expressiveness. Whole scenes were added to the Andrew Davies/Simon Langton 1995 BBC miniseries *Pride and Prejudice* to enhance Darcy's (Colin Firth's) barely restrained eroticism: he plays billiards, fences, and, memorably, swims. The Thompson/Lee *Sense and Sensibility* excavates the minor (in terms of age and textual appearance) Dashwood sister Margaret from Austen's novel as a foil for Hugh Grant's sympathetically comic, though sartorially buttoned-up Edward Ferrars; while Colonel Brandon's unsavoury novelistic reserve is transformed into a smouldering mix of Byronic adventure and sexual mystery, in which costume again exerts significant impact.

Where in the novels the modern reader finds in the hero someone placed awkwardly between a vacuum and a moral ideal, in the films the male protagonist's attractions are overspecified, and in particular his availability for pleasure. The effect of the difference is a sign of how large the marriage plot (or rather the sex plot)[44] looms in the cinematic contract with the viewer, which in turn explains why Austen's hurried, even embarrassed, narrative resolutions do not translate into effective film representation. For example, in reading *Emma* we can believe that the youthful, high-spirited Emma does not

[43] Hollywood in particular seems loathe to confront the often unpleasant inequalities of Austenian female friendship, like those portrayed in *Emma*. In McGrath's *Emma*, that between Emma Woodhouse (Gwyneth Paltrow) and Harriet Smith (Toni Collette) is levelled into an improbable and silly cosiness, a pair of empty-headed chums who enjoy hanging out together.

[44] Summing up the 'new approach to Jane Austen' as evidenced by screen adaptations of the 1990s, Giddings and Selby lay emphasis on the '*Pride and Prejudice* Factor' or what Sue Birtwistle, producer of the 1995 Davies screenplay, labelled the appeal of sex and money: 'When Darcy emerges from his swim in his wet shirt the fantasy is complete: sex and money made easy and wrapped in the respectable cloak of a classic. This was a new phenomenon.' (Giddings and Selby, *The Classic Serial on Television and Radio*, 122.)

recognize the older, staid Mr Knightley as lover until the substitute match-making plot (finding a husband for Harriet) is almost played out; in watching the film, whose romantic appeal is bound to the visual, even athletic, compatibility of hero and heroine, this knowledge cannot be suppressed beyond the opening frames because it is invisible neither to Emma nor the viewer. It is not only the viewer who is seduced by the look of the film.[45]

A comparable forestalling occurs in Patricia Rozema's *Mansfield Park*, where Fanny Price's complex emotional dysfunctionality (specifically, her slow growth to physical attractiveness and limited sociability), figured in the novel by her passivity and invisibility, are abolished by the 'look of the camera' and the obvious visual pleasure that both Edmund Bertram and Henry Crawford early take in her appearance and arch energy. But Rozema has clearly absorbed the lessons of feminist film criticism as of other recent influential academic discourses. Her answer to the implied simplification is to revision the core of the novel, transforming the pathological heroine into the autobiographical heroine. In a sense, this is yet another reading of Austen refracted through a reading of Charlotte Brontë. Austen-Leigh and Catherine Hubback had both turned to Brontë for critical purchase on their aunt's reticent materials; the Thompson/Lee *Sense and Sensibility* openly flirted with Brontë-derived visual imagery to enhance the appeal of Willoughby and Colonel Brandon (for example, in the Gothic accessory of the rearing horse).[46] Now in Rozema's script an elaborate intertextual mixing of mature Austen novel with juvenilia, passages from *Northanger Abbey*, her letters to Cassandra, and interpretations derived from the recent spate of biographies, and especially David Nokes's revisionist study, discloses an outspoken and anarchic Fanny Price who is Jane Austen's Jane Eyre. Fanny is the novelist's younger, scribbling self, encouraged in her writing of the juvenilia by Edmund Bertram and heard inventing the famous definition of history

[45] Debate around the gaze or exchange of looks which takes place in cinema, as well as the late entry of the female spectator into such arguments, is of great importance in understanding the visual pleasure within film and for the viewer. As in so many other instances, the filmic construction of relationships within the domestic sphere (the so-called women's film) must find different but equivalent means to convey the complex distribution of power invested in Austen's domestic environments. The double work done by female spectatorship, theorized by Laura Mulvey, Teresa de Lauretis, and E. Ann Kaplan is pertinent here, though so far little invoked by critics of film adaptations of Austen. See, for example, Mulvey's classic article, 'Visual Pleasure and Narrative Cinema' (1975), repr. in *Visual and Other Pleasures* (Basingstoke: Macmillan, 1989); de Lauretis, *Alice Doesn't: Feminism, Semiotics, Cinema* (Basingstoke: Macmillan, 1984); and Kaplan, *Looking for the Other: Feminism, Film, and the Imperial Gaze* (London and New York: Routledge, 1997).

[46] See Penny Gay, '*Sense and Sensibility* in a Postfeminist World: Sisterhood is still Powerful', in *Jane Austen On Screen*, 90–110.

from *Northanger Abbey*, Chapter 14 ('the men all so good for nothing, and hardly any women at all'). Later, in her filmic acceptance of Henry Crawford's marriage proposal, only to withdraw it the next day, she is Austen accepting Harris Bigg-Wither and the lure of material improvement.

As a means of developing an alternative but equivalent interiority for Austen's heroine, Rozema's large-scale colonization and reattribution of Austen's other writings is ingenious; the film's embodiment of Fanny's hidden life as author becomes in consequence an artistically expressive rather than a morbidly repressive device, and Fanny herself gains both authority and sympathy, something Austen's Fanny rarely achieves. It also shows how much can be done in film as in text-editing by attending to the possibilities inherent in a single phrase: in this case, Austen's uniquely attributive words 'My Fanny'.[47] As John Wiltshire suggests, Rozema's film is more than an adaptation, it 'reinvents' the novel.[48] By collapsing *Mansfield Park* so thoroughly into Austen's other writings and, more particularly, into the critical perspectives of their late twentieth-century post-feminist and post-colonial readings, Rozema has produced a romancing or anthology of 'Austen' for the new century. It is a dizzying feat whereby Austen's early anarchic authorial personality, conjured in film through Fanny's writing, is made to endorse the compelling political correctness of the reading of her novels within the late twentieth-century liberal academy.

But its ambition to combine the visual seductiveness of film's mass-market appeal with the latest and apparently most radical academic challenge to Austen's wholesome conservative status (specifically, the striving to represent filmically the basis of the Bertrams' wealth in slavery in Antigua) has the odd effect of making the production implode. Part of the problem is that Fanny Price's feisty makeover works against the shocking representation of Sir Thomas Bertram as sadist, just as the depiction of Mansfield Park itself (in the novel 'a spacious modern-built house') as a draughty, scarcely inhabited, Gothic ruin undermines the wider critique of colonial rapaciousness. In each case, filmic intervention exposes as a series of crude and confusing contrasts what the novel quietly (and disturbingly) contains. What is dysfunctional in the *society* of Austen's novel becomes in Rozema's adaptation merely a kind of *generic* disruption—rather like reading a set of annotations to the novel without the continuities of register and narrative provided by the novel itself.

[47] Austen uses the phrase only once, as the opening words of the second paragraph of the final chapter of *Mansfield Park*.

[48] Wiltshire, *Recreating Jane Austen*, 135.

28. The Dashwood women in a domestic scene which draws some of its charm from appearing also to recreate the all-female Chawton household of the Austens, from the Thompson/Lee *Sense and Sensibility*, Mirage/Columbia, 1995.
SEN023 BZ COLUMBIA / THE KOBAL COLLECTION

An ambitious failure in artistic terms, the film was, unsurprisingly, also a failure at the box office.[49]

When Jane Austen chose the novel as her medium the beginnings of a mass book culture witnessed a battle over the nature and limits of reading itself. In some quarters, the circulating library and its chief commodity, the novel, were heralded as inaugurating a new democratization of knowledge, driven by popular market forces rather than by élite ideological purposes. To its advocates, the novel appeared to celebrate the potential of subjective experience and therefore to challenge centralized authority. To its detractors, it represented the idle absorption of pre-packaged experience; it required less effort to read novels than other literary forms, and their totalizing perspectives deprived the reader of external points of view on their practices. Consolidating their mass

[49] 'Before it dropped off *Variety*'s listings in the issue of March 13–19, 2000 (11), it had last been shown to gross 4.68 million dollars in fourteen weeks—a far cry from Ang Lee's *Sense and Sensibility*, starring Emma Thompson, which grossed well over 100 million dollars', Jan Fergus, 'Two *Mansfield Parks*: Purist and Postmodern', in *Jane Austen On Screen*, 88.

appeal, the majority of novels were financed through a few powerful borrowing and vending outlets whose distributive mechanisms were assumed, by critics and enthusiasts alike, to simulate the circulatory systems of other aspects of society and human existence—the circulation of money through the public sector; of blood through the body; and, thanks to the replicatory power of the printing press, 'the moving phantasms of one man's delirium' through 'the barrenness of an hundred other brains'. To critics like Coleridge, popular novels marked the ascendancy of entertainment over instruction, a dangerously passive consumption of experience.[50]

Throughout Austen's writing career two men, William Lane and his successor, A. K. Newman, held a Hollywood-like grip on the novel's fortunes. Lane's success was based on three interrelated enterprises which together allowed him to control the market for three decades: the Minerva Library, the Minerva Press, and his activities as a commissioning publisher. From 1800 to 1829, Minerva held a dominant market share (estimated at 23 per cent) in new novel titles, far outstripping other primary fiction publishers. Lane was an acute businessman, switching early in life from poultry to books; controlling both production and distribution from his base in London's Leadenhall Street, he made a huge fortune. He had grasped that in an under-capitalized industry fiction was a lucrative product for which the fashion-conscious and the pleasure-seeking would pay highly; but that being an essentially ephemeral commodity, profit lay in circulation figures rather than in sales alone. He proceeded to saturate the market, offering for sale from his 'General Warehouse and Universal Repository of Literature' complete libraries, ranging from a hundred to ten thousand volumes, to jewellers, perfumers, tobacconists, purveyors of patent medicines, and haberdashers eager to extend their leisure-directed trades into book-lending; and he provided advice on how to set up in the lending business. It was thanks to Lane's entrepreneurial drive that commercial libraries, in existence in some urban centres since the early eighteenth century, penetrated to lesser provincial towns; by 1801 there were thought to be a thousand such libraries in England.[51]

Where Lane's symbiotic formula succeeded, its long-term effect on the market for and reputation of fiction is more debatable. The wholesale trade in

[50] Samuel Taylor Coleridge, *Biographia Literaria; or, Biographical Sketches of My Literary Life and Opinions*, ed. James Engell and W. Jackson Bate (1817; 2 vols., London: Routledge and Kegan Paul, 1983), i. 48–9; cf. H[ugh] Murray, *Morality of Fiction; or, An Inquiry into the Tendency of Ficitious Narratives, with Observations on Some of the Most Eminent* (Edinburgh: A. Constable and Co. and J. Anderson, 1805), 40.

[51] Garside *et al.*, *The English Novel 1770–1829*, ii. 83–6; and *Monthly Magazine*, 11 (1801), 238.

complete fiction libraries highlights the particular relationship to the material form of its manufacture which dogged the critical fortunes of the novel throughout the nineteenth century; after Lane, Charles Edward Mudie, who dominated the circulating library trade through the Victorian period, continued to influence by sheer economic clout the way the novel developed. The Minerva novel itself quickly assumed a corporate style with recognizable bibliographic codes or paratextual features which served both as self-advertisement and to anticipate how it would be read—to pre-engage the reader sensationally. Branding by layout and typographic design were not new: publishers engaged in the classic reprint trade were doing much the same to make recognizable commodities. But in Lane's productions, such devices as well-rehearsed formulaic titles and lurid frontispiece engravings displaying frenzied villains and swooning, scantily clad heroines—at a time when illustration was still a rarity in fiction—slipped over into self-parody even as they fuelled demand. His marketing strategies openly encouraged the identification of the formula-novel with women as authors and readers (a prospectus of 1798 lists ten 'particular and favourite Authors', all women)—the 'prolific ladies of the Minerva Press', as the *Critical Review* dubbed them in April 1808—and with a consumer-oriented practice. His methods included elaborate newspaper promotions of forthcoming titles, fly-leaf advertisements of future novels in published books, and even the puffing of the Minerva Press and its works in the text proper; all strategies which earned the charge of cynical trading.[52]

Austen wrote her novels as a form of critical engagement—with society and social relations but also with the genre itself. As novelist she took up a position from which to explore and expose opposing tendencies: roughly, the novelistic and the real. In the process she recalibrated the novel to the real as she saw it, at the same time questioning the basis in human psychology of any sustainable reality, of any permanent escape from romance and illusionment. Her spare conversational narratives read like nothing her contemporaries produced. They represent her ambition to take the novel in a new direction; but this does not mean that she was not anxious for immediate success and approval nor that she underrated the appeal of more sensational fiction. Instead, we see her attempting to moderate the power of popular fiction by containing it critically within her own quieter art. Her novels are written as elaborate patterns of difference and opposition in which the discordant

[52] Blakey, *The Minerva Press*, 91–3, 67, and 96–105.

elements vitally contribute to each other's construction, with the result that meaning never finally settles but remains at play across a range of possibilities.

In *Mansfield Park*, for example, Fanny Price exists as contrast to, and also finds her behaviour implicated in the kind of moral judgement made against, her cousin Maria Bertram, the passionate heroine of a far different romance. When Fanny refuses Henry Crawford's offer of marriage, her uncle Sir Thomas Bertram describes her conduct as 'wilful and perverse', imbued with 'that independence of spirit, which prevails so much in modern days'. In the novel and in the context of Fanny's habitual acquiesence, the charge appears unjust—more apt as anticipatory verdict on Maria's elopement with Henry. Nevertheless, it provides a clue to the way in which the life of the mind is so powerfully excavated in Austen's mature characters that it assumes an alternative existence. Beneath her modesty, Fanny Price is indeed as 'wilful and perverse' as the adulterous Maria, after her fashion, is pathetically conformist. If Austen's concentration on the everyday, in contrast to what Wordsworth called the fashion for 'frantic novels',[53] challenged the form to become a more complex critical medium for our romantic imaginings, it did so by driving those longings deeper (in psychological and structural terms) into the fabric of her texts. Her stories and her style of telling them are suggestive compounds of elements identified and denied, or as W. J. Harvey put it in a mid-twentieth-century essay on *Emma*: the written novel contains its unwritten twin whose shape is known only by the shadow it casts.'[54] By contrast, in its continuous supply of visual signals, cinema appears hypertrophically romantic; therefore, it might be argued, bound to flatten romance's subtle gradations and to dissolve any implied opposition to the mass genre whose devices Austen sought both to suppress and enlist.

A recent conceit for signalling film's intention to keep faith with the literary work is the use of the author's name in possessive relation to the film's title, or more accurately as the lead element in the title: Baz Luhrmann's *William Shakespeare's Romeo + Juliet* (1996), Kenneth Branagh's *Mary Shelley's Frankenstein* (1994), Andrew Davies's *Jane Austen's Emma* (1996), a branding device which vouches for authenticity even as it announces a more complicated system of ownership. A comparable declaration would be a Clarendon Press title-page on which R. W. Chapman authors Jane Austen in the same

[53] 'Preface' to *Lyrical Ballads* (1800), in *The Prose Works of William Wordsworth*, ed. W. J. B. Owen and Jane Worthington Smyser, 3 vols. (Oxford: Clarendon Press, 1974), i. 128.

[54] W. J. Harvey, 'The Plot of *Emma*', *Essays in Criticism*, 17 (1967), 55.

space as she vouches for his version of her text. In the afterlife of the film there is a further layer to be imposed, in the form of the spin-off book, the tie-in novel, which reaches the reader's hand and roused expectations as Jane Austen's Andrew Davies's *Jane Austen's Emma*. Tie-in sales of film-novels provide statistical data for the popularity of the film and not critical information about the appeal of the novel; and if in these circumstances the novel, film's diffuse other, pleases it may well be because it does not betray its filmic pre-text. In an earlier figuring of the relationship, favoured in 1940s and 1950s adaptations, the film opens with a shot of the open book, which is subsequently dissolved or wiped, gesturing towards a material rather than a moral transference of property in the text. In David Lean's *Great Expectations* (1946), for example, the shot of the novel's opening paragraph is accompanied by John Mills's adult Pip reading its words in a formal voice-over before a rising wind parodically animates the pages and renders them illegible, effectively signifying the novel's displacement by a more 'dynamic animation'.[55] In the books displayed as visual detail in film (for example, the heavy annotative uses to which volumes of poetry are put in the Thompson/Lee *Sense and Sensibility*) the incarnational form of the original text functions as just another heritage trapping.

The book wiped by the film and the author presiding over or initiating her work's transmogrification are both powerful instances of the adversarial complicity which persists in descriptions of the alliance between novel and film. The relationship was early imagined as vampiric, by which film both consumes and brings to life (destroys, inhabits, and reanimates) the novel. Virginia Woolf's famous dismissal of the film-novel coruscates with élitist scorn for and moral judgement of a medium whose conventions she levels with its most popular manifestation, the horror movie:

All the famous novels of the world with their well known characters and their famous scenes only asked to be put on the films. What could be easier, what could be simpler? The cinema fell upon its prey with immense rapacity and to this moment largely subsists upon the body of its unfortunate victim. But the results have been disastrous to both. The alliance is unnatural. Eye and brain are torn asunder ruthlessly as they try vainly to work in couples.[56]

[55] Elliott, *Rethinking the Novel/Film Debate*, 130. In some important ways, too, both devices figure the loosening of copyright which has supported the concept of authorship within modern literary culture and which film as a network of production exposes as problematic.

[56] Virginia Woolf, 'The Cinema' (1926), in *The Essays of Virginia Woolf*, 4, ed. McNeillie, 349–50.

Fifty years later, the Frankensteinian violation enacted in the process of adaptation was foregrounded in Anthony Burgess's cynical view that 'Every best-selling novel *has* to be turned into a film, the assumption being that the book itself whets an appetite for the true fulfilment—the verbal shadow turned into light, the word made flesh.'[57]

In the case of Austen's novels the shadowing of the precursor text which must constitute a significant part of the activity of scriptwriter and film-maker has led to an inevitable inversion of its emphases and values, among which is a raised visual awareness which also implies a more complete romantic illusion or the hypertrophic emancipation of its critically suppressed other. The different conditions of production of novel and film of course employ different signifying systems, and one cannot simply translate one system of signs (verbal) into another (visual) without confronting the implications of this difference. Woolf s complaint that cinema severs eye from brain contains the charge that film appeals too directly and simply to the emotions rather than engaging the intellect; it receives more rigorous formulation in George Bluestone's well-rehearsed formalist enquiry into the difference between 'perceptual knowledge' and 'conceptual imaging', a difference in kind, but 'not necessarily... in strength'. It is a difference which nevertheless accounts for a great deal: in a film spoken dialogue is attached to an image, and in the fusion of the two 'seeing... remains primary';[58] we continue to see when we cannot hear. In an Austen novel, especially in her mature works, the reverse is truer, and it makes a critical difference.

In a recent essay, Mary Favret sees issues of fidelity in the classic film-novel as dynamically infused with both 'animation and mortality'. Locating two 1995 Austen adaptations, the Thompson/Lee *Sense and Sensibility* and Dear/Michell *Persuasion*, within a reading of contemporary culture, with its 'postmodern appetite for' the styles and fashions of a dead past, she neatly links the dilemma to questions of fidelity to love as explored in the two novels: specifically, is Marianne's love for Willoughby/Anne's love for Wentworth 'an animating or a mortifying process'?[59] Favret's thesis implicitly challenges Woolf s criticism, with its simple assumption that the novel is a master system unavailable for sophisticated transposition, while nevertheless endorsing its

[57] Burgess, writing in 1975, is quoted in McFarlane, *Novel To Film*, 7.

[58] Bluestone, *Novels into Film*, 47 and 58.

[59] Mary A. Favret, 'Being True to Jane Austen', in *Victorian Afterlife: Postmodern Culture Rewrites the Nineteenth Century*, ed. John Kucich and Dianne F. Sadoff (Minneapolis and London: University of Minnesota Press, 2000), 64–6.

emotional logic. There are no simple answers; just as Elinor's tender sisterly care is transformed on screen into a 'lesbian vampire' encounter with death beside Marianne's sickbed, similarly in film's textual revisioning the 'consanguinity'[60] of film to novel is inevitably a Gothic bond. We might remind ourselves that on the dustjacket of the screenplay of *Sense and Sensibility* (writer Emma Thompson also took the part of Elinor Dashwood) the adaptation is described as 'a labour of love'. Where Woolf concludes that the love-relationship of film to novel is parasitic or melancholic, in that it involves a transference of affective power which can only diminish both parties, a new generation of film adapters and literary critics views the activity of filmic revisioning or reversioning as a two-way transfusion of energy.

Where modern consumer values ensured that Austen adaptations of the mid-1990s delivered up a heady cocktail of money, sex, and real estate, with or without period costume (Amy Heckerling's extraordinary relocation of *Emma* to contemporary Beverly Hills in *Clueless* (Paramount (1995)), there is the intriguing new possibility of a more complex cultural reanimation of her narratives of social manners when their stories are transposed to a non-Western setting. Gurinder Chadha's feature film *Bride and Prejudice* (Pathe and Miramax, 2004) exploits the film genres of Mumbai, London, and Los Angeles to mediate Austen's novel, in the process shifting its action from Regency England to modern-day India. The Bennets are a Sikh family, the Bakshis, living in a decaying former imperial residence in Amritsar. Bingley and Darcy arrive in town to attend a wedding: Bingley is a second-generation British Asian; Darcy, from Los Angeles, is the heir to a multi-million-dollar hotel chain. Wickham is a British backpacker, in search of the 'real India'; and best of all, Mr Collins, now Mr Kholi with a fortune made in Silicon Valley, has recently returned home to India to find a nice traditional wife. The resulting mix is a multilayered, hybrid form in which Bollywood spectacle and dance, exuberant performance and pastiche, and characters with diverse identities offer culturally different points of access into Austen's story. In establishing and moving across so many ethnic, geographic, and cultural boundaries (locations in Amritsar, London, and Los Angeles take the places of Longbourn, Netherfield, and Pemberley) it is likely that Chadha has found a way to mimic and so communicate the lively difference of Austen's social

[60] The word is used with some regularity by Wiltshire to identify the kinship between the disjunct forms which are the novel and its filmic representation, though his use is informed by psychoanalytic and Bloomian models of imitative and competitive relationship rather than Gothic romancing.

realities (the fact that they are not inaccessible but strange) to an audience who have all too easily reduced them to mere heritage consumables, a paradoxically hard-edged nostalgia for the materialism we (think we) have lost. If the miscegenation appears in some lights disrespectful of her novels' classic status, its hybrid product may nevertheless be Jane Austen's most effective ambassador in the twenty-first century, an enactment of the anthropological relativism which Lionel Trilling struggled to enlist in the 1970s.[61] Where the eye will not permit the mind to settle in a single register but shifts among different cultural codes and assumptions there is a chance that the sympathetic identification of Austen-land with our own wishes will not win out over the greater challenge of recognizing the altogether more complex nature of the lives texts lead.

[61] See Trilling's last essay, 'Why We Read Jane Austen', *Times Literary Supplement*, 5 March 1976, 250–2, and Ch. 1, 48-9.

Bibliography

MANUSCRIPT MATERIAL

Bodleian Library, Oxford

MS. Don. e. 7, holograph manuscript of *Volume the First*

MS. Eng. Misc. c.924, R. W. Chapman, 'Jane Austen Files'

MSS. Eng. Letters c.759–60, R. W. Chapman, Correspondence

MS. Eng. Letters e.150, Catherine Hubback, Correspondence

British Library, London

Add. MS. 59874, holograph manuscript of *Volume the Second*

MS. Egerton 3038, holograph manuscript fragment of *Persuasion*

Hampshire Record Office, Winchester

MS. 23M93, the Austen-Leigh papers:

MS. 23M93/64/4/2, a volume containing transcriptions in several unidentified hands of letters, poems, and short stories by Austen

MS. 23M93/66/2, letters to Caroline Austen, 1815–75

MS. 23M93/84/1, letters to Anna Lefroy, 1819–69

MS. 23M93/85/2, Fanny C. Lefroy, 'Family History'

MS. 23M93/86/3, letters to James Edward Austen-Leigh

MS. 23M93/87/3, letters to Emma Austen-Leigh

MS. 23M93/97/4, items found interleaved in R. A. Austen-Leigh's papers and published works

Jane Austen's House, Chawton

A copy in the hand of Cassandra Austen of the *Sanditon* manuscript

King's College, Cambridge

Holograph manuscript of *Sanditon*

Letter of 8 February 1925 from Mrs J. R. Sanders to 'the Secretary of the Oxford University Press' [R. W. Chapman], kept with the *Sanditon* MS

Letter of 28 October [1930] from M. Isabel Lefroy to R. W. Chapman, kept with the *Sanditon* MS

National Portrait Gallery, London

RWC/HH, a file of correspondence between R. W. Chapman and Henry Hake, 1932–48, containing typescripts made from letters (originals now missing) addressed to James Edward Austen-Leigh

Oxford University Press Archive, Oxford

LOGE000025, Correspondence relating to the Oxford edition of Jane Austen's Novels, 1912–87

PBED013422, Correspondence relating to the Works of Jane Austen, Volume 6, 1948–88

Pierpont Morgan Library, New York

MS. MA1034, holograph manuscript of *The Watsons*

MS. MA 1226, holograph manuscript of *Lady Susan*

MS. MA 2911, holograph manuscript of a letter from Jane Austen to Cassandra Austen, 14 September 1804

Queen Mary and Westfield College, University of London

Holograph manuscript of *The Watsons*

JANE AUSTEN

1st editions

Sense and Sensibility: A Novel, 3 vols. (London: T. Egerton, 1811)

Pride and Prejudice: A Novel, 3 vols. (London: T. Egerton, 1813)

Mansfield Park: A Novel, 3 vols. (London: T. Egerton, 1814)

Emma : A Novel, 3 vols. (London: John Murray, 1816)

Northanger Abbey and Persuasion, 4 vols. (London: John Murray, 1818)

Other early editions cited

Mansfield Park: A Novel, 3 vols., 2nd edn. (London: J. Murray, 1816)

Sense and Sensibility (followed by *Emma*, *Mansfield Park*, *Northanger Abbey and Persuasion*, *Pride and Prejudice*), Standard Novels series (London: Richard Bentley, 1833)

Sense and Sensibility, Railway Library (London: G. Routledge and Co., 1851)

Jane Austen's Works, Steventon Edition, 6 vols. (London: Richard Bentley & Son, 1882)

Sense and Sensibility, Routledge's Sixpenny Novels (London: G. Routledge and Sons, 1884)

The Novels of Jane Austen, ed. R. Brimley Johnson, 10 vols. (London: J. M. Dent, 1892)

Pride and Prejudice, with a preface by George Saintsbury and illustrations by Hugh Thomson (London: George Allen, 1894)

Northanger Abbey and Persuasion, with an introduction by Austin Dobson and illustrations by Hugh Thomson (London: Macmillan, 1897)

The Novels of Jane Austen, Hampshire Edition, with decorations by Miss Blanche MacManus, 6 vols. (London: R. Brimley Johnson, 1902)

Pride and Prejudice, ed. K. M. Metcalfe (London: Oxford University Press, 1912)

Love & Freindship and Other Early Works, now first printed from the original ms. by Jane Austen, with a preface by G. K. Chesterton (London: Chatto & Windus, 1922)

Northanger Abbey, ed. K. M. Metcalfe (Oxford: Clarendon Press, 1923)

R. W. Chapman's editions and their revisions

Prospectus advertising 1923 edition of *The Novels of Jane Austen* (Oxford: Clarendon Press, 1923)

The Novels of Jane Austen, ed. R. W. Chapman, 5 vols. (Oxford: Clarendon Press, 1923)

—— 'third edition' (1932–4), revised by Mary Lascelles, 5 vols. (Oxford: Oxford University Press, 1965–6)

Fragment of a Novel written by Jane Austen, January–March 1817 [ed. R. W. Chapman] (Oxford: Clarendon Press, 1925)

Jane Austen's Lady Susan: A Facsimile of the Manuscript in the Pierpont Morgan Library and the 1925 Printed Edition, preface by A. Walton Litz (New York and London: Garland Publishing, Inc., 1989)

The Manuscript Chapters of Persuasion [ed. R. W. Chapman] (*Two Chapters of Persuasion,* Oxford, 1926) (repr. London: Athlone Press, 1985)

Plan of a Novel, etc. [ed. R. W. Chapman] (Oxford: Clarendon Press, 1926)

The Watsons: A Fragment [ed. R. W. Chapman] (Oxford: Clarendon Press, 1927)

Volume the First, ed. R. W. C[hapman] (Oxford: Clarendon Press, 1933)

Volume the Third, ed. R. W. C[hapman] (Oxford: Clarendon Press, 1951)

Minor Works, The Works of Jane Austen, Vol. 6, ed. R. W. Chapman (1954), revised by B. C. Southam (Oxford: Oxford University Press, 1969)

Other modern editions cited

Jane Austen's Novels in the Oxford English Novels series, ed. James Kinsley (Oxford: Oxford University Press, 1970–1)

New Penguin Jane Austen (Harmondsworth, Middx.: Penguin, 1995–8): *Sense and Sensibility*, ed. Ros Ballaster (1995); *Pride and Prejudice*, ed. Vivien Jones (1996); *Mansfield Park*, ed. Kathryn Sutherland (1996); *Emma*, ed. Fiona Stafford (1996); *Northanger Abbey*, ed. Marilyn Butler (1995); *Persuasion*, ed. Gillian Beer (1998)

Mansfield Park, ed. Claudia L. Johnson (New York: W. W. Norton and Co., 1998)

Emma, ed. Stephen M. Parrish (1972; 3rd edn., New York: W. W. Norton and Co., 2000)

Northanger Abbey, Lady Susan, The Watsons, and Sanditon, ed. John Davie (Oxford: Oxford University Press, 1980)

Persuasion, ed. D. W. Harding (Harmondsworth, Middx.: Penguin, 1965)

Persuasion, ed. John Davie and introduced by Claude Rawson (Oxford: Oxford University Press, 1990)

Persuasion, ed. Patricia Meyer Spacks (New York: W. W. Norton and Co., 1995)

Sanditon: An Unfinished Novel [a facsimile reproduction of the manuscript], with an introduction by Brian Southam (Oxford: Clarendon Press, London: Scolar Press, 1975)

Jane Austen's 'Sir Charles Grandison', ed. Brian Southam (Oxford: Clarendon Press, 1981)

Catharine and Other Writings, ed. Margaret Anne Doody and Douglas Murray (Oxford: Oxford University Press, 1993)

Jane Austen's Evelyn, ed. Peter Sabor and others (Edmonton, Alberta: Juvenilia Press, 1999)

Other Jane Austen and primary reference works

Letters of Jane Austen, ed. Edward, Lord Brabourne, 2 vols. (London: Richard Bentley & Son, 1884)

Jane Austen's Letters, ed. R. W. Chapman, 2nd edn. (London: Oxford University Press, 1952)

—— ed. Deirdre Le Faye, 3rd edn. (Oxford: Oxford University Press, 1995)

Jane Austen's Manuscript Letters in Facsimile, ed. Jo Modert (Carbondale and Edwardsville: Southern Illinois University Press, 1990)

Austen-Leigh, J. E., *A Memoir of Jane Austen* (London: Richard Bentley, 1870)

—— *A Memoir of Jane Austen, to which is added Lady Susan and Fragments of Two Other Unfinished Tales by Miss Austen*, 2nd edn. (London: Richard Bentley & Son, 1871)

—— *A Memoir of Jane Austen and Other Family Recollections*, ed. Kathryn Sutherland (Oxford: Oxford University Press, 2002)

Austen-Leigh, R. A. (ed.), *Austen Papers, 1704–1856* (London: privately printed by Spottiswoode, Ballantyne and Co., 1942)

Austen-Leigh, William, and Austen-Leigh, Richard Arthur, *Jane Austen: Her Life and Letters. A Family Record* (London: Smith, Elder, and Co., 1913)

—— *Jane Austen: A Family Record*, revised and enlarged by Deirdre Le Faye (London: British Library, 1989)

Chapman, R. W., *Jane Austen: A Critical Bibliography*, 2nd edn. (Oxford: Clarendon Press, 1955)

—— *Jane Austen: Facts and Problems* (Oxford: Clarendon Press, 1948; repr. 1949)

Gilson, David, *A Bibliography of Jane Austen* (1982; corrected edn., Winchester: St Paul's Bibliographies, 1997).

Jane Austen Society Reports (1949–)

Johnson, R. Brimley, *Jane Austen: Her Life, Her Work, Her Family, and Her Critics* (London and Toronto: J. M. Dent and Sons, 1930)

Le Faye, Deirdre, *Jane Austen: A Family Record* (Cambridge: Cambridge University Press, 2004)

Southam, B. C., *Jane Austen: The Critical Heritage*, 2 vols. (London and New York: Routledge & Kegan Paul, 1968 and 1987)

OTHER WORKS CITED

Anon., 'Extracts from the Port-folio of a Man of Letters', *Monthly Magazine*, 11 (1801), 236–9

—— '*Heart of Midlothian*' [review of Walter Scott's novel], *British Review*, n.s., 12 (1818), 396–406

—— 'Jane Austen', *Temple Bar*, 64 (1882), 350–65

—— 'Miss Austen', *The Englishwoman's Domestic Magazine*, 2 (1866), 237–40; 278–82

—— Notice of Chapman's Edition of *The* Novels of Jane Austen, *London Mercury*, 9 (December 1923), 223

—— 'The Oxford Jane Austen' [a review of Chapman's edition], *Times Literary Supplement*, 1 November 1923, 725

Adams, Oscar Fay, *The Story of Jane Austen's Life* (Chicago: A. C. McClurg and Co., 1891)

Aitken, David, *Sleeping with Jane Austen* (Harpenden: No Exit Press, 2000)

Alberge Dalya, 'Put aside Pride and Prejudice, This is the Real Jane Austen', *The Times*, 11 December 2002, 13.

Allibone, S. Austin, *A Critical Dictionary of English Literature, and British and American Authors, Living and Deceased*, 3 vols. (Philadelphia and London: Childs and Peterson, and Trubner, 1859)

Altick, Richard D., *The English Common Reader: A Social History of the Mass Reading Public, 1800–1900* (1957; 2nd edn., Columbus, Ohio: Ohio State University Press, 1998)

Anderson, Benedict, *Imagined Communities: Reflections on the Origin and Spread of Nationalism* (1983; London and New York: Verso, 1991)

Andrew, Dudley, *Concepts in Film Theory* (Oxford and New York: Oxford University Press, 1984)

Armstrong, Nancy, *Desire and Domestic Fiction: A Political History of the Novel* (New York: Oxford University Press, 1987)

Attar, K. E., 'Jane Austen at King's College, Cambridge', *The Book Collector*, 51 (2002), 197–221

Austen-Leigh, Joan, 'New Light on JA's Refusal of Harris Bigg-Wither', *Persuasions*, 8 (1986), 34–6

Austen-Leigh, Mary Augusta, *Personal Aspects of Jane Austen* (London: John Murray, 1920)

Bakhtin, Mikhail, *Problems of Dostoevsky's Poetics*, ed. and trans. by Caryl Emerson (Manchester: Manchester University Press, 1984)

Baldick, Chris, *The Social Mission of English Criticism 1848–1932* (Oxford: Clarendon Press, 1983)

Barbauld, Mrs [Anna Laetitia], 'On the Origin and Progress of Novel-Writing', *The British Novelists* (New Edition, London: F. C. and J. Rivington *et al.*, 1820), Vol. 1.

Barchas, Janine, 'Sarah Fielding's Dashing Style and Eighteenth-Century Print Culture', *English Literary History*, 63 (1996), 633–56

Bate, Jonathan, *The Song of the Earth* (London: Picador, 2000)

Bellemin-Noël, Jean, *Le Texte et l'avant-texte* (Paris: Larousse, 1972)

Blakey, Dorothy, *The Minerva Press, 1790–1820* (London: Printed for the Bibliographical Society at the University Press, Oxford, 1939)

Blanchot, Maurice, *The Space of Literature*, trans. by Ann Smock (Lincoln and London: University of Nebraska Press, 1982)

Bluestone, George, *Novels into Film* (1957; Baltimore and London: Johns Hopkins University Press, 2003)

Bowers, Fredson, *Principles of Bibliographical Description* (Princeton: Princeton University Press, 1949)

—— 'Regularization and Normalization in Modern Critical Texts', *Studies in Bibliography*, 42 (1989), 79–102

—— 'Textual Criticism', in *The Aims and Methods of Scholarship in Modern Languages and Literatures*, ed. James Thorpe (New York: Modern Language Association of America, 1963), 23–42

—— *Textual and Literary Criticism* (Cambridge: Cambridge University Press, 1966)

Bradley, A. C., 'Jane Austen', *Essays and Studies By Members of the English Association*, 2 (1911), 7–36

Bray, Joe, 'Austen, "Enigmatic Lacunae" and the Art of Biography', in *Romantic Biography*, ed. Arthur Bradley and Alan Rawes (Aldershot, Hants: Ashgate, 2003), 58–73

Brilliant, Richard, *Portraiture* (London: Reaktion Books Ltd., 1991)

Brooke, Rupert, *The Letters of Rupert Brooke*, ed. Geoffrey Keynes (London: Faber & Faber, 1968)

—— *The Prose of Rupert Brooke*, ed. Christopher Hassall (London: Sidgwick and Jackson, 1956)

Brown, Edith, and Brown, Francis, *The Watsons* (London: Elkin Mathews and Marrot Ltd., 1928)

Brown, Mrs Francis, *Margaret Dashwood; or, Interference* (London: John Lane, the Bodley Head, 1929)

—— *Susan Price; or, Resolution* (London: John Lane, the Bodley Head, 1930)

Brown, Jane, *Spirits of Place: Five Famous Lives in their English Landscape* (London: Penguin, 2001)

Bull, Edward, *Hints and Directions for Authors* (London: Bull, 1842)

Burke, Seán, 'The Ethics of Signature', in *Authorship: From Plato to the Postmodern*, ed. Seán Burke (Edinburgh: Edinburgh University Press, 1995), 285–91

Burrows, J. F., *Computation into Criticism: A Study of Jane Austen's Novels and an Experiment in Method* (Oxford: Clarendon Press, 1987)

Butler, Marilyn, 'Disregarding Designs: Jane Austen's Sense of the Volume', *Jane Austen Society Collected Reports*, 1976–85 (Alton, Hants: Jane Austen Society, 1989), 99–114

—— *Jane Austen and the War of Ideas* (1975; revised edn., Oxford: Clarendon Press, 1987)

—— *Maria Edgeworth: A Literary Biography*, (Oxford: Clarendon Press, 1972)

Byrne, Paula, *Jane Austen and the Theatre* (London and New York: Hambledon, 2002)

Carter, John, and Pollard, Graham, *An Enquiry into the Nature of Certain Nineteenth-Century Pamphlets* (London: Constable, 1934)

Carlyle, Thomas, *The Collected Works of Thomas Carlyle*, 16 vols. (London: Chapman and Hall, 1858)

Castle, Terry, 'Sister-Sister', *London Review of Books*, 3 August 1995, 3–6

Cather, Willa, *The World and the Parish: Willa Cather's Articles and Reviews, 1893–1902*, ed. William M. Curtin, 2 vols. (Lincoln: University of Nebraska Press, 1970)

Cecil, David, *A Portrait of Jane Austen* (London: Constable and Co., 1978)

Chapman, R. W., *The Portrait of a Scholar and other Essays written in Macedonia 1916–1918* (London: Oxford University Press, 1920)

—— 'A Jane Austen Collection', *Times Literary Supplement*, 14 January 1926, 27

—— 'A Problem in Editorial Method', *Essays and Studies By Members of the English Association*, 27 (1941), 41–51

Clerihew, E. [Edmund Clerihew Bentley], *Biography for Beginners* (London: T. Werner Laurie, [1905/6])

Cohen, Philip (ed.), *Devils and Angels: Textual Editing and Literary Theory* (Charlottesville and London: University Press of Virginia, 1991)

Coleman, D. C., *The British Paper Industry, 1495–1860* (Oxford, 1958; repr. Westport, Conn.: Greenwood Press, 1975)

Coleridge, Samuel Taylor, *The Friend*, ed. Barbara E. Rooke, 2 vols. (London: Routledge & Kegan Paul, 1969)

—— *Biographia Literaria; or, Biographical Sketches of My Literary Life and Opinions*, ed. James Engell and W. Jackson Bate, 2 vols. (London: Routledge & Kegan Paul, 1983)

Committee of the Jane Austen Society, 'The Zoffany Portrait', in 'Report for the Year, 1973', *Jane Austen Society Collected Reports, 1966–75* (1977; reissued Alton, Hants: Jane Austen Society, 1999), 197–200

Copeland, Edward, *Women Writing About Money: Women's Fiction in England, 1790–1820* (Cambridge: Cambridge University Press, 1995)

Cornish, Francis Warre, *Jane Austen*, 'English Men of Letters' series (London: Macmillan, 1913)

Crashaw, Richard, *The Poems English, Latin, and Greek of Richard Crashaw*, ed. L. C. Martin (Oxford: Clarendon Press, 1927)

Dear, Nick, *Persuasion by Jane Austen, a Screenplay* (London: Methuen, 1996)

de Grazia, Margreta, 'The Essential Author and the Material Book', *Textual Practice*, 2 (1988), 69–86

—— *Shakespeare Verbatim: The Reproduction of Authenticity and the 1790 Apparatus* (Oxford: Clarendon Press, 1991)

—— and Peter Stallybrass, 'The Materiality of the Shakespearean Text', *Shakespeare Quarterly*, 44 (1993), 255–83

de Lauretis, Teresa, *Alice Doesn't: Feminism, Semiotics, Cinema* (Basingstoke and London: Macmillan, 1984)

Derry, Warren, 'Jane Austen', *Times Literary Supplement*, 29 December 1961, 929

Dickens, Charles, *The Letters of Charles Dickens*, 12 vols. (Oxford: Clarendon Press, 1965–2002), Vol. 9, ed. Graham Storey (1997)

Dictionary of National Biography, 1951–1960, ed. E. T. Williams and Helen M. Palmer (London: Oxford University Press, 1971)

Dooley, Allan C., *Author and Printer in Victorian England* (Charlottesville and London: University Press of Virginia, 1992)

Duckworth, Alistair M., *The Improvement of the Estate: A Study of Jane Austen's Novels* (1971; Baltimore and London: Johns Hopkins University Press, 1994)

Dunlop, John, *The History of Fiction* (London: Longman, Hurst, Rees, Orme, & Brown, 1814)

Eagleton, Terry, 'First-Class Fellow Traveller', review of Seán French, *Patrick Hamilton: A Life*, *London Review of Books*, 2 December 1993, 12

Eaves, Morris, ' "Why Don't They Leave It Alone?" Speculations on the Authority of the Audience in Editorial Theory', in *Cultural Artifacts and the Production of Meaning: The Page, The Image, and the Body*, ed. Margaret J. M. Ezell and Katherine O'Brien O'Keeffe (Ann Arbor: University of Michigan Press, 1994), 85–99.

Eggert, Paul, 'Document and Text: the "Life" of the Literary Work and the Capacities of Editing', *TEXT*, 7 (1994), 1–24

—— 'The Work Unravelled', *TEXT*, 11 (1998), 41–60

Eliot, George, *George Eliot's Life as Related in her Letters and Journals*, ed. J. W. Cross (1885; New York: AMS Press, 1965)

—— *The George Eliot Letters*, ed. Gordon Haight, 9 vols. (New Haven: Yale University Press, 1954–78)

Eliot, T. S., 'Euripides and Professor Murray', in *The Sacred Wood: Essays on Poetry and Criticism* (London: Methuen and Co., 1920)

Elliott, Kamilla, *Rethinking the Novel/Film Debate* (Cambridge: Cambridge University Press, 2003)

Elliott, Pauline, 'The Zoffany Portrait', in 'Report for the Year, 1991', in *Jane Austen Society Collected Reports, 1986–95* (Alton, Hants: Jane Austen Society, 1997), 215–17

Evans, Arthur, 'The Sixth Campaign at Knossos', *The Times*, 31 October 1905, 4.

Farrer, Reginald, 'A Jane Austen Celebration', *Times Literary Supplement*, 6 January 1916, 9.

Favret, Mary A., 'Being True to Jane Austen', in *Victorian Afterlife: Postmodern Culture Rewrites the Nineteenth Century*, ed. John Kucich and Dianne F. Sadoff (Minneapolis and London: University of Minnesota Press, 2000), 64–82

—— *Romantic Correspondence: Women, Politics, and the Fiction of Letters* (Cambridge: Cambridge University Press, 1993)

Fergus, Jan, *Jane Austen and the Didactic Novel* (Basingstoke and London: Macmillan, 1983)

—— *Jane Austen: A Literary Life* (Basingstoke and London: Macmillan, 1991).

Ferguson, Adam, *An Essay on the History of Civil Society* (1767), ed. Fania Oz-Salzberger (Cambridge: Cambridge University Press, 1995)

Ferrer, Daniel, 'The Open Space of the Draft Page: James Joyce and Modern Manuscripts', in *The Iconic Page in Manuscript, Print, and Digital Culture*, ed. George Bornstein and Theresa Tinkle (Ann Arbor: University of Michigan Press, 1998), 249–67

Finch, Casey, and Peter Bowen. '"The Tittle-Tattle of Highbury": Gossip and the Free Indirect Style in *Emma*', *Representations*, 31 (1990), 1–18

Fish, Stanley, *Is There a Text in this Class? The Authority of Interpretive Communities* (Cambridge, Mass.: Harvard University Press, 1980)

Flanders, Julia, 'The Body Encoded: Questions of Gender and the Electronic Text', in *Electronic Text: Investigations in Method and Theory*, ed. Kathryn Sutherland (Oxford: Clarendon Press, 1997), 127–43

Forster, E. M., *Howards End* (London: Edward Arnold, 1910)

—— *Aspects of the Novel* (1927; Harmondsworth, Middx.: Penguin, 1962)

—— *Abinger Harvest* (1936; Harmondsworth, Middx.: Penguin, 1967)

Friedman, Susan Stanford, 'The Return of the Repressed in Women's Narrative', *Journal of Narrative Technique*, 19 (1989), 141–56

Fussell, Paul, *The Great War and Modern Memory* (New York and London: Oxford University Press, 1975)

Gabler, Hans Walter, 'The Synchrony and Diachrony of Texts: Practice and Theory of the Critical Edition of James Joyce's *Ulysses*', *TEXT*, 1 (1984 for 1981), 305–26

Galperin, William H., *The Historical Austen* (Philadelphia: University of Pennsylvania Press, 2003)

Garside, Peter, *et al.* (eds.), *The English Novel 1770–1829: A Bibliographical Survey of Prose Fiction Published in the British Isles*, 2 vols. (Oxford: Oxford University Press, 2000)

Gaskell, E. C., *The Life of Charlotte Brontë*, ed. Alan Shelston (Harmondsworth, Middx.: Penguin, 1975)

Gaskell, Philip, *A New Introduction to Bibliography* (Oxford: Clarendon Press, 1972)

Geertz, Clifford, *Local Knowledge: Further Essays in Interpretive Anthropology* (1983; London: Fontana Press, 1993)

Genette, Gérard, *Paratexts: Thresholds of Interpretation* (in French as *Seuils* (1987)), trans. by Jane E. Lewin and Richard Macksey (Cambridge: Cambridge University Press, 1997)

Giddings, Robert, and Selby, Keith, *The Classic Serial on Television and Radio* (Basingstoke and New York: Palgrave, 2001)

Giddings, Robert, and Sheen, Erica (eds.), *The Classic Novel: From Page to Screen* (Manchester: Manchester University Press, 2000)

Gilbert, Sandra M., and Gubar, Susan, *The Madwoman in the Attic: The Woman Writer and the Nineteenth-Century Literary Imagination* (New Haven: Yale University Press, 1979)

Gilson, David, *Collected Articles and Introductions* (privately printed, 1998)

—— 'Jane Austen's Text: A Survey of Editions', *Review of English Studies*, n.s., 53 (2002), 61–85

Godwin, William, *Political and Philosophical Writings of William Godwin*, gen. ed. Mark Philp, 7 vols. (London: William Pickering, 1993)

Greetham, David C., *Textual Scholarship: An Introduction* (New York and London: Garland Publishing Inc., 1994)

—— *Theories of the Text* (Oxford: Oxford University Press, 1999)

Greg, Walter W., *The Calculus of Variants: An Essay on Textual Criticism* (Oxford: Clarendon Press, 1927)

—— *Collected Papers*, ed. J. C. Maxwell (Oxford: Clarendon Press, 1966)

—— 'The Rationale of Copy-Text', *Studies in Bibliography*, 3 (1950–1), 19–36

Grey, J. David (ed.), *Jane Austen's Beginnings: The Juvenilia and 'Lady Susan'* (Ann Arbor and London: UMI Research Press, 1989)

—— (ed.), *The Jane Austen Handbook* (London: Athlone Press, 1986)

Grigely, Joseph, *Textualterity: Art, Theory, and Textual Criticism* (Ann Arbor: University of Michigan Press, 1995)

Halperin, John, *The Life of Jane Austen* (1984; 3rd printing, Baltimore: Johns Hopkins University Press, 1996)

Hammond, Antony, 'The Noisy Comma: Searching for the Signal in Renaissance Dramatic Texts', in *Crisis in Editing: Texts of the English Renaissance*, ed. Randall McLeod (New York: AMS Press, Inc., 1994), 203–49

Hanaway, Lorraine, '"Janeite at 100"', *Persuasions*, 16 (1994), 28–9

Hanna, Ralph, 'Annotation as Social Practice' in *Annotation and Its Texts*, ed. Stephen A. Barney (New York: Oxford University Press, 1991), 178–84

Hansard, T. C., *Typographia* (London: Baldwin, Cradock, and Joy, 1825)

Hardy, Barbara, 'Properties and Possessions in Jane Austen's Novels', in *Jane Austen's Achievement*, ed. Juliet McMaster (Basingstoke and London: Macmillan, 1976), 79–105

Hardy, Thomas, *Tess of the d'Urbervilles*, ed. Juliet Grindle and Simon Gatrell (Oxford: Clarendon Press, 1983)

Harris, Wendell V., 'Canonicity', *Proceedings of the Modern Language Association of America*, 106 (1991), 110–21

Harvey, W. J., 'The Plot of *Emma*', *Essays in Criticism*, 17 (1967), 48–63

Hawk, Affable [Desmond MacCarthy], 'Current Literature: Books in General', *The New Statesman*, 22 (1923), 145

Hay, Louis, 'Die dritte Dimension der Literatur: Notizen zu einer "critique génétique"', *Poetica*, 16 (1984), 307–23

—— 'Genetic Editing, Past and Future: A Few Reflections by a User', *TEXT*, 3 (1987), 117–33

Hazlitt, William, *Complete Works*, ed. P. P. Howe, 21 vols. (London and Toronto: Dent, 1930–4)

Higson, Andrew, 'The Heritage Film and British Cinema', in *Dissolving Views: Key Writings on British Cinema*, ed. Andrew Higson (London and New York: Cassell, 1996), 232–48

Hill, Constance, *Jane Austen Her Homes and Her Friends* (1902; reissued London and New York: John Lane, 1904)

Hints to Authors in preparing Copy, with practical Directions for correcting Proof Sheets for the Press (8 pp., no date, but watermarked 1813)

Hodge, John, *Trainspotting & Shallow Grave* (London: Faber & Faber, 1996)

Holderness, Graham, Loughrey, Bryan, and Murphy, Andrew, '"What's the Matter?": Shakespeare and Textual Theory', *Textual Practice*, 9 (1995), 93–119

Holland, Jeanne, 'Scraps, Stamps, and Cutouts: Emily Dickinson's Domestic Technologies of Publication', in *Cultural Artifacts and the Production of Meaning: The Page, the Image, and the Body*, ed. Margaret J. M. Ezell and Katherine O'Brien O'Keeffe (Ann Arbor: University of Michigan Press, 1994), 139–81

Honan, Park, *Jane Austen: Her Life* (New York: Fawcett Columbine, 1987)

—— review of B. C. Southam's edition of *Jane Austen's 'Sir Charles Grandison'*, *Notes and Queries*, 228 (1983), 173–4

Hopkinson, David, 'A Niece of Jane Austen', *Notes and Queries*, 229 (1984), 470–1

Horner, Joyce M., *The English Women Novelists and their Connection with the Feminist Movement (1688–1797)* (Northampton, Mass.: Smith College Studies, 1930)

Howe, Susan, *The Birth-Mark: Unsettling the Wilderness in American Literary History* (Hanover and London: University Press of New England, 1993)

Hubback, John H., *Cross Currents in a Long Life* (privately printed, 1935)

—— and Edith C., *Jane Austen's Sailor Brothers: Being the Adventures of Sir Francis Austen, G.C.B., Admiral of the Fleet, and Rear-Admiral Charles Austen* (London: John Lane, 1906)

Hubback, Mrs [Catherine], *The Younger Sister. A Novel*, 3 vols. (London: Thomas Cautley Newby, 1850)

Hutcheon, Linda, *A Theory of Parody: The Teachings of Twentieth-Century Art Forms* (1985; reprinted New York and London: Routledge, 1991)

Isaac, Peter, 'Byron's Publisher and His "Spy": Constancy and Change among John Murray II's Printers, 1812–1831', *The Library*, 6th ser., 19 (1997), 1–24

Jack, Ian, 'Novels and those "Necessary Evils": Annotating the Brontës', *Essays in Criticism*, 32 (1982), 321–37

Jarrett-Kerr, Martin, 'The Mission of Eng. Lit.', *Times Literary Supplement*, 3 February 1984, 111

Jarvis, Simon, 'Sponge Cakes or Don Juan: Irony and Morality in Jane Austen's Life and Work', *Times Literary Supplement*, 12 September 1997, 3–4

Jed, Stephanie H., *Chaste Thinking: The Rape of Lucretia and the Birth of Humanism* (Bloomington and Indianapolis: Indiana University Press, 1989)

Jenkins, Elizabeth, *Jane Austen: A Biography* (London: Victor Gollancz, 1938)

Johnson, Claudia L., 'Austen Cults and Cultures', in *The Cambridge Companion to Jane Austen*, ed. Edward Copeland and Juliet McMaster (Cambridge: Cambridge University Press, 1997), 211–26

—— 'Fair Maid of Kent? The Arguments For (and Against) the Rice Portrait of Jane Austen', *Times Literary Supplement*, 13 March 1998, 14–15; and replies in *TLS*, 20 and 27 March, and 3 and 17 April 1998

Johnson, Samuel, *A Critical Edition of the Major Works*, ed. Donald Greene (Oxford: Oxford University Press, 1984)

—— *Johnson's Journey to the Western Islands of Scotland and Boswell's Journal of A Tour to the Hebrides with Samuel Johnson, LL.D.*, ed. R. W. Chapman (London: Oxford University Press, 1924)

—— 'Preface' (1765), in *Johnson on Shakespeare*, ed. Arthur Sherbo, Yale Edition of the Works of Samuel Johnson, Vol. 7 (New Haven and London: Yale University Press, 1968)

Joyce, James, *Finnegan's Wake* (1939; London: Faber & Faber, new edn., repr. 1960)

Kaplan, Deborah, *Jane Austen Among Women* (Baltimore and London: Johns Hopkins University Press, 1992)

—— 'Representing Two Cultures: Jane Austen's Letters', in *The Private Self: Theory and Practice of Women's Autobiographical Writings*, ed. Shari Benstock (London: Routledge, 1988), 211–29

Kaplan, E. Ann, *Looking for the Other: Feminism, Film, and the Imperial Gaze* (London and New York: Routledge, 1997)

Kavanagh, Julia, *English Women of Letters: Biographical Sketches*, 2 vols. (London: Hurst and Blackett, 1863)

Keats, John, *The Letters of John Keats*, ed. Hyder Edward Rollins, 2 vols. (Cambridge, Mass.: Harvard University Press, 1958)

Kebbel, T. E., 'Jane Austen at Home', *Fortnightly Review*, 43 (1885), 262–70

Kelly, Gary, 'Jane Austen's Real Business: The Novel, Literature, and Cultural Capital', in *Jane Austen's Business: Her World and Her Profession*, ed. Juliet McMaster and Bruce Stovel (Basingstoke and London: Macmillan, 1996), 154–67

Kermode, Frank, *The Sense of an Ending: Studies in the Theory of Fiction* (New York: Oxford University Press, 1967)

Keynes, Geoffrey, Kt., *The Gates of Memory* (Oxford: Clarendon Press, 1981)

—— *Jane Austen: A Bibliography* (London: Nonesuch Press, 1929)

—— 'The Text of *Mansfield Park*', *Times Literary Supplement*, 30 August 1923, 572

Kipling, Rudyard, 'The Janeites', *Debits and Credits* (London: Macmillan, 1926), 143–76

Knight, Fanny, *Fanny Knight's Diaries: Jane Austen through her Niece's Eyes*, ed. Deirdre Le Faye (Alton, Hants: Jane Austen Society, 2000)

Lamb, Charles, *The Letters of Charles and Mary Lamb*, ed. Edwin W. Marrs, Jr, 3 vols. (Ithaca and London: Cornell University Press, 1975)

—— *The Works of Charles Lamb*, ed. William Macdonald, 12 vols. (London: Dent, 1903)

Lane, Maggie, *Jane Austen's Family Through Five Generations* (London: Robert Hale, 1984)

Lascelles, Mary M., *Jane Austen and Her Art* (Oxford: Clarendon Press, 1939)

—— *Notions and Facts: Collected Criticism and Research* (Oxford: Clarendon Press, 1972)

—— '*Mansfield Park*', *Times Literary Supplement*, 21 October 1965, 946

Leader, Zacharay, *Revision and Romantic Authorship* (Oxford: Clarendon Press, 1996)

Leavis, F. R., *The Common Pursuit* (London: Chatto & Windus, 1952)

—— *For Continuity* (Cambridge: The Minority Press, 1933)

—— *The Great Tradition* (London: Chatto & Windus, 1948)

Leavis, Q. D., 'A Critical Theory of Jane Austen's Writings', *Scrutiny*, 10 and 12 (1941–5), repr. in *Collected Essays*, 1, *The Englishness of the English Novel*, ed. G. Singh (Cambridge: Cambridge University Press, 1983)

Leavis, Q. D., *Fiction and the Reading Public* (1932; Harmondsworth, Middx.: Penguin, 1979)

Le Faye, Deirdre, 'Anna Lefroy and Her Austen Family Letters', *Princeton University Library Chronicle*, 62 (2001), 519–62

—— '"The Business of Mothering": Two Austenian Dialogues', *The Book Collector*, 32 (1983), 296–314

—— *Jane Austen's 'Outlandish Cousin': The Life and Letters of Eliza de Feuillide* (London: British Library, 2002)

—— 'A Literary Portrait Re-examined: Jane Austen and Mary Anne Campion', *The Book Collector*, 45 (1996), 508–24

—— 'Lord Brabourne's Edition of Jane Austen's Letters', *Review of English Studies*, n.s., 52 (2001), 91–102

—— '*Sanditon*: Jane Austen's Manuscript and her Niece's Continuation', *Review of English Studies*, n.s., 38 (1987), 56–61

Lefroy, Anna, *Jane Austen's Sanditon: A Continuation by her Niece, together with 'Reminiscences of Aunt Jane'*, transcribed and edited by Mary Gaither Marshall (Chicago: Chiron Press, 1983)

[——] *Mary Hamilton* (1834; London: Elkin Mathews and Marrot Ltd., 1927)

[——] *The Winter's Tale* (London: James Burns, 1841)

Lefroy, F[anny] C., *The Force of Habit; or, The Story of Widow Monger* (London: Joseph Masters, 1861)

[——] *Hannah Lavender; or, Ladyhall* (London: Society for Promoting Christian Knowledge, 1857)

[——] 'Is it Just?', *Temple Bar*, 67 (1883), 270–84

[——] [Mary Lisle], *'Long, Long Ago': An Autobiography* (London: J. and C. Mozley, 1856)

[——] *My Three Aunts; or, Lowminster* (London: J. and C. Mozley, 1858)

—— *'Straight forward': and Patience Hart; or, The Dissembler* (London: J. and C. Mozley, 1860)

Leith, Sam, 'Modern Men Make the Search for Mr Darcy a Struggle', *Daily Telegraph*, 12 June 2004

Lewis, C. S., *Selected Literary Essays*, ed. Walter Hooper (Cambridge: Cambridge University Press, 1969)

Light, Alison, *Forever England: Femininity, Literature, and Conservatism between the Wars* (London: Routledge, 1991)

Litz, A. Walton, *Jane Austen: A Study of Her Artistic Development* (New York: Oxford University Press, 1965)

Lloyd, J. D. K., 'Jane Austen', *Times Literary Supplement*, 2 February 1962, 73

Loewenstein, Joseph F., 'Authentic Reproductions: The Material Origins of the New Bibliography', in *Textual Formations and Reformations*, ed. Laurie E. Maguire and Thomas L. Berger (Newark: University of Delaware Press, 1998), 23–44

Lucas, Victor, *Jane Austen* (Andover, Hants: Pitkin Unichrome Ltd., 1996)

Luckombe, Philip, *The History and Art of Printing* (London: J. Johnson, 1771)

Lynch, Deidre, 'At Home with Jane Austen', in *Cultural Institutions of the Novel*, ed. Deidre Lynch and William B. Warner (Durham and London: Duke University Press, 1996), 159–92

—— 'Homes and Haunts: Austen's and Mitford's English Idylls', *Proceedings of the Modern Language Association of America*, 115 (2000), 1103–8

Macaulay, Thomas Babington, Lord, *The Life and Letters of Lord Macaulay*, ed. George Otto Trevelyan, 2 vols. (London: Longmans, Green, and Co., 1876)

Macdonald, Gina, and Macdonald, Andrew F. (eds.), *Jane Austen On Screen*, (Cambridge: Cambridge University Press, 2003)

McDonald, Irene B., 'Contemporary Biography: Some Problems', *Persuasions*, 20 (1998), 61–8

McFarlane, Brian, *Novel To Film: An Introduction to the Theory of Adaptation* (Oxford: Clarendon Press, 1996)

McGann, Jerome J., *A Critique of Modern Textual Criticism* (Chicago: University of Chicago Press, 1983)

—— (ed.), *The New Oxford Book of Romantic Period Verse* (Oxford: Oxford University Press, 1993)

—— 'What Is Critical Editing?' and T. H. Howard-Hill's critical response, 'Theory and Praxis in the Social Approach to Editing', *TEXT*, 5 (1991), 15–29 and 31–46 (and McGann's response to the response, 47–8)

Macherey, Pierre, *A Theory of Literary Production* (*Pour une théorie de la production littéraire* (1966)), trans. by Geoffrey Wall (London, Henley, and Boston, Mass.: Routledge & Kegan Paul, 1978)

MacIntyre, Alasdair, *After Virtue: A Study in Moral Theory* (London: Duckworth, 1981)

McKenzie, D. F., *Bibliography and the Sociology of Texts* (1986; repr. Cambridge: Cambridge University Press, 1999)

—— 'Speech-Manuscript-Print', in *New Directions in Textual Studies*, ed. Dave Oliphant and Robin Bradford (Harry Ransom Humanities Research Center: University of Texas at Austin, 1990), 86–109

McKerrow, R. B. (ed.), *The Works of Thomas Nashe*, 5 vols. (London: A. H. Bullen and Sidgwick and Jackson, 1904–10)

McKusick, James C., 'John Clare and the Tyranny of Grammar', *Studies in Romanticism*, 33 (1994), 255–77

McLaverty, James, 'Issues of Identity and Utterance: An Intentionalist Response to "Textual Instability"', in *Devils and Angels: Textual Editing and Literary Theory*, ed. Philip Cohen (Charlottesville and London: University Press of Virginia, 1991), 134–51

McLaverty, James, 'The Mode of Existence of Literary Works of Art: The Case of the *Dunciad Variorum*', *Studies in Bibliography*, 37 (1986), 82–105

Malden, S. F., *Jane Austen* (Eminent Women Series) (London: W. H. Allen and Co., 1889)

Marcus, Laura, 'The Newness of the "New Biography": Biographical Theory and Practice in the Early Twentieth Century', in *Mapping Lives: The Uses of Biography*, ed. Peter France and William St Clair (Oxford: Oxford University Press for the British Academy, 2002), 193–218

Markham, Sarah, 'A Gardener's Question for Mrs Leigh Perrot', *Jane Austen Society Collected Reports, 1986–95* (Alton, Hants: Jane Austen Society, 1997), 213–14

Marsh, E., 'Some Notes on Miss Austen's Novels', *London Mercury*, 10 (1924), 189–93

Marsh, Madeleine, 'Ozias Humphrey and the Austens of Sevenoaks' and 'The Portrait', in 'Report for the Year, 1985', in *Jane Austen Society Collected Reports, 1976–85* (1989; reissued Alton, Hants: Jane Austen Society, 1994), 350–7

Marshall, Mary Gaither, 'Jane Austen's Legacy: Anna Austen Lefroy's Manuscript of *Sanditon*', *Persuasions*, 19 (1997), 226–8

Michaelson, Patricia Howell, *Speaking Volumes: Women, Reading, and Speech in the Age of Austen* (Stanford, Calif.: Stanford University Press, 2002)

Miller, D. A., *Jane Austen; or, The Secret of Style* (Princeton and Oxford: Princeton University Press, 2003)

Miller, Lucasta, *The Brontë Myth* (London: Jonathan Cape, 2001)

Mitford, Mary Russell, *Our Village*, with an introduction by Margaret Lane and illustrations by Joan Hassall (Oxford: Oxford University Press, 1982)

Mooneyham, Laura, *Romance, Language, and Education in Jane Austen's Novels* (New York: St Martin's Press, 1988)

Mulvey, Laura, 'Visual Pleasure and Narrative Cinema' (1975), repr. in *Visual and Other Pleasures* (Basingstoke: Macmillan, 1989)

Murphy, Andrew, ' "To Ferret Out Any Hidden Corruption": Shakespearean Editorial Metaphors', *TEXT*, 10 (1997), 202–19

Murray, H[ugh], *Morality of Fiction; or, An Inquiry into the Tendency of Fictitious Narratives, with Observations on Some of the Most Eminent* (Edinburgh: A. Constable and Co. and J. Anderson, 1805)

Myers, Mitzi, 'Shot from Canons; or, Maria Edgeworth and the Cultural Consumption of the Late Eighteenth-Century Woman Writer', in *The Consumption of Culture 1600–1800: Image, Object, Text*, ed. Ann Bermingham and John Brewer (London and New York: Routledge, 1995), 193–214

Nadel, Ira Bruce, *Biography: Fiction, Fact and Form* (Basingstoke and London: Macmillan, 1984)

Newman, A. K., *Catalogue of A. K. Newman and Co.'s Circulating Library... Consisting of a General Selection of Books in Every Department of Literature, and Particu-*

larly Embracing the Whole of the Modern Publications, 7 parts (London: Minerva Press, 1814–[19])

Nokes, David, *Jane Austen: A Life* (London: Fourth Estate, 1997)

Nowell-Smith, Simon (ed.), *Letters to Macmillan* (London: Macmillan, 1967)

Nunberg, Geoffrey, *The Linguistics of Punctuation* (Stanford, Calif.: Center for the Study of Language and Information, 1990)

Oliphant, M. O. W., 'The Ethics of Biography', *Contemporary Review*, 44 (1883), 76–93

[——] 'Miss Austen and Miss Mitford', *Blackwood's Edinburgh Magazine*, 107 (1870), 290–313

Olson, David R., *The World On Paper: The Conceptual and Cognitive Implications of Writing and Reading* (Cambridge: Cambridge University Press, 1994)

Page, Norman, *The Language of Jane Austen* (Oxford: Basil Blackwell, 1972)

Parkes, M. B., *Pause and Effect: An Introduction to the History of Punctuation in the West* (London: Scolar Press, 1992)

Parrish, Stephen, 'The Whig Interpretation of Literature', *TEXT*, 4 (1988), 343–50

Pechter, Edward, 'Making Love to our Employment; or, The Immateriality of Arguments about the Materiality of the Shakespearean Text', *Textual Practice*, 11 (1997), 51–67

Percy, Thomas (ed.), *Bishop Percy's Folio Manuscript*, ed. John W. Hales and Frederick J. Furnivall, 4 vols. (London: N. Trubner and Co., 1867–8)

Phillips, Adam, 'Appreciating Pater', in *Promises, Promises: Essays on Literature and Psychoanalysis* (London: Faber & Faber, 2000)

Phillipps, K. C., *Jane Austen's English* (London: Andre Deutsch, 1970)

Pilgrim, Constance, *Dear Jane: A Biographical Study of Jane Austen* (London: William Kimber, 1971)

—— 'The Zoffany Portrait: A Re-appraisal', in 'Report for the Year, 1974', *Jane Austen Society Collected Reports, 1966–75* (1977; reissued Alton, Hants: Jane Austen Society, 1999), 220–5

Pilbeam, Pamela M., *Madame Tussaud and the History of Waxworks* (London: Hambledon, 2003)

Piper, David, *Personality and the Portrait* (London: BBC Publications, 1973)

Pite, Ralph, *Hardy's Geography: Wessex and the Regional Novel* (Basingstoke: Palgrave Macmillan, 2002)

Platt, Arthur, *Nine Essays*, with a preface by A. E. Housman (Cambridge: Cambridge University Press, 1927)

Pollard, A. W., and Redgrave, G. R., *A Short-Title Catalogue of Books Printed in England, Scotland, and Ireland, and of English Books printed abroad, 1475–1640* (London: Bibliographical Society, 1926)

Price, Leah, *The Anthology and the Rise of the Novel, from Richardson to George Eliot* (Cambridge: Cambridge University Press, 2000)

Redford, Bruce, *Designing the Life of Johnson* (Oxford: Oxford University Press, 2002)

Reiman, Donald, *The Study of Modern Manuscripts: Public, Confidential, and Private* (Baltimore and London: Johns Hopkins University Press, 1993)

Richards, I. A., *Principles of Literary Criticism* (1924; London: Kegan Paul, Trench, Trubner & Co., 1934)

Rogers, Pat, ' "Caro Sposo": Mrs Elton, Burneys, Thrales, and Noels', *Review of English Studies*, n. s., 45 (1994), 70–5

—— 'Sposi in Surrey: Links between Jane Austen and Fanny Burney', *Times Literary Supplement*, 23 August 1996, 14–15

Sabor, Peter, 'James Edward Austen, Anna Lefroy, and the Interpolations to Jane Austen's "Volume the Third" ', *Notes and Queries*, 245 (2000), 304–6

—— and James-Cavan, Kathleen, 'Anna Lefroy's Continuation of *Sanditon*: Point and Counterpoint', *Persuasions*, 19 (1997), 229–43

Sadleir, Michael, *XIX Century Fiction: A Bibliographical Record based on his own Collection*, 2 vols. (London: Constable and Co., 1951)

Sales, Roger, *Jane Austen and Representations of Regency England* (London and New York: Routledge, 1994)

Samuel, Raphael, *Theatres of Memory*, Vol. 1 (London: Verso, 1994)

Sanders, J[anet] R., 'Sanditon', *Times Literary Supplement*, 19 February 1925, 120

Scott, Walter, *Guy Mannering*, ed. Peter Garside (Edinburgh: Edinburgh University Press, 1999)

[——] review of *Emma*, etc., *Quarterly Review*, 14 (1815), 188–201

Shields, Carol, *Jane Austen* (London: Weidenfeld & Nicolson, 2001)

Silver, Brenda R., 'Textual Criticism as Feminist Practice; or, Who's Afraid of Virginia Woolf, Part II', in *Representing Modernist Texts: Editing as Interpretation*, ed. George Bornstein (Ann Arbor: University of Michigan Press, 1991), 193–222

Siskin, Clifford, *The Work of Writing: Literature and Social Change in Britain, 1700–1830* (Baltimore and London: Johns Hopkins University Press, 1998)

Sisson, Rosemary Anne, *The Young Jane Austen* (London: Max Parrish, 1962)

Smiles, Samuel, *A Publisher and His Friends: Memoir and Correspondence of the late John Murray*, 2 vols., 2nd edn. (London: John Murray, 1891)

Smith, Adam, *An Inquiry into the Nature and Causes of the Wealth of Nations*, ed. R. H. Campbell, A. S. Skinner, and W. B. Todd, 2 vols. (Oxford: Clarendon Press, 1976)

Smith, C. Nowell, *The Origin and History of the Association* (English Association Pamphlet, London: Oxford University Press, 1942)

Smith, Stevie, *Novel on Yellow Paper, or Work it out for Yourself* (1936; London: Virago Press, 1980)

Sontag, Susan, *Illness as Metaphor* (1978; Harmondsworth, Middx.: Penguin, 1983)

—— *On Photography* (1977; Harmondsworth, Middx.: Penguin, 1979)

Sorensen, Janet, *The Grammar of Empire in Eighteenth-Century British Writing* (Cambridge: Cambridge University Press, 2000)

Southam, Brian C., 'Interpolations to Jane Austen's *Volume the Third*', *Notes and Queries*, 207 (1962), 185–7

—— 'Jane Austen', *Times Literary Supplement*, 19 January 1962, 41

—— *Jane Austen's Literary Manuscripts: A Study of the Novelist's Development through the Surviving Papers* (1964; rev. edn., London: Athlone Press, 2001)

—— 'The Manuscript of Jane Austen's *Volume the First*', *The Library*, 5th ser., 17 (1962), 232–7

Spielmann, M. H., and Jerrold, Walter, *Hugh Thomson: His Art, his Letters, his Humour, and his Charm* (London: A. and C. Black, 1931)

Stanford, Peter, 'True to the Word or the Spirit?' *Sunday Times*, 22 September 1996, Review Section, 5

Steiner, George, *After Babel* (Oxford: Oxford University Press, 1992)

Stillinger, Jack, *Coleridge and Textual Instability: The Multiple Versions of the Major Poems* (New York and Oxford: Oxford University Press, 1994)

Storey, Gladys, *Dickens and Daughter* (London: F. Muller Ltd., 1939)

Stower, Caleb, *The Printer's Grammar* (London: B. Crosby and Co., 1808)

Strachey, Lytton, *Eminent Victorians* (1918; repr. Harmondsworth, Middx.: Penguin, 1975)

Sulloway, Alison G., *Jane Austen and the Province of Womanhood* (Philadelphia: University of Pennsylvania Press, 1989)

Sutcliffe, Peter, *The Oxford University Press: An Informal History* (Oxford: Clarendon Press, 1978)

Sutherland, Kathryn, ' "Events ... have made us a World of Readers": Reader Relations 1780–1830', in *The Romantic Period*, ed. David B. Pirie (Penguin History of Literature, 5), (Harmondsworth, Middx.: Penguin, 1994), 1–48

—— 'Fictional Economies: Adam Smith, Walter Scott, and the Nineteenth-Century Novel', *English Literary History*, 54 (1987), 97–127

—— 'Jane Austen and the Invention of the Serious Modern Novel', in *The Cambridge Companion to English Literature, 1740–1830*, ed. Thomas Keymer and Jon Mee (Cambridge: Cambridge University Press, 2004), 244–62

—— 'Made in Scotland: The Edinburgh Edition of the Waverley Novels', *TEXT*, 14 (2002), 305–23

Tandon, Bharat, *Jane Austen and the Morality of Conversation* (London: Anthem Press, 2003)

Tanner, Tony, *Jane Austen* (Basingstoke and London: Macmillan, 1986)

Tanselle, G. Thomas, 'Editing without a Copy-Text', *Studies in Bibliography*, 47 (1994), 1–22

Tave, Stuart M., *Some Words of Jane Austen* (Chicago and London: University of Chicago Press, 1973)

Thomas, Edward, *The Last Sheaf* (London: Jonathan Cape, 1928)

Thomsen, Inger Sigrun, 'Words "Half-Dethroned": Jane Austen's Art of the Unspoken', in *Jane Austen's Business: Her World and Her Profession*, ed. Juliet McMaster and Bruce Stovel (Basingstoke and London: Macmillan, 1996), 95–106

Thomson, C. L., *Jane Austen: A Survey* (London: Horace Marshall and Son, 1929)

Tillotson, Kathleen, *Novels of the Eighteen-Forties* (1954; London: Oxford University Press, 1961)

—— 'Jane Austen', *Times Literary Supplement*, 17 September 1954, 591

Todd, Janet (ed.), *Jane Austen: New Perspectives; Women and Literature*, 3 (New York and London: Holmes and Meier Publishers Inc., 1983)

Todd, William B., *A Directory of Printers and Others in Allied Trades, London and Vicinity, 1800–1840* (London: Printing Historical Society, 1972)

Tompkins, J. M. S., *The Popular Novel in England, 1770–1800* (London: Constable, 1932)

Tomalin, Claire, *Jane Austen: A Life* (Harmondsworth, Middx.: Viking, 1997)

Trilling, Lionel, *The Opposing Self: Nine Essays in Criticism* (London: Secker and Warburg, 1955)

—— 'Why We Read Jane Austen', *Times Literary Supplement*, 5 March 1976, 250–2

Tucker, George Holbert, *A History of Jane Austen's Family* (rev. edn., Stroud, Glos.: Sutton Publishing Ltd., 1998)

Tuite, Clara, *Romantic Austen: Sexual Politics and the Literary Canon* (Cambridge: Cambridge University Press, 2002)

Tytler, Sarah [Henrietta Keddie], *Jane Austen and her Works* (London, Paris, and New York: Cassell, Petter, Galpin and Co., 1880)

Updike, John, 'One Cheer for Literary Biography', *New York Review of Books*, 4 February 1999, 3–5

Verrall, A. W., *Collected and Literary Essays, Classical and Modern*, ed. M. A. Bayfield and J. D. Duff (Cambridge: Cambridge University Press, 1913)

—— 'On the Printing of Jane Austen's Novels', *Cambridge Observer*, 1 (1892), 2–4

—— 'On Some Passages in Jane Austen's *Mansfield Park*', *Cambridge Review*, 15 (1893–4), 126–7, and 145–6

Vinaver, Eugène, 'Principles of Textual Emendation', in *Studies in French Language and Medieval Literature presented to Professor M. K. Pope* [ed., 'pupils, colleagues, and friends'] (Manchester: Manchester University Press, 1939), 351–69

Wagner, Tamara, 'Mrs Hubback's *The Younger Sister*: The Victorian Austen and the Phenomenon of the Austen Sequel', *The Victorian Web* (October 2003) http://www.victorianweb.org/victorian/authors/hubback/

Waldron, Mary, *Jane Austen and the Fiction of Her Time* (Cambridge: Cambridge University Press, 1999)

Walkley, A. B., 'The Novels of Jane Austen', *Edinburgh Review*, 239 (Jan. 1924), 27–40

Walsh, Marcus, *Shakespeare, Milton, and Eighteenth-Century Literary Editing: The Beginnings of Interpretative Scholarship* (Cambridge: Cambridge University Press, 1997)

Wayne, Valerie, 'The Sexual Politics of Textual Transmission', in *Textual Formations and Reformations*, ed. Laurie E. Maguire and Thomas L. Berger (Newark: University of Delaware Press, 1998), 179–210

Welsh, Irvine, *Trainspotting* (1993; London: Vintage, 1999)

Werner, Marta L., *Emily Dickinson's Open Folios: Scenes of Reading, Surfaces of Writing* (Ann Arbor: University of Michigan Press, 1995)

Wheeler, Richard James, *The Rice Portrait of Jane Austen: The Ill-Conceived Controversy* (Westerham, Kent: Codex Publications, 1996)

—— and Hammond, Margaret Campbell, *The Rice Portrait of Jane Austen: A Summary of Conclusive Evidence* (Sevenoaks: Codex Publications, 1997)

[Wilson, T.], *The Use of Circulating Libraries Considered; with Instructions for Opening and Conducting a Library, either upon a Large or Small Plan* (London and Bromley, Kent: J. Hamilton and T. Wilson, 1797)

Wiltshire, John, *Jane Austen and the Body: 'The Picture of Health'* (Cambridge: Cambridge University Press, 1992)

—— *Recreating Jane Austen* (Cambridge: Cambridge University Press, 2001)

Woolf, Virginia, *The Common Reader*, 1st ser. (London: Hogarth Press, 1925)

—— *The Common Reader*, 2nd ser. (London: Hogarth Press, 1932)

—— *The Complete Shorter Fiction*, ed. Susan Dick (rev. edn., London: Hogarth Press, 1989)

—— *The Death of the Moth and Other Essays* (1942; 5th impression, London: Hogarth Press, 1947)

—— *The Essays of Virginia Woolf*, ed. Andrew McNeillie, 4 vols. (London: Hogarth Press, 1986–94)

—— *Orlando: A Biography* (1928; London: Hogarth Press, 7th impression, 1954)

Wordsworth, William, *The Prelude: The Four Texts (1798, 1799, 1805, 1850)*, ed. Jonathan Wordsworth (Harmondsworth, Middx.: Penguin, 1995)

—— *The Prose Works of William Wordsworth*, ed. W. J. B. Owen and Jane Worthington Smyser, 3 vols. (Oxford: Clarendon Press, 1974)

Wright, Andrew, 'Jane Austen Adapted', *Nineteenth-Century Fiction*, 30 (1975–6), 421–53

Wroe, Martin, 'Hard Drugs and Heroine Addiction', *Observer*, 10 March 1996, 13

www.pemberley.com/janeinfo

Index